AF361490

Saddam Husayn and Islam, 1968–2003

Saddam Husayn and Islam, 1968–2003

Ba'thi Iraq from Secularism to Faith

Amatzia Baram

Woodrow Wilson Center Press
Washington, D.C.

Johns Hopkins University Press
Baltimore

Editorial Offices
Woodrow Wilson Center Press
Woodrow Wilson International Center for Scholars
One Woodrow Wilson Plaza
1300 Pennsylvania Avenue NW
Washington, DC 20004-3027
www.wilsoncenter.org

Order From
Johns Hopkins University Press
Hopkins Fulfillment Services
P.O. Box 50370
Baltimore, MD 21211-4370
Telephone 1-800-527-5487
www.press.jhu.edu/books/

2 4 6 8 9 7 5 3 1

Library of Congress Cataloging-in Publication Data

Baram, Amatzia, 1938–
  Saddam Husayn and Islam, 1968–2003 : Ba'thi Iraq from secularism to faith / Amatzia Baram.
    pages cm
  Includes bibliographical references and index.
  ISBN-13: 978-1-4214-1582-6
  1. Hussein, Saddam, 1937–2006. 2. Islam and politics—Iraq—20th century. 3. Iraq—Politics and government—1979–1991. 4. Iraq—Politics and government—1991–2003. I. Title.
  DS79.7.B375 2014
  324.2567'08309045—dc23
                    2014020675

Table of Contents

Preface

The idea to write about the Ba'th Party and Islam came to me between 1981 and 1982 while I was collecting material for my PhD dissertation in Durham and London, England. This topic eventually did not find its way into my dissertation. However, since the Ba'thi policy was of such interest and so unusual in the Arab-Islamic world, I never gave up on the notion that one day I would go back to this theme and devote a book to it.

Very early on, I was struck by the party's staunch secularism despite the cost it had to pay in terms of public support in Iraq. It compensated by introducing an extensive system of *al-tarhib wal-targhib*, "terrorizing and enticement," but the cost was undeniable. I was surprised to see how far this secularism went: during the first years of its regime, the Iraqi Ba'th Party allowed some intellectuals to argue in public treatises that God does not exist. Those treatises appeared in quaint intellectual magazines and volumes of forgotten lore that I found in the library of the School of Oriental and African Studies at the University of London. In the British Library at the British Museum, I found the Iraqi government official *Gazette* that poured the staunch Ba'thi secular worldview into a legal mold. I also came across muffled antireligious expressions in the regime's more popular literature, which I found in the archives at the Dayan Center in Tel Aviv University. Perhaps the most surprising detail was an invitation on the front page of the Ba'th Party daily *al-Thawra*, suggesting that newly married couples boost their fertility by spending their honeymoons at the government's expense in the towers of the reconstructed Babylonian Temple of Ishtar. As Ishtar was the Mesopotamian goddess of love and war, this was not mere atheism: this was a fascination with a heathen culture and a stab at Islam. Additional material of a similar nature, mainly in Baghdad-based communist magazines, was to be found in the central library of Durham University.

The next time I felt the urge to go back to the topic of the Ba'th Party and Islam came in 1989 when I was a Senior Fellow at the Woodrow Wilson International Center for Scholars in Washington, DC, and in 1990 when I was a Senior Associate Member at St. Antony's College of Oxford University. By then, I suspected that I was witnessing a sea-change in Baghdad—a retreat from secularism and a tilt toward religiosity. It was intriguing, even perplexing, and I was not certain that what I saw was more than an apparition. In fact, for a few years, even though some written evidence, the artistic visual images, and conversations I had with people who had just left Iraq seemed to suggest that at least outwardly Ba'thi Iraq was going Islamic, I classified all that under the category of "there is no such thing."

From time to time, though, a puzzling document or event forced me to think again. This was the case, for example, of the public announcement in 1989 that Michel 'Aflaq, the Christian founder of the Ba'th Party, had converted to Islam prior to his death. This statement was baffling, not mainly because it was not credible but because the Iraqi regime had felt the need to make such an announcement. And yet, I did not believe that the secular and by implication atheistic Ba'th Party under Saddam Husayn was going through conversion to Islam or pretending to do so—which, in terms of the party's public image, were the same thing. The U-turn seemed to me improbable because it meant that the party was betraying its most cherished tenet of faith: secular Arab nationalism. Since its inception, the Ba'th had fought fiercely against the Muslim Brotherhood. It treated the Brotherhood with the utmost contempt and considered their Salafi-Islamist worldview to be the most potent threat to the resurrection (*al-ba'th*) of the Arab nation. The Ba'th believed that the Brotherhood, who flaunted the Qur'an as their "doctrine," represented a primitive, backward remnant of the past that held back Arab progress and modernity. That the Ba'th were adopting—even if partially, even if merely for show—the very ideology of their nemesis was difficult for me to believe. Time and again, I checked and found that the old secular slogans were still everywhere in Iraq. Alcoholic drinks and promiscuous nightclubs were still flourishing in Baghdad. Just to be sure, I also checked the Syrian media. Despite Syria's close alliance with the Islamic regime in Tehran, there was no sign of a tilt toward Islam in Ba'thi Damascus. I therefore considered the signals coming from Baghdad as a false alarm, as irrelevant background "white" noise.

In ignoring Baghdad's momentous U-turn, I behaved much like one team member of the scientific mission headed by my childhood hero, the renowned Norwegian historian, ethnographer, zoologist, botanist, geographer, and adventurer Thor Heyerdahl (1914–2002). In his famous *The Kon-Tiki Expedition: By Raft Across the South Seas*, Heyerdahl describes a situation in which on one of the mornings the team found on the open part of the raft a deep-water fish that had jumped out of the water and become stranded there. They passed it around, gaping at it, as it was the most amazing creature that they had ever seen. In the end, one of the team members grabbed it by the tail and tossed it back into the ocean, saying, "There is no such fish."

Two additional sabbaticals at the Wilson Center (1994–95 and 2005) and two sabbaticals at the US Institute of Peace (1997–98 and 2003–4) gave me the opportunity to study more sources, meet more people, and publish very brief progress reports, and eventually convinced me that what looked like a public, high-profile U-turn, whatever its sincerity, was probably real and deserved a more comprehensive study regardless. Between 1995 and 1998, I decided to look for the kind of evidence that I had tossed back into the ocean over the years: the evidence I invite you to contemplate while reading this book. At the same time, however, when I read again Michel 'Aflaq's lectures— the founding scriptures of the Ba'th Party—I began to wonder: was his call for secularism a form of disguised atheism, or was it in fact Islamic religiosity in a sophisticated guise coming, very strangely, from a Christian intellectual? If the latter was the case, then the Islamic U-turn of the 1980s and 1990s was not a U-turn at all. Did Ba'th ideology from its first days mean anything real, or was it merely smoke and mirrors? But then, for more than a decade, 'Aflaq's disciples in Baghdad did enforce a secular system in the sense that they limited the cultural, legal, and educational role of Islam and the 'ulama to the best of their ability. So what was 'Aflaq really saying, how was he understood in the 1940s and 1950s, and how was he interpreted in the 1990s? Throughout the book, I ask this question and suggest answers, and I invite you to be the judge.

The last phase of collecting material for this book took place while I was teaching at the Department of Government at Georgetown University in 2010–11. This is where I became acquainted, for the first time, with the Conflict Records Research Center (CRRC) at the National Defense University. The documents that I found at the CRRC did not change the big picture, but all the same they added color and life to the open-source materials that I had gathered, and cast a bright ray of light on Saddam Husayn's decisionmaking process and debating style. The secret documents also enabled me to better understand a personality change in Saddam. Saddam's conversations with his lieutenants confirmed my two impressions: that some of his senior lieutenants did indeed believe in secularism, and that the first steps toward Islamization were taken out of cold, cynical calculation. Still, even though most of the party retained a secular worldview in their internal correspondence, outwardly the party did "convert" to Islamic religiosity, thus creating a kind of unresolved cognitive dissonance. As for Saddam, it seems that he went through a personal metamorphosis, and by the time the American troops entered Baghdad in 2003, he was already a changed man, in all probability a sort of born-again Muslim.

For me, a student for some thirty years of Iraqi history with special emphasis on the Ba'th regime, listening to the recordings of the dictator and his closest circle of sycophants was the experience of a lifetime. The CRRC proved to be an exciting time capsule. Sometimes, it was frightening and nauseating. This was the case, for example, when Saddam presented himself as a humanitarian while approving the cutting-off of deserters' ears with a knife in the field, even though he admitted that this would kill some six thousand men. Likewise sickening is his order to execute publicly hundreds of Shi'i marsh Arabs in their own villages. His nuclear strategy, too, was unsettling. Sometimes the recordings are bizarre, as when Saddam suggests studying the *Protocols of the Elders of Zion* "in order to understand the Jews better." Sometimes the recordings are hilarious, as when experienced and competent generals are forced to praise Saddam, who had never served in the military, for his military ingenuity; or when the Iraqi intelligence is warning Saddam about the Japanese Pokémon cartoon; or when Saddam is exposing his softer side and love for all humans when he tells his lieutenants a story of how he forgave one of his servants for stealing a jacket from him. Understandably, he could not allow the man to keep the jacket or his job, but being most merciful and compassionate he allowed the unfortunate servant to keep his head. Most instructive—though not surprising—is his way of telling his lieutenants what they must vote for; for example, for war with Iran or steps of Islamization. Most surprising are cases when some of his lieutenants explicitly express reluctance to accept the leader's dictates. Since they expressed their objections very politely indeed, they were not punished, but their objections were hopeless all the same.

I hope that the reader will find it of interest to follow Saddam and the Ba'th Party's tortuous road from what I now believe was secularism with a whiff of atheism to their conversion (whether real, virtual, or something in between) to Islam. In this book, I am trying to present what I believe to be the most relevant facts, delineate the trajectory of events, and suggest why the Ba'th regime embarked on this particular trajectory. I also discuss the way in which Saddam imagined Islam and his role in it, what he tried to do, and what the results were. It seems to me that in view of the revival of trends of Islamic religiosity in the Arab world following the upheavals of the 2011 "Arab Spring," Saddam's Islamization campaign—which I tend to see as the equivalent of burning a stretch of forest in order to stop a greater fire—is becoming relevant in many realms.

Acknowledgments

I would like to take this opportunity to express my gratitude to the people whose help made this book possible. At first those were the staffs of the School of Oriental and African Studies and Durham libraries, the British Library, and the Dayan Center at Tel-Aviv University, which has an extensive collection of Arabic newspaper and magazines. I am grateful to them, and in particular to the late Haim Gal at the Dayan Center, who spared no effort to assist me with my work. When I was in Durham, Peter Sluglett and the late Marion Farouk-Sluglett offered me warm hospitality and rare counseling on the Ba'th regime. I am very grateful for it. My stay in the United Kingdom in 1981–82, when the first documents used in this book were collected, was enabled by a grant from Stanley Bogen of New York and the Harry S. Truman Research Institute on Mt. Scopus at the Hebrew University of Jerusalem. I am indebted to both for their generous help.

To my many Iraqi interviewees who asked to remain anonymous, some of whom have become good friends, I am indebted. With all my heart, I wish that both they and their country will overcome the present tragic crisis and soon see a prosperous and peaceful Iraq.

The United States Institute of Peace (USIP) and the Woodrow Wilson International Center for Scholars, where I spent a few years as a senior fellow, are two remarkable congressional institutions, the perfect hunting grounds for any researcher who is seeking knowledge, political sagacity, and sound advice. I am deeply grateful to both for the invaluable opportunity they accorded me. In both centers, many staffers were of great help, and I ask their forgiveness for not mentioning all of them by name.

At the USIP, I am grateful in particular to Richard H. Solomon, who served as president when I did my research there, for his support and friendship. I owe debts of gratitude also to Joe Klaits, David Smock, Pamela Aal, Virginia Bouvier, Keith Bowen, Michael Dziedzik, Paul Hughes, Niel Kritz, Scott Lasensky, Charles Nelson, Robert Perito, Steve Riskin, Daniel Server, and Michael Lekson. Both Steven Heydemann and John Christ Jr. commented on the first draft of the manuscript. I am grateful for their advice.

I spent three periods as a Senior Fellow at the Wilson Center: in 1989–90 and 1994–95 at the Smithsonian Castle and then in 2005 in their new premises in the Ronald Reagan Building. I would like to express my gratitude to the Center for those unique opportunities to dedicate all my time to research in an environment of great scholarship, and for accepting this book for publication in 2013. In particular, I am indebted to Robert Litvak, with whom I have compared notes extensively throughout the years and from whom I have received constant support. In my conversations with Haleh Esfandiari at the Center, and with both her and Shaul Bakhash outside of it, I have benefited greatly from their profound understanding of the Islamic Republic of Iran. Zdeněk David was of tremendous help whenever I needed the library. Susan Nugent, Arlyn Charles, and Lindsay Collins rushed to my rescue whenever I needed guidance in the Center and in Washington, D.C. This book would not have seen the light of day had it not been for the managerial skills and editing wisdom of Joe Brinley and Shannon Granville of Woodrow Wilson Center Press, and Marjorie Pannell's editing talent, patience, and energy. For that, I am deeply grateful to all three of them.

In 1997, I spent several fruitful months at the Washington Institute for Near East Policy. There, too, I was received with warmth and support. I am grateful to the whole research community there, and especially to Robert Satloff, Patrick Clawson, Kenneth Pollack, and Mike Eisenstadt. Kenneth Pollack provided me with his valuable advice also in 2002–3 when I did research for a few months at the Brookings Institution's Saban Center for Middle East Policy. I am grateful to him, to Martin Indyk, and to the Saban Center for accepting me as one of them.

I want to thank Professor Robert Lieber and the Georgetown University Department of Government for their support, which enabled me to spend a day or two a week at the National Defense University's Conflict Records Research Center (CRRC), where I could read Saddam's documents and listen to his closed-door conversations with his military generals and party luminaries. At the CRRC, I was warmly received and extensively helped by

Lorry Fenner, David Palkki, Chris Alkhoury, Joseph Simmons, and Sabra Simmonds. I am indebted to them for their professionalism and camaraderie.

At various stages during the writing of this book, I was guided by and am indebted to two people who helped my thinking. While the conclusions are mine and only my responsibility, Dale Eickelman's and Phebe Marr's intellectual and professional guidance was invaluable. I am also indebted to two of my former PhD students, Noga Efrati and Ronen Zeidel, with whom I discussed parts of this book. There is nothing more satisfying for me as a teacher than to thank my students.

During all my sabbatical years in Washington, D.C., the friendship and encouragement of four persons was of great value for me. I am deeply thankful to Stuart Eizenstat and the late Fran Eizenstat for their wonderful hospitality and support. Like Stu and Fran, Peter Rosenblatt and the late Max Kampelman, too, were always happy to meet and discuss American policies in the Middle East. I am missing Fran and Max.

Last but not least, this book could not have been published without my wife Bonnie Belkin-Baram's solid and practical advice and endless patience, which enabled me to keep focused and continue my work in times of confusion and doubt.

List of Abbreviations

BRCC	Ba'th Regional Command Collection
CRRC	Conflict Records Research Center
GUIW	General Union of Iraqi Women
PAL	Pan Arab Leadership (of the Ba'th Party)
RCC	Revolutionary Command Council
RL	Regional Leadership (of the Ba'th Party)
SAIRI	Supreme Assembly of the Islamic Revolution in Iraq
USIP	United States Institute of Peace

Saddam Husayn and Islam, 1968–2003

Ethnographic Map of Iraq, 2003

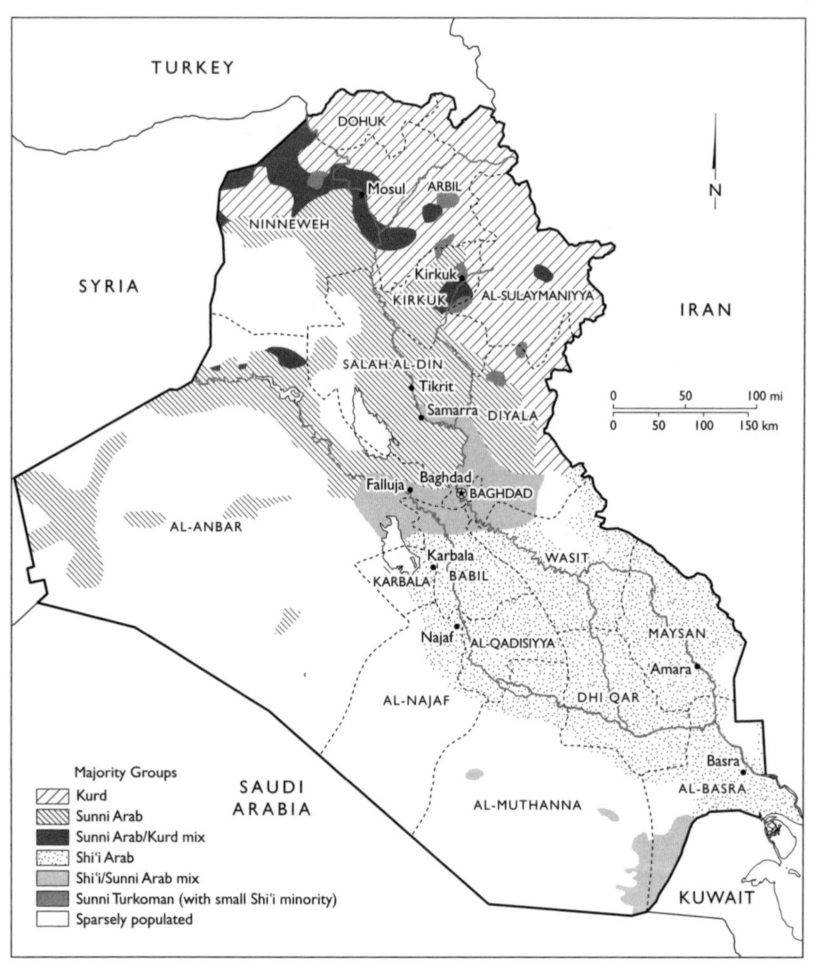

Introduction

This book portrays and analyzes the ideological, the intellectual, and to a large extent the emotional history of the Ba'th Party in Iraq through the lens of its single most important tenet of faith, secular Arabism. The Ba'th Party's holy trinity was "[Arab] Unity, Freedom, Socialism," meaning a socialistic society in an expansive united Arab state, allegedly democratic and free from colonial domination. However, all these ideals eventually flowed into one estuary: secularism (*al-'ilmaniyya*), a vision of a thoroughly modern and therefore secular Arab society in which religion was separated from state. This path was seen as the only way to true modernity. Without its secular content, the party ideology would have been an empty shell and would have failed to attract the kind of people that it did. Young men and (far fewer) women joined the party because it offered them a tantalizing vision of a formidable united Arab nation free from the shackles of Islamic religious duties and restrictions and from the grip of the Muslim clerics, the 'ulama.

During the first decades of the party's existence, Arab unity was a dream that not only gave meaning and direction to the members' political affiliation, but also seemed attainable in the near future. Since the mid-1960s, however, following a few painful failures, the dream of unity, while still a defining one, became a distant goal. As Saddam Husayn explained in 1975 to teachers who had been assigned to write school textbooks, "When we talk about the Arab homeland it is necessary that we do not forget to educate the Iraqi to be proud of . . . the Iraqi country in which he is living . . . [and which] is his tangible homeland . . . because the [united] Arab homeland . . . is still a goal in a state of [long-term] struggle. . . . This means that we must not drown in the principled pan-Arab [*al-qawmi al-mabda'i*] and forsake direct [Iraqi] patriotism."[1] This "principled" or theoretical vision remained unaltered until the end of Ba'th rule in Baghdad. Secularism was embedded in the party members' emotional and intellectual world. It was also an integral part of their daily lives and the daily conduct of the state. Most of the hard-core Ba'this led a secular lifestyle. Even to the more religious among them, keeping the politics and culture of their "tangible homeland" as far as possible from the rules of religion and the 'ulama was of great importance.

When the Ba'th Party took over in Baghdad in 1968, some minimal concessions to religion notwithstanding, it made great efforts to implement this ideology, to "indoctrinate" society (*al-taw'iya*),[2] or, as it was defined strictly in internal party documents, to "Ba'thize" it (*al-tab'ith*),[3] thus creating the "New Arab man."[4] While trying to impose its values, the Sunni-led party clashed widely with many circles, but mostly with the religious Shi'i masses and the establishment, which offered an alternative vision of the Iraqi nation and state. However, by 2003, when the Ba'th regime was destroyed by the invasion of the United States and its allies, Saddam Husayn, its leader, had already given up the vision of a secular society. Indeed, he went much further when he imposed important aspects of Islam on party and regime and nudged the country as a whole in the direction of Islamization.

The transformation was incomplete. For any highly ideological party, a U-turn hinged on a central tenet of faith is an incremental and agonizing journey. Much of the party's internal and public discourse retained its secular nature in the sense that it kept God out. One cannot find party documents that ascribe the "Islamization" of party and regime to a desire "to please God." Often the party officials used "Oldspeak"—utilitarian, pragmatic, secular arguments—to justify the regime's "Newspeak," an Islamic language and the Islamization of official practices. It may safely be assumed that most of the party's old guard did not really become piously religious overnight, but much of the public behavior of party and regime was Islamized.

An example is the treatment of the traditional principle according to which the future united Arab state would be "national," that is, secular rather than religious as demanded by the Islamists. In a closed-door meeting of the Pan-Arab Leadership in January 1995, Saddam announced that the Ba'th were no longer against the principle of a pan-Islamic state, provided that unification began with pan-Arab unity.[5] This vision came very close to that of Hasan al-Banna, the founder of the Muslim Brotherhood.

To retain a semblance of self-respect, the party kept parts of its old symbolism. Until 2003, and in contradiction to the new Islamic line, the two traditional party slogans of "Unity, Freedom, Socialism" and "One Arab nation with an eternal message" continued to appear on all the party's publications and internal documents. Likewise, at the start of every party congress the whole hall would get to its feet and chant the second slogan as one.[6] However, an Islamic layer was superimposed on the existing foundation, so much so that some party members asked in bewilderment whether Baghdad was becoming Riyadh.[7] By 2003, what remained of the old secular Ba'th Party was only an empty ideological shell. Baghdad did not become Riyadh, but it went a long way in that direction. Saddam's was an unusual interpretation of Islam, very different from those of al-Qa'ida, the Taliban, the Wahhabis, or the Muslim Brotherhood. There are some indications that whereas Saddam initiated the Islamization campaign as a pragmatic, even cynical step designed to win his regime mass support at home and in the Islamic world, in the end he personally may have become a born-again Muslim. This book explores the different stages in the Islamic metamorphosis or conversion of leader, party, and regime, and the causes behind it.

During the thirty-five years of Ba'th rule in Iraq, a profound transformation occurred in the relationship of state and mosque. But when, how, and why did a major secular Arab nationalist party that ruled over a major Arab state undertake a breathtaking *salto mortale* and strike a U-turn in its identity and belief system? This book first describes the original secular belief system of the nascent Ba'th Party when it was created in the 1940s and its historical and social background, then analyzes how this belief system was expressed in political practice in Iraq when the Ba'th came to power. The central question is how and why a movement that was established by a Christian and whose initial membership also included 'Alawites, Druze, and Sabeans executed such an Islamic about-face. Toward the end of Ba'th Party rule in Iraq, the political and cultural systems of Iraq reflected a strange and confusing cross between the old secular and the new Islamic practice and rhetoric.

The existing literature on Iraq's transformation helps move us in the direction of answers. Four previous studies of the Iraqi nation-state provide, each in its own way, a panoramic view and comprehensive analysis of the turbulent sixty- to eighty-year history of post–World War I Iraq: Hanna Batatu's *The Old Social Classes and the Revolutionary Movements of Iraq* (Princeton, 1978), Phebe Marr's *The Modern History of Iraq* (Westview, 3rd ed., 2011), Charles Tripp's *A History of Iraq* (Cambridge, 3rd ed., 2007), and Adeed Dawisha's *Iraq: A Political History from Independence to Occupation* (Cambridge, 2009). Valuable studies of Iraqi politics and society under Baʿth rule include Marion Farouk-Sluglett and Peter Sluglett's *Iraq since 1958: From Revolution to Dictatorship* (KPI, 1987) and David Baran's *Vivre la tyrannie et lui survivre: L'Irak en transition* (Mille et une nuits, 2004). For biographies of Saddam Husayn that also cover much of Baʿthi Iraq's history, see Said Aburish's *Saddam Hussein: The Politics of Revenge* (Bloomsbury, 2000) and Efraim Karsh and Inari Rautsi's *Saddam Hussein: A Political Biography* (Free Press, 1991). An excellent history of the Baʿth Party is John F. Devlin's *The Baʿth Party: A History from Its Origins to 1966* (Stanford, 1979).[8] Last but not least are several remarkable anthropological studies of Middle Eastern and Islamic societies, mainly Dale Eickelman's *The Middle East and Central Asia: An Anthropological Approach* (Prentice Hall, 2002), Michael Gilsenan's *Recognizing Islam: Religion and Society in the Modern Arab World* (Pantheon, 1982), and Ernest Gellner's *Muslim Society* (Cambridge, 1985). This book is about some sixty years of the Baʿth Party history in Syria and Iraq, but mostly about the thirty-five years (1968–2003) of the Iraqi Baʿth regime, one that left a very deep and possibly indelible mark on the people and the country and on their changing attitude to Islam.

The Limits of Baʿthi Dictatorship

Dictatorship is defined by the *Encyclopaedia Britannica* as a government in which "one person or a small group possesses absolute power without effective constitutional limitations." Political power in a dictatorship is maintained through the use of "intimidation, terror, and the suppression of basic civil liberties."[9] The Baʿth regime under Saddam Husayn fits well the definition and pattern of a dictatorship and shares also most of its characteristics with totalitarian dictatorships, but it was analogous rather than identical to those of Nazi Germany or Stalin's Soviet Union.[10] There is a fairly general impression that the Baʿth regime was so effectively dictatorial that it could and did destroy all vestiges of independent society and impose its values. This book is concerned with the relationship between a dictatorial regime and its society and between the regime's ideology and the belief systems of the society, but its main conclusion is counterintuitive. In the numerous discussions I had with Iraqis who lived in Baʿthi Iraq for many years and who knew their country and the Baʿth regime intimately, a clear-cut view emerged: Saddam was immensely powerful, and his rule was total and ruthless. He was always capable of rewarding those who collaborated with him such that in Iraq he could do anything he wanted. The historian Toby Dodge supports this popular view:

> Since seizing power in 1968 the Baʿth regime efficiently used extreme levels of violence and . . . patronage to co-opt or break any independent vestiges of civil society. Autonomous collective social structures beyond the control of the state simply do not exist. In their place society came to be dominated by . . . flexible networks of patronage and violence used to reshape Iraqi society in the image of Saddam Hussein and his regime.[11]

Paradoxically, I argue that the totalitarian omnipotence ascribed by so many to the Baʿth regime of Iraq never existed. There is no doubt as to the intention and effort invested in the attempt "to reshape Iraqi society in the image of Saddam Hussein and his regime." However, Saddam and his comrades failed in their endeavor.

Whether Saddam's system is defined as a mere dictatorship or as a totalitarian one, all the trappings of a totalitarian dictatorship were in place. Like other dictatorships, the Baʿth regime comprised a single ruling party, to which adults were expected to belong. According to Baʿthi leaders, by the end of 1989 party membership (including the lower ranks) had reached "over two million"[12]—definitely an inflated number. As the total population of Iraq then was around 17 million, party members would have represented almost 12 percent of the population. By September 2002 this number had made a quantum leap to close to four million, or 16.5 percent of the population.[13] If only people between the ages of fifteen and sixty-four are taken into consideration, then by 2002 at least 25 percent of all Iraqi adults were party members of various ranks. Even though this figure too is undoubtedly inflated, there is no reason to doubt that at least the lower membership ranks expanded substantially. Beginning in the mid-1970s, mass mobilization to join the party was a declared policy.[14] It exposed the recruits to massive doses of indoctrination, in addition to the indoctrination provided at all school levels. The regime had total control over formal education at all levels, including teaching jobs, stipends, and the employment of many graduates. For Arab (as distinct from Kurdish) professionals, students, and army officers, avoiding membership was possible but risky. The regime had also total control over the print media and almost exclusive control of television broadcasts: owning a satellite dish was illegal. The only television-based challenge came from the Iranian border, but the broadcast reached only limited zones. The party controlled all unions, and the state had control over culture[15] and the legal system, over parliament and all legislation, and over most central aspects of the economy, most critically over government employment and salaries, as well as budgetary allocations for government services and development.

Like other fierce dictatorships, the Ba'th too had an effective internal security system based on a number of competing intelligence organs that terrorized the citizenry and spied on each other.[16] A complex system of surveillance, rewards, and punishments was designed to cow the Iraqis.[17] In most cases, this system forced Iraqi citizens to self-police themselves, and as a result, in ordinary times political opposition was very weak. Saddam also had a fairly extensive terrorist network operating outside Iraq.[18] The regime initiated numerous mass parades and other mass gatherings, mainly on secular but also on religious occasions, as well as *bay'a* (the traditional Islamic oath of allegiance) signing ceremonies during which people pledged their loyalty to the president, sometimes signing with their blood. Through such mass gatherings and ceremonies the regime demonstrated its omnipotence to skeptics and would-be revolutionaries, who at least outwardly recognized its authority. Last but not least, a personality cult of unprecedented proportions in Iraq was launched soon after Saddam became president in 1979 and continued until his last day in power. In all this, Saddam and his regime were eager students of Stalin's totalitarian dictatorship, and somewhat less so of the Nazi and fascist systems in Germany and Italy, respectively.

Once the Ba'th came to power in 1968, Iraq's oil revenues, the major factor underpinning the economy, were entirely in the hands of the regime. In 1973–74, those revenues increased enormously, and the regime's totalitarian clout and self-confidence increased in tandem. However, by 1980, with the Iran-Iraq War in progress, the bonanza came to an end, and under the international embargo imposed by the United Nations Security Council in 1990–2003 the crisis deepened.[19] However, Ba'thi Iraq did not become less totalitarian. On the contrary: with fewer rewards to dispense, the regime tightened its grip on the population. And as the reward system weakened, the president, party, and regime began to lose confidence. This is where the totalitarian nature of the regime began to fray at the edges: it gave up nothing when it came to the tools of totalitarian control, but to stay in power the leadership ceded the party's most cherished tenet of faith, secular Arabism. Moreover, the party and the regime leaders themselves recognized their failure.

The Changing Ideology of a Totalitarian Regime

While the party was in power in Baghdad, Ba'th ideology went through three major transformations. All three represented the net result of a sophisticated form of interaction or "bargain" between a dictatorial regime and the society it governed during some thirty-five years of rule. Although the regime could execute or assassinate any individual, it was far from omnipotent. It fully recognized this fact, and rather than molding the public as it had intended, it adapted itself to the public's values, at least to an extent.

Some theoretical background on state-society relations helps set the context for understanding these transformations. The Italian communist intellectual Antonio Gramsci (1891–1937) saw the state not as a pure instrument of suppression by a ruling class. Rather, the state also initiates cultural and ideological activities designed to encourage the consent of the citizens.[20] In the Iraqi context, Pierre Darle, who spent more than a year cumulatively in Iraq between 1998 and 2001, noticed an ambiguity in the regime's policies. He identified it as resulting from some kind of implicit bargain between the regime and certain social powers.[21] The Middle East expert Achim Rohde has similarly observed, "Official discourse . . . reflects a certain implicit interaction between the ruler and his objects rather than a mere imposition of elite values from above."[22] However, this was not a development of the 1990s. Rather, it was true of Ba'thi Iraq from day one. Along with brutal suppression and attempted indoctrination, the party tried to win hearts and minds. It undertook the latter by championing what regime leaders believed to have been a popular cause, that of the "Arab revolution" against the "Zionist entity," Western "imperialism," Arab "reactionary forces," and even against 'Abd al-Nasir's "petty bourgeois mentality."[23] Likewise, to avoid a costly clash with the conservative religious circles the Ba'th decided to somewhat soften their secular tenet of faith, but only somewhat. Then, to avoid a clash with the Shi'is and the Kurds as well as with the tribal groups, they modified the nature of Arab unity. When it came to secularism, though, in the 1990s the bargain was of a different order of magnitude.

Two Early Metamorphoses

The first of the three major ideological-political metamorphoses came mere months after the Ba'th Party gained power. It replaced Syrian political philosopher Michel 'Aflaq's traditional Ba'thi egalitarian and integrative Arab nationalism with a Mesopotamian-inspired, Iraq-centered, hegemonic and federative pan-Arabism. The new ideology was meant first to assure the Shi'is and Kurds that Iraq would not melt in an Arab crucible in which they would be lost in a Sunni-Arab multitude. Second, the concept of an eternal Iraq at the head of the Arab world was designed to ward off any expectation that the Iraqi Ba'th would give up power in favor of Cairo or Damascus.[24] Finally: the "Iraq first" faction in the party needed to give substance to an Iraqi national identity. They found it waiting, buried in the alluvial plains of ancient Mesopotamia. As all pre-Islamic civilizations were usually considered by Islamic tradition to be *Jahiliyya*, or ages of barbarism and ignorance, looking for national Iraqi roots in heathen Mesopotamia accentuated the party's secular credo.[25]

The second bargain was with the tribes. The classical Ba'th concept of an Arab nation was based exclusively on the literary Arabic language and the language-related culture and history. All traditional subnational identities— tribe, sect, religion, geographic region, even the Arab nation-states—were viewed as obstacles on the way to pan-Arab unification, and therefore illegitimate. From late 1969, though, Vice President Saddam Husayn recruited the tribes. He manipulated them, and for their part they often manipulated Baghdad. The regime's tolerance of such manipulation represented its recognition of the limits to its power.[26]

The Final Metamorphosis: Islamization as a Bargain with Society

In a secret meeting in 1986, the Ba'th leadership succumbed for the first time to Islamism when it decided to try cooperation with the powerful Egyptian and Sudanese Muslim Brotherhood. Within a few years, this move had produced profound ramifications for state public policies and for the party's identity. The U-turn from a secular state to an Islamist one was reported in the West in 1996, but that study, based exclusively on open sources, was no more than an extremely brief progress report.[27] An excellent study of the incorporation of Islamic themes into the regime's rhetoric, Ofra Bengio's *Saddam's Word: Political Discourse in Iraq* (Oxford University Press, 1998), came out two years later.[28] And yet much of Saddam Husayn's "Islamized" rhetoric, some of it quite surprising, has remained unexplored by scholars. An equally first-rate study, Rohde's *State-Society Relations in Ba'thist Iraq*, expanded the treatment of Islamization in Iraq to the fields of gender and culture,[29] though it too leaves much to be explored. The broader metamorphosis of the regime in critical realms such as the legal and educational systems, intellectual pursuits, Islamic institutions, Sunni-Shi'i relations, the official terminology, state symbolism, foreign relations, and the changing balance between the party officials and the competing clerical elite remained unstudied. The classified internal documents of the regime, including the leader's audio recordings of his secret meetings, became available to researchers only in 2009, and since then they have been scrutinized very little from this angle.[30]

Ba'th Original Secularism and Its Collapse

Since the 1950s, little research has been carried out on the extraordinary depth of Ba'th secularism during the party's founding years, even though the open-source material was available to all. Likewise, little was known about the baffling degree of ambiguity of Ba'th secularism, or of the party's secular policies during the first fifteen or so years of Ba'th rule in Baghdad. Finally, nothing at all was written regarding the decision-making processes that guided the course of Islamization. Until the early 1980s, Saddam and his Ba'th regime were bent on creating the "New Arab Man": a secular, modern, and scientific Iraqi person for whom Islam would serve merely as historical inspiration. They imposed their approach on Iraqi culture, law, education, and media, helped by many like-minded non-Ba'thi intellectuals and artists—and then they capitulated. Not only did they abandon their efforts to change society, but they jumped, in a calculating and even cynical way, on the bandwagon of the public's growing religiosity. The party's defiantly secular "message" became officially "the Message of Islam."

The Ba'th surrender was the result of accumulating pressure over some two decades. The change was not complete, however. At a personal level, most of the Ba'th leadership seemed to have remained as secular as before. Indeed, in the 1990s party members complained that Baghdad was becoming Riyadh, seemingly mirroring Saudi Arabia in its Islamization efforts. This grumble was greatly exaggerated: Baghdad did not become Riyadh. And yet the party's public surrender was profound and indeed a "bargain" with society. Saddam's never was the all-powerful, all-consuming dictatorship that many believed it to be. State-society relations were not a one-way street. In the last analysis, the regime was influenced by what it considered to be the balance of power and conviction between itself and Iraqi society, mainly the Shi'i population.

The Baʿth Conversion and the Arab Spring

While a major historical development such as the Islamization of a secular party and regime is in itself of great interest, the questions this book addresses are not only of historical interest; they are also of great contemporary relevance in view of the evolution and aftermath of the Arab uprisings of 2011–13. After some of the dust had settled, in all the Arab states where the uprisings had rocked or changed the regimes, Islamic movements became more prominent, in some cases the most prominent. In Egypt and Tunisia, where the uprisings were most successful and democratic elections were held, Islamic parties scored the greatest wins. As of the time of writing, the summer of 2013–14, the jury is still out on Libya and Syria, but Islamic movements are quite prominent. In Jordan, the regime was not challenged with arms, but the strongest opposition has come from Islamic parties. As is evident from both the open-source material and the secret discussions between Saddam and his party luminaries, available as recordings in 2009, the Iraqi president was aware of a similar trend in Iraq and the Arab world long before the Arab uprisings of 2011–12.

In Saddam's Iraq there was no way that the *mukhabarat*—the national intelligence service or secret police—could discreetly report some Iraqis' negative views of the president. Any such explicitly negative view was punishable by imprisonment, even death. An agent simply could not gather such information without immediately arresting every offender or risking his own life for failing to do so.[31] However, as long as politically correct language was used, social reporting was adequate. Between 1980 and 1986, the president learned that the Iraqi people were returning to the mosque. Since those reports described to him a reality that he reviled, one must conclude that his *mukhabarat* did not try to sugarcoat the bitter pills, and told him what they truly believed to be happening in society. As a result, by the second half of the 1980s Saddam had already placed one foot on the Islamic bandwagon. Saddam was not oblivious to Shiʿi resentment, either. Even before his "return" to Islam, he offered the Iraqi people an integrative identity that included a Sunni-Shiʿi ecumenical component. His archrival, the Najaf-based Ayatollah Muhammad Baqir al-Sadr, whom Saddam had executed in 1980, had embarked on a similar ecumenical endeavor before his death. Both men failed. These competing identities are explored in subsequent chapters.

Methodology

This study proceeds as a historical study with an emphasis on the textual analysis of documents, but it also employs methods borrowed from other disciplines, such as anthropology and political science. If some sixty-five years of Ba'th existence and thirty-five years of Ba'th rule in Iraq may be said to constitute a *longue durée*, then this book is indeed concerned with a long stretch of the history of a major Arab political party and state. Where relevant, the discussion briefly looks back to earlier eras, to the history of the Ottoman Empire and the Hashimite monarchy. Most of the processes studied here occurred in slow motion, and only when they are seen through a long prism of time, beginning with the origins of the party in the 1940s, can they be identified and understood. With the end of Ba'th rule in Baghdad in 2003 and what looks like the twilight of Ba'th rule in Damascus, now seems an appropriate time to take stock of the history of this movement. This is particularly so when it comes to the apple of the Ba'th eye, secular Arabism, which in the second decade of the twenty-first century seems to be lying in ruins.

Historians typically try to answer the following sorts of questions: What happened? When and how did it happen? What were the motivating forces behind it? How are the facts of the matter connected? At the same time, the historian strives to craft an interpretation of the facts that is not arbitrary but the soundest one possible. Therefore, at the same time that this study endeavors to chart the *longue durée*, it also pays attention to facts and provides a detailed analysis of the political and cultural activity during each period, which we may characterize as the birth of the party, its first fifteen or so years in power in Iraq, the transitional years of the 1980s, and the era of Islamization that followed.

How and why the Ba'th regime and state-mosque relations changed during the years 1968–2003 is often veiled. Even the ways in which high-profile events influenced the regime often seem mysterious to this day. The regime's secret documents, recently made available at the Conflict Records Research Center in Washington, DC, provide much new information about the deliberations of the innermost power circles of the regime, but much more remains unknown. Analyzing how key events inexorably pushed the ruling party to abandon its cherished ideal of a secular Arabism came to resemble the work of astronomers identifying the existence of a planet from disturbances in the behavior of the sun it circles. The behavior of the sun—in this case, Saddam and his ruling regime—its movements, and changes in its light patterns provide indirect evidence of the existence of the planet. The changes in the public behavior of the regime during and after each crisis, or even when no crisis could be observed, provide evidence that those crises and developments pushed leader and regime in a certain direction. An example of an important change that came as a result of the unseen hand of society's attitude was the sudden disappearance of atheist treatises from Ba'thi intellectual magazines. Until 1975, many such studies were published, but then they vanished. Not until a decade later did Saddam offer even a cryptic explanation. Why was atheism struck from the intellectual magazines? This book reports the developments and, where there is no clear evidence regarding the causes of the change, it suggests some answers, based on the available information.

Chapter 1 analyzes the radically secular point of departure of the party's founders in the 1940s and 1950s. It also attempts to expose the intended equivocality of the party's ideology, which could simultaneously be interpreted as either straightforward atheism or fundamentalist Islamism. Chapter 2 describes the first one and a half decades of Ba'th rule in Baghdad. During this period, the party, making limited concessions to Islam, showed remarkable tenacity in keeping religion largely out of politics and even largely out of education, law, and culture. Chapter 3 analyzes the reasons for the estrangement between the Ba'th Party and the majority of the Shi'i community, an estrangement that went beyond anything seen in Iraq under the previous regimes. The chapter then surveys and analyzes the confrontations between the regime and the religious Shi'i circles between 1969 and 1980. Of special interest is the regime's little-known provocative intellectual and ideological response to those confrontations.

Chapter 4 describes the impact in Iraq of Ayatollah Ruhollah Khomeini's 1979 victory in Iran. The discussion analyzes the two crucial closed-door discussions of the Iraqi leadership that led to the Iran-Iraq War (1980–88). It tries to answer the questions, why did Iraq decide to go to war, and what role did religion play in this decision? The chapter also surveys and analyzes the war period and beyond: the regime's blade-running between secularism and religiosity during the 1980s and up to the Gulf War of 1991. Finally, the chapter investigates the causes of the tilt toward Islam and its manifestations.

Chapter 5 examines Saddam's decision making on the eve of the 1990 invasion and during the occupation of and retreat from Kuwait. It focuses on the apparent beginning of the Iraqi president's personal religious metamorphosis and how it was influenced by the momentous events of 1990–91. This chapter also discusses the Shi'i revolt of March 1991 against the Ba'th regime. As this revolt has already been discussed by a number of sources, its brief treatment here mainly adds social analysis. Finally, the regime's understanding of the revolt and the revolt's impact on regime-Shi'i relations, subjects still largely unexplored (and misunderstood) elsewhere in any significant way, are dealt with in detail. Much of the analysis in this chapter is based on the newly released secret documents of the Ba'th regime, combined with the regime's open-source material. Indeed, because misleading traps are an organic part of the internal Ba'thi sources, only by combining them with the regime's open sources can a researcher hope to understand Ba'thi Iraq. Part of this chapter, therefore, is concerned with casting light on the pitfalls that await those who rely exclusively or almost exclusively on internal regime sources.

Chapters 6 and 7 are dedicated to Saddam's 1993–2003 "faith campaign" and its results. This campaign was the culmination of the regime's conversion process. There is evidence in both publicly available and classified sources that Saddam probably personally became a born-again Muslim, though of a unique kind. What he initiated as a cynical strategy or bargain designed to win public support seems to have overtaken him on a personal level. The concluding chapter offers a few new insights: the limits to state "enticement and terrorizing" (*al-targhib wal-tarhib*); the dialectical impact of a successful mass recruitment to the party; Saddam, Stalin, and Hitler in the context of ideology change; and a postscript on the effect of the faith campaign on post-Ba'thi Iraq.

Interview Sources

Although the interviews represent a very small part of this book, they add depth and experiential value. Between Iraq's 1990 invasion of Kuwait and 2013 I was able to interview a fairly large number of knowledgeable Iraqis who had lived in Iraq under Ba'th Party rule. They included ex–Ba'th Party members, ex-regime journalists, Da'wa Party members and Supreme Assembly of the Islamic Revolution in Iraq (SAIRI) members, Communist Party members, academics, and others. Without exception, all the interviewees agreed to a conversation only on the condition of anonymity. As long as Iraq was under Ba'th rule, the interviewees' families could be harmed; after the demise of the Ba'th regime, any interview with an Israeli scholar was likely to draw the attention of the extremist Shi'i and Sunni militias alike. I respected their wishes. All the information from interviews quoted in this book, however, was cross-checked against other sources to verify its reliability, and facts that could not be corroborated from a second source were not included.

Notes on Arabic-English Transliteration and Usage

This book follows the convention of romanizing and using accepted Western spellings of Iraqi words in common use, such as madrasa, ayatollah, hijab, and fatwa. Ramadan and other major religious observances, such as 'Ashura, al-Arba'in, and 'Id al-Fitr, are also romanized. Arabic geographical names also generally appear in accepted Western spellings to aid in identification. Names for some clerical positions, such as 'ulama and khatib, are romanized analogous to the treatment of père or padre, as is the designation shari'a to indicate Islamic moral and religious laws. The body of religious writings known as the Hadith is not italicized, in keeping with the treatment of the Bible and the Qur'an; an individual *hadith* is italicized.

The spelling of personal names reflects the current academic practice of reproducing closely the name in the original language. This practice results, for example, in the use of Husayn as Saddam's family name (in fact, this is his father's name) throughout, of Asad instead of Assad, and of Mohammed Morsi as Muhammad Mursi.

Arabic transliteration is kept as simple and consistent as possible. Diacritical signs for long vowels and those differentiating between letters that sound similar to Western ears were eliminated, with one exception: in cases where a long *a* vowel is important. In such cases, this text uses a doubled *a*—for example, *Aal*, to differentiate between the word for "clan" and the definite article *al-*. Otherwise, both the long and short *a*, *u*, and *i* will appear as only one letter. Arabic letters that sound similar to Western ears (even though they sound very different to Arabic speakers) appear as one English letter to simplify the transliteration. The English letter *z* thus represents two different Arabic letters (*zayn* and *za*), as does the English combination *dh* (for the Arabic letters *dhal* and *dhad*). The same applies to the English letters *h* and *s*, which each represent two different Arabic letters (see the list following the glossary on page 413).

The guttural Arabic letter *'ayn* is transliterated as '. Except in a few cases, the Arabic letter *hamzah* will appear only in the middle of a word as '. The Arabic letter *ta marbutah*, which appears at the end of feminine words, does not appear at all (for example, *al-Thawra* instead of *al-Thawrah*). When the consonant *ya* has a doubling sign (*shadda*), it will appear as *yy* (as in *al-Jumhuriyya*).

The term "imam" has two different meanings. One is the leader of prayer in a mosque, in which case the term appears with a lowercase *i*. The other refers to one of the twelve historical holy leaders of the Twelver Shi'a, in which case the term appears with capital *I*. As Arabic has no capital letters, this distinction is unique to this English transliteration.

Chapter 1
A Radical Nationalist Movement Is Born

Romance, mystery, drama—this is the stuff of any nationalist salvation-drama. It is important, because it helps to teach us "who we are," to impart the sense of being a link in a chain which stretches back over the generations to bind us to our ancestors and our descendants. . . . It teaches us "where we are" and "who we should be," if we are to "recover ourselves." By conveying the atmosphere and drama of past epochs in the life of the community, we "re-live" the lives and times of our forbears and make ourselves part of "a community of fate."

—Anthony D. Smith, *The Ethnic Origins of Nations*

The Historical Setting

As defined by its historical sources, the Arab Ba'th (Resurrection) Party was born to breathe new life into the ancient Arab nation and redeem it by uniting all the Arab countries into a vast pan-Arab state and restoring the breathtaking glory of the Arab past. Its first and most important ideologue and founding father, Michel 'Aflaq, did indeed offer his young and enthusiastic disciples romance, mystery, and drama. He told them who they were, who they should be, and where should they lead their "community of fate," and they followed him with elation and adoration.

According to its founders, the party came into being in Damascus in 1940. In fact, political activity by the party's founders began a few years earlier. Still, it was only on April 7, 1947, that the party's First Pan-Arab (or National) Congress approved the Ba'th Constitution (*al-Dustur*). This date is the party's official anniversary, celebrated annually in Iraq until 2002: Ba'thi Baghdad fell on April 8, 2003, one day after the party's fifty-sixth anniversary. In Ba'thi Syria, too—where the party still holds power, however tenuously, as these lines are being written—the anniversary is celebrated on this date.

The 1920s, 1930s, and 1940s were years of tremendous intellectual fervor in the Arab world, and in particular among the Arabs of the Middle East. By the end of World War I, the Ottoman Empire was no more. Until then almost all Sunni Muslims—Turks, Arabs, Kurds, and others—saw the Ottoman sultan (*khalifa*) as a legitimate ruler, the protector of Islam. Provided that one mastered Turkish, the language of bureaucracy, one's ethnicity or mother tongue mattered little; religion was almost everything. When it came to religious minorities, the Ottoman Empire created mainly semiautonomous communities based on religion rather than on ethnicity or territory. When the empire crumbled, the sultan's Muslim Arab subjects were left without their traditional focus of political identity. The confusion increased when Kemal Atatürk abolished both the sultanate (in 1922) and the caliphate (in 1924) and, no less significantly, when he introduced his secular reforms in Turkey. Many remained attached to Islam as the cornerstone of their political identity. Some established Islamic political parties. Intellectuals such as Rashid Ridha (1865–1935) even developed the notion of a rejuvenated Arab caliphate.

Most political movements and elites, however, moved on. At first, they were led mostly by young Arab ex-Ottoman elites, who, much like Atatürk and his elite, had already been influenced by some European ideas, prominently secularism. Even though none of the elites went as far as Atatürk did in moving toward secularism, they were the people who formed the backbone of the new Arab regimes, the Iraqi and Jordanian monarchies and the Syrian republic. The Egyptian monarchy and its political parties, particularly the Wafd, were not much different. A large part of the younger, post-Ottoman generation of political activists was also essentially secular. The defeat of the Muslim sword represented to them the failure of Islam as a political rallying cry. They looked feverishly for a new identity that would promise dignity and a place under the international sun. Not surprisingly, most of the ideas they developed were adapted from the victorious European world. Even Germany, which had been defeated in the war, was considered an integral part of Europe. Learning from it made sense to those Arabs who dreamed of a vast, language-based state that would revive the glory of the Arab golden age. Some nationalist romantic flavor could not hurt, either. German post-Kantian national philosophers such as Johann Gottlieb Fichte (1762–1814) became particularly in vogue.[1] These young ex-Ottoman and later post-Ottoman elites sought to modernize their countries.

Pan-Arabism was not the only secular identity that was competing for hearts and minds. Some of the new politicians and movements followed the pattern of French patriotism, which was based mainly on the notion of the territorial homeland, *la patrie*. The most conspicuous among these movements was Antun Sa'ada's Syrian Social Nationalist Party. Established in 1932, the Syrian Social Nationalist Party envisioned a Syrian nation-state that would extend "historical" Syria from the Turkish border to the Sinai Peninsula and from the Mediterranean to the Euphrates. Sa'ada later extended the borders of "natural Syria" to include Cyprus and Iraq. A different approach was that of the Arab communist parties. As elsewhere in the world, the Arab communists accepted as legitimate for the foreseeable future the existing national borders, specifically those of the post-Ottoman states as delineated by the colonialist powers. Their political anti-Western and social struggle was to be pursued within the existing borders. To the Ba'th leadership, however, all these were dangerous concepts. From the late 1930s, when its two founders discussed a program for a political party, they had a far more ambitious vision. They found a source of inspiration in the idea of German nationalism that was eventually implemented by Otto von Bismarck. Rather than religious affinity or some geographic borders or landmarks defining a nation, for the Ba'thists the Arab language and culture were to provide the defining political identity and unifying force behind the new state. This meant essentially two things. First, the language defined the borders. If Arabism was the uniting force, then the united state was to extend over all the Arabic-speaking states and thus encompass the entirety of the huge land mass lying between the Persian Gulf and the Atlantic Ocean. This is a breathtaking expanse and a potentially huge source of power no less awe-inspiring than the defunct Ottoman Empire, except that the state's identity was to be grounded in the secular notion of language rather than in Islam. Second, the secular nature of such a state promised to guarantee complete equality among all Arabic speakers, be they Sunni Muslims, Shi'i Muslims, Christians of any denomination, Druze, 'Alawites—indeed, theoretically, even Arab Jews. The first proponent of this concept was the Arab senior ex-Ottoman official Sati' al-Husri. In the 1920s, under the wing of King Faysal I of Iraq, he developed this ideology and disseminated it through the Iraqi educational system. The Ba'th founders introduced some changes to al-Husri's theory, but it essentially remained attached to the main principle of a secular language-based nationalism.

Another banner raised by all the anti–status-quo political movements in the Arab Middle East after the demise of the Ottoman Empire was the anticolonialist struggle. No European colonial power could possibly gain a legitimacy that would come even close to that which had been enjoyed by the Ottoman sultan-khalifah. The European powers managed to find local collaborators among the ex-Ottoman elites, but the lack of legitimacy of the colonial powers contaminated the local ruling elites who collaborated with them. It was no wonder, then, that the young men who joined the various opposition political movements, whether Islamists, communists, Syrian nationalists, or pan-Arabs, were virulently anticolonialist, sometimes even anti-Western. The fledgling Ba'th Party was no exception.

One more historical development helps explain the secular worldview of the communists, the Syrian nationalists, and the pan-Arabists. Paradoxically, it was the largely secular educational system that was introduced in the 1920s by the hated European overlords and their local collaborators that influenced many high school and college students. Thus, even though they were quite fiercely anticolonialists, they nonetheless identified with many European-inspired values, most conspicuously secular nationalism.

A Radical Nationalist Movement Is Born

The main intellectual driving force behind the establishment of the party was a Damascus-born and Sorbonne-educated Greek Orthodox school-teacher named Michel 'Aflaq. His cofounder was another Sorbonne-educated Damascene, Salah al-Din al-Baytar, a Sunni Muslim. A significant contribution to the party's thinking was provided by yet another Sorbonne graduate, Zaki Arsuzi, an 'Alawite from Alexandretta, although he himself never joined 'Aflaq's Ba'th Party. In 1939, he established his own minuscule al-Hizb al-Qawmi al-'Arabi, the Arab National Party, and in 1940, he changed its name to al-Ba'th al-'Arabi, the Arab Resurrection. Many of his disciples eventually joined 'Aflaq's organization. At first the latter was called Harakat al-Ihya, the Movement of Revitalization, but in 1943 'Aflaq changed it to Harakat al-Ba'th al-'Arabi, the Arab Resurrection Movement. For decades, 'Aflaq and Arsuzi argued vehemently over who had come up first with both the name and the ideology of their respective parties, but in reality they influenced each other. There were some important ideological differences between them: 'Aflaq emphasized mainly Arab history, including Islam, as a source of inspiration, while Arsuzi avoided Islam altogether and, along with some mystical components, emphasized mainly the Arabic language as an expression of Arab identity and ingenuity. Their main political messages, however, were identical. They preached struggle against the French (and other European) rule and total commitment to the political unification of all the Arab lands. Once united, the Arab states and peoples (*shu'ub*) would cease to exist; all would melt and mix in a huge crucible, and a new, pan-Arab amalgam would come into being.

In 1953, 'Aflaq's Arab Ba'th Party in Syria merged with the antifeudalist Arab Socialist Party of Akram al-Hurani, a Hama-based Sunni Muslim, scion of a family of impoverished landowners and a seasoned politician. The union was named Hizb al-Ba'th al-'Arabi al-Ishtiraki, the Arab Ba'th Socialist Party. In 1942, 'Aflaq and Baytar had only twelve followers, apparently all of them their Damascus high school students, but during the 1940s the party managed to expand from Damascus to Lataqiya, Homs, Halab (Aleppo), and Banyas.[2] In the late 1940s it also established small branches in Iraq, Jordan, and Lebanon.[3] The membership now included some university students as well, and, with the unification with al-Hurani, some peasants in Hama. A few workers, too, joined the party, though it remained essentially a small movement and a city and town phenomenon, appealing mainly to middle-class and lower-middle-class young men, and a very small number of young women, who were educated in the secular state system of the French Mandate. In 1954, for the first time, a member of the party, the cofounder Salah al-Din al-Baytar, managed to be elected as a member of parliament. In 1958, the party was the main moving force behind the Syrian initiative to unite Syria with 'Abd al-Nasir's Egypt. In a moment of enthusiasm but also desperation as a result of fear of the growing influence of the Syrian Communist Party and of a possible Turkish military strike, the party accepted all the conditions presented by 'Abd al-Nasir. These conditions included dissolution of the party in Syria. It also implied recognition of Egyptian supremacy in the union, as 'Abd al-Nasir was to be the sole head of state. However, the party's leaders soon found themselves completely marginalized in the United Arab Republic by the Egyptian leader. The Syrian military officers, too, found themselves subordinate to their Egyptian parallels, and the Syrian economy became subservient to the Egyptian one. This was the beginning of antileadership sentiment among the younger generation of party members, mainly disgruntled army officers, who held 'Aflaq and Baytar responsible for the dissolution and the dire straits in which they found themselves. In September 1961, led by a combination of army officers and civilian politicians, Syria seceded from the United Arab Republic, to the consternation of the Egyptian president. Despite their frustration at the way the Egyptian leader had treated them, though, 'Aflaq and Baytar did not openly support the secession, even though they likely did not mourn, it either. Indeed, Baytar soon became the prime minister of the newly separated Syria, if not for long. Akram al-Hurani, the third point of the Ba'thi leadership triangle, supported the secession openly and vociferously and left the newly resurrected Resurrection (Ba'th) Party. The rift between the young officers, most of whom hailed from the rural 'Allawi and Druze communities, and the civilian (mostly urban) old guard surfaced in the party a few years later. This happened after the Ba'th came to power in Damascus in a March 1963 military coup d'état. One month earlier, in February 1963, the party had come to power in Baghdad, too, but was ousted from power by pro–'Abd al-Nasir army officers after nine months of rule.

Back in Ba'thi-controlled Damascus in March 1963, at first the party's old guard held considerable sway (Baytar became foreign minister), but gradually it found itself on the defensive. After a series of internal power struggles, partly explained in ideological terms as a confrontation between "leftist" officers and "right-wing" civilians, on February 23, 1966, the party's military officers executed a new coup d'état. Led by the colonels Salah Jadid and Hafiz al-Asad, and working in cooperation with other officers, such as Mustafa Talas (eventually to become Syria's minister of defense), and some "leftist" civilians, they ousted the old guard from power. 'Aflaq and Baytar were expelled from the party and from Syria. 'Aflaq spent the next few years in Lebanon and South America; Baytar in Lebanon and Paris.

In 1968, the party came to power in Baghdad for the second time, but, happily for 'Aflaq, this was the branch of the "rightist" party loyal to him. They were mostly civilians, mostly hailed from Sunni families, and were bitterly opposed to the "leftist" and essentially military and 'Alawite-supremacy Ba'thi regime ruling in Damascus. 'Aflaq was immediately invited to Baghdad. It took him more than two years to make up his mind: only as late as 1971 did he oblige.[4] The reasons for his hesitation to leave Beirut can only be guessed at: Baghdad is hot and humid in summer and wet and cold in winter, while Lebanon has one of the best climates in the Arab world. The political climate in Baghdad was equally uninviting: to entrench itself, the highly unpopular Ba'th regime there introduced a system of terror unprecedented even in Iraq. 'Aflaq must have realized that even though he would head the Baghdad-sponsored Pan-Arab (or National) Leadership (or Command, *al-qiyada al-qawmiyya*), his leadership would be purely symbolic, leaving all the decisions to the Iraqi "branch," the Regional Leadership (or Command, *al-qiyada al-qutriyya*). When he at long last arrived, he became known there as *al-Ab al-Mu'assis* (the

Founding Father). When addressed personally by the senior party officials, it was always as *ustadh*, meaning professor or teacher. Until his death in 1989, 'Aflaq enjoyed high status and lavish material perks in exchange for bestowing Ba'thi legitimacy on the party and leadership in Baghdad. During the first one-and-a-half decades or so of Ba'th rule, his stamp of approval was of great importance to the Baghdad-based Ba'th regime, mainly in its political struggle against Ba'thi Damascus and Nasirist Cairo. However, it was a rubber stamp. Even when crucial policies that clashed head-on with party doctrine were adopted, 'Aflaq had no way of protesting, let alone preventing their adoption. 'Aflaq's gift of legitimacy to Ba'thi Baghdad in its battle against pan-Arab secular regimes, though, did not come without a cost. In its struggle against Shi'i and Sunni Islamist circles, the Ba'th regime was embarrassed when the religious groups accused it of being led by a Christian "infidel" and "Crusader" who was also a "missionary" and an "agent" of Western colonialism.[5]

The largely 'Alawite-controlled Ba'th regime in Damascus for its part adopted the 'Alawite Zaki Arsuzi as its ideological inspiration and legitimizing authority. With very brief lulls, the bitter rivalry between the two Ba'th branches continued until 1998. As for 'Aflaq, as he must have guessed, throughout his Baghdad years he served as a pure figurehead, having no influence over the regime's decisions. If silence is evidence, since the early 1970s he was unhappy about the shift from egalitarian and amalgamative to hegemonic, Iraqi-centered and federative pan-Arabism. Likewise, he must have resented Saddam Husayn's search for particular Iraqi historical roots in the glory that was pre-Arab Mesopotamia. While he supported Iraq in its war against Iran in the 1980s, from the recorded secret discussion in which Saddam and his top advisers decided on reopening the dispute with Iran over the Shatt al-Arab, it seems that 'Aflaq was not consulted.[6] It is quite possible that he also resented the attack on Iran in September 1980, as it placed the Palestinian issue on the back burner. He spent his last years in a golden cage, unable to protect the party he had created from the gradual Islamization initiated by Saddam Husayn beginning in the second half of the 1980s.[7]

'Aflaq died in late June 1989. He was converted to Islam posthumously by his Iraqi disciples.[8] His colleague Baytar, while still supportive of the regime in Baghdad against its Damascus rival, relinquished political activity and settled in Paris. In 1980, he was assassinated there, most likely by agents of Damascus. As their young Ba'thi disciples ascended to supreme power in Iraq and Syria, the party's founding fathers ended their lives in despondency and tragedy.

The Foundation of Party Ideology: The Holy Trinity (Unity, Freedom, Socialism) and Beyond

Arab Unity (*al-wahda al-ʿarabiyya*)

At its inception in the 1940s, the Baʿth Party adopted a number of principles that, notwithstanding some significant modifications in the 1970s, remained staples of its doctrine in Iraq until well into the early 1990s. In varying degrees, these principles were soon incorporated into the theories of other pan-Arab movements, notably that of Egypt's Gamal ʿAbd al-Nasir. The party's most important principle was Arab national unity, which envisioned the unification of all the Arab states, *min al-muhit ila al-khalij*, from the Atlantic Ocean in the west to the Persian Gulf (or, in Baʿth vernacular, the Gulf of Basra) in the east, and from the Taurus Mountains in the north, separating Turkish and Arabic speakers, to the Indian Ocean in the south. All Arabic speakers represent "One nation with an eternal message" (*umma ʿarabiyya wahida dhat risala khalida*). In their huge united state, the Arabs would rise from their ashes and fulfill their worldwide secular "eternal message" of civilization and enlightenment (for what is meant by "secular," see below). ʿAflaq never discussed the message in more than the most general terms. This was only one of his deliberate ambiguities. In the Qurʾan, and in Arabic in general, *risala* is understood in the first place as God's Islamic Message, delivered to mankind through his *rasul*, the Messenger, the Prophet Muhammad.[9] ʿAflaq chose this term knowing well that many Muslim Arabs would mistake his for an Islamic Message. "One Arab nation" is similarly loaded with double meaning. *Umma* for a nation is based on the Qurʾan and appears there in different contexts, but the most important and memorable one is that of the Islamic nation. The Qurʾan says of the Muslims, "You are the best nation created for Mankind [*kuntum khayr umma ukhrijat lil-nas*]."[10] Indeed, even the expression "One [Islamic] nation" (*umma wahida*) appears there.[11] Could ʿAflaq, the well-read intellectual, possibly not have known that? Furthermore, in the 1940s and 1950s, most Muslim Arabs understood "Arab" as coextensive with "Muslim" or "Islamic." The Prophet was an Arab, the Qurʾan was given in Arabic, the Arabs were the first Muslims and those who carried the Message to the world, and they identified themselves with the Islamic Message or mission. To many, therefore, "one Arab nation" meant "one Muslim nation." ʿAflaq was most likely aware of this as well. His choice of terms could hardly have been accidental: he could have chosen "*shaʿb*" ("a people") or "*qawm*" ("a tribe" or "a nation"), both nonreligious designations, but he chose otherwise.

In his lectures, 'Aflaq never clearly defined what Arab nationalism was based on. He preferred vague formulas such as "love [for the nation] before anything else [*al-hubb qabla kull shay*]." This concept may have borrowed from that of agape promulgated in the teachings of Saint Augustine, the fourth-century bishop of Hippo, among other early Christian thinkers. Nevertheless, Arab nationalism was defined in the 1947 Constitution clearly in terms of the Arabic language, Arab culture, and history. Whether he meant it or not, 'Aflaq's insistence on love, or a requirement that a person feel a deep sense of belonging to the nation as a precondition, helped the party exclude Arabic-speaking Jews, as they were considered at least passive supporters of Zionism, a competing national movement.[12] Very little thought was given to the issue of other ethnolingual groups living in Arab countries as minorities, such as the Kurds or the Berbers. When referring to the Berbers, 'Aflaq accused imperialists of inciting them against the Arabs. In reality, he insisted, the Berbers were fully fledged Arabs, having lost all their original cultural characteristics:

> In the Arab West there is an element, called Berber. This element is amalgamated [*yamtaziju*] with the Arabs' total amalgamation. . . . [North Africa] from the Arab conquest to this very day has been one land, one religion, one culture and one language and one interest. . . . Therefore . . . the [Arab] land in its East and West has one name, one language and one nationalism.[13]

As for the Kurds, 'Aflaq similarly asked, "Why are the Kurds afraid . . . of Arabism?" His answer was the same: because of the policies of the British and the French. In reality, he claimed, the Kurds wanted the same things the Arabs did, liberation from social and foreign oppression. As long as they did not challenge the united Arab state they would be allowed to study their language, he promised.[14] In other words, if they demanded self-determination they would be crushed and forced to abandon their language and culture. In later years, when the party was in power in Iraq, the unresolved issue of the Kurdish minority and its political rights came to haunt it. As for the Shi'a of Iraq and Lebanon, the vast majority of whom spoke Arabic, there was no reason, at least in theory, why they should not fit well into the Ba'th national mold. Indeed, during the Ba'th Party's early years in Iraq, young Shi'i men occupied the most important leadership positions in the party. From 1968 on in Iraq, though, most Shi'is were alienated from the Ba'th regime, which failed to create an ambience of equal opportunity (see chapter 3).

Freedom (*huriyya*)

Another principle of the young party was freedom or liberty (*huriyya*), meaning chiefly a relentless struggle against Western imperialism or colonialism and its influence on the Arab world. This struggle entailed opposition to Western strategic pacts and to the local collaborative or *compere* classes, the feudalists (*al-iqta'*) and large capitalists. In the party's constitution and in the writings of party leaders such as Munif al-Razzaz, liberal parliamentary democracy too came under the rubric of "freedom."[15] Indeed, in an ideological sparring with Egypt's Gamal 'Abd al-Nasir in unity negotiations in the spring of 1963, Michel 'Aflaq emphasized the democracy aspect of "freedom," which, he argued, was absent in Egypt yet present in Ba'th tradition. And yet the Ba'th constitution also makes it clear that no political platform other than pan-Arabism and no political organization other than pan-Arab ones would be allowed. This non-democratic principle was later used to legitimize Ba'th dictatorship. In its name, the regime harshly coerced communists, Islamists, liberals, and even Ba'th Party luminaries who challenged the stronger party faction led by President Bakr and his deputy, Saddam, and later by Saddam himself.

Socialism (*ishtirakiyya*)

A further principle was a mild form of socialism, combining both Fabian and etatist influences. Up to the early 1960s, however, socialism was perceived merely as an expediency, designed to draw the deprived social classes into the camp of Arab unity. At the Sixth Pan-Arab (National) Congress in October 1963, when the party was already in power in Syria and Iraq, it placed socialism on a level equal to unity. It also adopted a quasi-Marxist terminology, using expressions such as "class struggle" and "popular democracy." Indeed, the Soviet political system, a dictatorship of one party claiming to represent the interests of the "laboring masses," appealed to the young, radical party members. From that moment the principle of liberal parliamentary democracy, however ambivalently articulated in the party's 1947 Constitution, became identified with social exploitation, a petty bourgeois mentality, and Western imperialism.

Fascism and Nazism as Remote Inspirations

An influence on the nascent party that deserves mention was a combination of Sufi, fascist, and Nazi sentiments. No trace of that can be found in official party ideology, but it appears in personal memoirs. According to Sami al-Jundi, one of the party's founders, such sentiments were very real and potent among the young members, but they also could be gleaned from the intellectual interests of at least Michel 'Aflaq himself.[16] Fascist influences can be detected in al-Jundi's account of his days in Zaki Arsuzi's party, al-Hizb al-Qawmi al-'Arabi. The party believed in the principle that "the Arabs have one sole leader [za'im], who expresses the potentialities of the Arab nation as a whole, represents them and expresses them in the best way." Arsuzi's disciples explained these ideas in terms of traditional Sufi values. Al-Jundi tells us that Arsuzi bestowed on the leadership "a Sufi meaning, influenced by his 'Alawi upbringing." The leader is not only a politician, he is also "the summit of the virtues of the nation," expressing all its energies and potential for heroic and spiritual contributions. As al-Jundi saw it, this leader's image was a secular modern form of Imam al-Zaman, the Shi'i Imam Mahdi, the Expected Imam who would be revealed at the end of time to save humanity "because he is the political and religious ruler. The leader is the creator of ideas and state." It may be suggested that Arsuzi saw himself, if not as the incarnation of the Shi'i Imam Mahdi, then at least as a Sufi shaykh in whom his followers recognized a divine and superhuman leader. Some medieval Shi'i and Sufi influences are indeed there, but in the same place al-Jundi also disclosed that during the early 1940s the party was influenced by "Nazism and fascism," which could easily mean that the attachment to the idea of a sole and omniscient leader was not based exclusively on Sufi and 'Allawi concepts. The secular worldview of the Ba'th may also serve as indication that the source of inspiration was at least in part a contemporary European one.

Al-Jundi describes a meeting that took place in Damascus on November 29, 1940, at which Zaki Arsuzi spoke to a gathering of members of his party about democracy, communism, and Nazism. "He started with Descartes and ended with [Houston Stewart] Chamberlain," the ferociously anti-Jewish, proto-Nazi author of *The Foundations of the Nineteenth Century*. Describing the atmosphere among the young men who joined the party that, by late 1940, was already called *Hizb al-Ba'th al-'Arabi*, al-Jundi wrote:

We were racists ['irqiyyin], enthusiastic about Nazism. We were reading its books and intellectual sources, and especially [Friedrich] Nietzsche's *Thus Spoke Zarathustra* (his least understood, most enigmatic work), [Johann Gottlieb] Fichte's *Lectures to the German Nation* and Chamberlain's *Foundations of the 19th Century* . . . and we were the first ones to contemplate the translation [into Arabic] of [Adolf Hitler's] *Mein Kampf.* He who lived during that period [the years of World War II] in Damascus could appreciate the inclination of the Arab people towards Nazism. . . .The defeated one loves the victorious one . . . even though we were a different trend [or school, *madhhab*].[17]

Al-Jundi also reports that the youth of the Ba'th Party were looking for Alfred Rosenberg's *The Myth of the Twentieth Century*, a vitriolic anti-Jewish and racist "Nordic" Nazi manifesto that, among other themes, also popularized *The Protocols of the Elders of Zion.* They could find only a French version of the book, in the library of Michel 'Aflaq, who in turn had borrowed it from one of his students.[18] Although many anti-Semitic articles and books appeared both in Ba'thi Iraq and in Ba'thi Syria,[19] and anti-Semitic comments appeared often during the 1980s in the secret documents and recordings of the Iraqi party leadership,[20] no such references appeared in 'Aflaq's lectures and writings or in the party's 1947 Constitution. At the same time, however, other party documents from the 1940s did contain anti-Jewish texts.[21]

The Foundation of Party Ideology: Secularism and What Lies Beneath

Although it was not included in the Ba'th Party trinity of unity, freedom, and socialism, yet another tenet of party faith was the separation of religion from politics: secularism (*al-'ilmaniyya*). In a Muslim country, this notion came naturally to a Christian intellectual such as 'Aflaq and his Druze and 'Alawite disciples, but less naturally to the Muslim masses. And yet confining Islam to the mosque did appeal to secular-minded Muslim high school and university students and young Damascene intellectuals who were educated in the French-inspired secular government schools. Even the older generation of Iraqi politicians, people like Nuri al-Sa'id, Taha and Yasin al-Hashimi, Jamil al-Midfa'i, Prince Faysal, and their Syrian counterparts, all of them post-Ottoman officers, officials, and princes, were inclined in the same direction as a result of their connection to the Ottoman reformers. Some of 'Aflaq's and Arsuzi's disciples were influenced by Western thinkers such as the French philosopher Ernest M. Renan, who regarded Islam as an impediment to progress. When Mustafa Kemal Atatürk abolished the caliphate and separated mosque from state, this served as inspiration to many Arab politicians. However, unlike the communists and members of Antun Sa'ada's Syrian Social Nationalist Party, who turned to atheism, both the ex-Ottoman politicians and the younger generation of Western-educated Arabs avoided a rift with the more traditional masses by paying lip service to Islam and religious faith in general while striving simultaneously to defuse Islam as a political and even social force. The principle of separation of mosque and state had promising potential in the Iraqi context, as it could ease the integration of secularly minded Shi'is as well as Christian Arabs into the political system. The party therefore adopted Western-style secular nationalism and fused it with an ambition for national grandeur, virulent anti-imperialism, and moderate socialism. The potency of this amalgam was illustrated in the early 1960s when the party came to power in Baghdad and Damascus and became a force to be reckoned with in Jordan and Lebanon.

Between Secularism and Faux Islamism

With respect to state-mosque relations, the legacy of Michel 'Aflaq, the Christian-born founder of the Ba'th, was profoundly ambivalent. At one extreme end of the lectures that he delivered in the coffee shops and cultural clubs of Damascus and Beirut in the 1940s and 1950s, he demonstrated staunch secularism. Occasionally it even came with hints of atheism. At the other extreme, however, his lectures created the illusion of a deep Islamic religiosity. Coming from a Christian, this was a baffling message. Yet this bizarre ideological cocktail, rather than baffling the party avant-garde, was fully understood by most of them and served the fledgling party well. There were two ways that the party's hard core understood this message. Many, probably most, understood that the Islamic piety implied by the founder was a kind of *taqiyya*, or precautionary dissimulation, meant to deceive the public into thinking that the Ba'th was a traditional party that embraced Islam. Sami al-Jundi and Saddam Husayn belonged to this category. Others, the more traditional members, saw this kind of ambivalence as a comforting assurance that the party was not atheistic and was even somehow part of the culture of Islam.[22] This is the only way to understand how a fairly religious youth like 'Izzat Ibrahim al-Duri could join the party in 1959 at age seventeen. He was attracted by the party's young and ultra-activist image and by its exciting pan-Arab vision, and he needed assurance that the party was somehow religious. He remained religious throughout his career. 'Izzat Ibrahim, though, was an exception. Most members were strictly secular: they did not pray regularly, they rarely attended the mosque, and many consumed alcoholic drinks. For many years, when it was in opposition, the party's blatant secularism, let alone atheism, avoided detection and, therefore, much criticism, hostility, and even persecution. That way it could operate without creating too much allergic reaction in the body of Islamic societies. The party could even hope to—and did—attract to its outer circumference traditional people who did not suspect its true nature. Over time, at least some of them could be gradually converted.

What made this possible was that the party was constructed from its early days in concentric circles, with a clear hierarchy extending across four levels or ranks, starting with three lower levels of "supporters" and ending with the top tier of "full" or "active" members. Full members were in no doubt that their leader had created a secular party. If any of them had any doubt about it in the first years, it was dispelled by the 1947 Constitution. The Constitution was read and discussed extensively by the hard core but attracted relatively little attention from the rank and file, certainly far less attention than did the founding leader's inspiring rhetoric.

The ambiguity in mosque-state relations extended to the other main slogan of the party, "One Arab nation with an eternal message." To the majority of Muslim Arabs, *al-risala* (the message) sounded like the Message of Islam, brought by the Messenger of God (*rasul allah*) Muhammad. To the initiated Ba'this, it sounded not only secular—being language-based rather than religion-based nationalism—but also like a challenge to Islam. If the sacred term *umma* is now attached to European-style nationalism, this means that behind it lurks an intention not just to secularize a religious term but to take Islam's place as the force that motivates and unites the Arabs. Most Muslim Arabs, even though they were aware of the existence of Christian Arabs and of non-Arab Muslims, still closely identified Arabism with Islam. Some did not even consider the Arab Christians to be full-fledged Arabs. Indeed, Michel 'Aflaq himself made it clear that, to be full-fledged Arabs, Christians had to admire the Prophet and Islam, owing to Islam's "important role in shaping Arab history and Arab nationalism."[23] Even more emphatically, he insisted that "the connection between Islam and Arabism is unlike that of any religion to any nationalism." In this he ignored at least three national groups, Jews, Armenians, and Hindus, but he never claimed the mantle of an uninvolved historian. "The Christian Arabs will know, when their nationalism is fully awakened within them," he promised, "that Islam to them is national culture and it is necessary for them to be immersed in it, and they should cherish Islam as the most precious thing in their Arabism." And while he admitted that "the situation at present is far from this belief," he made a far-reaching demand on "the new generation of Christian Arabs." They must "achieve it . . . and sacrifice for it."[24] This insistence on the duty of Christian Arabs to worship Islam, designed apparently to find grace in the eyes of the Muslim majority, could easily be understood as a call for conversion to Islam. In the same lecture, 'Aflaq emphasized that the Ba'th movement was against atheism (*al-ilhad*). As emerged from interviews with an Iraqi Shi'i al-Da'wa activist,[25] in the early 1960s they believed that 'Aflaq himself actually converted to Islam and that, unlike the Communist Party, the Ba'th was indeed a religious party. Though some other religious minorities, such as Druze and 'Alawites, joined the party en masse, Christians did not. They feared that with pan-Arabism, Islam would creep in no matter what 'Aflaq's real intention was, and his lavish lip service to Islam and the Prophet scared them.

There was also a diametrically opposed aspect of 'Aflaq's approach to religion that became apparent when he stressed that Islam should be admired as a mere spiritual movement rather than as a set of religious duties. Those who listened to him carefully had to conclude that the special place of Islam in 'Aflaq's thinking was strictly as a part of history. Whether or not 'Aflaq was a religious person, the religiosity he offered to his disciples, most of whom were young secular Muslims (that is, born to Muslim families), was ethereal, theoretical, and devoid of any concrete substance:

> Maybe we [Ba'this] are not seen praying with the ones who pray, or fasting with the ones who fast, but we believe in God because we are in dire need and painful yearning for Him: our burden is heavy, our road arduous, and our destination is far away.[26]

In Islam, fulfilling one's duties to God (*al-'ibadat*) and to society (*al-mu'amalat*) is the most important aspect of religion. The Five Pillars of Islam—saying the *shahada*, praying, observing the Ramadan fast, carrying out the pilgrimage (*haj*) to Mecca, and paying the religious tax (*zakat*)—are practical "thou shalt do" instructions. Believers must "order what is a duty [*al-amr bil-ma'ruf*]," and the five duties therefore are the individual duty (*fardh 'ayn*) of every believer. Another practical duty is "forbidding what is forbidden [*al-nahi 'an al-munkar*]," that is, avoiding and preventing certain practices such as consuming alcohol, eating pork, using hallucinatory and similar drugs, and gambling. A Muslim who does not practice—does not pray, does not fast during the month of Ramadan, or consumes alcohol—is regarded by most as a bad

Muslim or even as a nonbeliever. An important component in Islam is the public sphere: every Muslim must be *seen* by his or her peers as fulfilling "what is a duty" and must not be seen as performing "the forbidden." This is how Islamic communities function. To suggest that the members of the movement perhaps neither fast nor pray or frequent the mosque is to suggest that perhaps they are not practicing Muslims at all. 'Aflaq's young secular Muslim disciples, however, were thrilled about all this. It rendered the Islamic clergy, whom they despised, unnecessary; it freed them from the duties of a religious Muslim and from what they saw as an oppressive and depressing belief in an omnipresent, demanding, and ferocious God.[27] At the same time, it created around them an aura of Islamic spirituality without forcing them into a mold of exhausting practices they considered tedious and passé. Furthermore, 'Aflaq's admiration for Islamic Arab history—which was different from practicing the religion—legitimized their deep emotional attachment to that history. The glory that was the Arab Islamic golden age and its heroes—the Prophet; the four Rightly Guided Caliphs; the remarkable military commanders of early Islam, such as Khalid bin al-Walid, 'Amr bin al-'As, al-Qa'qaa, and al-Muthanna bin al-Haritha; the breathtaking 'Abbasid Empire; and the magnificent victories of Salah al-Din al-Ayyubi (Saladin) over the hated Crusaders—represented an integral part of their identity. Saddam Husayn, his party comrades, and his army generals, all of them representing this generation of secular pan-Arabs and Ba'this, may serve as typical examples. To justify his policies, Saddam often leaned against the practices of early Islamic heroes. In the most important moment of his career to that point, after he had executed hundreds of senior party members and military officers whom he accused of collaboration with Syria against him, Saddam used various examples from the history of early Islam to demonstrate that even the greatest were on occasion faced with betrayal. Some of the *Sahaba*, the Prophet's closest companions, betrayed Muhammad before he entered Mecca. Others supported the People of Apostacy (*Ahl al-Ridda*) in their revolt against Caliph Abu Bakr, and yet others supported Mu'awiya against the (legitimate) Caliph 'Ali, even though "Imam Ali carried all the meanings of honor and the spirit of the Islamic Message," while Mu'awiya "fought for the needs of this world." Saddam's point was that like those great historical Muslims, he too was faced with betrayal coming from very senior and close colleagues, while the masses remained supportive of him, as was the case with the Prophet and his successors.[28]

In private discussions, too, Saddam often compared his and Iraq's experiences to the Prophet's and early Muslim events and military exploits. For example, in a typical private discussion with his military commanders during the early phase of the Iran-Iraq War—that is, in his most secular period, when he was very close to atheism—he and the officers compared their war against Iran with the battles of early Islam. This particular discussion created the impression that Saddam actually was living at the same time in seventh-century Arabia and twentieth-century Iraq. He became very emotional when discussing with his General Staff the unfortunate end of the career of Khalid bin al-Walid and the death of great heroes: "I am miserable and feel pain," he said with great emotion, "because of the [unjust] removal of Khalid from command and the martyrdom of Hamza" (the Prophet's uncle, who died in 627 during the battle of Uhud and earned the title *asad allah wa rasulihi*, "the Lion of God and of His Messenger"). The discussion with his senior military officers is detailed, and officers relate also to other early Islamic military heroes such as 'Umar (the second caliph), 'Amr bin al-'As, and others.[29] Saddam's voice betrays great emotion, and the recording is very convincing: he truly grieved Khalid's tragedy. Both Saddam's propaganda machine and the internal party guidelines often presented him as a latter-day Saladin.[30] This powerful identity component was given full support by 'Aflaq, at the expense of religious duties and the role of religion in the running of the state.

'Aflaq was very clear when he described his vision for the future united Arab state. As he visualized it, it would "treat equally all its citizens and respect their religious freedom" because the Ba'th "looks at the various religions as equal, respecting and revering them equally." "Islam," he told his disciples, will be "equal to other religions in the [future united] Arab state." This clearly excluded the possibility that the state would declare any religion the official one. However, as discussed in chapter 2, when his disciples came to power in Iraq in 1968 they did declare Islam the official religion of the state. As 'Aflaq described it, the secularization of the state would "free religion from [the influence of] political circumstances" and enable it to flourish and exert a positive moral influence on people.[31] This argument for separating state and mosque, whatever its virtue, is totally alien to Islam. When discussing the values that should inspire the citizens of the future united Arab state, 'Aflaq was again clear:

The State . . . will be established on a social foundation, being Arab nationalism, and a moral foundation being freedom. . . . The secular nature of the State [*'ilmaniyyat al-dawla*] . . . is nothing but a striving to preserve the spiritual and moral orientation [of religion]. . . . [This is] a condition among the conditions of the resurrection [*Ba'th*] of the nation.[32]

In March 1968, Shibli al-ʿAysami went one step further. ʿAysami was a longtime Druze colleague of ʿAflaq and from late 1968 a member of the Baghdad-based Pan-Arab (National) Leadership of the party. He published in Beirut a book that was republished a few times during the 1970s by a pro-Iraqi publishing house. In the book he attacked the Islamists of his time (such as the Muslim Brotherhood) head-on for obstructing the course of the Arab revolution. Those "intellectual circles," he argued, believed that "the reason for all the inflictions and retardation [of the Arabs] is the lack of adherence to the traditions of the past [read: Islam] and that the road to salvation and resurrection is to be found in a return to the by-gone heritage [*al-turath al-ghabir*]." ʿAysami accused such "counterrevolutionary forces" of being "petrified and zealous," spreading "mythological" ideas, and in this way helping to keep Arab society in a state of intellectual and social retardation.[33] For a Druze it was relatively easy to attack the Islamists, but the sentiment was shared by his Muslim colleagues.

The party's founding constitution was even more coherently secular than ʿAflaq. Islam is not mentioned explicitly even once in the whole text. Where there is an oblique reference to Islam it is in a negative way, where the constitution attacks religious practices that prevent the unity of all the speakers of Arabic:

> The pan-Arab bond [*al-rabita al-qawmiyya*] is the only bond existing in the Arab state . . . which struggles against all other loyalties, [against] religious schools' fanaticism (or bigotry), [against] religious sectarianism [*al-ʿasabiyyat al-madhhabiyya wal-taʾifiyya*].[34]

In other words, the Baʿth constitution warns against Islamic extremism of all kinds, Sunni and Shiʿi alike, in Arab society, but has not one word suggesting a positive role for religion.

Grassroots Ambivalence, Confusion, and Secularism

When describing Grand Ayatollah Muhsin al-Hakim in his memoirs, the Shiʿi Hani al-Fukayki, who was one of the first members of the party, characterized him and the Shiʿi Najaf University (*al-hawza*) as "conservative right-wing forces whose goals clash with the party's way and policies."[35] While the young Baʿthis of the 1940s, 1950s, and 1960s had a high-school-level knowledge of Islamic history, its military commanders, military exploits, and great scientists, philosophers, and poets, most of them had very little knowledge of Islam.[36] The information the Sunni members had about the Shi'a was almost nonexistent. The Shi'i members were far more knowledgeable and, unlike their Sunni colleagues, some of them even participated actively in important religious occasions such as the 'Ashura. And yet they too were looking for something beyond religion.[37] As explained by Fukayki, it was not acceptable to criticize those religious ceremonies or to judge the cultural and social traditions that went with them, but only for purely tactical reasons: it was seen as attacking things considered holy. "We, the leadership of the party, avoided any confrontation with the traditions and the culture [read: the Shi'i rites] of the eras of tyranny, fearing that this would prevent the spread of our party." During the party's formative years its leadership believed that "changing the ruling regime will solve all the problems and that colonialism and imperialism are the reason for our backwardness," including such religious practices as self-flagellation.[38] In other words, the party leaders believed that once monarchy was replaced by the Ba'th revolutionary rule, Islam with its old rites and clerics would disappear. Colonialism and its collaborative corrupt Arab elites, they believed, were the only forces that breathed life into the religion of clerics' authority and "thou shalt do." Saddam himself occasionally gave vent to his hatred for the "men of religion," whom he was usually careful not to call 'ulama, because this title implied scientific knowledge.

Despite its tactical maneuvers designed to deceive the masses and even some of its own members into thinking that the party was religious, the party was indeed secular. Its leaders saw themselves and their secular message as replacing the Messenger and his Message. At the same time they also admired the Messenger and saw themselves as continuing his Message in their own way. As Fukayki described it, the young Ba'this saw themselves as "little prophets," redeeming the Arab nation in the modern age. This filled them with great elation and enthusiasm, as they felt they were following in the footsteps of the Prophet. At the same time, however, theirs was a secular nationalist faith and movement.[39] This kind of ambiguity, even intended confusion, made it possible for many members to feel at the same time modern, secular, and revolutionary and also spiritually Muslim believers. Some were closer to the secular or even atheistic pole, others were closer to the Islamic pole. Most were in the middle.

That 'Aflaq was a Christian did not make it easy for the party to recruit young Muslim men. "Michel 'Aflaq being a Christian stopped many and was used against the party in the conservative circles," remembered Fukayki.[40] And yet the young Muslim men who did join the party knew why: they rejected Islam as a religion, and ʿAflaq accepted it as history. The Iraqi branch of the party remained loyal to its founder until the day he died in 1989. This was the ultimate litmus test: only secular youth could possibly join a party that was established and led by a Christian. Only secular young people could remain loyal to a party that was continuously and vociferously accused by the Islamists of heresy, atheism, and service to Christian missionaries and to the Christian imperialists.

Early Baʿth "Sufism" and Implied Atheism

Reflecting on the early years of the Baʿth Party, Sami al-Jundi, one of ʿAflaq's young disciples who later became prominent in the party, wrote:

> We were living in this hope [of the establishment of Arab unity], alien to our society . . . revolting against all the old values. . . . We were atheists regarding all the ceremonies, relations and religions, looking for battle in every place . . . society oppressed us so we challenged it. . . . We were accused of atheism [*al-ilhad*], and this was true, too, despite all that the Baʿthis later claimed apologetically. We believed in the religious *feeling*, in the Sufism [mysticism] of the religions, and in their total human striving, and as for the religion of others, we were against it.[41]

Some of ʿAflaq's lectures of the 1940s and 1950s are masterpieces of equivocation and deception, masquerading blatant atheism. They include even a call to replace Islam and the Prophet with the modern message and leadership of the Baʿth Party. Had it been understood for what it really was, the party would have been declared blasphemous and the lives of its members would have been in great danger. This is precisely why the essence of the message was disguised so brilliantly, to be fully understood only by the initiated. The party's founding Constitution of April 1947 calls on the members to "return to the [Arab] nation its link with its glorious past."[42] On the face of it both expressions could be seen as a call to the Baʿth youth to become Salafis by imitating the Prophet and his way of life. But this was the precise opposite of what was intended, and here too the party's avant-garde understood it well. At the end of the above-mentioned sentence in the Constitution, the leadership provides a deciphering key for the perplexed: the Constitution appeals to party members "to aspire to a future [even] more glorious and exemplary [*amjad wa amthal*]" than the Arabs had ever achieved.[43]

To a religious Sunni Muslim, such a call is sheer blasphemy. According to the orthodox Islamic Sunni viewpoint, the Prophetic era (and often also the era when the four Rightly Guided Caliphs who followed him ruled over the Islamic community) represents absolute perfection. This is therefore the absolute peak that humans can aspire to. The very best a Muslim can do is endeavor to return to those days and ways. Thus, in the eyes of religious Muslims, a promise to surpass the Prophet's era is sacrilege. In one of his speeches 'Aflaq went even further, demanding that his followers "recognize the past," meaning the Prophet's days, "without [however] considering it perfect." The "past" to 'Aflaq was merely a "phase that cannot be returned to, though it can influence. . . . It is our duty to transcend it."[44] In the eyes of Sunni Islam, again, any claim that one can surpass the Prophet's legacy is blasphemy. In Shi'i eyes, the Prophet was not perfect because, among other omissions, he failed to insist that Imam 'Ali, his paternal cousin and son-in-law, was his legitimate replacement. Likewise, Shi'a Islam believes that 'Ali and the ten Imams who followed him had much work to do to complete missing links after the Prophet's death. The twelfth Imam is expected to return by the end of days and complete the work. However, Shi'is too believe that the "past"—namely, the combined teachings of the Prophet and the eleven Imams—were indeed perfection incarnate, to be crowned only by the twelfth, the Imam Mahdi.

The founding 1947 Constitution introduces yet another concept in this respect that is clearly meant to mislead the uninitiated. "The Arab [rather than Islamic] nation is carrying out an *eternal mission* [*risala khalida*] which appears in [ever]-renewed and accomplished forms in the [various] historical phases."[45] As was pointed out earlier, the "eternal mission" was interpreted by many outsiders as simply Islam, because the Prophet is also called *rasul allah*, "God's Messenger," but the Constitution meant something very different: Islam is only one message among many, all of them equally important, that the Arabs have carried to humanity since remote antiquity. To decipher the Constitution's code, one must return to 'Aflaq. In 1946, one year before the Constitution was formulated, he suggested that it was the Arab nation (rather than God) that "expressed itself . . . in . . . Muhammad's religion," in the same way that it had expressed itself before in "the enactment of Hammurabi, in *Jahili* [pre-Islamic Arab] poetry . . . and in the culture [and science] of [Caliph] al-Ma'mun's era."[46] To 'Aflaq, then, Islam was only like froth on the waves, floating above the miles-deep ocean of a far more ancient and glorious Arab history. 'Aflaq did not worry too much about the fact that Hammurabi was a Babylonian, not an Arab. Worse still, to devout Muslims the history of the pre-Islamic era (*Jahiliyya*) is anathema, as it represents barbarity, ignorance, and idolatry. To a traditional Muslim, equating "Muhammad's religion"—God is somehow missing here—with the lawmaking of a heathen king like Hammurabi or with the poetry of *Jahili* idol worshippers is profanity. In the same vein, in another of his lectures, while assuring his listeners that "there is no fear that Arab nationalism will clash with religion" because both were the result of Allah's will (but so, one could argue, is Marxism), 'Aflaq also said that "religion [read: Islam] represents the ingenuity of Arab nationalism."[47] In other words, Islam's greatness is the result of Arab, rather than God's, greatness.

'Aflaq further implied that he and his disciples, the Ba'th avant-garde, were as great as the Prophet and his supporters, the *Sahaba*, and that they, the Ba'th, were the only true incarnation of Arab ingenuity in the modern age. In other words, to him Islam was no longer needed as a social-political-ideological force. In fact, as such in the twentieth century it was playing a negative role. However, the way 'Aflaq broke this news to the public was designed to confuse the outsider, whereas the party members easily saw through his equivocations. In one of the earliest lectures he ever recorded, 'Aflaq exclaimed, "Muhammad was all the Arabs, so let all the Arabs today be Muhammad," and "the young generation today represents the same thing that Islam did in its heyday."[48] In the same lecture, he elaborated:

> Islam was born out of suffering, the suffering of Arabism. This suffering has returned to the lands of the Arabs so deep and hard that the Arabs of the *Jahiliyya* never knew. What is more appropriate than that a purifying and reconstructing revolution would be resurrected [*tub'athu*] within us today, like the one whose banner Islam carried. . . . We [Ba'this] are the new Arab generation.[49]

While a student at the Sorbonne, 'Aflaq was close to the French Communist Party and was well acquainted with Vladimir Lenin's teachings. Back in Syria, he often harped on Leninist pathfinding or pioneering "professional revolutionaries," except that he never mentioned Lenin. Like the Prophet's close supporters, he told his followers, the Ba'th youth too dedicated their whole lives to the party's political struggle, and they too were sure to be victorious. Like their predecessors at the dawn of Islam, who were "small in numbers," the Ba'this too were a small, chosen elite who had "invisible troops" fighting on their side: "the true interests of the Arab nation."[50]

What does it all mean? It could be construed as the traditional expectation from every Muslim to imitate the Prophet's practices. A listener unacquainted with 'Aflaq's background could easily be misled, as indeed many were, to think that the charismatic ideologue was urging his disciples to purify Islam and resurrect it. But these calls can equally be seen as a claim that the party was coming up with an entirely new message, thus replacing the Prophet and the Qur'an and taking on the same role of uniting and leading the Arabs that the Prophet did in the seventh century. That the latter is the correct interpretation is evident from a few more of 'Aflaq's thoughts. In 1946, for example, he advised his disciples:

> In the past, religion expressed the Arab Message [Mission, *risala*], which was based on human principles. Does that mean that that Message [Mission] cannot be [secular] nationalist-pan-Arab? . . . And is the Message [Mission] something that ends at a certain time, or is it something that is being renewed and perfected [*tatajaddad wa tataka-mal*] with life?[51]

This is an amazingly bold assertion: it means that today, the Arab mission (or message) is not religion but rather secular nationalism, because in the modern age Islam has lost its political relevance. Again, in Muslim eyes this is sacrilege: Islam regards the Prophet as *khatim* (or *khatm*) *al-anbiya*, the Seal of the Prophets. To declare that Muhammad's Message was not the last one, as well as to insist that the Prophet's Message, namely, God's word, is anything but perfect and that it should be "perfected," is unacceptable to any traditional Sunni Muslim. The case of a young political officer in the Syrian military under the Ba'th regimes may serve as an indication that 'Aflaq's mission (or message) was clear to the initiated. In 1967, Lieutenant Ibrahim Khalas published an article in the army's journal in which he announced that the party would "create the New Arab Man." If creating a man were not atheistic enough, the young intellectual officer added that "the new socialist revolutionary Man . . . believes in man and man only." This New Man "[believes] that God, the religions, feudalism, imperialism, the fat cats and all the values that dominated the former society are nothing but mummies embalmed in the museum of history."[52] Before it appeared in print, the article had to go through rigorous censorship, and indeed the military did not see any problem with it until Syria saw mass demonstrations against it. The regime immediately sacked the officer. Rumor had it that he was executed.

To sum up, there is little doubt that in 'Aflaq's thinking, state and mosque were to be completely separated, and the "eternal message [mission]" that was to guide the future of the united Arab state was secular Arab nationalism. 'Aflaq even implied that he did not believe in the existence of God. And yet his insistence that the party was against atheism, the lavish tribute to Islam, even if only as part of Arab history and memory, and to the Prophet, even though he carefully defined him as "Arab" rather than as the Muslim Messenger, left a wake of ideological ambiguity. The very fact that a secular, let alone a Christian, ideologue ceaselessly equated the inception of his movement with the dawn of Islam and himself and his party members with the Prophet and his first supporters created deliberate confusion. The hard core of party activists understood well his coded message, but the Arab masses did not. This way the party not only avoided public criticism, but even had a chance of attracting the traditional masses, who gullibly believed it was a religious party. This left the party a safety hatch through which in Iraq—but not in Syria—it eventually escaped from its increasingly unpopular secularism back into Islam. Posthumously this ambiguity caught up with 'Aflaq himself when, at his death in 1989, the party announced that before he died he had secretly converted to Islam.

The Ba'th: A Civil Religion?

From its inception, Ba'thi secular nationalism had some aspects of what is known in sociological studies as "civil religion," namely, a set of quasi-religious attitudes, beliefs, rituals, and symbols that tie members of a political community together. But how civil or secular was it? To what extent was it detached from Islam? 'Aflaq and his colleagues created a world of ideals, symbols, and organizations, among them the party's exciting slogans, 'Aflaq's lectures in Damascus coffee shops to his eager disciples, and the party's membership system and congresses, which translated those ideals into action. To its hard-core membership it was all a "secular religion," but Ba'th secularism was different from European secularism (*laïcité*, laicism). Unlike Europe, by the middle of the twentieth century most of the Muslim Arab world was still religious to varying degrees, having not yet gone through a long process like the European Enlightenment and its secular offshoots. As a result, while Michel 'Aflaq's young Ba'thi followers were dreaming of secularizing their society, they themselves were going through a still incomplete secular revolution and, equally as important, they were aware of their religious environment and therefore were ready for a limited compromise.

The concept of a civil religion, as originally formulated by Jean-Jacques Rousseau, referred to the virtues that citizens need to serve the state. The elaboration of the concept most suitable for our purpose is that of Robert N. Bellah, who found in the US attachment to secular elements such as the flag, the Constitution, the Founding Fathers, the annual holiday calendar, and certain social values a similar kind of civil religion. Bellah also recognized that belief in a supreme deity may be part of civil religion as long as it does not have a particular or sectarian coloration. This was indeed the American Founding Fathers' religiosity, at least as enshrined in the US Constitution.[53] Before the Ba'th Party came to power, it was not in a position to impose rituals and symbols on the state, but the fledgling movement was inspired by its own symbols and values. The founder, Michel 'Aflaq, insisted that the Ba'th were no atheists; they believed in a supreme deity, but 'Aflaq was very clear that the party's religion was not connected to the mosque or the church. He likely formulated this approach in line with some Western examples he was aware of, such as the national philosophy of the German post-Kantians and perhaps even the experience of the United States. His approach to religion is perfectly accommodated by the theoretical mold that Bellah suggested one generation later.

'Aflaq provided an emotional even more than a rational-intellectual stimulus. One component he emphasized was the romanticism of his Arabism. When asked by his disciples to define Arab nationalism for them, he delivered his most often quoted saying: "*Al-qawmiyya allati nunadi biha hiya hubb qabla kull shay*" (The pan-Arab nationalism we are calling for is love before anything else), meaning love for the nation.[54] Beyond its romantic connotation, this expression strongly recalls a central Christian concept of God from John 4:8: "God is love." As mentioned earlier, Saint Augustine and other early Christian theologians developed the concept of agape. God does not merely love; he *is* love itself. 'Aflaq's pan-Arab nationalism is love itself. Therefore, the young Ba'thi is to be the embodiment of love for the nation.

'Aflaq inspired his followers to ecstasy through his enchanting language and the living style and personality of a secular prophet or a charismatic Sufi shaykh. As is evident in al-Jundi's memoirs, Ba'th Party members lived in a state of secular religiosity and Sufi-like ecstasy. As al-Jundi put it, "We believed in the religious feeling" of Arab nationalism and "in the Sufism of the religions."[55] Hani al-Fukayki, who in the early 1960s was a member of the Iraqi regional leadership and the party's politburo, recalled that despite the rising star of Egypt's 'Abd al-Nasir in the 1950s, this "did not detract" from the way in which party members saw 'Aflaq. They saw him "as a god with a holy countenance. . . . When we sat in front of him we felt that we were in the presence of Jesus, possessed by his speech and enchanting words and by his Sufi style."[56]

But ʿAflaq did more. Fukayki remembered:

When I read his [ʿAflaq's] booklet "Memory of the Arab Messenger" I was transfixed by his language and when he came to its end saying "As Muhammad was all the Arabs, let all the Arabs [today] be Muhammad" I shivered . . . as if I heard the [Islamic] revelation again . . . and I saw in my mind the . . . perfection and omniscience and loftiness and prophecy in every Baʿthi. . . . And despite my belief in secularism I found no difference between Arab nationalism and Islam, because our Eternal Message, like [that of] little prophets, is the resurrection of the Arab nation and renewing its spirit so that it will become ingenious again as it ingeniously created Islam.[57]

Fukayki was indeed a secularist, but even in his case, in what he heard and read from ʿAflaq, the line separating nationalist Arab ecstasy and Islamic passion was fuzzy. What he heard could have been interpreted equally as straightforward Islamism or as blatant blasphemy because it meant the deification of secular Arabism and the Baʿth Party as its messenger. There is no doubt that the hard core of the party, Fukayki included, ended up on the blasphemous side, but it seems they were not fully cognizant of it, or possibly they were reluctant to fully admit it to themselves. They were enchanted by ʿAflaq's equivocal rhetoric blurring the line between Islam and Arabism. They still saw themselves as Muslims, but of a newly inspired, young and glorious breed, discarding the dead weight of fossilized rites and "superstitions" and of the ossified ʿulama. Seeing themselves as "little prophets" and ʿAflaq as a prophet was sheer blasphemy from any Islamic point of view, but not to them. They saw themselves as the prophets of a new age and a new quasi-Islamic religion. Benedict Anderson's theory may help us here: a national movement aligns itself, he suggested, with "the large cultural system that preceded it, out of which—as well as against which—it came into being."[58] In this sense, ʿAflaq aligned his nationalism with the Islamic religion that he came to marginalize if not destroy.

Fukayki saw himself as a Prophet's Companion, or "little prophet," following a great latter-day new Prophet of a new Arab age and a new sacred message and mission that would bring back to life the quasi-dead Arab nation in its state of barely suspended animation. If we consult Anthony Smith, then, by projecting this image to his followers 'Aflaq created "a temporal and terrestrial drama of salvation"[59] and successfully disseminated it among the young generation of his time. As Smith observed, the "civil religion" that national movements create enables the individual to link himself or herself to a "community of history and destiny." In this way "the individual hopes to achieve a measure of immortality which will preserve his or her person and achievements from oblivion; they will live on and bear fruit in the community." "Ethnic nationalism becomes a 'surrogate' religion," Smith argued. This kind of civil religion "aims to overcome the sense of futility engendered by the removal of any vision of existence after death by linking individuals to persisting communities." Smith wrote of an era when "the ethnic past of the community has been sundered from its religious anchorage; and men and women have had to look elsewhere for the immortality which so many desire."[60] They expected to find their immortality in the memory of the nation.

In the Arab Islamic world, though, the ethnic past of the community has been sundered from its religious anchorage only partially, if at all, and only in small sections of society. In the case of 'Aflaq himself, such sundering was easy: he was a Christian-born atheist. For many if not all of his Muslim disciples, though, the Arab ethnic past was never fully severed from the Islamic past. Even those who were inclined toward atheism—and they were many—saw themselves as secular or irreligious Muslims. Islamic history was organically fused into their identity. When he created a civil national religion, therefore, 'Aflaq had to take it into account, and he did: his was a credo in which atheistic hints and Islamist insinuations appeared and disappeared in a dazzling display of rhetorical fireworks. One component, though, and a central one to all three Abrahamic religions, was completely missing from his credo—the hereafter. Throughout his intellectual activity 'Aflaq never mentioned paradise and hell. In the end, therefore, through an "argument of silence," there may be no doubt that, at its core, his nationalism offered a "terrestrial salvation," not a heavenly one. His disciples did not miss the heavenly promise. As shown in chapter 5, many years later one of them, Saddam Husayn, began to promise heaven to his hapless soldiers in Kuwait who were dying by the thousands under the relentless blows of the American war machine. This was the strongest indication to date that Husayn was embarking on a totally new ideology, even identity: Islamic religiosity.

As Michael Gilsenan reminds us, to the young Arab generation of Yemen of the 1950s, even those among them who were religious, the 'ulama, the sharifs, and other clerical functionaries "were not only obstacles to independence [from colonialism] but had nothing to do with a true Islam, which had no need of sheriffs . . . or of deference to a religious hierarchy."[61] In another part of the Arab world at the same time poor religious villagers were refusing to believe "that anyone acted for anything other than personal interests, whatever the vocabulary of religion . . . that was used. . . . At the heart of reality might lie the core truth of religion but who knew where that heart of reality lay or how to discover it. All this made for a multiplicity of interpretations, questionings and almost theatrical social encounters."[62] Gilsenan here refers to the crisis of Islam in Akkar, a Sunni Arab region in northern Lebanon, but the same may also be said of the large cities of Syria and Lebanon in the 1940s and 1950s. ʿAflaq's disciples went one step further than the revolutionary young Yemenis and Lebanese peasants observed by Gilsenan. Not only did they lose faith in the ʿulama, they lost faith in traditional Islam, and their search for "the core truth" led them in a different direction, toward a secular religion fused with yearnings to replicate the wonder that was Muhammad, "*al-rasul al-ʿArabi*," the "Arab Messenger," the messenger of Arab ingenuity and glory.

Upon coming to power the party introduced and imposed a more "classical" or Western-inspired "civil religion" designed to enhance (or create) a united Iraqi people loyal to its secular and modernizing (though undemocratic) ruling party. They introduced a new Revolution Day, Baʿth Party Day, Ramadan Revolution Day (commemorating the 1963 Baʿth takeover), the Mosul and Babylon Mesopotamian-inspired Spring and Fall Festivals, Oil Nationalization Day, *Shahid* Day, Saddam's birthday (a royal tradition), ceremonies of swearing allegiance (*bayʿa*) to Saddam,[63] the Call (*al-nidaa*) Day, to mark the invasion of Kuwait, the Flag (*al-raya*) Day, to celebrate the people's protection of the presidential palaces, the Great March (*al-zahf al-kabir*) Day, commemorating Saddam's "election" as president in October 1995, and many others. All were designed to create a reservoir of grand secular or secularized national Iraqi occasions and ceremonies. Beginning in 1979, they were mostly connected to the personality cult of Saddam, the ultimate Iraqi Arab.[64] Within the party the regime kept the tradition of (no longer democratic) elections to the various positions, party congresses, and ceremonies. An impressive example is a videotape, mentioned earlier, from around 1992 showing the opening of an Extraordinary Party Congress. The members, around three hundred of them, are standing in an auditorium with Saddam facing them, and the whole crowd is chanting together the party's traditional slogan: "One Arab nation with an eternal message!"[65] Even in the Islamic 1990s, all those national days and ceremonies were still there and still secular, though they had to compete for public attention with the gushing torrent of Islamic symbols and activities.

The Ba'th Genesis, the Shi'a, and Pan-Arabism

Kan'an Makiya argued that "Pan Arabism is rooted not only in Islam, but in the Sunni sect that embraces the overwhelming majority of Arabic-speaking Muslims."[66] How was Ba'thi secular pan-Arabism received in the Arab parts of Iraq and Syria? Is, or was, pan-Arabism necessarily Sunni? In Iraq, between its inception and 2003, demography changed little. Some 80 percent of the population consisted of Arabs, but some 75 percent of all Arabs belonged to the Shi'i sect. Since the early days of the monarchy, for the Shi'i community of Iraq the pan-Arab vision of integrative unity was unappealing, for two mutually reinforcing reasons. One was that the Hashimite pan-Arab ideology as formulated mainly by Director of Education Sati' al-Husri promised to drown the Shi'a in a Sunni-majority pan-Arab crucible. In Iraq they had at least a chance of one day translating their majority into equality, even hegemony, but in a pan-Arab state there could be no such hope. The other was that well before any Arab unity was to be accomplished, the monarchy's Arab nationalism was seen as a trap, designed to attract Shi'i Arab support merely to eternalize Sunni hegemony. Demands for Sunni-Shi'i equality, let alone for the majority rights of the Shi'a, were often defined by the Sunni Arab ruling elite as "sectarianism" (*al-ta'ifiyya*), and the proponents of sectarian justice were accused of fanning division among Arabs. Sometimes such proponents of Shi'i rights were even called *shu'ubiyyun*, a medieval concept that in its contemporary usage may be translated as "Arab haters" of Persian stock. Even during the first Ba'th rule (1963), senior Shi'i Ba'thi leaders were reluctant to support Shi'i communal demands or even to help the Najaf *mujtahids* to present requests to the regime lest they be accused of sectarianism.[67] Finally, the Shi'a community of Iraq was more religious than the Sunni one. Ba'this and even Communist Party members in the south of Iraq in the 1950s often participated in the various religious ceremonies of 'Ashura and other important occasions.[68] Ba'thi secular Arabism, therefore, appealed more to young Sunnis than to their Shi'i counterparts. Ba'th secularism, disguised as it was, could still be gleaned, and this kept many young Shi'is in Iraq at arm's length from the party.[69] The Shi'i perception did not change much under the postmonarchy regimes. And yet, as will be shown below, in Iraq, before it came to power and lost it in 1963, the Ba'th Party was an important exception. In Syria, even as late as 2012 the Ba'th was not "rooted . . . in the Sunni sect." The 'Alawites in Syria were a small (12 percent or so) and unpopular minority, not even considered to be Muslims by many. Most of them were quite secular to begin with. For them, language-based equality in the Syrian state was a way out of their minority status. In the promised united Arab state they stood to lose nothing, as even in Syria they had never had a chance to be more than a small minority. Borrowing from Karl Marx's *Communist Manifesto*, one might say that by supporting pan-Arabism the 'Alawites of Syria had "nothing to lose but their chains," while they had "a world to win." Indeed, even before Arab unity was achieved, secular Arabism served the 'Alawites well. Once they achieved a hegemonic position through the party's military supporters, they could argue that the sectarian affinity of much of the military commanders, senior intelligence officials, and government employees was irrelevant, as they were all Arabs.

Ostensibly the party had no particular point of departure regarding the Shi'a; the terms "Sunni" or "Shi'i" appear nowhere in early Ba'th tracts. However, if an argument by silence is indeed an argument, then the party had a clear position. In the first place, its secular Arabism held a great promise of sectarian equality both in Syria and Iraq. Second, whenever 'Aflaq related to the Arab golden age he emphasized the Prophet's lifetime. This was not a coincidence. After the Prophet's death, the Muslim community became embroiled in inheritance disputes that gave rise to the Sunni-Shi'i divide that, at times, was acrimonious. 'Aflaq wisely skirted this dispute, and because both Sunnis and Shi'is accept the Qur'an as the foundation of Islam, this issue could be laid to rest, or so 'Aflaq seemed to have believed. In Syria, Sunni Arabs represent around 60 percent of the population, and pan-Arabism could indeed be seen by the population as "rooted not only in Islam, but in the Sunni sect," as Makiya suggests, but in reality this was not at all the case. Throughout the party's existence there, in addition to Sunnis, 'Alawites and Druze (both offshoots of the Shi'a) as well as Christians joined the party. Beginning in 1966, in fact, in Damascus a coalition of religious minorities with a meaningful participation of Sunni Arabs even achieved hegemony.

In Iraq, despite the hurdles mentioned above, until the early 1960s the party attracted almost as many Shi'is as Sunnis. As shown by Ronen Zeidel, the party already existed in 1946–47, but only in 1948–49 did it have for the first time a few score members and a recognizable structure and leadership. By

1952, the total number of party members was 170 (Hanna Batatu reported only some fifty).[70] The religious identity of 124 is known. Fifty-five (44%) were Sunni Arabs, forty-five (36%) were Shiʻi Arabs, five (4%) were Christians, and nineteen (15%) were non-Iraqi Arabs of various sects and religions. When it comes to the leadership members between 1948 and 1952 (between four and seven members in each leadership), 43 percent were Sunnis, 33 percent were Shiʻis, and 23 percent came from other Arab countries. As for the secretaries general, the first two (both in 1948–49) were Syrian ʻAlawites, and thereafter they all were Iraqis: two, Saʻdun Hamadi and Fuʼad al-Rikabi, were Shiʻis and one, ʻAbd al-Rahman Dhamin, was a Sunni.[71] Until November 1963, there was always a considerable Shiʻi component in the Baʻth and its leadership. Shiʻis, Christians, and Sibaʻis (Sabians) in Iraq and ʻAlawites, Christians, and Druze in Syria who joined the party saw in it a chance for equality with the Sunnis, whose sect was the hegemonic community in both countries. In an anti–status-quo party that considered language rather than sect or religious affinity as the criterion for nationhood, it made sense for non-Sunnis to join. Many secular Iraqi Shiʻis who objected to pan-Arabism joined the Communist Party for a similar reason: it was an anti–status-quo party that demanded complete equality on the basis of Iraqi citizenship. After the Baʻth Party lost power in November 1963, the Shiʻi membership gradually declined, mainly as the result of persecutions by the ʻArif regime and a political split between pro- and anti-Damascus factions. When in 1968 the "rightist" or anti-Damascus faction of the party came to power again in Baghdad, the Shiʻis were poorly represented there.

During his rule, Saddam tried to balance terror with temptation: he recruited many Shiʻis to the party and elevated Shiʻis to senior positions. For the same reason, Saddam also promoted the Mesopotamian-Iraqi identity and vision. This vision included replacing the Arab crucible dream with a limited federal union of the existing Arab states led by Iraq. Saddam even tried to promote an ecumenical Sunni-Shiʻi Islam. The promise of Sunni-Shiʻi equality remained for many years, hanging low in the sky in the distance, the Arab equivalent of the shining city on a hill, shimmering, alluring, beguiling. By 1991, though, it had become clear to the regime that its love offensive, incomplete and limited in its execution, had failed.

Chapter 2
The Ba'th in Power, 1968–80:
Fortress Secularism

The Ba'th Ruling Regime between Secularism and Islam

During the first fifteen years or so of its rule in Iraq, the Ba'th regime demonstrated fairly convincing attachment to the party's secular ideological tradition. However, having come to power in a large country where most of the population was traditional, even during its secular years the regime felt obliged to make some concessions to Islam that involved retreats from its secular credo. The party leadership believed that those would be merely tactical retreats. It dreamed of the "New Iraqi Man" (*al-insan al-'Iraqi al-jadid*), a thoroughly modern, secular, and nationalistic (patriotic Iraqi and pan-Arab) breed, but it also realized that creating this new man would take time. The most crucial and urgent compromise, one the regime powers considered an absolute must simply to stay in power, was imposing state control over all the Islamic institutions in the land. It seems likely that the regime never seriously considered actual separation of state and mosque. What the leadership had in mind to do, and did do, was to impose state control over the mosque. This had three operational aspects. First, it meant keeping the 'ulama out of antiregime politics. Second, it meant encouraging the religious establishment to lend religious legitimacy to the regime's policies when such support was necessary. Finally, it meant keeping Islam out of regime ideology and, as much as was reasonably possible, out of state education, culture, the legal system, and state symbolism. Until the second half of the 1980s, the Ba'th regime managed to do all this successfully, even though it met with some opposition from individual clerics and their flocks.

The concessions to Islam that the regime made were limited and unavoidable if the Ba'this did not wish to confront public religiosity head-on. As a result, Iraq became a land of dichotomy. On the popular level of religious festivals and general deference to Islam, the regime paid the requisite lip service. However, Islam was almost absent from the realm of high culture, and occasionally was even attacked. This was the case, for example, in the more programmatic political speeches of the leaders and in the resolutions of party conferences. Regime-sponsored art was preoccupied with resurrecting the civilizations of ancient Mesopotamia, and the age of pre-Islamic culture (*Jahiliyya*) in the Arabian Peninsula was similarly portrayed in a very positive fashion. In between the demotic and the high cultural levels, however, was a vast territory of ambivalence that included lawmaking, the constitution, and education. The regime recognized certain aspects of Islamic traditions when enacting laws and issuing government regulations. At the same time, it largely steered clear of imposing shari'a law. In instances in which public expectations were high that the government would indeed impose shari'a law, the regime sometimes tried to navigate a middle course. It demanded adherence to Islam in public but left legal safety hatches as long as the offenders did not flaunt their non-Islamic practices. This approach created a bizarre chimera in the legal sphere. A conspicuous example was the imposition of Islamic rules of fasting during the month of Ramadan. Ostensibly, every Iraqi had to adhere to the Islamic rules, but so many legal loopholes were available that the laws made a mockery of the holy month. There can be little doubt that making such legal avoidance possible was the regime's intention.

Secularizing the Constitution:
The First Two Constitutions, 1968 and 1970

A typical—and confusing—case of ambivalence is that of the Iraqi constitutions under the Ba'th. Within the first two years of gaining power, the Ba'th regime introduced two provisional constitutions.[1] The first was made public some two months after the party came to power in a bloodless coup d'état. The second was issued some two years later and remained in force until the regime's demise in 2003. The differences between the two were meaningful in a number of areas, but the most significant difference was the place of Islam. The first Provisional Constitution assigned Islam a central role. It was formulated mainly under the influence of the elderly President Ahmad Hasan al-Bakr (born 1925), who was known to be personally very religious. Bakr was also a latecomer to the Ba'th Party, having joined it in 1960. Saddam, by comparison, was twelve years younger but had joined the party some four years earlier. (It was common knowledge that Bakr joined the Ba'th because of his pan-Arab rather than secular convictions.) The second Provisional Constitution represented a shift toward a more secular state and was introduced mainly under the influence of the young vice president and deputy chairman of the Revolutionary Command Council (RCC), Saddam Husayn, and the younger generation of party leadership. Another factor that may have contributed to the Islamic nature of the first constitution was the haste with which it was assembled. To save time, large parts of the constitution of the previous regime, that of the religious 'Arif brothers, were simply copied and inserted into the new document. Indeed, on issues of state-mosque relations the Ba'thi first Provisional (or Interim, *mu'aqqat*) Constitution and the 'Arif brothers' Provisional Constitution were practically identical.[2] In view of the lively constitutional debates that began in Iraq in 2003 and the Arab revolutions of 2011 in Egypt, Tunisia, Libya, Morocco, and other Arab states, the evolution of the Islamic versus secular components of the Iraqi constitution under the Ba'th regime is of particular interest.

The preamble to the first Provisional Constitution (1968) emphasized religiosity, but of the same ethereal kind so popular with Michel 'Aflaq, the party's Christian-born Syrian founder: "After relying on God and the faithful citizens of the nation . . . a righteous group of the nation that believes in God *and in the aims of the Arabic nation* . . . has carried out the . . . Revolution of the 17th of July 1968 . . . seeking all the help of Almighty God" (emphasis added). Even this nonbinding spirituality, though, vanished together with the preamble to the second Provisional Constitution (1970).

Article 1 of the first Provisional Constitution stipulated: "The Republic of Iraq is a People's democratic state [a terminology borrowed from the Eastern European "popular democracies"] deriving the principles of its democracy and popularity from Arab heritage and the Islamic spirit." In the Second Provisional Constitution, Islam was dropped altogether, and even "heritage" was omitted. Instead, Article 1 read: "Iraq is a sovereign people's democratic republic. Its principal aim is to fulfill the United Arab State and to establish the socialist system." Article 4 of the earlier document made it clear that "Islam is the State religion [*al-Islam din al-dawla*] and it is the *fundamental basis* for its constitution" (emphasis added). This wording also implied that shari'a law would be the foundation of its enactment. In Article 4 of the 1970 Constitution, Islam was demoted. It was still defined as "the religion of the state," but there was no mention of it as a basis for the constitution.

Article 8 of the 1968 document defined the family as "the basic unit of society whose principles are religion, morals and patriotism." The equivalent in the 1970 document was Article 11: "The family is the nucleus of society. The state shall guarantee its protection and support and shall foster maternity and childhood." Religion is gone altogether. Inheritance is defined in Article 17b in the 1968 text as "a right determined by Islamic Law." This is the reason given why the regime recognized it as legitimate. In the text of the 1970 document, the Islamic legitimization of inheritance was dropped. It said only, "Inheritance is a right organized by law" (Article 17). Finally, Article 57 in the 1968 Constitution spelled out the oath of the president and that of his deputies, to wit: "I swear by Almighty God to be sincere to my religion [*dini*], my homeland and my nation and to safeguard the Republican regime." In the 1970 Constitution, the equivalent oath, found in Article 60, reads: "I swear by Almighty God, my honor and belief [*mu'taqadi*] to preserve the republican regime . . . and fulfill the aims of the Arab nation in unity, freedom and socialism." Unlike "religion," "belief" may—and often does—refer to party doctrine. God thus remains in the 1970 Constitution, but except for Article 4, Islam and "religion" are gone.

In 1970, there was only one constitution of an Arab state with a Muslim majority in which Islam was not defined as the state religion, that of Tunisia. As for Iraq itself, during the monarchy Islam was defined as "the official religion of the state,"[3] and even General 'Abd al-Karim Qasim, the most secular ruler in Iraqi history, included this clause in his otherwise perfectly secular constitution.[4] It seems clear that in the 1970 Constitution, by not dropping the final mention of Islam, the Ba'th regime decided not to risk too great a confrontation with Iraq's traditional circles, Sunnis as well as Shi'is, but Islam was removed from all other parts of the constitution.[5]

Under the Ba'th in Iraq, the secular changes between the first and the second Interim Constitutions seem, perhaps, marginal and purely symbolic, but they reflected the true convictions of the young generation of Ba'this. They were by majority truly secular, some even atheists, and during the first fifteen years of their rule they remained more or less faithful to their convictions.

Two Examples of the Treatment of the Forbidden

Alcohol Consumption

One of the best-known verses in the Qur'an reads, "Ye are the best community that hath been raised up for mankind: ye enjoin right conduct and forbid indecency" (*kuntum khayr umma ukhrijat lil-nas, ta'muruna bil-ma'ruf wa tanhawna 'an al-munkar*) (*Sura 3, Aal 'Imran, Aaya* 110). One of the most important "indecencies" or "thou shall not do" instructions in the Qur'an applies to the consumption of alcoholic drinks. In many Muslim states, however, one can easily find alcoholic drinks, and Iraq was no exception. Under the monarchy, not only were there liquor shops, but alcoholic drinks could be procured in many bars and hotels across Baghdad. Indeed, an elaborate system of laws regulated bars, pubs, and other places where alcoholic drinks could be served and sold. For example, in 1931 an important liquor law was promulgated dealing with the places where such drinks could be provided. The 1931 Law No. 56 dealt with customs duties on alcoholic products; the 1937 Law No. 17 dealt with liquor excise duties, and there were many more. The regimes of General Qasim and the 'Arif brothers did not abolish these laws, but rather introduced some technical amendments, and the Ba'th inherited the same system. The Ba'th regime, being more secular than its immediate predecessor, issued a large number of laws and regulations applying to alcoholic drinks.[6] None of them forbade Muslims from frequenting the bars, pubs, and liquor shops. There were only a few days in the year on which some limitations were imposed, but these restrictions only highlighted the fact that on at least 320 days of the year, everybody above the age of eighteen in Iraq was free to consume alcoholic drinks to their heart's content, privately as well as publicly.

Prostitution

Another major sin in Islam is adultery and prostitution (*al-zana*). Even though Islamic law makes it difficult to convict a person of this crime, theoretically the punishment is death by stoning. Yet under the monarchy, there were brothels in Baghdad, in particular a large one in Mahallat al-Maydan, in front of the main entrance to the Ministry of Defense.[7] Badr Shakir al-Sayyab (died 1964), arguably Iraq's greatest free-verse poet, describes Baghdad as a "big brothel."[8] No doubt the great poet meant "brothel" in a much wider sense, but there are hints in the poem that he also meant something more literal. As many Jewish Iraqis who had lived in Baghdad under the monarchy and General Qasim and with whom I spoke confirmed, the state went halfway toward legalizing at least the central brothel by forcing the women there to undergo periodic medical checks.[9] When General Qasim came to power, he issued a special law outlawing prostitution that imposed heavy prison sentences on procurers, and ordered the establishment of compulsory rehabilitation centers for prostitutes.[10] According to my interview subjects, Qasim tried to force the former prostitutes to learn how to sew and in this way make an honest living, but his efforts failed miserably. There is no indication that the ʿArif brothers or the Baʿth regime after them did much to stop prostitution. Indeed, interviews I conducted with people who lived in Baghdad or had visited Iraq at the time confirmed that under the Baʿth, prostitution thrived. In addition to private enterprise in this field, young women were often recruited into prostitution by the intelligence services as a way to obtain information from selected foreign visitors. Not surprisingly, there is no trace of this tactic in the legal system. In 1994, as part of the Islamization campaign, prostitution was outlawed and made punishable by death.[11] This too may serve as an indication that the phenomenon had existed on a fairly large scale, for had it not been, there would have been no need to outlaw it.

Women's Legal Status

Our view of the woman [will be achieved through] . . . the total change [*al-taghyir al-shamil*] in society. . . . Limiting the role of woman and compressing her in society according to bourgeois-feudal thinking that considers her exclusive role to be at home . . . is denying her humanity and the spirit of innovation and annulling her intellectual energies. . . . [We must] overcome the retarded bourgeois-feudal-totalitarian mentality. . . . Liberating the woman totally . . . according to the world view in which we believe will be achieved through the political, economic and cultural liberation of society as a whole.

—Saddam Husayn, speaking at an International
Women's Year conference, 1975[12]

If the woman is not free and politically aware and educated our society will remain backward and shackled.

—Saddam Husayn, speaking at the Third Congress of the
Ba'th Women's Union, April 17, 1971[13]

Throughout the monarchy, personal status issues for Muslims—legal questions related to family issues such as marriage, divorce, inheritance, and child custody—were settled in shari'a courts according to Islamic law. Christians and Jews settled their affairs in their own religious courts.[14] As for Sunni-Shi'i legal differences, according to the monarchy constitution, justice "shall be administered in the shari'a courts in accordance with the terms of the shari'a doctrine peculiar to each of the Islamic sects [the Sunna and the Shi'a]. . . . The *qadhi* [religious judge] shall be a member of the sect to which the majority of the inhabitants of the place to which he is appointed belong, maintaining the appointment of both Sunni and Ja'fari [Shi'i] *qadhi*s in the cities of Baghdad and Basra" (Article 77). In this way, the monarchy introduced an important change to the Ottoman legal system by allowing Islamic Shi'i courts to function on an equal basis with Sunni ones. However, throughout the monarchy there was no law of personal status, despite some attempts to enact one. General 'Abd al-Karim Qasim, who toppled the monarchy on July 14, 1958, was a thoroughly secular army officer. One of his first major legal reforms was the introduction of a law of personal status that, while shari'a in most part, in certain aspects was based on European law.[15] One of the most important clauses of the new law was Article 74, which stipulated complete equality between males and females in respect to inheritance. Another deviation from Islamic law was Article 3c, which forbade polygamy except with the permission of a judge. Infringement of that clause was punishable by up to one year of imprisonment or a fine of 100 dinars (the equivalent of 100 British pounds), and the marriage would be annulled. Under the monarchy, in many shari'a courts a civil judge, a graduate of Baghdad's University Law School, fulfilled the role of a religious judge (*qadhi*). This did not pose a great threat to the religious establishment: as long as there was no supra-shar'i law of personal status, regardless of who the judge was, all matters of personal status were settled according to the shari'a. In practice, most people turned to their community's clerics rather than to the state shari'a courts. Once there was a state law, the danger was that more and more people would turn to state courts and abandon the independent clergy. This could certainly be the case with women, who could receive better rulings in state courts. The Shi'i *mujtahids* in particular were worried because most of them depended for their living on the community rather than on the state. Thus, the clerics had strong reservations not only because they objected to non-shar'i legislation but also because it threatened their socioeconomic position. When criticized, Qasim justified the equality between men and women in matters of inheritance he had introduced in his law by arguing that, even under the monarchy, and before it the Ottomans, not all the divine laws were followed by the contemporary law in Iraq. According to the Qur'an, he argued, theft had been punishable by amputation of the hand, but the modern lawmaker thought otherwise.[16]

Throughout the rule of General Qasim, the supreme *marja'* (religious authority), Grand Ayatollah Muhsin al-Hakim, continually asked the benevolent dictator to return to the status quo under the monarchy, namely, to the rules of the shari'a, and to return exclusive authority in matters of Muslims' personal status to the shari'a courts, but his solicitation was to no avail.[17] On February 8, 1963, as soon as the Ba'th Party toppled—and killed—Qasim and took over the government, with General 'Abd al-Salam 'Arif as a figurehead president, Ayatollah Hakim called on the regime to annul Qasim's law. There was disagreement in the party over what to do.[18] Still, two days later the new rulers abolished Article 74 of Qasim's law, the section dealing with inheritance, replacing it with a clause that greatly resembled the Shi'i law of inheritance. In addition, the 1963 law stipulated that, even if bigamy was practiced illegally, once a couple was married, the marriage could not be declared null and void by a court.[19] The automatic annulment was dropped, probably because the regime was unwilling to confront the clergy, whose commonplace interpretation of the shari'a was that marrying up to four women was legal. The religious establishment was not fully satisfied with the change because the clergy wanted to abolish the law as a whole, thus leaving all matters of personal status exclusively to the 'ulama.[20] The first Ba'th regime, however, was unwilling to make further concessions, especially if it meant bestowing on the clerics the sole responsibility for interpreting the shari'a, thus denying such responsibility to nonclerical judges. Enacting such a concession would have meant giving up a stronghold that gave the government power at the expense of the religious establishment. In keeping with Shi'i jurisdiction, the new clause in the Law of Personal Status gave preference to heirs from the nuclear family at the expense of the agnatic tribal heirs.[21] Thus, women who belonged to the nuclear family, such as a daughter whose father had died, came before men outside it (such as the deceased man's father or paternal uncles). The new clause did not confer male-female equality in inheritance, which is widely believed to be prevented by a Qur'anic verse (*Aaya*), but it did give females more than Sunni interpretations of the verse did. With minor changes, this law remained in force until 2003.

Under the second Ba'th regime (1968–2003), in addition to the various civil and criminal courts, the Shar'i courts were retained and were very active. They included Sunni and Shi'i versions of a regular, lower instance court (*mahakim al-qadha' al-shar'i*) and also Sunni and Shi'i versions of higher courts (*majlis al-tamyiz al-shar'i*). These courts dealt with personal status issues of Muslims and with religious endowments, *awqaf*. The two shar'i *tamyiz* courts were the highest courts. They were situated in the capital city, and each consisted of a president and two members. If a shar'i court had no religious judge (*qadhi*), the civil judge of the civil court in that town, if he was a Muslim, served as a judge.[22] For personal status issues, people could turn either to the civil courts or to the shar'i courts. While both were obliged to follow the Law of Personal Status, interpretations were often different, as the civil courts' rulings were more generous to women than the shar'i courts' rulings.

Promise and Disappointment

When addressing the issue of women's equality, the Eighth Iraqi Regional Party Congress of 1974 presented a secular and progressive platform. Indeed, this platform could have been interpreted as expressing an intention to return to the controversial articles of Qasim's law: "One of the main aims of the Party," the resolution declared, "is the liberation of women from the chains of economic, social and legal anachronism," the latter meaning shari'a inequalities. "The social, cultural and economic backwardness of Arab women," the resolution stated, "is a major obstacle to contemporary Arab revival. It casts a dark shadow on most aspects of the life of society and does direct harm to such fundamental matters as children's education, the construction of the new society and the release of the Arab people's creative energies." This observation could easily be endorsed by any Western sociologist. "There can be no genuine radical change of Arab society toward unity, liberty and socialism while women remain inferior and unequal partners of men, in law, in theory and in practice," the resolution added. In this way the resolution tied together the four greatest ideals of the party, for legal equality between men and women was synonymous with secularism. Finally, the resolution could not resist a stab at the Islamists, including the conservative 'ulama, whether Sunni or Shi'i: "It is the party's duty to bring down the reactionary and backward trends and ideas that diminish woman's worth."[23]

A daring approach to women's status was articulated by a female intellectual soon after the 1974 party congress. In a 1975 article published in the most prestigious intellectual magazine in Baghdad, the author, Bushra Bustani, used the Qur'an interpretation of the early twentieth-century Egyptian Grand Mufti and Islamic reformer Muhammad ʿAbduh against fundamentalists like the Muslim Brotherhood and their radical spokesman, Sayyid Qutb, even turning Qutb's own concept of *Jahiliyya* against him. Bravely, she presented the ʿulama and fundamentalists as heathen reactionaries by pointing out that, while Islam was originally "a mighty revolution" in favor of women, the men managed later to deviate from it "in order to turn it into a weapon against woman." Thus, Bustani claimed, society in the Islamic world had in fact reverted to *Jahiliyya*. In line with *Jahili* tribal traditions, false Muslims singled out the woman as a potential cause of family shame. As a result, whereas Islam originally equated man and woman, and both bore the same punishment for adultery, this equality was no more. Also, during the late ʿAbbasid era, women started to "withdraw into the home," and the veil was forced on them. But in fact, echoing ʿAbduh, Bustani pointed out that, from an Islamic perspective, the veil was a forbidden "innovation" (*bidʿa*). It was true that the Qur'an says: "And stay in your houses. Adorn not yourselves with the adornment of the *Jahiliyya*" (*Sura* 33, *al-Ahzab*, *Aaya* 33). But this injunction has to do explicitly with the Prophet's wives, not with all women. Women, Bustani insisted, are not frail creatures and do not need men's guardianship. They are strong, independent. It was the Baʿth Party's obligation, she wrote, to protect Iraqi women from "man's [legal] oppression." Thus, "replacing the Law of Personal Status [with a more progressive one] is a must that cannot be avoided." This was what socialist revolutions had done. It was up to the party to "expose . . . the forces of reaction and exploitation" that oppressed women.[24] The article went far in explicitly demanding a secular law that would guarantee perfect gender equality. It was probably encouraged by the party, perhaps by the vice president himself, as a trial balloon following the implied promises of gender legal equality made at the party congress. In reality, though, almost nothing happened. The trial balloon was punctured, but by whom?

Some two years later, in a speech at a symposium that discussed legal reform, Saddam Husayn backtracked. He explained that his retreat from enacting laws that would guarantee "the elementary rights of women" was the result of opposition from "counterrevolutionaries," people who adopted "a narrow and distorted interpretation of religion," to oppose social progress on the path of the revolution. And while the party had to continue its work in educating the masses, it had little choice but to relent on this issue, for otherwise it would have alienated "a section of our people—who so far have been with us." If the party were to insist on women's total equality, he explained, it would arouse "a hostile attitude to the Revolution." Therefore, "it is not necessary to hurry in initiating matters . . . which may conceivably cause us substantial losses."[25] Had it been only a dispute with 'ulama, the regime might have stuck to its guns, but the source of objection that scared Saddam likely came from many Iraqi men, including many party members. There was no difference in this case between Sunnis and Shi'is: men in both sects were unwilling to give up their relative advantage. Together with the conservative objection of most of the religious establishment, the opposition from men doomed Saddam's egalitarian initiative. As the second most powerful person in Iraq, on his way to becoming the next president, he needed the solid support of the party. He was therefore reluctant to confront such opposition over women's equality. While secularism as a whole was of tremendous importance and even became a hallmark of the party, women's equality was only one aspect of it and, in light of the opposition to it, it was expendable.

The promise of a perfectly secular law was abandoned. Indeed, even the more daring parts of Qasim's Law of Personal Status were never resurrected. Still, the regime did introduce some small improvements in women's legal status. In 1978, ten years after it came to power, the Ba'th regime at long last issued its First Amendment to the Law of Personal Status.[26] To placate the conservative (mainly tribal) circles, the new law lowered the minimum age of marriage from sixteen to fifteen years, though a judge's permission was required for such a marriage (Clause 8). More progressively, it forbade the guardian or any relative to force marriage, and forced marriages were declared null and void as long as no intercourse had taken place. Similarly, no relative was allowed to prevent marriage between people whom the law recognized as fit (Clause 9). This annulled the tribal tradition according to which an unmarried woman's paternal cousin had the right of first rejection. If there had been intercourse, willing or unwilling, then the marriage was legally binding, but the woman could turn to the courts to demand a divorce (Clause 40). The new law, while not forbidding bigamy if approved by a state court, punished with three to five years' imprisonment such bigamy if not approved by a court (Clause 10). Similarly, it defined such a second marriage as a sufficient reason for the first wife to turn to the court and demand a divorce (Clause 40).

Another improvement in women's rights was introduced in early 1980, when the Fourth Amendment to the Law of Personal Status stipulated that a woman could disobey her husband without being considered "rebellious" (*nashizan*) if the husband did not see to it that their home was within a reasonable distance of the woman's place of employment, so that she could "reconcile her obligations at home with those at work." This clause (2B) is clearly outside the shari'a. To drive this difference home, it is explained that while the amendment was "in harmony with . . . the Islamic shari'a" (though of course it was not), it also conformed "with the spirit of the times" and with Ba'thi principles. Finally, the RCC explained that the amendment was in the spirit of "the ancient Iraqi constitutions, particularly the Hammurabi Constitution."[27] Selecting a *Jahili* polytheist lawgiver as a model for personal status enactment represented a deliberate affront to Islam, in line with the wider Mesopotamian trend. It would seem that, having decided that a return to the most controversial aspects of Qasim's law was too costly in terms of support from Iraqi men, Saddam wanted at least to have some satisfaction by offending the 'ulama.

In the War: Male Chauvinism Rules the Waves

The war with Iran (1980–88), which was expected to elevate the regime's prestige at home and abroad to unprecedented heights,[28] produced the opposite results. The offensive achieved little, and the number of war casualties mounted rapidly. Under the impact of the war, the regime took a few steps away from greater male-female equality. For example, in late 1980 it issued the Sixth Amendment to the Law of Personal Status, which fully legalized marrying a widow as a second wife.[29] A few years later, the RCC issued a resolution allowing a man to remarry his divorced spouse even if, in the meantime, he had married another woman.[30] This kind of bigamy no longer required court permission. During the war, some legislation was enacted that favored women. For example, in 1985 a law was issued instructing that a man who divorced his wife arbitrarily had to pay her compensation.[31] The more important changes, though, while ostensibly in women's favor, were in reality directed against them. A woman could ask for a divorce if her husband was convicted of high treason. The court was instructed in such a case to ensure that the woman received "all her rights," such as her postponed dowry and alimony.[32] Another resolution adopted in the middle of the war stipulated that a woman could ask for a divorce if her husband was a foreign citizen who had stayed out of Iraq for more than three years, whether of his own volition or because the state prevented him from entering. Even the husband's desertion from military service for more than six months or shirking recruitment or his defection to the other (Iranian) side were regarded as sufficient reasons to ask for divorce.[33] In many cases, women did not wish to divorce their husbands even if the regime considered them traitors, but under the new laws they were forced to divorce them.

Until its downfall in 2003, the Baʿth regime did not annul the core of the Law of Personal Status: it did not deny nonclerical judges and non-sharʿi courts the right to deal with issues of personal status. The historical irony is that the institution that changed it back into the sharʿi mold was the Iraqi Governing Council (IGC), largely consisting of exiled dissidents who returned to Iraq in 2003 on the bayonets of the Allied troops. Many of them had spent many years in the West and were well acquainted with women's rights there. Others had spent many years in Iran, where the infringement of these rights was clear to all. Yet others had spent time in Baʿthi Syria, where women's status was similar to that in Baʿthi Iraq until the mid-1980s. And yet many of them collaborated with the Shiʿi fundamentalist president of the IGC, ʿAbd al-ʿAziz al-Hakim, the leader of the Supreme Assembly of the Islamic Revolution in Iraq (SAIRI), to pass Decree No. 137 on December 29, 2003. The decree stipulated: "The provisions of the shariʿa shall be implemented with respect to cases concerning marriage, engagement, marriage contracts, legal competence . . . marital rights . . . alimony, divorce . . . wills, bequeathals, *waqf* and inheritance"— in short, all matters of personal status. Worse still, the decree made it clear that "this law shall be implemented in all religious courts (personal status) in line with the provisions of the schools [*madhahib*] of Islamic thought." In other words, civil courts could no longer get involved.[34] The senior Coalition Provisional Authority representative in Baghdad, Paul Bremmer, vetoed the decree, and it was later repealed as a result of the activism of one of the three women representatives to the IGC, but the conservatives on the council were unrepentant and promised to raise the issue again in the permanent constitution. When I mentioned this in a conversation with a very senior SAIRI representative in Europe in 2004, he insisted that women under the temporarily abolished decree would be far better off than under Saddam, because owing to liberation they no longer would need to worry about their husbands, sons, and fathers being dragged into Saddam's dungeons. His conviction that a return to the shariʿa, as happened under the monarchy, was the right thing to do was absolute.

Culture and Identity: A Fascination with Pagan Civilizations

Homeland that spreads wing to the horizon
and clads itself in civilizations as mark of honor
Blessed is the Land of Mesopotamia, homeland wherein
Splendor and resolve, majesty and grandeur [. . .]
Babylon inside us, Assyria is ours
and with us history is filled with glow [. . .]
O the flying columns of the Ba'th, O the lion of the thicket
March like horror toward the decisive victory [. . .]
You will always be to the Arabs a shield O Iraq
and suns that turn the night into morning.

—The 1981 new Iraqi anthem, by Shafiq al-Kamali[35]

In 1969, Saddam, by then already the power behind President Ahmad Hasan al-Bakr, embarked on a unique cultural and later political campaign designed to persuade the Iraqi people that they were the legitimate genetic offspring and cultural heirs of the great civilizations of ancient Mesopotamia. This campaign represented a major departure from the Ba'th Party's pan-Arab credo. Saddam undertook it as the result of essentially three different yet mutually enforcing motives: his personal fascination with the glory that was Mesopotamia, a hard-nosed political analysis, and, finally, a wish to accentuate the party's secularism, if not atheism.

Unlike President Bakr and his generation, as children and youth Saddam and his generation went through the Iraqi state education that, under British pressure, from 1941 forsook its previous pan-Arab emphasis and instead highlighted ancient Mesopotamia.[36] Saddam absorbed pan-Arab and anti-British sentiments in the streets of Tikrit and Baghdad, and in his maternal uncle's home (Khayr Allah Talfah's military career was nipped in the bud because he participated in the 1941 revolt). But he also was captivated by stories of the exploits of the great Mesopotamian kings. As a young man he was already inclined toward secularism, or he never would have joined a party that was established by a Christian. Thus, for him, pre-Islamic Mesopotamia was a legitimate, even exciting source of identity building. The result was a chimera: pan-Arabism with a twist of Iraqi uniqueness and hegemony.

But there were also, and likely prominent, political motivations behind Saddam's Mesopotamian campaign. The Shi'a and the Kurds of Iraq were wary of amalgamative pan-Arabism, as it promised to drown them in an ocean of Sunni Arabs. An everlasting Mesopotamian-based Iraqi territorial nationalism was designed to allay their fears and offer them a glorious future of equal membership in an Iraqi-led Arab empire. And since nationalism is in need of pride in its history and a source of inspiration for an equally bright future, Saddam felt that the dazzling scientific and cultural achievements of the Sumerians, Babylonians, and other Mesopotamians were ideal sources for such pride and hope. Indeed, he made it clear that, being the heir of those civilizations, the modern Iraqi people were the natural leader of all the Arabs. The RCC once condensed this concept into one sentence when it announced the invasion of Kuwait: "Oh great Iraqi people, pearl of the Arabs' crown [*lu'lu'at taj al-'Arab*] and symbol of their might and pride."[37]

Another goal behind the drive to promote the Mesopotamian connection was more narrowly defined, but it was of crucial strategic importance. Soon after the party came to power, in July 1968, its traditional obsession with the pan-Arab revolution became a liability. On the one hand, delegitimizing all Arab states and inter-Arab borders legitimized Ba'thi Iraq's constant meddling in the domestic affairs of other Arab states. This was no mere theoretical principle. Baghdad actively supported revolutionary forces in many Arab countries, which created an atmosphere of constant crisis in Iraq's relations with almost all the Arab states precisely when it needed Arab support in its 1969–75 confrontation with Iran. Moreover, diehards like 'Abd al-Khaliq al-Samarra'i and 'Aziz al-Sayyid Jasim, but even President Bakr himself, who took the party's ideology seriously, demanded that all of Iraq's potential be invested in the single most important Arab issue, the Palestinian front, regardless of the consequences to Iraq itself and to the Ba'th rule there. Iraq, the diehards announced, had to be ready to sacrifice itself on the altar of pan-Arab interests, and the liberation of Palestine was of paramount importance. The hope was that through such revolutionary Arab involvement, Baghdad would gain Arab prestige that it could use to change Arab regimes. However, in a post–Six-Day War situation, this strategy was tantamount to suicide. Israel enjoyed an overwhelming strategic advantage over the Arab armies. Iraq's 18,000-strong expeditionary force in Jordan, with no effective air cover and 700 miles of a bad desert road leading away from Baghdad, could not afford an all-out confrontation even as part of an Arab coalition, let alone on its own. The promise that Iraq would destroy Israel and "liberate Palestine" and the commitment to place the Iraqi Salah al-Din forces in Jordan "under the command" of the Palestine Liberation Organization turned Baghdad into the darling of the revolutionary Arab movements, but Baghdad stood to lose one-third of its military force precisely when it needed every soldier on the Iran-Iraq border.

In September 1970, King Husayn of Jordan unleashed his troops against the Palestinian armed organizations, while Baʿthi Syria tried to help the Palestinians. The Iraqi Salah al-Din expeditionary force was ordered to withdraw a few miles east of the Damascus-Amman road into the desert and keep its nose clean. The decision to remain out of the fray proved to be a propaganda disaster, as Baghdad drew down on itself the ire and contempt of the Arab revolutionary circles. It ignited a deadly confrontation within the Baʿth leadership between the radicals, who demanded intervention no matter the cost, and the pragmatists, led by President Bakr, Vice President Saddam Husayn, and ex-defense minister and RCC member Hardan ʿAbd al-Ghaffar al-Tikriti. ʿAbd al-Khaliq al-Samarraʾi, who had urged throwing everything that Iraq had at the Palestinian front, was jailed and later executed. There was no escape from changing the regime's political priorities. To justify at least some part of Iraqi egotism and self-preservation, even at the expense of general Arab interests, it was necessary to fully legitimize the Iraqi state and nation and strengthen the Iraqi identity at the expense of the pan-Arab one. The Mesopotamian roots proved very useful in this respect. Indeed, in July 1971 Iraq withdrew its troops from Jordan, and from then on Saddam endeavored to persuade the Iraqis that Iraq had to come first, even if it meant postponing the liberation of Palestine. Iraq's Arab adventurism also backfired. The regime needed a breathing space. From the early 1970s, it sought to improve relations with all Arab regimes save Baʿthi Syria. This, too, was justified by the need to concentrate on the immediate interests of the Iraqi nation-state before Iraq emerged once more into the Arab arena. Again, in building legitimacy for the Iraqi national state, a nationalism of blood and soil based on ancient territorial ethnocultural roots was seen as an asset. Baʿthi Iraq remained pan-Arab in the same way that Joseph Stalin's Soviet Union remained committed to a world proletarian revolution. Following in Stalin's footsteps, Saddam defined the new scale of priorities as "socialism in one country."[38]

All this made perfect sense, but it had one apparent flaw: all Mesopotamian civilizations were pagan, regarded by Islam as *Jahiliyya* and therefore as ignorant and backward. To Saddam and his colleagues, however, the pagan status was a bonus. By adopting those civilizations as role models, they demonstrated clearly their secular leaning. Until the early 1980s, the regime did not hesitate even to resurrect pagan rites, though under the guise of cultural activity. For example, in Mosul in March 1969 Saddam initiated a spring festival, which persisted until his regime was toppled in 2003. More provocative was an announcement on the first page of the party's daily in 1979 that recruited pagan fertility rites to Saddam's push to increase the population of Iraq. Thus, following the completion of the reconstruction of a part of Nebuchadnezzar's Babylon, the daily announced:

> It became possible for every bride and bridegroom to spend their honeymoon in one of the towers of the Temple of Ishtar, the ancient Babylonians' goddess of love. Some parts of this temple are being reconstructed now, prepared to become an archeological and tourist site for this purpose. In it there is all the atmosphere of love and marriage ceremonies which prevailed during the days of the historical city of Babylon when it flourished some 3,000 years ago.[39]

For Ishtar, the goddess of sex, fertility, and war, to be anointed the symbol of fertility in Ba'thi Iraq was a shocking sacrilege. Clearly, in the 1970s the Ba'this were happy to shock the traditionalists.

Similar shocks were frequent and appeared in a variety of ways. For example, in 1976 one of the most important literary critics in Iraq published an article in which he praised the *Jahiliyya* when he claimed that "Arab paganism" (*al-wathniyya al-'Arabiyya*) was not a deformed religion. In reality it was an "original" (*asila*), integral part of Arab culture.[40] In the field of contemporary art, too, Mesopotamian themes became omnipresent. Mesopotamian figures such as the Sumerian Princess, Hammurabi, Nebuchadnezzar, and many others inspired Iraqi artists, who were encouraged by the regime.[41]

With the rise of Ayatollah Ruhollah Khomeini to power in Iran in 1979, the stirrings of a Shi'i revolt in Iraq, and the Iran-Iraq War in the 1980s, Saddam threw a new component into the cocktail of his Iraqi territorial nationalism, the Shi'i holy cities. In a speech in 1981, Saddam declared Iraqi territory sacred because it contained the soil of Najaf and Karbala, the same soil that had absorbed the pure blood of the Imams 'Ali and al-Husayn, spilled in defense of Islam's lofty principles.[42] This was a revised, "Shi'ified" version of his earlier blood-and-soil nationalism adapted to the political necessity of the time, for he needed to attract more Shi'i support. And yet, even after he initiated his Islamic faith campaign in the early 1990s, Saddam did not forsake his attachment to the greatness of pagan Mesopotamia as a source of Iraqi unity, pride, and promise.[43]

Until the mid-1980s, the regime's eagerness to demonstrate its disdain for Islamic codes of conduct was so great that even medieval Islamic figures were brought forward to challenge Islam. For example, in 1972, with the aid of government funding, one of Iraq's greatest sculptors, Isma'il Fattah al-Turk, created a huge bronze statue of the medieval Islamic court poet Abu Nuwas. The statue was erected, appropriately enough, in Abu Nuwas Street, a popular thoroughfare on the bank of the Tigris River that boasted coffee shops and high-class restaurants. In a large public ceremony, the mayor of Baghdad unveiled the monument. The 'Abbasid poet, who wrote of wine and male love, is seen holding a glass of wine as large as a bucket. The monument was described as weighing one and one-half tons and rising to a height of two and one-half meters, on a base two meters high. On the sides of the monument, one of Abu Nuwas's famous wine poems was etched. It begins, "The wine [glass] is making the rounds between us with its golden beads."[44] This was a political declaration of the first order that the regime considered the Islamic ban, at least on alcoholic drinks, irrelevant.

According to one of Saddam's generals who was also a party member, during the Iran-Iraq War (1980–88) one could always find whisky in the officers' mess.[45] Indeed, already in the early days of the party, before it came to power, members consumed alcohol socially, though it was considered in bad taste to get drunk.[46] Drinking may have served as a kind of a screening mechanism, used to filter out Islamists. To demonstrate its secularism and objection to religious conservative values, the regime also allowed a degree of promiscuity in the media. Until the late 1980s, the daily papers and magazines were full of photographs of scantily clad, attractive women, mostly Western film actresses and models. Even as late as 1988, one could come across photographs of young, attractive women wearing revealing clothing. For example, in the April 1988 issue of the armed forces magazine, under the headline "Stars on Earth," the shapely French Korean film actress Nina Kleib appears half naked and tied up in a rope that covers very little, looking at the viewer pleadingly with gazelle eyes, apparently waiting for an Iraqi war hero to release her from her bondage.[47] Such examples were numerous and widespread in the daily press, too.[48] To an Islamist, the Ba'th knew, a naked woman, whether Iraqi or not, is a naked woman. This provocative material was a sword that cut both ways. It was designed to taunt the conservative circles and at the same time to demonstrate to party members that nothing had changed, and that the party's antireligious policy was alive and well.

This Ba'thi cultural style did not go without criticism. Surprisingly, such criticism came from within the educational establishment. A professor of education pointed out that Islam was not observed in society. Far worse: nonbelief in God, he complained, was regarded as some kind of sick humor. Among the educated classes, he claimed, there was an "animosity [to Islam] that deafens the ears." Hinting at the Ba'th (and communist) approach, he reported bitterly that "there is stabbing Islam and accusing it of being petrified or reactionary or opium," and noted that many educated people felt that the ideas imported from the West and from the Soviet Union were better, and that Islam had "exhausted itself in some period in history." Indeed, this was precisely the Ba'thi approach. To this, the professor protested, one should add the "aversion of the intellectuals toward Islam out of ignorance or hatred," as well as the spread of immodest attire, nudity, and sexual promiscuity in popular films.[49] The professor further complained that in the markets and bookshops one could find "books of atheism," apparently Marxist books. There were "entertainment houses," frequented by many, and there was a "white slave trade," by which he meant the "female dancers and singers" in the various bars. There is little doubt that in this he also included prostitution. Finally, Iraqi cities were full of liquor shops, and the government allowed bets on horse races and lotteries, both forbidden by Islam. Under such circumstances, the educator sighed, it was no wonder that Islamic studies were far from what they should be.[50] The best students were running away from Islamic studies. Only those who could not get accepted anywhere else turned to them, and even they were relatively few.[51] To make sure he was not targeted by the regime, which was, of course, responsible for all those corrupting phenomena, the professor insisted that it was the Jews who were introducing sexual corruption to Iraq. His source for that was *The Protocols of the Elders of Zion*.[52] In 1974, though, there were only a few hundred Jews left in Iraq, and they were completely isolated socially.

It is an enigma why such criticism was allowed. At the same time, there is no reason to doubt the veracity of these reports. It is important, though, to point out that the secular and to an extent promiscuous atmosphere was particularly typical of Baghdad, or rather the modern parts of Baghdad. In the west Baghdad neighborhood of Kazimiyya, which was built around an important Shi'i shrine, and in the poor Shi'i neighborhood of Saddam City in east Baghdad, the dress code was conservative Islamic and the places looked very traditional. The same applied to the holy cities of Najaf and Karbala. In Basra and middle-size towns like Falluja in the Sunni area and in similar-size Shi'i towns in the Shi'i south, the scene was more a mix of tradition and modernity.

The Status of Islamic Studies in School Curricula, Textbooks, and Children's Magazines

We are striving to turn the young child into a center of radiation inside his family . . . so he can . . . introduce a positive change . . . [toward] the Revolution's meanings. . . . If the father does not know this new behavior/attitude . . . the young pupil will create in the family a new example of life that is connected to the principles of the Ba'th.

—Saddam Husayn at the Ministry of Patriotic Education, July 10, 1977[53]

Our central slogan, "Let us win the youth to guarantee the future" . . . has its demands . . . preparing the cadre that will lead the youth.

—Saddam Husayn to the Youth Union, February 15, 1976[54]

School Curricula and Islam

According to a study published in 1974 by 'Abd Tufiq al-Hashimi, a professor on the Faculty of Education, the Department of Pedagogy (*kuliyyat al-tarbiya, qism al-tarbiya wa turuq al-tadris*) of Baghdad University, at least until that year Islamic studies had been in terrible shape in Ba'thi Iraq at all levels below university. Hashimi, who published his book in Baghdad, complained that Islamic education was "glaringly neglected," which raised "questions and surprise." Books used at the primary school level were shallow and poorly written, he reported. They were at least twenty-five years old and related to Islam in a way that left it completely detached from real life. Textbooks used in other disciplines, by contrast, had been rewritten or revised every few years. The status of religious studies in the schools was extremely low. Religion classes typically provided an opportunity for "leisure [and] relaxation." "These classes usually took place in the last hours of the school day, "when both pupils and teachers are weary." The teachers therefore often sent pupils home instead of teaching, or the religion classes were accepted as "classes of laziness and slumber . . . or a place for . . . [pursuing] pastimes."[55]

Worse still, Hashimi complained, because schoolmasters were appointing every available teacher to teach religion, religion was being taught by teachers who were in no position to inspire the children or to direct them toward the love of Islam:

> [Teaching Islam is delegated] to people who essentially do not believe in Islam as a faith . . . and a regime [of life]. This is happening because some of the teachers may believe in a non-Islamic faith, be it a heavenly one or a mundane one [Ba'thism? Marxism?]. Their character may be very free, some of them drink wine or gamble or have a way of life that brings shame on Islam, and some of them believe in loyalty, ideological or sentimental, to a non-Islamic system [secularism?]. How can religion be resurrected by its enemies who would like to destroy it or those who hate it or are ignorant of it?[56]

Furthermore, even if a youngster was eager to study and teach Islam, teachers' preparation in that field was extremely poor: only one hour per week was dedicated to Islamic studies in the various teachers' colleges, and not until 1973 did the colleges start dedicating one hour per week to the pedagogical aspect of teaching Islam.[57]

Insofar as by the early seventies every schoolteacher was carefully vetted by the fully "Ba'thized" Ministry of Education, this was a barely disguised attack not only on Ba'thi (and communist) teachers but also on the regime itself as an enemy of Islam. After all, it was the Ba'thi Ministry of Education that appointed those supposedly anti-Muslim teachers and severely neglected Islamic teaching. It is surprising that the regime allowed the publication of such a book. Two different explanations can be offered. One is that the study was not vetted carefully enough before it was published, and its anti-Ba'thi twist went unnoticed by the authorities. A second is that the regime desired bad publicity in this realm, and in an involuted way it was sending an indirect message to educators that Islam was and should be a very low priority and that it should be studied from an external, that is, critical point of view. This explanation is less likely than the first, but is still plausible because the book was directed mainly at professional teachers and educators rather than at the general public.

Hashimi further complained that the government examinations at the end of primary school seemed to give Islam a respectable place in the sense that knowledge of Islam represented up to 30 percent of the final grade. However, it came under the heading of Arab language. This fit well into Ba'th ideology, which looked at Islam as an instrument for the preservation of the Arabic language following the decline of the Arab Islamic civilization. But the professor did not like it at all. "This," he wrote, was "as if religion were too low to have its own independent degree or as if it were subservient to the language." The historical reality, Hashimi observed, was the reverse: "It is the language which developed to serve religion and help the understanding of its Qur'an and its Hadith." Many students and parents underestimated the importance of religious studies, he complained.[58]

Roughly the same problems plagued Islamic studies in the intermediate and secondary schools. Few teachers had attained an adequate teaching level. Some graduates of the Islamic Jurisdiction Faculty (*kuliyyat al-shari'a*, a Sunni university-level school) did not know how to teach, apparently because they had been groomed to become preachers and imams in mosques. Those who graduated from the Faculty of Education, the Department of Arab Language, on the other hand, perhaps knew how to teach some subjects, but were described as "ignoramuses" in Islam. Worse still, in many of these cases Islam was being taught by teachers who were even worse than the primary schoolteachers: "Some of them gamble, some are drunkards, and some are buffoons." They too did not believe in Islam but rather in "imported faiths." Here, too, in high school only one hour a week was dedicated to Islam. Even more surprising to the professor, Islam was completely absent from the matriculation examinations.[59]

In a study written by another Iraqi academic a few years later, the poor rating of religious studies remained essentially the same. Thus, for example, in the academic year 1979–80, the weekly schedule for primary schools included only two hours for religious education in all grades. This was the same amount of time as was spent on physical education and only half the time dedicated to English language study in the fifth and sixth grades. Arabic language, mathematics, social and national education, science, and health education received much more.[60] In intermediate schools in 1979–80, religious education received only one hour per week in all grades, far less than Arabic (six hours), English (five to six hours), history (two hours), geography (two hours), mathematics (three hours), art education (one to three hours), and physical education (two to three hours).[61] In agricultural high schools, Islam and Arabic together received two hours. In industrial high schools religion received only one hour, and in commercial high schools there were no Islamic studies classes at all.[62] Finally, among the Ministry of Education's officially defined general objectives of education, by 1979–80 religion was not mentioned even once. The closest that the Ministry of Education came to religion was when it articulated the "reactivation of the Arab cultural inheritance" as an educational goal.[63]

General School Textbooks and Islam

Textbooks dedicated to teaching Islam were, of course, available in schools. Still, as detailed earlier, during the 1970s and apparently also most of the 1980s, little time was given to Islamic studies. Also, many of the teachers were reportedly secular or even atheists. This situation remained unchanged until Saddam initiated his faith campaign, at which point Islamic studies went through a period of catching up at a breakneck pace (see chapter 6). Of interest now is the place of Islam in books that taught general social values before the faith campaign got under way. The most typical was a primary-school-level series titled "Pan-Arab and Socialist Education" (*Al-Tarbiya al-Qawmiyya wal-Ishirakiyya*), which provided the basic facts about the Baʿth Party and informed students of the most fundamental ideals the party believed in. Islam is there, but merely as an important part of a glorious Arab history that had begun long before the Prophet was born.[64] When the books discuss the party's slogan, "One Arab nation with an eternal message," the "message" is "an eternal human message that was exposed in the past through the Arab nation's civilizing role that spread its light to the whole world. . . . Today [this message] is manifest in the struggle of the nation for liberation and unity." The Arab message in world history started with "the history of the ancient civilizations," like that of Mesopotamia, the Nile, Syria, and Yemen, "and after the revolution of Islam the Arabs built a civilization, a greater one than which mankind had not known, when it comes to its values and morality or . . . literary influence and scientific production." Today, the text continues, "the eternal message of the nation is embodied in this idealistic endeavor towards rejuvenation and resurrection so that the nation will return to its leading position in human civilization." The message is also embodied in the struggle for Arab unity and liberation, and to defeat "all the expressions of division, retardation and exploitation."[65] In other words, even though Islam is part of Arab history, there is nothing religious in the party's "message" (*risala*).

The only bow to Islamic piety is to be found in the last pages of the book, which are dedicated to the ideal student, who is the "role model of the class" (*qudwat al-saff*). The Prophet's way of life is suggested as the supreme example that ought to be followed. The model pupil ought to be patriotic, ready to defend his country and the Arab nation; he must endeavor to become a good student; he must be disciplined.[66] The model pupil is not required, however, to have faith in God or to follow any religious duties, and the mosque and God are completely absent throughout the series. This was no coincidence: in the resolutions of the Eighth Regional Congress of January 1974, when discussing the party's aims in education, Islam was not mentioned even once. The principles mentioned were "socialism and national revolution."[67] Michel 'Aflaq, by then already living in Baghdad, was no doubt proud of his Iraqi disciples' approach to Islam. This secular approach, designed to treat both sects equally, had one problematic angle: the series suggested not only the Prophet but also all four Rightly Guided Caliphs as historical role models. In this way, the book clearly adopted the Sunni interpretation of history (for a detailed analysis, see chapter 6).

Children's Magazines and Islamic Values

In a professional statistical study by the Ministry of Culture and Arts of the values mentioned in the only two children's magazines in Iraq during the 1970s, an Iraqi professor of education reached the conclusion that Islam was almost absent. Furthermore, whereas religion was still present in 1970, if not very conspicuously, by 1976 religion had vanished altogether. The two magazines were the monthly *Majallati* and the weekly *al-Mizmar*. Both were published by the Ministry of Culture and Arts.[68] It was notable that the cluster of values in which religion was included, "Moral Values," was statistically last among all the clusters, appearing the fewest times in the children's magazines. And within that cluster of values, religion came last, after justice, morality, truth, and obedience.[69] The author presented a critical trend: whereas in 1970 religion placed twenty-first out of forty-five values, by 1973 it was in the forty-second place, and in 1976 it was dead last, sharing the forty-fourth place with "not dominating [people]" (*al-la-saytara*). Neither value was mentioned even once in either magazine throughout the year.[70] It seems that in the Ba'thi state, children were supposed to understand that nondomination and Islam were equally passé. Finally, efforts to replace religion with values such as "knowledge," "freedom of the homeland," "Arab unity," "socialist ownership," "altruism," and "social security" all went up steeply between 1970 and 1976.[71]

A Whiff of Atheism

The first half of the 1970s saw the publication of a large number of articles that implied atheism. While not officially limited to party members, the articles appeared only in highbrow magazines, not easily available to the general public. The more or less atheistic articles were written in a Marxist spirit, serving also to demonstrate that the Ba'th were no less progressive, scientific, and revolutionary than their competition, the Iraqi Communist Party. The most important such magazine was *al-Muthaqqaf al-'Arabi* (*The Arab Intellectual*), issued in Baghdad between 1970 and 1975 and also read outside Iraq. The atheist whiff became a rarity after 1975 with the discontinuation of *al-Muthaqqaf al-'Arabi*, and disappeared altogether after 1980. As implied by Saddam a few years later, it proved to be detrimental to the public image of the ruling party.

One example of the implied atheism of the first half of the 1970s is an article published in 1974 by a Marxist-inclined Iraqi intellectual. He was permitted to publish a theoretical discussion explaining how history ought to be studied. He criticized medieval Islamic historians for failing to understand the "dialectical connection between the development of social forces and change of social production relations." They did not understand the "natural historical determinism that derives from the natural laws which move history." They explained history in terms of "metaphysical, mythological reasons." In other words, they totally ignored the infallibility of Karl Marx's historical and dialectical materialism, as any decent historian could have told them, because they explained historical developments and events in terms of God's will. All that they wrote, the Marxist intellectual went on, was designed to support the ruler's "divine right to rule, [he] being the shadow of God on earth as [the 'Abbasid caliph] Abu Ja'far al-Mansur claimed to be." Also, the Islamic historians, for example the 'Abbasid-era al-Tabari, saw all revolutionary movements as negative and destructive, whereas some of the revolutionary movements actually represented progressive struggles for social liberation, the author wrote. One example of such a progressive movement was the ninth century CE anti-'Abbasid revolution of the *Zunuj*, the black slaves, whose leader was unjustly described by 'Abbasid historians as wicked. The Marxist intellectual complained that unbiased medieval Islamic writing was hard to come by when it concerned the "eruptions of oppressed peoples and the exploited, revolutionary masses."[72] The same author also dared to launch an attack on the greatest Islamic medieval theologian and mystic, Abu Hamid Muhammad al-Ghazali, a frequent target of Ba'thi attacks. As the Marxist saw it, in his *Tahafut al-Falasafa* (*The Defeat of Philosophy*), Ghazali "helped the transcendental metaphysical [faith] [*al-mithaliyya al-ghaybiyya*] spread," and in this way he helped "freeze [free] thinking." In the twentieth century, he was happy to report, Arab intellectuals became aware of and attracted to "the [right] progressive ideas," mainly to [Marxist] "dialectical materialism."[73]

Another theoretician opened his article by quoting approvingly the thought of a Polish Marxist whose writings had been translated into Arabic by the Ba'thi Dar al-Tali'a publication house in Beirut in 1971. In the ancient Greek era (he quoted the Pole), owing to the nature of production, which was essentially a slavery system, and the lack of scientific data, the materialistic philosophy could not win the day. In the medieval era, the Catholic Church used religion to support the feudalists. The development of production forces in the modern age, however, inevitably created the scientific thinking of materialistic philosophy, which became the basis for modern rationalism.[74] Speaking for himself, the Iraqi author then argued that the principles of Copernicus, Bruno, Galileo, Hobbs, Descartes, Spinoza, and other rationalists contributed substantially to the struggle against "metaphysics" (read: religion). These great rationalists' success was achieved "through the theoretical vindication of atheism [*ilhad*]." Hegel contributed dialectics, and Marx added to it materialism. Marx and Lenin showed the way toward a perfectly rational and materialistic philosophy. They presented the final solution to the question of which came first, "the material world or the spirit [*awlawiyyat al-wujud aw al-wa'i*]."[75] The only way to understand this article is that matter came before spirit, and thus the world of matter preceded God. In other words, God did not create the universe; rather, man created God. The author summed up his lengthy treatise by stating emphatically that the struggle of his time was "between a rotting world" of religion and other metaphysical beliefs "that is ready for the fall, and . . . a new world that will be created by the vast masses."[76]

In another philosophical treatise dealing with "human freedom" and the issue of a causative connection between natural phenomena, the author argued that all natural phenomena have natural and material causes. The article stated that, in contradistinction to the claims of theologians such as Muhammad al-Ghazali, there existed no supernatural force that could make things happen. In the same vein, the author argued for total and unimpeded human freedom in choosing man's course.[77] The only way this position could be understood was by recognizing that no religious duties were ordained by a deity. Rather, they were invented by man. In another article the same author argued explicitly that "matter . . . is what produced life. . . . Essence [*al-mahiyya*, the human spirit], then, is not to be found outside of matter." This implies the nonexistence of God and an afterlife. The author argued very forcefully for Darwinist theories, with some Marxist undertones, including specifying that "[material] existence preceded consciousness [*asbaqiyyat al-ka'in 'ala al-wa'i*]."[78]

Even more poignantly, in an anthropological study published in 1980, a Shi‘i Ba‘thi author pointed out that in the (Shi‘i) village he studied, al-Sharsh, south of al-Qurna on the Tigris, the struggle was no longer between the tribal groups of which the village consisted. Rather, it was

> a struggle between *the old, which is based on religion* and tribal tradition [*al-‘urf*] and *the new, based on liberation from* [*al-takhallus min*] *the shackles of religion* and traditional customs, and on finding a social mechanism for life that will be more flexible.[79]

No wonder that, when mocking the party, the enemies of the Ba‘th invented for it an oath of allegiance: "*Uqsimu bil-Ba‘th ilahan la sharika lahu, wa bil-‘uruba ingilan wa Qur’anan*" (I swear in the Ba‘th as God who has no copartner, and in Arabism as the New Testament and Qur’an). More wicked tongues invented for the party a more offensive oath: "*La ilaha illa al-Ba‘th wa ‘Aflaq rasul al-Ba‘th*" (There is no God but the Ba‘th and ‘Aflaq is the Messenger of the Ba‘th).

Religious Holidays as a Balancing Act

Religious and Secular Holidays between Tradition and Ba‘thi Practice

In terms of religious and secular national holidays, that is, days on which school students and their teachers, state officials, and workers in the public and mixed sectors were to have a day off, the legal system under the Ba‘th regime largely followed in the footsteps of previous Iraqi regimes.[80] Previous regimes, too, had shown respect for Islam by declaring all major Islamic festivals national holidays. However, the Ba‘th also recognized the main holidays of other religions. In this way they remained essentially within a secular framework. Under the monarchy, three days of holiday were allocated for ‘Id al-Fitr (between 1 and 3 Shawal), at the end of the fasting month of Ramadan. Four days were declared holiday for ‘Id al-Adhha, at the end of the *haj*, the pilgrimage to Mecca (between 10 and 13 Dhu al-Hijja). One day was dedicated to the Prophet's birthday (12 Rabi‘ al-Awwal). Even though the royal house and most of the state officialdom were Sunnis, the monarchy made a meaningful gesture to its Shi‘i majority: one day was declared a national holiday on ‘Ashura (10 Muharram), the most important day in the Shi‘i calendar. Friday was the weekly day of rest, but at least until 1936 Saturday was a bank holiday, apparently as a result of the Jewish ownership of most private banks. The monarchy had very few secular holidays: one day for King Faysal's birthday (March 21) and one more day to celebrate the 1933 coronation of King Ghazi (September 8), which included a military parade under the king's auspices.[81] Army Day on January 6 was also celebrated but was not declared a day off other obligations.

Under Generals 'Abd al-Karim Qasim (1958–63) and 'Abd al-Salam 'Arif (1963–66) and his brother 'Abd al-Rahman 'Arif (1966–68), with the exception of the monarch's birthday and coronation, national holidays remained essentially the same. They included every Friday. This made sense, not only because Islam was declared the state religion but also because at least 90 percent of all Iraqis were Muslims. The same three-day holiday for 'Id al-Fitr remained; four days for 'Id al-Adhha and a day for the Prophet's birthday were also retained. Beginning in 1958, one day was added for the new Islamic (*Hijri*) year (1 Muharram). The 'Ashura, too, was retained as a national holiday. Secular holidays under Qasim were July 14, commemorating the 1958 revolution that toppled the monarchy, and Army Day on January 6. The 'Arifs continued those holidays and added February 8 (14 Ramadan), celebrating the coup d'état that toppled General Qasim in 1963. In 1964, 'Abd al-Salam 'Arif adopted socialism as part of his preparation for unification with 'Abd al-Nasir's Egypt. This prompted him to declare May 1, International Workers' Day, as a brand-new holiday (and a very secular one at that). When it came to non-Muslim communities, Christians received December 25 and January 1 as holidays (on such a day, Christian teachers and other government officials were allowed a day off work). Jews received one day on Yom Kippur, two days at Sukkot (Pentecost), and two days at Passover.[82]

Under the Ba'th, Law No. 110 of 1972 retained all the Muslim holidays precisely as they were under the 'Arifs, including 'Ashura on 10 Muharram. By 1972, regime-Shi'i relations were tense; the party had already experienced antiregime 'Ashura mass demonstrations and thus was aware of the explosive potential of the day. Even if the regime had wanted not to recognize 'Ashura, however, the Ba'th could not have taken this step. If previous regimes had recognized it, they were obliged to recognize it as well, or the decision not to would have been considered akin to a declaration of war. The party considered the self-flagellation and other rites of 'Ashura to be primitive, bizarre anthropological relics from days gone by,[83] but there is no evidence that the Ba'th regime ever considered excluding it from the calendar. Almost from its first day in power, the party went to great effort to recruit Shi'i members to its lower echelons, and filtering out *'Ashura* would have been seen by even the most secular Shi'i members as an offense. The regime, however, implied that it did not consider Iraq to be a Shi'i-majority state by excluding other Shi'i holidays that could undermine Sunni legitimacy. For example, the birthday of the Imam Mahdi on 15 Sha'ban, as well as 'Id al-Ghadir—marking the day on which, according to Shi'i interpretation, the Prophet announced Imam 'Ali as his successor—were celebrated in Iran with great publicity but were not recognized as holidays in Iraq. At the same time, Imam 'Ali's and Imam Husayn's birthdays and 'Ali's death were mentioned in the press, even though the days were not national days of commemoration. The special connection that the regime created between the two imams and Saddam's tribe explains this unusual mention.

For Christians, Christmas remained a holiday, as well as January 1, which was upgraded to an all-Iraqi holiday. In addition, two days were declared holidays for Christians only at Easter. Surprisingly, despite the ongoing official anti-Semitic (or, more accurately, anti-Jewish) campaign and the fact that, by 1972, few Jews remained in Iraq, there was no change in the holidays recognized for Jews. Yet Christians did not get Sundays or Jews Saturdays as holidays. New holidays were recognized for two other ancient minorities: the Sabeans received six days of holiday and the Yezidis received fourteen days.[84] Even though, with the exception of Newruz (New Year in the solar Persian and Kurdish calendar and the Spring Festival), non-Islamic holidays did not enjoy the same status as Islamic ones, by recognizing them the regime made the statement that all religions were equal (or roughly so). Christian or Jewish or other non-Islamic holidays applied only to small minorities, and entitling only these groups and no one else to have a free day can easily be explained as a secular approach.

Secular holidays were at first few, but in terms of state-mosque relations two of them were nonetheless meaningful. The Kurdish holiday of Newruz on March 21 was made a national holiday for all Iraqis. Official acceptance of what was a pagan pre-Islamic celebration was not only a symbolic step toward including the Kurds but also a manifestation of a secular frame of mind. Likewise, the January 1 holiday could be and widely was seen not only as a Christian religious holiday but also as an all-Iraqi occasion. A full-fledged national holiday on a Christian holiday demonstrated that under the Ba'th, the beginning of the Christian Gregorian year carried the same weight as 1 Muharram, the beginning of the Islamic year. This was a very meaningful statement. Other secular national days were inspired by contemporary political events and followed the mold of the previous postmonarchy regimes in Iraq, but also of Gamal 'Abd al-Nasir's Egypt and Syria under the Ba'th regime. The celebrations on May 1 signaled the party's commitment to socialism, a concept vehemently rejected by the religious parties, Sunni as well as Shi'i, because it was widely (though mistakenly) perceived as rooted in the atheist tradition of communism. On January 6, as under all previous regimes, Ba'thi Iraq celebrated Army Day. February 8 marked the toppling of Qasim, July 14 celebrated Qasim's revolution against the monarchy, and July 17 and 30 marked the Ba'th revolutions, or the two phases of the 1968 coup d'état.

Beginning in 1979, Saddam as president added a crushing number of national holidays to mark victories in the Iran-Iraq War and to celebrate the 1991 *umm al-ma'arik* (Mother of All Battles), as well as myriad other Ba'th regime occasions. The most telling among the new holidays was his birthday, April 28 (1937). Celebrating it nationwide was unprecedented in postmonarchy Iraq and a clear sign that the "republican" president considered himself to be some kind of royalty. The newspapers congratulated him on their front pages, radio and television broadcasts were dedicated to his life story, he was shown on television dressed in a white suit with a white tie and white shoes and socks, children met with him in the Republican Palace and sang birthday songs for him, and he was raised to the level of the Redeemer.[85] Such latter-day holidays, however, had no bearing on mosque-state relations, being designed to elevate the status of Saddam.

Celebrating the 'Ids, Ba'th Style

Throughout the Ba'th party's rule, the state "nationalized" the main Islamic occasions: 'Id al-Adhha or 'Id al-Qurban (the Sacrifice Celebration, starting on 10 Dhu al-Hijja); 'Id al-Fitr (the Celebration of the Breaking of the Fast at the end of the month-long Ramadan fasting); *iftar* (fast-breaking) dinners during Ramadan evenings; *al-mawlid al-nabawi* (the Prophet's birthday); Badr Day, commemorating a great victory of the Muslims over the pagans of Mecca in 624 CE; *laylat al-isra' wal-mi'raj*, the Night of the Journey and Ascendancy to Heaven, during which the Prophet rode on a magic winged horse to the "Furthest Mosque" (*al-masjid al-aqsa*), from where he ascended to heaven and then returned; *laylat al-qadar* (The Night of the Divine Decree, on which the Qur'an was revealed and descended from heaven), and similar events. The party and the Ministry of Awqaf (Endowments) organized public meetings and dinners related to each particular festival. Lavish *iftar* dinners for hundreds of citizens were organized throughout the month of Ramadan, sponsored by and with the participation of regime luminaries.[86] In this way, many times throughout the year the regime and party demonstrated respect for Islamic values in the hope that this would win them the support of the traditional masses. The consistent pursuit of this policy over thirty-five years suggests that it bore fruit and met with approval from at least some of the Iraqi Muslim public.

A Slight Bow to the Mosque: Ramadan Fasting and Its Mutations

Following in the footsteps of the 'Arif regime, some Shar'i rules forbidding public fast-breaking (*al-iftar al-'alani*) during the day were occasionally announced just before the month of Ramadan. To placate the Shi'a, some restrictions on public entertainment were also imposed during the first ten days of Muharram, leading to the most central Shi'i day of commemoration, 10 Muharram.[87] On the surface, all this activity focused on restrictions and permissions around important holidays created the impression of a traditional and religious regime, but more often than not it was for show, as the restrictions were far from the shar'i standard. In fact, rather than demonstrating regime piety, Ramadan restrictions, however maintained over the course of Ba'th rule, might serve as the best litmus test of the regime's self-confidence. The degree of "respect for the holiness of Ramadan" fluctuated continuously. When the regime felt weak and vulnerable, it imposed more restrictions, or at least imposed the existing ones more strictly. When it felt omnipotent, it let its hair down, relaxed those restrictions, and allowed itself to be more in harmony with the separation of mosque and state.

When the Ba'th regime came to power, it imposed more or less the same restrictions as 'Abd al-Rahman 'Arif's regime had done, even though it went contrary to the Ba'th regime's secular credo (the 'Arif brothers never pretended to represent a secular worldview). During its first two years in power, the Ba'th regime was extremely unpopular and felt very insecure. As a result, it added some restrictions to those imposed by 'Arif. Thus, in November 1968, on the regime's first Ramadan, the Ba'thi Ministry of Labor and Social Affairs issued a communiqué emphasizing "the duty of . . . adhering to everything that will guard Ramadan's holiness and sacredness." The ministry announced that it was necessary to prevent completely any public breaking of the fast. In practical terms this meant "the closure of all *coffeehouses* [*al-maqahi*], the casinos, the bars, the shops and places where liquors are consumed and bought"—all this during daytime. By implication, the restrictions meant that alcoholic drinks could be consumed in public places in the evenings and, of course, any time before and after the month of Ramadan, but this was the case under all the previous regimes, and anyway it was a separate issue. In addition, all places where drinks were sold (*bay al-martabat*) and all restaurants in official, semiofficial, public, or commercial institutions were to be closed during the day (the regulations also applied to mobile food vendors). Again, these institutions were allowed to reopen in the evenings after dark. There were only a few exceptions to the regulations: hotels with the two highest ratings; centers of tourism; and restaurants, coffee shops, and hotels on the railway system, at airports, and in ports. Except for the expensive hotels in town, all the other exceptions were more or less in line with the shari'a, because travelers are allowed to postpone the Ramadan fasting. To compensate for it, a person is instructed to fast a similar number of days when he or she is home, after the end of Ramadan.[88] This explains the permission to keep restaurants open in airports, in the railroad system, and in ports. On three days *and* nights, however, all the entertainment and dancing centers (*al-malahi wal-maraqis*), and all bars and shops where liquors were consumed and bought, were to close. These nights were the nineteenth, twenty-first, and twenty-seventh of Ramadan. There were no explanations, but every Shi'i knew that the first day was the day when Imam 'Ali was stabbed in his Friday Mosque in his capital city of Kufa in 661 CE, and the second was the day on which he died. The third was the all-Islamic Night of the Divine Decree (*laylat al-qadar*). The Ba'th initially allowed fewer exceptions than did the 'Arif regime: the latter had allowed the governor of each governorate to exempt "those restaurants deemed highly necessary."[89] One year later, in 1969, the Ba'th regime allowed itself to follow the 'Arif regime to the letter, in that it allowed the governors to exempt from the restrictions those institutions regarded as "absolutely essential."[90]

For the next two years, nothing changed.[91] In 1972, however, something changed. Governors were allowed to exempt "popular restaurants" without their having to be particularly essential. Furthermore, in a typical Ba'thi sly backhand blow to religion, the governor of Baghdad allowed restaurants on "secondary streets" to remain open during the day with no limitations at all. Moreover, the governor allowed even restaurants on the main streets to remain open during the day, provided that they had an entrance from a secondary street and kept their main door locked and the windows facing the main street covered.[92] The restrictions applying to the rest of the country remained as before and unchanged until 1981.[93]

The years 1972–79 were good years for the regime. The regime leaders destroyed their most dangerous enemies—the communists, the pro-Syrian Ba'this, and Iranian agents; they signed an important agreement with the Soviet Union; and they managed to terrorize the population sufficiently to cow all but the most ardent Shi'i fundamentalists. In 1974–75, their oil revenues quadrupled. Their self-confidence was growing, and with it their secular policies.

A marked change in the opposite direction occurred during the Iran-Iraq War. The war did not go well. Casualties mounted; many soldiers deserted; the economy suffered. In 1982 the Iraqi army was beaten back inside Iraq's borders, and the regime's popularity fell to a record low. No less problematic, the public began to frequent the mosques more than ever before. Now the regime's mouthpiece claimed that "adhering to the rites of this month" was a patriotic Iraqi duty as much as a religious one. This would buttress Islam, "which the Persian enemy wants to twist and derail." Also, keeping to the rules of Ramadan would "strengthen the will to prevail" in the war. The governors were instructed to allow popular restaurants to open only in cases of "extreme need" and in "the smallest number possible." In addition to closures on the nights of 19, 21, and 27 Ramadan, places of entertainment and dancing were to be closed completely also on one extra night, that of 17 Ramadan. This was to commemorate the victory of the Muslim armies under the Prophet in the battle of Badr in 624 CE. Badr was chosen because it represented a victory of the believers over the pagans, and the Ba'th regime promised the same kind of victory against the "Persian Zoroastrian priest" Khomeini. During the days of Ramadan other than those four, the places of entertainment were to be closed only during the day, but in June 1981 dark fell very late, about 10:30 p.m., so the thirsty Ba'this and some others had to wait a long time.[94]

Toward the end of the war, restrictions became even more stringent: this time, all places of entertainment, the social clubs (*al-muntadiyat*), places where liquor could be consumed or purchased, and dance halls in hotels (and, apparently, all other dance halls) were to be closed for the whole month, day and night. It was stressed that throughout the month, day and night, no alcoholic drinks could be consumed (in public), and all bars would be closed. Still, the defiant Ba'thi spirit was not completely dead: top-tier restaurants in town and tourist restaurants on the roads could remain open, provided that the windows and doors were covered. Restaurants in the factories could also be kept open, apparently so as not to affect the war effort, as could a small number of restaurants at the center of each governorate (*muhafaza*), district (*qadha*), and subdivision of a province (*nahiya*), provided that all were camouflaged in the same manner.[95] In the 1990s, the restrictions were announced by the Presidential Bureau, a clear upgrade of authority, but the rules remained the same.[96] Beginning in 1994, when the regime placed severe limitations on alcohol consumption, clubs, and other forms of entertainment during the year, many of the Ramadan restrictions became redundant.

Certain conclusions concerning state-mosque relations and the power of the state with respect to religious bodies can be drawn from the ebb and tide of restrictions surrounding religious holidays. When the party felt vulnerable and shari'a-wise, not without some flaws, Ramadan restrictions were extensive. This was the case from 1968 to 1970. In 1972–80, the regime felt progressively more secure, even omnipotent. Those years saw a marked relaxation of Ramadan restrictions, one of the litmus tests of regime self-confidence. When Ayatollah Khomeini returned to Tehran in February 1979, life did not change immediately, and the regime, still confident, stuck tenaciously to its secular ways. As documents and recordings that have recently become available reveal, in a secret discussion with his lieutenants six days before the Iraqi invasion of Iran in September 1980, Saddam's launching of a military offensive against Iran was a sign of a triumphal state of mind more than anything else.[97] By the second half of the 1980s, the tide had turned. The unsuccessful war against an Islamist regime that had accused the Ba'th of atheism rattled the Iraqi regime. Saddam himself admitted in another secret meeting that Khomeini's accusations that the Ba'th were enemies of Islam had hurt the party.[98] This was the pivotal moment when the Ba'th regime began losing confidence in itself and in its secular credo. Toward the end of the Iran-Iraq War, the Ramadan restrictions became particularly severe. These restrictions, which the public associated with Saudi demands in return for Saudi financial aid, were abhorred by secular Iraqis, including many party members.[99] However, the restrictions likely had little to do with Saudi financial support. If developments during the early 1990s are any evidence (see chapters 5 and 6), the increased restrictions were simply a trial balloon floated by the regime to test the public's reaction to gradual Islamization in times of national crisis. Although secular Iraqis were annoyed, the religious strictures were popular with the more traditional public, or the "born-again" Muslims. As a result, Saddam decided to stay the Islamic course. As discussed in chapters 5 and 6, the increased restrictions during Ramadan were soon followed by a far more comprehensive campaign of Islamization.

Chapter 3
The Other Islam:
Regime-Shi'i Relations, 1968–79

The Sunni-Shi'i Divide: Structural or Intentional?

Under the Ba'th, Iraq's Sunni-Shi'i-Kurdish cleavage was not absolute, nor was it always the most important fault line in Iraqi society. Class divisions between rich and poor in Baghdad, for example, often blurred the Sunni-Shi'i distinction. Senior Shi'i party officials and the Shi'i rich who lived in al-Rashid or al-Ma'mun quarters in Baghdad—and there were more than just a few of them—were far closer to their Sunni peers than to their poverty-stricken and still largely tribal coreligionists in Saddam City. Iraq's established traditional merchant class, in which Shi'is had long enjoyed a strong presence, was for the most part absent from religious movements opposing the Ba'th. As success in big commerce depended on contacts in the government and the party, some upwardly mobile Shi'is flourished by identifying themselves to varying degrees with the regime.[1] Similarly, the differences between the more cosmopolitan old-time residents of the capital and other major towns and the partially tribal villagers or the poorer newcomers to the cities were deep and meaningful, in many cases overriding ethnic and sectarian dividing lines. For example, while most of the population of the Shi'i cities supported the March 1991 antiregime uprising, some rural tribes supported the regime, and many others remained on the sidelines, waiting to see who would come out on top. This urban-rural difference became a major consideration in the shaping of the regime's postrevolt policies, when it fairly successfully recruited Shi'i tribes and shaykhs.[2] Nonetheless, the Sunni-Shi'i chasm has been of great importance throughout the history of the Iraqi state, and under the Ba'th more so than under any other regime.

There is an ongoing debate among students of Iraqi history between "structuralists" and "intentionalists" regarding the nature of the Sunni-Shi'i-Kurdish conflict in Iraq.[3] As this book is concerned with state-mosque relations, the Kurds, a Muslim ethnic group, are essentially outside the scope of the discussion, leaving the Sunni-Shi'i fracture as a focal point.[4] The structuralist versus intentionalist debate comes down to the following: How much of the Sunni-Shi'i divide can be explained as the result of structural historical socioreligious developments or, conversely, attributed to immediate political circumstances or intentional manipulation? Under the Ba'th, I believe, both kinds of explanations were at work. The Sunni-Shi'i divide is not unique to the Ba'th era; it dates back a long way, to the dawn of the Iraqi nation-state. This divide, however, appeared only after an initial impressive show of Sunni-Shi'i unity that took place even before the establishment of the monarchy (August 1921–July 1958). In a major 1920 uprising against the British rule, there was no Sunni-Shi'i antagonism. On the contrary, there was some limited Sunni cooperation with the Shi'i anti-British revolt, though almost all the fighting was done in the south by Shi'i tribes. When the Shi'i revolt was over and the British were bleeding, the Shi'i tribes were devastated, and the Sunni Arab elite of Baghdad and Mosul were handed the reins of government on a silver platter.[5]

The first sectarian incident that could be interpreted as indicative of a structural antagonism took place less than two years later, during the first year of the reign of King Faysal I (1921–33). Sati' al-Husri, the king's director of education (1921–27), noted in his memoirs that on the first day of 'Ashura, which was commemorated under the monarchy, the king and his entourage attended the Shi'i passion play mourning the killing of Imam Husayn (*marasim 'azaa al-Husayn*) at al-Kazimayn. "Hundreds" participated actively in the play, according to al-Husri, and "thousands" watched and accompanied the unfolding story with heavily charged emotions. There were two camps in the play, one of the holy Imam Husayn and the other of "al-Husayn's murderer," the reviled Sa'd bin Abihi. Whenever the murderer showed up on his horse, "roaring screams of curses came out of the throats" of the audience, "especially the women's." Then al-Husri noticed that the brand-new national flag of the Iraqi monarchy was meticulously accompanying the murderer's camp. Whenever the equestrian murderer appeared with the monarchy's flag-bearer accompanying him, both were showered with heated curses. Al-Husri was shocked: "The Iraqi flag was riding with the pageant of the horse-rider whom the people were cursing!" he fumed. (It should be remembered that even though the king was regarded as a descendant of the Prophet and Imam Husayn, he was a Sunni.) As the king was seated too far away, al-Husri immediately turned to a nearby courtier, told him about the outrage, and instructed him to order the organizers to make sure that the national flag was glued to Imam Husayn's group. The organizers gave the right instruction, but the equestrian Imam Husayn "pushed him [the national flag-bearer] away forcefully." Whenever the flag carrier tried to move again near Imam Husayn, the latter "pushed him away again, showing signs of extreme rage." When al-Husri realized that his efforts were in vain, he ordered the flag removed altogether. On the way back to the palace, al-Husri told the king about the incident. The king said that he was completely unaware of it, but commended al-Husri for his initiative.[6] It stands to reason that the king was fully aware of what had happened but chose to ignore it, for it was beneath him to get involved in a skirmish. Whatever the case, the king was made aware of a major problem he had with around 50 percent of his citizens even before he completed his first year on the throne.

In March 1933, King Faysal I sent a confidential memorandum to his top officials arguing that "Iraq is a monarchy ruled by a Sunni-Arab government . . . ruling over . . . an ignorant Shi'i majority. . . . The oppression they suffered from the Turkish rule . . . opened a deep trench within the Arab people, who are split between these two sects. Regrettably, all this moved this [Shi'i] majority . . . to believe that they are oppressed because they are Shi'is." Shi'i antiregime circles often told the simple people that "the taxes are on the Shi'i, and death is for the Shi'i, and the jobs are for the Sunni."[7] While Faysal did not agree with these complaints, he described them accurately. He was worried that what he termed incitement was working, and tried to change this reality by incorporating Shi'is into the state system, but he was a realist, and aimed only for what he believed he could achieve.[8] Having come from outside Iraq, he depended heavily on the support of his Sunni bureaucrats, and they were averse to allowing Shi'is in meaningful numbers into the government system. After a brutal suppression of the next Shi'i tribal revolts of 1935–36, some Shi'i demonstrations and complaints notwithstanding, throughout the monarchical era no major confrontations took place, even though the Shi'is were indeed in an inferior position.

Yet the underprivileged position of the Shi'a was not the only cause for Shi'a-regime political tension. The nascent Iraqi state was afflicted with a far older structural problem. In the first place, King Faysal's ruling elite did not trust the Shi'a: they suspected them of being hostile to Iraq and Arabism, and of being an Iranian fifth column.[9] When it came to the Shi'a, even had they been far better off than they were in Iraq, the mere difference in terms of identity would have meant that a Sunni king, even if a Hashimite *sharif,* ruling over a Shi'i majority would still face a challenge. No strong community of identity—and the Shi'a of Iraq were indeed a strong such community—accepts an outside ruler willingly. But the particular doctrine and historical tradition of the Shi'a made such acceptance even more difficult: historically speaking, even Shi'i rulers were not fully legitimate in the eyes of, or accepted by, the Shi'i community. As noted by Etan Kohlberg, a historian of medieval Shi'ism, and Michael Gilsenan, an anthropologist of contemporary Islamic societies, in Shi'i doctrine and tradition, at least since the rise of the Shi'i Qajars to power in Shi'i Iran at the end of the eighteenth century, the only fully legitimate rule has been that of the twelfth Imam, the Expected Imam Mahdi (*al-mahdi al-muntazar*), whose appearance (*al-zuhur*) will take place at the end of time. Even though the Qajars were Shi'i rulers, their authority was therefore never fully recognized.[10] Since at least the eighteenth century, the dominant rule in Shi'i theological-political tradition has been that, in the absence of the Imam Mahdi, the 'ulama are regarded as the source of authority. And yet even the 'ulama have not been all-powerful and immune to challenge.[11] Not surprisingly, then, the Sunni-hegemonic regimes of Iraq since 1920–21 were never seen by the Shi'i majority and their 'ulama as fully legitimate. This was certainly a built-in structural problem for any Sunni ruler in Iraq.

Reviving Historical Antagonisms

In addition to the need to satisfy a legitimacy requirement, there was the potential clash of identities between Sunnis and Shi'is arising out of historical memory and theology. The well-known 1927 case of Anis al-Nusuli's school textbook that was pro-Umayyad and portrayed 'Ali in an unfavorable light is just one example. The incident threatened to trigger a violent intersectarian crisis and was defused only by a difficult decision King Faysal I made to satisfy the hurt feelings of the Shi'is.[12] This clash could lie dormant, and Iraq indeed saw years of fruitful, even harmonious coexistence and cooperation between the sects, including intermarriages, but history is etched in people's memory and becomes a part of their identity. In times of crisis old historical grievances and bitter memories often rise up from the dust and ashes of the long-dead past. As the Shi'a see it, 'Ali's right to the caliphate was usurped by the first three caliphs. The brutal murder of his son, Imam Husayn, and many of his family at the hands of the "Sunni" Umayyad army in 680 CE "had a profound impact on Imami consciousness and became a focal point for the martyrdom motif which is so characteristic of Imami Shi'ism," according to Kohlberg. To this day, "the active participation of the faithful in the grief of Husayn . . . is considered a religious obligation." The obverse side of the loyalty (*al-wilaya*) to 'Ali and his descendants, the eleven Imams, is "the utter rejection [*bara'a*] of their opponents."[13] However, those opponents—the first three caliphs and their supporters, as well as later caliphs who were believed to have persecuted the Shi'i Imams and their community—were seen by the Sunnis as perfectly legitimate, indeed, even as role model caliphs.[14]

That the historical heroes of the Sunni-hegemonic community of Iraq were seen as despicable villains by the Shi'i majority stood in the way of achieving national unity. It posed another structural barrier. Some ruling regimes tried to manipulate al-Husayn's memory to win Shi'i support, but had little success. Some Shi'i opposition leaders manipulated the memory of al-Husayn's martyrdom to enhance antiregime and, by insinuation, anti-Sunni sentiments.[15] These leaders took advantage of religious commemoration days such as the Tasu'a, the 'Ashura, and the Arba'in to whip up antiregime sentiments. And yet, as Gilsenan has noted, the cultural tradition in his study areas of mourning the death of Imam Husayn was not "merely a kind of emotive window dressing. . . . It was of enormous power in summoning up the founding myth of the community, focusing on a primordial identity now put at risk in a very real sense by new modes of domination, and concentrating opposition to the rulers. For all strata could find in their own experience different critical areas of correspondence with those martyred [in 680 CE] by the unjust and unbelieving."[16] For their part, the ruling regimes also manipulated the Sunni-Shi'i divide when it suited them.

And yet, following the brutal suppression of a series of Shi'i tribal revolts in 1935–36, and some Shi'i demonstrations and complaints notwithstanding, throughout the monarchical era no major intersectarian confrontations took place. In the last decade of the monarchy, Sunni-Shi'i relations became more relaxed, in part because Shi'is found it easier to join the ruling elite, and did so in growing numbers. As well, after the 1950–52 exodus of the Jews from Iraq, many Shi'is found work in the private sector, moving into the vacated niches, thus improving their socioeconomic status.

The Rise of the Ba'th Party

The process of integrating Shi'is into government service was enhanced under the rule of General 'Abd al-Karim Qasim (1958–63), who also devoted resources to building homes for the poorest Shi'i families in Baghdad's slums. Moreover, politically, Qasim kept Iraq at arm's length from 'Abd al-Nasir's Egypt and Arab unity plans. Most Shi'is welcomed this policy, as they feared Arab unification, which threatened to drown them in a Sunni majority. Moreover, Qasim's mother was a Shi'i Fayli Kurd, and he was seen as half Shi'i himself (in Arab tradition, the mother's side is still of great importance, even though the society is patriarchal). Qasim's mother's side seems to have played a role in reducing Shi'i alienation. All this may explain why, even though the Shi'i 'ulama spearheaded the struggle against Qasim's secular Law of Personal Status and denounced his cooperation with the Communist Party, under Qasim Iraq did not see Shi'i mass demonstrations, and nothing like a revolt. In fact, when the Ba'th Party and part of the military executed the February 1963 coup against Qasim, many working-class Shi'is who were grateful to him for his social policies rushed to his aid. Qasim, though, was reluctant to issue weapons to the supportive masses and to the Communist Party, and this became his doom.[17]

The main force behind the new regime was the Ba'th Party, which consisted mostly of little-known civilians. For prestige purposes, they anointed General 'Abd al-Salam 'Arif, a well-known pro-Egyptian military man, as a titular president. Their rule was brief. Nine months later, in November 1963, they lost power to General 'Arif and a military junta. Under 'Abd al-Salam 'Arif (1963–66), Shi'is were again marginalized, and they widely saw him as a Sunni bigot. Ayatollah al-'Askari told a revolutionary Shi'i magazine a story of regime horrors and Shi'i redemption during 'Abd al-Salam 'Arif's era. According to the ayatollah, with the help of Egypt's 'Abd al-Nasir, another Sunni Arab dictator, 'Arif planned "to strike at the followers of the school of the Prophet's family," namely, the Iraqi Shi'a. The ayatollah insisted that the two reviled and feared Sunni dictators were adamant on destroying the Iraqi Shi'a in a Satanic anti-Shi'i holocaust. The Shi'is were saved by the swift action of Mahdi al-Hakim, the ingenious son of the chief *marja'* (religious authority) of the Shi'i community, and by divine intervention.[18] This and other horror stories were baseless, but they reflected real paranoia and a true sentiment. Limited protests against the 'Arif regime occurred during the Shi'i holy days, but only one confrontation with the regime took place. During an Arba'in procession in June 1965, marchers chanted antiregime refrains. In a battle with the police, three marchers and two policemen were killed.[19]

Shi'i-Regime Alienation and Saddam's Rise to Power

The Ba'th Party came to power for the second time in a coup d'état on July 17, 1968. President 'Abd al-Rahman 'Arif (1966–68), the brother of the previous president, 'Abd al-Salam, who had died in a helicopter crash, was sent into a long exile in Turkey. Two weeks later, on July 30, the Ba'th removed from their positions all the senior officers who had helped them execute the coup, but whom the Ba'this did not trust. Within a few months, the powerful Ba'thi president, General Ahmad Hasan al-Bakr, had appointed his tribesman, a little-known young civilian Ba'thi activist by the name of Saddam Husayn al-Tikriti, to the position of czar of internal security. By November 1969, Bakr had promoted Saddam to the positions of vice president, deputy chairman of the Revolutionary Command Council (RCC), and deputy secretary general of the Regional Leadership. Saddam became the second most powerful man at the top, but when it came to security policy, including how to deal with Shi'i opposition to the regime, he was the main authority. By 1971, having managed to drive his chief rivals from the corridors of power, Saddam had also managed to partially marginalize even President Bakr. By then, Saddam was the most important decision-maker in Baghdad in all the strategic realms, including internal security; the military; and relations with the Western oil companies, Iran, the Arab world, and the superpowers (mainly the Soviet Union and France). Policy regarding religion and culture, too, became his domain. In July 1979, he became president, and in one stroke eliminated all the real and perceived opposition to his leadership within the party. Hundreds of senior party members and military officers were executed. After that, no real opposition inside the party to Saddam's decisions was possible.

The Demographic Foundation of Shi'i-Regime Alienation

Under the second Ba'th rule (1968–2003), regime-Shi'a relations reached the deepest crisis ever experienced in modern Iraq. The revolt of March 1991, and even the riots of 1969, 1977, and 1979, discussed later in the chapter, had no parallels in pre-Ba'th Iraqi history since 1936. There are a few mutually supportive reasons for the failure of the Ba'th regime to reduce the tension with a large part of the Shi'i community, or at least to keep it low, as it had been under the 'Arif brothers. As a result of this failure, regime-Shi'i relations deteriorated quickly, and the 1970s saw a few head-on confrontations. In 1991, the unrest exploded in a mass revolt. To fully understand why regime-Shi'i relations were so tense under the Ba'th, it is necessary to look first at the country's demography.

According to the British Population Census of 1919–20, the Shi'a represented 52.4 percent of Iraq's population (1,494,015 out of 2,849,282 people).[20] Almost all were Arabs; Persians, Kurds, Indians, and others represented no more than 6 percent of the total Shi'i population. The British 1932 reassessment produced similar results, 56.3 percent.[21] The censuses made it very clear that, with the exception of Basra and some small towns (such as Zubayr), the south was more than 90 percent Shi'i Arab, Baghdad and the center-north (a triangle between the capital, the Syrian border, and Mosul) were essentially Sunni Arab, and the north and northeast, especially the mountainous area, were Kurdish. Since then, official censuses carried out by the various regimes in Baghdad in 1947, 1957, 1965, 1977, 1987, and 1997 have been careful to avoid any mention of the Sunni-Shi'i divide because it could imply a division within the Arab community. After the 2003 downfall of the Ba'th regime, no census was conducted. The 2005, 2009, and 2010 election campaigns could not provide accurate data regarding this division.[22]

All the available evidence, however, underscores the observation that these demographic proportions have changed little in the past eighty-odd years. It is quite possible that today, the Shi'a represent between 50 and 55 percent of the population. The Kurds, some 90 percent of them Sunni Muslims, are believed to represent 17 to 18 percent, and Sunni Arabs around 20 percent. The rest are small minorities: Arabic-speaking Chaldeans, Aramaic-speaking Assyrians, Kurdish-speaking Yezidis, Turkomans (split between Sunnis and Shi'is), and others, such as the Siba'is. Almost all Jews left Iraq between 1950 and the first half of the 1970s.[23] What did change is one aspect of the distribution of the three main communities within Iraq. As a result of very little circular migration (from a Shi'i province to a Sunni Arab or Kurdish one, and vice versa),[24] the communal concentrations in the provinces remain much as they were in the 1920s and 1930s. The only exception is oil-rich Kirkuk, where the regime drove the Kurds out and introduced Arabs, mostly Shi'is, in their stead.[25]

When it comes to the capital city, however, a major change has occurred. According to the 1920 census, most of Baghdad's inhabitants were Sunni Arabs, and only 21.6 percent were Shi'is. However, after the Jewish exodus in 1950–51 and four decades of heavy migration, mainly from Kut, 'Amara, and generally the lower Tigris Valley, Baghdad became a majority-Shi'i town. Masses of new arrivals were added to the population of the traditional Shi'i neighborhoods such as Kazimiyya and vast shanty towns. The large, poor al-Thawra Shi'i quarter (from 1982 Saddam City, and from April 2003 Sadr City) alone numbered close to 1.5 million inhabitants in 1983–84.[26] At the time, Baghdad's population as a whole was around four million.[27] Thus, in 1984, the Shi'i slum quarter known as Saddam City alone represented around one-third and possibly a little more of the total capital's population. And there were other, fairly large Shi'i quarters.[28] In the mid-1980s, an innovative study, based on statistical analysis of indirect information that appeared in the Iraqi daily press, concluded that the Shi'is represented some 68 percent of the capital's population.[29] The mass migration from the war zones in the south to Baghdad during and after the Iran-Iraq War must have added momentum to this demographic trend. It is reasonable to suggest that, in 1990, the Shi'a represented around 70 percent of the population of Baghdad. With the Kurds accounting for 5 to 10 percent of the city's population, Sunni Arabs represented a fairly small proportion.

Politically speaking, this means that the ruling elite's natural Sunni Arab base of support in the capital has been shrinking continuously and significantly since the early 1930s, and especially since the 1970s. In a country in which the capital city is by far the most important (indeed, practically the only important) administrative, military, industrial, communication, and cultural center, this means that since the 1970s the ruling elite, consisting mostly of Sunni Arabs but also of some Shi'is, has been living under a growing state of siege. Most of the city's population consisted of traditional to very religious and poor Shi'is. This overlap of the social, the cultural, and the denominational presented the essentially Sunni Arab secular and economically comfortable to wealthy ruling elite with a serious problem. After the 1991 uprising, this reality became more threatening than ever before. The secret documents following the revolt testify that the regime's elite was fully aware of it. For example, Saddam met with Baghdad-based Shi'i tribal shaykhs and warned them darkly against supporting any new insurrection.[30]

Root Causes of the Ba'th-Shi'i Estrangement

There were at least six different root causes of the Ba'th regime–Shi'i estrangement. They ranged from sectarian differences, through the Ba'thi blatant secularism, the regime's obsession with control, a threatening geostrategic reality, and the existence of a well-entrenched competing communal leadership for the Shi'a, to the pedigree of the regime's leadership. The regime's efforts to win hearts and minds proved inadequate to satisfy even minimal Shi'i expectations. Between 1969 and 1977, small-scale confrontations erupted almost every year in the south. Then, encouraged by Ayatollah Khomeini's 1979 ascent to power in Tehran, the more religious segments of the Shi'a of the Iraqi south revolted again, looking for an "Iraqi Khomeini." The Iran-Iraq War (1980–88) brought Shi'i and Sunni Iraqis together to fight shoulder to shoulder against Shi'i Iran, but it also deepened the muted alienation between large segments of the Shi'i community and the Ba'th regime. Throughout Ba'th rule, the Shi'i population oscillated from collaboration to apathy to confrontation. In 1991, after the defeat of the Iraqi army in the Gulf War, the Shi'a launched their last major revolt, which ended disastrously.

Sectarian identity. From the point of view of the more religious Shi'i population, there were good reasons for the second Ba'th regime's lack of popularity. That the regime was essentially Sunni while most of the population was Shi'i was only one factor, but it was perhaps the most important one, for their interests and worldviews diverged in critical ways. As early as June 1969, a mere eleven months into Ba'th rule, Shi'i demonstrators were already demanding a Shi'i government.[31] This drive did not fade with time. Ten years later, Shi'i opposition sources reported numerous calls for the establishment of an Islamic Republic in Iraq.[32] Fifteen years later, interviews with young revolutionaries who had fled Iraq after the failure of the 1991 uprising confirmed that their intention had been to establish a Shi'i Islamic republic of Iraq.[33] Sectarian identity and the correlative desire to have a government more aligned with majority interests was an unmitigated factor in the sustained conflict between the regime and the Shi'i population.

Secularism. The Shi'i religious community was more conservative and less secular than the second Ba'th regime, which, by contrast, until the late 1980s was more committed to secular politics and culture than either the monarchy or the 'Arif brothers had been. Adding insult to injury, the Ba'th regime resolved to demonstrate that it was more socialistic than the 'Arif regime and mandated additional nationalizations and land reforms, even though under the 'Arif brothers the Shi'i religious establishment had strongly objected to any socialist steps, a historical fact the Ba'th regime chose to ignore.

Centralization. The Ba'th regime embarked on a single-minded project of extreme centralization, thus denying the Shi'i establishment much of its autonomy within the nation-state. Having lost power to General 'Abd al-Salam 'Arif in 1963, in 1968 the Ba'this were adamant about securing total control over all societal cells: schools, universities, religious madrasas, mosques, workers' and professional unions, youth movements, religious and other charity organizations—indeed, the party even endeavored to penetrate the tribes and the nuclear families. This necessitated, among other measures, at least the partial control of *al-hawzat al-ʿilmiyya*, the Shiʿi "Circles of Learning" in the religious universities of Najaf and Karbala. The Baʿth regime sent spies to report on the content of the textbooks and the teaching in classes; it could and sometimes did close madrasas or transfer their management to supportive ʿulama. It limited the stay of foreign students or denied entry altogether; it spied on the citizens who frequented the *husayniyya* (small Shiʿa mosques or congregation halls) "too often"; it limited participation in various rites, and banned some rites altogether, on commemoration days. As a further measure, between 1969 and 1972 the regime issued legal regulations for the management of the contributions received by the *ʿatabat* (shrines) from the Shiʿi faithful. Such oversight of monies denied the clergy much of their independent decision making about the contributions and opened the door to possible confiscation of some of the donations.[34] Since their educational and financial autonomy were the most precious assets of the Shiʿi clergy, this was a sure recipe for a confrontation.

As part of its obsession with control, the new regime made another mistake in the religious arena. Rather than leave the Shiʿi clergy alone, the regime demanded that it take sides in the conflict between Iraq and the shah's and later Khomeini's Iran whenever the two neighbors clashed, and clash they often did. The Baʿth inherited from previous regimes concern over Shiʿi loyalty, but under Saddam as czar of internal security this concern underwent a quantum leap upward, and with it came greater pressures on the clerics to demonstrate political support. The combination of secularization, centralization, and political demands was too much for the Shiʿi religious leadership and its followers and produced great bitterness and outbreaks of protest.

Ancestry. A far less tangible but still relevant reason for estrangement was ancestry. The royal Hashimite house was generally believed to represent the line of descent of the Prophet Muhammad, his cousin and son-in-law ʿAli, and his grandson al-Husayn, the latter being the first and third Shiʿi Imams. In Sunni terms, they were sharifs; in Shiʿi terms, they were *sada* (plural of *sayyid*). While not quite turning reservation and a sense of being underprivileged into devotion, this pedigree helped the Sunni royal family win some support in Shiʿi circles. Though he himself was a Sunni Arab, Qasim was half Shiʿi. The ʿArif brothers had no useful family connection, but, though Sunnis, they were seen as personally devout Muslims. The Ba'th leaders, Bakr and Saddam, similarly had no useful pedigree that could leaven the Shi'i estrangement. When Saddam claimed that his (and Bakr's) tribe, al-bu Nasir, were *sada*, this was not believed. Bakr never made such a claim.

Competing leaderships. From the Ba'th point of view, the *mujtahids* of the Shi'i holy cities of Najaf and Karbala (and to a lesser extent Kazimayn, today a quarter of Baghdad, and Samarra) were a dangerous competing elite. The Sunni religious leadership was far less dangerous in their eyes, but it too represented a threat. Under the previous regimes, Iraq had had a grand mufti (also called *mufti al-'Iraq*).[35] A few years into its rule, the Ba'th regime quietly dismissed the grand mufti of Iraq and never appointed a new one.[36] The intention was that there would be no central Sunni authority to issue fatwas. However, the Ba'th could not do the same with the senior Shi'i 'ulama because the latter were not state officials; their power and resources came from the voluntary contributions of their flock. As a result, the Sunni community was left without an overarching, high-level religious leadership. Instead, it was supposed to see the Ba'th Party as its leader. In the Shi'i community, the party tried to do the same, and eventually Shi'i party membership swelled, but this was not enough. The regime would have preferred to remove the religious leadership, but it could not fire an *ayat allah* (ayatollah). Killing one was possible, and was done on a few occasions, but such extreme measures always risked an eruption of the popular uprisings the regime was trying to avoid. Therefore, the regime was always wary of the competition coming from the Shi'i clerics, who enjoyed a strong and popular leadership. Their leadership style represented the precise opposite of that of the Ba'th, for they did not need to coerce followers. In fact, following them was sometimes dangerous, and yet they had a following. They did not need to buy off their flocks with money and material assets; instead, they received from their followers voluntary contributions. Finally, they did not need to invent a new organization complete with ideology, media, hierarchy, ceremonies, and meeting centers: they had the mosque, the *husayniyya*, the madrasa, and even their private homes, all traditional institutions, highly respected by their public. And they were opposed both to Ba'thi secularizing, centralizing policies and to the attempts to nationalize or at least somehow control their economic and educational assets. They offered their flock a worldview, identity, and leadership style diametrically opposed to the Ba'th Party's. They had to be muzzled at all costs. Antagonism thus was built in.

The geostrategic component. Geostrategic relations also pushed the two sides toward repeated confrontations. Iraq is sandwiched between Iran, a powerful

Shi'i-majority state, and Syria, which since 1966 has been under a Ba'th regime hostile to Iraq. As for the Iranian threat, throughout its rule the Ba'th regime saw in the Shi'a a potential fifth column. For the most part, this was a misperception, but in some cases it was true. A senior ex-official of the Iranian SAVAK, or secret service, under the shah reported to me that, until his master signed the 1975 Algiers Agreement with Saddam, Muhammad Baqir al-Hakim, the son of the leading ayatollah of Iraq, worked for him. In 1975, the shah ordered him to end those activities.[37] This information could not be corroborated, but the interviewee had no reason to provide false information. Even if true, though, this was not much of a threat, but when it came to domestic threats, Ba'thi Baghdad was always prone to overreacting. From 1979, Ba'thi suspicions were justified: Khomeini had many open supporters in the Shi'i centers of Iraq, including the al-Da'wa Islamic Party and its mentor, Ayatollah Muhammad Baqir al-Sadr.

As for Damascus, until 1979 the main threat Baghdad feared was pro-Syrian Ba'th infiltration. The rival Ba'th regime threatened Baghdad's Ba'thi legitimacy. After 1979, the threat changed but was no less potent: the 'Alawite ruling elite presented itself as Shi'i and hosted Da'wa and other Shi'i opposition leaders. This cooperation had actually begun even earlier: in 1973, the Najaf-trained imam Musa Sadr of Lebanon declared the 'Alawites to be Shi'a. Also, in the second half of the 1970s at least one senior Iraqi Shi'i cleric, the Najaf-born and Karbala-educated Ayatollah Hasan al-Shirazi, worked in Syria, reportedly converting 'Alawites to Shi'i Islam. This way, despite the secularism of the Syrian Ba'th, a loose political alliance between Damascus and important circles in the Shi'i holy cities of Iraq was forged, in addition to the questionable theological bond between the two sects.[38] Beginning in 1980, Iraqi Shi'i armed opposition groups started to operate from Iran against the Iraqi regime, and from 1982 Shi'i fundamentalist opposition movements established offices in secular Damascus as well.[39] Clearly, their allergy to secularism was triggered only when they were in Sunni-controlled Iraq.[40]

The influence on the Iraqi Shi'i opposition of the geographic proximity of a Shi'i Iran and a "Shi'i" Syria was intoxicating. It created a false sense of omnipotence—false because neither Iran nor Syria ever came to the rescue of the Iraqi Shi'is in any meaningful way, even when they were being killed in the tens of thousands. Still, the hope that help would be forthcoming pushed the opposition to take unreasonable risks. This happened especially in 1979, 1991, and 1998–99. The Ba'th regime, for its part, felt threatened by the combination of domestic potential enemies collaborating with hostile neighbors and responded with extreme brutality, resulting in a widening gulf between the two sides.

Regime Strategies for Winning Shi'i Hearts and Minds

The first major confrontation between the Ba'th regime and the Shi'i religious establishment and its supporters erupted in June 1969 and lasted until the fall of that year. From that time, the south saw frequent clashes between the regime and the Shi'a. In addition to its repressive tactics, the regime sought to find ways to win Shi'i hearts and minds, or at least to blunt Shi'i opposition. Some of the strategies were adopted early on, between 1969 and the early 1970s, and remained in place until the fall of the regime in 2003. Others were enjoined later, as the regime adapted to new developments.

The strategies fell basically into three categories. One was coercion. This strategy is described in more detail later, in the discussion of the main clashes between the regime and the Shi'a. The regime resorted at first to mass expulsion of Iraqi Shi'is, whom it defined as "Persians." Later, it executed or assassinated individual 'ulama and executed members of the Da'wa Islamic Party and "saboteurs," and evacuated many scores of marsh Arab villages. In the end, in response to a mass revolt, it dried out much of the marshland and resorted to mass murder in Najaf, Karbala, and other cities. Another was the use of symbolism as expressed in the mass media. The media had to demonstrate that the regime was supporting Shi'i values, holy places, and clerics, and that the last were in support of the regime. The third strategy entailed creating more tangible, "real life" policies that could demonstrate that the regime was practicing the equal treatment of both sects, not just preaching it. For example, the regime recruited many Shi'is to the ranks of the ruling party. It also had to demonstrate that it was providing equal government services and opportunity for both communities in terms of state and party positions. Here, too, media exposure was crucial. Paradoxically, because efforts to provide equal opportunity could imply a chasm separating Arabs, only rarely did the media use the expressions "Sunna" and "Shi'a." Instead, the media—newspapers, radio and TV programs—used coded language, such as "the south" instead of "the Shi'i population." The public understood those hints well.

Support for Shi'i 'Ulama and 'Ulama Support for the Regime

A prominent media campaign tactic designed to win the support of the Shi'i community was to provide publicity for those Shi'i clerics who offered support for the regime. This clerical support was often expressed in messages of gratitude following regime-supplied material support for the clerics and the shrines. Usually, no names were mentioned, but occasionally the regime did mention specific Shi'i 'ulama by name. Almost as a rule, they were lower-level clerics. Between 1969 and 1975, they supported the regime and denounced the shah of Iran, his Zionist allies, his American masters, and his "spies" in Iraq, who were spreading "racist [Persian Shi'i] sectarianism."[41] From 1980, they supported the regime against Ayatollah Khomeini. Similarly, at the height of the 1969 confrontation between the regime and the *marja'iyya* of Najaf, the regime announced that the clerics of Karbala province (*Liwa'*), which at the time included Najaf, would receive land in special neighborhoods to build homes, and that the religious madrasas would be exempt from paying water and electricity bills. A group of clerics, whose names were not disclosed, and who were on a visit to the presidential palace, expressed their deep gratitude.[42] However, when no names were mentioned, the public became suspicious, and the regime failed to deliver the message of clerical support.

A similar initiative that won full media coverage came following massive antiregime demonstrations in February 1977. The regime issued a new Law of the Service of Men of Religion that turned them all into government officials, with a rise in salaries between 50 and 100 percent and all the social benefits involved.[43] In this crisis, too, and throughout the Ba'th rule, many 'ulama were lured or coerced (or both) to express support for the regime.[44] Senior clerics could stay silent, as Muhsin al-Hakim did in 1969, Abu al-Qasim al-Kho'i did from the 1970s to the 1980s, and 'Ali al-Sistani did in the 1990s. Nevertheless, under exceptional circumstances they too were forced to publicly support the regime. Thus, for example, after he supported the great Shi'i revolt against the Ba'th in March 1991, the supreme *marja'* Abu al-Qasim al-Kho'i was brought to Baghdad and from there forced to denounce the revolt.[45] Similarly, a few months before the 2003 American invasion of Iraq, the regime managed to coerce Grand Ayatollah 'Ali al-Sistani, the widely recognized *marja' taqlid*, to denounce "anyone helping America in its plans to attack Iraq."[46] Those clerics considered too defiant or whose families were deeply involved in the opposition were deported, executed, or assassinated. As far as can be ascertained, though, the *mujtahids'* support for the regime failed to achieve its main goal, for it was believed by all that those *mujtahids* practiced *taqiyya* (precautionary dissimulation), regarded as a religious duty when one's life is in danger. Still, the deeper message that came through was that the community should follow the lead of the clerics and avoid a confrontation. In that respect, the regime scored some success. Sometimes Saddam and his lieutenants fell into their own trap, as they were misled by the Shi'i passivity, mistaking it for support.[47]

Support for the Holy Shrines

To demonstrate that Shi'i values were dear to their hearts, beginning in the 1970s Ba'thi politicians reported that the state was spending large sums of money on the holy shrines (*al-'atabat al-muqaddasa*) in Najaf and Karbala.[48] Providing other religious services, such as building mosques and improving services for pilgrims to the shrines, received substantial media exposure as well.[49] Closer scrutiny reveals, however, that except for the shrines of Najaf and Karbala, which clearly received much official support, spending on Shi'i mosques and smaller congregation halls (*al-husayniyyat*) was far lower than the amount spent on Sunni ones. By the second half of the 1980s, in the Sunni areas there was one mosque per every 3,253 people, while in the Shi'i ones it was one per every 8,854 people. As late as 2001, there is regime confirmation that things had not improved: in January of that year, none other than 'Uday Saddam Husayn, who enjoyed taunting Saddam but used good information to do so, strongly criticized the Ministry of Endowments (*Awqaf*) for being unfair in its policy of the building of mosques in areas with a Shi'i majority.[50] Indeed, the ministers of *awqaf* were all Sunnis, and this too, to the extent that they could decide freely where to build mosques, may have influenced their preferences.[51] Still, by spending substantial sums on the main Shi'i shrines the regime scored two points: every dinar counted more because it was a high-profile expenditure, and controlling the devout was far easier since they were concentrated in fewer venues.

Sunni-Shi'i "Ecumenism"

Saddam also attempted to use symbolism to create the impression that he was constructing an ecumenical Sunni-Shi'i Islam. To a very limited degree, the Ba'thi construct was indeed ecumenical but, as the Ba'th were unable to truly bridge the gulf, this practice tended to accentuate the differences. One tactic to force the semblance of a bridge was to insist that there was no difference between the Sunna and the Shi'a, and therefore there was no room for any feelings of discrimination. In 1991, for example, following the great Shi'i uprising, the elder son of the Ba'quba-based Ayatollah 'Abd al-Karim Khan al-Madani disclosed to the party daily that his father had told him many years ago, "By God, I am a Sunni! By God, I am a Shi'i!"[52] A few months later, Saddam himself quoted Madani, who reportedly said, "All the Muslims of Iraq belong to the Sunna because all of them believe in the Tradition [*Sunna*] of God's Messenger . . . and all of them belong to the Faction [*Shi'a*] of Imam 'Ali . . . [because] they are . . . with the principles of Imam 'Ali and not with those [the Umayyad caliphs] who opposed them, and they are with the principles of our Imam Husayn."[53] The claim that theologically there was no difference between the sects was wrong, of course. Whereas in respect to substantive law the differences were insignificant, the overall picture delineated by Saddam glossed over substantial differences and conflicts with respect to theology and historiography, and also ignored serious Shi'i historical and contemporary grievances.[54] The Sunni community did not pay much attention to this ecumenical attempt, mainly because its understanding of Shi'i Islam was limited. In the Shi'i community, though, many paid attention to Madani's claim, but it never took root: Madani was not regarded as very senior, and in any event, the Shi'i historical complaints against the Sunna were familiar to every Shi'i. Glossing over them could not be convincing. Madani's declaration was seen as *taqiyya*. But Saddam also tried a more subtle ecumenical approach: by publicly supporting the cause of the first Shi'i Imams in their struggle against their "Sunni" enemies, the Umayyads, he hoped to win Shi'i hearts.

Between 'Ali and Mu'awiya: Saddam Supports the Shi'i Narrative

Another way of creating the impression that the two sects in Iraq were one was through an official media campaign designed to demonstrate that choice parts of the Shi'i historiography represented an integral part of the Iraqi national pantheon. Thus, Saddam's response to Khomeini's rise to power in Iran came in mid-July 1979 and thereafter was part of the regime's efforts to win over the Shi'i masses. Immediately after he assumed the presidency, in a speech printed by the government dailies under the bold red headline "An Appointment with History," Saddam took sides in the crucial historical-theological dispute between the Sunna and the Shi'a. He described 'Ali ibn Abi Talib, the fourth Muslim caliph and first Shi'i Imam, as representing "faith" and "the heavenly values," and Mu'awiya, the Umayyad caliph who the Shi'a believe usurped the caliphate from 'Ali, as representing "treachery and deviation."[55] Mu'awiya has never been very popular in the Sunni community, as he has been regarded as insufficiently religious. In Iraq he was even less popular, because while 'Ali ruled from Kufa in southern Iraq, Mu'awiya ruled from Damascus, and under him and his Umayyad dynasty Iraq became marginalized. Yet Sunni Islam regards the Umayyads as legitimate caliphs, while the Shi'is see them as usurpers and criminals who are burning eternally in hell. For Saddam, it was a bold step to take 'Ali's and al-Husayn's side as he did, but he did not take a great risk: the Sunnis understood his reasons, and accusing Mu'awiya of mundane motives could hardly be seen as sacrilege.

Saddam's public identification with Imams 'Ali and Husayn, the leading figures in Shi'i identity and faith, continued in his public and confidential records alike in later years. For example, in a meeting with Shi'i shaykhs in Saddam City following the Shi'i revolt of March 1991, he compared his decision to fight the superior American coalition in Kuwait with the decision of Imam Husayn to fight the Umayyads despite the overwhelming military advantage the latter had. Saddam implied that, like Imam Husayn, he too was fully aware of the military gap but that, like the Imam, he went to war to defend sacred principles: Iraq's right to Kuwait and defying imperialism.[56] In the same way, in a closed-door meeting with graduates of a high-level party seminar in July 1999 at which both Sunni and Shi'i members were present, when emphasizing the need to win the people's hearts, he reminded his listeners: "There is a historical saying by one of the Arabs" according to which during the confrontation between 'Ali and Mu'awiya the people said, "Our hearts are with Imam 'Ali, but our stomachs are with Mu'awiya's table [*inna qulubana ma'a al-Imam 'ali, wa ma'idatana ma'a ma'idat Mu'awiya*]." The important thing, he explained, was not how many people were in his camp, for Mu'awiya had more supporters than 'Ali, but rather that the leader "expresses the conscience of his people [*an yakun mu'abbiran 'an dhamir sha'bihi*]."[57] In many closed-door meetings Saddam tried to drive home his view that Imam and Caliph 'Ali was very close to Caliphs Abu Bakr, 'Umar, and 'Uthman by emphasizing that he had named some of his children after his three predecessors. He also frequently emphasized that 'Umar was used to consulting 'Ali about religious issues.[58] This seems to have meant that the ecumenical inclination, partial as it was, went deep and was of great importance to Saddam not only politically but also emotionally.

Nationalization of Shi'i Commemoration Days and Imams

An additional symbolism measure, but one with some potential, that the regime put in place to create the impression of an ecumenical creed and win over the Shi'a was the adoption, or nationalization, of Shi'i commemoration days and festivals and the heroes and holy towns associated with them. The most important example is the 'Ashura, which falls on the tenth day of the month of Muharram and on which in 680 CE Imam Husayn ibn 'Ali, the third Imam of the Shi'a, was beheaded at the hands of "Sunni" Umayyad troops in Karbala. Along with secular national celebrations, the 'Ashura was traditionally recognized as a national day in Iraq.[59] Beginning in 1973, the state organized public rallies on that day during which parallels were drawn between the martyrdom of Imam Husayn and the struggle of the Ba'th Party's revolution against the enemies of the Arabs.[60] At the same time, though, the regime had a problem: 'Ashura and al-Arba'in (the fortieth day after Imam Husayn's martyrdom) were the preferred occasions for antiregime demonstrations. The regime could not always ban all gatherings on those days, so it walked a tightrope by occasionally banning the Husayni mass processions (*al-mawakib al-Husayniyya*) in memory of the imam or banning certain practices on those days. In addition to the Shi'i commemoration days, following the rise of Ayatollah Khomeini to power in Iran in February 1979, the regime also "nationalized" the birthdays of the first and third Imams. The president's representatives would go down to Najaf and Karbala, where great public rallies were organized at the shrines. As a rule, the president's message connected Imams 'Ali's and Husayn's "principles" and "values" with those of the Ba'th regime, including "revolution," "Arabism, and Islam."[61] During the Iran-Iraq War, the regime continued to celebrate with great fanfare the birthdays of the two Imams, emphasizing their Arabism and contrasting it with Khomeini's Persian anti-Arab sentiment and hostility to Islam. 'Ali's victory over the "treasonous Jews" of Khaybar, too, was praised, and the contemporary alliance between "the Zionists and Khomeini's clique" was thrown into the mix as well.[62] After Saddam became president in July 1979, the Iraqi media identified the Imams' "values" with those of their "grandson" (or "offspring," *hafid*), "our Magnificent Leader-Commander, the Struggling President Saddam Husayn, may God Protect and Defend Him."[63] On February 19, 1982, Saddam paid a visit to Najaf and prayed at 'Ali's shrine. Ever since, until the end of Ba'th rule, every February 19 the province of Najaf celebrated Province Day.[64] In April 1987, vice president 'Izzat Ibrahim al-Duri delivered the president's message for the celebrations marking the birthday of Imam Husayn in Karbala, and that day has since been celebrated as Province Day for Karbala.[65] The presidential power trips apparently achieved two goals. First, they demonstrated even to the opposition who was the boss, and second, they may have helped Shi'i party members resolve their cognitive dissonance by showing them that their president respected their history.

The two Imams were as a rule given the title of "Imam," as the Shi'a would do. Sometimes, 'Ali would also be given the title of Amir al-Mu'minin (Leader or Prince of the Faithful or the Believers), a title the Sunnis give to all caliphs but which the Shi'a reserve for 'Ali. This, too, was a sign of respect. Even more significant was the president's message in 1988, in which he described 'Ali in much the same way the Shi'i 'ulama would have done: his growing up in the Prophet's household and therefore his absorption of Islam in its purest form from early childhood; the advice he provided to his three predecessors, the Rightly Guided Caliphs, "especially to 'Umar," on Islamic and military matters alike until, whenever confronted with an intricate problem, 'Umar used to say, "This is a problem that has no 'Ali to solve it" (*qadhiyya wala Aba Hasan laha*).[66] While the Shi'a had been harping on those historical facts to accentuate 'Ali's exclusive suitability to become the first caliph, Saddam had a different goal in mind. He attempted to bridge the Sunni-Shi'i divide by demonstrating that 'Ali and 'Umar were very close and that therefore 'Umar, whom the Sunnis admire but the Shi'a revile, must not be seen by the latter as a negative figure. By quoting the *hadith* that stated that 'Ali's understanding of Islam was superior to that of 'Umar and the other two caliphs, Saddam presented himself as an unbiased, broad-minded, even pro-'Ali Muslim. As such, he hoped to win Shi'i sympathy, even though he did not challenge 'Umar's right to the caliphate and, therefore, remained a Sunni.

While the president's messages on the birthday occasions usually included references to 'Umar, surprisingly, the regime allowed the Shi'i citizens who sent congratulations to the president on religious occasions to omit 'Umar's name as long as they mentioned non-Shi'i historical military leaders such as Khalid bin al-Walid and Salah al-Din al-Ayyubi (Saladin).[67] This permission was meant to demonstrate tolerance. Another facet of the regime's approach to the Shi'i Imams was the wide publicity given to leaders' visits to their shrines and tombs. These visits and prayers at the shrines of Najaf and Karbala were designed to create the impression that the two sects were in fact one.[68] Finally, as mentioned above, every year on the nineteenth and twenty-first of the month of Ramadan all the Iraqi press paid homage to Imam 'Ali by mourning his 661 CE death at the hands of the Khariji fanatic Ibn Muljam. There were, however, clear limits. The birthdays of other Shi'i imams were mentioned only rarely, and that of the Imam Mahdi, the Vanished and Expected Imam (*al-imam al-gha'ib, al-imam al-muntazar*), on 15 Sha'ban, a central day for the Shi'a, was not mentioned even once. The Sunnis do not recognize the concept of the Vanished Imam, who disappeared in the ninth century CE and whose return (*al-raj'a*) is expected. A recognition of this tenet of faith would have been interpreted as conversion to Shi'ism, *al-tashayyu'*.

Saddam as a Newly Minted *Sayyid*

A far more daring attempt to connect the regime's leadership to the greatest Shi'i historical heroes was inaugurated in 1971, when Saddam's family began to promote the notion that they and their tribe, al-bu Nasir, were offspring of the Prophet, of his cousin and son-in-law 'Ali, the first Shi'i Imam, and of al-Husayn, the third Imam.[69] From the time he became president in 1979, this was part of Saddam's official biography. On ideological and possibly emotional levels, from 1979 on Saddam demonstrated in public speeches and private meetings his wholehearted support for the first and third Shi'i Imams in their historical battles against their enemies, whom the Sunnis regard as legitimate rulers. Already in his first speech as president, Saddam compared the "conspirators" against him in the party, whom he accused of serving Damascus, to the Damascus-based Caliph Mu'awiya, who fought against the Iraq-based Imam 'Ali. In his speech, Saddam claimed to represent Imam 'Ali's values and accused those "conspiring" against him of serving the Syrian arch-villain Hafiz al-Asad, a latter-day representative of Mu'awiya and his values.[70] This was a clever ploy, because many of the purged "conspirators" were Shi'is, and being accused of supporting Asad-Mu'awiya was extremely offensive. It is not clear to what extent this attachment to 'Ali helped Saddam's image in Shi'i eyes at the time. Years later, after he had crushed with much bloodshed the March 1991 Shi'i revolt, when he met privately with the tribal shaykhs Saddam again drew parallels between himself and Imam 'Ali and compared those who revolted against him to Mu'awiya.[71]

The president remained consistent in his efforts to win Shi'i sympathy through such symbolic gestures. There is no reason to doubt his sincerity when it came to his love for 'Ali and disdain for Mu'awiya. 'Ali represented Iraq; Mu'awiya represented Syria. In claiming a Prophetic pedigree Saddam was trying to follow in the footsteps of the Hashemite royal family. His family tree, showing his Prophetic ancestry, was painted in gold on one of the main doors of the shrine of Imam 'Ali in Najaf. It is far from certain that even if Saddam's claim had been credible it would have helped legitimize him as ruler of Iraq, but matters never reached that point. The credibility of Saddam's claim in the Shi'i community was extremely low, yet challenging it in Iraq was unthinkable. To Saddam, his pedigree connection to the two Shi'i Imams was genuinely important. In a Saddam-Asad meeting in 1978 as part of unification discussions when Saddam was still vice president, Asad ridiculed this claim. As reported later by Saddam to his cabinet ministers in a closed-door meeting, Asad said, "We cannot reach an understanding with al-Husayn's [grand-]son [*ihna mush qadirin natafaham ma'a ibn al-Husayn*]." To which Saddam retorted, deeply offended: "Had *he* been from the Prophet's dynasty! And why is he ridiculing [Imam] al-Husayn? [*Idha kana huwa min salalat al-rasul! Wa limadha yastakhiff bil-Husayn?*] Al-Husayn is grandson of the Prophet!"[72] Asad, of course, was not ridiculing the Imam but rather Saddam for his claim. Saddam's "special relation" to Najaf and Karbala, provinces that were the resting places of his "ancestors," was often mentioned by him, by the media, and even by collaborative Shi'i 'ulama on many Shi'i occasions.[73]

Apparently, Saddam's attachment to his Prophetic pedigree reached absurd proportions when in 2000 the RCC reportedly issued a directive that disallowed anyone other than Saddam to claim a pedigree going back to the family of Imam 'Ali. Offenders were to receive a seven-year term of imprisonment.[74] This was an absurd decision. In the Shi'i south, there were whole tribes of *sada*, and many senior Shi'i clerics, such as 'Ali al-Sistani, were considered *sada*. Moreover, every man in Saddam's tribe was a *sayyid*, according to Saddam's family tree. Implementing such an RCC decision was therefore somewhat tricky.

Efforts to Drive a Wedge between the Iraqi and Iranian Shi'a

The flip side of the regime's strategy of forging a kind of ecumenical Sunni-Shi'i Islam inside Iraq was a two-pronged effort. The first part entailed manipulating the ethnocultural Arab-Persian divide to drive a wedge between Arab Iraqis and Persian Iranians. The second part required demonstrating that, as distinct from Arab Shi'a, Khomeini's Persian Shi'a was heretic. The secular racial anti-Persian propaganda had been launched as early as 1969, at the beginning of the dispute with the shah over the Shatt al-Arab. However, as soon as Khomeini rose to power in Tehran, the problem of Iraqi Shi'i identification with his religious ideology became acute.

In a secret meeting of vice president Saddam Husayn with some Sunni members of the RCC in May or June 1979, this danger was the focus of discussion. The meeting was convened to discuss the Arabs of Khozestan (Arabestan), but the discussion soon drifted to the Shi'a of Iraq and the lure of Khomeini. The Sunni members of the RCC present revealed substantial ignorance of Shi'i Islam, its theology, and its doctrine. Some, for example, had never heard of the concept of the Imam Mahdi until just before the meeting.[75] Many years later, in another closed-door meeting with his most senior lieutenants, Saddam admitted that as a young man he was unaware of the differences between the Sunna and the Shi'a. Only when in Cairo as an exile did he realize that the issue was of some significance and that the Egyptians knew more about it than he did; they asked whether he was a Sunni or a Shi'i. This issue, he said, had never been discussed in his hometown of Tikrit.[76] This confession was credible. Sunnis who lived separately from Shi'is were usually unfamiliar with Shi'i historiography and even more so with Shi'i theology. The case with the Shi'is is very different: they have always been fully aware of the Sunni approach to early Islamic history after the Prophet's death, and they strongly dislike it.

Ignorant as they were regarding Shi'i eschatology, in the same 1979 meeting the senior Ba'this demonstrated good political judgment: they quickly identified a useful policy that could derive from understanding the Shi'a better. Presenting Khomeini's position in 1979 as "totally incompatible with the *Ja'fari* [Shi'i] doctrine," a knowledgeable participant suggested, was an excellent way to delegitimize him in Iraqi Shi'i eyes. Ayatollah (Muhammad Kazim) Shari'at-Madari, he knew, had announced that Khomeini's concept of "the rule of the jurist" (*wilayat al-faqih*) was a deviation from Shi'i Islam. Therefore, according to Iran's greatest religious scholar, Khomeini's status as head of state represented blasphemy. The participants decided that the Ba'th needed to use it at home against Khomeini. More broadly, Saddam argued in the meeting that Iranian Shi'ism was "an Arab religious doctrine adapted in a Persian fashion [*'aqida diniyya 'arabiyya mukayyafa farisiyyan*]."[77] In other words, a regime propaganda campaign should be designed to destroy the connection between Arab and Persian Shi'ism by exposing the latter's falsehood. This propaganda strategy was indeed launched in the early 1980s and continued well into the 1990s. For example, in a programmatic speech discussing the evil Iranians, Saddam argued that while the Arabs adopted Shi'ism early, and "out of a strong conviction . . . and not by force," the Persians were forced to do that much later, in the early sixteenth century, by Shah Isma'il al-Safawi. Therefore, he explained, Persian Shi'ism was in fact a "separate new religion" that kept only a Shi'i "façade."[78] In other words, Persian Shi'ism was apostasy.

In the 1979 highly secret meeting of only part of the RCC, Saddam also suggested a way to fight the Iranian religious-sectarian-Shi'i influence that was more in line with secular Ba'thi thinking. What needed to be done, he explained, was "to fortify our people in Arab nationalism [*tahsin Sha'bana qawmiyyan*]" and in Iraqi patriotism (*al-wataniyya*). This way, Saddam hoped, "an Arab-Ja'fari (Shi'i)" identity would be created "separated from the Iranian Shi'a."[79] Saddam related ostensibly to the Shi'i Arabs of Arabestan, but he could also be understood as implying that the Shi'is of Iraq were not yet fully Arab in their minds either. Indeed, there is a strong impression from the audiotapes that even when the participants were talking about the Arabs of Arabestan they actually meant the Shi'a of Iraq. For example, at the beginning of the discussion, Taha Yasin Ramadhan reports that many in Iraq were saying that the Arabs of Khozestan (Arabestan) were not Arab at all. This was bizarre because since 1969, Iraq had been demanding for those Arabs the right of self-determination, at Iran's expense. Worse still, many of the Shi'i Arab tribes of Khozestan belonged to the same Shi'i Arab tribes that lived on the Iraqi side of the border. This was most conspicuously the case for the Khaza'il. Ramadhan was talking about the Shi'is of Khozestan but thinking about the marsh Shi'is of Iraq. Saddam eventually opined that the tribes in Khozestan (Arabestan—and therefore definitely in Iraq) were all Arab, but his admission that "an Arab Ja'fari" identity was still to be born was an admission of failure. It seemed that to him, after eleven years of Ba'th rule, and fifty-nine years after the establishment of the Arab-majority Iraqi state, the Arab identity of the Iraqi Shi'is was still in question. Saddam and his lieutenants were aware that driving a wedge between the Iraqi Arab Shi'is and their Iranian Persian coreligionists was a tall order.

Another way to win the respect of the Shi'is, believed to be the more religious segment of Iraqi society, was to demonstrate Islamic piety. Beginning in the early-to-mid 1980s, when the war against the Islamic Republic of Iran was not going well and in the face of Iranian accusations that the Ba'th were atheists and enemies of Islam, Saddam embarked on a slow-motion project designed to "convert" the party and regime to Islam. This subject is discussed in chapter 6.

Anti-Zionism and Anti-Imperialism as National Glue

An additional symbolic policy designed to legitimize the Ba'th in Shi'i eyes was anti-Zionism, which often spilled over into anti-Semitism. From the first day of Ba'th rule, to cement Sunni-Shi'i unity the Ba'thi leaders directed much of their anti-Zionist propaganda at the Shi'a. The public hanging and display of Jewish "spies" for Israel, Iran, and others between January 1969 and January 1970 was meant for the benefit of the population as a whole, but it was also meant to bond the Shi'i and Sunni Arabs in the face of a common enemy. Baghdad Radio called the hangings "a courageous first step toward the liberation of Palestine,"[80] Palestine being a Shi'i-Sunni common denominator.

Surprisingly, at least Cairo and Rabat were critical of this gory spectacle[81]—so much so that the Iraqi regime complained that it received "no Arab support for the hanging of spies."[82]

On acceding to power, the party was both very small (numbering a few hundred members) and extremely unpopular because of its horrible track record from 1963. The regime felt that after the crushing Arab defeat in June 1967, anti-Semitism and anti-Zionism, mixed with a heavy dose of anti-American propaganda and paranoia, were sure to prompt a degree of publicly acclaimed legitimacy. After the eruption of the April 1969 confrontation with Iran, much of the Ba'thi propaganda was dedicated to demonstrating that the Iranians were Zionists and imperialist agents. This propaganda was clearly aimed at the Shi'is; Sunni Arab Iraqis had never associated themselves with Iran, and there was never a need to wean them from Iranian sympathies. The regime's media argued that, because Iraq was by far the most (or the only) ardent anti-Israeli Arab power, the shah was increasing the pressure on Iraq as a way of easing the military pressure on Israel. Indeed, to achieve this American-sponsored conspiracy, the Iraqi media speculated, the shah would even risk a military confrontation with Iraq. Iran, the media said, hoped that a confrontation over the Shatt al-Arab would force Iraq to withdraw its Salah al-Din Dispatch Forces from the Jordan Valley, where they were inflicting "heavy blows" on Israel.[83] Ascribing such altruism to the shah of Iran was quite remarkable, but he was an ally of the United States, and this propaganda course would have made sense to many. In his speeches directed at his Shi'i citizens, President al-Bakr (1968–79) also equated the heroism of the Iraqi units fighting Israel on the Jordan River with that of "al-Husayn and his grandfather [the Prophet]" and their struggle.[84] Beginning in 1979, the Ba'th propaganda machine started accusing Khomeini of similar subservience to the Zionists. At the time, I believed those accusations were likely mere propaganda, and that the Ba'thi leaders knew better. That was a mistake. At least some in the regime's leadership truly believed that Khomeini was an American and Israeli agent.[85]

The Tangibles, Part I: Economic Development and Services

The regime deemed symbolism to be extremely important and devoted considerable resources to it, but it also undertook more tangible steps to win the Shi'i population's support. During the second half of the 1970s, when oil revenues quadrupled, the regime substantially upgraded the infrastructure and the social services provided to the southern provinces. Reports of development projects in the Shi'i areas appeared frequently in the press, and there is no doubt that meaningful development actually took place, especially electrification, potable water projects and road building, and improvements in social services such as education and health. The political background to these developments became particularly obvious after the February 1977 mass demonstration against the regime and the sudden end of the shah's rule in Iran in 1979. Thus, a few months after the 1977 riots, even the communist weekly was compelled to give great exposure to infrastructure development in the Five-Year Development Plan for 1976–80 in the southern (Shi'i) provinces.[86] Days after Khomeini returned to Tehran, Saddam Husayn (then vice president) announced with great fanfare that, even though there was a good chance of finding oil in the Shi'i al-Thawra quarter (which had served as an excuse for leaving it in its squalid state), for the first time since Qasim's days the regime had decided to improve the infrastructure for the benefit of its inhabitants.[87] As reported by many visitors, the living conditions there did indeed improve, although the quarter remained extremely poor and neglected.

That such development of infrastructure and social services was of high priority to the regime is also evident from a private conversation that took place sometime between July 1979 and mid-1980 between Saddam and his top advisers. The meeting was dedicated to rural development, but the discussion turned to the reconstruction and massive expansion of Baghdad. The participants paid particular attention to the Shi'i mega-neighborhood of Madinat al-Thawra, with the intention of moving its one million residents to new satellite towns.[88] Such a program was extremely expensive, but Iraq at the time had officially $30 billion in reserves in foreign banks, and possibly more elsewhere. The Iran-Iraq War rendered those plans unfeasible, but there is no reason to doubt their initial seriousness: Saddam and most of the leadership expected the war to last for no more than a few days, and victory to be total.[89] Until 1981–82, when money ran out, the regime continued to make great efforts to counter the Iranian propaganda with development, social services, and subsidies all over Iraq, and apparently, particularly in the Shi'i south.[90]

The Tangibles, Part II: Shi'i Representation in the Top Institutions, and Its Limits

Another important concrete—as distinct from purely symbolic—strategy by which the regime sought to win legitimacy in Shi'i eyes was by opening government service to Shi'is. Many Shi'i party members rose to mid-level positions and participated regularly in the party's security and other duties. To the very end, the Ba'th regime allowed more Shi'is to rise to senior positions than either the monarchy or the 'Arif brothers had, including representation in the top military ranks, and those Shi'is were ready to serve. All this is notable, but it creates the false impression of an egalitarian integration of Shi'is into the party system. The written documents, though, do not tell the whole story. There is evidence in the regime's open sources that this inclusion, important as it was, fell short of comprehensive equal opportunity. A degree of subtle discrimination seems to have existed, but the written documents could not admit such an embarrassing fact. Therefore, the vast majority of both the classified written and open-source documents papered over the Sunni-Shi'i difference. However, to win support, the regime also wanted the Shi'is to be able to identify their coreligionists at the top. Careful reading of an adequate amount of open-source material complements the findings in the classified sources as it reveals critical hints regarding the sectarian backgrounds of the senior politicians. Such hints include, for example, the full name of the politician, his birthplace, and the trajectory of his party advancement. The public had to guess, however, and so it did. A critical eye is needed, and the classified documents must be checked against the daily newspapers of the time, where such personal profiles of senior politicians appeared regularly. Otherwise scholars could be misled into overstating Sunni-Shi'i equality and harmony in party and regime.[91]

Shi'is in the Power Elite

Upon acceding to power in 1968, the Ba'th Party was confronted with a problem: secular Shi'i-Arab nationalists who were not against the Ba'th realized there was not one Shi'i among the members of the two top institutions in the land, the all-powerful Revolutionary Command Council and the Regional (all-Iraqi) Leadership of the Ba'th Party. Even in government, the third institution from the top, Shi'is were few and far between. In the senior command of the armed forces, too, Shi'i officers were a rare phenomenon. Shi'is were to be found in the lower echelons of the party's hierarchy in the Shi'i provinces, but this created an impression of Sunni hegemony through Shi'i agents rather than equality. This means that during the first decade of Ba'th rule, secularly inclined Shi'is had reasons for estrangement from the regime.[92]

In the mid- to late 1970s, Shi'is entered the more senior echelons of state bureaucracy and party hierarchy, but no complete equality was achieved. With respect to the RCC, the highest decisionmaking body in the land, the first

Shi'i members appeared there in March 1977: at least five but probably eight members were then Shi'is (23–40%). Some of these Shi'is also held senior executive positions as secretaries of party *tanzimat*, the unit immediately below the Regional Leadership, usually with responsibility for three governorates, or as government ministers with important portfolios, such as commerce, industry, and planning. Thereafter, Shi'i membership in the RCC was always significant. For example, in the RCC of July–August 1986, Shi'is represented between 22 and 33 percent. Yet Shi'i representation in the RCC was still clearly less than the share of Shi'is in the Arab population of Iraq, which was around two Sunnis for every five Shi'is. The Kurds, being non-Arab, infrequently joined the Ba'th Party.

Shi'i representation in the various governments in the 1970s and 1980s was more substantial but still less than their share in the general population. For example, in the first Ba'thi government following the July 30, 1968, coup, only 12.5 percent of the ministers were Shi'is. This percentage remained roughly the same until May 1972, when it rose to around 19 percent. In the governments of May 1976 and January 1977, the Shi'i share rose to around 25 percent. Between the early 1980s and 1987, the Shi'i share went down to around 20 percent.[93] Until 1990, Shi'is did not become ministers of defense, and even then only once: in December 1990, the Shi'i four-star general, Sa'di Tu'ma 'Abbas al-Jubburi, was appointed minister of defense.[94] Having lost the Gulf War, he was, as might have been expected, fired. In the late 1990s, a Shi'i general, 'Abd al-Wahid Shanan Aal Ribat, was appointed chief of staff. This was an important appointment, but again, an exceptional case. Shi'is never became ministers of the interior. Defense and Interior were the two most important government portfolios, far more important than the premiership. Indeed, in the late 1980s and early 1990s Iraq had two Shi'i prime ministers. This was a significant gesture, but their real weight was very limited.

The Regional Leadership

For the first time since 1966, the party's January 1974 Eighth Regional Congress elected Shi'i members to the Regional Leadership, the party's top institution in the country. In the January 1977 elections, the number of Shi'i Arabs in the Regional Leadership at least doubled, from three to anywhere between six and ten out of twenty-three members. Their proportional share, too, at least doubled, rising to anywhere between 26 and 43 percent. Between July 1979 and June 1982, there were between three and six Shi'ites out of fifteen Regional Leadership members (between 20 and 40 percent). Between June 1982 and early 1986 there were between six and seven Shi'is out of fifteen Regional Leadership members (40 to 47 percent).[95] As was the case for the RCC, this was definitely a meaningful representation, demonstrating Saddam's resolve to win mass Shi'i support through inclusion. Yet in the Regional Leadership, as in the RCC, the Shi'i share fell short of equality. There is some evidence that the glass ceiling, or the bottleneck that made it difficult for Shi'is to rise higher, was at the middle to senior level of *shu'ba*, a party section. Some Shi'is managed to go higher, but advancement was easier for Sunni Arabs.[96]

The Lower Echelons of the Party

On the lower rungs of the party ladder, Shi'i members were very likely a majority. In the first place, they were in clear majority in the Iraqi Arab population, which meant that if the regime wanted to embark on mass recruitment, the masses were Shi'i. In addition, recruiting many young Shi'is made considerable sense as part of the regime's effort to blunt the anti-Ba'th sentiment on the Shi'i street. These assumptions are supported by the major thrust of party expansion between 1976 and 1989. Altogether eleven new party branches (*furu'*) were created. Of those branches, five were created in the Shi'i south, four in Baghdad, and two in the Kurdish governorates. Not one new branch was created in the Sunni Arab governorates. Insofar as by the mid-1980s around 60 percent of Baghdad's population were Shi'i, there is every reason to believe that most of the new recruits were indeed Shi'is.[97] In 1976, the total number of members was reported to be 500,000, many of whom were already regarded as unreliable party members.[98] By the early 1980s, their number had apparently reached 1.5 million.[99] In 1986, it was reportedly 1.6 million.[100] In 1989, in a lengthy senior leadership debate in which Saddam too participated, it was assessed to be between 1.5 million and 2 million.[101] It is quite clear that the party leaders themselves did not really know the precise figures, but the expansion was still impressive—so much so that during the senior leadership debate, Saddam expressed doubts as to the commitment of the new recruits.[102]

Why did young Shi'is join the Ba'th Party? Many were coerced, others saw it as a faster track to a career, and some may have identified with the ideal of Shi'i-Sunni Arab equality and Arab nationalism in general. But even Saddam recognized that the rapid expansion of the party's lower ranks with the recruitment of many who were not truly Ba'this jeopardized the party's ideological purity. This problem came to haunt the party leaders following Ayatollah Khomeini's rise to power in Tehran in 1979: in a party regional congress in 1982, the leadership admitted in alarm that many young party members had begun to frequent mosques. The report provides hints that those young people were overwhelmingly Shi'is.[103]

The Tribal Policy Approach to the Shi'a

An additional sociopolitical tool adopted by the regime to co-opt Shi'i leaders was a tribal policy that went contrary to party doctrine. After the confrontations of 1969, Saddam as vice president and deputy chairman of the RCC in charge of domestic security reached the conclusion that rather than confronting them, he needed to co-opt the shaykhs. In doing so, he was following in the footsteps of the British Mandate and the monarchy. He also, if unknowingly, followed a saying by Colonel T. E. Lawrence—Lawrence of Arabia—that indirect rule would make it possible "to make more bricks with less straw," the expensive "straw" representing government troops. Already by the early 1970s, tribal shaykhs, Shi'is as well as Sunnis, were being wooed with small monetary gifts, some land, and special treatment, including personal visits by the vice president, Saddam Husayn. Those who refused to collaborate were pushed aside and their place taken by "black sheep," more compliant members of the shaykhly family. Those considered dangerous were killed, usually by poisoning. Much like the Ottomans, the British, and the monarchy, the Ba'th regime manipulated the tribes in many ways, sometimes even creating new tribes. The shaykhs were given weapons. They received financial support that enabled them to raise small private armies, and the regime distributed state land to them. Personal ties with the president, the result of occasional visits to the Republican Palace and presidential visits to the tribal domains, became an important component in the new political arrangement. This made it possible for the shaykhs to bypass the regular and impersonal bureaucratic system. In most cases, this arrangement created some degree of compliance. For their part, the tribes, too, often tried and sometimes succeeded in manipulating the regime to do their bidding, but both sides benefited from this cooperation. The party's ideological commitment to a brave new socialist, modern, and national society lost out.[104]

A Shi'i Counterstrategy: Baqir al-Sadr's Ecumenical Endeavor

It is not clear which of the two nemeses first embarked on his ecumenical endeavor. Saddam launched his ecumenical campaign in early August 1979 and Ayatollah Muhammad Baqir al-Sadr, the charismatic leader of the Shi'i activist circles, did the same sometime between June 1979 and early April 1980. And yet there can be no doubt that one of them was responding to the other. While Saddam aimed at the heart of Iraqi Shi'i identity, Sadr did the same, aiming his communiqué at the Sunnis of Iraq. Without meaningful Sunni support, the Shi'is could not topple the Ba'th regime. Much like Saddam, Sadr therefore resorted to Sunni-Shi'i ecumenism by evoking Sunni symbols. Because of his support for Khomeini in June 1979, he was placed under house arrest in Najaf, where he remained until his execution in Baghdad in April 1980.

Following in Khomeini's footsteps, Sadr sent three recorded messages from his house arrest, the most important of which was the third one, which was recorded sometime between mid-July 1979 and early April 1980. It called on all the sons of the Iraqi people, "Arabs and Kurds, Sunnis and Shi'is," to unite against "the ruling despots . . . [who] desecrate Islam, 'Ali and 'Umar alike" and who "fill the land with alcoholic drinks, pigs' fields, and all kinds of abominations." He besought his people to build a "noble, free Iraq, where Islamic justice will abound and human dignity will reign." He called on all Sunnis and Shi'is who were pious Muslims to unite against the Ba'th. Indeed, Sadr even made an effort to bridge the theological and emotional gap between the two sects. He proclaimed Abu Bakr and 'Umar, two of the three Rightly Guided Caliphs who preceded Imam 'Ali, to be pious Muslims. This was nothing short of a revolution in Shi'i theology. Traditionally, Shi'a regards the two as base usurpers who are burning in hell for denying 'Ali his right to the caliphate. Sadr went so far with his ecumenical impulse that he promised that Shi'is were ready to fight against the apostate Ba'th regime even under pious Sunni leaders, as Imam 'Ali had done under 'Umar.

> O my dear Iraqi people . . . I am with you my Sunni brother and son as much as I am with you my Shi'a brother and son. . . . I want to say to you, [Sunnis], the sons of Abu Bakr and 'Umar. . . . The Sunni rule which was represented by the Rightly Guided Caliphs caused Imam 'Ali to carry the sword defending it. . . . [Legitimate] Sunni rule does not mean the rule of a person who has descended from Sunni parents [like Saddam] but it

means the rule of Abu Bakr and Umar which has been challenged by the tyrannical rulers of Iraq today. . . . They [the Ba'th] violate Islam and they abuse Ali and 'Umar alike. . . . They have dropped the religious ceremonies which were protected by Abu Bakr and Umar.[105]

Another innovative, even revolutionary element in this communiqué is the emphasis on Iraqi nationalism or patriotism, which had never before appeared in Sadr's writings. There is no doubt that Sadr was "corresponding" with Saddam: by 1979, it had become clear that the president was emphasizing Iraqi identity at the expense of Arab identity. Sadr followed in his footsteps, placing an emphasis on Iraqi identity at the expense of pan-Islam or pan-Shi'a. His acceptance of Abu Bakr and 'Umar as legitimate Muslims, however, was partial. He defined the first three Rightly Guided Caliphs as "Muslims" rather than as "Believers" (*mu'minin*). In Shi'i sources, Sunnis may be called Muslims, but in the full awareness that this is a kind of *taqiyya* because they are imperfect followers of Islam. After all, they deviated from God's instruction to anoint 'Ali as the Prophet's heir. The only real Muslims are the Shi'is, and they are indeed regarded as "Believers."[106]

Furthermore, anyone who took the trouble to read Sadr's earlier writings could have found very critical views of 'Umar and the 'Abbasid caliph Harun al-Rashid. 'Umar was castigated for his harsh treatment of Fatima, the Prophet's daughter and 'Ali's wife, as well as for rejecting the Prophet's deathbed wish to provide one more point of guidance to the community, "after which you shall not go astray." Apparently guessing that the Prophet intended to appoint 'Ali as his heir, 'Umar prevented this, arguing that "his pain [or ailment] has overcome him." As Sadr saw it, 'Umar represented a highly problematic trend in early Islam, that of rejecting clear Qur'anic texts and opposing the Prophet's decisions.[107] Likewise, Sadr's lectures in Najaf would have bred a profound feeling of unease even in very pious Sunnis. In a series of lectures at the *hawza al-'ilmiyya* in the mid-1960s, he addressed the issue of devotion and sacrifice on the altar of true Islam. His supreme example was, naturally, 'Ali ibn Abi Talib, the first Shi'i Imam. 'Ali sacrificed everything for true Islam, asking for nothing in return. Sadr compared him to Caliph Harun al-Rashid, in front of whom "the temporal world knelt. . . . The world of Harun al-Rashid was tremendous. . . . *Harun al-Rashid whom we are cursing day and night* [author's italics] because he sank in love for the temporal world, lofty castles . . . luxuries . . . leadership, caliphate. . . . [However], to keep this world he arrested Musa bin Ja'far [al-Kazim, the seventh Imam of the Shi'is]."[108] According to the Shi'i narrative, Harun al-Rashid ordered that Musa al-Kazim, who had been his prisoner for several years, be poisoned. Cursing Rashid and accusing him of killing Musa al-Kazim is definitely something no Sunni can possibly be indifferent to, especially in Iraq. Iraqi Sunnis are particularly proud of the golden age of Harun al-Rashid, who ruled the vast 'Abbasid Empire from Baghdad. But this is not all.

In his introduction to the history of the Shi'a written by 'Abd Allah al-Fayyadh, Sadr exposed his views that "following an instruction from God," the Prophet chose 'Ali to succeed him, "represent[ing] both the intellectual *marja'iyya* [the supreme religious authority] and the political leadership."[109] Indeed, Sunnis would have felt completely estranged had they heard Sadr's views on the historical and political role not only of 'Ali but also of all the other Shi'i Imams. By implication, he bared his plans for the modern Shi'is of Iraq through the description of the historical role of the Imams. The Imams, he narrated, were both the supreme spiritual and political leaders. They opted for political passivity only because they did not yet have a sufficient number of devoted troops, but they were working to raise such an army. Sadr implied that the Shi'a, following in their footsteps, were only waiting for the moment when they would have a sufficient force to carry out a Shi'i revolution. In the same place, Sadr also defined the Sunni rule after 'Ali's death as a "deviation" (*al-inhiraf*),[110] for not only the Umayyad but also the 'Abbasid Caliphate was non-Islamic. This was very offensive to all Sunnis.

All this leaves doubt as to Sadr's true intentions. Was it still possible that in 1979 he was ready for true Shi'i-Sunni cooperation, equality, and even for Sunni supremacy, provided that shari'a was enforced? Perhaps, but this assumption becomes even more doubtful in view of his support for Khomeini's principle of the absolute "rule of the [religious] jurist" (*wilayat al-faqih*). In February 1979, on Khomeini's return to Tehran, in response to a petition from Shi'i 'ulama he wrote a draft constitution for the Islamic revolution in Iran. In the absence of the Hidden Imam, he wrote,

the Rightly Guided *Marja'iyya* is the legitimate expression of Islam and the [individual] *marja'* is legally the General Deputy of the [Expected] Imam. Based on that . . . the *marja'* is the supreme representative of the state and the supreme commander of the armed forces. . . . [He decides about] the individuals that will run for the position of chief of the executive authority. . . . [He will] decide regarding the constitutional legitimacy of the laws prepared by the Council [of Representatives].[111]

By emphasizing that the *marja*, an exclusively Shiʿi title, was the leader of Islam in general, Sadr implied that he was also the preeminent leader of all Sunnis. This is far from ecumenism. In fact, the very concept of clerical political leadership is alien to Sunni Islam. Even some leading Shiʿi *mujtahid*s such as Ayatollah Shariʿat-Madari rejected it.

Sadr left therefore an ambiguous legacy. Probably the best way to understand him is to follow his disciples and ascertain how they understood this legacy. In some cases, they are ecumenical.[112] More often than not, however, Sadr's disciples, including al-Hakim himself, moved back to the particular Shiʿi pole.[113] In September 1990, a senior member of the Daʿwa in Europe described to me his party's unambiguous vision for a post-Baʿth Iraq. Whereas in 1990, Iraq was united like a donkey and its rider, the donkey being the Shiʿa and the rider being the Sunna, he wished Iraq to stay united, and all he wanted to change was who was the donkey and who was the rider. This view was not merely his personal one, but was quite broadly shared. The Daʿwa was a close-knit organization with a highly disciplined membership. A personal view like that could not be allowed. Indeed, in May 2004, soon after the Iraqi Governing Council and the Iraq Provisional Authority issued the provisional constitution, or the Law for the Administration of Iraq in the Transitional Period, one of Sadr's disciples who was based in Qom had a different proposal. Grand Ayatollah Kazim al-Husayni al-Haʾiri published his own draft for an Iraqi constitution, and it was almost a carbon copy of Muhammad Baqir al-Sadr's 1979 draft constitution for Iran.[114] Haʾiri followed Sadr's example in placing a heavy emphasis on Iraqi patriotism, but all vestiges of ecumenism had disappeared. His draft was meant to establish clear-cut Shiʿi sovereignty and domination.

In Haʾiri's draft constitution Islam is the official religion of the state, but "the official school" (*al-madhhab al-rasmi*) is the "Twelver Jaʿfari" one, that is, the Shiʿi school that believes in the twelve Imams, because "the majority of the Iraqis belong to this school" (appropriately, Article 12). The president of the republic, being the head of the executive branch and the supreme commander of the armed forces, must, among other things, "believe . . . in the principles of the Islamic Republic [of Iran] and in the official school of the regime"—that is, he must be a Shiʿi (Article 112, Clause 7). One may dismiss this proposal as the production of an irrelevant and isolated cleric, but Haʾiri was one of Daʿwa's leading ʿulama and, by 2005, Muqtada Sadr's senior clerical patron, admired by many Iraqi Shiʿis.

In the last analysis, both Saddam and Sadr failed. Saddam's ecumenical efforts had no chance of success because he could not adopt the complete Shiʿi historiography and theology, including *al-bara'a*, or "denunciation," declaring Abu Bakr, 'Umar, and 'Uthman, as well as the Umayyads and 'Abbasids, sinners and enemies of God. No less important, he failed to fulfill the expectations of the Shi'i majority for Shi'i-Sunni equality. As for Sadr, at the time his message reached only a few in Iraq, Shi'is or Sunnis. It became known to wider audiences only after his death, during the media campaign that accompanied the Iran-Iraq War. By then the lines were clearly drawn: any Sunni cooperation with the Da'wa, if successful in toppling the Ba'th regime, risked an Iranian occupation of Iraq. The most interesting aspects of the identities the two leaders offered to the Iraqi people were the timing and the uncanny similarity between their solutions, but also the differences. Sadr published his two volumes of an ecumenical all-Islamic study, *Falsafatuna* (*Our Philosophy*), in 1959, and *Iqtisaduna* (*Our Economics*), in 1961. Both were aimed mainly at combating Marxism and, to an extent, capitalism. The books had nothing to do with the Ba'th; they were part of the struggle against the powerful communists. The ecumenical component in both books was a silent one: there was no mention of the Shi'i-Sunni dispute, and the arguments were all-Islamic. In 1963, the Ba'th practically eliminated the communists through a bloody massacre, and Sadr's need to combat communism receded. His written production in the next few years was very Shi'i with strong anti-Sunni components. It took him most of the 1970s to respond to two strategies that the Ba'th had adopted between 1969 and the early 1970s: the cultivation of territorial Iraqi patriotism and a kind of ecumenism through the incorporation of Shi'i heroes into the national pantheon. Belatedly, he addressed both issues in his two last communiqués,[115] but he was executed before he could develop his response. His disciples continued his territorial Iraqi theme but rejected his ecumenical attempt.[116] The similarities, including whiffs of ecumenism and an emphasis on Iraqi patriotism, were secondary to the differences, and the differences were profound. Saddam was nurturing secular Iraqi nationalism, based in part on heathen civilizations. Sadr tried to foster shari'a-based Iraqi identity. And yet Sadr never assaulted Saddam's Mesopotamian trend. Very likely, he too had a soft spot for the glory that was pre-Islamic Iraq. Finally, that the regime paid close attention to Sadr's 1979 ecumenical initiative is evident from Saddam's above-mentioned 1980s ecumenical projects, but Manal Yunis, head of the party-affiliated Implementing Bureau of the General Union of Iraqi Women, actually copied Sadr verbatim. In a message to the president on International Women's Day, she congratulated him in the name of "the Sisters of the Two Rivers, Daughters of 'Ali, 'Umar and al-Husayn."[117]

Regime-Shi'i Confrontations, 1969–79: A Pattern Is Set

Less than one year into Ba'th rule, the first confrontation with the Shi'a erupted. In later years, the Da'wa Islamic Party played a fairly central role in pushing the Shi'i community to protest regime policies, but not this time. The Da'wa was established under the monarchy in the fall of 1957,[118] and in 1968 it was still concentrating on its own organization and recruitment and on building educational institutions, mainly libraries. This it did with the indirect help of Grand Ayatollah Muhsin al-Hakim, the *marja' taqlid* or Source of Emulation for all the Shi'is in Iraq and most Shi'is in the world. The party was peaceful, though highly secretive. The Ba'th regime was too busy assassinating and executing real and perceived pro-Iranian and pro-Syrian agents and communist activists and hanging Jewish "spies" in the public square to pay full attention to the Da'wa or the Shi'i clerics. Until the spring of 1969, religious Shi'i activities such as gatherings on commemoration days were allowed even at Baghdad University, where the Da'wa organized them openly and regularly.[119]

The Start of the Confrontations

The first confrontation between the Ba'th regime and the Shi'i establishment came as a spin-off from two developments. One was the April 1969 confrontation with the shah's Iran over sovereignty in the Shatt al-Arab waterway. The other was the expansion of the land reform. When the crisis with Iran erupted, the Ba'thi security organs suspected the Da'wa, but also the clerics and their madrasa students, of sympathy for Iran. In June 1969, to nip any support for Iran in the bud, the regime placed all religious education under supervision. Since most Shi'i religious education was concentrated in Najaf and Karbala, those towns reacted most severely.[120] To demonstrate to the Shi'i masses which side they should support, the regime also tried to coerce Grand Ayatollah Muhsin al-Hakim to declare the Shah "infidel."[121] Al-Hakim turned down the suggestion, arguing that the clergy must not get involved in politics. In making such an argument, he was quoting to the Ba'th a chapter from their own book: no less a figure than Michel 'Aflaq had insisted as early as the mid-1940s on *'ilmaniyyat al-dawla*, "the secularism of the state"—in other words, that religion and state ought to be separated. The regime did not take kindly to this joke. In retaliation, it declared al-Hakim's elder son, Mahdi, who was a member of the Da'wa, a fugitive traitor and an American spy, and imprisoned the Karbala-based Ayatollah Hasan al-Shirazi, accusing him too of espionage for the United States.[122]

According to another version, the order of events was somewhat different. In early 1969, the Ba'th regime nationalized all private education in Iraq. This angered the Shi'i clergy but did not immediately start a revolt. The regime also confiscated a few million Iraqi dinars, a huge sum in those days, representing all the financial contributions designated for establishing Kufa University, a Shi'i institution that was to teach sciences in Kufa, a suburb of Najaf. The project had been initiated by secular Shi'i businessmen, mainly merchants, but also with the participation of some mullas. The would-be founders, including the well-known architect Makiya, were arrested and interrogated. This was not necessarily an anti-Shi'a step: the Jesuit American Baghdad College, an excellent intermediate and high school, was also nationalized. Then, in a television announcement, a large monetary prize was promised to whoever helped capture "the spy Mahdi Muhsin [al-Hakim]." This prompted many Shi'is to phone each other and ponder what this meant. People went to the mosques to talk to each other about it. There was tremendous tension in the air. Many people established contact with Grand Ayatollah Muhsin al-Hakim. The population of Madinat al-Thawra (later Saddam City) sent representatives to the *marja'* and told him that they were ready to start a revolt. The Ba'th Party was then very weak, and the impression was that success was possible. But al-Hakim strongly objected. When my interviewee, "Abu Layth," met Mahdi al-Hakim later outside Iraq, Mahdi told him that there were two reasons for avoiding war: the *marja'* feared that "a Shi'i soldier will kill Shi'i revolutionaries." Also, he was "not sure that a revolt would lead to a better government." Mahdi al-Hakim and Salih Kubba, another Shi'i accused of spying, were smuggled out to Saudi Arabia because they had been warned about the arrest warrant a few hours before it was made public.[123] The two versions are not mutually exclusive; in fact, they are mutually reinforcing. But that was not all.

The *marja'iyya* also came out against new socialist measures, including deepening the land reform at the expense of the old landowners; nationalizing industries, banks, and some segments of domestic and foreign trade; and an alleged official plan to license the sale of alcoholic drinks and to open places of entertainment in Najaf and Karbala. Such places were never opened, but the government introduced in Najaf a mixed school and a tourist resort with a lake (Buhayrat Razaza) where women wore minimal bathing costumes (the resort was later closed down). Between real steps, reversed steps, and rumors, the public in the holy cities, encouraged by the clergy, took to the streets in protest. Government repression led to further protests and further complaints that the regime was aiming at the destruction of the centers of "Islamic learning."

There were a number of tribal uprisings in the south, most notably the revolt of the Mayah tribal federation near 'Amara and Kut in protest of the land reform. It is not clear exactly what they were protesting against. After all, the regime was trying to win them over by distributing the shaykhs' lands to the peasants. Apparently, the new regime did not understand the importance of the shaykh to the tribe. In many tribes, the shaykhs were essential for a number of social needs, such as arbitration, mediation, and even social and economic help in times of need. Not all shaykhs were large landowners and cruel absentee landlords; some were popular with their tribesmen and were seen as indispensable. The tribal peasants wanted their shaykh to have enough land so that he could finance his *mudif* (guest house), which won the tribe respect from the neighbors and the government, and with his relative wealth he could also help a family in distress. The Ba'th activists, on the other hand, saw most shaykhs as "bad," as did their sources of inspiration, the European anthropologists. Those Ba'this who recognized the shaykhs' popularity saw in them yet another competing elite and were out to cut them down to size. Either way, the tribes did not like it. Extending the land reform represented as well a blow to the religious establishment, which received donations from the shaykhs.

In 1969, at least one major clash between demonstrators and the security forces in Najaf led to bloodshed. There were many arrests, deportations, and a few fatalities. Centers of Shi'i culture and learning were closed, and many 'ulama and students of religion fled the country.[124] Despite its opposition to the regime's policies, though, during this confrontation the *marja'iyya* under Hakim opposed a mass revolt and made only defensive and limited demands. In doing so, the religious leaders refused to be drawn into a dangerous vortex by the more militant masses. During the demonstrations the masses shouted radical slogans like "*Maku wali illa 'Ali wa-nurid qa'id Ja'fari*" (There is no Master but 'Ali [the first Shi'i Imam] and we want a Shi'i leader),[125] a goal that Hakim did not support. Another indication of the *marja'iyya*'s modus operandi in 1969 was that they did not hesitate to swallow their pride and turn for help to the pope, to Bertrand Russell, to Jean-Paul Sartre, to the secretary-general of the UN, and to the Sunni shaykh al-Azhar in Cairo. The fact that many 'ulama fled the country before the regime could lay its hands on them is further evidence of their pragmatism. Among those who sneaked out of Iraq were Ayatollah Muhammad al-Husayni al-Shirazi and, more surprisingly, *Hujjat al-Islam* Muhammad Baqir al-Sadr. Sadr's biographer insists that his "journey" to Lebanon was merely in pursuit of his duty, as he engaged in "secret" propaganda there in support of the *marja'iyya* of the holy cities.[126] Indeed, his activities there were so secret that he did not come to the notice of the Lebanese press and was allowed soon afterward to return to Najaf without any reprisals. It is quite obvious that Sadr, Shirazi, and Mahdi al-Hakim, as well as seven other senior *mujtahids* and some one thousand students of religion, decided to act wisely rather than heroically and keep at a safe distance until the storm subsided.[127] The same decision was reflected in the flat denial that Hakim had at any time issued a fatwa against the "infidel atheist Ba'th government."[128]

By contrast, in 1979–80, under the intoxicating influence of Khomeini's successful revolution, Muhammad Baqir al-Sadr openly delegitimized the regime and left little room for accommodation. But that time had not yet arrived. The 1969 confrontation abated after a few months. The truce began with an appeal by Muhsin al-Hakim to President Ahmad Hasan al-Bakr to release Ayatollah Hasan al-Shirazi, and with an open letter from the *marja'iyya* of the two holy cities to the president, listing their grievances.[129] By late September, following a diplomatic crisis with Lebanon that had a large Shi'i community, the regime allowed a delegation of Lebanese journalists and Sunni and Shi'i 'ulama to visit southern Iraq and see that it was peaceful.[130] Next, President Bakr marched at the head of the funeral of Muhsin al-Hakim, and the Iraqi official press lavishly praised the deceased *marja'*.[131] As reported by a person who was present, the Shi'i masses who followed the coffin of the deceased *marja'* were not conciliatory at all and shouted anti-Ba'th slogans like "*Hak isma' ya kha'in, sayyid Mahdi mu jasus* (Take it! Listen, O traitor, the Offspring of the Prophet Mahdi [al-Hakim] is not a spy!). This was chanted in the style of *hosa*, the traditional tribal war dance and chanting. A sinister decision by Saddam during that crisis that infuriated people was to execute a wealthy Shi'i Pakistani merchant, 'Abd al-Husayn Jita, for "spying for Israel." The public was told that Jita was in fact Jewish, but it was well known that he was Shi'i and had contributed substantial funds to building Shi'i mosques.[132]

Even before Grand Ayatollah al-Hakim's death, the Iraqi authorities undertook a few conciliatory steps. For example, the regime announced in November 1969 that it would soon celebrate the millennial anniversary of the establishment of Najaf as a religious study center. This, it was explained, would be the "practical translation of the belief of the 17th July [Ba'thi] Revolutionaries in the tremendous importance of religion and knowledge in our social life." Reportedly, the "respectable men of religion" received the announcement with "tremendous gratitude and enthusiasm."[133] The Ba'thi media usually and Saddam Husayn as a rule avoided the title "'ulama," because it also means "scientists" or "knowledgeable people," and preferred the expression *rijal al-din*. While these gestures were unlikely to fool a seasoned political observer, they were made in the hope that at least Shi'i regime supporters would see them as gestures to Shi'i values.

All this does not mean that Hakim was a quietist. Judging from the fact that he and his sons worked hand in hand with the most influential of the activist 'ulama, Muhammad Baqir al-Sadr, and from the description in the Lebanese press of his leadership of the Iraqi Shi'i community during the crisis of 1969, Hakim was a tough leader. His vigorous political and media campaigns presented the Ba'th regime in a bad light in the Arab world and set Iraq and Lebanon on a collision course. Iraq needed the Lebanese ports for its imports and, in addition, did not wish to push that country into Syria's sphere of influence. Hakim's policy was totally different from, for example, that of Ayatollah 'Ali Kashif al-Ghita, who during the confrontation headed a mission to Lebanon sent out by the Iraqi government to refute all anti-Ba'th accusations.[134] Despite his caution, Hakim was admired by Shi'i radicals, both during his lifetime and with the hindsight of the 1980s.[135] In fact, Hakim was a pragmatic activist who very ably managed a crisis not entirely of his own making. Mindful of the limitations of his community, he sparred expertly with a hostile, agitated, insecure, and thus trigger-happy secular Sunni regime. He won on two counts: the regime retreated temporarily from its decision to control fully the religious universities of Najaf and Karbala, and it ceased (again temporarily) to persecute those senior *mujtahid*s who remained in Iraq and refused to denounce Iran. Hakim also lost on two counts: first, even though it changed its policy regarding tribal shaykhs, the regime went ahead with its "socialist" policies all over the country, and second, some of the 'ulama who fled the country, including Mahdi, were never allowed back. This was a blow to the *hawzat*. Eventually, Mahdi al-Hakim was assassinated in exile.

The regime also scored some gains in that it managed to coerce some Shi'i 'ulama such as 'Ali Kashif al-Ghita to sign on publicly to its political causes. Ayatollah Muhammad al-Baghdadi al-Hasani, for example, issued a fatwa according to which the Shatt al-Arab belonged to Iraq. He called on all "Iraqi Muslims" to fight against "the [Iranian] *Kafara* [Infidels]—the enemies of the

Muslims," and warned that some Muslims (Iraqi Shi'is) had been deceived by imperialism, and so had turned against their own brothers. Likewise, lesser 'ulama such as 'Abd al-Hakim al-Musawi and Muhammad Jawad al-Sahlani expressed support for the regime, and the more senior *mujtahid* Mir Muhammad al-Qazwini for his part denounced "any spying of one Muslim against his Muslim brother." "Anyone who tries to spy on his people for the benefit of imperialism and the Zionists," he proclaimed, was an "enemy of God and his religion and deserves to die." Qazwini also prayed for President Bakr's health.[136] By the late 1980s, the Ba'th leadership had reached the conclusion that the Shi'i 'ulama led by Kashif al-Ghita, who openly served the regime, were ineffective because the Shi'i community ignored them, but the regime continued using them anyway.[137] One might consider Kashif al-Ghita, Qazwini, and their docile colleagues quietists, but it would be a mistake to brand all of them collectively as collaborators: they had to weigh the interests of the community and the *hawza*, the Shi'i religious "university" of the holy cities, as well as their personal safety, against the urge to confront the regime. Each of them individually decided to what extent to practice the traditional strategy of *taqiyya*, or precautionary dissimulation.

The appellation "quietist," perhaps even "collaborator," might suit another ayatollah who was present at the time in Najaf as a political exile, Ruhollah al-Musawi al-Khomeini. Throughout the period of tension, the Lebanese press mentioned many names of senior and less senior *mujtahids* who were in one way or another involved in the confrontation with the regime. Many of these, like the Shirazis, were of Iranian origin, and some had Iranian nationality. Khomeini's name was not mentioned once. In fact, when the Ba'th regime was cracking down on the Shi'i *hawza* of Najaf in a manner unknown in Iraqi history, the Iraqi press reported that Shabib al-Maliki, the provincial governor of Karbala, paid a three-hour visit to Najaf and met with some of its clerics, including Khomeini. The clerics were reported to have wished the governor and the president "success and good luck." They strongly denounced the "treason" of the "agent Iranian rulers" who initiated the Shatt al-Arab waterway crisis, which only served "imperialism and its world Zionist creation that attacked our holy places in Palestine," and they "stressed their total support" for government efforts "to eliminate the spies and the agents of imperialism."[138] Two days later, in an interview with the junior cleric 'alama Musa al-Musawi, grandson of the admired Ayatollah Abu al-Hasan al-Musawi, Ayatollah Khomeini supported the Ba'th regime in its confrontation with the Iranian shah.[139] It may be argued that the regime's media quoted those clerics falsely, but the report carefully avoided mentioning the names of the *marja' taqlid* Muhsin al-Hakim or of *Hujjat al-Islam* Muhammad Baqir al-Sadr, as well as those of other clerics who were known to be in opposition to the regime. Had the newspaper mentioned their names, the credibility gap would have rendered the whole publication ineffective, even very damaging to the Ba'th. Mentioning Khomeini twice as a supporter of the Ba'th, however, was credible enough. Indeed, soon after the 1969 conflict subsided, Khomeini even gave an interview to the Iraqi government newspaper on the symbolic occasion of Imam Husayn's birthday in which he supported the Ba'th policy of nonparticipation in the Rabat Islamic conference. His inherent radical-ism could be gleaned from his vehement opposition to the repair of al-Aqsa mosque in Jerusalem after the 1969 fire there because "the ashes of the ancient mosque should remain in front of the eyes of all Muslims to remind them of the crimes of Zionism in Islamic [as distinct from Arab] Palestine."[140] In 1969, this radicalism was not aimed against, but in support of the, Ba'th. No doubt he was in a vulnerable position; as a prominent political exile from Iran, his stay in Iraq depended on the goodwill of the Ba'th. But then, some Shi'i activ-ists, Arab as well as Iranian, risked not only deportation but their lives in 1969 and later, and indeed, already in 1969 many 'ulama and their students were exiled to Iran. In later years a few of them paid with their lives. Khomeini, the fiery activist, chose a different trajectory: To settle his accounts with the shah, he supported the Ba'th.

For a few months in 1969, the *hawzat* of Najaf and Karbala were in total disarray. This started thirty years of regime-Shi'a estrangement and confronta-tion. The persecution of the clergy, the supervision of their funds, and the partial nationalization of their autonomous education system offended even the less orthodox Shi'is because these measures touched on their sense of identity. In their eyes, the regime had exposed itself as hating Shi'i tradition and values. When in later years the regime forbade or limited religious Shi'i mass assemblies and processions on 'Ashura and the Arba'in, this impression was enhanced.

The Confrontations of the 1970s

The combination of measures targeting the Shi'a succeeded in creating a twi-light situation. Many joined the lower ranks of the ruling party, some out of conviction, some to upgrade their socioeconomic status, some to avoid per-secution. A handful became active, even senior members, while others joined the Da'wa Islamic Party, the most important organized Shi'i revolutionary movement until 1982. The Da'wa was established in October 1957 by the young charismatic cleric Muhammad Baqir al-Sadr (1933–80) and a small group of young mullas and laymen.[141] The main force driving the establishment of the Da'wa was the wish to combat the growing influence of the communists in Iraq and even in Najaf.[142] The purpose of the party was to attract the young generation back to Shi'i Islam. It was organized as a clandestine body, yet under the regimes of 'Abd al-Karim Qasim, 'Abd al-Salam, and 'Abd al-Rahman 'Arif it operated openly. Under the Ba'th, its activities were at first tolerated, but in late 1969, as part of the first Shi'i-regime confrontation, the party was banned.[143]

Most of the Shi'i community, however, remained uncommitted, hovering between disinterest and estrangement. Yet almost every year, there was some upheaval in the Shi'i south. A new upheaval occurred in 1970, for unclear reasons. In December 1971–January 1972, as a result of a new Iraqi-Iranian confrontation over three strategic islands in the Gulf, there was another wave of arrests, and reportedly no fewer than 30,000 people were exiled to Iran.[144] In 1972, one of the founders of the Da'wa, 'Abd al-Sahib Dakhil, was executed.[145] The year 1974 saw another upheaval. It started again with a confrontation on the Iraqi-Iranian border.[146] The regime immediately tightened its domestic security. The Shi'i opposition reported that the religious processions of 'Ashura (on February 2 that year) had turned into mass demonstrations against the Ba'th regime.[147] Even though there was no clear evidence of collusion between Iran and the Iraqi Shi'a, the regime worried about the combination of domestic Shi'i unrest and a confrontation with Iran. There was no explicit official admission of riots, but an unusual wave of support communiqués for the regime and against "the enemies of the Revolution," denouncing "treason" (*ghadar*) from within and "aggression" (*al-'udhwan*) from without, appeared, mainly from the Shi'i provinces. The government, for its part, announced its firm resolve to "raise the standard of living" in the south, and the people expressed their enthusiastic gratitude.[148]

In 1974, the regime had another reason for concern. The Kurdish revolt, supported by Iran, the United States, and Israel, had reached a stage at which whole Iranian artillery brigades dressed in Kurdish attire were entering Iraqi Kurdistan in support of the Kurds.[149] A few dangers combined to force Iraq to offer Iran a major concession over sovereignty of the Shatt al-Arab River in southern Iraq. The danger of the two countries sliding involuntarily into a major military confrontation in the north was one possibility. The Iraqi suspicions that the shah was somehow involved with the Shi'i riots was another;

confrontations both in the north and in the south were too much for the regime, especially because at the same time, the Soviets decided to limit exports of weapons to Iraq. In this way domestic intercommunal strife played a major role in one of the most important foreign policy decisions made by the Ba'th regime, the signing of the March 6, 1975, Algiers Agreement between the shah of Iran and Saddam Husayn.

The regime's crackdown on the Shi'a was severe. It imposed limitations on religious gatherings. Five Da'wa leaders were executed, and Sadr was arrested for a brief period.[150] According to an Iranian report, these executions were again accompanied by arrests and deportations of students of religion and the closure of religious institutions.[151] In this new moment of crisis, Sadr proved that his political radicalism was matched by very cautious tactics: to avoid a major crackdown on the *hawza* he safely distanced himself from the Da'wa by issuing a fatwa forbidding 'ulama from joining any "party organization."[152] Again, the regime announced its intention to embark on many development projects in the south, and 2,263 peasant families were promised land in the Basra area.[153] Some Shi'i clerics expressed gratitude and declared their total allegiance to the principles shared by Imam Husayn and the Ba'th revolution,[154] and the crisis was over.

The Crisis of 1977

In 1977, the demonstrations were prompted by a government ban on the processions for the annual Ziyara (Visitation) of the Arba'in (the fortieth day after the martyrdom of Imam Husayn). The procession usually left Najaf on foot and entered Karbala (where al-Husayn is buried) some three days later.[155] According to another source, the regime tried to control the processions and place at their heads Shi'i Ba'this. The "heads" of the processions, usually nonpolitical citizens, turned down the regime's instructions. The processions numbered tens of thousands of people.[156] The frustration of the populace could no longer be contained, and this sparked the great crisis of that year. The Da'wa and other activists launched the march all the same, chanting *hosa*-style antiregime slogans.[157] Beginning in the early seventies, the regime also forbade the carrying of knives and swords during the processions, implements with which men wounded their backs and heads in a display of religious zeal. They even forbade the popular storytellers from reciting in public the moving story of al-Husayn and his tragic end. Amazingly, on the radio the regime was broadcasting the *shabiya*, the drama of the Battle of

Karbala and of Imam Husayn's heroic death. However, it was broadcast on the Tasu'a, one day before the 'Ashura, and was forbidden during the 'Ashura. The regime also cracked down on the ceremonial preparations of the *qima*, the special commemoration dish of meat, rice, and grains that people contribute for the benefit of the pilgrims (usually, each column of pilgrims coming from a different town prepares it for itself). The dish is prepared in large pots in the street and is given out for free. People who were preparing it were sometimes arrested. The reason was that the more free food was available, the more participants would be attracted to the area.

Some additional practices connected with the commemoration days were forbidden. For example, the *radud*, the popular poets who read in a poetic style the story of al-Husayn, were forbidden to perform as usual, and some of the poets were arrested. In 1976, the Ba'th branch of Najaf went through a crisis when the secretary of the branch, a Shi'i party old-timer, strongly criticized some senior party officials who had come from Baghdad to talk to the Najaf members. The old-timer was deeply upset by the limitations the regime imposed and asked the senior visitors, "Why should you be against Imam Husayn?" As a result, the party changed tack. It emphasized with greater vigor the similarity between Imam Husayn and his legacy and the party's ideals. Thereafter the party began hanging leaflets on the walls quoting none other than the party's Christian founder, Michel 'Aflaq, who said, "*Ta'allamtu min al-Husayn Kayfa akun mithalan lil-huriyya* [From al-Husayn, I have learned how to become an example of liberty]." This was the Ba'thi interpretation of the Imam's legacy, and it appealed to some, because it was more modern and more easily understood than the style used by the old school of the 'ulama.[158]

Most strangely, even though officially speaking the day of 'Ashura was a national holiday, reportedly anyone who did not show up for work on that day was punished. The explanation for this bizarre approach may be that in the government's calendar, the tenth day of Muharram holiday fell one day before the day that the Shi'i clerics considered to be the tenth. In other words, on the ninth of Muharram (the Tasu'a) the state commemorated the tenth of Muharram, and people had a free day, to the chagrin of the Shi'i religious establishment. The reason for that was simple: the regime did everything it could to dissuade people from participating in the ceremonies and processions, which were often used for antiregime demonstrations. A senior Shi'i Ba'th Party member, the governor of Karbala, Shabib al-Maliki, once pleaded with President Bakr to commemorate the tenth of Muharram on the tenth of

Muharram. Bakr agreed, and this made people very happy, but it was a one-time variance, and things went back to their usual state the next year.[159]

In February 1977, for the first time, the Iraqi media explicitly admitted that large-scale demonstrations had taken place in the south and gave full publicity to the disciplinary measures adopted by the regime, including executions and arrests. In a mass procession from Najaf to Karbala earlier in that month, many in the crowd processing had chanted anti-Ba'th slogans. Some reported that Kurdish guerrillas, deported to the south during the Ba'th Arabization campaign, had supplied the Shi'is with weapons and that members of the military had defected to side with the demonstrators.[160] The security forces tried to stop them along the way, especially in Karbala. Al-Husayn's shrine was closed down. Ayatollah Muhammad Baqir al-Sadr, the young activist, instructed the marchers not to provoke the regime. Nevertheless, the activists did enter Karbala, and clashed with the security forces there. The result was at least seven dead and thousands detained.[161]

The regime denied that it had tried to stop the march, and blamed the uprising on foreign forces. "Imperialists" and "Zionists" were accused of planting provocateurs among the marching masses that shouted anti-Ba'thi slogans and fired on a police station. In 1977, though, relations with Iran were very good, following the near complete implementation of the March 1975 Algiers Agreement. This time, therefore, the Ba'th regime could not blame the demonstrations on Iran, nor could it hide the riots. The regime accused Syria of sending agents to bomb the holy shrines of Karbala and Najaf when they were teeming with pilgrims. The regime even produced a sixteen-year-old Syrian boy and charged him with planting a bomb in Karbala's al-Husayn's tomb on the day of Arba'in. This was an elegant way to explain why the regime shut down the Karbala shrine on such an important day—to protect the pilgrims. Other Syrian agents were said to have been hiding in Iraq, waiting for an opportunity "to blow the [Shi'i] faithful to pieces."[162] Even though the term "Shi'a" was never mentioned, it was sufficient to mention Karbala as the main target and *Ziyarat al-Arba'in*, a unique Shi'i occasion, and to have mainly Shi'i clerics condemn Damascus for the public to get the message. The language of these and other public condemnations was of particular importance. President Asad and his regime were accused of *inhiraf* (deviation) from the *haqq* (truth generally, but also, in a religious context, God), and of *ridda* (apostasy), which again could be seen as deviating from true Ba'thism but, when coming from a Shi'i cleric, could only mean deviation from Islam. Qur'anic verses, too, were quoted, promising the *kuffar* (infidels, atheists, nonbelievers) "devastation."[163] By implication, this meant something that the Syrian Sunni Muslim Brotherhood had been saying explicitly, that Damascus was ruled by a heretic sect that had seceded from true Islam, and thus its members deserved to die.[164] By implication, again, this meant that Baghdad's struggle against Asad and his regime was a continuation of the famous *Hurub al-Ridda* (the Apostasy Wars) fought after the Prophet's death by Caliph Abu Bakr against the tribes that had abandoned Islam.

That a staunchly secular regime would sponsor such religious propaganda is evidence of a deep sense of alarm in Baghdad: the Shi'i demonstrations, combined with a split in the ruling party, had shaken the very foundations of the regime. The incident also exposed once again the Ba'th regime's deep need for a reliable object of hate on which to blame its rift with meaningful circles within its Shi'i population. In early 1977, the Arab-Israeli conflict was momentarily dormant, and relations with Iran were good, but hostility with the Ba'th regime in Damascus remained as intense as ever. It thus seemed a suitable scapegoat. By 1977 some Iraqi Shi'i clerics were already declaring the 'Alawites of Syria to be Shi'a. Baghdad was out to demolish the new legitimacy accorded Asad and his sect by presenting them as Shi'i killers and desecrators of Shi'i shrines.

As a result of the 1977 riots, the party went through its first crisis over its sectarian policy. The regime established a senior special court to try the instigators. Two of its members were Shi'i party old-timers and one was a Sunni. Saddam Husayn reportedly expected between fifty and one hundred executions.[165] However, the court was lenient: only eight were sentenced to death and fifteen to life imprisonment, including Muhammad Baqir al-Hakim, son of the late Grand Ayatollah Muhsin al-Hakim and the future leader of SAIRI, the Supreme Assembly of the Islamic Revolution of Iraq, established in Tehran in 1982. All the other defendants were released because they were "simple people" who had become victims of "social deceptions."[166] A few weeks later two of the judges, Fulayyih Hasan Jasim, a Shi'i from Diyala and a member of the highest party institution, the Regional Leadership, and Dr. 'Izzat Mustafa, a Sunni Arab from 'Anna, a physician, a cabinet minister, and a member of both the Regional Leadership and the RCC, were accused of failing in their party duties and lacking faith in the party's ideals. They were summarily dismissed from their party positions and disappeared from the public eye.[167] This massive tremor at the top of the regime's leadership reflected a deep rift. Some, reportedly including President Bakr, wanted to pacify the Shi'a through relative leniency, and some even recommended making meaningful concessions to the Islamists. Saddam's circle favored harsh measures. By 1977, though, Saddam was already the strongman in Baghdad. His control of the domestic security system was total, and he had an automatic majority in the two top institutes, the RCC and the Regional Iraqi Leadership.[168] President Bakr was already under unofficial house arrest, with a cloud of doom hanging over him. It is not clear whether the majority of senior Shi'is in the party were in favor of leniency. If they were, and if they had voiced their views, this could have been an additional reason for the far more extensive purge Saddam initiated in July–August 1979 when he became president.

The 1977 crisis also demonstrated the regime's tremendous reluctance to admit that its problems with the Shi'a stemmed from domestic rather than external sources. This denial started at the top of the power structure and permeated all the way to the lowest echelons of the party and internal security apparatus. When Shi'i suspects were being interrogated, the interrogators (some of them themselves Shi'is) knew precisely what the bosses wanted to hear, and they extracted the "right" confessions from the unfortunate prisoners. The bosses liked nothing better than to hear that the antiregime demonstrations had been instigated by a foreign power, especially a power they suspected of maintaining ties with "their" Shi'is. When this "information" reached the top, it further enhanced paranoia and animosity toward those outside powers. After 1977, flocking to Karbala on some religious occasions was still permitted, but only under heavy surveillance and only in cars (not on foot), and on an individual basis rather than in large groups. The severe clashes of February 1977 marked the end of the very large processions of the 'Ashura and Arba'in, along with some other religious traditions. The regime was unwilling to risk another such confrontation.[169]

The regime sealed the 1977 confrontation with two final episodes. One was a high-profile visit by then vice president Saddam Husayn to Najaf and Karbala. Saddam promised major renovation and development of the Shi'i holy places, and for the first time he officially announced that he was an off-spring of the Prophet and Imams 'Ali and Husayn: "If any of you has one connection with Imams 'Ali and Husayn," he announced, "we [read: "I"] have two connections [spiritual and a bloodline]. . . . They are our [read: my] ances-tors [*ajdaduna*]."[170] In fact, as discussed earlier, the first time that Saddam's pedigree as a *sayyid* (in the Shi'i tradition) or Hashimi *sharif* (in the Sunni one) was mentioned occurred in 1971 in a book dedicated to his maternal uncle, Khayr Allah Tilfah. It provided a full family tree for the tribe of al-bu Nasir.[171] The book won very little public attention, however, and there was a need to publicize the new information in a high-profile speech. The second episode was a series of programmatic speeches by Saddam in which he declared the Islamic Shari'a passé. While paying some unavoidable lip service, rather than giving in to the Islamic pressure, which came mainly from the Shi'i 'ulama and community, he declared war on Islam, Sunni and Shi'i alike.

Saddam Responds to Religious Shi'i Riots: Declaring the Shari'a *passer de mode*

An explanation for this defiance may be a combination of a sense of the Shi'i threat at home with a sense of great power elsewhere: the economy was booming, government services everywhere were being rapidly upgraded, the Kurdish revolt had been crushed in 1975, and foreign relations were at an all-time zenith, as Iran, Turkey, Jordan, Saudi Arabia, and the Gulf states were all on friendly terms with Ba'thi Iraq. Saddam felt that the combination of harsh repression and economic development, as Iraqis defined it—"terrorizing and enticement" (*al-tarhib wal-targhib*)—could get the Shi'a to cooperate with the regime. He saw no need to make any concessions to the mullas or to party members who went soft. Defending secularism became a means to fight a dangerous competing leadership, the Shi'i clerical class, but secularism was of crucial importance in its own right, just as it was an essential component of the party's identity. Saddam drew his legitimacy from Michel 'Aflaq, the Christian founder of the party, and there is much evidence that his commitment to secularism was anything but cynical. He seemed to have identified with this principle wholeheartedly and saw in any challenge to it a challenge to him personally and to his leadership.

In late 1977, therefore, it made sense to Saddam to respond to the religious riots by addressing the relationship between Islam and politics. The deputy RCC chairman and vice president was defiant. When it came to the Islamist anti-Ba'th struggle, Sunni Arab 'ulama and fundamentalists were few. They were aware that even had they been able to topple the regime, they would only have been clearing the way for the Shi'i majority to assume power. In view of the historical estrangement between the sects and the traditional Sunni Arab fear in Iraq of Iranian Shi'i influence dating back to the days of the monarchy, an end to Sunni Arab hegemony in Iraq was too much to sacrifice, even on the altar of Islamic rule. Saddam's secular offensive was therefore directed mainly at the Shi'a.

In view of his attachment to pre-Islamic Mesopotamia, the content of his 1977 lectures, and the permission he gave to publish atheist articles in prestigious Ba'thi magazines, it is very likely that Saddam was close to atheism, but he had to deny it so as not to alienate the religious majority in Iraq. Like 'Aflaq before him, Saddam dissociated himself from atheism (*al-ilhad*). Still, in his lectures he had to draw a clear line between the Ba'th and the religious parties. He therefore warned against any attempt to imitate the religious parties and mix religion and politics: "We should go back to the origin of our ideology: be proud of religion, without, [however,] adopting policies for religion." "Our party is with faith [*al-iman*], but it is not a religious party, nor should it be one." His main message was daring: "We should not force our treatment of the present worldly aspects of life into a framework of religious jurisprudence." Clarifying, he said: "The current social problems . . . are quite different from those of the early Islamic times, when the [shari'a] rules of jurisprudence were laid down. . . . [These rules] cannot be the rules of present life."[172] In another lecture, he even implied, much as his mentor 'Aflaq had, that the Ba'th came to replace Islam in the modern age: "Islam is the soul of the Arab nation. However, we derive . . . from Islam . . . lessons to express *in a new theory*—the Arab Ba'th Socialist Party['s] . . . revolution, progress and social construction" (emphasis added).[173] This could mean only one thing: the Ba'this were offering a new and different approach to life from what Islam had to offer. They were building something new. Were they really taking some lessons from Islam? What were those lessons? Saddam remained silent, but if, as he announced, the Shari'a was out and "socialism," "revolution," "progress," and Muslim-Christian-Druze secular Arabism represented the new "social construction," then Islam being "the soul of the Arab nation" and the "lessons" were nothing but a convenient rhetorical cover for a de facto departure from Islam.

Saddam rejected altogether the possibility of imposing the Shari'a, as demanded by the fundamentalists; he warned that if the state and the party followed the religious "reactionary line" by building modern life on "the teachings of ancient jurisprudence," it would only lead to conflict between Sunnis and Shi'is owing to "existing differences between the sects."[174] As noted earlier, however, the differences between the Sunna and the Shi'a in terms of substantive law are minor, and therefore a mixed Sunni-Shi'i Islamist state could easily have resolved all differences of jurisprudence. An elegant way to do this would have been to allow every individual to turn to a Shi'i or Sunni shari'a court as he or she pleased, as was the case under the monarchy. If Saddam was worried, or pretended to be worried, about the legal aspect, then he was barking up the wrong tree, and he must have known this. Far more difficult to diffuse would have been the issues of history, theology, and identity. Theoretically, at least, in a state based on a divided Islam rather than on the common Arabic language, conflict over the interpretation of history was unavoidable. The state would need to define history's saints and villains. Were the first three caliphs base criminals who usurped the caliphate from Imam 'Ali, or were they upright role models? Were the Umayyads and the 'Abbasids legitimate caliphs, or were they, too, despicable villains? Were the Shi'is treated fairly throughout history by the Sunni majority? Not that Saddam himself found a magic solution to these questions; his ruling elite, while integrating Shi'is, still relied more heavily on Sunni Arabs. Likewise, school textbooks under the Ba'th were written essentially in a Sunni spirit. Yet as long as religious studies were limited and considered an inferior discipline, all these painful controversies could be, and indeed were, kept at the periphery of the national attention. Theoretically, secular Arabism therefore offered a better common denominator than Islam. In that, Saddam was right. In his lectures, Saddam made it clear to the mullas that, rather than accept the rioters' demand to Islamize the state, he would actually eliminate Islamic law and replace it with modern, secular Ba'thi legislation. The meaning of what he said was an open challenge to the very core of Islam, Sunni as well as Shi'i—namely, a challenge to the belief that the God-given Shari'a is eternal. Coming from the vice president of an Islamic state whose constitution recognized Islam as the official religion of the state, this was incredible.

In a more tactical and calculating way, Saddam also made an effort to persuade his party members that they only stood to lose from Islamization. The very warning was the first indication that already by 1977, there were members for whom the party's secular worldview and practice had become a burden. Any meaningful concessions to Islam, Saddam argued, would inevitably lead the party to lose its soul, and eventually to lose power. The confused membership and the public alike would no longer be able to tell the difference between the Ba'th and the fundamentalists, and the party would be lost. If it went Islamic, he insisted, the Ba'th had no chance of beating the religious parties at their own game: "The religious forces of reaction will take over the leadership in such a case, because every . . . ideology has its own leaders. . . . Leaders from reactionary circles . . . are more specialized in this field."[175] It is not clear that this analysis was correct. Had it not been for the American invasion of 2003, Saddam and his domesticated and "Islamized" Ba'th Party would probably have remained in power much longer. At least there were no signs that the Islamic campaign, which lasted for more than a decade, jeopardized the party's rule. In fact, the faith campaign of the 1990s proved popular in the Sunni camp, and the Shi'is were too weak to revolt against it (see chapter 6). The party took no risks: the conversion to Islam notwithstanding, the internal security system continued to follow carefully all the usual suspects, Sunnis as well as Shi'is, making sure that the extended religious freedom would not be used to build opposition groups.

If Saddam's 1977 tracts provided the prescription, that is, replacing the Shari'a with Ba'thi enactment, Shibli al-'Aysami, the senior Syrian member of the Baghdad-based Pan-Arab Leadership, provided the diagnosis. A daring book he published in 1977 diagnosed the condition of Islam in the modern age. Islam as a potent faith, he wrote, was over. No man, he insisted, would henceforth be willing to risk his life for the promise of heaven. This was so because "the era in which we are living is not the era of the prophets and miracles. Magic, mystical and Sufi thinking is no longer useful, because [our era] is typified by rationalism and science." Medieval Islamic theology was "an affliction." The rational philosophy of Ibn Rushd (Averroës, died 1198) represented "the Arab-Islamic rational revolution" after the irrational days of the Prophet and the four Rightly Guided Caliphs. Aysami therefore did not reject wholesale the Islamic civilization, only its relevance to the modern age: "only" Islam's jurisprudence, its supernatural components and its rites, namely, Islam as a living religion. Today, he explained, the ingenuity of the Arab nation no longer appeared in Islam. Rather, it "appears through the emergence of the revolutionary Arab movement and in its avant-garde . . . the Ba'th." In other words, the Ba'th had come to replace Islam. "The Arab eternal message in the party's slogan," he summed up, "does not mean any particular religious message . . . rather it is the Arab nation's struggle toward progress . . . during successive historical phases."[176] It is difficult to imagine a more effective way to diminish Islam than to consider it to be as great as the *Jahiliyya*, but this was what 'Aysami did.

The regime's antireligious thrust in 1977also manifested in the introduction of new laws. The most important one was the Law of Reforming the Legal System (*qanun islah al-nizam al-qanuni*). In it, lawmakers aspired to give expression only to "socialist values, Arab nationalism and democracy," with religion left out completely.[177] In a closed-door meeting in late 1980 with his senior military commanders, Saddam remained committed to the party's doctrine, though with some modification. The meeting was convened to discuss the conduct of the Iran-Iraq War. Suddenly, Saddam strayed into a different set of issues that were preoccupying him: Khomeini's message, the role of the clerics, and the crisis of Islam. Saddam could not ignore Khomeini's religious lure. His views therefore were an exercise in dialectical contradictions. He claimed to be protecting Islam from Khomeini's corrupting influence, but he did this in a surprisingly secular way. The Ba'th, Saddam insisted, "reject atheism," but Khomeini "will make atheism easier" by turning Islam into "superstitions" (*khurafat*) and Shi'i "sectarianism." This would keep people away from Islam. Saddam thus presented himself to his officers as a defender of true Islam. But what kind of Islam was he defending? "Allah," he proclaimed, "is neither Sunni nor Shi'i, He is neither Catholic nor Protestant [*Allah la huwa Sunni wala Shi'i, la huwa kathuliki wa la brotostanti*]." What Saddam delineated to his senior military commanders was an ecumenical Sunni-Shi'i and even Muslim-Christian religion, spiritual and ethereal.[178] This was consistent with the Ba'thi approach to religion as it appeared in 'Aflaq's theory in the 1940s and 1950s. Saddam and his old-time colleagues were secular and hostile to the clerics; some even inclined toward atheism.

Is it possible that at the same time they also believed in this ethereal, purely spiritual Islam, free from 'ulama, free from Sunni-Shi'i sectarianism and even Muslim-Christian antagonism, as well as from Shari'a and "superstitions"? Such a possibility definitely exists. More likely, however, while attached to Islamic Arab history, they were not religious in any sense of the word, but they had to pretend to be religious for public consumption. They were practical men and therefore recognized that the Arab public was religious. At the same time, it would seem that the majority truly believed that religion was passé and that the Arab future was their future: secular, scientific, and rational, with no room for "superstitions," which to them was apparently a code word for the supernatural and, therefore, God.

Medieval Islamic Historiography in Defense of Ba'th Rule, Arabism, and the Sunna

Starting in the second half of the 1970s, regime establishment historians were adamant about defending the 'Abbasid Caliphate golden age (between the middle of the eighth century and the middle of the tenth century CE) against its detractors. The 'Abbasid Caliphate served as a punching bag—or whipping boy—for many left-wing non-pan-Arab antiregime intellectuals, who could not launch direct attacks on the Ba'th. The regime opened the way for such indirect attacks by adopting the 'Abbasid golden age as the best example of the glory that was the Arab Islamic civilization at its pinnacle. After Saddam Husayn became president, he was often equated with great 'Abbasids such as al-Mu'tasim and Harun al-Rashid. Earlier Arab Islamic eras too, certainly the Arab Islamic expansion under the first four caliphs, were a source of great pride for the Ba'th, not because of the religious aspect but rather because of those eras' place in Arab history. Between 1972 and 1979, the Iraqi Communist Party was allowed to operate openly as a result of an Iraqi-Soviet rapprochement. The Iraqi communists saw this as carte blanche to criticize the Ba'th petty bourgeois mentality, which expressed itself in the regime's socioeconomic and pan-Arab policies, but they were careful to do this through nasty attacks on the 'Abbasids. Many of the Marxist detractors hailed from Shi'i backgrounds. When they criticized the Arab conquests under the first three caliphs or the 'Abbasids, the strong impression is that they were settling a Shi'i account with the hegemonic Sunni historiography. Under the Ba'th, the establishment historians therefore were trusted with the defense at the same time of Arabism, the regime, and the Sunni approach to Islamic history. Thus, for example, when criticizing the Shi'i Marxist historian Husayn Qasim al-'Aziz for presenting the 'Abbasid Caliphate in a negative light, Iraq's leading historian, the Sunni Arab intellectual Faruq 'Umar Fawzi (henceforth Faruq 'Umar), complained that the Marxist's account was damaging the Arab self-view: "Does the Arab reader find in the . . . [Marxist's] book what strengthens his pride in his positive values? The . . . book is hard on our Arab history."[179] Faruq 'Umar expressed deep disappointment at the way 'Aziz described the Arab expansion in the seventh century CE. While 'Aziz saw the early Arab Islamic expansion into Iraq, Syria, and Egypt under the first three caliphs as "an act of occupation" (*ihtilal*), designed to "acquire the wealth of the occupied countries," in defense of Arab history, Faruq 'Umar saw in it nothing but "an act of liberation of lands in which Arab tribes had been dwelling and which the Sassanid [Persians] and the Byzantines robbed."[180] In this particular article, Faruq 'Umar's arguments are extremely weak and his motivation is too obviously political, but in most of his other publications (see below) he proved himself to be an adept historian. He always served the party line, and likely also his own personal inclination, but while doing so he demonstrated impressive proficiency. Defending the Arab caliphate at all costs led occasionally to anti-Persian and anti-Turkish twists, because the blame for problems that arose during the 'Abbasid rule could not be laid at the door of the Arabs.

Another goal of the establishment historians was combating contemporary antiregime political movements, mainly the Shi'i revolutionary ones such as the Daʻwa Islamic Party, through appealing to medieval history. When regime-sponsored historians criticized medieval revolutionary anti-Umayyad and anti-ʻAbbasid movements, though, they were faced with a problem. The Baʻth regime defined itself as the July 17–30 Revolution (*Thawrat 17–30 Tammuz*). As it was itself a "revolution," its politicians and historians had some difficulty denouncing medieval revolutionaries. In the Iraq of the early 1970s, Marxist and communist historians were still allowed, therefore, to describe such medieval movements, many of them either Shiʻi or containing some Shiʻi components, as idealistic and just liberation movements that fought against the oppression of the caliphate. Leaving things at that could, however, easily be interpreted as implying support for contemporary anti-Baʻthi revolts, and apparently this was precisely what the communists meant. The task of the Baʻthi historians since the mid-1970s was, therefore, to reverse that tide. They needed to delegitimize even the anti-Umayyad revolts, let alone the anti-ʻAbbasid revolts, by proving that they were dangerously extreme, or cruel, or cynical, or sexually and financially corrupt, or all the above, and thus destructive. The regime's historians, though, needed to demonstrate that there was one positive medieval revolution, the ʻAbbasid Daʻwa, which in 749–50 CE destroyed the Umayyads and brought the ʻAbbasids to power. After all, the Baʻth regime in Baghdad saw itself as the latter-day incarnation of the Baghdad-based ʻAbbasid Caliphate golden age struggling against Baʻthi Damascus, the latter-day incarnation of Umayyad Damascus.

In the course of delegitimizing practically all the medieval revolutionary movements, some historians went so far as to imply that the Shiʻi doctrine and eschatology were illegitimate because they were based on Persian pre-Islamic concepts. Still, because it appeared in highbrow Baʻth-sponsored magazines and learned books of history, it did not create a crisis, even inside the party. The Marxist historians, for their part, published their articles mainly in the communist monthly *al-Thaqafa al-Jadida*. In a treatise analyzing an important anti-ʻAbbasid movement, the Babikiyya-Kharamiyya (circa 799–837 CE),[181] Faruq ʻUmar attacked Marxist dialectical materialism typical of communist Arab intellectuals. These Marxist intellectuals, Faruq ʻUmar argued, presented the Kharamiyya movement as if it had "led for over twenty years a heroic and arduous liberating struggle against the ruling classes and the [ʻAbbasid] Caliphate." The intellectuals also claimed that the movement had "well-defined revolutionary social programs." According to those Marxists, the Kharamiyya fought against "oppression and exploitation" by disobeying the feudalists and the government and by declining to pay taxes.

The Moscow-inspired doctoral dissertation by 'Aziz angered Faruq 'Umar to no end. He castigated not only the Iraqi Shi'i Marxist but also his Soviet mentor. As he saw it, all those Marxists, Iraqi and Soviet alike, had come to false conclusions because of their anti-Arab bias. Faruq 'Umar here quoted medieval historians such as Baghdadi, Maqdisi, Ibn al-Jawzi, Shaharistani, Biruni, Tabari, and Ibn al-Athir, and lamented the fact that 'Aziz and his Soviet mentor were defaming in the dissertation such "pioneering historians" (*al-mu'arrikhin al-ruwwad*), especially Tabari and Maqdisi, accusing them of partiality. Faruq 'Umar pointed out (correctly) that Babik, the movement's leader, was not Azerbaijani and did not fight for the liberation of his "occupied homeland." The revolution was not that of the Azerbaijani "people" (*sha'b*) against its Arab oppressors, but rather a revolt of a hodgepodge of elements, including Arabs, and it was not exactly an Azerbaijani phenomenon. Furthermore, while the Marxist 'Aziz regarded the Babikiyya as "a peasant uprising against tyranny and oppression . . . one of the greatest of the popular uprisings of peasants," Faruq 'Umar pointed out (correctly again) that the feudalists actually joined the revolt and that it was also supported by the Byzantine emperor, and yet 'Aziz defined it as "class struggle."[182]

In Faruq 'Umar's view, the Babikiyya-Kharamiyya was typified by an "inclination toward sexual promiscuity" (*al-ibahiyya*) and forsook "the known social values." Rather than fighting for oppressed peasants, it was extremely violent and spilled much blood to achieve its goals. Its leader, Babik al-Kharami, was said to have "tortured people" and set settlements on fire. Their ultimate goal was to eradicate Arab Islam, returning the pre-Islamic Persian religions and "grabbing the empire from the hands of the Arabs and returning it to the emperors of Persia." The movement was Persian-inspired. It was like a more developed *mazdaqiyya* and a version of Zoroastrianism, both pre-Islamic Persian religions. Some medieval historians reported that they shared their women, a claim that Faruq 'Umar seemed to accept at face value. But Faruq 'Umar went much further, coming dangerously close to declaring the Shi'a heretics. This heathen movement, he reported, also saw in their leaders prophets, and believed in their return. They "predicted the arrival of the Savior [*al-Munqidh*] in the personality of a previous leader or religious reformer." This belief in the "Savior hero" and his return, argued Faruq 'Umar, was adopted by other movements, such as the one led by "the 'Allawi [Shi'i] revolutionary, Muhammad [Ibn 'Abd Allah, Dhu] al-Nafs al-Zakiyya (who revolted against the 'Abbasids in Hijaz in 762 CE), who claimed that he was the Expected Mahdi (*al-Mahdi al-Muntazar*).[183] In this way, Faruq 'Umar launched a frontal attack on Shi'i eschatology. Writing, on the pages of the leading Baʻthi intellectual magazine, that the Shiʻi concept of the Return of the Imam Mahdi is rooted in pagan Persian beliefs is extraordinary.

A few months later the prolific Faruq ʻUmar set out to demolish yet another Shiʻi historical hero.[184] He portrayed al-Mukhtar (bin Abu ʻUbayd) al-Thaqafi, who fought against the Umayyad rule in Iraq (685–87 CE) in the name of the Prophet's family (*Ahl al-Bayt*), as a cynical politician and religious hypocrite who betrayed Islam. Faruq ʻUmar described Mukhtar as cynical also in religious terms, as he adopted different religious slogans according to political expediency. Mukhtar, Faruq ʻUmar claimed, returned to "*Jahili* rites," and even resorted to religious trickery. He was a politician "who used all styles and who raised [all] sorts of slogans in order to achieve power and influence." Faruq ʻUmar pointed out (correctly) that at the same time that al-Mukhtar rose up in revolt, the moderate Shiʻis, such as Muhammad bin al-Hanafiyah (637–700 CE, half-brother of al-Hasan and al-Husayn, the second and third Shiʻi Imams), in whose name Mukhtar fought, were opposed to him. Again correctly, Faruq ʻUmar observed that some moderate Shiʻis accused Mukhtar of being *dajjal*, the Shiʻi equivalent of a false messiah or Antichrist. Faruq ʻUmar ignored, however, the very real possibility that those Shiʻis who criticized Mukhtar practiced *taqiyya* to save their lives. He admitted, however, that in later years the Shiʻa started to consider him a great leader because he killed Imam Husayn's murderers and claimed to have represented the Prophet's family. As Faruq ʻUmar saw it, "Al-Mukhtar's doctrine [*ʻaqida*] went beyond the moderate Shiʻa to extremism. . . . He was no longer a revolutionary for the sake of the pro-ʻAli [Shiʻi] cause and avenging the Prophet's family, but, rather, he became a leader of a religious group that came to be known as al-Mukhtariyya, or al-Kaysaʻiyya, or Khashabiyya."[185] The subtext of Faruq ʻUmar's treatise seems to be that the contemporary Shiʻi Daʻwa Islamic Party was a cynical, extremist, and deviant movement that even the mainstream Shiʻis regarded as illegitimate. And yet throughout history Mukhtar has been a popular hero in Shiʻi tradition. Attacking him this way could not please the Iraqi Shiʻa. Strangely, though, Faruq ʻUmar did not accuse Mukhtar and his supporters of introducing the concept of the Mahdi, his occultation (*al-ghayba*), and his return (*al-rajʻa*), even though they were the ones who introduced it into Shiʻi Islam.

Soon after Khomeini's rise to power, Faruq ʻUmar again disclosed his approach to Persians, Arab Islam, Arabism, and Shiʻism. Abu Muslim al-Khurasani, the son of a Persian father and a slave mother, and arguably the most important leader of the ʻAbbasid campaign, the Daʻwa, that brought them to power, never dreamed that he would fall into the jaws of Faruq ʻUmar. According to him,

Abu Muslim was plotting against the 'Abbasids after he helped them achieve power in 749–50 CE, and thus Caliph al-Mansur had no choice but to assassinate him when he was a guest in the caliph's tent in al-Mada'in (Ctesiphon). Faruq 'Umar's claim has no serious basis in history. The assassination remains a mystery. Faruq 'Umar further portrayed the Persians as both anti-Arab and anti-Muslim. Their political goal was to break up the great 'Abbasid Arab-Islamic Empire. This goal, however, destructive as it was, represented only a small part of their scheme. Far more devastating was their intent to destroy Arab Islam and replace it with ancient Persian religious doctrines. Here too the whole concept of the "savior hero" (*al-Batal al-Munqidh*) or the "expected savior" (*al-Munqidh al-Muntazar*), who has never died and "who will return to this world and fill it with justice after it had been filled with oppression," is presented as a Persian, pre-Islamic, and anti-Muslim concept.[186] This was yet another forceful assault on the Shi'i concept of the Expected Imam, who vanished in 874 CE and who will return at the end of time to redeem the Shi'a and the world.

Whether or not these descriptions are historically correct, by depicting Dhu al-Nafs al-Zakiyya, a medieval Shi'i revolutionary who rose against the Umayyad rule and who is highly popular among contemporary Shi'is, as a self-serving megalomaniac, Faruq 'Umar was in fact attacking Shi'i historiography. Presenting al-Mukhtar al-Thaqafi, who similarly is seen as a positive figure, as a rascal was no less of a challenge. More dangerously: the majority sect among the Shi'a, the "Twelvers," believe in the return (*al-raj'a*) of the twelfth Imam, the Expected Mahdi. By describing the return of the savior hero as rooted in heathen Persian pre-Islamic traditions, Faruq 'Umar implied that the very core of Shi'i theology and eschatology derived from heathen origins. The reason why this implication did not result in disturbances in Shi'i areas is that *Afaq 'Arabiyya* was read only by secular intellectuals and some equally secular Ba'thi political officers. Even though it was available in university libraries, there is no evidence that many students consulted it. This magazine served as a platform for the exchange of ideas within a limited circle in Iraq, and it was exported to the Sunni Arab world, where it served as the most important vehicle for the Iraqi-Ba'thi intellectual-political message. The message the regime reserved for the popular masses, delivered in Saddam's speeches and in the daily newspapers, was a very different one. Short of accepting the Shi'i concepts of the exclusive right of Imam 'Ali ibn Abi Talib and his offspring to the caliphate and the return of the twelfth Imam as Mahdi, the regime included Imams 'Ali and al-Husayn in the Iraqi national pantheon, and paid them lavish tribute.

Chapter 4
The Impact of War, 1980–88

The Islamic Revolution in Iran and the Iraqi Shiʻa, 1979–80

Under the shah, while the Iraqi Shiʻi clergy retained contacts with their Iranian colleagues, contacts with the secular regime in Tehran were very limited. The shah persecuted many of the Iranian clergy and antagonized his religious public. However, by persecuting the Iraqi Shiʻi ʻulama and students of religion and driving many across the border into Iran, the Baʻth regime enhanced Shiʻi Iraqi-Iranian solidarity, creating a time bomb where one had hardly existed before. After the March 1975 Algiers Agreement and greatly improved Iraqi-Iranian relations, cross-border Shiʻi cooperation almost disappeared, but as soon as Ayatollah Ruhollah Khomeini came to power in Tehran, things changed radically. This time the Baʻth regime did not need to invent or imagine a foreign danger. Days after Khomeini returned to Tehran, mass demonstrations of support erupted in Najaf and quickly spread to other cities.[1] In Iraqi-Iranian relations there was no precedent for such a development. A few weeks after he arrived in Tehran, Khomeini added fuel to the fire by calling on the Iraqi masses to topple the "infidel" Baʻth regime. As demonstrations in Iraq gained momentum, two of the regime's most senior security officials, Interior Minister Saʻdun Shakir and Chief of General Security General Fadhil al-Barrak (a member of Saddam's tribe), rushed to Najaf to disperse the crowd. Indeed, Najaf, the seat of the charismatic Ayatollah Muhammad Baqir al-Sadr, became the focal point for pro-Khomeini antiregime activities, including demonstrations, leaflets, and graffiti. One such graffito read, "Naʻam lil-islam, la li ʻAflaq wa Saddam" (Yes to Islam, No to ʻAflaq and Saddam). Khomeini's posters, too, appeared on the walls. Sadr himself inspired the delegations that came to see him from all the Shi'i areas and urged them to "perform their Islamic duty," and according to some sources he actually instructed them to go out in the streets and demonstrate.[2] Shi'i opposition sources report numerous calls for the establishment of an Islamic republic in Iraq under an "Iraqi Khomeini," whom many identified in Muhammad Baqir al-Sadr.[3]

The regime's concern grew to near panic. The opposition reported that the general public had started to exhibit growing religiosity, including more women wearing the hijab and more people attending mosques.[4] This description was given credibility by the Ba'th Party report that the party itself was affected. The resolutions of the Ninth Ba'th Party Regional Congress, convened in June 1982, severely criticized Ba'th Party members for displaying too much Islamic fervor.[5] Around May 1979, following the regime's crackdown on the demonstrators, Sadr felt that his life was in danger and contemplated doing as he had done in 1969, flee the country. When Khomeini learned of those plans, he was quick to react. He sent Sadr a message instructing him to stay. "I do not regard it as appropriate," he wrote, "that you leave Najaf . . . and I am worried about it [Najaf without you]." Sadr immediately changed his plans. In a message he sent to Khomeini on June 1, 1979, he did not deny that he had intended to leave Iraq but assured Khomeini that he fully appreciated his "paternal interest" in the holy city and that his "directive" (*tawjih*) to stay gave Sadr "spiritual encouragement."[6] The Ba'th intercepted those messages. They suspected Khomeini of planning to appoint Sadr as the Source of Emulation (*marja' taqlid*) for the Iraqis instead of Grand Ayatollah Abu al-Qasim al-Kho'i, who was not one of Khomeini's followers.

June 1979 was a watershed. After he decided to obey Khomeini and stay, Sadr also decided to pull out all the stops and charge ahead, regardless of consequences. From early June on, Sadr behaved as though possessed. The day he replied to Khomeini, Sadr gave the last of a series of lectures to his students in Najaf. In that lecture he said, "My father did not live any longer than I have lived now. My brother did not live any longer than I have lived. By now I have had my full share of life. It is [therefore] most logical that I should die at the age at which my father. . . [and] brother died."[7] In early June there were renewed demonstrations, sparked by the news of Sadr's correspondence with Khomeini and his decision to stay in Najaf. The Ba'th response was mass arrests. Sadr then called for a general strike in protest. On June 12, responding to an anti-Khomeini insurgency in Khozestan (Arabestan) that many believed had been instigated by Iraq, Sadr sent a telegram to the "Arabs living in Iran" urging them to support Khomeini and Islam.[8] By implication, this meant rejecting Ba'thism and Arab nationalism as un-Islamic. The next day Sadr was arrested.

Sadr had given the regime good reasons to fear him. According to Shi'i opposition sources, when he realized that the brutal suppression of the demonstrations by the regime "made the Iraqi individual think twice before starting any anti-government demonstration," rendering street demonstrations "almost impossible," and after he had accepted Khomeini's instructions to stay in Najaf, he "decided to break through the barrier of fear." He issued a fatwa forbidding Muslims to be members of the Ba'th Party; he announced his "total support" for Khomeini's revolution; and in another fatwa he allowed the shedding of the blood of "the headless arrows of the regime," meaning the regime's security forces. Moreover, he gave permission to disregard Shar'i rules if this was necessary in order to purchase arms or engage in other *jihad* activities. Whatever this meant, it certainly could be interpreted as a declaration of *jihad* against the regime. Finally, Sadr instructed his followers to encourage popular delegations to come to him from the various parts of Iraq to express their support. At the point where, as the Da'wa itself put it, "the barrier of fear started to crumble, and people started to demonstrate again," Sadr was arrested. The arrest in turn provoked mass demonstrations. These events coincided with 'Ali's birthday, giving the demonstrations added impetus. When the government realized the extent of the demonstrations, it released Sadr the same day. Khomeini immediately added fuel to the fire by sending Sadr a message of total support. Sadr apparently perceived his release as a sign of government weakness and encouraged the masses to step up the demonstrations. Indeed, a day later his sister, Bint al-Huda, led a women's demonstration to 'Ali's tomb in Najaf. Other demonstrations erupted elsewhere. For the first time since 1968, Madinat al-Thawra, the huge Shi'i quarter in northeast Baghdad, was teeming with antiregime activity, including attacks on regime targets. The Shi'i Islamic revolution was now surrounding the Ba'this in their capital city, where Shi'is represented among at least 50 percent of the population. This led to severe clashes with the security forces. Some opposition sources reported "tens of thousands" of arrests. Others reported eight thousand arrests. By July 1979, eighty-six executions had been reported by Islamist sources.[9]

In February there had been a carrot: President Bakr (in fact, Saddam) instructed the ministers of commerce and irrigation to supply all the needs of the southern provinces for food staples and consumer goods, and to expedite irrigation projects there. The president also promised "special fatherly patronage of the provinces of Najaf and Karbala."[10] Later the regime resorted mainly to coercion. By mid-June 1979, when things had heated up, the authorities still tried to avoid public overreaction by putting Sadr under house arrest in Najaf rather than imprisoning him. He could still receive guests, but the visitors were watched by the mukhabarat. As is evident from a secret consultation in May or June 1979, Saddam and his advisers were clearly undecided what to do about Sadr, and about the Shi'i population in general. Crackdowns generated more demonstrations, so at that stage they decided to look for ways to counter Khomeini's propaganda.[11] Sadr's house arrest, however, did not prevent him from reasserting in a telephone conversation his support for Khomeini, speaking of him as "a lighthouse of Islam" and the guardian of the "monotheistic religion." On June 16, 1979, Sadr, following Khomeini's example, recorded his first taped message to the Iraqi people. He accused the regime of imposing its rule on the Iraqi people "by force of iron and fire," yet his message, a combination of protest, warning, and appeal, stopped short of an explicit call for the overthrow of the Ba'th. His second message, recorded on July 6, 1979, sounded a very different note. In it Sadr branded the regime "bloody murderers" and "despots" who, panicking at the sound of the people's growl, arrested, tortured, and executed "tens of thousands" of Iraqis, starting with the 'ulama. He accused it of forcing the Iraqi people to comply with "Aflaq and other agents of the [Christian] mission and imperialism" rather than keep faith with Muhammad and 'Ali. The duty of every Muslim in Iraq, he went on, was to do his utmost, including giving his life, to rid Iraq of the Ba'thi "nightmare." He concluded, "I have decided on martyrdom, and this may be the last you hear from me. The gates of heaven have already opened to greet the [ascending] columns of martyrs!"[12]

Sadr's third and last message, recorded sometime between mid-July 1979 and early April 1980, was his first ecumenical Shi'i-Sunni appeal. In previous years he had often expressed clear-cut Shi'i anti-Sunni views, but now he needed Sunni Islamist cooperation. Without it the Shi'i opposition had no chance of toppling the Ba'th regime. In his last message Sadr called on all sons of the Iraqi people, "Arabs and Kurds, Sunnis and Shi'is," to unite against "the ruling despots . . . [who] desecrate Islam, 'Ali['s] and 'Umar['s] alike," and who "fill the land with alcoholic drinks, pigs' fields and all kinds of abominations."[13] As he had said to his disciples a few years earlier, Sadr was prepared for martyrdom; he hoped that his death would be fused with the memory of the martyrdom of Imam Husayn and would spur the Shi'i masses to revolt.

When sporadic demonstrations and armed attacks on party and government installations continued through the second half of 1979, Saddam, now president, decided to increase the pressure. The first step was a law enacted by the Revolutionary Command Council (RCC) on March 31, 1980, decreeing the death penalty for everyone who had at any time belonged to the Da'wa Party or had helped disseminate its ideas.[14] On April 4, 1980, an attempt was made on the life of Tariq 'Aziz, one of Saddam's most trusted lieutenants, while he attended a public rally at Mustansiriyya University. He was wounded in his right arm but survived the attack. Two students, however, died. A day later at their funeral another student was killed by a hand grenade. Rumor had it that the operations were carried out by a small Karbala-based group, Munazzamat al-'Amal al-Islami (the Organization of Islamic Action), headed by the Shirazi family. Still, it could also have been the Da'wa. Saddam saw this as a personal affront coming from Khomeini. On that day Sadr and his sister were brought from Najaf to Baghdad. When Sadr refused to denounce Khomeini publicly, he and his sister were executed, based on the new law against the Da'wa.[15] Just to make sure that Munazzamat al-'Amal al-Islami paid a price, too, in May 1980 Ayatollah Hasan al-Shirazi was assassinated in Lebanon.[16] The Organization of Islamic Action emerged, according to outside sources, sometime between 1979 and 1980. According to its own sources, the organization was established under a different name in Karbala by the Shirazi brothers in the early 1960s, and its military branch was born in 1976. Whatever the case, it was a smaller body than the Da'wa, though it was based on the same organizational principles of clandestine activity. Although its founders, the Shirazi brothers, continued to provide religious inspiration for a few years, the organization's everyday activities were managed by the brothers Muhammad Taqi and Hadi al-Mudarrisi.[17]

The Ba'th regime's suppression was not limited to the Shi'i elite, however. Iraqi authorities announced that "every Iranian family whose unfaithfulness toward the Revolution and the homeland was proven [were to be] deported even if they carried Iraqi citizenship."[18] Indeed, a 1980 RCC directive mandated the deportation of all "Iranians," whether possessing Iraqi citizenship or simply residing in Iraq. Furthermore, families some members of which possessed Iraq citizenship but others did not would be expelled, on the principle of "family reunion beyond the border." The result was the dislocation of at least 100,000 Iraqi Shi'is to Syria and Iran.[19] The most convincing sign that the backbone of the radical Shi'i movement had been broken by these ruthless measures was that while Sadr's arrest had led to disorder and mass demonstrations, his execution a year later triggered no mass protests. The Shi'i opposition press had nothing to report, and Khomeini expressed his distress at the lack of reaction (which seemed to have shocked him more than the actual execution). In a message to the Iraqi people, he wrote:

> It is not surprising that the late Sadr and his wronged sister gained martyrdom, but it is surprising that the Muslim nations, especially the noble nation of Iraq and the tribes of the Tigris and the Euphrates and the brave [Shi'i] university youth and the other dear youth of Iraq accept these great calamities, which are inflicted upon Islam and upon the family of the Prophet [Sadr was a *sayyid*] . . . with indifference, and thus give the chance to the damned Ba'th Party to martyr their glories one after the other.[20]

Cynics could interpret Khomeini's messages as evidence that he was interested in Sadr's martyrdom in the hope that this would push the Shi'i masses to start a mass revolt. This is unlikely, but whatever the case, no revolt took place. The regime realized that the radical Shi'i opposition was paralyzed, no longer able to mobilize the masses. This explains the difference in the attitude toward the Shi'i threat between the secret discussion of Saddam and his advisers in May or June 1979 and the meeting in September 1980. At the first meeting there was a sense of alarm; at the second the issue was treated only as a side issue, still a problem but not an immediate danger.[21] During the war, on May 20, 1983, 130 members of Hakim's family were arrested and six were executed. Among the victims were three of Muhammad Baqir al-Hakim's brothers and three of his nephews. A fourth brother was sent to Tehran with a written demand ordering Hakim to stop all anti-Ba'thi activities.[22] This time, too, there were reports in the Shi'i press of demonstrations in Iran, in London, Kuwait, Bahrain, and Beirut, and even in Lebanon's Nabatiyya, which was under Israeli occupation, but not in Iraq. Another indication of the collapse of the opposition was the fact that from mid-1980 on, reports in *al-Da'wa Chronicle* on demonstrations and civil disorders in Iraq became more and more infrequent. The last reported mass demonstrations in Najaf, Karbala, al-Thawra, Kut, and Samarra took place between April and July 1981. For the Shi'i opposition's press, which had occasionally exaggerated the scope of earlier demonstrations, this was a tacit admission of declining public protest. There is no better way of learning about the situation as it looked to the radical Shi'is themselves than from the conclusion that the Da'wa drew from the events of 1979–80:

> The uprising was successful, but come to think of it we realized that hastiness and the lack of short-term and long-term goals caused some

people to hesitate. . . . People did not know what the imam [Sadr] had wanted from these delegations he received and what the aim had been. Moreover, no plans had been drawn up with a view to counter the various reactions that the authorities . . . were likely to have. Furthermore, no actions had been planned as alternatives . . . panic and lack of preparation were evident . . . the probabilities of the imam's arrest [were not] studied carefully before it happened.[23]

Four years later, the party admitted that the confrontation with the regime in 1979–80 had taxed the party far too heavily. "Tens of thousands of its members" were lost (very likely meaning supporters; the party was highly selective in recruiting members, but it did have thousands of supporters), and the party became completely disoriented. At long last it understood that "there are differences between conditions in Iraq and Iran. The formula that worked in Iran would not have the same effect in Iraq."[24] What that statement probably meant was that the security forces were mainly Sunni. The Shi'is among them were Ba'thi old-timers who had already burned their bridges with the majority of the Shi'i public. Unlike the shah's army, they were ready to go all the way, and Saddam, not being the shah, ordered them to do just that. Muhammad Baqir al-Hakim, the spokesman for the Supreme Assembly of the Islamic Revolution in Iraq (SAIRI), also reported that the call-up of Shi'i youngsters to the army once Iraq invaded Iran, no less than the brutal suppression, completely prevented mass demonstrations in Iraq.[25] The Da'wa drew the conclusion that in the future, the only means of action should be covert activity.

To Fight or Not to Fight? Two Secret Leadership Meetings on the Eve of the Invasion of Iran

Following Saddam's 1975 Algiers Agreement with the shah of Iran, Iraqi-Iranian relations improved very quickly and reached a surprising level of cooperation. After the agreement the shah stopped all aid to the Kurdish rebellion and, as emerged from an interview with a senior Iranian ex-intelligence (SAVAK) official, the Iranians also instructed their agents in the Shi'i population of Iraq to cease all activities.[26] On the Iraqi side a member of the RCC reported in a meeting in May or June 1979 that after the Algiers Agreement with Iran, Iraq had ceased all clandestine Ba'th activities in Khozestan (Arabestan).[27] Another early sign of improved relations was a royal visit to Iraq by the shah's sister.

Even more indicative was Saddam's 1978 agreeing, at the shah's request, to force Ayatollah Khomeini to leave Iraq, where he had been in political exile. This move, of course, proved to be a fatal mistake for the shah and a disastrous decision for Saddam, for the ayatollah could send his messages to Iran from France far more easily than he had done from Najaf. The rest is history.

The First Secret Meeting: The Decision Not to Fight

Between early May and July 15, 1979, before Saddam became president and before the full force of the *mukhabarat* was deployed against the Shi'i pro-Khomeini demonstrators, a few members of the RCC met to discuss the situation. The main subject of discussion was the findings of a committee that Saddam Husayn had charged with studying what should be done about the Arabs of Arabestan. The ignorance of all the participants regarding the most elementary concepts of Shi'i theology indicates that all present were Sunnis, which means that the Shi'i RCC members had not been invited. In May–June 1979 at least five of the twenty-two members of the RCC were Shi'i. Their absence was in itself a sign of a gathering storm. Soon after this meeting Saddam initiated his most sweeping purge, in which two of the five purged—and executed—RCC members were indeed Shi'is.[28] The most urgent issue was a mysterious anti-Iranian revolt that was simmering in Arabestan. The discussion also dealt with the crisis with Iran, but beneath it all was deep concern over the growing domestic threat coming from Shi'i pro-Khomeini elements in Iraq. Saddam was by then still *al-sayyid al-na'ib*, the Lord (and Descended of the Prophet) Vice President. In the conversation he and his colleagues demonstrated patience, good judgment, and restraint, as well as cunning.

The meeting was opened by Taha Yasin Ramadhan, who reported that many in Iraq were not certain that the people of Arabestan were Arab at all. Saddam eventually decided that they were indeed Arab, but Ramadhan's doubt in itself was bizarre in the extreme: since 1969, when Ba'thi Iraq had clashed with Iran over the Shatt al-Arab waterway, and until the 1975 Iraqi-Iranian Algiers Agreement, the Iraqi side had been adamant that Khozestan (Arabestan) was Arab land inhabited by pure Arabs. How could Ramadhan possibly forget this? The technical reason seems to have been his reluctance to extend direct and open support to the revolutionaries: if the Arabestanis were Arabs, then such support had to be extended regardless of the consequences, as the party pretended to do in the case of the Palestinians. Ramadhan was very clear: if Iraq decided to provide such support, it would be dragged into a disastrous war with Iran:

"I truly and personally do not support the decision to engage in war against Iran," Ramadhan spoke with perceptible conviction in his voice. "I do not think that it has reached the time or occasion to do so under the assumption that Iran is now weak, and that it will be strong in two years," and therefore that the time to attack was now. The revolt, he opined, was a trap set by the Iranian regime or another enemy of Iraq, such as Israel, to draw Iraq into an ill-advised war. In all probability, though, Ramadhan had a deeper reason for voicing his doubt. It should be remembered that the Arabs of Arabestan were all Shi'is and as such could be suspected of Shi'i-Iranian loyalties. Ramadhan did not say what his view was: were they Arabs or Persians? This was strange, as it had to do with many Iraqi Shi'is no less so than with those of Arabestan. Many tribes on both sides of the border are the same, especially the most important one, the Khaza'il. Doubting the "Arabness" of Arabestan tribes means doubting the Arab identity of most or all the Iraqi tribes on the southern Tigris and the Shatt River. Ramadhan's ostensibly innocent report on what the public in Iraq was asking was powerful evidence of the estrangement between the Ba'th and at least part of the Shi'i population in 1979.

The participants were puzzled as to who was behind the Arabestan revolt. Conspiracy theories abounded. One was an elaborate theory suggesting that it was a Jimmy Carter machination together with the remnants of the Iranian SAVAK, designed to distance Iraq from its struggle against Anwar Sadat's peace with Israel and humiliate it. The United States was suspected of inciting the Persians to slaughter the Arabs of Arabestan. If it stayed aloof, Iraq would be seen by all the Arabs as betraying Arabism. All agreed that Iraq must not fall into this clever American-Israeli-Khomeini trap. If Iraq intervened to save the Arabs of Arabestan, it would provide Khomeini with justification to drag it into war and keep it busy, unable to foil the crime of Camp David.[29]

"I am not for sending Iraqis to [help the revolutionaries in] Arabestan, honestly, unless you are planning to fight Iran in two days or a month," Ramadhan warned. If anyone was interested in war, "what is the objective of fighting Iran? What is the benefit? I do not know," he concluded. Ramadhan was well informed: he pointed out that the Iranian regime was embroiled in domestic struggles between competing elites and difficulties with ethnic and religious minorities that could bring it down without any Iraqi involvement. Iran should be left to stew in its own juice, he concluded.[30] This was a brilliant analysis. Ramadhan was a practical man; already by May–June 1979 he was fully aware of the danger to the Ba'th regime coming from the Shi'i pro-Iranian revolutionaries. He was probably not looking forward to having more of the same problem if Iraq annexed Arabestan. To him, Arabestan was a poisoned apple. Even when one of the participants commented presciently, "The clash with the present [Iranian] regime is a future reality that we must face now or within two years," he too agreed that Iraq must not be dragged into it at a timing chosen by the Americans.[31]

All present agreed that Iraq should help the revolt only covertly. That way it would inflict damage on Iran without, however, dragging Iraq into a war. This, the participants believed, could be achieved through building strong clandestine Ba'th and underground militia organizations there, providing them with financial support, training non-Iraqi volunteers, and supplying them with American and German weapons that could not be traced back to Iraq (the latter idea amused the comrades tremendously). In 1976 the same was done in Syria with great success, Ramadhan reported.[32] And yet all this had to be done in great secrecy. "I hope that the brothers on the committee" (that studied Arabestan), Ramadhan concluded, "take into consideration all possible measures that will keep a direct war between Iraq and Iran away for now." Saddam concurred: "Any association between the Arabestan revolt and Iraq will cause a great harm. . . . People there should not assume that Iraq is the driving force behind this revolt. . . . The name of Iraq should not be mentioned because it would mean that we will be dragged into a war during this period." Saddam objected to war because he realized that the whole Arab world was "currently with Khomeini," and thus attacking him would damage Iraq's reputation. "I am against openly sending Iraqis" to Arabestan, he added. And again he warned that Iraq must not "be dragged into a war with Iran at this period of time [*annu ninjar lilharb fi hadhihi al-fitra ma'a Iran*]."[33] The fact that Saddam repeated this warning a few times during the discussion is significant, because it seems to indicate that this was his genuine opinion. He and his comrades were ready to fight Iran, but only until the last Arabestani. The contrast between his view in mid-1979, when he was vice president, and in September 1980, when he was president (see below), is puzzling.

Saddam's realism, too, was impressive. When one of the members suggested that Khomeini "has no system" or "understanding" of the international arena, Saddam warned his colleagues not to underestimate Khomeini, as he had managed to turn himself into a "symbol" (*ramz*) of the revolution.[34] He was persistent, Saddam commented, he had leadership qualities, and he intended to do exactly what he said.[35] One of the participants also very tellingly cautioned that, because the Iranian leader "has influence even in our Iraq" (*hatta fi 'Iraqina yilqa ta'thir*), this meant that "we must take our people in account when every [negative] comment is made" about the ayatollah.[36] In other words, to avoid a rift with the Shi'a of Iraq, the regime should avoid offensive expressions when criticizing Khomeini. This advice was at first adhered to, but a few months later Khomeini had already won the sobriquets of "deceiver" or "false messiah" (*dajjal*, the Islamic equivalent of the Antichrist), and similarly unendearing nicknames.

The reluctance to go to war was not for lack of suspicion that Khomeini was trying to incite the Iraqi Shi'a against their government. One of the participants brought up the issue of the letter sent from Khomeini to Muhammad Baqir al-Sadr in June 1979 ordering him to stay in Najaf: "If it is true, it is considered an intervention in the internal affairs [of Iraq]," he warned. Saddam guessed why Khomeini had ordered Sadr to stay in Najaf: "The plan is to remove [the quietist Abu al-Qasim] al-Kho'i from the position of religious leadership [*'azl Kho'i min al-Marja'iyya*] and replace him with al-Sadr."[37] Even had Sadr kept quiet, which he did not, Saddam's suspicion that Khomeini had anointed Sadr meant Sadr's doom. Kho'i objected to Khomeini's concept of "the rule of the [religious] jurist," as well as to his political activism in general. He saw it as his duty to preserve the Shi'i community, shield it from persecution, and provide it with legal and spiritual guidance. Even twelve years later he was against the 1991 antiregime revolt, and it started without his blessing. Only after he could not stop it did he reluctantly join it. Sadr, by contrast, was a political activist and a staunch supporter of Khomeini's political concepts.

While the Sunni Ba'thi leaders understood well the danger that Khomeini represented to their regime at home, their ignorance regarding Shi'i theology is surprising. One of the members of the committee charged with studying the situation in Arabestan reported that six weeks earlier he had known "very little" about the "Ja'faris" (Shi'is). Only recently had he learned that "they are always waiting [for the Imam Mahdi]." When they had a chance to come to power they would begin to argue about who would be the ruler, he had learned and (correctly) explained, because the Shi'i doctrine did not allow for any fully legitimate ruler except for the Mahdi. At the time, he reported, again correctly, Ayatollah Shari'at-Madari was opposing Khomeini because he was against the rule of the clerics.[38] Demonstrating the participants' recognition of their ignorance regarding things Shi'i, another one of them suggested, "Maybe our comrades in Najaf" would know more about the division between Khomeini and Shari'at-Madari and its theological roots.[39] While this committee member still misunderstood the reason why Shari'at-Madari and Kho'i objected to Khomeini's principle of "the rule of the jurist," he was right in pointing out that they did.

Having realized that his party luminaries were ignorant about the religion of the majority of their citizens, Saddam then encouraged them to learn: "For the occasion, comrades, I would like the members of the leadership to read about the Shi'i ideology," he suggested. "This will give us a picture to help us when solving the problems of our [Shi'i] people to see the origins behind them. Of course," he cautioned, "we shall be solving them [the problems] through the use of Ba'th ideology, not by using the religious ideology, but [what we learn will help] to figure out what the most effective formulas are within the Ba'ath ideology to apply at the [right] time and place." Saddam then suggested that all read Khomeini's book, *Al-Hukuma al-Islamiyya* (The Islamic Government), and promised to provide copies. To understand the Shi'a better, as well as the sects that branched out from the Shi'a, such as the "'Alawites and the Druze," a member suggested that all read a concise book, *Islam bila madhahib* (Islam without Schools), by Waqi' al-Zaylani.

The committee members realized the potential of using this split between Khomeini and his critics to demonstrate to the Iraqi Shi'is that Khomeini's position was "totally incompatible with the Ja'fari (Shi'i) doctrine." Saddam was hopeful that through Arab education, the regime would "fortify our people in the sense of Arab nationalism [*tahsin Sha'bana qawmiyyan*]" and Iraqi patriotism, in order to neutralize the sectarian Shi'i message coming from Tehran. Saddam was talking alternately about the Arabs of Arabestan and the Iraqi Shi'a, but there can be little doubt that when he expected "an Arab-Ja'fari [Shi'i]" identity to be created, he also meant the Iraqi Shi'a, who, because of their link to Iran, were not yet Arab enough. And yet all the fears of Khomeini's sway in Iraq were insufficient to push the Iraqi leadership to engage him in war. Ramadhan implied that there were senior Iraqis who wanted war because they felt that Iraq's military advantage was short-lived and had to be exploited immediately, but he and all the other participants in the meeting were against it. The reasons given by Ramadhan and Saddam as to why war would be a mistake were sound. In the first place, Khomeini was indeed very popular in the Arab world, owing to his support for the Palestinian cause. War against him would damage Iraq's prestige and its claim to spearhead the struggle against Israel. Second, having been prodded by Ayatollah Sadr, under house arrest in Najaf, to rise against the Ba'th, the Shi'a were in open revolt. An attack on Iran at such a moment, before the Shi'a were brought under control, was very risky. This reason was mentioned only in a roundabout way during the meeting, but it was unmistakable all the same. Third, the meeting took place a few weeks before Saddam's purge of his rivals among the leadership. The vice president could not embark on a major war effort before he he was able to take over the presidency and send his less than fully trusted party comrades to face the firing squad. Finally, Khomeini was indeed facing strong opposition at home. As suggested by Ramadhan, attacking Iran might therefore be unnecessary, as the Iranian regime might crumble under its own weight. Even though most of these reasons for caution were still relevant, all went unmentioned in the crucial prewar meeting fifteen months later.

Fifteen Months Later: The Decision to Go to War

The single most important bit of evidence available regarding Iraqi ambitions, concerns, and plans prior to the war with Iran is a September 16, 1980, recorded discussion among Saddam, the RCC, and the party's Regional Leadership, the two highest decision-making institutions in the land.[40] This discussion took place one day before the Iraqi president made his public speech in the National Assembly declaring the 1975 Algiers Agreement settling border issues between Iraq and Iran null and void. At the meeting Saddam explained his motivation for the next day's declaration and what he believed to be the most likely results of such a declaration. Not all those present agreed with the president's assessments and predictions, but unsurprisingly, in the end the unanimous decision was to adopt his plan. The change of atmosphere between the two meetings was palpable. In June 1979 the discussion was egalitarian and free-flowing. No one's view was more important than any other participant's, or so it seems. Though there were some slight nuances, the general consensus was that war with Iran at that time would be a disaster, and that with Khomeini in Tehran, the Arab society of Iraq, including Arabestan, was split between the two Islamic sects, an issue that demanded much attention and sensitivity. The term "Ja'fari" was used, it being a soft version of "Shi'i," as a way of presenting the Shi'a as merely a fifth legal "school" (*madhhab*) in Islam, in addition to the four Sunni schools. The meeting in September 1980, by contrast, coming after the most brutal purges in the party's history in which hundreds of senior "comrades" and military officers were executed, was more orchestrated. Now Saddam was president—an all-powerful one at that—and he had just demonstrated what could befall anyone who opposed him. The discussion was clearly hierarchical. The consensus to support Saddam's initiative, that is, to annul the 1975 Algiers Agreement and risk war with Iran, was reached under duress, not as a result of a free-flowing discussion. Moreover, it was diametrically opposed to the consensus reached in the 1979 meeting.

Why the U-Turn?

There were few significant changes between May 1979 and September 1980 in terms of the Iraqi military advantage. The Iranian long-term strategic advantages in terms of manpower, territory, and economic assets had not changed, either, and the participants in the secret meeting were aware of it. The chances for regime disintegration in Tehran even without war were also similarly unchanged. The public's pro-Khomeini sentiment in the Arab world and the Iraqi Shi'i identification with Tehran remained as before. But some things had changed. Border clashes were escalating, and the Iraqi side had demonstrated its advantage. Also, by 1980 Khomeini had managed to alienate the Gulf Arabs and the Soviet Union, and theoretically Iraq could expect some support from those sides. The Iran hostage crisis with the United States (November 4, 1979, to January 20, 1981) could be seen as a bonus. Indeed, unbeknownst to the participants (Saddam did not bother to inform them), as General Alexander Haig told his president later, King Fahd of Saudi Arabia had told Saddam that "President Carter gave the Iraqis a green light to launch the war against Iran."[41] It is very doubtful that Carter actually asked Fahd to tell Saddam that the United States would support an Iraqi offensive. There is no record of it, but Fahd may have invented the American support in order to push Saddam to war.

Be it as it may, even though most felt that the "international circumstances" were favorable, the participants were suspicious of the Arab regimes, the Soviet Union, and the United States. The United States was seen as an enemy of Iraq and Khomeini's sponsor. The hostage crisis was perceived as a way to camouflage a Carter-Khomeini secret love affair. Thus the explanation for why Saddam should have wanted to go to war hinged mainly on domestic developments. The Shi'i opposition in Iraq had burned out, but with Khomeini as a source of inspiration it could rise from the ashes. This danger is implied in the secret discussion, and toppling or humiliating Khomeini seemed to the participants a good solution. Most important, however, was that Saddam had become the sole leader. As vice president he was careful and calculating. Somehow he had managed to shift responsibility for regime failures to President Bakr and take credit for all the successes, such as the 1972 agreement with the Soviet Union and the nationalization of oil, the 1975 crushing of the Kurdish revolt, and the 1974–80 petrodollar bonanza. As president, however, everything was his responsibility, and he took Khomeini's offensive behavior personally. To him, Iraq's widely perceived military advantage meant that Khomeini had to behave, and if he did not, he had to be severely punished. As Saddam put it in the secret meeting, strategic "flexibility" (*muruna*) was justifiable only when Iraq was at a military disadvantage. This was the case in 1975 but was no longer true in 1980. Furthermore, as is evident in the recording of the discussion, Saddam aspired to leadership of the Arab world, a mirage that had beguiled many before him. He dreamed of donning the mantle of Gamal 'Abd al-Nasir,[42] and a decisive victory over Khomeini seemed the shortest route to achieving this dream. As all checks and balances in Baghdad had disappeared, there was no stopping him.

Saddam's legal excuse for dissociating himself and Iraq from the Algiers Agreement was his (false) interpretation of Iranian declarations according to which they no longer supported the agreement. Saddam also insisted that since February 1979, Iran had abrogated the agreement in practice. This claim was closer to the truth: Khomeini had inspired the "people" of Iraq to revolt, and had supported the Iraqi Kurds. As Saddam saw it, Iraq was therefore no longer bound by the agreement. However, not only did the Iraqi president did not see the Iranian behavior as a disaster, he saw in it a golden opportunity. To him, Iran's behavior provided Iraq with international legitimacy to abrogate the agreement and return the Shatt al-Arab waterway to Iraqi sovereignty. This would mean that Tehran would have to recognize Iraq's sovereignty over most of the Shatt, all the way to the eastern (Iranian) bank. Tehran would have to agree that Iranian ships bound for Khorramshahr and Abadan would hoist the Iraqi flag, hire an Iraqi pilot, and pay Iraq passage fees. Before he was very politely challenged, Saddam also believed that Iran would recognize its military inferiority and therefore, however reluctantly, accept the new reality. Once challenged on this point he agreed that the Iranians might put up opposition, but he had no doubt that they would easily be defeated. Khomeini would be toppled, or at least thoroughly humiliated. Another participant, 'Ali Hasan al-Majid ("Abu Hasan"), suggested that because of Iran's long-term strategic advantages, war might be a bad idea, but after Saddam showed signs of displeasure Majid did not press this point. Yet his comments and the uncertainty about the international situation led all the participants to agree that the war had to be won quickly and decisively. And everyone seemed to agree that this could be achieved. Even if the Arab governments opposed the war, if the Iraqi victory was quick and decisive it was thought that "the Arab people will be ecstatic [*sa yakhruj min al-qumqum*, literally: "they will jump out of the kettle"]." Then the regimes would have no choice but to follow the street.[43]

Iraq's Broader Ambitions

One of the participants, Deputy Chairman of the RCC ʿIzzat Ibrahim, provided the wider context: "This is our chance. This is a historical chance. It does not mean only getting back the Shatt al-Arab. . . . Rather, it means much more . . . it means that Iraq has moved from one level to another," namely, "to the highest level [*ila mustawa ʿaali*]." Iraq will "create positive Arab and international influence without parallel and without limits . . . mainly on the Arab people and regimes." Iraq could take major steps "to accomplish its goals *within the country* and [on] the pan-Arab [level] in addition to its advantage . . . in building the ideological revolutionary armed forces that will be built as the armed forces of the Arab nation" (emphasis added). Success would elevate Iraq "psychologically, militarily and technologically in one big leap to a very superior level [*mustawa raqi jiddan*]." Through victory, Iraq would thus "save a lot of time [that would otherwise be spent] in achieving this level," and all this could be done in "twenty or fifteen days." ʿIzzat Ibrahim was not just a member of both top institutions, or just deputy chairman of the RCC. Since 1969 he had been his master's voice. It may safely be assumed that his breathtaking prediction represented Saddam's thinking: total victory would catapult Baʿthi Iraq (and Saddam) into Gulf and Arab leadership and world power. The deputy also predicted that it would have a positive influence "*on our domestic people* [ʿala Shaʿbina al-dakhili]" (emphasis added).[44] By that he undoubtedly meant the Kurds and the Shiʿis, and the latter more than the former. They were the ones most influenced by Khomeini's revolution, they represented around 50 percent of the Iraqi population, and they populated the vast area between landlocked Baghdad and the high seas.

An argument for going to war that was not mentioned at the meeting but that became perhaps the most central one during the war was the Lebanese syndrome. As the war dragged on, the regime was forced to develop convincing arguments to explain why it had rushed into such a risky confrontation; after all, neither Iraq's existence nor the Baʿth rule was in jeopardy. In a 1987 analysis issued by the Department of Political Orientation (*daʾirat al-tawjih al-siyasi*) of the Ministry of Defense and directed to the army's chief of staff, the department provided a new reason for the war that was to be disseminated among the senior military personnel. According to this explanation, the Iranians and the Zionists had been aiming at creating a (Shiʿi) ministate in Basra and, following that, a few other ministates in Iraq. Imperialism and world Zionism had removed the shah and anointed Khomeini in order that he destroy Iraq for them. The idea was to drive wedges between Iraq's Kurds, Sunnis, and Shiʻis. This left Iraq no option but a military offensive. Iraq had to act preemptively because, unlike Iran, it did not have strategic depth.[45] In my interviews with Iraqi army officers who had fought in the war, all saw these arguments as convincing. These were men who found themselves commanding troops in a grinding war they did not choose and could not escape. To resolve their cognitive dissonance, they had to find a reason for the war. The need to thwart Shiʻi secession with Iranian help was such a reason. Khomeini assisted Saddam in convincing many Iraqis of the veracity of the argument that Iran was aiming at splitting Iraq, starting with a Shiʻi mini-state in Basra. Beginning in July 1982, Iran was indeed trying to conquer Basra, and later (April 1986–April 1987) it called a whole series of its military offensives "Karbala."

Finally, but very significantly, missing altogether were the Arabs of Khozestan (Arabestan). In anti-Iranian propaganda disseminated just before and during the war, their right to self-determination as Arabs was frequently hailed,[46] but nothing was said about it in the prewar meeting, nor were they mentioned as potential support for an Iraqi invasion. The Iraqi leaders had been warned in the secret meeting of 1979 that the Arabs of Arabestan could not be relied on. The propaganda use of the language-based Arab common denominator notwithstanding, they did not expect any meaningful support from the Arabs of Arabestan, nor were they truly interested in them. Had Iraq been able to hold on to Arabestan, the local Arabs' right to self-determination would have been used to legitimize it, as indeed it was during the war. However, the combined impression from transcripts of the two meetings, in 1979 and in 1980, is that the Iraqi regime was not interested in the people of Arabestan; it had enough unhappy Shiʻis at home already. And as it happened, no Arabestan Arab support of the invading troops ever developed. Keeping the territory of oil-rich Arabestan was another matter altogether. Already in the 1979 discussion Saddam had made clear that if Iraq succeeded in occupying this area, it had to hold on to it.

Very strangely, what emerges in this prewar discussion is that while everyone was aware of the danger of a lengthy war of attrition, no one realized the danger of attacking a country in the throes of a revolution. Even though the Baʻthi leadership saw themselves as revolutionaries, none of them was truly a revolutionary because none of them had ever participated in a true revolution. Both in 1963 in Iraq and Syria and again in 1968 in Iraq, the Baʻth Party took over through coups d'état. The Baʻthis were successful conspirators and bureaucrats of repression, but they were not revolutionaries, and they could not understand what a true revolution does to a nation. As a result, they did not understand the huge élan released in revolutionary situations. Likewise, the Iraqi leadership was oblivious to Iranian nationalism. In the 1979 discussion much attention was paid to Khomeini's vulnerability to the ethnic divisions in Iran, and it was decided to enhance those divisions, but no one mentioned the national Persian identity and cohesion. It may be that this oversight was the result of a subconscious sense on the part of the Iraqi leadership that Iraq lacked a cohesive national identity and therefore ascribed the same deficiency to Iran. Once attacked, however, Iran showed remarkable cohesion. The Iraqi leadership was oblivious to yet another development in Iran: Khomeini's radical Shiʻi Islam instilled great enthusiasm in the masses. During the war the Iranian military exploited it to the full. Only a year or two later the Baʻth regime began to recognize the power of Islam.[47]

The Last Stand of Fortress Secularism: The Ninth Baʻth Party Congress, 1982

Why Convene a Congress?

Beginning in 1972, the regime felt progressively more secure in its seat. By 1973, it had roundly defeated its most dangerous enemies, the communists, the pro-Syrian Baʻthists and pro-Iranian, pro-Western officers, and the internal anti-Tikriti coup d'état of the Shiʻi security deputy czar Nazim Czar. The quadrupling of oil revenues in 1973–75 further increased the regime's confidence, and with it came secularizing steps. During those years the tactical alliance with the defeated communists, which was necessary to improve relations with the Soviet Union, allowed the communists to publish a weekly and a monthly magazine. This pushed the regime to compete with them on their own turf, on the ground of explicit and implied atheism. On another front, since the spring of 1975, Kurdistan Iraq had been kept securely underfoot. This too added much to the regime's confidence. By 1977–78, the regime had successfully contained as well the Shiʻi Islamists, mainly Hizb al-Daʻwa, through a combination of violence and, buoyed by the incredible bounty of the new oil revenues, relatively generous rewards through economic development. In the 1970s Saddam, as the czar of domestic security, also dealt crippling blows to the two Sunni Arab fundamentalist movements, the Muslim

Brotherhood (known as al-Hizb al-Islami al-ʻIraqi, the Iraqi Islamic Party) and the Liberation Party (Hizb al-Tahrir).[48] By early 1980 Saddam, now president, reigned supreme. And yet Ayatollah Khomeini's return to Tehran in February 1979, and following it the need to once again use violence to crush the Shiʻi demonstrations, sounded the alarm. The regime stuck tenaciously to its secular guns, but the secret discussions for which transcripts are available provide evidence that it was worried all the same.

In May or June 1979, members of the RCC were warned about Khomeini's great influence over the Iraqi Shiʻis.[49] By December of the same year the regime was seriously concerned about the growing religiosity of the "Iraqi youth."[50] From the secret document it is clear that it was the Shiʻi youth that represented the main problem. In a special meeting of the Supreme Council for State Security in which Saddam Husayn, the interior minister, the director of General Security (*al-Amn al-ʻAmm*), and others participated, the gathering dealt with "the inclination of the youth towards belonging to the reactionary religious movements." No details are provided in the document of the party's countermeasures except for one: female party members, who came under the appellation "the Glorious Baʻthi Females [*al-Baʻthiyyat al-majidat*]," were to be instructed to participate in all the *ta'azi* (mourning) and other religious Shiʻi occasions to establish "good connections" with the women who performed the special vocal calls that expressed happiness or mourning (*al-malaliyyat*). The party girls, *al-Baʻthiyyat*, were supposed to give the *malaliyyat* monetary gifts in order to turn them to support the party and provide its security apparatus with information on troublesome people.[51] The details made it clear that the fear was mainly of the growing religiosity among the Shiʻi youth. Though he was militarily on the eve of war, Saddam's confidence in victory was absolute. He and his lieutenants believed they had a good chance to topple Khomeini's regime, or at least to defeat the ayatollah thoroughly, and expected this would take care of the problem of "our domestic people."[52]

But the war went badly. The May–June 1982 withdrawal from almost all Iranian territories changed the earlier perceptions radically. By the mid-1980s Saddam had admitted in another secret meeting that Khomeini's accusations that the Baʻth were enemies of Islam had hurt the party badly.[53] In the second half of the 1980s the Baʻth regime gradually lost its confidence, and with it, its confidence in its secular credo. But before that the regime launched a heroic if doomed rear-guard battle against the rising Islamist tide.

The Resolutions of the Ninth Regional Party Congress

Despite the sense of resolve and conviction, even defiance, that reverberates through his 1977 series of lectures, Saddam Husayn also transmitted a sense of foreboding. He admitted that most Iraqis were more traditional than the Ba'th Party, and that the party's secular policy therefore might not have been popular with many. There was a need, he said, to "convince the whole people and transform them" along the party's secular line; there was a need to "enhance the leading role of our party in moving and transforming and directing society." Saddam instructed the party cadres, "[You must not] give up your . . . leadership in . . . education." "Ambiguity . . . should not be our means of winning over the majority." Yet he cautioned his party members that possibly "the majority of your people" might support the Islamists. In such a case, he advised, "you have to act skillfully" by refraining from offending the sensitivities of the masses.[54] This sense of foreboding was fully justified. The defeat of the Iraqi army meant for many Iraqis that something was very wrong with the ruling party and its ideology, and very right with Khomeini's Islamism. Islam started to be identified with power. Saddam felt the need to shore up the morale of party members and stop the slide toward an Islamic alternative to Ba'th rule. This he did by convening the Ninth Regional Ba'th Party Congress of June 1982.[55]

The resolutions from the congress were surprising. A central topic of the resolutions was "the religious-political phenomenon in Iraq." The resolutions discussed frankly for the first time in the history of the Ba'th Party the nature of the Iraqi people and the Islamization of Iraqi society. When the resolutions got specific and complained that the "religious-political parties" were "based on sectarian grounds,"[56] they left no room for doubt that this was mainly a Shi'i phenomenon: almost as a rule, accusations of "sectarianism" (*al-ta'ifiyya*) were directed at Shi'i antiregime activists. If any doubt remained, the resolutions decipher the code: "One of the most active of such parties . . . was the so-called al-Da'wa, which has so well-known sectarian nature." They and anti-Arab Persian and "Persianized" elements in the *hawza* were inciting people against the regime, "relying on aid coming from Iran."[57] The attendees deplored the rise of "ultra-religiosity" (*al-tadayyun*) among Iraqi youth in general and the Shi'a in particular, and ascribed it to the defeat of the pan-Arab movement. The Iraqi people, too, were to blame. The Iraqi character, the resolutions held, was traditionally "charged with the passion of extremism and reaction[ary feelings]. Such a negative attitude may change into a hostile one if it is exploited by malicious and organized forces seeking . . . to obstruct and wreck the course of the [Ba'th] Revolution." Indeed, "the Da'wa Party had exploited the feelings of anxiety and loss by [of] certain circles of youth and incited them in a fanatic, religious and sectarian manner against the Party and the Revolution."[58] The resolutions could hardly have been more explicit in accusing the Shi'i youth of religious-sectarian animosity toward the state. Many young (Shi'i) people were easy prey because they were confused. They sought quick and radical solutions, and turned to terrorism. The Ba'th Party admitted that its regime was vulnerable owing to a number of crises inside the party, including stagnation, lack of revolutionary zeal, and ideological confusion. This situation had alienated a part of the youth. When alienated this way, "religion and religious attitudes" would attract "this kind of [Shi'i] youth." Such a negative phenomenon had existed before, but it had become much more evident following Khomeini's rise to power in Iran, the resolutions observed.[59] This was a deeply embarrassing admission of failure. But the resolutions went further. Most shocking, the congress even detailed what kind of ideological confusion was undermining the Ba'th and why:

> Some party members began to practice religious rites in a superficial manner. Religious concepts began gradually to overcome party concepts . . . in thought and practice. . . . The religious aspect began to spread . . . among certain Party members who started to imitate senior party members, imagining that the party leadership demanded it. . . . Moreover, some party members started to make the practice of religious rites a standard of Party assessment [of dedication to the Ba'th]. . . . They began to carry out religious practices to satisfy their superiors who themselves carried out such practices and asked their comrades to follow suit in order that they could advance their position in the Party and Revolution.[60]

The "state of confusion in party ranks" became so great that the young members were asking an absurd question: for a party member to be a serious Ba'thi, did he have to practice religious ceremonies? The answer was, alas, in many cases, in the affirmative. The resolutions of the Ninth Regional Ba'th Party Congress lamented the spread of this horrific process down to the lowest rungs of the party, where young members joined. This hit at the very heart of the problem, the secularism of future generations of the party. Indeed, this phenomenon permeated to the lowest levels of party membership, the *ansar* and *mu'ayyidin.* This brought about "a state of relative entanglement between the base of the Party and those of religious-political [read: funda-mentalistic] parties." An intermingling of the party's junior base and the base of the religious-political (or fundamentalist) parties presented the Ba'th with a major challenge, because individuals from both extreme ends of society—young and inexperienced Ba'this and Da'wa supporters—met at the same mosques, and their ideologies "became close to each other."[61]

This unbelievable confession exposed existential fear. The party was falling apart. In the first place, the party's upper echleons, most likely in the Shi'i areas, had been penetrated by the hostile ideology and the alien, feared, and occasionally derided practice of Islamic "*al-amr bil-ma'ruf,*" "ordering what is right." Worse still, it had been abandoned by its young members, mainly the Shi'i and less so but, still, also Sunni ones, in favor of the Islamist groups. By merely frequenting the mosque, those inexperienced young members or can-didates (a Ba'thi remained a candidate for a number of years before becoming a full party member) were exposed to truly religious Muslims. This was seen by the party as a devastating encounter: the young Ba'this were arriving at the mosque carrying the load of the party's message and doctrine of secular Arab and Iraqi nationalism, while the fundamentalists arrived there with an Islamic message, and, as the party implied, the Islamic message won every time.

What had happened to the eternally haughty and triumphalist Ba'th? One of two different developments may have occurred. It is possible that parts of the leadership genuinely lost their faith in the Ba'th extreme secularism, cer-tainly in its atheism, and became more or less religious. Alternatively—and this is what the congress's resolutions hint at—some senior Shi'i members smelled the Ba'th defeat at the hands of Khomeini's Iran and were already hedging their bets. A few more blows to the Ba'th regime's military in the battle for Basra and they would have jumped ship. The young and inexperi-enced candidates were different: observing the old-timers in the party, they were led to believe that this was the party line. But the danger to the party's identity was even greater: when the Ba'th entered into a "Popular Front" (*al-Jabha al-Sha'biyya*) with the communists and some small groups in the early 1970s, they made sure all contacts were kept to the senior-most level. Old-time senior Ba'this could be relied on to repulse any communist attempt to recruit them. Young candidates were forbidden to mix with communists; they were seen as half-baked, and as such vulnerable. In this the Ba'th followed in the footsteps of the Bolshevik Party under Vladimir Lenin. Now, however, the Ba'th leadership admitted that it had lost control over such encounters between their young generation and Islamists. What all this meant was for them both simple and alarming: each visit to the mosque by each junior party candidate represented a threat. The greatest danger came from the Shi'i membership. Defection to the Da'wa or any other such militant political group could mean penetration of the Ba'th and an unacceptable breach of internal security. At the same time, the Ba'th regime could not do what it had done vis-à-vis meetings with members of the Communist Party: it could not issue a sweeping instruction forbidding visits to the mosque. After all, the regime was on the record as being against atheism. This dilemma was solved only in part by keeping an eye on members who showed up "too often" in the mosque, but what "too often" meant was left to the security organs to decide.

While some very limited rhetorical concessions to Islam may be traced already in 1981–82, even had he wanted to, in 1982 Saddam was unable to make any major concessions to religious public opinion, for such concessions, made in a moment of a crushing military defeat, would have been seen as a sign of weakness and surrender. The result could have been total disintegration of the party and the regime's internal security structure in the south, where it rested to a large extent on Shi'i party members. A few years later Saddam could afford covert concessions (see below on the July 1986 secret meeting), and by 1988–89 he could afford public concessions. This happened after Khomeini admitted defeat when he described the August 1988 cease-fire with Iraq as poison. One year later Khomeini died. But even then the concessions to Islam were limited. It was only when the American military appeared poised for a major offensive against Iraq on the Kuwaiti-Saudi border that the rhetoric of the president and his media began to undergo deep changes. But in 1982, this was still unthinkable.

Regime-Shi'i Relations in the War

In closed-door meetings of the political leadership and in his highly classified discussions with his military commanders in the 1990s, Saddam said that the Shi'i uprising of March 1991 following the military defeat in Kuwait could not have been foreseen. "The main reason [for the surprise] I believe was perhaps the total trust in the [Iraqi] people [*al-thiqa al-mutlaqa fi al-Sha'b*]. I mean in the sense of inability to imagine what would happen . . . a state [of mind] that led [us] not to expect . . . such a possibility ['adam tawaqqu' . . . *hadha al-ihtiyal*]."[62] Saddam's surprise was part of a far wider-reaching phenomenon:

his army officers too were oblivious to the Shi'i problem they had. In a secret discussion with senior officers during the 1991 Shi'i revolt, a very senior officer reported to the president two phenomena that should not have come as a surprise, but did so all the same. First, he told Saddam that officers were afraid to report bad news about the sagging morale of the troops because they were deathly afraid they would be punished for the report. Second, he admitted that when the government forces moved into the Karbala area during the Shi'i revolt, they were shocked when they encountered extreme hostility from the local population.[63]

This inability to expect a Shi'i revolt against regime and state may be explained in terms of the regime's decision-making and thinking during the Iran-Iraq War. Throughout the war the regime had some problems with a few Shi'i marsh Arab tribes (*al-ma'dan*) in the marsh areas on the border with Iran. The regime's response was harsh: a large number of villages were evacuated; the population was sent deeper into Iraq, usually around Basra; and very modest compensations were paid.[64] There were also executions of marsh Arabs for antiregime activities and of Shi'i revolutionaries during the war under the law against al-Da'wa.[65] Apart from that, however, the only signs of a negative Shi'i approach to the war were the many desertions and the many instances of washing and preparation of dead fighters' bodies according to Islamic rites by bereaved Shi'i families. In Islamic tradition, the body of a warrior who dies in a holy war need not be washed because the dust of the battlefield is regarded as purifying. By washing their battle dead, the families indicated that they did not see the war as *jihad*. Those expressions of reservations, though, were purely passive. The Shi'i population of Iraq fought against Iran for two mutually reinforcing reasons. In the first place, desertion meant death or mutilation, often mutilation that resulted in death. Saddam himself reported to his colleagues that he had at first rejected the government's suggestion to mutilate deserters. After a while, though, he consented that an ear could be chopped off first-time offenders, then the other ear would be separated from the heads of recidivists, and that such mutliations were to be performed with a knife and under field conditions rather than in hospital. Saddam explained his initial reluctance by his realization that through such a practice, "we shall be killing five or six thousand men," apparently from the resulting infection. Like the humanitarian that he was, he bemoaned the need to do this. "What kind of people are those" (*ma huwa naw' hadha al-bashar*), he asked in bewilderment, people who cannot do the right thing—serve in the military, fight for leadership and country—unless such a punishment is hanging over their heads? But he was convinced that his decision was the right one when he saw that right away, two thousand deserters reported to duty "voluntarily" in Basra alone (a Shiʻi area) as a result of the new law.[66] It is safe to suggest that most of them were Shiʻis. Summary executions for desertion had been introduced even earlier.[67]

Another reason for fighting in the war was a very different one. The Iraqi Shiʻa, by majority, felt Arab. Their attitude toward Persians was ambivalent: they were coreligionists, but because of historical Persian-Arab cultural alienation and even a degree of mutual disrespect, they refused to be subjugated by Persians. Indeed, since the age of modern nationalism the Shiʻis of Iraq have represented an anomaly: they have been a Shiʻi minority in a Sunni Arabic-speaking world, but also an Arab minority in the Shiʻi Farsi-speaking world. Some chose the Persian side, moving across the border and fighting alongside the Iranian troops. Those who stayed fought, however reluctantly, as Iraqi soldiers. When you are swamped by gushing human waves of Iranian soldiers with their Kalashnikov rifles blazing, you don't have much time to clarify to yourself whether you are first Shiʻi or first Iraqi: you shoot. Some, though, fought well and excelled. For the most part they were tribal young men. Unlike their urban coreligionists, tribal Shiʻis were trusted by the regime. As Saddam saw it, Persian religious-cultural-political influence in the holy Iraqi cities and in parts of Baghdad represented a threat, but the Shiʻi Iraqi tribal countryside was Arab and could be trusted.

The long war necessitated general conscription. Despite the war's unpopularity with the Shiʻis of Iraq, by mass mobilizing young Shiʻi men the regime deprived the Daʻwa and other opposition movements of manpower. The war also created an atmosphere that was conducive to the imposition of more draconian emergency measures than before. All this made it very difficult for the Shiʻi opposition to operate, and turned hundreds of thousands of young Shiʻi men into a regime-captive audience, exposing them to an intense bombardment of party doctrine by the Baʻth political officers. This did not turn them into supporters of the regime, but it did temporarily limit the impact of the opposition. In addition, Shiʻi soldiers who defected to the Iranian side or were captured were not treated well by the Iranians. This convinced them that Shiʻi solidarity had its limits.[68] Still, the majority stayed and fought, but fighting a war they did not want to fight created an agonizing dilemma, which in turn increased their hatred of the regime, something the regime failed to see.

Wartime Military Promotions: Redressing the Sectarian Imbalance?

According to a count that I conducted throughout the 1980s, based on interviews with intelligence officers in the West and numerous newspaper reports in the Iraqi press, as well as Iraqi TV footage, of forty-six two-star generals in the Iraqi Army and Republican Guard whose sectarian affiliation was known, twenty-four (52.2%) were Sunnis, sixteen (34.8%) were Shi'ites, and six (13%) were Kurds. Of twenty-nine three-star generals whose sectarian and ethnic affiliation was known, sixteen (55.2%) were Sunnis, eight (27.6%) were Shi'ites, two of whom served also as corps (*faylaq*, usually consisting of three to four divisions) commanders, and five (17.2%) were Kurds. These were the most prominent active-service officers who won the greatest exposure in the Iraqi media, but they are likely a representative sample. The most conspicuous Shi'i officer under the Ba'th was the four-star general 'Abd al-Wahid Shanan Aal Ribat. He hailed from the small Ribat tribe, part of al-Samawa al-Gharbiyyin (Western Samawais), from the vicinity of al-Samawa (the tribe is also to be found near Basra, Nasiriyya, and Hilla).[69] His last position in the armed forces was chief of the General Staff until December 1999, when he was retired (for the second time) and made governor of Baghdad, in itself not a minor position.[70] During the last phase of the Iran-Iraq War he commanded Infantry Division 11, and was often decorated.[71] After the Iran-Iraq War he served as commander of the "Baghdad" Division of the Republican Guard,[72] the first Shi'i commander of a Republican Guard division. In the early 1990s he became the commander of the Fourth Corps, placing his command post near his tribal domain in al-Samawa.[73] In the mid-1990s he served as assistant chief of staff for operations.[74] Another very high-profile Shi'i officer was the four-star general Sa'di Tu'ma 'Abbas al-Jubburi, who served as assistant chief of staff for training in 1987[75] and as minister of defense between December 1990 and March 1991. In other words, he was charged with conducting the military campaign during the Gulf War in which only defeat could be expected. There were many others.[76]

Although the promotion and prominence given to some two dozen Shi'i officers (and probably more whose sectarian affiliation I could not ascertain) during the Iran-Iraq War were unprecedented, a few qualifying facts should be borne in mind. First, no Shi'i officer ever rose to general in the Iraqi Air Force. Second, only Shi'i men with a clear tribal background could aspire to a prominent military career. In Saddam's view, tribal Shi'is were less "contaminated" by Persian influence. Those who hailed from a large Shi'i town and had no tribal affiliation could at most reach the rank of captain, and none of them could hope to become an aviator (the number of Shiʻi fighter pilots was small, in any case). Shiʻi recruits were sent overwhelmingly to the infantry, and only rarely to the tank corps. As a result, they suffered particularly heavy losses. Armored and other technological units were seen as less expendable. Casualties would have been horrendous even had the Shiʻis been spread evenly across all units: as most Kurds were either exempt from military service (being regarded as a potential fifth column) or served in a purely Kurdish militia (called the Saladin Force by the regime and *Juhush* or *Jash*, "Young Donkeys," by the Kurdish nationalists), the ratio of Sunni Arabs to Shiʻi Arabs in the regular armed forces was between 1:3 and 1:4. When added to the fact that infantry units were particularly exposed, it is no wonder that the Shiʻi population, which in any case was ambivalent about the war against Shiʻi Iran, was traumatized by the casualties. Finally, even though under Saddam, Shiʻis were allowed to rise to important military positions more often than before, in view of their massive contribution to the war effort and losses in it, this advancement was modest. One way to demonstrate it is by comparing their prominence with that of the Tikritis, who hailed from Saddam's hometown. At least as reflected in the random sample of public sources I surveyed in the 1980s, the number and share of Shiʻi general officers in the regular armed forces were roughly equal to those of the Tikritis, although the Shiʻa represented just over 50 percent of the population of Iraq and 66 to 75 percent of the men in the regular military, whereas Tikrit was a small provincial town of no more than 50,000. Indeed, the Tikriti officers were a subject of envy even within the Sunni Arab officer corps. Because of Saddam's attachment to and heavy reliance on his tribal and regional roots, they were usually promoted faster than their contemporaries.

Executions of Shiʻi Clerics

In addition to government financial support for Shiʻi ʻulama and for the great shrines, as reported by the media, the regime applied also the whip. The arrests and executions in 1983 of members of the Hakim family were unusual in the sense that they were not motivated by a need to put down any revolt. There was none. The barbaric executions were meant solely to compel the Tehran-based Hakims, mainly Muhammad Baqir and ʻAbd al-ʻAziz, to quit their opposition activity in Iran at the head of the SAIRI. Indeed, the last Hakim brother was sent to Tehran with a written demand ordering the Hakims to stop all anti-Ba'thi activities.[77] Here the Ba'th regime failed: the Hakim brothers continued their work in Iran and even established a military wing, the Badr Brigade. They returned to Iraq with their political party and military wing in late April 2003. The executions denied the Shi'i community important secondary level spiritual leaders and frightened people, but they did not seriously affect the opposition inside Iraq, simply because by 1983 this opposition had already been rendered ineffectual. And yet the fear of the demonic power and influence of the *hawza* (the religious university) of Najaf over the Shi'i masses preoccupied the Ba'th regime during and after the Iran-Iraq War.

What to Do about Kho'i and the *Hawza*?

> The *hawza* was essentially established to distribute money and separate the [Shi'i] people from the state.[78]

Internal documents produced by very high-level committees between 1983 and 1988 show the regime's deep hostility toward and concern about the *hawza* (here referring to the religious university in Najaf and Karbala, including all the professors and schools, or madrasas) and its leader, *marja' taqlid* Grand Ayatollah Abu al-Qasim al-Kho'i, and its influence over the Shi'i masses.[79] The great importance of those deliberations is suggested by the fact that some of the committees studying the *hawza* and suggesting solutions were headed by Saddam's deputy, 'Izzat Ibrahim al-Duri; his first paternal cousin and henchman, 'Ali Hasan al-Majid (later nicknamed 'Ali al-Kimyawi, or "Chemical Ali"); and his tribesman, security chief General Fadhil al-Barrak. Other participants included the most senior Shi'i party members, including the venerable old-timer Regional Leadership and RCC member Sa'dun Hamadi. Some comments came from Saddam himself.

The party officials worried mainly about two different dangers. One was the long-term anti-Ba'th influence of the *hawza* under Kho'i on the Shi'i population. Another and more tangible threat was that of a mass revolt, or at least open protest, which could have resulted, they feared, from mass participation in the Shi'i religious commemorations. The regime made significant efforts to reduce the number of active participants in the commemorative gatherings but with limited success.[80]

According to the party's reports between 1983 and 1988, the crimes of Kho'i and his close circle were numerous. For example, they spoke in Farsi among themselves; they gave financial help to pilgrims; Kho'i's followers practiced the banned chest-beating and crying; and Kho'i never attended the *Fatiha* prayers for the dead in battle. Worse: much like his predecessor, Muhsin al-Hakim, Kho'i too refused to endorse the regime's position against Iran. 'Izzat Ibrahim quoted a statement that the *marja* had made to him: "Do you want me to evaluate [read: criticize] Khomeini? Then I must evaluate Iraq as well!"[81] It is not surprising, then, that Saddam regarded the *hawza* as being "unfriendly at best."[82] The most important questions regarding the *hawza* considered by the Ba'th officials were, first, should Grand Ayatollah Kho'i and the *hawza* itself stay in Iraq or should they, or at least all the Persian and other non-Arab 'ulama and students, be expelled? And second, either way, could the regime take full control of the *hawza*'s schools and fully integrate them into the government educational system? As an alternative, could a pro-Ba'th Arab, as distinct from a Persian *marja*, be prepared to take over the *hawza*, and who might that person be?

The most radical suggestion regarding the *hawza* came from a Shi'i Regional Leadership member, who called for complete state control of Shi'i religious education and the closing of all nongovernmental religious schools. As part of the strategy, he suggested "banishing the [Persian] pollutants" from Iraq.[83] A Sunni old security hand and member of the RCC and Regional Leadership was more moderate, recommending the "transfer of the *hawza* from the Persian element to the Arabs." Fadhil al-Barrak, the Sunni senior security official, poured cold water on the notions of his enthusiastic colleagues. "There are 493 Iranians and they make up the entire *hawza* cadre. If they were deported it would be the end of the *hawza* existence in Iraq," he said.[84] 'Izzat Ibrahim cautioned, "We do not want to end religion, because we cannot."[85] What he meant was, "We cannot eradicate *Shi'i* Islam." In the March 1988 memorandum to Saddam the decision was that until an Arab was able to head the *hawza*, "keeping al-Kho'i and not harassing the *hawza*" was necessary, as "deporting him will lead to the removal of the *hawza* from Iraq to Iran."[86] The binding conclusion was that the *hawza* would remain in Iraq, "but it must not run contrary to the Revolution's goals."[87] 'Izzat Ibrahim further warned that there were limits to the regime's ability to introduce changes into the curricula and texbooks of the *hawza*.[88] Another aspect of the same conclusion was provided by General Fadhil al-Barrak, the security professional. Barrak explained that closing down the *hawza* would be useless because "al-Da'wa Party is everywhere in Iraq," not only in the Hawza's schools.[89] So the *hawza* was allowed to stay, but by the mid- to late 1980s it was already a shadow of its former self. When the Ba'th came to power the number of students and faculty in Najaf and Karbala was a few thousand, with a large number of schools. By 1988 Najaf was reported to have only 465 students in two schools, and Karbala had no schools at all.[90] This was the result of two decades of very strict supervision of every cleric, deportations, arrests, executions, and other forms of pressure.

What about an Arab chief *marja'*? The Sunni RCC member Sa'dun Shakir said, "No one will be in contact with any religious leader who receives money from the government . . . even if he is [Prophet] Muhammad [himself]." 'Izzat Ibrahim noted that Kashif al-Ghita was "burnt as soon as he was recognized as a collaborator with the state, and this will be the fate of anyone who works with the state." Of another senior cleric, he said, "We transformed [him] into a rat." He concluded that any support for a proregime Shi'i cleric would therefore have to be highly secretive. The Ba'this also understood that, much as they wanted to see an Arab *marja'* at the head of the *hawza*, an Arab *marja'* would not necessarily be regime-friendly. 'Izzat Ibrahim warned that "replacing a Persian by an Arab will not solve the problem." If Ayatollah Muhammad (Muhammad Sadiq) al-Sadr (Muqtada's father) ascended to the *hawza* leadership, 'Izzat Ibrahim warned presciently, he would be "worse than al-Kho'i, because he is harsher than al-Kho'i." He would thus cause "a disaster."[91] Despite some efforts on the part of the regime, yet another bitter truth was that, as Fadhil al-Barrak confessed, after twenty years of Ba'th rule "we do not have one qualified scholar to control the *hawza*; our system cannot prepare one scholar."[92] So an Arab *marja' taqlid* was not an option for the time being.

Some Conclusions from the Regime's *Hawza* Deliberations

Based on the Ba'thi discussions and memoranda reported by 'Abbas Kadhim, a few conclusions may be suggested. In the first place, the regime's fear in the mid- to late 1980s of Shi'i mass riots was justified and not exaggerated. Iraq was at war with a Shi'i enemy that was popular with its own Shi'is, and spontaneous eruptions, even though they never occurred, were still likely. Seeing Kho'i as an instigator, if only a potential instigator, of riots was, however, a mistake. There was no evidence that Kho'i, or before him Hakim, even though he was definitely more confrontational, ever incited the masses to demonstrate against the regime. The mass demonstrations of 1969 and the 1970s were reported by the revolutionaries themselves to be the result of a combination of spontaneous action and Da'wa organization. Kho'i, for his part, encouraged people to participate in the commemorative ceremonies and gatherings. This worried the Ba'this a great deal, but this was his narrowly defined religious duty. In view of Kho'i's political quietism, the Ba'th fear of and obsession with him and the *hawza* were greatly exaggerated, verging on paranoia.

Second, the Ba'thi leaders recognized a few bitter truths. One was an explicit admission that if they closed down the *hawza*, all the Shi'i spiritual leadership would inexorably move to Qom, Iran. Already in their 1979 discussion the Ba'this expressed an awareness that Kho'i was less radical than Baqir al-Sadr, and they believed that Khomeini wanted the latter to replace the former. By the late 1980s they were probably also aware that Kho'i disagreed with Khomeini over the rule of the jurist. Either way, if Najaf lost to Qom, this would have meant losing to Khomeini. This was unacceptable. After considering the alternatives, the Ba'this resigned themselves to the idea that for the time being, the *hawza* under the "Persian" Kho'i would be allowed to remain uncooperative as long as it did not actively preach against the regime. And yet they kept looking for an Arab *marja' taqlid*! The obsession with an Arab *marja'* was a trap, and the regime paid a price for it.

After his death in 1992, Kho'i was succeeded by another Persian, 'Ali al-Sistani. However reluctantly, the regime learned to live with him too, but the regime's search for a cooperative Arab ayatollah continued. This search was the result of shamanistic thinking, the victory of ideology over experience. The Ba'thi old-timers could not part from the conviction that an Arab would always, or almost always, be an Arab nationalist. Ayatollah Hakim was an Arab, but an active opponent. His sons Mahdi, 'Abd al-Hakim, and 'Abd al-'Aziz even joined the opposition. His protégé, Muhammad Baqir al-Sadr, another Arab Iraqi cleric, posed such a threat that Saddam decided to execute him. So much for Arab ayatollahs. On the other hand, Kho'i, while a Persian, was a passive opponent of the regime, and, unlike Baqir al-Sadr, he was also an opponent of Khomeini. Because of a language problem (he spoke Arabic with a heavy Persian accent), his direct communication with the Shi'i Arab masses was very limited. Why take the trouble of replacing him with an Arab like Sadiq al-Sadr, who was potentially far more dangerous? The leaders' hate for Persians blinded them.

Another unpleasant truth was that the *hawza* was not as central in deciding the attitude of the Shi'i masses as the Ba'th Party leaders had convinced themselves. While it was convenient for the Ba'th luminaries to explicitly blame almost everything on the *hawza*, Fadhil al-Barrak's comment was evidence that they had reached the conclusion that anti-regime sentiments were "everywhere" in the Shi'i community. This meant that the regime's top security experts understood well that, with or without the *hawza*, almost twenty years after the Ba'th takeover the party was deeply unpopular with the Iraqi Shi'a. Although such things were said strictly in closed-door meetings, they were still an impressive admission of failure. The shrinking of the *hawza* as reported by the regime's intelligence was a sweeping indication. The regime tried to hide the relentless pressure on the *hawza* behind its lavish support for the three main shrines in Najaf and Karbala and the support given to some clerics. This support was reported to the public in the open media, but the decline of the *hawza* was too steep for the Shi'i public not to notice. This further alienated the more religious segments of the Shi'i population.

Yet another unpleasant fact the Ba'this had to act on was that any connection known to the public between an ayatollah and the regime was poison for both. As the Ba'thi open media showed, the regime managed to recruit some 'ulama, but they were almost exclusively junior. The failure of the senior pro-Ba'th Shi'i 'ulama meant that in the future, if the party decided to support an Arab ayatollah to replace al-Kho'i or another "Persian" *marja*', it would need to approach a non-Ba'thi, or even an ostensibly anti-Ba'thi figure. To avoid being branded a collaborator and therefore being "burnt," the candidate would need to demonstrate his independence of the regime. The regime leaders would therefore have to rely on a secret understanding with the candidate, or have no understanding at all and just hope for the best. In this context, 'Izzat Ibrahim's warning against trusting Muhammad Sadiq al-Sadr, the quietist cousin of Baqir al-Sadr, may be understood in two different ways. Either 'Izzat Ibrahim saw through Sadr, realizing that he indeed presented a great threat, or he did not want to expose even to his most senior comrades his and Saddam's plans to secretly support Sadr, an Arab-Iraqi *'alim*, in his rise to the top. As discussed below, this is what happened with Ayatollah Muhammad Sadiq al-Sadr, Muqtada's father.

Finally, from the discussions in the high-level party committees. the impression is that, with the exception of Sa'dun Hammadi, it was the senior Shi'i officials who offered the most radical solutions for dealing with the *hawza*. By comparison, the Sunni officials were practical, more ready to admit the regime's failures and act on them. It is possible that more than their Sunni peers, the senior Shi'is felt they had to prove their staunch loyalty to the Ba'th.

Regime Delusions

It is difficult to explain why, despite its fears of Shi'i unrest in the 1970s and 1980s, the regime was taken by surprise by the Shi'i revolt of March 1991. One reason may be the absence of any significant revolts or mass demonstrations in the 1980s. This situation could have been misinterpreted by leader and regime as growing acceptance on the part of the Shi'a. The reason for the heightened fears in the 1980s was the unrest of the 1970s. The Ba'this worried that if, with the shah in Tehran, the Iraqi Shi'a were restive, with Khomeini in Tehran they would be doubly so. When unrest did not manifest, the door was open to a self-delusional process. Indeed, along with fear of the bad influence of the *hawza* on the Shi'i masses in the internal documents of the war and immediately following it we find a delusional description of the Shi'i attitude toward the regime. Thus, for example, in a 1989 discussion among the top leaders, one of the participants commented that during the war, "even though many believed that Iraq was in a tough spot, our people remained faithful to its pledge of loyalty." Saddam responded by saying that this was "an expression of freedom [*ta'bir 'an al-huriyya*]." Saddam complained that some people "say about Saddam Husayn that he is detached from his [Iraqi Shi'i] people [*ma'zul 'an sha'bihi*]." In response, he suggested, "We shall put up as a candidate [*nurashshih*—himself] before the Shi'a of Iraq and he [Khomeini] will present [himself] as a candidate for the Iranians, and we shall calculate and see the percentage and see who will win [more support] from the people. Free elections!"[93] In highly classified internal documents from the war, party analysis produced for the benefit of the senior members expressed the same kind of views. For example, in a 1987 document sent by the minister of defense, Department of Political Orientation, to the chief of staff and designed to inform the senior military officers, the party bosses explained that despite Khomeini's efforts to split the Iraqi people into Sunnis, Shi'is, and Kurds, "Iraqis of all sects are standing together" and "sectarianism will not prevail." All of the Iraqis, the minister wrote, "are united in the faith in God. Old sensitivities disappeared and the belonging is to pan-Arab nationalism, neither to tribe nor to city nor to sectarianism."[94] Such a text might reasonably be expected to appear in public propaganda, and indeed did appear there. However, for the Sunni-Shi'i divide not to be discussed in an open and honest way in the most highly classified documents, intended only for the internal discussion of the top leadership, was evidence of either fear to deviate from the party's political correctness or, just as likely, genuine self-delusion. Political correctness often leads to erroneous analysis because it prevents free thinking. Indeed, it could be that political correctness led to delusions when the leaders became brainwashed by their own propaganda. Also, as noted earlier, the *mukhabarat* could not report any antiregime expressions, let alone criticism of the leader, without arresting the offenders, and the punishments were severe. This fact created a dual inhibition: on the one hand, people were very careful whenever they said anything about the regime. Certainly they did not feel free to express their views. This denied the *mukhabarat* an important means to measure public opinion. On the other hand, local government agents who had many friends and family in their area of responsibility were often reluctant to report a transgression that was sure to lead to severe consequences. This dual inhibition against expressing opinions and gathering information goes some way toward explaining the regime's blind spot. The effect was devastating: when an issue is not discussed openly even among decision makers, it is pushed to the furthest edge of awareness, and without awareness there is no action. The regime was caught by surprise by the Shi'i revolt of March 1991. Saddam nearly lost the Iraqi south as a result, and his reaction was barbaric. The scars that this reaction left on the Shi'i population of Iraq have not healed even in the post-Ba'th era.

The Islamization of Rhetoric, 1980–88

[Saddam Husayn,] our historical, ingenious, Jihad-launching leadership, fighting for the future of our Iraqi people and elevating our monotheistic Islamic religion, guided by the Message of Eternal Islam.

—*Al-Jumhuriyya*, a telegram to Saddam from a celebration of the Prophet's birthday[95]

Beginning in the early 1980s, four main developments could be seen in the regime's public record. All of them were the result of the ideological battle with Khomeini and the Iran-Iraq War, and all pointed in the same direction, toward an increasingly Islamic posture on the part of the regime. First, the regime's official language began to evolve into an Islamic one. Second, anti-Persian literature began to dominate history books and school textbooks. The anti-Persian motif was a matter of race, not religion, but as Persians were known to be of the Shi'i persuasion, the anti-Shi'i subtext was evident. Third, a new, Islamic layer was added on top of the old secular symbols of the state. Fourth, in the early 1980s the government's support for religious institutions and 'ulama of both sects was upgraded. Toward the end of the war such support receded with the dwindling of the state's financial resources.

Al-Qadisiyya as a Religious Battle Cry

Even before the actual war between Iraq and Iran began, in the propaganda battle against Khomeini the regime had already deviated to some extent from extent its commitment to secular Arabism when, in January 1980, it presented itself as the defender not only of Arabs against Persians but also of Islam against apostacy. A good example is the most important film ever produced by the Ba'th regime, an epic movie, *Al-Qadisiyya*. The film described fairly accurately and in a technically reasonable fashion the Arab Islamic historical account of the most important battle of early Islam outside the Arabian Peninsula. The Battle of Qadisiyya between the Arab Islamic army and that of the Zoroastrian Sassanid Persian Empire took place in southern Iraq around 636 CE. Even though the Persian army, commanded by General Rustam, was far larger and better equipped and had the aid of a few elephants, the Muslim Arabs under Sa'd bin Abi Waqqas were victorious. The victory opened the Arabs' way to the Sassanid capital, Ctisphon (Ctesiphon)-Seleucia (later, al-Mada'in), some 70 kilometers south of today's Baghdad. The Persian emperor, Yazdajird III, having lost his capital city and state treasure to the Muslims, never recovered. After conquering the rest of Mesopotamia, the Arabs climbed the Zagros Mountains and swept through the Iranian plateau.[96] The film conveyed three messages. The first was that a new Arab-Persian and Muslim-Zoroastrian war was coming. The Ba'th were not only defending Arabism against the racial enemy (Rustam was a redhead in the film, a typical Arab image of Persians, *al-'Ajam*), they were also defending true Islam because the Persians under Khomeini were still Zoroastrian. This was a new kind of message for a secular party. It also risked antagonizing the Iraqi Shi'a, as it could be interpreted as identifying the Shi'a as Zoroastrianism. The second message was that all Arabs, therefore, in Iraq, Iran, and the Arab world had to unite, as they had in Qadisiyya. Indeed, Saddam himself, one day before he sent his troops to war, urged all the Arabs to support Iraq, as was their moral duty to their common nation, against any non-Arab enemy.[97] The third message of the film, as was fitting for the "classical" Ba'th Party, promoted women's support for the war effort. In the heat of the war, though, this message of gender equality evaporated. The film and a growing number of media references to the battle of Qadisiyya provided a sufficient indication that Saddam was getting ready for war.[98]

When small-scale military confrontations erupted along the border in early September 1980, the press warned the other side, "This is the hour for settling the account, O Persian midgets." It promised that the account would be settled by "the offspring of Qadisiyya and Saddam of the Ba'th."[99] Following Saddam's announcement that the March 1975 Iraqi-Iranian Algiers Agreement regarding the Shatt al-Arab waterway was null and void, but before Iraq launched its military offensive, the press had already predicted a "Qadisiyya," which would be won by "the Knights of the Arabs and their Commander Saddam Husayn."[100] At this stage, though, God was still absent. As soon as Iraq launched eleven of its twelve army divisions into Iran, the war was branded by the Iraqi media "the Second Qadisiyya" and "Saddam's Qadisiyya."[101] The regime's propaganda machine was tireless in its efforts to convince the Iraqi people, this time very explicitly, that history was repeating itself, that they were the modern incarnation of the Muslim Arabs who had won the first Qadisiyya battle against the Zoroastrian Persians, and that as then, they were destined to win it. Qadisiyya was everywhere: a huge panorama was created at at enormous cost describing the historical battle, and schoolchildren were taken to gawk at it. Saddam was depicted in numerous posters and murals hugging Sa'd bin Abi Waqqas and the Qadisiyya warrior, the poet al-Qa'qa', to demonstrate that he was the latter-day commander of the victorious Arab Islamic armies. On a money note of 25 dinars he was shown in a field marshal's uniform, commanding the battle of the first Qadisiyya, and in posters he was shown on a tank, commanding the battles of both the first and second Qadisiyyas. The communiqués of the General Command of the Armed Forces told of victories "over the Zoroastrian enemy's forces [*quwat al-'adu al-majusi*]."[102] In numerous other ways the regime endeavored to mobilize the public for the war effort under the banner of Qadisiyya, from Qadisiyya festivals and gatherings to the awarding of the Qadisiyya Sword, the highest military decoration, in impressive ceremonies that were broadcast on TV and appeared in the daily press on the front pages.[103]

Anti-Persian Medieval Historiography in the Service of the War Effort

For the benefit of the intellectuals and university students, the regime's historians rewrote early medieval Islamic history to convey a strong anti-Persian bias. This trend had no explicit religious or sectarian cutting edge, for until the early sixteenth century most Persians were Sunnis anyway. And yet the attacks on the Persians as a historically anti-Arab, corrupt, power-hungry, and treacherous nation implied that they were bound to corrupt any culture and religion they adopted. Of particular interest was the historiography of the ʿAbbasid era, owing to the efforts made by the regime to force a close identification of Khomeini with pre-Islamic Zoroastrian Persia, on the one hand, and with the Baʿth regime and the ʿAbbasids on the other. Saddam was often compared to Caliph al-Mansur and even acquired the moniker "al-Mansur" (The One Whom God Makes Victorious). More rarely, he was equated with Caliph Harun al-Rashid.[104] One example suffices to show why: the puzzling case of the Barmakids.

An outstanding episode in the regime's attempt to absolve the ʿAbbasids (and by implication the Arabs) of all charges of incompetence, betrayal, and raw lust for power and to lay precisely those same accusations on the doorstep of the Persians was the elimination of the Barmakids (*al-Baramika*), the prominent family of (Sunni) viziers of Persian stock who served Caliph Harun al-Rashid (786–809 CE).[105] One member of the family, Harun al-Rashid's most loyal and competent official, Jaʿfar bin Yahya, was executed, and other family members met a similarly tragic end in 803 CE on the caliph's order. Important medieval historians, including Tabari, mention a family sex scandal, but as a secondary reason for the downfall of the Barmakids. Instead they suggest reasons of state for the downfall, including the Barmakids' growing power and popularity, which threatened the caliph. Later and more popular sources, apparently looking for a good story (and some Persian ones, possibly identifying with a Persian vizier), report that the caliph's wrath was the result mainly of a family sex scandal involving his beautiful and bright sister, ʿAbbasa, and his vizier, Jaʿfar.[106]

None other than Saddam himself indicated to the Iraqi historians that the Barmakids were a key historical case in the struggle against the Persians and their agents in Iraq. In Saddam's world the Barmakids stood for every kind of fifth column. Thus, when he spoke of the ʿArif coup d'état against the Baʿth rule in 1963 he called it "a Baramika infiltration . . . in an Arab guise." The same applied to the military coup in Syria against the Baʿthi civilian flank in 1966. "The Baramika are still here even if their root is not necessarily Persian," he explained, referring to the danger of treason from within the party ranks.[107] The Baʿthi historians who wrote about the downfall of the Barmakids therefore omitted mention of the sex scandal and the ensuing personal vendetta, and concentrated exclusively on reasons of state. One historian accused the Barmakids of financially supporting Persian anti-'Abbasid revolt movements in order to turn the 'Abbasid Arab Islamic state into a Persian Zoroastrian one.[108] Faruq 'Umar Fawzi is more sophisticated, but his conclusions are essentially the same. He implies that the vizier, Ja'far bin Yahya al-Barmaki, had some sinister mesmerizing influence over Harun al-Rashid that enabled him to "overcome" and isolate him. Barmaki became the commander of the caliph's personal guard and his chief adviser. He actually controlled all the central power nexuses of the state. But the most serious of his transgressions was the favoritism he showed toward Persia (*bilad faris*) at the expense of the empire as a whole. Furthermore, the Barmakids spent the central treasury's resources on an army they had raised in the east that was loyal only to them. In this way "they sowed the first seed" for the disintegration of the 'Abbasid Empire. Faruq 'Umar does not even mention that the caliph had Yahya killed and the other Barmakids arrested for life; in his account, they were just "stopped." All these activities against the state were the result of the anti-Arab "Persian complex" that they and other prominent Persians before them could not resist.[109] It was indeed a severe accusation, coming as it did from a serious historian.

Faruq 'Umar's criticism of the Marxist historians in the 1970s with regard to their ideological and anachronistic approach to medieval history was sound. Then he expressed his views with honesty. That his academic views in their main contours fit into the Ba'th regime's political agenda of defending the 'Abbasid cause against revolutionary movements was a fortunate coincidence for him. In 1977 the conflict with the shah's Iran was over, and the regime was indifferent to positive views of Persians. In those days Faruq 'Umar was free to express his true views about the Barmakids with no official interference. They appeared in a very positive light in his writings, while he criticized Harun al-Rashid severely for his immaturity and weakness. In fact, when reading Faruq 'Umar's 1977 account, one might even draw the conclusion that those were indeed the Barmakids who saved the 'Abbasid Empire from disintegration during Rashid's first sixteen years in power. The caliph in fact withdrew from politics and responsibility and left it all to the Barmakids. "Then," Faruq 'Umar told his readers in 1977, "all of a sudden, he [Rashid] veered and unleashed against them a side blow because of their growing influence."[110] The mid-1980s were a very different era: now Saddam harnessed all his intellectuals to the war effort against Khomeini's Iran (Persia) and its Iraqi Shi'i supporters, and any remnant of professional impartiality had to disappear. Faruq 'Umar had no choice, but even in 1987 he retained a degree of his old secular worldview. His writings were vitriolic, anti-Persian, but he did not buy into the regime's Islamic-Zoroastrian confrontation fantasy.[111]

Persians in School Textbooks

Vilifying the "Persian" Baramika did not remain on the level of intellectual pastime. Very quickly it showed up in school textbooks. Thus, for example, a textbook on Arab and Islamic history for the second grade intermediate school recounts the story of the ruthless elimination of the family of viziers:

> Harun al-Rashid . . . showed great resolve in confronting the [state's] enemies and those who conspired against its unity . . . on the inside. They were non-Arabs, like the Persian Baramika who exploited their high positions in the state and tried to conspire against it owing to their Persian racist fanaticism, and [al-Rashid] eliminated them and saved the state from their evil and plots.[112]

Indeed, school textbooks of the 1980s were a rich source of anti-Persian diatribes. Before the Baramika there were other Persians who plotted "against the Arab Islamic state in order to weaken, and then topple it." They "adopted a number of measures, including twisting the teaching of the monotheistic Islamic religion and the Arab language, the language of the Qur'an . . . and starting civil wars."[113] More specifically, Persians were accused of responsibility for the assassination of three of the first four Rightly Guided Caliphs. First was the Persian Zoroastrian Abu Lu'lu'a Fayruz, who murdered the second caliph, 'Umar bin al-Khattab. Other Persians started the chaos and civil wars that led to the assassinations of 'Uthman bin 'Affan, the third caliph, and 'Ali ibn Abi Talib, the fourth caliph.[114] (In fact, however, the assassinations of 'Uthman and 'Ali had nothing to do with Persians.) Persian "lustful appetite," coveting Arab lands "on the eastern flank of the Arab homeland . . . for a number of centuries," was described in detail as well in a series of textbooks titled *The Modern and Contemporary History of the Arab Homeland*.[115]

From an Anti-Persian to a Religious Assault

In his private discussions with his lieutenants in the war, Saddam usually remained cryptic and analytical, merely accusing Khomeini of "superstitions" and "sectarianism."[116] "Superstitions" meant in all probability the belief in the future return (*al-raj'a*) of the Imam Mahdi, a fundamental Shi'i tenet of faith, but Saddam did not elaborate. In its public media the regime could not settle for such restraint for long. Legally, in May 1980, in response to the attempted assassination of Tariq 'Aziz, the RCC issued Resolution No. 666, which was written in coded language, as almost all official documents were. It legalized the "dropping" of Iraqi citizenship from "any Iraqi of foreign origin" for disloyalty to the Iraqi homeland, people, and revolution.[117] This resolution was applied almost exclusively to real and perceived Shi'i opponents of the regime who had a Persian ancestor or an Arab one who held Persian rather than Ottoman citizenship before 1920.

Despite the risk of offending the Iraqi Shi'a, in response to Khomeini's accusations that the Ba'th were enemies of God and Islam, full-blooded Islamic anti-Iranian propaganda had to be adopted, and with it came full-blooded Islamic rhetoric in areas not directly connected to Iran or the war. The difference between the propaganda war against the shah in the 1970s and against Khomeini in the 1980s was striking. In the 1970s the shah was accused of Persian hatred for Arabs; the Persians were portrayed as covetous, expansionists, and generally extremely unpleasant; and the shah was accused of promoting reactionary antisocialist feudalism and capitalism, of doglike servitude to imperialism, and of Zionism to the degree that he was ready to commit suicide to help Israel, as well as of raw aggression, but no explicit religious themes were brought up. The shah for his part also refrained from religious offensives. Both sides were secular and felt uncomfortable with an explicitly religious war. Because of the sectarian division in Iraq, the Ba'this were even less inclined than the shah to awaken the sleeping lion of religion. To ward off any sympathy toward Shi'i Iran, the Ba'th Party offered its Shi'is Arabism, socialism (whatever that meant), and its fiery anti-Western and anti-Zionist credo, and considered that sufficient. Khomeini was a different case altogether: his most powerful weapon against the Ba'th was Islam. Since the early 1980s, therefore, the Ba'th regime had responded in kind, attacking him for his "deviant" Islam. Ba'th ideology notwithstanding, the logical way to complement this assault was to portray the Ba'th as guardians of true Islam.

Khomeini as Antichrist

To try to drive a wedge between Persian and Arab Iraqi Shi'is, the main thrust of the Iraqi propaganda attack entailed depicting Khomeini as a *daj-jal* ("trickster" or "deceiver," akin to the Antichrist) who deviated from Islam

178

and created an apostate Persian version of the Shi'a. The best way to damage Khomeini's reputation was to recruit Iraqi Arab Shi'i 'ulama to denounce him as un-Islamic. This was indeed done amply during the Iran-Iraq War. Low-level Shi'i clerics in Najaf and Karbala joined the fray. The rulers of Iran were accused of equating Khomeini with the Prophet, of designs to control Mecca, and of atrocious expressions of "trickery" (*al-sha'wadha*), blasphemy, and atheism.[118] Sunni as well as Shi'i clerics and, reportedly, Shi'i pilgrims to the holy shrines, along with all sorts of "southern" (that is, Shi'i) "masses," denounced Khomeini as "the Great Imposter" or "Antichrist" (*al-dajjal al-kabir*), or just "the Imposter," while his little helpers Khamenei and Rafsanjani were branded "the Small Imposters." The Iranian leaders were described as *kuffar* (nonbelievers), "the Imposters of Qom and Tehran" and "enemies of Allah, Mankind and history." They were accused of "attacking the unity of all Muslims and the teachings of the Islamic shari'a," of "apostasy" (*ridda*), and of "black hatred toward Arabism and Islam." Khomeini's regime was branded "the regime of the barbarians (also idol worshippers, *al-jahla*) and analphabets in Tehran."[119] In the resolutions of the Second Popular Islamic Conference, convened in Baghdad in April 1985, the three hundred assembled clerics and intellectuals assailed Tehran using fairly extreme Islamic vocabulary: "The rulers of Iran are oppressive tyrants, corrupt Enemies of God, His Messenger and all the Muslims, not just of Iraq. . . . From now on they should be called the Tyrannical [or: Perverse, or prostituting, or covetous] Clique [*al-fi'a al-baghiya*]."[120] And while the Iraqis and Saddam their leader were characterized as "offspring of the Prophet and his jihad warriors," Khomeini and his "tyrannical clique" were dubbed "offspring of Kisra [the title of Persian Sassanid emperors] and Rustam [the commander of the Persian army, defeated by the Muslims]," or simply "Zoroastrians" and "Magian priests" (*Majus*).[121] More rarely, Khomeini was also accused of being a "*zindiq*" (an atheist, a heretic).[122]

Occasionally the Iraqi media would latch on to an outrage the Iranian mullas said (or were said to have said), and all hell would break loose. This was the case, for example, when in May 1981, on the occasion of Imam 'Ali's birthday, the Iraqi media reported that "Khomeini the Trickster announced that Imam 'Ali's remains are not to be found in his shrine in Najaf." According to this information, Khomeini insisted that 'Ali's body was in Qom, Iran. Iraqi 'ulama, both Shi'is and Sunnis, strongly denounced this announcement, some of them characterizing Khomeini as a Zoroastrian priest, but the names of the clerics mentioned by the Iraqi media did not include that of any senior Shi'i cleric.[123] There can be little doubt that the Shi'i clerics were forced to make those announcements, and that the public understood it well, but the clerics' "collaboration" with the regime sent a message to the masses all the same—that passivity was advised. The regime seems to have interpreted this passivity as support. This was a serious mistake.

The Islamization of General Rhetoric

Once the ideological inhibition disappeared, the rhetoric coming from the regime's media assumed progressively more Islamic overtones in areas not directly connected with Iran as well. The reason behind it was the regime's decision to jump on the bandwagon of the growing religiosity in the Iraqi public. As described to me by a young Iraqi intellectual who had lived in Baghdad and served in the military during the war, first the Shi'a "returned" to the mosque. Then the Sunnis did too. The propaganda pouring out of Shi'i Iran, followed by information that seeped into Iraq about the high fighting spirit of the Iranian Pasdaran and Besij, aroused Shi'i admiration despite the reservations many Shi'is had regarding Iran, and proved the power of religion. Even though the Sunnis feared Iran, many of them, too, were eventually caught up in the lure of the power that is Islam, except in their case it was Sunni Islam. Many young women started wearing the hijab, often against the best advice of their parents, and the regime did not lag far behind.[124]

The new Islamic expressions in the Iraqi media were numerous; here only a few examples will be provided. Already by the early 1980s expressions like "a secular state" had disappeared.[125] The regime laid heavier emphasis than before on its objection to atheism; regime luminaries laced their speeches with progressively more Islamic terminology. Since the early 1980s Saddam had been using more religious terminology in his public speeches, and by early 1982 he had started speaking of "*jihad*" and of "men who are believers" (*al-rijal al-mu'minin*), ending his speeches with Islamic formulas such as "God bless you [*hayakum Alla*]," "God will defend and protect you and lead you on the road to victory [*hafazakum wa ra'akum . . . 'ala tariq al-nasr*]," and the like—blessings he had not used before.[126] Military communiqués more often started with the *basmala* religious formula. In 1984 the masses celebrating the Prophet's birthday portrayed Saddam as "our historical, ingenious, Jihad-launching leadership, fighting for the future of our Iraqi people and elevating our monotheistic Islamic religion, guided by the Message [*al-risala*] of Eternal Islam."[127] This was the first time 'Aflaq's secular "eternal message" (*risala khalida*) was turned 180 degrees to become the Message of Islam. It was encouraged by the media but had not yet been done by a Ba'thi official. An additional facet of the incremental Islamization of the public sphere was that religious occasions and festivals received more media attention than before. While the Islamization of the legal and educational systems had to wait for a deeper crisis, already by late 1981 the regime had commenced Islamic activities abroad. Strangely for a secular regime, in November the Ministry of Endowments announced that under Saddam's instructions, Iraq had begun "to spread the Islamic religion in the world and establish stronger ties with Muslims . . . in the world" by extending to them "support and generous material aid." This aid included money contributions to Islamic communities in Japan, Brazil, Australia, Britain, the United States, France, Italy, Sri Lanka, India, Pakistan, and Bangladesh.[128] In a state facing looming financial disaster, this was an astonishing admission of the depth of need for international Islamic support. This was no longer 'Aflaq's separation between religion and state.

Anti-Shi'i Allusions

From anti-Persian literature the distance to anti-Shi'i allusions was not far. Some of the attacks on Khomeini's claim to be a Muslim could easily backfire, as they were also indirect attacks on the Shi'a in general. An interview with the Sunni Iraqi Minister of Endowments and Religious Affairs may serve as an example of this kind of pitfall, if pitfall it was. There were no negative repercussions, because the interview was conducted by a secular magazine published in Beirut and Europe, and it never reached Iraq. A question that cannot be answered without more information from the internal documents is whether the interview was an indication of growing anti-Shi'i sentiment among the leadership. One year into the war, while on a visit to London, the minister gave an interview to Beirut's *al-Dustur.* He reported that a [Sunni] Islamic conference in the British capital had just denounced Khomeini's regime for "transgressions." Khomeini's first transgression, the minister explained, was to have taken for himself the blasphemous title of ayatollah (Sign of God). "In Islam such a title does not exist, nor does such a title exist in other religions," the minister insisted. This was a barb directed at the Shi'a in general. The second transgression was that two months after he came to power, Khomeini announced "that Islam as a religion has not yet been completed [*lam yak-tamil ba'd*]," that the Message of Islam and the venerable Qur'an were still incomplete (*naqisa*), and that the Expected Mahdi "would appear in order to complete this Message." Whether Khomeini was quoted correctly or not, what was ascribed to him is part of the Shiʻi doctrine, and many Shiʻis were aware of it. The very existence of the twelfth Imam as the ultimate Redeemer is challenged by the Sunnis. Those who know enough about the Shiʻa also resent the name given to him in Shiʻi tradition: Muhammad, with the byname al-Qasim, this being the combined name reserved exclusively for the Prophet.[129] According to one of the most authoritative medieval Shiʻi sources, the Imam Mahdi will come with a new book and a new shariʻa.[130] Some Shiʻi medieval sources also accuse ʻUthman, the third caliph, of omitting pro-ʻAli references when he assembled the Qurʻan.[131] Whether Khomeini in fact said it or not, by castigating him for having suggested that the Qurʻan was "incomplete," the Baʻthi minister simultaneously attacked Shiʻi tradition. The minister even accused Khomeini of falsifying parts of the Qurʻan. As a result of all of these transgressions, the minister insisted, "We are fighting to guard the essence of the monotheistic Islamic religion."[132] For a Baʻthi official to position himself as the defender of Islam merely one year into the war was the clearest evidence that, under the heavy hammer blows of Khomeini's propaganda, the Baʻth regime was slowly changing its spots.

The Arabs as Leaders of Islam

In its attempt to drive a wedge between the Shiʻi Arabs of Iraq and the Shiʻi Persians, the Baʻth regime endeavored to convince its Shiʻa that only the Arabs were the source of true Islam. The Prophet was an Arab, the Qurʻan was given to mankind in Arabic on Arab soil, and the Arabs were the first carriers of the Islamic mission. The Persians therefore ought to recognize Arab seniority. Thematically this was a new concept, producing a vulgar version of the teachings of Salafi thinkers of the early twentieth century such as ʻAbd al-Rahman al-Kawakibi and Rashid Ridha. In many of his public speeches as well as in private meetings with the leadership, Saddam insisted that the Arabs were the only leaders of Islam. Not surprisingly, these principles were fully elaborated for the first time a few months into the war in a presidential speech to "men of religion" (*rijal al-din*) in Najaf and Karbala.[133] Sixteen years later Saddam still stuck to his Arab-Islamic mission guns when he told his people that Arab Shiʻism was born "out of a strong conviction." It is "based on love of the Prophet Muhammad's descendants . . . and . . . on their principles and practices, while Persian Shiʻism is a false credo imposed on them by the Safawi Shah Ismaʻil in the sixteenth century. Arab Shiʻism was "merely a way of interpretation . . . within the context of the same religion" as that of

Sunni Islam, but Persian Shi'ism was "a new religion," keeping only an Islamic "façade." The rulers of Tehran, even those who came after Khomeini, "are not the Shi'ites of 'Ali and al-Husayn." Unlike all other Muslims, Saddam argued, who "have always viewed the Arabs as rescuers," Persian Shi'ism was hateful of the Arabs.[134] In other words, only Arabs were true Shi'is; only they could "naturally" love the Arab Prophet's family [*ahl al-bayt*], including the twelve Shi'i Imams. Persians like Khomeini, his successor Khamenei, and others could not be and could not really understand the Shi'a, nor could they love the Imams and their Arab descendants.

Military Symbols in the War

Military Units: The "Return" to Islam and a Sunni Tilt

Two indicia are of interest in the case of military symbolism.[135] One was where the military fell in terms of the Shi'i-Sunni balance. The regime's attempt to walk a tightrope may be discerned here, but being essentially a Sunni-hegemonic regime, it could hardly avoid a Sunni tilt. The other index is the extent to which the military gave in to all-Islamic religious pressures, as exemplified by referencing God rather than medieval heroes of Islam in naming military units. The memory of medieval Muslim warriors and battles may be seen as secular because even the most secular party members of Muslim background were still attached to such heroes and battles as part of their cultural identity. In this respect, the year 1986 represents a watershed. Until 1985–86, the names of military corps, divisions, and military operations were God-free. In 1986 the change began, and God appeared.

Iraq entered the war with twelve army divisions. The names of all of them were acceptable to Sunnis, but three were called after heroes detested by the Shi'a: The First Mechanized Division was named after Abu 'Ubayda, who supported the first caliph, Abu Bakr. The Seventh Infantry Division was named after Caliph al-Mansur, an 'Abbasid ruler whom the Shi'a dislike, and the 12th Armored Division was named after al-Nu'man bin Bashir, who was a staunch enemy of 'Ali. Later, Bashir became a governor under the Umayyad Mu'awiya and then under his son Yazid, whose troops murdered Imam Husayn. Only the al-Miqdad 11th Infantry Division, created in the late 1970s and named after a Companion of the Prophet, was perfectly acceptable to the Sunna but also admired by the Shi'a, as he was a staunch supporter of 'Ali. As for the secular-religious balance, until 1980 no divisions incorporated a reference to God in their name, and even though the symbolism in the army was mainly Sunni-inspired, it was still secular.

During the Iran-Iraq War, Iraq created some seventy new divisions. A better Sunni-Shiʻi balance was struck than before, as Shiʻi conscripts filled the ranks of the new divisions, and winning Shiʻi hearts in general became a high priority. Still, a certain Sunni tilt remained.

During the war years the ground forces were organized mainly in seven corps, or *fayaliq* (each comprising three or more divisions), all of them new. The corps were mostly named after famous medieval Islamic victories that are admired by Sunnis and acceptable to Shiʻis. The First Corps was the only one that could displease Shiʻis in its naming; it was called al-Rashid Forces, after the ʻAbbasid caliph whom the Shiʻa accused of jailing and poisoning the seventh Shiʻi Imam, Musa al-Kazim. As for a secular-religious balance in naming units, it passed the 1986 test: only the name of the First Special *faylaq*, created as late as 1987, was to include God. It was named Allahu Akbar, a sign of the approaching Islamicized era. With respect to the long list of new divisions and other units (brigades, battalions, commando units, military camps), naming took into account Shiʻi sensitivities, but a certain imbalance remained, manifested in two ways. First, all the Shiʻi heroes and other symbols that the regime chose to include in the pool of divisional names were acceptable to and occasionally even admired by the Sunnis, certainly in Iraq. This means that when it came to Sunnis, the regime was taking no risks. Second, some Sunni heroes chosen were unpopular with the Shiʻa. Here the regime evinced its old and unchanging preference for Sunni identity. A few examples will demonstrate the Sunni tilt. Division 15, al-Faruq, was named after the second caliph, ʻUmar, seen as a great hero and role model by the Sunnis but regarded by the Shiʻites as a lowly usurper who denied ʻAli his right to the caliphate and abused ʻAli's wife, Fatima. To sugarcoat this bitter pill for the Shiʻis, Division 16, Dhu al-Fiqar, was named after a mythological sword used by both the Prophet and ʻAli—a revered all-Islamic symbol. Division 21 was named after Muslim bin ʻAqil bin Abi Talib (died 680 CE). He was Imam Husayn's cousin and supporter who died in a Shiʻi (pro-Husayn) revolt in the Kufa area. He is seen by the Shiʻa as the first martyr and is believed to be buried in Kufa, where many Shiʻites visit his tomb. The Sunnis are indifferent to him. Armored Division 17, al-ʻAbbas, could have been named either after the Prophet's uncle, who is respected by both sects, or after the fierce half-brother of Imam Husayn, admired by the

Shi'a and acceptable to the Sunnis. Remarkably, one of Iran's major operations against Iraq during the war was also named after him. In other words, both Khomeini and Saddam decided that his memory could bring them Shi'i support. Division 24 was named after the 'Abbasid caliph al-Mu'tasim (ruled 833–842 CE), disliked by the Shi'a, but Division 26 was named after 'Ammar bin Yasir, known as one of the "two right hands of 'Ali." He is a Shi'i hero, but again, one acceptable to the Sunnis. However, when the next division was established it was named after (abu Bakr) al-Siddiq, the first caliph, whom the Shi'ites revile, and the division included a tank battalion named Dhu al-Nurayn, after the third caliph, 'Uthman bin 'Affan, whom the Shi'a despise. To balance it off, Division 28 was called al-Hasan, after the second Shi'i Imam, and Division 31 was named after Imam Husayn.

As for secular versus religious names, 1986 again was the watershed. From then on a few units received straightforward religious names, such as al-Jihad, Allahu Akbar, and al-Shahid; most important, a mechanized division of the Republican Guard was named Tawakkalna 'Ala Allah (In God We Trust). To balance the Islamic religious naming, Republican Guard units were also named after pagan Mesopotamian heroes. For example, two Republican Guard divisions were named Nebuchadnezzar (infantry and commando) and Hammurabi (armored). Around 1987 the Second Special Infantry Division of the regular army was still called Gilgamesh, after the mythological mid-third-millennium BCE pagan king of Uruk. A clear sign of the changing hues of the regime's ideology was the fact that while pagan Mesopotamia was not out, Allah was definitely in.

Symbolic Names for Weapons

The mix of pagan Mesopotamian and all-Islamic historical symbols was typical also when it came to weapons systems. An Iraqi short-range missile and an Iraqi (Soviet-style) tank were called *Asad Babil* (the Lion of Babylon). An air-to-air missile was called *Ababil* (Swarms of Flying Creatures), to remind the public of the *sura* of the Elephant and God's pre-Islamic support for the Arabs against the Abyssinians. Two medium-range missiles were named after Imam Husayn and his ferocious brother al-'Abbas.[136] So far, at least, the Iraqi weapons systems names were secular and, this time, with a tilt toward the Shi'a, but without offending the Sunnis.

Units of the Popular Army (*al-jaysh al-sha'bi*), the Party Militia

The militia was created by the Ba'th Party in February 1970,[137] and was commanded throughout its existence by RCC member (later vice president) Taha Yasin Ramadhan. In the war it sent units to the battlefront. Their names were different from those of army units in the sense that they celebrated more perfectly secular events, connected with the party and with personalities devoid of any historical Islamic connotation. Likewise, hailing from specific regions, they carried special messages for the Shi'a. For example, there was a unit from Shi'i Maysan called Seventeen Tammuz (July), commemorating the ascendancy of the Ba'th to power in 1968. This was meant to remind the Shi'is that the Ba'th revolution was for them. Another unit from al-Muthanna Shi'i governorate was called "1920," after the great all-Iraqi (but mainly Shi'i) revolt against the British occupation. In Ba'thi (and pre-Ba'thi) historiography, the 1920 revolt was a symbol of the national Iraqi Sunni-Shi'i anti-imperialist struggle. All this was perfectly in harmony with classical party ideology. Another interesting aspect of the popular army's units was that often, those that hailed from Shi'i areas in the south had names that could be seen favorably by the Shi'i population, such as a unit named after al-Husayn from Dhi Qar, or units named after lesser Shi'i saints, such as Musa bin Nusayr, from Babil (al-Hilla), or Muslim bin 'Aqil, from Najaf. For good measure, however, another unit from Shi'i Babil was called al-Siddiq, after Abu Bakr, the first caliph hated by the Shi'a. That was a deliberate affront, a reminder that no one should even consider partitioning Iraq along sectarian lines. No "Godly" units at all were incorporated into the party's Popular Army. The party was the most difficult fortress for Saddam's Islamist about-face to conquer. The Popular Army therefore never had "Allah" units.

Names of Military Operations

Iraqi units conducted hundreds of military operations. Each operation, at least from the level of brigade up, received a code name. Unlike the computer-generated code names used by most Western militaries, in Ba'thist Iraq all code names had an ideological edge. Many were derived from state secular rites, such as April 1987, "*al-Milad al-Maymun*" (the Fortunate Birth), celebrating Saddam Husayn's birthday. Another such name was "*al-Hisad al-Akbar*" (the Great Harvest), to celebrate the huge losses the Iraqi army inflicted on the Iranians in the south in January 1987. For the benefit of the Shi'a, in

January 1981 the Iraqi army launched Operation al-Husayn, the Lord of Martyrs (*Sayyid al-Shuhada*), commemorating the third Shi'i Imam. An operation under a similar name, Operation al-Shuhuda (*Sayyid al-Shuhada*), was launched in July 1987 in the Majnun Islands by the 6th Army Group.

The year 1985 saw the appearance of Allah on the battlefield. For example, in January 1985 the Iraqi army launched Operation *Nasr Allah* (God's Victory) in the Majnun swamps. One month later Operation *Sayf Allah* (God's Sword) was launched by the 2nd Army Group in Mehran. In the same month and the same area the same corps also launched Operation *Tawakkalta 'Ala Allah* (You Trust in God).

To sum up, with respect to getting God into the names of units and operations, 1985 and the second half of the 1980s saw a clear shift toward religion. This is why the crucial meeting of the Pan-Arab Leadership of July 1986 should not have come as a complete surprise. With respect to a Sunni-Shi'i balance in the names of military units, weapons, and operations, the Ba'th regime did devise a more equitable pantheon than its predecessors. It still chose a few figures admired by the Sunnis and reviled by the Shi'is, though admittedly it was difficult for a Sunni-hegemonic regime to leap over figures such as the first caliphs or the 'Abbasid golden age. At the same time the regime avoided those figures the Shi'is hated most, such as Mu'awiya and Yazid. Was satisfying both Sunnis and Shi'is impossible? Not necessarily. The regime could have chosen only all-Islamic, Arab, or Iraqi geographic and historical names or concepts that had a universally positive connotation. Mecca, al-Madina, Jerusalem, al-Shahid, Victory, or names of historical noncontroversial war leaders such as al-Muthanna, Tariq bin Ziyad (conqueror of al-Andalus), or Khalid bin al-Walid would have suited. Alternatively, the regime could have departed from the British tradition of naming units and settled for numbers. Instead, while its choices represented a soft Sunni tilt, the tilt could still be discerned. On the other hand, most Shi'i soldiers whom I spoke with did not pay much attention to their units' names. They just wanted to go home.

Islamic Institutions in the War

Soon after the beginning of the Iran-Iraq War the regime conducted its economic policy as if there were no tomorrow. Although the leadership was convinced that victory was close, it also recognized that the war was unpopular with most people (the Shi'is in particlar), and therefore that any economic hardships would be difficult to explain. Significantly, the budgets for religious institutions and activities increased by leaps and bounds. The state doubled its contribution to the budget of the Ministry of Endowments from 5 million Iraqi dinars (around $15 million) in 1979 to 10.9 million dinars (around $30 million) in 1981. The ministry had usually paid most of its expenses from its own revenues, but now the state treasury was to participate in more than 75 percent of the ministry's budget. This was an amazing act of generosity, or subsidy. A look at the items that were to be augmented substantially between the 1980 and 1981 budgets is telling. Payments of all kinds (salaries, grants, social security, and so forth) to workers and officials in Sunni religious establishments increased from 1.57 million to 2.61 million dinars. The same kinds of payments to "officials and workers" at the Shi'i shrines and other Shi'i mosques and religious institutions were doubled, from 2.4 million to 5.05 million dinars. The building and renovation of small Shi'i mosques (*al-husayniyyat*), a new item, received 1 million dinars. To demonstrate the Ba'th secular credo, the same amount was also allocated for the first time to Christian religious institutions. The establishment and renovation of other "religious institutions" (apparently Sunni) went up from 0.45 million to 3 million dinars. Politically understandable but ideologically a major sin, the budget for "Religious Guidance," that is, Ba'thi-inspired religious indoctrination, increased from 37,000 to 300,000 dinars.[138] At this point also the Ministry of Endowments (Awqaf) became the Ministry of Endowments and Religious Affairs and was charged with the additional responsibility of religious-patriotic indoctrination. This new assignment was performed by a large number of clerics and officials who operated the Committees of Religious Indoctrination (*lajan al-taw'iya al-diniyya*).[139] To demonstrate his deep attachment to things Islamic, the president also decided that the Ministry of Endowments and Religious Affairs would be the only one tied directly to the president rather than to the prime minister. As a result, as the minister proudly reported, "All our requests . . . are presented to the president directly. Consequently the assignments of the ministry are easy to achieve."[140]

Regime Support for the Shi'i Shrines

One year into the Iran-Iraq War the Iraqi minister of endowments and religious affairs reported that his ministry had been instructed by Saddam to invite advisers from abroad and start extensive construction operations on the Najaf and Karbala shrines.[141] According to the *sadin* (sexton) of Imam Husayn's shrine in Karbala, between 1980 and 1984 the president had visited the place a number of times and ordered "unlimited spending," which "demonstrate the depth of his spiritual ties to the Message of the Prophet Muhammad, the Pure Imams and their struggling life and values." Despite the difficult war conditions, the *sadin* emphasized, the shrine's court was greatly expanded and paved with Italian marble, air conditioning was installed in the tomb, with new electric and water systems, and the president contributed here, as in Najaf, very expensive chandeliers to replace the old ones. Before the Ba'th revolution, the *sadin* disclosed, the people "belonging" to the shrine received only "symbolic" salaries, and they numbered only fifteen, but in 1984 they already numbered seventy-five and were receiving real salaries, like state officials, and they received plots of land for housing. Similar improvements were also introduced to the shrine of al-'Abbas in Karbala.[142] Judging by the press reports, Karbala received the lion's share of the government's generosity, with Najaf lagging behind.[143]

Najaf, too, received some official attention. In early 1984 the Iraqi press reported that, on the president's instructions, Imam 'Ali's shrine in Najaf had been provided with new floor tiles of Italian marble and other major improvements. The Friday Mosque of Kufa, (belonging to Muhammad Sadiq al-Sadr, Muqtada's father), was reported to have been refurbished for the second time since 1981. I could find no reports of new Shi'i mosques being built, but well-known tombs of lesser Shi'i saints were reconstructed, including those of the Prophet's Companions Muslim bin 'Aqil (a cousin and supporter of Imam Husayn) and Hani bin 'Urwa (a Yemeni chief who died fighting for Imam Husayn). The regime reported regularly on civic investments, true or imagined, in the province of Najaf: new roads, kindergartens, hospitals, and new apartments; and 25,000 families received plots of land on which to build their homes. Naturally, a number of Shi'i clerics were quoted as having thanked the president for the generosity he showed toward the city where the Imam 'Ali, his ancestor, was buried.[144]

Regime Support for Sunni Mosques

While the regime invested in existing Shi'i mosques, its "Sunni" investments went mostly toward building new ones. Between 1979 and 1985 the government established eight extravagant (Sunni) Saddam Husayn Friday Mosques in all parts of Iraq.[145] The two most central mosques of Baghdad were to be refurbished, too: the tomb and mosque of Shaykh 'Abd al-Qadir al-Kaylani (Gaylani) and the Abu Hanifa tomb and mosque. The instructions were to pave the floors of all these holy tombs with marble, and this alone was expected to cost 1.5 million dinars.[146] Between 1983 and 1985, government contributions to all religious institutions began to decline as a result of the impact of the war on the economy, but when compared to expenditures during the late 1960s and early 1970s they were nevertheless high, even when inflation is taken into account.[147]

The First Major Breach in the Wall of Fortress Secularism: The July 1986 Secret Meeting of the Pan-Arab Leadership

On a hot summer day in July 1986, Michel ʿAflaq and Saddam Husayn, the secretary general of the Baghdad-based Pan-Arab Leadership of the Baʿth Party and his deputy, convened in Baghdad the regime's highest ideological echelon for an extraordinary closed-door meeting.[148] On the surface, this meeting was designed exclusively to discuss improving Iraq's relations with the Sunni Islamist world by ending the enmity with two strong Islamist movements, and therefore it had nothing to do with domestic affairs. The audio tapes of the conversation, however, reveal that much more was at stake, or so at least some of the participants feared. The nearly complete recording of the discussion enables the researcher to analyze not only *what* was said and *when*, but also *how* it was said, that is, the emotional charge behind each speaker's words. The recording also provides the listener with the context of each opinion: how the discussion evolved, how the view of one participant influenced or was influenced by those of others, what views dominated at first and how they changed. The order of the debate therefore is of consequence. This was an agonizing, even a traumatic discussion, as it forced the party old-timers to agree to a reviled U-turn in the party's practice. As some of the party's luminaries seemed to have feared, while Saddam appeared only to suggest (while in fact imposing) an about-face in Iraq's foreign policy, this was bound to have crucial ramifications also for the regime's domestic policy, its ideology, and its very identity. The recording suggests that emotionally, this U-turn was more painful for the party veterans than any other party strategy change discussed in a high-level meeting for which a recording is available. The party old-timers' fears were well founded. Saddam, by then also president of Iraq, as well as secretary general of the Iraqi party Regional (or Country) Leadership (*al-qiyada al-qutriyya*), suggested a truce and even some tacit alliance with both the Sudanese and the Egyptian Muslim Brotherhood.[149] After many years of open hostility, this policy reversal would mean that for the first time in its history, the militantly secular Ba'th Party would cease all attacks against, and even cooperate with, very strong Islamist movements.

Since its establishment in Syria in the early 1940s, the Ba'th Party had had three strong rivals: the Communist Party, Antun Sa'ada's Syrian Social Nationalist Party, and the Islamist parties, mainly the Muslim Brotherhood. In Iraq, the bitter rivalry with the Islamic circles emerged in June 1969. Major confrontations with the religious establishment of Najaf and with some Shi'i tribes represented the main challenges to the nascent regime, but the Ba'th wrath was also directed toward the small and marginal radical Sunni parties such as Hizb al-Tahrir and the Muslim Brotherhood. This included arrests and even executions. The Ba'th regime fought the Islamists on a number of fronts, among the most important of which was an ideological struggle designed to demonstrate the absurdity of running a modern state along Islamic Shar'i lines. Thus, any cooperation with an Islamist political party was a clear-cut deviation from party doctrine. Moreover, secularism no less than Arabism was an integral part of the emotional DNA, or identity, of the party leaders. Any Muslim man who since his youth has followed a Christian political guru is emotionally secular even before he is ideologically committed to secularism.

The first crack in the regime's staunchly secular wall was the decision to cooperate closely with the Syrian Muslim Brotherhood. Cooperation with an Islamist movement against a perfectly secular Arab regime represented a serious ideological deviation. In practical terms, however, this was a minor crack in the wall of secularism and could be kept secret. Also, and no less important, like the Iraqi Communist Party, with which the Ba'th established a "front" between 1972 and 1979, the Syrian Muslim Brotherhood was very weak. While the Communists were entirely dependent on Ba'thi goodwill, the Syrian Muslim Brotherhood was heavily reliant on actual Iraqi-Ba'thi support. Thus they could be seen—and were seen—in Baghdad as little helpers in a bitter struggle against the rival Ba'th regime of Damascus rather than as an enemy, let alone a threat. Furthermore, the Iraqi Ba'th regime was Sunni-hegemonic, challenged mainly by Shi'i Islamists, and the Syrian Muslim Brotherhood was exclusively Sunni, challenging an 'Alawite pseudo-Shi'i regime. The sectarian common denominator helped cooperation between the two movements. Even though the de facto alliance may have begun a few years earlier, the earliest secret Iraqi document recording this alliance between Baghdad and the Syrian Muslim Brotherhood dates from September 1982.[150] Why cooperate? By 1982 Iraqi-Syrian inter-Ba'thi rivalry had reached its zenith. Earlier in that year Syria's alliance with Iran had been cemented, and Syria had cut off the Iraqi oil pipeline from Kirkuk to Banias, on the Syrian Mediterranean shore. Having lost their outlets to the Persian Gulf during the first days of the Iran-Iraq War, the Iraqis depended greatly on the Syrian pipeline, and the damage to Iraq's war economy was substantial. Early in September 1982 the Muslim Brotherhood of Syria, too, had a very convincing reason to cement relations with Ba'thi Iraq: the Asad regime in Damascus cracked down on them ferociously and in al-Hama alone killed between 20,000 and 30,000 people.

Late in September 1982 the most senior leaders of the Syrian Muslim Brotherhood arrived secretly in Baghdad for strategic talks. The initial intention was to establish a political front consisting mainly of the two parties, but also of additional Syrian anti-Asad ex-Ba'thi political groups, such as supporters of Colonel Salah Jadid, who ruled Syria between 1966 and 1969–70, and the Ba'thi old-timer Akram Horani. The representatives of the Syrian Muslim Brotherhood under the ideologue Sa'id Hawa and of the Baghdad-based Pan-Arab Leadership under Vice President Taha Yasin Ramadhan met in Baghdad. The talks were friendly but bizarre, even comical, as the two sides seemed at first to completely misunderstand each other. Ramadhan explained to his Muslim Brotherhood interlocutors that the constitution of the joint action front that the Muslim Brotherhood suggested was explicitly Islamist, as it said that Islam would be the "sole source" (*al-masdar al-wahid*) for enactment. Therefore, he explained, the Ba'th, who were against a religious state, could not accept it. His Muslim Brotherhood counterpart rejected this analysis and insisted that "sole source" did not mean a religious state at all. Ramadhan, exasperated, pointed out that "linguistically speaking," a sole source is a sole source, and that therefore it was unacceptable to the Ba'th. Dead end! However, the two partners decided not to raise this subject again, and the negotiations continued.

There can be no doubt that the Syrian Muslim Brotherhood was interested in forging an alliance with the Ba'th, but the joint constitution was meant to be made public. The Muslim Brotherhood had to preserve its reputation as an Islamic party, because this was the only way in which it could attract wide public support in the majority-Sunni community of Syria. Islamist anti-'Alawite propaganda was too powerful a weapon to give up. Presenting the 'Alawis-Nusayris as *ahl-al-ridda* (apostates)—as it was indeed doing—and as such unfit to rule over an Islamic state according to the shari'a served their struggle well. To them, therefore, the source of enactment had to be the shari'a. The Ba'th, for their part, simply could not overlook such a crucial issue. Ramadhan was an experienced negotiator used to accepting all sorts of creative ideological compromises, Saddam's fascination with ancient pre-Arab and non-Arab Mesopotamia being just one example, but this was too much even for him. Betraying the party's modernizing, secular worldview was unthinkable. He too had to protect his party's reputation, and even more, its identity. The Baghdad-based Pan-Arab Leadership included three Christians and one Druze, and going publicly Islamic was out of the question. In the end, the whole idea of a joint constitution was dropped because neither side agreed to recognize the other's final political goal, a secular nationalist or an Islamic religious state. And yet Saddam was adamant about not allowing ideological differences to obstruct when it came to such a crucial strategic interest, that of weakening, hopefully even toppling, a sworn enemy, Asad's regime. The idea of a united front was thus off, but cooperation was on, if strictly secretly.[151]

The very decision to host in Baghdad a senior Muslim Brotherhood delegation, even if the delegation was from a weak and relatively moderate branch, was evidence of a realization in Baghdad as early as 1982 that Iraq was in trouble. The Ba'th regime needed new allies. Indeed, in the spring of 1982 Iraqi forces retreated from almost all the territories they had conquered in Iran and dug in inside Iraq along the Iraqi-Iranian border. This was an admission of partial defeat, because Khomeini rejected out of hand Saddam's offer of a cease-fire and initiated a few large-scale offensives into Iraq. New allies, however, could be found only in the Sunni world. Saddam therefore followed in Asad's footsteps. In his foreign relations Asad had decided to sacrifice the principle of secularism on the altar of sectarian cooperation with Khomeini's Islamic Republic. In 1982 Saddam did the same with the Sunni Syrian Muslim Brotherhood. The latter, for its part, followed in Khomeini's footsteps when it decided to ignored the staunch secularism of the Iraqi Ba'th. Befriending the Syrian Muslim Brotherhood, therefore, even though the association was maintained in strict secrecy, was a central war decision. Had the new alliance been able to topple the regime in Damascus, this action could have opened up to Iraq not only the valuable pipeline but also a number of supply routes to the Mediterranean. The best-case scenario would also have meant some military support from Syria to Iraq, certainly support in terms of weapons and ammunition supplies, as both countries depended on Soviet-made weaponry. The alliance with the Muslim Brotherhood underscored a core characteristic of the Iraqi Ba'th regime: when push came to shove, expediency and survival were far more important than ideological purity. Ideology still mattered, in that the party could not give up publicly its commitment to secularism, but toppling the Baʿth regime in Damascus was so important that it justified a covert political deal with an ideological arch-enemy. However, except for the top leadership very few in the party were aware of the alliance with the Muslim Brotherhood. Even more important, until the Islamization process that began in the early 1980s and flourished in the 1990s, the ideological concessions the party made, while meaningful, were not profound. Switching from ʿAflaq's secular, egalitarian, and integrative pan-Arabism to Saddam's secular, Iraqi-hegemonic, federative pan-Arabism was not a revolution. Even encouraging tribal values and organization could somehow be streamlined when presented as a return to authentic traditional Arab values and identities, and it was. Tossing secularism overboard was a far more difficult and sensitive issue because it meant changing a whole way of life. It was also humiliating because it was an admission that everything the party had done and preached for before was a colossal blunder. But the 1982 alliance with the Syrian Muslim Brotherhood was a small step that was seen as purely tactical. Eventually this alliance failed to achieve its goal. The Syrian side was far too weak for any Iraqi support to enable it to topple the Syrian Baʿth regime. Still, the alliance was just the beginning of a far more profound metamorphosis that was launched at the 1986 secret meeting of the Pan-Arab Leadership.

In 1986 Iraq was still conducting an existential defensive war against a radical Islamist regime, that of Khomeini's Iran. At such a moment, having to cooperate with two other radical Islamist political forces, this time powerful and independent ones, was humiliating. If it came out, it could demolish party morale and confidence. Like the 1982 meetings, the 1986 Pan-Arab Leadership meeting and decision too were secret, but the foreign policy change suggested by Saddam was too extreme and far-reaching to remain secret for long. Secretary General Michel ʿAflaq was in all probability a full partner to Saddam's decision; he chaired the meeting, and he had to at least know the issues to be discussed. Since objection on ʿAflaq's part to the new policy could at the very least be deeply embarrassing for all, if not an insurmountable obstacle, it is more than likely that he and Saddam met before the discussion. ʿAflaq, appearing in the written translation as a mysterious "Unidentified Male One" (UM1), seems to have been persuaded to support the president's initiative: he indeed showed support, but he was clearly worried. Because the the Pan-Arab Leadership was a pan-Arab rather than an Iraqi body, ʿAflaq and the Pan-Arab Leadership were rarely involved in the day-to-day political decisions. Their realm was exclusively party ideology and party activities in other Arab states. But this time Saddam's initiative, while clearly political, involved both party ideology and the political activities of the party branches outside Iraq, so there was no avoiding a discussion by the Pan-Arab Leadership. In addition to the secretary general, there was no way that party old-timers from Syria, the Druze Shibli al-'Aysami and the Christian Ilyas Farah, and the party leader in Sudan, Badr al-Din Muzaffar, the member supposed to implement the new policy, could be kept out of the meeting. Another Christian member, Tariq 'Aziz, could not be kept out either. In the Pan-Arab Leadership he carried more weight than most other Iraqi members, as he was highly regarded as a Ba'thi ideologue.[152]

But why such a sudden ideological about-face? Like 1982, 1986 was a bad year for the Iraqi Ba'th regime. Iraq had just lost the Faw Peninsula and with it the limited access it still had to the Gulf. The Shatt al-'Arab waterway had been closed to navigation since the beginning of the Iran-Iraq War. Iraq confronted an uncompromising Iran in a seemingly unending war. Internationally, many speculated that Iraq was losing the war. The propaganda machine of Ayatollah Khomeini was extremely effective in portraying the Iraqi regime as atheistic and an enemy of Islam. The degree to which it hurt was demonstrated in the meeting when one of the participants (his voice could not be identified) suggested that Iraq should ask the most influential—but also most moderate—Syrian Muslim Brotherhood leaders, Sa'id Hawa and 'Adnan Sa'd al-Din, with whom Baghdad already had good relations, to save the Ba'th image. He suggested that the Syrian Muslim Brotherhood leaders would be asked to tell their colleagues in Sudan and Egypt that Michel 'Aflaq, the Ba'th founder, "is not an atheist [mu mulhid]" and "provide them with examples" from 'Aflaq's and Saddam's speeches in which they insist that the Ba'th are "believers" (mu'minin). The suggestion met with approval. Indeed, Saddam himself admitted that the accusations of atheism coming from Iran were hurting the regime.[153]

The discussion exposed acute ambivalence. The Christian Tariq 'Aziz came late to the meeting. He had not been pre-prepared, and he did not hear Saddam's remarks that implied that opposition to improved relations with the Muslim Brotherhood was not an option. He did not realize that he was actually responding to the boss. He thus launched a head-on assault on Saddam's proposal. His voice sounded very tense, very agitated. It was quite clear that 'Aziz was reading into the truce with the Muslim Brotherhood far more than what met the eye, a mere foreign policy issue. He rested his opposition on the solid ground of Saddam's own programmatic speeches in 1977. 'Aziz reminded his colleagues that Saddam had clearly presented the party's position regarding religion, and that this position was diametrically opposed to the position of the Muslim Brotherhood. He also reminded the leadership members that while the Ba'th were committed to a "democratic national pan-Arab state" (*dawla dimuqratiyya qawmiyya*), a crucial tenet of Ba'thi faith, the Muslim Brotherhood was fighting for a "religious state" (*al-dawla al-diniyya*). All present had to be aware that only in a "national" language-based state could Christians, let alone Druze, 'Alawites, and other non-Islamic minorities, participate as equals. Furthermore, they also had to be fully aware that in Iraq, this was the best principle that promised Sunni-Shi'i equality, and those Shi'is who joined the party before it came to power had joined it thanks to this principle. An alliance or even just a truce with the Muslim Brotherhood could mean eventually accepting their opposite principle of an Islamic state, and 'Aziz was deeply disturbed by such a prospect. Was he unnecessarily concerned? It took the party some nine years, but it did indeed eventually reach precisely the point that 'Aziz feared so much. In January 1995, in a closed-door meeting of the Pan-Arab Leadership, Saddam hammered the last nail into the coffin of the party's secular ideology when he announced that the Ba'th Party was no longer against the principle of a pan-Islamic state, provided that unification began with pan-Arab unity.[154] In other words, even if Arab unity should come first, he agreed that Islam, rather than Arabism or the Arabic language and Arab culture, could be the uniting principle for the future state. This vision came very close to that of Hasan al-Banna, the founder of the Muslim Brotherhood movement. At the same time, however, until 2003, and in total contradiction to the new Islamic line, the party endlessly repeated its commitment to a secular united pan-Arab state. One of the two party slogans, "Unity, Freedom, Socialism," continued to appear on all the party's publications and internal documents. Moreover, at the opening of every party congress and mass meeting the whole hall would get to its feet and chant as one, "One Arab nation with an eternal message."[155] The result was a chimera, a confusing cross between old and new.

'Aziz further reminded his colleagues that the reason why Saddam had defined the Ba'th doctrine so clearly and publicly "in the 1970s" was that "we had a powerful religious movement that hit us with bullets, namely: they staged armed demonstrations and hit us with bombs [*ya'ni, tutalli'u muzaharat musallaha wa gamat tadhrubu 'alayna qanabil*], so it became imperative . . . that we present against them an ideological position, in addition to mass public and even repressive [*qam'iyya*] steps."[156] 'Aziz saw no difference between Iranian and Arab, Sunni and Shi'i, Islamists: his hatred for and fear of them all came out very clearly. To 'Aziz, the Syrian Muslim Brotherhood, with whom he and his colleagues had had relations for a few years, was an exception. The membership included "enlightened men like ʿAdnan Saʿd al-Din," and they were fighting against "atheists like the ʿAlawites." In Damascus, he explained, there was "an infidel rule, they are *Nusayris* [ʿAlawites] and also atheists." Fighting a regime like that was a must, said ʿAziz, in the presence of the Christians ʿAflaq and Ilyas Farah and the Druze Shibli al-ʿAysami, all of them, like ʿAziz himself, equally "infidels" in Islamist eyes. But, he continued, the Muslim Brotherhood of Egypt was fighting against Mubarak, that is, against "Muslim people," people who, unlike the ʿAlawites, "fast and pray" and who "believe in Islam," and whose moral behavior was "wholesome." The same applied to the (more or less secular) rulers of Sudan (Sadiq al-Mahdi) and Jordan (King Husayn). ʿAziz may have forgotten that in the 1940s ʿAflaq had insisted that the Baʿthis did not necessarily have to pray or fast during the month of Ramadan. He also conveniently forgot that the religion of an Arab had been irrelevant when it came to the Baʿth doctrine: all speakers of Arabic who loved the Arab nation had been regarded as equally legitimate Arab nationalists. After all, "Love before anything else" (*al-hubb qabla kull shay*) represented to Michel ʿAflaq the foundation of Arab nationalism.[157]

ʿAziz pressed on. The Muslim Brotherhood in Egypt was not "struggling against an infidel rule," like that of the Syrian Baʿth. It was fighting against "a civil regular [or normative, or normal] regime [*nizam madani iʿtiyadi*] and want[ed] to topple it!" In other words, the Egyptian Muslim Brotherhood was trying to topple a "normative" regime, much like that of the Baʿth in Iraq. To ʿAziz, this was unacceptable. With few exceptions, he pointed out, all the Islamic groups, Sunnis as well as Shiʿis, considered Khomeini's Iran an "example to be emulated." Because of Khomeini, people had begun to believe that a religious state, which at first had seemed impossible to achieve, was doable. That phenomenon, ʿAziz implied, was very dangerous for the Baʿth and its vision. Very emotionally, he then said: "I believe in my heart, from the heart [*qalbiyyan ana aʿtaqidu, qalbiyyan*], that it is impossible that a person would believe in the religious state unless he [also] considers the Iranian experience as an ally in some form or another [*tajriba halifa bi shikl ou bi aakhar*]." In other words, to ʿAziz, with the exception of the Syrian Muslim Brotherhood, all Islamists were at least passive allies of Iran and sworn enemies of Baʿthi Iraq.

In 1986, many years before the Sunni-Shiʿi divide in the Arab world became acute following the so-called Arab Spring, this observation was essentially correct. The Egyptian Muslim Brotherhood supported Khomeini soon after he came to power. Already in 1979–80, *al-Daʿwa*, the main mouthpiece of the

Egyptian Muslim Brotherhood, often supported the "Islamic Revolution."[158] On the Iraqi invasion of Iran and during the Iran-Iraq War, the Egyptian Muslim Brotherhood had criticized both Khomeini and Saddam for wasting Muslim resources on war between Muslims, but Saddam clearly received the lion's share of the blame. Also, when the Muslim Brotherhood censured Khomeini for the war, it was mostly implicitly. As for the Ba'th, in August 1979, for example, soon after both Khomeini and Saddam became heads of state, the Egyptian Muslim Brotherhood's magazine began attacking the new Iraqi president as an enemy of Islam. No such curse words were ever used against Khomeini. In January 1980, together with other secular Arab dictators, Saddam was called "murderer" (*al-Saffah*). In July 1980, he was lumped together with the devil incarnate, President Asad of Syria. From 1987, the main attacks on the Baghdad-based Ba'th regime were concerned with the mass murder of the (Sunni) Kurds. Throughout the Iran-Iraq war the Egyptian Muslim Brotherhood was quite hostile to the Baghdad-based Ba'th, and only the Ba'th regime in Damascus was attacked more.[159] All this gives credence to the emotional criticism unleashed by 'Aziz against the idea of befriending at least the Egyptian Muslim Brotherhood. The Sudanese Muslim Brotherhood, though, was less critical of the Ba'th than their Egyptian colleagues.

'Aziz was again close to the mark in his warning that Khomeini's Islamic Republic demonstrated to traditional Muslims of both sects that such a state was feasible. The example of an Islamic state and rule, rather than the Shi'i leader himself, was a source of inspiration and as such dangerous to the Ba'th. It could strengthen the (Sunni) Muslim Brotherhood inside and outside Iraq, let alone the Shi'i Iraqi Islamists. Indeed, three years later, in 1989, a military coup d'état brought the Islamists to power in the Sudan. And even though the subject was so sensitivite he did not mention it, the whole meeting is evidence that 'Aziz and his colleagues were aware that Khomeini's Islamic Republic demonstrated to the Muslim masses, Sunnis and Shi'is alike, the mighty energies that political Islam could release. In that too, Khomeini served as inspiration even to Sunni Islamists, who otherwise could not trust him and his regime.

Whatever the accuracy of his arguments, 'Aziz was desperate to bring up any reasonable persuasions he could mobilize to forestall an alliance with the Muslim Brotherhood. Both as a Ba'thi old-timer who truly believed in the secular message of his party and as a Christian, he could not trust the Brotherhood. More immediately and pragmatically, he warned that if the Ba'th were to make common cause with the Muslim Brotherhood, it would earn the enmity of the ruling regimes in Egypt and Sudan. However, justifying the alliance with the Syrian Muslim Brotherhood because it was fighting an 'Alawite sect that deviated from Islam was a betrayal of the same Ba'thi principle he was trying to protect—secularism.

Why did 'Aziz not describe things simply the way they were? He could have said that Baghdad could befriend the Syrian Muslim Brotherhood because the group represented no threat and because it was an enemy of Baghdad's nemesis, Ba'thi Damascus, while the Egyptian and Jordanian regimes had supported Iraq in the Iran-Iraq War. Why did he choose instead to pay lip service to Islam? It seems that he recognized a new atmosphere or a new inclination of the leader. At the same time that he was fighting tooth and nail against normalizing relations with the Sudanese and Egyptian Muslim Brotherhood and its adverse consequences, his very use of the term "infidel" in relation to the 'Alawites and his support for semisecular Sunni regimes because they were also semireligious reflected the incremental Islamization of the party's rhetoric. It would seem that, to placate Saddam, whom 'Aziz knew very well, and to protect party secularism, he used an Islamic "Newspeak." Still, by attacking Asad for his parents' religion, 'Aziz himself betrayed his party's deepest ideological and emotional commitment. Eventually, once he realized that the whole idea was Saddam's, he relented.

The Sudanese member of the Pan-Arab Leadership, Badr al-Din Muzaffar, who was expected to make the first move once he returned home, was extremely reluctant to do so, though he lacked the courage to reject Saddam's new policy. Still, he was very clear: "[On] the religious state . . . in the Arab homeland, it is impossible that it will be other than a sectarian [*ta'ifiyya*] or *madhhab*-related state that will split, rather than unite [society]. . . . We have to raise this issue, which is a critique of their thinking. This is a sufficient reason for them to open a campaign [against us]. Shall we carry [a campaign] out [against them] or not?" In other words, Muzaffar, who came from a Sunni-Muslim background, warned of a Sunni-Shi'i and Muslim-Christian split, let alone a Sunni-'Alawi and Sunni-Druze split, the moment the Arab world relinquished the Arabic language as the sole criterion for political identity and future unification.

This was when 'Aflaq made his first contribution. While not rejecting Saddam's idea, he was skeptical: "If we compromise, they [the Muslim Brotherhood] are not going to compromise this much." Therefore the Ba'this would be at a disadvantage. Then, from his higher vantage point, he sent a message that sounded like a severe warning: "We are supposedly getting close to setting up a strategy for decades." And he drew some lines in the sand: "We have to set up the basic lines: the religious current is not our enemy, not our enemy, but we are different. We want to dialogue with it and support those who are not so bad or wrong [among them. And yet,] the particularity of each country should be reviewed where this strategy will be implemented. Implementation [must be] realistic and gradual."[160] At a minimum, this was not wholehearted support.

'Aflaq agreed with Muzaffar, who was wary of an immediate U-turn. "It will be natural for our comrades in Sudan not to be able to jump from one situation to another. It requires an appropriate amount of time." But 'Aflaq was not going to confront Saddam: "When we understand the strategic guidelines," apparently as designed by Saddam, he summed up, "we will have no other choice but to proceed along these lines, *even for the long run.*"[161] Meaningful reservations notwithstanding, Aflaq was ready, therefore, for a strategic shift. Why? As a secular Christian, he should never have allowed his own creation to compromise on such a central principle as equality among all speakers of Arabic, which meant keeping religion out of politics as much as possible. A strategic alliance with the Muslim Brotherhood had to lead to a profound compromise over this principle.

Several lines of argument can be adduced to explain 'Aflaq's apparent acceptance of a shift. In the first place, 'Aflaq must have been fully aware that he could not prevent Saddam from implementing the new policy. He knew his own weakness. Objection would have been useless, and a confrontation dangerous. Even he personally was not safe: rumors of the poisoning of retired President Ahmad Hasan al-Bakr abounded. A state funeral would be small consolation. Party members who might have joined him could meet the same fate as the opposition to Saddam in 1979, the firing squad. Second, even had 'Aflaq not expected any such dire consequences, a split in the party could have serious consequences. This was particularly the case in time of war. 'Aflaq must have been as aware as Saddam was of the danger to the regime coming from the Iranian propaganda success fused with an impressive Iranian military success. The accusations of atheism and hostility to Islam leveled against the Ba'th by Khomeini and the Egyptian Muslim Brotherhood undermined the regime's ideological legitimacy at home. The Iranian occupation of al-Faw and the incessant offensives elsewhere that the Iraqi forces were pushing back with great difficulty seriously tarnished the Ba'th regime's image as powerful and capable of defeating its external and domestic enemies. This fusion of slow-motion defeat on the battlefield of ideas and on the battlefields along the Iraqi-Iranian border threatened to be an explosive combination. Third, 'Aflaq's approach could encompass compromise. Aflaq cared very much about the fate of the Baghdad-based Baʻth regime, whose members were his only supporters. Even during the founding years of the 1940s, to secure the success of his fledgling movement ʻAflaq had been ready to compromise over the approach to Islam. By 1986, during the secret meeting at which Saddam introduced the U-turn, Aflaq was ready for a deeper compromise to secure the survival of his Baʻthi disciples.

It was clear, though, that he was deeply conflicted. On the one hand, he saw it as possibly a strategic change; on the other, he predicted that the rivalry with the Muslim Brotherhood was likely to return. Indeed, in a later part of the discussion ʻAflaq cautioned, contradicting himself in the process: "We will clash [with the Islamists] in many other stages . . . during this long journey [of the party]." And yet he agreed that there was no reason to antagonize the Muslim Brotherhood now. "They [the Muslim Brotherhood] are not required to be deeply aware of and have great knowledge of the Baʻth ideology. They look at some superficial aspects and see it as easy to fight, if it [the Baʻth] places itself in their way," he said. Therefore the party should emphasize those aspects pointing to a commonality of purpose with the Islamists, such as anti-imperialism, socialism, Arab unity, and democracy. ʻAflaq felt that the Muslim Brotherhood was not acquainted with those aspects and needed to be made aware of them, which might create a common denominator.

What about the party's secularism? Even though under his guidance since its inception the party had done precisely that, ʻAflaq did not suggest *taqiyya*, or precautionary dissimulation. On the contrary: "[We should] announce our thoughts" that the Baʻth Party is against "the religious state issue," he said. Indeed, he soon delved into modern Arab history and explained why, on its inception, the party was sympathetic to Islam. At the time the party corrected a historical "flaw" in the thinking of earlier Arab nationalists who worked under the Ottomans. Because they were struggling against an Islamic caliphate, the early Arab nationalists had to dissociate themselves completely from Islam. But the Baʻth Party was born in the midst of the struggle against Western (Christian) imperialism in the Levant, and therefore it was only natural that the party should make Islam "the most important thing in its platform." Here ʻAflaq grossly inflated the centrality of Islam to the historical Baʻth doctrine in order to demolish Islam in the contemporary party. Making Islam "the most important thing," ʻAflaq continued, "was inspired by the [needs of the] historical stage. I mean: we expressed the popular . . . need [for Islam] *without having the intention to do it*. Without being aware—" and here Saddam completed the sentence: "of its reasons." Amazingly, on the eve of dragging their party screaming and kicking into Islam, the founding father and his disciple the president were criticizing themselves for historically giving Islam too large a role in party doctrine. Indeed, eventually 'Aflaq's real view came through loud and clear: "If the [Muslim Brotherhood] is about to come to power, this becomes a national battle and we ally with anyone who prevents this danger," he said, in no uncertain terms.[162] In other words, 'Aflaq consented to a purely tactical alliance, and only as long as the Muslim Brotherhood represented an ineffectual opposition to the regimes. Once it endangered the regimes, the deal was off. It is not at all clear how this condition could be reconciled with his earlier warning that the alliance was likely to last for decades. What is clear, though, is that 'Aflaq was deeply conflicted. He seemed to have suspected that all this was heading toward Islamization; he abhorred it and tried to make sure this would not happen, but he also realized that he could not prevent the first step, an alliance with the Muslim Brotherhood.

Saddam felt that the atmosphere was not encouraging. Shrewdly, he tried to please his comrades by demonstrating to them his staunch adherence to Ba'th ideology and his strong reservations regarding the Muslim Brotherhood. In this way his new policy could not be interpreted as more than mere tactic, a matter of urgent necessity that could be reversed easily once conditions changed. In other words: while 'Aziz used Islamic "Newspeak" to prevent the party from sliding toward Islam, Saddam used the party's strictly secular "Oldspeak" to push the Ba'th, knowingly or not, into Islam. First he announced, "We do not stop our ideological struggle, [do not] stop our work to attract [people] to our thinking [*ihna mu nuqif nidhalana al-idiuluji, [mu] nuqif 'amaliyyat al-istiqtab ila fikrina*] . . . but . . . in forms connected to our [present] conditions." Not only did he not attack 'Aziz for his anti-Islamist views: he actually praised him. "Comrade Tariq came late, so we agree with all the concepts he mentioned *as a general principle*." "We wanted to talk about the *stages* in addition to the ideological and historical backgrounds," he explained, meaning that the urgent needs of the present phase, rather than long-term planning, demanded friendship with the Muslim Brotherhood. Nonetheless, Saddam assured his colleagues, "If it [the Islamist movement] launches a battle against us, we will launch a battle against it. And if it reaches power or gets close to it," he agreed with 'Aflaq, "we would launch a battle against it. And if it gets closer to power alone, we would be forced to advance [against it] . . . to expose them." But otherwise, he argued, there was no need for it. In an attempt to assure his colleagues that he was still fully committed to the traditional party ideals, loves, and hates, Saddam readily admitted that the Islamists were pretty unpleasant: "When an unveiled woman is walking, they torture her [*timshi safira yuʿadhdhibuha*]" and make ugly threats against her, he complained. The Muslim Brotherhood was attacking the Baʿth, he said, claiming that at that time in Iraq, more women than before were unveiled. They were right, he confirmed, but he was proud of it: this was the result of the fact that Iraqi women were better educated, were working out of the home, and had greater buying power. "So the veil is no longer suitable for school, college, or factory," he argued.

"Our movement bets on the nation's readiness for renaissance," declared ʿAflaq in this context, thus implying that removing the veil was part of the renaissance. "Of course," Saddam agreed. The Islamists, ʿAflaq continued, "are against the renaissance [*dhidd al-nuhudh*] of the Arabs, no matter how much they veil," to which the comrades laughed heartily. Both ʿAflaq and Saddam were full of disdain: the Muslim Brotherhood was "morally corrupt [*fasidin*] even before they achieved power," Saddam opined. "The best people and the best brains among them," ʿAflaq added quite disgustedly, "are the ones who write something that the [Baʿth] Party had already approached—" and here he was interrupted by Saddam: "Forty years ago!" ʿAflaq, always the professor, *al-Ustadh*, corrected his disciple: "Fifty *or* forty years [ago]. These are the best [among them]. This means they do not have—" and here Saddam interrupted him again: "There is no innovation [*ma fi ibtikar*]." ʿAflaq agreed: "Indeed."

Here Saddam made a remarkable point. All the Muslim Brotherhood knew, he said dismissively, was "to read the Qurʾan from cover to cover and say, 'This is my doctrine' [*hadhihi ʿaqidati*]! This is no innovation! Life cannot gain anything from this!" In other words, he made it clear that in 1986 as in 1977, he remained deeply committed to the secular tradition of the party, which saw no role for the shariʿa in the contemporary world. "Also," he added, "Among humankind, they [the Muslim Brotherhood] are the most dictatorial!" This was very touching, coming from him. "They consider you weak and they devour you [*hum akthar nas diktaturiyyin humma! . . . istadʿafuka wa akaluka!*]." In short, the Muslim Brotherhood simply could not be trusted. Saddam went one step further than any other participant: "We can also tell them that they are our brothers but their talk about the religious state is an attack against us." The whole discussion was the result of a moment of crisis for the Iraqi regime: Saddam explained that the Baʿth badly needed the support of the Muslim Brotherhood, rather than the other way around. In such a situation he could not possibly have believed that the Baʿth would be able to impose on the Muslim Brotherhood a change of the latter's most cherished tenet of faith. Unless we consider Saddam to be a complete fool, he had to know that such an expectation would have rendered the whole overture to the Muslim Brotherhood hopeless. His promise to fight the Muslim Brotherhood if it did not cease to preach for an Islamic state therefore was a ruse, designed to paralyze any opposition to his policy.[163] Indeed, in reality the Muslim Brotherhood remained committed to the concept of an Islamic state, and Saddam remained committed to his idea of improving relations with them.

As Saddam explained, the need for the Muslim Brotherhood's seal of approval was not merely a matter of foreign policy; such a seal was needed badly at home. He warned, "We must reduce the views that accuse us of atheism." "There is a public that is being influenced by what the men of religion [*rijal al-din*] are saying." The "men of religion" had "power to influence the people. Their ticket now has risen [*waraqathum ghalat*]," and in people's eyes they had become "more precious than before [*saru aghla min qablu*]." All this, Saddam insisted, had to be taken into account.[164] It is not clear where this information came from; I found no internal intelligence report that dealt with this subject. Still, while explicit criticism of government and leader was punished severely, the *mukhabarat* apparently followed and reported on general public moods without punishing anyone.[165] Saddam did not elaborate, but his observation could easily be understood as an admission that the regime must adapt even beyond befriending the Muslim Brotherhood; it needed to add some Islamic components to its policies and make more efforts to entice the clerics. Saddam carefully avoided the term "'ulama"—"religious scientists" or "scholars"—as this implied science, and he was not going to honor those people whom he saw as witch doctors by connecting them with science. Bribing them, however, was another matter altogether.

A particular target for the Pan-Arab Leadership's members' hate and fear was Hasan al-Turabi, the leader of the Sudanese Muslim Brotherhood. This made sense. The Egyptian *Murshid 'Amm* (General Guide) was little known outside Egypt, while Turabi was a celebrity. Presciently, 'Aziz warned that Turabi "wants to rule the Sudan" and was not likely to "relinquish his ideological struggle," no matter what the Ba'th did. So how, he wondered, could the Ba'th branch in Sudan relinquish its struggle against the Muslim Brotherhood? There was no response. And yet, when summing up the meeting, Saddam insisted that the party could gain more by befriending the Muslim Brotherhood than by antagonizing it.[166] And that was that.

Three years later, Turabi as the general secretary of the Sudanese National Islamic Front was indeed the brains behind an Islamist military coup d'état in

Sudan. The profound change that was introduced at the 1986 secret meeting of the Pan-Arab Leadership was demonstrated when, contrary to all the promises, following the invasion of Kuwait and the Gulf War, in July 1991 Turabi, on a fully publicized official visit during one of Saddam's international Islamic conferences, was already seated in front of Saddam in Baghdad. In their private conversation, which was never made public, he was polite and offensive at the same time. "Thank God," he told Saddam, "that relations with you are good." He wished that Iraq would "overcome the crisis," but he also warned: "You are under a psychological siege [*muhasarun nafsiyyan*]." Smelling blood, he immediately went for the jugular: with amazing chutzpah, he added that this siege psychology was the result of the fact that "the Ba'th Party is detached from Islam [*munqata' 'an al-islam*]." Being fully aware of Saddam's struggle against Islamist parties, he explained that when the state itself is "leading the religious guidance" there is "no need [meaning room] for religious parties." In view of Saddam's policy in the 1990s, Saddam probably understood Turabi to have confirmed that if the state Islamized itself, he would be fully justified in suppressing all nongovernmental Sunni and Shi'i religious opposition parties such as the Da'wa, or the Iraqi Muslim Brotherhood or Salafis. Saddam, though, had to protect his party and leadership, and thus he could not appear repentant. He replied that he was proud of everything the party had done.[167] However, in less than two years he followed his guest's advice lock, stock, and barrel. The Islamist opposition groups did not disappear, but neither did the *mukhabarat*, Saddam's internal security apparatus.

Confessing the Blunder of Secularism

A few months after the 1986 secret meeting of the Pan-Arab Leadership, Saddam decided to disclose to the public some of the issues that had been discussed. However, in his speech he went much further, for he made the astonishing admission of a Ba'th historical blunder. First, and now publicly, he opened the way for cooperation with the Muslim Brotherhood by portraying the organization as benign. Saddam drew a separating line between religious-political movements in the Arab world and in Iran. He defined the Iranian and Iranian-inspired religious movements—which apparently included the Iraqi Shi'i ones—as anti-Arab (*shu'ubi*)[168] and deviating from true Islam. At the same time he explained that Arab Islamists were not necessarily negative. This was because the Arabs understood Islam intuitively and deeply; after all, Islam was given to them in the first place. "We should not be misled to think that religious movements . . . in the Arab world are the offshoot of Khomeini," he insisted. Since the Shiʻi revolutionary movements, Arab and Persian alike, were clearly excluded, Saddam could only be understood as legitimizing the Muslim Brotherhood and similar Sunni movements. He was clearly preparing the grounds for a rapprochement not just with the Egyptian and Sudanese but also with the Iraqi Muslim Brotherhood. Indeed, in late 1986 he allowed the leader of the Iraqi Muslim Brotherhood, Muhsin ʻAbd al-Hamid, to return to Iraq from Europe and even teach Qurʼan interpretation at Baghdad University. Then in his speech Saddam leaped far beyond the decisions of the July 1986 meeting of the Pan-Arab Leadership. Performing his most amazing ideological *salto mortale* since he became president, he criticized himself and the Baʻth Party for distancing themselves from Islam and alienating the clerics. He chose to do this in a somewhat roundabout way, but there was no mistaking his self-criticism. He analyzed the reasons why all the post-independence Arab regimes were in crisis and why the secular nature of the regime of the shah of Iran guaranteed its demise. By criticizing the shah's secularism, he implied that the Baʻthis too would face the same fate if they did not return to Islam.[169]

Following political independence, he explained, all the new Arab regimes "relied on the minority of intellectuals. The drive to realize economic, scientific and technological development has led to a greater role by technocrats and to dominance of their concepts and values at the expense of . . . popular ones." This created a wide gap between "what is necessary," namely, modernization, and the "[religious] nature of the people." Therefore a gulf had been created between "the governments" and "the people." The result was "violent rejection" on the part of the masses. From this resulted another problematic development: "the religious current became more appealing." Such was particularly but not exclusively the case, Saddam argued, with the regime of the shah of Iran. The shah had committed "a grave mistake when he thought that he could build up a modern state through copying alien thought . . . . He opted for an alien opinion and practice which had no roots in his own country. . . . [He] handed over control to a group of technocrats who were educated along Western thought and behavior, imagining that that group alone could make his dream [of modernization] come true." As Saddam now realized, the shah and, by implication, the Baʻth had "failed to grasp that development cannot be one-sided and that if it relies on economic and scientific bases alone it will be doomed." Much of the modernization the shah introduced also "collided partly with the clergy and their way of dealing with the people." The result was that the people and the clergy were "all united against the shah."

Worse still, the shah encouraged "currents and groups that were considered atheists by . . . the majority of the Iranians." There could hardly be a more precise description of the Ba'th regime's policies, defined now as mistaken. To soften the blow, Saddam still paid lip service to old party ideals when he warned against involving religion in politics, but this went against the tenor and content of his whole speech.[170] There could be no doubt which direction he would follow.

The Conversion of Michel 'Aflaq

That something strange was happening in Baghdad became evident to the party membership in June 1989 when Baghdad announced the death of Michel 'Aflaq. The Pan-Arab Leadership of the party published a communiqué that left many party members speechless: "The late 'Aflaq . . . embraced Islam as his religion [prior to his death]. He and his comrades in the command did not want to announce this, out of . . . concern that this . . . would be given a political interpretation."[171] Had the party not wanted to give it "a political interpretation," the leadership could simply have refrained from any mention of this conversion. As was disclosed to me by a Western ambassador who had served in Baghdad at the time, 'Aflaq's elder son had told her that he was unaware of his father's conversion.[172] Whether 'Aflaq's deathbed conversion was true or ginned up for expediency by the Ba'th leadership, the publicity it received amounted to an ideological and political explosion. There could be no doubt as to what it meant: Saddam and the party were already prepared for a turn to Islam. The Ba'th Party could no longer risk any further deterioration in its public image as a result of the embarrassing fact that its founding father, *al-Ab al-Mu'assis*, was a Christian. At the same time, Saddam's personal conduct began to change as he started to demonstrate Islamic piety in his dealings with foreign diplomats, relying on them to spread the word. As relayed to me by another Western ambassador who served in Baghdad in the mid- to late 1980s, in the middle of an important discussion with the Iraqi president in 1988 the latter apologized, left to pray in a separate room, and returned after a few minutes as good as new.[173]

There were additional signs that the Ba'th regime was going Islamic. On January 14, 1991, one day before the UN ultimatum elapsed, in a meeting of the General Command of the Armed Forces, "the leader president . . . ordered that the phrase 'God is great' be added to the Iraqi flag." Thus, in an act that was clearly unconstitutional (the RCC was not involved at all, let alone the party leadership or the parliament), "the Iraqi flag [became] the banner of *jihad* and faith . . . against the infidel horde." In a Prophetic *hadith* style the president's eyes were said to have "lit up, and he traced with his venerable hand the phrase 'God is great' on it [the flag]."[174]

There seem to have been two mutually reinforcing reasons for this death blow to the party's doctrine of separation of state and mosque. First, by this act Saddam sought to portray himself as a devout Muslim. This was supposed to bolster his legitimacy in the eyes of the masses after his decision to stay in Kuwait and risk war had surprised many. As was usually the case with him, there had to be a personal stamp on the innovation, as part of his ongoing cult of personality. When he "resurrected" Babylon in the late 1970s, the country was made aware of it when his image appeared everywhere together with those of Nebuchadnezzar and Hammurabi, and his name was inscribed on every tenth brick. In the same way now, it had to be his personal handwriting. Second, it is very likely that Saddam believed that, if defending Kuwait for leader and party was insufficiently inspiring, the masses would be more willing to risk their lives for God. The new flag made no difference in that respect; to most soldiers, Kuwait was not Iraq. But Saddam was not completely mistaken. That he was prescient became clear when, after the 2003 American conquest of Iraq, a new national flag was designed to replace the Ba'thi one, and no one dared remove God from the new banner. The post-Ba'th flag retained the pan-Arab colors of red, white, green, and black, but it also retained the *takbir*, the Islamic "*Allahu Akbar*." Aptly, though, Saddam's handwriting was replaced with Kufic script.

Chapter 5
From War to War, 1988–93

The Disintegration of the Soviet Bloc, and Islamization

The inconclusive end to the Iran-Iraq War and the deep economic crisis that followed hurt the regime and delivered a blow to its self-confidence.[1] The next blow came in 1989–90, when the Soviet Union and the regimes of Eastern Europe began to crumble one after another. Since 1968, the Ba'th Party had established its governing system on the Eastern European example of *al-dimuqratiyya al-sha'biyya*, or popular democracy, as distinct from Western liberal democracy. The violent death of the Romanian dictator Nicolae Ceauşescu in December 1989 rattled the Ba'this even more. In a spasmodic reaction to the slow disintegration of the Eastern bloc, they began to look for differences between the Iraqi and the communist systems that would explain why the Ba'th would not be next.

The regime provided chiefly two answers. First, unlike the communist regimes, Iraq was a democratic country, and it was embarking on a further democratization process. During the first half of 1990, the press was allowed to discuss democratization steps, even Western democracy as an option.[2] The leadership itself discussed some measures to enhance democracy, such as disbanding the Revolutionary Command Council (RCC) and allowing a multiparty system. The draft 1990 Constitution was part of this quest.[3] It is doubtful that Saddam seriously considered democratization; most likely, this discussion was a tactical measure to absorb possible shock waves that the regime anticipated from the combination of the socio-economic crisis of expectations (the regime had promised a quick economic recovery at the end of the war) and the events occurring in Eastern Europe.

Soon after, Iraqi troops conquered Kuwait, and talk of democratization died with barely a whimper.

The second answer to the question of how the Baʻth regime differed from the communist world was Islam. The crisis of communism, the Baʻthi media explained, had nothing to do with economic decline. Rather, it was the result of the essence of communism: the Baʻthis were believers, while the communists were materialists and atheists. Therefore, the communist regimes were bound to be short-lived. The materialistic West would soon meet the same fate, the media promised.[4] A full-fledged Islamization effort, though, could wait. First, Saddam had to try to extricate himself from the socioeconomic Gordian knot he had crafted. As if imitating the proverbial solution of Alexander the Great, Saddam decided to simply sever the knot of his postwar economic and strategic quandary with his sword—except that he was no Alexander the Great.

The Kuwait Crisis and Saddam's Direct Line to God

The 1991 Gulf War has been studied and analyzed by many, including the commanders of the Allied forces. A recent and impressive addition to the literature is Pesach Malovany's 2009 *Milhamot Bavel ha-Hadashah* (*The Wars of Modern Babylon*), which addresses how the Iraqi commanders saw the war.[5] Here, I will consider only the impact of the war on Saddam's attitude toward Islam and God, as the evidence suggests that this was the time when Saddam's personal metamorphosis began. The extent of this metamorphosis may be illuminated by comparing Saddam's rhetoric after the invasion with the language of his draft permanent constitution written just before the invasion.

The July 1990 new draft constitution was published in the Iraqi press for the public to consider three days before Saddam ordered his tank divisions into Kuwait.[6] The timing of the publication seemed intended to distract the Iraqi populace from the military maneuvers. Still, of great importance was the fact that Saddam was not sure that his party was ready for a constitutional thrust into religiosity: the new constitution was as secular as the 1970 one. Article 5 retained the definition that "Islam is the official religion of the state," but elsewhere there was no mention of Islam. When the draft mentioned the values that inspire the Iraqi family, it pointed to the "legacy" (*turath*) and the "civilizational values" of the Iraqi people (*qiyamihi al-khadhariyya*), a clear reference to the pre-Islamic civilizations of Mesopotamia, as well as to the "deep-rooted, noble values [*qiyam*] of Arab tradition," but it did not mention Islam

(Article 23). When it discussed the right to private ownership and inheritance, it did not mention religion as the basis for it (Articles 30, 32, and 36). The values that most closely approached religion were those intended to inspire the Iraqi citizen when he "defend[ed] his homeland and its unity." Such defense was defined as "a sacred duty" (*wajib muqaddas*). "Martyrdom [or "heroic death," *al-istishhad*] for the sake of the [Iraqi] homeland and the [Arab] nation is a supreme honor." Martyrdom for God was absent. Also, the state would therefore endeavor to encourage the "patriotic [Iraqi], pan-Arab social and moral values" that might lead to such sacrifice (Article 25), but evidently no religious values were to prompt people to risk their lives. The media were to promote the principles of the Ba'th revolution and the "sublime values" that emerged from "Saddam's Glorious *Qadisiyya*" (the Iran-Iraq War), mainly "the values of martyrdom and total sacrifice [*al-fida' wal-tadhhiya*]" (Article 55). *Istishhad* and *fida'* have strongly religious connotations, as they refer to dying in a *jihad*, a holy war, but the context could hardly be more secular. The citizens were expected to sacrifice themselves for Iraq, Saddam, and the Arabs, not to find grace in the eyes of the Lord or to defend Islam. No heaven was promised as reward. Instead, martyrs were promised purely worldly eternity: the admiration of the people, an eternal place in their collective memory, and support for the families of the fallen (Article 25).

The candidate for the presidency had to be "a believer" (*mu'min*), but the belief itself is not made clear, except for belief in the principles of the Ba'th revolution. Those principles were, for example, that Saddam's Qadisiyya (the Iran-Iraq War) was "the only way to guard the land, water, sky, security and holy things [*muqaddasat*] of Iraq," whatever the latter meant. Likewise, the candidate had to believe in socialism and democracy, but no religion was mentioned (Article 83). The same applied to the oath of the president and other senior politicians. They were required to swear on "God almighty, my honor and belief" (*Allah al-'azim . . . sharafi wa mu'taqadi*), in precisely the same way as was stipulated in the 1970 Constitution (Articles 85, 152, and 156). When the legal system was discussed, shari'a was not mentioned at all. Instead, a secular contemporary term was used, "the rule of law" (*al-mashru'iyya*) (Articles 69–80). Finally, a new body was instituted that was supposed to replace the RCC, called the *Shura*, or "consultative council," which would also make laws. This is an Islamic Qur'anic concept, but the *Shura* was a perfectly secular being: its members were not required to have any religious qualifications. Thus, this was a secular constitution. Three days after it was published, however, Iraq invaded Kuwait, and six months later, in preparation for the Allies' assault, Saddam added to the national Iraqi flag the words *"Allahu Akbar"* (God is Great). But this belongs to a new era in Ba'th history, one taken up later in the chapter.

The Occupation

The decision to occupy the whole of Kuwait rather than, as had been discussed by the party leadership a few weeks earlier, to conquer only the two islands of Warba and Bubyan and a few miles of the border, stunned the leadership. The RCC and the Regional Leadership were told of the decision four hours before the invasion. Preparations for a large-scale maneuver had already begun in the early spring of 1990. In mid-July, Saddam secretly met with his cousins Husayn Kamil and 'Ali Hasan al-Majid ("Chemical Ali"). The only professional military man present was the fourth man, General Iyad Khalifa al-Rawi, commander of the Republican Guard. Saddam disclosed to them that he had decided to occupy the whole of Kuwait, and they immediately consented. The rest of the military were not informed. According to Sa'd al-Bazzaz, then editor in chief of *al-Jumhuriyya*, the General Staff and the minister of defense learned of the decision only from public radio broadcasts.[7] According to an Iraqi brigadier general who later defected to the West, he was attached to the Republican Guard two days before the invasion because he knew Kuwait well, and that was when he heard about the invasion. At that stage, around ten people knew about it, most of them Republican Guard officers who needed to know for operational reasons. They were never consulted; they were just given orders to prepare for the campaign.[8] Indeed, in a talk with his closest lieutenants in 1995, Saddam himself had boasted that secrecy was so tight that even his minister of defense and chief of the General Staff did not know about the invasion.[9] When the political leadership was informed about the change of plans, Tariq 'Aziz gathered up enough courage to ask why. Saddam replied, "Because it makes no difference." The leadership immediately consented. They then followed a practice known as providing "pink [that is, optimistic] information," assuring Saddam that his decision was the right one and that everything would be fine.[10] Another demonstration of Saddam's use of the collective leadership as rubber stamp, but also of his need for this kind of rubber stamp, was his secret urgent meeting with his cabinet on August 4, 1990, two days after the occupation of Kuwait. Saddam claimed that "God made us victorious" (*nassarana allah*) in Kuwait. He also claimed elatedly that "the branch [has] returned to the source and the part to the whole." Then he asked the ministers for their opinion as to whether future relations between Iraq and Kuwait should be federative or a state of complete integration (*hala indimajiyya kamila*). This was a clear enough hint of how Saddam would like things to be, and the government, without much ado, adopted the concept of a wholly integrated state.[11]

Why Invade?

Saddam was desperate to do something spectacular to save his sagging prestige. Democratization was out of the question, but even Islamization did not appeal to him as yet. A real military victory at long last, a conquest, new financial resources, strategic gains such as a deep-water harbor and new oil fields so that even Iran would have to take notice—those were worthy goals. An elevated seat at the table of oil producers and, last but not least, fulfillment of an old nationalist Iraqi desire to annex Kuwait that was "severed from Iraq with British scissors"—those, too, were respectable goals. If all were achieved, they would in one stroke deliver Saddam from his economic woes and launch him into the position he always desired, a giant among his Arab brethren midgets. The similarity to his state of mind in September 1980, when he believed that a few days of war would have the same effect, is striking. Saddam was moving in circles, each circle higher in risk and potential reward, each circle more of a gamble. However, when it dawned on him that the initial military success could still end badly, Saddam looked for a way to shield himself against self-doubt and the doubts of his lieutenants. If it all failed, he needed to blame the invasion on someone. Similarly, to maintain his confidence in victory, he needed something or someone reliable to pin his hopes on. The answer to both needs was God.

A Direct Line to God

Five days after his troops occupied Kuwait, Saddam was still justifiably delighted with the military operation.[12] Politically, however, things were not going well. The occupation was opposed by most Arabs, as well as by the Western nations. Arab League majority denunciation and UN Security Council demands under Chapter Seven for an immediate withdrawal of Iraqi troops from Kuwait came crashing down on his head in quick succession. The United States received permission to deploy troops on Saudi soil. Saddam also failed to tap into Kuwait's $100 billion in foreign assets, and the socioeconomic crisis threatened to become more acute with new wartime expenditures and an international embargo in place. Even though he was far from certain that the United States would go to war—he put the likelihood at 50 percent[13]—he had to prepare for it, nonetheless, and he did.[14]

Saddam maintained an appearance of optimism, but he was not blind. With the possibility of war against a superpower, now was the time for Saddam to rely on God. Thus, from a new angle Islam was again invoked as a convenient way for Saddam to regain confidence and stoke public legitimacy. In a closed-door meeting with his commanders five days into the occupation of Kuwait, Saddam made it impossible for them to as much as hint at criticism, for that way lay their assassination. Saddam blocked any notion of criticism when he explained that "it was God who showed us [read: me] the path. Our brain was worthless in this matter: it was God who guided us. . . . God has blessed us."[15] This was the first time Saddam claimed a direct line to God. It would not be the last.

Much like the transcript of his private August 7 meeting with his generals, Saddam's public speeches are indicative of his changing moods in a gathering storm, which would soon enough manifest as Desert Storm. In late October and early November 1990, Saddam for the first time repeated in public what he had told his military commanders behind closed doors. Addressing *mukhabarat* reports that people were frightened by the huge gamble he was making with Iraq, Saddam declared, "If God wills something there is no stopping His will. . . . We all believe that what God wants us to do is not to feel angry with Him irrespective of . . . the situation we are in."[16] In other words, the whole adventure was God's responsibility, and the Iraqis must not be angry with God even if he sent them into a battle already lost. "God Almighty willed what he willed," he explained, and with the Iraqi occupation of Kuwait, God had "rid the nation of this conspiring and filthy hotbed" in Kuwait.[17] Saddam, thus, merely served as God's scourge. As a peaceful exit from Kuwait was too humiliating for him but staying was extremely dangerous, Saddam had to involve God in his decision to stay put.

There is every reason to believe that at first, Saddam's claim to a direct line to God was cynical and utilitarian. The ploy did not work very well, but it was designed to neutralize criticism and increase his public appeal at home and in the Arab street. Saddam's craving for the admiration of the Arab street was well known to his lieutenants. It stemmed from two mutually reinforcing needs. In the first place, it emanated from his profound emotional need for genuine mass love and awe. In a 1992 Pan-Arab Leadership meeting, for example, a Shi'i leadership member who had just returned from hospitalization in Jordan told his comrades that everyone in the hospital had the utmost love and admiration for Saddam, and even sick people who were in bad shape would ask him, "How is Saddam? How does Saddam feel?" Those were mainly Jordanians, the party leader reported, but also Somalis, Sudanese, and Algerians, and even Syrians, including some "from the governing party" in Syria. He knew well how to please his boss.[18] Second, Saddam often expressed his belief in the power of the Arab street. He addressed the Arab masses above the heads of the Arab regimes in the belief that the Arab street could and would force the Arab regimes to support him.[19]

Nine days before the UN ultimatum expired, Saddam assured the Iraqis and the Arabs that if the Americans attacked, the ensuing battle would be "the will of God Almighty; the will of Man in it is merely obedience . . . to what God wants and accepts."[20] Indeed, the Iraqi president characterized himself as merely "one of the faithful subjects of God," meekly obeying God's instructions. In an open letter to Egypt's Mubarak, the Iraqi president referred to himself as "the slave of God" (*'abd Allah*) and as "the humble servant of God," who was an orphan born to a poor peasant family. "The good slaves of God" are more capable of understanding God's will than is Mubarak," he asserted.[21] On another occasion he described himself and his close associates as "a group of God-fearing mortals . . . aspiring to please the Almighty."[22] As far as I could ascertain, this was the first time Saddam used this expression. Whether Saddam truly believed in what he said, dedicating oneself to pleasing God is the most binding expression of religiosity.

However, the Iraqi president resorted to God only when he was depressed. In a meeting with his senior military officers on January 13, 1991, two days before the UN ultimatum elapsed, Saddam was in an optimistic and jovial mood for no obvious reason. Just in case he had to leave Kuwait, the Kuwaiti oil wells were ready to be blown up. But he was satisfied that his troops were in place and that his minuscule navy was ready to release sea mines into the Gulf, and he was celebrating the ineptitude of the Americans. "Would the Americans be able to do anything if we capture twenty thousand of them?" he asked.[23] He was brimming with self-confidence again. God was not there.

However, the next day, January 14, 1991, one day before the Allied ultimatum elapsed, Saddam remembered God again and added "*Allahu Akbar*" to the Iraqi flag. Why? Perhaps his mood changed suddenly and he became depressed again. Putting God on the flag may have been his version of an antidepressant. Alternatively, this addition to the flag may have been planned for some time as a morale booster for the troops. Whatever the case, this was his first public admission that the Baʻth Party's long adherence to the separation of state and mosque was over. From being confined to one sentence in the constitution, Islam had now emerged to claim a place on the national flag, the most visible state symbol.

Even a few weeks into the war, Saddam seemed to be still oscillating violently between elation and depression. When he was manic, and therefore very optimistic and confident, he assigned God no or little role. This was again the case in his open—and very offensive—letter to the American president on January 17, the first day of the war. A haughty Saddam made it clear that he was continuing Caliph Harun al-Rashid's tradition of cursing Christian rulers and promising them doom.[24] Feeling confident, he emphasized Arab history more than God's will. However, after a month in which the Iraqi troops came under heavy air attack and it dawned on the Iraqi president that the war was going badly, Saddam emphasized that the Iraqis would not "relinquish their role, which God has for them." Indeed, as the Iraqi president described it, the "faithful, struggling, patient, great Iraqi people" were "the true model whom God . . . has chosen to play the role that He wants and with which He is satisfied." In fact, he disclosed, "their place with God Almighty is getting firmer and more." God would secure for them an exalted place "in life and the afterlife," Saddam assured the soldiers who he had sent to fight a superior enemy and die for him.[25] Talking about the afterlife was another first, an unprecedented rhetorical U-turn for Saddam.

After a few more days of bombardment, things got worse. Saddam sent a secret message to the Baʻth Senior Cadre (*al-kadir al-mutaqqaddam*) in the armed forces. Quoting from the Qurʾan, he assured them that God had promised to guard his messengers "and those who believed." Therefore, there was no reason to worry. God had a purpose when he allowed such a devastating war: "He [God] is accompanying the Muslim victory with sacrifices for his sake, so that the [Islamic] principles will grow deeper in the souls [*an yusahiba nasr al-muslimin tadhhiyyat fi sabilihi li tataʻammaq al-mabadi fi al-nufus*]." Even the Prophet himself had won his battles only after paying a heavy price in casualties and battlefield setbacks, so there was no way that the battle would not be won.

Now that Saddam had God safely on his side, he could turn to the other reason for his message. Worried about mass desertions under the relentless Allied aerial bombardment, and fearing that his professional officers would be too lenient on deserters, Saddam decided to authorize the Baʻth political officers at the front (a Soviet-style practice) to punish soldiers for any offenses. He bestowed on them an authority similar to that of the field commanders, each according to his rank in the party. "Remember, my dear comrades, the manifest divine wisdom of God's Book," he reminded his audience. God created heaven, but he also created hell to deter would-be offenders. Saddam explained that he was following in God's footsteps: like God, the party commissars were authorized to implement the punishment aspect.[26] On February 24, the day on which the Allies' ground offensive began, Saddam sent an even more alarming message to the secretary and members of the party's Forward Headquarters of the General (Military) Command (*al-maqarr al-mutaqaddam lil-qiyada al-'amma*) in Basra Province. "This is a test [by God], and what a test! [*annahu imtihan, wa ayy imtihan!*]," he wrote. "Except that this is the test that Allah wanted in order to elevate the Believers' position [*illa annahu al-imtihan alladhi aradahu Allah li yazid makanat al-mu'minin irtiqa'an*]." In other words: Saddam knew that God wanted the Iraqi soldiers to die in agony in order to make them better Muslims. This battle, he also reported, was desired by God to augment the enemies' defeat and to "increase the weight and agony of their punishment" in this world and "the next" (*al-aakhira*).[27] One day later, at 8.30 p.m. on February 25, Saddam issued his order of withdrawal from "the Province of Kuwait," and "as soon as possible." This was very depressing. Therefore, God had to be there too: the withdrawal could not have been ordered one hour earlier, only at that exact time, after "the Believing Men performed what they did on the road of the tremendous jihad battles." In other words, after a sufficient number of soldiers had died.[28]

The grave danger that the war with Kuwait posed to the Ba'th regime pushed Saddam to introduce a related innovation. Until the war, the Iraqi president had never mentioned heaven or paradise in the context of an afterlife, but now he did. As he was in close touch with God, he knew something important about the afterlife. Throughout the Kuwait crisis, he besought his soldiers and countrymen to sacrifice their souls because their place in heaven was secure. The most forceful emphasis on the great future awaiting the Iraqi soldiers in the afterlife came in an open message to King Fahd of Saudi Arabia one day before the UN Security Council ultimatum elapsed. "You know, or rather I suppose that you know," Saddam warned the Saudi king, "that this war, should it break out, will have its own results and the Iraqis' sacrifice for it will be a ladder to heaven. . . . Where will the ladder of the Saudi losses lead?"[29] This promise eventually became a stock item in Saddam's speeches during and after the war.[30] On Revolution Day 1993, he promised it again.[31] Choosing a strange occasion, the party's birthday, Saddam promised paradise in a speech to tribal shaykhs.[32] Choosing a strange stage, Saddam had the party daily open its pages to an *'alim*, Shaykh Jasim al-Jubburi, who assured the party members that *shahid*s do not in fact die but rather are very much alive in paradise, and all they want is to go back to earth to fight and die again.[33]

Saddam's secret and public messages during the occupation of Kuwait indicated to his underlings that a new policy had been ushered in: God was in; secularism was out. They also indicate that under the blows of outrageous fortune in Kuwait, the Iraqi president set out on the journey of a personal metamorphosis from atheism to religiosity. When he decided there was nothing more he could do to avoid disaster, it seems that from the total self-reliance that brought him to the pinnacle of power in Iraq, Saddam shifted to a growing reliance on God to save him. The personal metamorphosis complemented well the utilitarian reasons that had provided the initial thrust toward Islamization.

The Kuwait Crisis and Saddam as a Mahdi

To legitimize the invasion and annexation of Kuwait, Saddam and the Iraqi media eventually adopted the motif of Saddam as a latter-day Mahdi. Now that the Iraqi leader knew what God's will was, it was his responsibility to see that God's will was enforced. The Arab and Islamic worlds were going through a profound crisis and needed to be purged of moral and religious corruption, with the Kuwaiti rulers being the first target. Had Saddam invaded Kuwait in 1980 he would most likely have purged the "corrupt" emir in the name of Iraqi interests, socialism, and pan-Arab nationalism. Now, however, above his role as champion of the Iraqi right to Kuwait and of Arabism, he presented himself as God's blazing sword that would redeem Islam and, through Islam, humanity at large. His hatred for Khomeini and the Persians, his animosity toward all Islamist movements, and his disdain for the clerics, too, occasionally surfaced in Saddam's newfound messianic mission.

Under the combined intoxicating influence of a dizzying sense of opportunity and the recognition of a great danger and the need for Arab and Islamic support, Saddam implied that he saw himself as a new Arab Mahdi whose sacred mission was not only to purge the Arab and Islamic world but, even more important, to reform Islam and lead the way to salvation. In Sunni tradition, every *Hijri* century a Mahdi, or "religious innovator" (*mujaddid al-din*), will come and renew the spirit of Islam. Some see this Mahdi also as a military genius who will return Islam with the sword to its rightful place under the global sun.[34] In early November 1990, three months into the occupation and annexation of Kuwait, Saddam elaborated on his role as the one who would resurrect Islam. "Islam," he explained, "has been transformed into a state of routine and bureaucracy, practiced by the majority according to the technical device of the minority," the 'ulama and the political Islamic parties. The majority of the people received from that minority routine instructions regarding rituals but were neglecting the essence. Religious guidance had been "stripped of the . . . basic spirit." One way to resurrect Islam was through *jihad*, which, having liberated Kuwait, would next spill into Mecca, al-Madina, and Jerusalem. Through *jihad*, Saddam insisted, the true spirit of Islam would return, and Iraq would lead this spiritual Islamic revival.[35]

The Kuwaiti rulers, Saddam pounded home, had been economically and sexually corrupt. This, he knew, angered God. The rulers of Kuwait hoarded so many women that "some of them became unable to recognize their own children." The situation had become so bad that one Kuwaiti shaykh wanted to marry a sexy young girl whom he coveted until his courtiers told him that she was his own daughter. Saddam branded the Kuwaiti rulers "Croesuses" (*Qaruniyyin*), after Qarun-Korah, the biblical Qur'anic magnate who angered God and was punished when the land swallowed him.[36] Saddam's preoccupation with sex shone through his messianic speeches. "You all know," Saddam reminded his audience, "that some Arab emirs and kings go to Islamic and Arab states . . . [where] they line up women to choose some of them for their entourage . . . and for the Emir himself. Is this the Islam that God Almighty wanted for mankind?"[37] The Saudi princes and their ilk were living in opulence, while in Egypt many people were living in cemeteries and in Sudan people were starving. "Is this Islam? Is this God's religion?" he asked in astounded disbelief."[38] Kuwait "has been returned to the Faith," he promised Egypt's Mubarak, after the emirs had forced the Egyptian girls "to become prostitutes and provide services to the rich Gulf Arabs."[39] "Our army was charged [by God] to purify the land of Kuwait from the filth and the traitors,"[40] he disclosed. The Saudis, too, infuriated him. "The princes of the ruling family are traveling abroad to indulge themselves in womanizing and drinking."[41] (Saddam seems to have forgotten that Iraqis did not need to go abroad to purchase alcoholic drinks.) Likewise, the Saudis "challenged God when they placed Mecca and the tomb of the Prophet Muhammad under foreign protection," forgetting that they had asked for protection from him.

Logically, then, Saddam called for a *jihad* against the *kuffar* (nonbelievers, the Americans) and *munafiqun* (hypocrites, the pro-Western Arabs) who are trying to "extinguish the flame of Islam."[42] In their modern usage, both expressions are heavily loaded with religious fanaticism. By far the most devastating way to defame the Saudi and Kuwaiti royal houses, though, was to claim that they had a Jewish pedigree.[43] Indeed, 'Uday Saddam Husayn's daily *Babil* found a new name for the Kuwaiti ruling family: "The Jews of the Gulf" (*yahud al-khalij*).[44] Another Saddam-designed way to revive Islam was to return to the Qur'an and the Sunna—"the action of Prophet Muhammad."[45] As will be shown below, the faith campaign later (1993–2003) emphasized the teaching of the Qur'an and the Prophet's Hadith, or Sunna. Saddam here was following in the footsteps of Islamic reformers of the early twentieth century, such as the Grand Mufti of Egypt Muhammad 'Abduh (died 1905) and after him Hasan al-Banna, founder of the Muslim Brotherhood (died 1949), who demanded reopening the gates of *ijtihad*, namely, allowing fatwas based on the two original sources of Islam rather than on later jurisprudence. Even though in his Islamic mode he was as distant from them as could possibly be imagined, Saddam also followed Banna and his intellectual successor Sayyid Qutb in two other respects: like them, he was a layman, and like them, he was highly critical of the 'ulama. It is very likely that he was fully aware that Banna's and Qutb's religious opinions, while not recognized as full-fledged fatwas, were nonetheless far more influential than any fatwa issued by the 'ulama. As Saddam had no religious education, though, his attack on the 'ulama, his ambition to take their place and to leap over thirteen hundred years of jurisprudence, was extraordinary.

Saddam seems to have gone even higher than portraying himself as Mahdi when he encouraged his National Assembly to equate him with the Prophet. The Assembly passed a law establishing a special committee to oversee the writing of Saddam's official biography. The Assembly rejected a proposal to call the biography "Book" (*sifr*), preferring "Life Story" (*sira*), the same term given to the Prophet's biography. It explained its choice by saying that the biography was intended to keep Saddam's memory alive "for hundreds of years."[46] During the occupation of Kuwait, a Ba'thi intellectual announced that, for the first time since the days of the Prophet, all the Muslim "believers" were again united under Saddam's leadership.[47] In 2002, Saddam's sycophants elevated their champion to the level of God when a party document detailed Saddam's ninety-nine "beautiful names," mimicking the Islamic tradition of *al-asmaa al-husna*, God's ninety-nine "beautiful names."[48]

To sum up, in an attempt to legitimize the conquest of Kuwait, Saddam presented himself first as the sword that would put an end to Kuwaiti and Saudi moral corruption, but quickly expanded his vision to breathtaking proportions. Overnight, he became the solution to the crisis of Islam, Sunni and Shi'i alike, the world over. The fossilized "men of religion," the Khomeinists and the Islamist movements, used Islam as a political tool, and the 'ulama froze it and turned it into meaningless ceremonies. As a result, religion had deteriorated and reached a crisis state, but Saddam would redeem it. He seems to have genuinely believed that he had the solution: a synthesis of the original soul of pregovernment Ba'thi modernity, spirituality, and free thinking, on the one hand, and on the other, deep faith and devotion directed to God without the mediation of the 'ulama and with Saddam and Iraq as the radiant core. Saddam's solution was, of course, chiefly a strategic tool intended to legitimate the annexation of Kuwait at least in the poverty-stricken Arab Islamic street, to defeat the Islamist movements inside Iraq but also in the greater Islamic world, and to reeducate the 'ulama or render them unnecessary. As he presented and very likely believed it, Saddam Husayn's Islam was a reformist, modern, and enlightened religion. Below this rhetoric lay his core attitude, which appeared more clearly later: namely, that his interpretation of Islam was the only legitimate one.

The March 1991 Shi'i Revolt

The Revolt

The Iran-Iraq War raged mainly in the south and north, and with it came devastation. When the guns fell silent, much of the north was de facto separated from Iraq. The Gulf Arab money had run dry, and reconstruction in the south was extremely slow, almost imperceptible. This created a deep sense of frustration. In addition, while war casualties affected people from all sectors of Iraqi society, the Shi'i conscripts bore the brunt of it. They served mainly in the infantry units, and these units suffered the heaviest casualties. This was another reason for frustration. It is true that most Shi'is saw themselves as both Arabs and Iraqis and were averse to the idea of an Iranian occupation of Iraq, but nonetheless they were deeply disturbed by being forced to fight and kill their Iranian coreligionists. Because the economic recovery was weak, unemployment was high throughout Iraq, and Shi'is suffered from it most, because getting a government job, while not easy for anyone, was easier for Sunnis. Throughout the Iran-Iraq War, in response to Shiʻi opposition attacks against government targets, Shiʻi activists were executed.[49] Occasionally, the property of people suspected of supporting the Daʻwa was confiscated, and it is not at all clear that this confiscation was justified.[50] Those acts exacerbated the sense of alienation, but the Shiʻi community resented it even more when many Shiʻi villagers were forced to leave their homes in the marshes near the Iranian border.[51] The many arrests and the executions of nonpolitical clerics from the Hakim family could terrorize the Shiʻis but could not prevent a backlash once the regime looked weak. In March 1991, as soon as the Gulf War guns had fallen silent, the most massive Shiʻi revolt since 1920 began and nearly left Saddam Husayn's regime without the Iraqi south. Within a few days, the regime's forces and party organizations in the entire south had collapsed. The south was out of Baghdad's control. As mentioned earlier, Saddam admitted his complete surprise in closed-door meetings, but later also stated it publicly.[52] During the Shiʻi uprising, Saddam Husayn himself, in order to mobilize every ounce of support among both Sunni and Shiʻi Arabs, predicted darkly—again, first privately and then publicly—that Iraq might split and become a "second Lebanon."[53] He admitted that such a calamity had not happened in Iraq for hundreds of years.[54]

The "Intifada," or "*Intifadat Shaʻban*" as it was called by the more religious circles,[55] was started by disaffected soldiers who retreated from the Kuwait front and who felt betrayed by their own leadership. It began in the Basra area on March 1, 1991, and spread to Suq al-Shuyukh the next day, then west and north to the holy cities. Then it spread east to ʻAmara and Kut, then north to Hilla, some 70 kilometers south of Baghdad.[56] By mid-March, nearly all the towns of the Shiʻi south had joined the revolt. According to antiregime sources, some eighty towns were involved.[57] When the Shiʻi revolutionaries took over, they frequently executed Baʻth Party members (most of them Shiʻis as well), and sometimes even their families. In some cases, even doctors and administrative workers in government offices were killed because of their association with the regime.[58] During the revolt, many exaggerated reports emanated from government sources, designed to cause panic and turn the population against the revolutionaries. However, many reports of atrocities also came from impartial observers and from the supporters of the revolutionaries.[59]

Within this regime-Shiʻi confrontation, then, was an element of Shiʻi-on-Shiʻi internecine warfare. The regime took full advantage of these atrocities, made them public, and amplified them. The shock waves that passed through

222

the affluent parts of Baghdad (where many Shi'is lived) and the Sunni Arab areas were massive. The regime fed this sense of shock and disaster with reports that 30,000 Iranians had penetrated into southern Iraq during the Gulf War, and that, following the cease-fire with the Allied forces, within 48 hours 20,000 more had flocked in.[60.]Those figures were grossly inflated, but some did infiltrate from Iran, mainly Iraqi Shi'i Islamists who had lived in Iran, fighting alongside the Iranian army. According to sources sympathetic to the revolutionaries who interviewed people who had managed to escape from the south, hundreds of Iraqi expatriates did indeed penetrate into southern Iraq from Iran. They were mostly part of the Badr brigade—the private army of Ayatollah Muhammad Baqir al-Hakim—and they committed atrocities and gave the revolt its fundamentalist radical image, which put off not only the Sunnis but also many Shi'is.[61] In the course of the revolt, the Badr Brigade soldiers who had crossed into Iraq and other Shi'i groups attacked liquor stores, casinos, and other sites deemed "un-Islamic."[62] I myself interviewed a group of four young Iraqi expatriates and one middle-aged one who had started the revolt in Hilla and eventually fled to Saudi Arabia, then became naturalized US citizens. The young men admitted that they themselves had decided to hang ultraradical Islamist slogans in the city streets, slogans such as "No to the East, No to the West, / We want an Islamic republic." This information infuriated the middle-aged Shi'i intellectual. He exploded and shouted at the young men, saying that because of this kind of extreme propaganda, many Shi'is had turned to help Saddam, and the Americans were reluctant to help. He himself had thought that Saddam's agents had put up these provocative slogans.[63] Thus, between inexcusable atrocities committed against real and perceived Ba'thists and the partial Islamization of the revolution in the streets, the Intifada lost much of the support it might have received otherwise.

There was one religious authority who could have changed things for the better: the ninety-year-old Grand Ayatollah Abu al-Qasim al-Kho'i. Kho'i at first rejected calls for revolt because he did not think it could succeed. To discourage the young firebrands who demanded revolution in his hometown, Najaf, Kho'i traveled from Najaf to Karbala in his black sedan to visit the tomb of Imam Husayn. This was on the fifteenth of the Islamic month of Sha'ban, the birthday of the Imam Mahdi. In this journey, he joined hundreds of thousands of pilgrims. This time, the regime was too busy licking its wounds from the Gulf War to prevent the *mawakib* (processions). On seeing his limousine, ecstatic pilgrims began to shout: "Speak to us! Speak to us!" Al-Kho'i immediately turned around and returned to Najaf, but by the time he arrived, the

223

Najaf revolt was already on.[64] When the Intifada started despite his warnings, he decided reluctantly to join it. He was old and weak, and served only as a symbolic figure, but many in the south admired him, partly because he was a great jurist and partly because he had not been political; with the right help, he stood an excellent chance of uniting most of the population behind him. Like his disciple and successor 'Ali al-Sistani, Kho'i was a moderate. Unlike Khomeini, he believed that the religious establishment should not get involved in politics. When Khomeini, residing in Najaf as an exile, supported the Ba'th regime against Iran (1969–75), Kho'i remained uninvolved and kept at arm's length from the Iranian ayatollah. Unlike the much younger radical Iraqi ayatollah Muhammad Baqir al-Sadr, Kho'i never supported the Islamic revolution in Tehran, either. Though a proud Iraqi (of Azeri extraction), he was not anti-American or anti-Iranian, and he was ready to receive help from both. However, when he asked for such help, both turned him down. Kho'i sent his elder son, 'Abd al-Majid, to the American camp to beseech General Norman Schwarzkopf to help the Intifada. He managed to cross the lines, but the American general never saw him. The French delayed him first, then he was allowed to go to the American camp, but there he was detained. Two very senior American officials admitted to this author that they did not know anything about this desperate mission.[65] An admired but nonpolitical cleric, Kho'i could have provided what Iraq needed most: a principled, popular, and peaceful leader of the Shi'i community who could prevent further atrocities and stand up to both Saddam and the clergy ruling in Tehran. He may have also been the only Shi'i figure who could have helped bring about true post-Ba'thi Sunni-Shi'i and religious-secular rapprochement, because he was essentially against the mixing of religion with the affairs of the state.

On the third day of the Intifada, Kho'i issued a fatwa prohibiting looting of private and public property and "maiming." He also ordered the burial of animal and human corpses that had been strewn in the streets of Najaf. He authorized a Supreme Committee, composed of nine leading clerics from different seminaries in Najaf, to act in his name; the committee succeeded in limiting the scope of the destruction within the city. When the regime managed to reassert control in the city later in the month, however, helicopter-borne government storm troopers disguised as Iranian Revolutionary Guards absconded with the elderly ayatollah to Baghdad and forced him to appear on television to denounce the insurrection. Kho'i spent the last seventeen months of his life under house arrest in Kufa.[66] His son 'Abd al-Majid Kho'i ended up in London, where he managed the Kho'i Foundation, a thoroughly modern, enlightened educational establishment free of hate for the West, for non-Muslims and non-Shi'is. He was in constant touch with the British government, and immediately after Najaf was conquered by US troops in 2003 he was escorted there by the Americans. A few days later, on April 10, 2003, he was murdered. According to a judicial inquiry, the order came from Muqtada al-Sadr. Muqtada never stood trial for this murder.

The violence and Islamization of the Intifada caused many who were critical of Saddam to remain on the sidelines or even help the government troops. Whether they were horrified by the atrocities or feared Shi'i or Persian dominance or saw in it a way to return to positions of authority, many retired and out-of-favor generals offered their support to Saddam. Even General Mahir 'Abd Rashid—"Rommel of the Arabs," as many called him—Saddam's in-law and tribesman, who had been under house arrest since 1988, volunteered to lead units against the revolution.[67] As for the more general picture, although almost all the towns of the Shi'i south were Ba'th-free, and much of Kurdistan was also in revolt, the Sunni triangle (the provinces of Salah al-Din, Anbar, and some of Ta'mim and Diyala) was quiet. The way in which the Republican Guard put down the uprising left the Shi'i south in a state of shock and panic. It was widely believed that tanks crews used Shi'i women and children as live shields when they attacked Shi'i cities.[68] Regardless of the veracity of this belief, the artillery, the tank corps, and helicopter gunships leveled whole city quarters. Thousands of civilians were rounded up in public squares. Many were executed on the spot; others were arrested, tortured, and killed.[69] Between combatants and noncombatants, the regime's forces reportedly killed between 25,000 and 100,000 people.[70] The Iraqi forces acted under the command of army generals, mainly from the Republican Guard, but the most prominent civilians above them were Saddam's son-in-law and paternal second cousin Husayn Kamil and his paternal cousins 'Ali Hasan al-Majid ("Chemical Ali") and Kamil Yasin Rashid al-Tikriti, RCC deputy chairman 'Izzat Ibrahim al-Duri, and the Shi'i senior party officials Muhammad Hamza al-Zubaydi and Mizban Khadar Hadi.[71] A tribal Shi'i general, 'Abd al-Wahid Shanan Aal Ribbat, commanding a Republican Guard division, was among the more conspicuous commanders who suppressed the Intifada. Since all the bridges had been destroyed by the US Air Force, Aal Ribbat's Shi'i tribe helped his division cross the river. The high level of the officials assigned to suppress the revolt was clear evidence of the extreme danger it posed to the regime. Never before had the Ba'th regime assigned such an impressive gallery of butchers to such a mission. At a certain point, when the going was tough, Saddam ordered the use of chemical bombs.

However, because the bombs were dropped from helicopters rather than from fixed-wing jet fighters as they should have been, they did not explode.

Participation in the revolt was uneven. By and large, the cities revolted. Local revolutionary councils took over, though coordination between the various towns was minimal. The tribes in the countryside were slow to join in. Most of them waited to see which way the battle would go. Some joined the revolutionaries; others supported the regime.[72] This rift may be explained in terms of the different degrees of religiosity and the previous relations between the regime and the towns and tribes. The tribes were less religious and less in touch with the clergy than the towns were. Also, the Da'wa had never had much presence in the villages, and the Supreme Assembly of the Islamic Revolution in Iraq (SAIRI), created during the war, was unable to establish a meaningful presence there either. In addition, since 1969–70 Saddam as RCC deputy chairman and internal security czar had taken it upon himself to co-opt the tribes and their shaykhs. His efforts, which sometimes entailed application of extreme versions of his notorious system of "terrorizing and enticement," were quite successful. By the 1980s, those tribes that had opposed the regime had lost their defiant shaykhs and Saddam had imposed on them his own supporters. Those who cooperated with him were rewarded, and many tribes became dependent on his largesse. The most troublesome marsh tribes had already been removed from the Iranian border and resettled in the Kirkuk and Basra areas. Some, but not all of them, joined the revolt.

Saddam's Message to the Iraqis

Some two weeks into the Shi'i revolt, on March 16, Saddam publicly addressed its existence for the first time. He was still in the midst of efforts to suppress the revolt, and his speech on the radio could be heard only in Baghdad and its environs and abroad because of the Gulf War damage to the antennas. The newspapers, too, could only reach Baghdad. In Saddam's presidential archive, the speech can be read in full.[73] The president blamed much of the revolt on the failure of communication and transportation as a result of the war. The south was in chaos, with no electricity or other services. The party's word thus did not reach the people, and the enemy controlled the propaganda field. By implication, Saddam put much of the blame on his party officials in the south. Saddam forgot, though, to mention that the United States had called on the Iraqi people to topple the regime and that, near the end of the Gulf War, a number of foreign broadcast stations had informed the Iraqis that their president and his family were already on their way on jetliners to Algiers. Saddam also forgot to mention that the strong impression in the south at the end of the Gulf War was that the regime was finished. This influenced many to join the revolt. Obviously, Saddam could never admit publicly that much of the Shiʿi population hated his regime to begin with and was only waiting for an opportunity to topple it.

The revolt failed chiefly because it had no effective central command. Among other consequences of the chaos was a shortage of ammunition. Large munition dumps were lying in the desert, behind the American lines, but when the rebels asked to be allowed to go there they were turned down by the American commanders, who had no orders in that respect and who also feared that the insurgents' forces had been infiltrated by Saddam's men, who could use this ammunition against US forces.[74] Another reason for the failure was that the rebels misjudged the regime's power, believing that the Iraqi military had been decimated in the war. Yet another mistake the revolutionaries made was assuming that the United States would not allow Saddam to use air power against them. These assumptions proved wrong. Saddam managed to reorganize the Republican Guard at tremendous speed, mainly because it had not been seriously affected by the war: it was left with some 700 operational Soviet-made T72 tanks. Moreover, the United States and United Kingdom did not limit Saddam's use of helicopter gunships. Finally, the rebels received practically no support from Iran. The Iranians were unwilling to be drawn into a new war with Iraq or into a confrontation with the United States. The Shiʿi rebels were on their own, and hopelessly outgunned.

Who were the revolutionaries? Here Saddam fed his people the party line. First, he branded the revolt "*safhat al-ghadr wal-khiyana*" (the Pages of Betrayal and Treason). This became the phrase by which the regime's propaganda referred to the revolt from then on. Who were these traitors? It was rare, he said, that "known people or from known families" (*anas maʿrufun au min usar wa ʿawaʾil maʿrufa*) participated. Many of them were widely described as "*ibn fulana*" (son of his mother)—that is, people "whose fathers have no weight." "In this description there is no [intention] to degrade the woman," he quickly added, remembering that he himself was "*ibn sabha*," as his father had died before he was born. Rather, he explained, it referred to people who suffered from "family disintegration . . . and absence of a chain of responsibility [*tasalsul al-masʿuliyya*] in the family and lack of a systematic arrangement for building submissiveness and obedience to the head . . . of the family [*ʿadam intizam binaa al-taʿa wal-imtithal ila raʾis wa rabb al-ʿaʾila*]." They were "riffraff" (*ghawghaa*). In other words, Saddam expected his people to transfer to him their obedience to their fathers, but this could work only with people who had grown up in normal families and had had decent childhoods and responsible fathers. The revolutionaries, he analyzed, had never enjoyed such an upbringing.[75] Strangely, when describing the revolutionary "riffraff," Saddam accurately described his own childhood.

In Saddam's meetings with Shiʻi tribal shaykhs in the poor neighborhood of Saddam City a few months later, the shayhks played his own concepts back to him.[76] In his March 16, 1991, speech, Saddam pointed out also that military personnel could not reach their units. They were good patriots, but they feared punishment for desertion, and this pushed them to join the revolt. This was true. What Saddam forgot to say was that the soldiers' fear of punishment was the result of his decision during the Iran-Iraq War to execute deserters or cut off their ears. The fear of such punishments was so great that many soldiers were not ready to push their luck and report for duty after their units were disrupted or destroyed. According to Saddam, there were also infiltrators from Iran, some of them Iranian, others Iraqis of Iranian background or Daʻwa members who had left for Iran. This, too, was true, even though the number of infiltrators was altogether between a few hundred and a few thousand. Still, as Saddam saw it, only "circles of low consciousness and shaky social structure" were influenced by them. On the other hand, he explained, the participation of "even one Iraqi intellectual [*muthaqqaf*] was not recorded." This, of course, was false. Far more accurately, the president reported that, with the exception of some in the marsh areas (Ahwar), the villages did not participate in the insurrection, and some even helped the government troops.

The speech breathes victory. By mid-March, most of the south had been reconquered, but the sense of surprise and shock could not be mistaken, either. What Saddam could not admit was that the majority of the Shiʻis did not accept him and his party as legitimate rulers. The Baʻth had a nonsectarian ideology, but in practice, despite their efforts, they had failed to implement it or to give the Shiʻa a true sense of equality. Their blatant secularism did not help, either: many Shiʻis were religious and resented it. From then on, Saddam's main ideological-emotional goal became to reduce Shiʻi (and to an extent Sunni) alienation by Islamizing the party and the state, and to do so in a way that would be as ecumenically Sunni-Shiʻi as possible. However, he failed again, and for three main reasons. First, his media and educational system remained biased in favor of the Sunni approach, though in a subtle way. Second, he treated the Shiʻis from then on with greater suspicion than ever before, something they could not miss. Finally, for lack of resources, and perhaps out of revenge, there was very little reconstruction in the south.

The Aftershocks

Saddam's Formula: The Unity of the Diverse

Seventeen months after the March 1991 Shiʻi uprising, the most traumatic event in the history of the Iraqi state until then, the president discussed the Sunni-Shiʻi divide in the most alarming and detailed, though not necessarily the most frank, fashion in the regime's history. The Eighth Regional Party Congress resolutions of 1974 had dealt with that issue more candidly and with far less sense of alarm and detail. The main thrust of the president's speech was an unprecedented effort to convince the Iraqis that the Sunni-Shiʻi difference did not affect the patriotic unity of all Iraqis. The very need to address this issue in such detail and urgency was evidence of the depth of the crisis.[77] "O formidable Iraqi people!" Saddam dramatically opened his address. "Our enemies . . . divide the Iraqis according to the sects/schools [*madhahib*] of the one religion [Islam]." The enemies were saying: "This one is an Arab, that one is a Kurd . . . this one is a Sunni and that one is a *Jaʻfari* [Shiʻi]." Saddam offered an alternative formula, the unity of the diverse: "We know, O brothers, that our [Iraqi] people, like the peoples of the world, are made up of a variety of religions and . . . nationalities." However, "our people are one and . . . one state . . . more than six thousand years old," he insisted. That he needed to rub it in again after he had been promoting the ancient Mesopotamian national myth since 1969 was a bad sign: the myth had not taken hold in the minds of the populace.

In desperation, Saddam threw out every additional argument that could demonstrate not only the unity of the Iraqi people but also, and most important, Sunni-Shiʻi unity. He insisted that in the Iran-Iraq War, Iraqi Shiʻis and Sunnis had fought shoulder to shoulder against the Iranian Shiʻi state. Saddam then reminded the Shiʻa that he was tied to them by a unique bond, invoking his alleged genealogy as the descendant of the Prophet and the Shiʻi Imams, Ali and al-Husayn. Then, he bitterly complained that his detractors were accusing his regime of discrimination against Shiʻis in terms of government jobs and development funds and that he preferred his hometown Tikrit. He flatly denied such charges and argued that just because he was born to a

Sunni family in Tikrit did not mean that he was biased. Rather, he was "for the formidable Iraq as a whole." He also brought up the ecumenical argument quoting the government-sponsored Shi'i cleric, 'Abd al-Karim al-Madani, who had argued that there was no religious difference between Sunnis and Shi'is in Iraq. The Iraqi president then plunged into the realm of popular Islam by reminding his audience that Sunni and Shi'i Iraqis alike were visiting the Shi'i holy tombs. Finally, Saddam reminded his people that many Iraqi tribes were split between Sunnis and Shi'is. Even al-bu Nasir, his own tribe, he disclosed, had a Shi'i branch in Babil (Hilla), Dhi Qar, Karbala, and Najaf.[78]

How much truth lay behind Saddam's arguments? That Shi'is and Sunnis fought shoulder to shoulder was true, and many Shi'is had patriotic sentiments. Still, they were highly ambivalent about the war. The number of Shi'i deserters was substantial, and barbaric coercion was needed to keep many of them from defecting. The sweeping denial of inequality could not change reality. Saddam was fully aware of Shi'i bitterness, but he had no simple solution. As for the claim that theologically there was no difference between the two sects, this claim was false.[79] Saddam's account that both sects visited the Shi'i shrines was correct, and the visits demonstrated some Sunni-Shi'i contact points. And yet this meant less than met the eye. To most Sunnis, 'Ali and al-Husayn are holy men and very positive historical figures. Visiting their tombs to ask for their intercession was and is fairly commonplace. And yet, unlike the Shi'is, Sunnis have never seen them as superhuman heroes or Imams. As for what visitations mean in general, they are indeed evidence of some cultural-historical common denominator, but this common denominator is easily eclipsed by negative components of identity. Over the generations, many Muslims, Christians, and Jews alike had visited the same places in Iraq where Jewish prophets were believed to be buried—Daniel's tomb near Kirkuk, Ezekiel's shrine at al-Kifl, and Ezra's tomb in al-'Uzayr, near Basra. And yet those were three different religions.

With respect to anthropological details, Saddam's account of mixed Sunni-Shi'i tribes was accurate enough; there are many such tribes in Iraq, and the intermingling of populations often helped soften sectarian tensions. In times of sectarian strife, Sunni and Shi'i branches of the same tribe usually treated each other very well. But unlike what Saddam argued, this was insufficient to create harmony between the sects on the wider, all-Iraqi level. Relations between Sunni and Shi'i Arabs in modern Iraq are multifaceted. They include many periods of cooperation and even cases of integration. However, Saddam's denial that there was a Sunni-Shi'i divide or a regime-Shi'i rift was strong evidence that, on the contrary, he was painfully aware of such differences, and that his earlier analysis that the revolutionaries were just riffraff sons-of-their-mothers missed the point.

The Regime's Political Reaction to the Revolt: The Party and Its Shi'i Members

The revolt left the Ba'th Party in deep crisis. This was admitted by the regime's open media.[80] The party's Tenth Regional Congress of September 1991 was convened to deal with this crisis. It elected sixteen members to the new Regional Leadership. Three Shi'i members of the previous Regional Leadership were dismissed. One was Dr. Sa'dun Hamadi, an economist and one of the most veteran members. He had had nothing to do with the failure to prevent the revolt. Another, Hasan 'Ali al-'Amiri, was accused of being part of the failure in the south. The third, 'Abd al-Hasan Rahi Aal Fir'awn, was also in the south, in charge of two governorates. He was later put on trial for neglect.[81] Only two Shi'i members from the previous Regional Leadership, Muhammad Hamza al-Zubaydi and Mizban Khadhar Hadi, remained in the new one. The places of the three Shi'is who were sacked were taken by six new members, all of them Sunnis.[82] From a Regional Leadership with five Shi'is out of fifteen members (33.3%), the new Regional Leadership now had two Shi'is out of seventeen members (11.8%). It was easy to find a few senior Shi'i officials who were dedicated to the party and who had been courageous and resourceful during the revolt, but Saddam wanted to demonstrate his anti-Shi'i wrath. Typical of Saddam, once his anger cooled, he tried to correct his mistake: the next congress of October 1992 and some subsequent changes raised the Shi'i representation, but not to the prerevolt level. The same phenomenon repeated itself when it came to senior nominations for Ba'th Party organizations (*tanzimat*), a party region combining two to three governorates. Sunni Arab party apparatchiks replaced all the Shi'i ones. Shi'i province governors, too, all but disappeared. This stark imbalance was addressed partially in 1992 and then in 1995, but there is no mistaking the crisis of confidence between the regime and its own staunch Shi'i stalwarts.[83]

The regime daily press reported much of what happened to the mid-level and senior party officials during the revolt of 1991: some were killed, some fought, some fled. Lists of the party's *shuhada* (martyrs) who died at the hands of the revolutionaries, between 1,600 and 2,500 in all, appeared in the daily press almost every day. However, very little is known about the many low-level "follower" (*mu'ayyid*) and "supporter" (*nasir*) party members. Their numbers were impressive: by 1986 the total number of members of all ranks was just over 1.6 million, out of which some 1,576,000 belonged to those two lowest categories.[84] The number of Shi'is among them, or that of members who lived in the south, is not known, but it was considerable, many tens of thousands— and yet we hear very little about them. What we know is that some fought, while others fled and waited in the quiet countryside to see which way the battle would go. Yet others fled north. Some managed to hide in plain sight, some died, and some crossed the lines.[85] The regime itself admitted that the party's militia, the Popular Army, made no significant contribution to the suppression of the revolt.[86] It would seem that when the revolt exploded, most of the Shi'i rank and file in the south melted away. Before the revolt, then, Saddam's inclusion policy succeeded quantitatively, but as the revolt showed, qualitatively it was a very limited success.

In a roundabout way, much of the blame for the regime's failure during the initial stage of the revolt in the south was laid at the door of the Shi'i party members there. The only senior official who was put on trial for neglect and failure was the Shi'i Aal Fir'awn. His name but not his sectarian affiliation was made public, but the public could not miss it.[87] The Iraqi general Ra'd Hamdani later described Saddam's postrevolt state of mind as being "obsessed with the possibility" of a new Shi'i revolt. There was apparently an atmosphere of "paranoia about the Shi'is after the 1991 intifada."[88] In view of the heavy price they paid when they were caught between the party and the revolutionaries,[89] this had to cause much gloom among Shi'i party old-timers. If it existed, though, neither the open media nor the classified documents could give expression to such a malaise. And yet the full members could not leave. They had already "crossed the Rubicon" when they rose in the party's hierarchy. For them, the die was cast, and there was no turning back. From the Shi'i majority's point of view, they were collaborators, and in the party a complex structure of discipline, threats, and rewards, combined in many cases with a sense of commitment, kept them in.

Junior members could either return later or stop showing up for party meetings. After the great uprising, the party experienced a crisis that the open media admitted. There is no doubt that many members at the lower ranks, very likely most of them Shi'is, left the party,[90] to return a few years later. The party reported that by 2002 its membership at the lowest echelons had swollen from 1.58 million in 1986 to 3.43 million.[91] Even though these figures look inflated, the expansion itself is not in doubt. It is likely that before recruiting new members, people who had been members before the revolt and who did not cross the lines were readmitted first. Then new recruits were added.

Why join, or rejoin? When it became clear that the regime had survived, a young Shiʻi member who decided to join could expect, from the outset, insurance against the whims of the intelligence organizations that were hunting for revolutionaries. Membership also held a promise of some, if limited, economic relief, which was very important under the international embargo,[92] and easier upward mobility. Finally, it is possible that, despite the brutal suppression of the uprising, some joined because they still believed that a pan-Arab party offered Shiʻi-Sunni equality. Because Saddam had already indicated, through speeches, new laws, and symbolism (such as adding *"Allahu Akbar"* to the national flag), that the Baʻth was going Islamic, this made it easier for more traditional young people to join. Such mass recruitment of less secularly inclined young men and women in turn helped push the leader to embrace Islam faster and in a more ostentatious fashion. All this kept the system going, if not quite on an even keel.

Shiʻis in the Military

From the limited information on the most senior officers in active service, it seems there was a reaction to the uprising in this realm, too, even though the reaction was delayed and limited. A decline in Shiʻi representation took place between 1993–94 and 1999. In 1999, not one of the five corps commanders was Shiʻi, whereas in 1993–94 there had always been one Shiʻi corps commander.[93] While one could still find Shiʻi generals in important positions (for example, Brigadier General Khalaf al-Khafaji, Commander of the 20th Army division, and possibly Major General ʻAbbas Hasan Jabr, Commander of the Fifth Mechanized Army division), there was still a decline in Shiʻi representation at that level, too.[94] Information about the Iraqi Air Force is scant. According to a Shiʻi Iraqi pilot major who defected in the mid-1990s, the number of Shiʻi pilots was extremely low to begin with, and all of them were removed from flying missions after the Shiʻi revolt of March 1991 for fear they would fly their jet fighters to Iran.[95]

Was the Sunni-Shiʻi Chasm Overstated by Open-Source Historians?

Is it possible, as Joseph Sassoon suggests, that many of the studies of Iraqi history under the Baʻth that were based only on open-source documents "overstated the Sunni-Shi'i chasm"?[96] Part of the answer requires looking at Saddam's punishment policy, about which Sassoon writes, "The [classified Ba'th] documents clearly indicate that Saddam Hussein was almost 'egalitarian' in his treatment of anyone considered or suspected of disloyalty."[97] In view of what was described above, this was not the case. It is correct to say that Saddam imprisoned, tortured, or killed anyone whom he considered to represent a threat, whether Sunnis, Shi'is, or Kurds. In that, he was indeed egalitarian. Had the majority of the Shi'i Arab community been as supportive of Saddam and the Ba'th regime as was the majority of the Sunni-Arab community, there would have been no massacres or deportations of Shi'is. But, for reasons explored in chapter 3, this was not the case. The proof of that is plentiful both in the open sources and in the classified sources. A fairly small number of Sunni Arabs, but at different times large numbers of Shi'i Arabs and Kurds, were real or perceived opponents of the regime, and punishments were inflicted accordingly. The clearest evidence that many Shi'is did not accept the Ba'th regime as a legitimate rule is the March 1991 uprising. The uprising engulfed all the Shi'i and Kurdish governorates, but not even one Sunni governorate. The open sources tell us that the uprisings were suppressed by mass killings, and that mass killings and mass graves were reserved for Shi'is and Kurds.[98] And yet, even though many internal documents of the Ba'th regime report the suppression of the revolt, I could not find a single word about this massacre. This does not mean that the massacre never took place.[99]

The 1991 bloodbath is unprecedented in Iraqi history. By comparison, when Saddam crushed a revolt by the Sunni al-bu Nimr tribe and other Dulaymis in and around Ramadi and Abu Ghraib in mid-May to June 1995, he was aware that if he did not want to lose the Dulaym tribal federation (*qabila*), which represented much of his power base, he needed to show restraint. The result was a few hundred tribesmen killed.[100] For the families, every murdered son is equally painful, but the different proportions may serve as evidence of very different punishment levels. In addition to his perception of the extreme danger that a Shi'i revolt represented, it may also be that the Iraqi president felt that the mass participation of the Shi'a in the revolt deserved a special "lesson," and that he could punish the Shi'a most severely and get away with it. It seems that Saddam felt that the Shi'is betrayed his trust: he had made great efforts to integrate (or domesticate) them, and they were ungrateful.[101]

There were additional cases of severe punishments inflicted specifically on Shi'i populations. The mass deportations of "Persians" (including Iraqi Shi'i citizens with some Persian ancestry) in 1969 were reported mainly in the independent Lebanese press. Another wave began in 1979–80, as reported even by the internal regime sources.[102] Likewise, there were mass evacuations of Shi'i marsh-dwellers during the Iran-Iraq War, and the number evacuated increased greatly following the Shi'i 1991 revolt. These evacuations, too, were reported in the internal Ba'thi documents. At first, the relocations of marsh villages were not motivated by malice. New research based on Ba'th classified documents shows that, at least in the 1970s, with the wish to relocate some of the marsh Arabs there was also a strong interest in bringing them into the modern age (and, no doubt, under state control) and concern for their well-being. An intelligence source even praised the marsh Arabs for being less religious (read: less fanatically Shi'i) than the people of Najaf and Karbala. That meant that the regime had sectarian problems with Najaf and Karbala, but not with the marsh Arabs. The decisions to evacuate marsh villages and tribes were made out of security considerations that trumped everything else but also, to an extent, out of modernization considerations, and extensive and apparently genuine development plans were made for the evacuees.[103] Later, during the Iran-Iraq War and following the 1991 revolt, the cross-border activities of the marsh Arabs presented a far greater challenge. Along with some compensation for the evacuees, Saddam applied draconian measures to deter the (Shi'i) marsh people from collaborating with Iran. Those measures ranged from public executions to a harsh siege and massive forced relocations: finally, in the early to mid-1990s, much of the marsh area was drained.[104] Such harsh policies were never considered necessary in the Sunni Arab areas. If one acknowledges that the Ba'th regime was Sunni-hegemonic, then both the mass antiregime Shi'i riots and the regime's draconian responses are evidence that Saddam's punishment policy was grossly nonegalitarian. This may serve as one indication that "the Sunni-Shi'i chasm" was not "overstated" by those historians who had access only to open sources.

Even beyond the suppression and collective punishments, the newly released confidential documents support the analysis of those historians who recognized the tragic "chasm" between the Shi'a and the Sunna in Ba'thi Iraq. All a researcher need do is ask the right questions, then study the right files. (Ariel Ahram and Abbas Kadhim have done so in their recent studies, cited in the above paragraph.) Only if a researcher is aware of the Ba'th's deep suspicion of the Shi'i *hawza* (religious university) or of the challenge that the marsh Arabs presented to the regime will the researcher look up the internal files focusing on those topics. Those files expose the fact that already in the 1980s, long before the great revolt of 1991, the Shi'i estrangement deeply worried the regime. As a result, the top officials and internal security operatives spent much time, intellectual energy, and manpower on devising ways to minimize the *hawza* and its influence and, in another realm, to seal the border with Iran, at a heavy cost to the Shi'i marsh Arabs.[105] In fact, as shown above, even as early as 1979 the Ba'thi leadership was fully aware of the existence of what it saw as a Shi'i pro-Khomeini time bomb in its own backyard.[106] Between 1991 and 2003, Saddam's closed-door discussions with his generals and senior party officials show that a new Shi'i revolt remained high on his list of threats (see chapter 6). All this may be found in the Ba'th internal documents.

The internal documents can be misleading because they are subject to strict self-censorship. For example, I have never come across internal reports of Sunni-Shi'i conflicts within the party. Maybe there were none: as suggested above, those Shi'is who joined the party and reached the middle level of *firqa* (division) membership, let alone more senior positions, crossed the Rubicon. As demonstrated in Kadhim's study of the *hawza*, clerics who were known to be collaborators with the Ba'th regime were ostracized by many of their sect. Most likely, these officials were regarded with the same suspicions and had no way back. If anyone had any doubt, the treatment of Ba'th officials by the revolutionaries in 1991 demonstrated this attitude. Confronting their Sunni party comrades therefore over sectarian policy or discrimination was risky. If senior Shi'i party members objected, for example, to the 1991 carnage, they could not protest, lest they be suspected of disloyalty and "sectarianism" (*al-ta'ifiyya*). Saddam's punishment of members of the party tribunal of 1977 for being insufficiently harsh on Shi'i revolutionaries was etched in everyone's memory. Furthermore, even if there were any disagreements with sectarian undertones, the inclination, even in the most confidential written documents, was to occlude such disagreements because they threatened the most cherished tenet of Ba'thi faith: the unity and equality of all Arabic speakers, regardless of religion or sect. A good example of the secret documents' silence is the case of the party congress of September 1991, which reduced the percentage representation of Shi'is in the Regional Leadership from 33 percent to 11 percent and completely screened out Shi'is at the level of heads of Ba'th Party organizations (*tanzimat*), the second-highest party level. No party document mentioned it as a sectarian issue: the public was provided with the names of those dismissed and those who were promoted, but people were left to draw their own conclusions. A scholar unfamiliar with the subject may not notice this steep decline in the Shi'i representation and may therefore conclude that all was well.[107] But all was not well.

236

More often than not, the Ba'thi documents are written in a politically correct language. Whether in public sources or in internal documents, except for fairly rare cases there was no criticism of the Shi'a as a religion or as a community. Indeed, even the terms "Shi'i" or "Shi'a," as well as "Sunnis" and "Sunna," are rare. The great Shi'i uprising of 1991 is called "*safhat al-ghadr wal-khiyana*" (the Chapters—or Pages—of Betrayal and Treason), with no mention of its Shi'i nature.[108] Saddam himself in his March 16, 1991, speech during the revolt does not use the term "Shi'a" even once.[109] Similarly, many of the written classified sources tell the reader that Da'wa Party activists were executed, without mentioning that the Da'wa was a Shi'i party. Rather, the Da'wa members are identified as "Iranian agents," "traitors," "criminals," or "saboteurs." To denote the Shi'i south, the documents almost as a rule use "the South" or "the Middle Euphrates," or similar geographic descriptions, rather than "Shi'is." Everyone in the party, of course, understood perfectly well that the discussion was about the Shi'a, but the preference was to avoid explicitly mentioning this fact.

A few additional examples demonstrate this preference to leave the sect issue unmentioned. After the 1991 Shi'i revolt, the *mukhabarat* outsourced the investigation of the reasons for the uprising in "Basra" and its environs to the University of Basra. The extensive report the university produced is otherwise mostly solid, but it does not mention the terms "Shi'i" or "Ja'fari" even once, nor does it discuss the challenge of the sectarian identity, probably the greatest contributor to the revolt.[110] Another example is an audio-tape of a top-secret meeting of the party's Pan-Arab Leadership to discuss the situation of the party in the south following the same revolt. Saddam was extremely pleased. The situation of the party and of security in general in "Basra" (a 90 percent Shi'i city) was excellent, he reported, as good as in Baghdad. (This could hardly be good news because, at the time, Baghdad was cause for concern.) One of the luminaries assured him that the whole Shi'i area was behind him: "The *south*," he exclaimed, "is your south and the people in the south are your people [*al-janub janubak wal-sha'b bil-janub sha'bak*]." The speaker admitted that there were "difficulties" in the "south" that stemmed from "objective reasons of some of our comrades" (meaning incompetence), but "we find there a people with the Leader, a people that is not neutral, at all! Under the worst circumstances, the people were with the Leader Saddam Husayn and the party." Saddam admitted that "the Pages of Betrayal and Treason"—that is, the Shi'i revolt—"were more difficult than the page that preceded them"—in other words, more difficult than the 1991 Gulf War.[111]

And yet the terms "Shi'i" and "Ja'fari" never came up in the whole discussion. Saddam's disclosure is embarrassing for him, and therefore I see no reason to doubt its sincerity. This is additional evidence that he saw the Shi'i problem as a formidable challenge. The same admission is implied, as shown above, when, without explicitly mentioning the Shi'a, the Iraqi media regularly reported on Saddam's extensive efforts to win Shi'i hearts and minds through the inclusion of Shi'i heroes in the Iraqi national pantheon, and the ostentatious financial support for the Shi'i shrines. By way of comparison, because Kurds are not Arabs, "Kurd" and "Kurdish" appear often both in open-source and in classified documents. This consistent practice could be misleading and suggests there was something about the Sunni-Shi'i rift that alarmed the Ba'this, so much so that they tried to paper it over in their documents and in most classified conversations. The terrifying specter, "the thing whose name must not be mentioned," was the possibility that with a frank and open discussion of the Shi'i-Sunni divide and ways to bridge it, someone might deduce that the apple of the Ba'thi eye, language-based Arabism, was a fantasy, a mirage.

As distinct from secret written documents and the open regime media, some recorded secret conversations between Saddam and his senior party officials and military officers regarding the Shi'a were not politically correct, showing clearly that the leaders were indeed fully aware of the magnitude of the Shi'i challenge. As noted above, in one of the earliest recordings available at the Conflict Records Research Center (CRRC), the regime's most senior officials explicitly acknowledge that "their" Shi'a were bewitched by their most dangerous nemesis, Ayatollah Khomeini.[112] A government meeting sometime in the mid-1990s exposed a degree of hostility that I had not detected before. It is not clear whether Shi'i ministers were present at the meeting. If they were, then their voice was not heard. Saddam and a colleague recalled a visit they had paid as young men to Najaf and Karbala before the Ba'th came to power. They had heard some prayers in which people said about Imam Husayn, "May God curse a nation that murdered him." This angered Saddam, as he saw in it "an insult to the entire Arab nation," which in fact admired al-Husayn. In Karbala, he realized that "no one speaks Arabic anymore." "The Arabs were accommodating the Persians and speaking Persian. What is that?" Saddam asked in disgust. He also saw a local market there called "the Arab Market," as if the Arabs were a minority and the rest of the city was Persian. This was "an insult," he exclaimed. In the same discussion the "Persians" were accused of trying to convert Sunnis to the Shi'a and even of claiming that they had managed to convert the pope to Shi'i Islam. In Karbala, Saddam complained,

"Persians" were trying to convert people. A minister told his colleagues that in Algeria, Khomeini was using similarities with the Sunni Maliki School to convert to Shi'ism. Another minister insisted that any Persian influence on Arabs was being rejected, and therefore the Zaydi Shi'is of Yemen were not contaminated. The whole atmosphere of that discussion was heavily anti-Shi'i, not just anti-Persian.[113] It would seem, then, that despite their limitations, the classified documents can yield much evidence that under the Ba'th, especially from 1991 on, the Shi'i-Sunni chasm was quite profound and the ruling elite was fully aware of it. The leaders attempted to bridge the chasm, but it was mainly their obsession with control and security and their excessive violence that rendered those efforts largely unsuccessful. Partial successes were scored in two areas, in party membership at the lower and middle rungs and in Saddam's tribal initiative.

The Shi'i Tribes Again

Following the 1991 Gulf War and the Shi'i revolt, the regime's tribal policy went through an enormous change. Iraq had lost much of its armed forces in the war. The March 1991 Shi'i revolt further destabilized the south, especially the border areas with Iran. The regime security authorities saw the constant stream of infiltrators into and out of Iran—some smugglers, others antiregime elements—as a meaningful threat. Around the marsh areas, where refugees from the uprising and army deserters mingled with the local Shi'i marsh-dwelling tribes, this became a particularly difficult challenge for the regime. They harassed army units and sometimes even innocent passers-by. The single most important event occurred on December 12, 1996, when members of the Shi'i guerrilla group Fifteen Sha'ban, named for the anniversary of the beginning of the 1991 uprising and the birthday of the Imam Mahdi, managed to ambush 'Uday Saddam Husayn on the streets of Baghdad and wound him severely. The membership of Fifteen Sha'ban had participated in the 1991 revolt and later gravitated to the marshes. The group attacked low-level party officials and army units around Basra before deciding to stalk a much more important target in Baghdad. Although they escaped the immediate scene, the regime managed to track down the perpetrators in exile in Jordan and Iran, torturing and executing many of the group's members and their families in retaliation.[114]

Beginning in the early 1990s, the regime embarked on a huge operation designed to deny the guerrillas their safe haven. Vast resources and precious spare parts were dedicated to digging colossal canals in the south, with the ostensible aim of irrigation and agricultural drainage. In reality, however, the "Mother of Battles River," "Loyalty to the Leader River," "Saddam's River," and especially the "Glory River" were designed mainly to curb the guerrilla activities. The main area drained was west of the Shatt al-Arab and the Euphrates, between Basra in the south and Qal'at Salih in the north (with al-Qurna in the middle).[115] The damage to the lifestyle of the marsh Arabs and to the environment was extensive, with an estimated 200,000 to 250,000 people uprooted, some of whom were sent to the Kirkuk area as part of the government's Arabization campaign of the Kurdish north.[116] Many others found their way to Basra, where they became a destabilizing social element. These operations did not make a meaningful difference in security, however, because guerrilla operations were low-key to start with and remained so afterward. Still, 40,000 Iraqi soldiers (five to six divisions) were dispatched to pacify the south.[117]

Saddam had to think creatively how to guard the border areas with Iran on the cheap. His solution was to arm those Shi'i tribes that had proved loyal, or had not proved disloyal, during the March 1991 Shi'i revolt. Until the CRRC archive was opened, there was good information in the Iraqi press regarding the final result of his decision. Eventually, the tribes were given weapons, including old Howitzers, troop carriers, mortars, and heavy machine guns (which some of them used against each other, to Saddam's consternation). The government also turned a blind eye to tribal smuggling operations, which the tribes saw as a semilegitimate form of import-export trade. They responded by generally keeping their side of the bargain, guarding the border with Iran against hostile infiltration even as smuggling continued.[118] The CRRC archive provides important details on the discussion between Saddam and his generals that led to a new security policy.

To police the border areas, Saddam wanted his military commanders to recruit some Shi'i tribal shaykhs, especially those of the lower Tigris, the areas straddling the Iraqi-Iranian border, to serve as guardians of the frontier. The commanders objected because they could not trust the (Shi'i) marsh tribes. Echoing Taha Yasin Ramadhan's comment back in 1979, one of the officers even said angrily that those tribes "are not Arab at all" but rather "*ajami*" (Persians). Saddam was unimpressed. When the commanders relented, they suggested that the tribal units be composed of a mixture of men from a few tribes each. This way they would watch each other and report on each other. Saddam patiently told them that he knew the tribes better (an undeniable fact) and insisted that the only way he could hold a tribe and a shaykh responsible was if the whole unit came from one tribe. There is no conclusion to the discussion.[119] Still, from the Iraqi press we know that Saddam's view, which this time was the correct one, prevailed. In the 1990s, all these policies emerged into the full light of the Iraqi media, and Saddam also elevated tribal values to the level of national ideals.[120]

In 2003, following the American invasion, Saddam issued an urgent order to the members of the Regional Leadership and to the military units relevant to the south.[121] He reported that the southern tribes had asked him for heavy weapons to fight the invading Americans: "They request support in terms of anti-armor weapons and medium machine guns." He was, however, very careful not to allow such powerful weapons to be given again to tribes, loyal, as he claimed, that they were. Whereas in the early 1990s, tribes were indeed given medium and heavy weapons, Saddam later allowed only government units to have such weapons. In the final analysis, with the US troops marching north, he did not trust the tribes. Thus, to defend Iraq, he decided, the lightly armed tribal units would work jointly with the more heavily armed state bodies. Saddam was always fully aware of the ancient rule that you can hire a tribe, but you can never buy one. The tribes are usually pragmatic, putting their own interests first. Saddam was right. In the end, the tribes were reluctant to commit suicide for him and remained on the sidelines.

Meeting with the Shaykhs

Part of Saddam's tribal policy was to meet with Shi'i tribal shaykhs to discuss the revolt, to express support for their values, and to encourage them to be loyal to him—and to deliver threats if they were not. One such meeting is recorded in great detail.[122] It took place in Saddam City in late 1991, and its main focus was on those who participated in the March revolt. As befitting an ecumenical leader, Saddam opened by asking whether he was not right to suggest that all present agree that behavior should be in line with the principles of the Qur'an. No one disagreed. After all, the Qur'an is accepted by both sects. He also emphasized the fact that all present were Muslim and "very Arab, coming from prominent families, shaykhly families." No one disagreed. There was no need to ask from what tribe or faith they came, he said, as long as those were the common denominators. Then he tried to explain his decision to stay in Kuwait and fight. That this was necessary provides evidence that the war was not popular. He assured the Shi'i shaykhs, "Why are we proud in the situation of [Imam] Husayn?" The Imam, after all, seemed to have made the wrong military

241

assessment when he decided to confront the Umayyad army in Karbala, as he was accompanied by only seventy-two supporters. And yet he decided to fight. He lost the battle, Saddam explained, but won the historical glory of a courageous fighter for his correct principles. He and his supporters died, but they were considered to be "the true believers, and this is why we are [read: I am] very proud of al-Husayn." Had it not been for his courage, he would have been remembered only as a son of Imam Ali. He died for his faith, but also for his Arabism, because a true Arab would prefer death to humiliating retreat. "He knew that if he withdrew this would mean that he was afraid and that his faith was weak, and this would be interpreted that as a man . . . he . . . [was] a weak leader in the face of insurgency." Here, Saddam reached the furthest frontier of Sunni-Shi'i ecumenism. He identified completely with the Shi'i interpretation of Islam when it came to the struggle between the Syrian caliph Yazid and the martyred Imam. Saddam equated himself with the martyred Imam and left no room for speculation: he explained that even though Iraq paid dearly for this, he could not withdraw peacefully from Kuwait for the same kind of reasons. This was a preposterous comparison. The Iraqi annexation of a sister Arab state was no lofty tenet of Shi'i and Islamic faith, and Saddam had sent hundreds of thousands of reluctant, demoralized Iraqis, mostly Shi'is, to die for his pride while keeping himself safe. Still, one shaykh supported the Iraqi claim to Kuwait and the need to demand this right "until death." The shaykh also insisted that the Iranians were not real Muslims and Shi'is, and that the Iraqi Shi'a would never betray Saddam. Saddam compared the Ba'th revolution to the Prophet's Message, insisting that in the same way that the Arabs chose Islam over *Jahiliyya*, so the present shaykhs chose the Ba'th revolution over the pre-Ba'th era. Equating the merit of the Ba'th with the merit of Islam was a bit presumptuous, but no one disagreed.

One of the shaykhs asked that Saddam not be angry with them. The shaykh argued that despite problems in March 1991 and in the Iran-Iraq War, he and his colleagues had supported the regime. Saddam replied, "I am not angry with you. Had I been angry I would have told you that." However, right after that he said, "I *am* angry because I know that you might lose your lives and the lives of your children because of the behavior of certain people [revolutionaries]. At the time, you covered up for them." So he *was* angry after all. The barely veiled threat was that turning a blind eye to insurrection would cost the lives of the shaykhs and their families. Under the soft kid glove of support for Shi'i values was a fist of steel. Saddam admitted that among 10,000 people, there might be some "bad people," but he wondered why. Who were they?

Then came the main message: "We must warn them [and you] and direct them to the right path." This was what early Islam had done, Saddam insisted. After the Prophet's death, he narrated, under Caliph Abu Bakr, Salama, a "false" prophet, had "declared himself to be a prophet." The Muslims brought the deviant tribes back to Islam, but only after "they chopped off the heads of 10,000 people with the sword." In this way they rid the Islamic community of many bad people, "including those who treasured the Qur'an." In other words, even people who followed the Qur'an but defied the Islamic nation's leadership were put to the sword. This was a false historical account, but it was necessary in order to justify the killing of anti-Ba'th revolutionaries who claimed that they were good Muslims. Those who were allowed to live, Saddam insisted, returned to Islam not out of conviction but rather "because they were afraid of the swords." This was an admission that he did not believe that the chiefs were loyal to him and that he knew that they were obeying him out of fear, but that was okay with him as long as they supported him. Indeed, Saddam compared himself to the first caliph also in his warning against neutrality: Islam, he said, was not saved in the days of Abu Bakr, the first caliph, by "neutral" swords. In Iraq, too, if people were not neutral and should "raise their swords to kill the sick individuals, I shall not be angry" he promised. Then Saddam added, "I shall blame you only if, God forbid, something shameful happens and no one is executed [by you]. Then I will be forced to blame you."

As to the question of who the revolutionaries were, one of the shaykhs explained that they were *breikiyya* and *mabrikiyya* (effeminate men, feminine-looking dancers). It was also suggested that all of them were *mutiyerchiyya* (literally owners of pigeons, a derogatory expression in Iraq for cheats, rascals, and arrant knaves, because pigeon owners used to steal pigeons from each other). It was also suggested that the rabble-rousers were coming from a very lowly social background and that they were called *ibn fulana* (son of his mother). Saddam, who thereby received back from the shaykhs his own earlier definition of who the rebels were, was pleased: "Thank God that there was not even one among them from a prominent family," he said. But then he remembered, as he had done before, that he himself was *ibn fulana*. Again, he immediately retracted his words halfway and explained that the Ba'th revolution needed every good person, no matter who his parents were, but that it was still good to know that no important families were involved.

What angered him most about the information regarding the rebels was that they were an effeminate kind of rebel. There was anger in his voice, but his words were angry enough. He said, "Whoever dyes his hair and wears makeup like women is effeminate [*akhnath*]." And he fired the most devastating weapon in his ecumenical arsenal: "Imam Ali," he said, "issued his first fatwa" in this regard. The Imam ordered, "We should climb to the highest point, throw him . . . and let him fall down head first." To Saddam, "this was a great fatwa."[123] In another part of the meeting, he could not forget about the transvestites. Again, he quoted Imam 'Ali, who advised how to treat such a person: "We shall begin where the problem began: and hit him [the transvestite] on the head." In keeping with Imam 'Ali's approach, Saddam demanded that the tribal shaykhs kill even transvestites who had no connection to the revolt: "I ask for your help regarding those who dye their hair and wear women's clothes. This is shame to the Iraqis and against Islam. If a Syrian or an Egyptian or a Moroccan will see these people, they will laugh and say: 'What is this? Is this a man or a woman?' The Iraqis are not like that. The Iraqis are real men." "It is a sin to leave them alive [*haram yutrukhum ahya*]." He would not drop the issue. "You should slaughter them with your own hands. Those people who dye their hair and wear red lipstick like women, I say you must slaughter them and hold me responsible for it." He just could not calm down. One of the shaykhs, clearly unimpressed with the "fatwa," replied, "We are afraid that this would be a crime." To which Saddam said, sealing the matter: "I take full responsibility for it [*birugbti, 'ala rugbati*, "on my neck"] and it is not a crime." One of the shaykhs had the temerity to tell Saddam, "We have more important problems" than transvestites, but in the end all the shaykhs agreed with the president: "You are right, *Sayyid!*"[124]

The details of that meeting are important because such meetings represented a common feature of the president's activities following the uprising. Many of the elements that appeared in this meeting appeared also in Saddam's public speeches, though in a muffled way. The homage to Shi'i and Arab values was important to demonstrate that all Iraqi Arabs were united and that the regime was identifying with much of the Shi'i historical narrative. Justifying the suicidal war against America by equating it with Imam Husayn's battle of Karbala was a stretch, but a clever one: through the ages, Shi'i scholars have debated the Imam's reasons for fighting such a hopeless battle, but all Shi'is admire him and mourn his tragic death. When Saddam implied that in Kuwait he was following in Imam Husayn's footsteps, the shaykhs likely resented this comparison, but there was nothing they could do about it. Invoking Arab values of valor was a vastly exaggerated claim: Arab tribes do not fight to the death just to protect a small portion of their domain. And yet it sounded reasonable to argue that one must not look cowardly. On different occasions Saddam alternately emphasized heroic intransigence and political "flexibility." In the Kuwaiti case, he explained that his religious ideals, combined with Arab "tribal honor" (*al-sharaf al-'asha'iri*), left him no choice but to stick to his guns.[125] Whatever they thought about this, there was no way that the shaykhs could disagree.

As for defining the rebels, presenting them all as transvestites and riffraff was an elegant way to avoid the truth: they, or many of them, were normal but frustrated and angry young Shi'is. As for Saddam's intense hate for transvestites, it seems to have been something very deep in his psychology and personal background involving his sense of manhood. He apparently saw their behavior as ridiculing Iraqi manhood. Saddam saw himself as the incarnation of a virile, masculine Iraq, so this was a deep personal offense and an unforgivable crime to him. Finally, the most important message of the meeting was a stern warning to the shaykhs not to allow members of their tribes to rise against the regime again. In many similar meetings Saddam demanded that the shaykhs kill or turn in rebels, deserters, and other offenders against the state.[126] This was a demand not recognized by true tribal tradition: if a tribesman's behavior is endangering the tribe, a tribe may decide to allow the shedding of his blood (*hadr al-dam*) with no risk of revenge or "blood feud" (*al-tha'r*), but the tribe itself is not supposed to kill or turn in the outcast.

Outsourcing the Analysis of the Revolt to Basra University

Some seven months after the revolt, the University of Basra, in cooperation with the Intelligence Directorate of the Southern Region, prepared a classified study of the revolt and the revolutionaries. Its importance was demonstrated by the addressee: the National Security Council of the RCC, the highest policymaking body in the land. Titled "The Face of Betrayal and Treason," the report was extensive and, even though unavoidably tinted with Saddam's politically correct terminology, it was the best thing that could be found in the classified Iraqi material.[127] It centered almost exclusively on the revolt in Basra and was based on interviews with 402 prisoners, all of whom had participated in the revolt. "Two questionnaires were used as a basis to gather the information. The target was the discovery of the nature of the participants in the . . . [rebellious] acts, and their motives." It was reported that most of the city-dwelling tribes in Basra participated, and the participation of the (forcibly uprooted) immigrants from Maysan and Dhi Qar (marsh tribes), too, was conspicuous. Still, most of the participants—tribal or not, immigrants or not—came from heavily populated areas, that is, from the city itself, not from the rural hinterland. The instigators, representing "20 to 30 percent" of the revolutionaries, were "Iranian intelligence and its agents who were [originally] from Al-Basra," that is, Shiʻi Iraqis who had fled to Iran. They "attempted to contact some of the leaders of the tribes and prominent persons of Al-Basra." We are not told how successful they were. A very important though not surprising fact uncovered by the study was that 60 percent of the revolutionaries had only an elementary education or were uneducated. But this also means that people with a secondary and higher education represented some 40 percent of the participants. Of most importance to the party commissars, however, the report insisted that "most of them [the participants in the revolt] had little national allegiance" to Iraq and Arabism. More seriously, "income did not have any effect on the participants"; that is, some educated middle-class people were involved. This was not exactly Saddam's "riffraff" and "sons of their mothers," even though, to be on the safe side, the report repeats these derogatory expressions. Further, "Most . . . had experience in the use of weapons." This could mean that many had served in the Iraqi military during the Iran-Iraq War. If so, then they were patriots after all. This whole issue of previous service in the armed forces is left out completely, apparently not by coincidence.

With regard to the age of the participants, the study reported that "a sizable proportion of adolescents and youths participated. The largest proportion was of young men between the ages of eighteen and thirty-five." Those who were not Iranian, or Iraqi "agents" of Iran, some 70 to 80 percent of the revolutionaries, especially the younger men, "were dragged along by . . . collective behavior and curiosity." The report admits, however, that "some were drawn by hatred of the regime and the Party." Why? There is no attempt to find out or to report the committee's findings.

The Basra academic-plus-intelligence team found that two developments pushed the rebels to act. One consisted of "objective causes, represented by the enormity of the American-Atlantic-Zionist assault on Iraq [in the Gulf War], and the role of Iran as an implementing and financing party." Another consisted of "subjective causes . . . failures [of] . . . the National and Party organization . . . linked to the lives of the citizens and the services offered to them, the [regime's failure] to absorb the psychological breakdown of a soldier during the withdrawal from Kuwait." Some officials were even accused of "corruption." The public, mainly in the eastern border provinces, thus succumbed to concentrated "psychological warfare," including "black hate" launched by Iran. There was no attempt to analyze why they had succumbed so easily.

Both the objective and the subjective reasons given are realistic. The general shock of the defeat, the large number of traumatized soldiers detached from units that no longer existed, the political chaos and disintegration of services, and the near-total failure of the party and provincial administration to reorganize security and restart those services were very real. (Indeed, Saddam had a few party officials, including one at the very top, removed and arrested, possibly even executed, for their failures.) The psychological warfare, too, was there: the United States called on the people to topple the regime, and Iran did its part too. Also, Baghdad Radio was silenced in the south. The report insisted, though, that the "rioting and rabble-rousing do not represent the attitude of the Iraqi public at large toward the leadership and the Party." If so, then the study remains silent as to why all those blows led to a mass revolt rather than to a mass voluntary community action to reconstruct the shattered system. In his conversation with the tribal shaykhs in Saddam City described earlier, the president himself provided the answer, to wit: in the south it was fear rather than loyalty to the Baʿth that had always kept much of the Shiʿi population in check, and when that fear was gone, a revolt occurred naturally. However, such a conclusion was far too dangerous to express.

The suggestions for preventing a new revolt were no less revealing. The study group demanded a much more comprehensive and tightly organized security organization involving close cooperation between the party and the *mukhabarat*, the recruitment of many more citizens to civil defense units, and tighter control of the border with Iran. Concerning socioeconomic issues, the recommendations were extensive. There was an urgent need for "economic growth . . . [better] education and communication." More specifically, the study group urged the regime "to deal with the black market, the rise in prices of basic commodities." Food staples had to become far more easily available. The private sector had to be supported so it could play "a leading role in service to society." Finally, the state had to "create suitable opportunities for work for the unemployed."[128] In other words, the existing socialist, highly centralized economy had failed, and it had to be replaced by a combination of more government subsidies and development on the one hand and much more freedom for private enterprise on the other. This was a remarkably bold recommendation and a politically risky one for the committee to make. Still, missing altogether were ideological or religious or communal reasons for the revolt. The term "Shiʿi" does not appear even once. Apparently, an explicit mention of the Shiʿa was too much, even for an academic study. This and other internal reports chose not to articulate the possibility that the Daʿwa and other revolutionaries had been created by Iraqi Shiʿites independent of foreign powers.[129]

The economic recommendations were not followed. In the mid-1990s, Saddam tried to encourage the private sector, but soon admitted his failure. As he complained, his *mukhabarat* breathed down the necks of new entrepreneurs until they chased them away. Under the international embargo, and with priority given to the regime's security pillars and the illicit purchase of new armaments,[130] unemployment could hardly be reduced and better services were unaffordable. Even compensations to bereaved families suffered. During the war and after, the regime made an effort to compensate families that had lost a son, a brother, or a father. The press placed special emphasis on southern (Shiʿi) families. At first, they were given cars and often also plots of land and loans to build their homes. Under the embargo, when there was less money and importing cars became very difficult, they were given some money and land, but the decline in support was substantial.[131]

New Security Measures in the South

The recommendation that was followed very effectively was in the realm of internal security. This was done with great vigor until the regime's downfall in 2003, even though the Baʿthi internal system suffered from a serious case of split personality. On the one hand, Saddam encouraged flattery and sanguine reports; on the other, he had to take precautions against a repeat of the uprising. The flattery is evident in the above-mentioned Pan-Arab Leadership meeting in 1992 at which a Shiʿi member assured the president, "The south [of Iraq] is your south, and the people in the south are your people." The people "are not neutral. They support Saddam Husayn and the party."[132] In the same way, in a meeting with graduates of a course for senior party members in 1999, Saddam was told by members stories that were believed to cause him happiness. According to one member from Saddam City, when a (Shiʿi) man received the news that his second son had just died in the war, he forbade his wife to cry before he checked and saw that his son was hit from the front. This meant that the son had died fighting the Persian enemy. The man then told his wife to express joy (*an tuhalhil*), rejoicing in the fact that her son "died as *shahid* in defense of the dear homeland." In other words, the Shiʿis preferred their country over their sect. Another member told Saddam all sorts of miracle stories about how the president's portraits were saved in fires while everything else around was burnt to ashes. Saddam was pleased indeed, and saw in it evidence of the Shiʿis' belief in their president. Another Shiʿi party member told the president that a (Shi'i) senior member of a *shu'ba* asked to execute with his own hands his brother for a crime that the latter had committed, and he carried out the killing while proudly wearing the party's uniform, so great was the devotion of members to the party.[133]

At the same time, as a 2002 party document reveals, cooperation between the party and the intelligence community was substantially upgraded, new party-armed and intelligence units were created, and surveillance was greatly enhanced. Extreme new security measures were introduced to control the crowd during the Shi'i commemoration days. The party branches (*furu'*) cooperated very closely with the *mukhabarat*. Every party unit had its strictly defined locations where it was to position its members in town and on the roads leading to town. Instructions as to who was to be stopped were very specific. Thus, for example, the 2002 instructions to the party branch (*far'*) of Karbala to prepare for the 'Ashura commemoration were prescribed to the level of each section (*shu'ba*). There were to be checkpoints on all roads leading to town three days before the occasion. "Evil ones" had to be deterred from even trying to enter the town. The number of non-Iraqis allowed in had to be limited. Buses bringing young men from other provinces (such as Najaf, Baghdad, or Basra) were to be checked carefully because the passengers might be "agents." Arrests were to be made. It was permissible to completely forbid young men from coming. Funerals would be allowed, but no postfuneral gatherings. No free food was to be allowed, as it would attract large crowds. Security detachments were to be positioned on the roofs overlooking Imam Husayn's shrine, and part of the shrine was to become a security command post. Each of the twelve sections of the Karbala branch was to be responsible for a section of the city. Female party members were to mingle with the crowd inside the shrines and report anything unusual. Their duties included arresting people who spread rumors, an affliction of a regime that rarely told its citizens the truth. The Karbala Security Administration (*mudiriyyat al-amn*), together with party security, would send around a large number of informants who would pray in every *husayniyya* (small local Shi'i mosque) and report on what went on there. The military was to prepare disposal teams to deal with the possibility of unexploded charges.[134] These reports serve as additional evidence of the regime's belief that the Shi'i population, or large segments thereof, represented a serious threat. In contrast to their complacency in 1991, in later years Saddam and his lieutenants took no chances. Such extensive security preparations could not have gone unnoticed by the Shi'i side and, while serving as a deterrent, must have also caused further alienation and resentment.

Chapter 6
Saddam's Faith Campaign, 1993–2003: Imagining Islam and Jumping on Its Bandwagon

We feel we need support, we need peace, so we pray. . . . Everybody seeks a refuge somewhere. . . . I turned to God.

—A young Iraqi

Iraq has always been a secular state and the Ba'th has always been a secular party. . . . But [now] we are aiming at a better understanding of religion as a factor uniting people.

—'Abd al-Razzaq al-Hashimi, a senior party official[1]

Voluntary Islamization and the Devastation of the Middle Class

'Abd al-Razzaq al-Hashimi's explanation in the second epigraph above represents the perfectly secular "Oldspeak," for it excludes God from the reasoning for the faith campaign. It reflects the reality of a crisis that necessitated a strong medicine, and this medicine was bitter for a secular party. After two devastating wars, and reeling under the blows of the international embargo, between 1992 and 1994 the Iraqi economy deteriorated at an accelerating pace. The press reported the failure of the regime's agricultural policy, which had resulted in great suffering of the populace.[2] *Babil*, an Iraqi daily newspaper owned by Saddam Husayn's son 'Uday, kept accusing the government of ineptitude since it was unable to arrest inflation.[3] In May 1994, Saddam realized that he

251

had to deal with the inflationary pressures before the whole Iraqi economy reached the point of no return. His first step was to take over the premiership and impose draconian punishments for profiteers, thieves, and corrupt officials, while simultaneously releasing various commodities from the government stores into the market at reduced prices. The result was an impressive success, but it was short-lived. The dinar exchange rate remained stable for a while, but in September 1994 it started to nosedive again. In late September the Ministry of Trade announced that to save government resources, most food rations would be cut by 33 to 50 percent.[4] This angered the impoverished public. Between February and March 1995, the dinar lost 36 percent of its value and, with some fluctuations, continued to fall. The public complained bitterly about food price hikes. For example, the prices of fresh food products such as eggs and meat were reported to have nearly doubled within a few days in late July 1994.[5] In December 1995, a letter to the editor of *Babil* sent by a "group of citizens" complained that while their salaries were 3,120 dinars per month, one kilogram of potatoes cost 500 dinars, one kilogram of onions cost 550 dinars, a kilogram of cauliflower cost 200 dinars, and the same price was also asked for one kilogram of eggplant and beets. The concerned citizens asked, "So what shall we eat?" The answer: "Eat air."[6] Inflation peaked in January 1996: within two weeks the dinar went from 2,556 per dollar to 3,000 per dollar, a drop of almost 15 percent. The price hike, which was unusual even in Iraq of the mid-1990s, produced massive public outrage and panic.[7] That the regime allowed such information to appear in the media was remarkable, demonstrating that it needed to provide a safety valve and win some credibility.

Under the international embargo in the early to mid-1990s the Iraqi middle class was crushed. People sold their furniture and other household items, sometimes even their homes, to pay for food and meet other basic needs.[8] This was one reason for a new wave of religiosity. The political uncertainty, the fear of another war, the rising crime rate, and the general atmosphere of hopelessness were additional reasons. As reported by a visiting journalist in early 2002, "More and more Iraqis are going to the mosque; more and more Iraqi women are wearing the veil. This is an unusual phenomenon in a country that has always been staunchly secular and is ruled by the secular Ba'th Party. But for Iraqis, struggling with life after two wars and 12 years of sanctions, religion is slowly becoming a refuge." As a young Iraqi explained it, "We feel we need support, we need peace, so we pray. . . . Everybody seeks a refuge somewhere. Some people here turned to art, I turned to God."[9] 'Abd al-Razzaq al-Hashimi, a senior party official, explained the regime's Islamic twist as a result of a perfectly rational decision:

> Iraq has always been a secular state and the Ba'th has always been a secular party. . . . But [now] we are aiming at a better understanding of religion as a factor uniting people. It's very important when the country is under threat, so that the people are united around the leadership and around the objectives of this leadership [Islam].[10]

This public mood, the beginning of which could be traced back to the 1980s, explains Saddam's decision to launch his faith campaign and "Islamize" Ba'thi Iraq. But what kind of Islam did the Iraqi president have in mind?

Launching the Faith Campaign: Qur'an and Ecumenism

The most revealing answer to the question of what kind of Islam was planned by the Iraqi president came in an interview given to a foreign journalist by a man who should have known, the vice president of Saddam University for Islamic Studies. In 2002, Shaykh 'Abd al-Ghafur al Qaysi described Saddam and his religious role as the university would have it very clearly: "He [Saddam] is our example, our school in religion and faith."[11] Islam has four "schools" of jurisprudence (*madhahib*), and the Shi'a is regarded by some as a fifth one. By adding Saddam as the sixth school and the one relevant to Iraq, the shaykh exposed at least what he believed to be Saddam's ambition. Through his faith campaign, Saddam endeavored to reinvent himself as the supreme religious authority for all Sunni Iraqis, and later for the entire Sunni Muslim world. While he made use of those Sunni clerics who did not defy him, his ultimate goal was to create a new generation of young Sunni clerics who would see in him their supreme religious authority, the only one able to interpret God's will. In this way, he hoped eventually to rid at least Iraq of the "old" Sunni clerical establishment. As for the Shi'a, the situation was far more complex. Maybe he hoped to achieve the same goal with them too, but judging from the evidence, when it came to the Shi'a, he was far more down to earth. His policy was limited to convincing them that the regime and the party had gone Islamic, and that the president's Islam was ecumenical because it incorporated much Shi'i symbolism into the national pantheon and because he was a great supporter of the shrines of Najaf and Karbala. He tried to promote at least one government-sponsored ayatollah to the level of *marja taqlid* (Supreme Authority, or Source of Emulation), but he settled for the Persian Grand Ayatollah 'Ali al-Sistani and his quietist colleagues. His demand of the Shi'i clerics was limited to preventing religious riots and antiregime incitement in the mosques and *husayniyyat* (Shi'i congregation halls) and during the festivals and commemoration days. He tolerated the quietist, nonpolitical clerics because had he destroyed them, it would have guaranteed mass riots at home and enabled Iran's Qom to replace Najaf as the focus of all the Shi'a in the world. Saddam structured his faith campaign accordingly. At a certain point, he seems to have begun to believe in his own story, imagining that he was in direct communication with God and that his mission was to introduce a revived form of Islam and adapt it to the modern age. If he did not really believe this, he presented a convincing front.

The faith campaign was launched on June 1, 1993. Significantly, Saddam used the term "faith," *iman*, rather than "Islam." In so doing, he continued Michel 'Aflaq's tradition of choosing ambiguous terms for the party's most cherished mantras. Like "*risala*," "*Umma*," and "the Arab Prophet," "faith" too can be interpreted both as "Islam" and as faith in the party's "message" (or mission). A little later the party's message was defined explicitly as Islam, and the faith campaign could not be understood in any other way, but at first Saddam preferred to affix an equivocal label to his new prescription medicine. Perhaps he feared that at the first taste, his party old-timers would find it too bitter, and balk.

As the first stage of his faith campaign, Saddam launched a massive educational effort to turn the study of the Qur'an and the Hadith into a national focus. Saddam's obsession with doubling or tripling the amount of time spent studying the Qur'an in all Iraqi schools, even forcing the senior party members to take Qur'an classes, was motivated by two mutually reinforcing reasons. First, he believed, with good reason, that the Qur'an could serve as common ground for Sunnis and Shi'is. Some Shi'i medieval authorities had reservations about a few Qur'anic *aayas*, from which, they believed, small but significant parts had been omitted by Caliph Uthman to mask the fact that the Prophet had appointed 'Ali as his heir.[12] And yet throughout the centuries the Qur'an still served as the most important common platform for both sects.[13] When he declared his faith campaign, Saddam implied that he was fully aware of it. When he met with educators, he explained that it was important "to study only the Qur'an and not everything around it," meaning later jurisprudence that to some extent separated Sunnis from Shi'is, the historical controversy that followed the Prophet's death, and the theology that emanated from this controversy.[14] Even more clearly, the president explained that he had chosen the Qur'an "because in our society there is more than . . . one interpretation [*ijtihad*] of the one religion [Islam]. . . .Therefore, we must remain with the most basic essentials" that represented the common denominator.[15] His earlier manifestations of love for Imams ʿAli and al-Husayn and the revulsion he expressed toward ʿAli's nemesis Muʿawiya the Umayyad caliph, in addition to his fascination with *ijtihad*, leave little doubt that as part of his role as *mujaddid al-din* he was trying to create an ecumenical Shiʿi-Sunni Islam. This was exactly what had happened in 1979–80 with his own nemesis, Ayatollah Muhammad Baqir al-Sadr. As is well known, part of Saddam's idea of Islamic revival derived its inspiration from earlier calls to "open the gates of *ijtihad*" and return jurisprudence to the Qur'an and Hadith, calls sounded by the Grand Mufti of Egypt Muhammad ʿAbduh and by Hasan al-Banna, founder of the Egyptian Muslim Brotherhood. However, Saddam's new Islam had two additional facets that were made possible by his status as dictator. The first was the imposition of Qur'an and Hadith studies to a hitherto unknown degree in Iraq. Then came the imposition of shariʿa law in many walks of life. At the same time, however, the regime still allowed non-sharʿi freedoms that most other Islamic reformers, such as Banna, the Wahhabis, and Sayyid Qutb, strongly denounced and would never have allowed.

The opening salvos of Islamization in fact preceded the faith campaign. In mid-1990, the Saddam Center for the Reciting of the Qur'an was established at the (Sunni) Imam al-Aʿzam Mosque in Baghdad. Its graduates were to supervise Qur'an reciting courses in mosques all over Iraq.[16] Furthermore, beginning in late summer 1990, after the Iraqi invasion of Kuwait, Qur'an reciting courses were given to male and female high school students during the summer break, and only in mosques.[17] By the summer of 1992, reportedly some 60,000 students were taking Qur'an memorization courses in mosques, taught by the center's teachers and graduates.[18] This was unheard of in Iraqi history. It not only gave Qur'an reciting a dominant place in the educational system, but it also placed students (at the expense of their school holidays) for months every year in the mosques, precisely what the 1982 Eighth National Baʿth Party Congress had sought to prevent. In August 1992, the president instructed the Ministry of Education to make sure every teacher underwent a new examination testing his or her knowledge of Islam.[19] This edict applied to all teachers, no matter what subject they taught—another first in the history of Iraq. At a subsequent meeting of Saddam with educators to discuss primary and secondary education, Saddam instructed the teachers to start teaching the Qur'an beginning in the first grade of primary school.[20] Since the president ordered that five million students in Iraqi schools should spend more time on the Qur'an,[21] the results were bizarre. Parents complained that the choice of verses (*aayas*) was idiotic. They were chosen according to their length, with the shortest ones taught, without regard for content. And the content was often baffling to young children. The newly recruited teachers taught six-year-olds about issues of personal status and the fires of hell. The children were utterly confused and suffered from nightmares.[22] An analysis of the content of those books found the parents' complaints fully justified, even mild.

By June 1994, the Ministry of Endowments (Awqaf) had produced 60,000 new Qur'an books.[23] Since Qur'an studies had been greatly expanded in all schools,[24] and since adults also underwent Qur'an recitation (*hafz al-Qur'an*) classes in all parts of Iraq,[25] many new Qur'an teachers were required. However, teaching the Qur'an is particularly difficult for persons without an appropriate background. Study of the Qur'an had been intentionally neglected under Ba'th rule, and because of its low status, few teachers chose to specialize in it. The Ministry of Education leaped to the rescue. It immediately announced that it would prepare 30,000 Qur'an and Islam teachers.[26] The academic level of the new recruits, though, was embarrassing. Up to December 1993, 11,500 male and female Qur'an teachers (at a minimum) were reportedly actually prepared.[27] The president ordered that Qur'an and religion teachers be given a monthly allowance of 100–150 Iraqi dinars over and above their regular salary.[28] This step elevated Qur'an teachers above other teachers and turned them into objects of envy, as the increased pay apparently redeemed Qur'an classes from their perennial inferiority in the eyes of students. To turn Qur'an studies into a prestigious subject, the Ministry of Education also included study of the Qur'an as a required subject on the general matriculation examination, another first for Iraq. The universities, a bastion of traditional Ba'thi ideology, objected. They saw in this move a misplaced emphasis and a waste of precious class time. They were supported by the private daily newspaper of 'Uday Saddam Husayn, but to no avail: Husayn père would not be swayed.[29] The obsession with reciting the Qur'an reached its apogee when prisoners (apparently nonpolitical ones) who had learned the whole Qur'an by heart were released from jail and their criminal records were wiped clean. The sentences of prisoners who managed to memorize only parts of the Book were reduced in proportion to how much they had learned.[30]

A spin-off of the Islamization of schools was the Ministry of Education's decision to separate boys from girls in schools beginning in the fifth grade. The parents accepted the change without complaint, but the ministry without warning instead imposed the separation beginning in the first grade. This move forced schools to hold classes in two shifts, often separating brothers and sisters. It also forced the schools to build provisional partition walls. Schoolmasters took advantage of the new setup to squeeze the funds for physical changes to the classrooms out of the impoverished parents. Parents had to pay 10,000 Iraqi dinars per child, and the public complained bitterly about this corruption.[31]

Senior Sunni and less senior Shiʿi clerics enthusiastically supported the president's initiative.[32] It is not clear to what extent their enthusiasm was genuine, but perhaps it was; after all, for both sects the Qurʾan represented the foundation of the faith. No less important, the Qurʾan courses and the enhanced centrality of the Qurʾan in Iraq's education and sociocultural life provided a major boost to the status of the ʿulama and their material well-being. The need for Qurʾan teachers became so great that professional clerics and even junior students of religion from both sects became a hot commodity on the education job market. Rewarded with the highest salaries in the system, they had little to complain about. This was one more reason for Saddam to initiate the campaign: as early as the 1986 closed-door meeting of the Pan-Arab Leadership, he had observed that the popularity and influence of "the men of religion" (*rijal al-din*) had just taken a significant leap upward.[33] During the faith campaign he acted on it: by upgrading their socioeconomic status, he could hope to buy off the clerics, and through them gain much-needed public support. In light of his expressed dislike of any and all clerics, this policy can only be seen as a cynical step: Saddam's strong dislike for "men of religion" did not suddenly metamorphose into love.

To equip the Iraqi masses with the linguistic proficiency necessary for Qurʾan studies, another part of the faith campaign entailed an education campaign designed to improve the level of adults' and children's literary Arabic. This step, too, could be seen as an ecumenical or national enterprise, designed to bring Sunni and Shiʿi Arabs together. As an added fillip, every letter and petition to the president had to be written in "pure literary Arabic, with refined style and fluency of expression. It is also preferred that the petition include quotations from the holy Qurʾan. . . . The body of the petition should also include well-known Arabic sayings and proverbs."[34] The vast majority of Iraqis were unable to comply. This opened the door to the services of paid petition writers, an ancient profession that had almost disappeared in Iraq with advancing literacy. Literacy is one thing, supreme eloquence quite another.

Qur'an Study and the Party Elite

In a mid-1990s notebook belonging to a low-level party member in which the member entered the party principles as he was taught them, I found an explanation for the imposition of Qur'an studies on the senior party membership. "What led the Leadership [read: Saddam] to teach the holy Qur'an to the senior cadres [*al-kadr al-mutaqaddam*] [of the party]," he wrote, was the intention that "it will be a [guiding] light in their work as well as in deepening the faith [*ta'miq al-iman*] thus boosting . . . the inherited spiritual values [*al-qiyam al-ruhiyya*] and the profound meanings of this eternal legacy [*al-turath al-khalid*]."[35] The other reasons he was given, and wrote down, were just as nebulous and grandiloquent, and all indicated that party ideals no longer sufficed. This imposition began with the party's top echelon, to set an example, but as the notebook shows, the lowest echelons of membership were made fully aware of it. The senior leadership alone, and all of it, from members of *far'* (branches) and *maktab* (organization bureaus) right up to the top, the Regional Leadership, was forced to study the Qur'an and the Hadith in an amazingly thorough way; courses lasted up to two years.[36]

In a private meeting with a minor Sudanese cabinet minister in 2002, Saddam made a humiliating effort to impress his Islamist guest with his born-again Islamic credentials. "Because the [faith] campaign went very smoothly," Saddam complained, "our Arab and Muslim brothers did not notice the extent of the upheaval [*al-inqilab*] that we caused in the life of the Iraqi people."[37] And he went into the details with a vengeance:

> Our pupils and students study religion from the first grade of primary school to the end of high school. All the judges [*al-qudhat*] have learned the Prophet's Tradition [*al-sunna al-nabawiyya*] and the Blessed Qur'an, and anyone who failed [the final examination] is excluded from the bench. And the same applies to the top cadre of the state and the party [*kadir al-dawla wal-hizb*], and according to the level of the results [of the tests] the fate of each of them is decided. And the latest issue we decided about is that the big merchants [*al-tujar*] will

study the jurisprudence of the *shar'i* interhuman instructions [*fiqh al-mu'ammalat*] and that they will be examined, and their fate, too, will be decided according to the results.[38]

Indeed, a mere few days before Saddam's private meeting with the Sudanese minister, the Iraqi president announced to his government in a closed-door meeting his decision regarding the merchants and, apparently, other businessmen as well.[39] This decision was made in preparation for his meeting with the Sudanese guest, but forcing the party's luminaries to study Qur'an and be tested on it came much earlier, probably in 1996.

On July 20, 1998, 'Izzat Ibrahim al-Duri, Saddam's number two, and many regime dignitaries participated in a celebration to mark the end of the third graduating Faith Class (*al-Dawra al-'Imaniyya*) of the most senior party leadership at the Saddam Higher Institute for the Study of the Blessed Qur'an and the Prophet's Esteemed Sunna (*ma'had saddam al-'aali li-dirasat al-Qur'an al-karim wal sunna al-nabawiyya al-sharifa*), founded in 1994. The celebration was described as part of "the Great Patriotic Faith Campaign" that had been "ordered and led" by the "Historical Leader Saddam Husayn."[40] A few months later, after the summer holiday, in October, 'Izzat Ibrahim celebrated the beginning of the academic year of the fourth Faith Class.[41] The mere presence of the regime's number two at the celebrations of a party educational institution was an indication of its importance.

Indeed, unusually, the Saddam Higher Institute did not come under the Ministry of Endowments (Awqaf) or the Ministry of Education, or any other government ministry. Rather, it was an integral part of the party's secretariat, alongside the party's military, financial, information, and other departments. By early 2000, the institute had branches in Baghdad, Basra, and Mosul and had already produced around a thousand graduates, many of them "full" (or "active") party members, that being the fourth and highest rank of party membership.[42] In 2002 alone, 241 graduates were members of *far'* and *shu'ba* (sections), or middle senior members. The students were middle-aged and older, as senior members would indeed be. They were given one or two years to spend full-time at the institute. There were also shorter courses of six months taught at the institute for many more party members that were sent by their party branches. All graduates received diplomas. Apparently most of them were given the study period of six months free to be able to dedicate themselves completely to study. A central focus of the institute was a Ba'thi-inspired or Saddam-inspired Qur'an interpretation.

Dissertations were dedicated to, among other subjects, Saddam's public record relevant to the faith campaign.[43] This was one of the fulfillments of Saddam's promise made during the Kuwait crisis to revive Islam through a new interpretation of the Qur'an and the Hadith. In this he followed in the footsteps of Sayyid Qutb, whose six-volume Qur'an interpretation was hugely popular.[44] Saddam's advantage over Sayyid Qutb was, of course, that he could impose his Qur'an interpretation on a whole nation. Eventually the Iraqi interpretation never came out in print, but the Saddam Higher Institute taught at least some of it. One of the graduates emphasized that the course, by teaching him the Qur'an and the Sunna, deepened "the original aspects of the party's principle."[45]

Three years later, in October 2001, 'Izzat Ibrahim himself addressed the seventh class of graduates. He assured his listeners that the Ba'th was not an Islamic "religious party," but neither was it (any longer) "a traditional revolutionary [read: secular] party" either. "We are the party of the Islamic Message [*risala*] and of the Arab Message," he declared. Then he added that Saddam, following in Caliph 'Umar's footsteps, would further expand Qur'an studies, and thus more such centers would be established.[46] 'Izzat sent two messages in his brief speech. By presenting Caliph 'Umar as Saddam's inspiration, he was hinting to the Shi'i members, who represented a significant proportion of the graduates, that their sensitivities did not deserve attention. 'Umar is the early caliph most hated by the Shi'a. More generally, he dealt the coup de grâce to Michel 'Aflaq's ideology. When 'Aflaq used "*risala*" and similar terms, he meant that Islam was a historical memory, while the party's "message" was a language-based secular Arab national socialist-humanitarian and thoroughly modern message to the world. To him, and to the Iraqi Ba'th regime until the early 1980s, this was the only answer to the needs of the Arabs and humanity in the modern age. Now, however, it was clear to all that secular party ideology was out, and "*risala*" meant Arab-led Islam with Iraq at the helm. Indeed, Saddam hammered the last nail in the coffin of the party's secular ideology when he announced, at a January 1995 closed-door meeting of the Pan-Arab Leadership, that the Ba'th leadership was no longer against the principle of a state that would unite all the Muslim world, provided that unification began with pan-Arab unity.[47] This was in fact the original position of the Egyptian Muslim Brotherhood under the leadership of Hasan al-Banna. The secular Arab national state was passé.

Nepotism and the Prophet's Legacy

In the early 1990s, two trends converged in Saddam's policy. Within his close circle, he began to rely progressively more on his cousins at the expense of the party's old-timers. On the national level, he embarked on his Islamic project. To legitimize his nepotism, the president recruited the Prophet. In an address on the occasion of the Prophet's birthday in late 1991, the Iraqi president argued that God chose the Prophet because he came from an exalted family in Mecca, that of ʿAbd al-Muttalib, "Guardian of the Kaʿba and Master of Quraysh." Muhammad's subsequent shining qualities, Saddam argued, were a development of "the qualities and features inherited from the Prophet's . . . family affiliation." The same applied to Moses, who received God's consent to appoint his brother, Harun (Aaron), as his spokesman. In both the Baʿth Party and the Iraqi state, Saddam declared, "no one should be allowed to emerge in the links of leadership" if he does not come "from a good origin," if he is not "the branch of a tree that bears good fruit."[48] Saddam, of course, and his tribe hailed from the Prophet's family. Since only blue-blooded Iraqis could be in the leadership, this was a farewell to Baʿth socialism, egalitarianism, and modernity. There was no response from the rest of the leadership, none of whom had a Prophetic pedigree or even a shaykhly one.

Limitations on Entertainment and Spirits

By 1991, some partial shariʿa measures had already been introduced. For example, the government established the Iraqi Islamic Bank.[49] In the same vein, the RCC decided to deduct from taxable income any sum donated to the poor, according to the Islamic principle of *zakat* (alms).[50] In mid-June 1993, Saddam announced the launch of the faith campaign[51] that would introduce major changes into the lives of all Iraqis. In September 1993, the Ministry of the Interior closed down twenty-nine of Baghdad's forty-five nightclubs and all but five discothèques. The remaining ones were limited to five areas in the capital: Liberation (Tahrir) and Aviators' (Tayran) Squares, Abu Nuwas and Nidhal Streets, and a street leading to the military camp of al-Rashid. The Iraqi president knew that outlawing spirits altogether would cause outrage even in a dispirited and tamed Baʿth Party and military. Therefore he never tried to ban the sale of liquor. However, the *public* consumption of alcohol was banned in all parts of Iraq, punishable by one month of imprisonment.[52]

In an interview with an Iraqi major general who had served under Saddam, the general reported that, since the early 1990s, while one could no longer drink in the officers' mess, it was a well-known secret that officers kept whiskey and arak in their offices in the drawers of their desks.[53] In the holy Shi'i cities of Najaf and Karbala and in the Sunni quarter of A'zamiyya, where important mosques are to be found, spirits of all kinds were completely out of bounds. Only non-Muslims were allowed to sell spirits. Liquor stores were not allowed within 150 meters of mosques, schools, and hospitals, and strangely, such stores had to bear "Iraqi or Arab names" rather than Western ones.[54] All the same, however, alcoholic drinks were legally available in all the other towns, including the major towns of Mosul and Basra.

Mosques or Butter?

In a country devastated by two wars and a massive revolt in which many family homes were destroyed and much of the infrastructure was ruined, in a country under severe international embargo, a huge construction effort had nevertheless been under way since 1991 as a major dimension of Saddam's Islamization of the country. The building effort was dedicated almost exclusively to the construction of new mosques and religious institutions. The most elaborate mosques were the costly President Leader Friday Mosques (*jawami' al-ra'is al-qa'id*), built almost solely in Sunni governorates.[55] Probably the most ambitious of those mosques was the Baghdad "Mother of All Battles" Mosque (*jami' umm al-ma'arik*). The cornerstone was laid in 1993,[56] and the mosque was completed in 2001. The mosque's structure is brimming with defiant anti-American symbolism. The minarets are built to resemble ballistic missiles sitting on launch pads. There are eight of them, four each 37 meters high and another four 28 meters high, resembling huge machine gun barrels aimed at the US and British warplanes flying over the no-fly zones. There were also references to Saddam's biography: the idea was to commemorate in this way Saddam's birthday on April 28, 1937. Dhahir al-'Anni, director of information for the mosque, also reported that "over three years, the president gave us a total of 28 liters of his own blood, which has been mixed with chemicals to produce [the ink for] this handwritten Qur'an of 605 pages." The construction of the mosques was characterized as part of the faith campaign. On the huge dome of the mosque the word "*La*" (No) was inscribed, for American pilots to see and dread. As pointed out by Al-'Anni, this was "the biggest 'no' ever given to the Americans." On a massive stone bas-relief showing the map of the Arab homeland, Iraq appears as a large rock carved with the portraits of the martyrs who gave their lives in the Mother of All Battles. It would seem that this was meant to indicate that Iraq was the only Arab country that opposed world imperialism and, of course, paid dearly for it.[57] Following the downfall of the Ba'th regime the name was changed to Umm al-Qura, the Mother of All Villages, the same name as the one given to the city of Mecca, and it remained in Sunni hands, serving as the headquarters of the Muslim 'Ulama Committee (Hay'at al-'Ulama al-Muslimin), a radical legal Islamist anti-American group.

In May 1994, Saddam decided to embark on another ambitious and costly project to establish the Great State Mosque (*jami' al-dawla al-kabir*), meant to be one of the biggest in the world, on the grounds of the Horsemanship Club (*nadi al-Furusiyya*) in al-Mansur quarter in the heart of Baghdad. It was supposed to have a prayer space for 20,000 people. The mosque, Saddam explained, ought to be "commensurate with Baghdad's pan-Arab and spiritual place" in the eyes of the Arabs and Muslims.[58] In the army, although the officers were not instructed to study the Qur'an, every unit from the level of the brigade up was encouraged to build a mosque at its permanent camp, a project that had never been embarked on before the 1990s.[59] The president also instructed the Horsemanship Club to stop all gambling, as it went contrary to "our deep-rooted Arab [read: Islamic] traditions."[60] The gigantic mosque was never completed. This did not mean that the regime neglected less extravagant projects of building and renovating mosques. Many scores of mosques, mostly in the Sunni areas, were promised, and quite a few were built, some in honor of Saddam's lieutenants.[61] Nor were the clerics neglected: to celebrate the Ba'th Party's birthday, in 1992 the president allotted 283 plots of land for Muslim but also for some Christian clerics.[62]

In 2002, one year before the collapse of the Ba'th regime, Shaykh 'Abd al-Ghafur al Qaysi, vice president of Saddam University for Islamic Studies in Baghdad, exposed the extreme degree of the regime's commitment to honor the president and his obsession with building mosques at the expense of the devastated Iraqi economy. He boasted that every year, in honor of the Iraqi leader's birthday on April 28, a new mosque was inaugurated and construction was started on another one.[63] It is noteworthy, though, that in addition to the frenzied construction of new mosques, Saddam also made sure that a few new churches were built and others were repaired.[64] In that as well as in a few other important aspects, he was very different from people like Banna, Qutb, Mulla Omar, or Osama bin Laden. Saddam expressed his wish to demonstrate that he was not a Muslim bigot also by delivering a special speech every Christmas.[65]

Other Islamic Institutions

Already in 1985 the regime had established the mixed Sunni-Shi'i Higher Islamic Institute for the Preparation of Imams and Khatibs (preachers) under the same Ministry of Endowments.[66] Its goal was to prepare the clerics in a way that "will be in harmony with the aims of the [Ba'th] Revolution." To sift out any undesirable element like Da'wa sympathizers and other unreliable people, it was stipulated that only Iraqis both of whose parents were Iraqi by birth could become students.[67] There was no difficulty in finding Iranian ancestry for undesirable persons. Under the faith campaign, in addition to the Ba'th Party's Saddam Higher Institute for the Study of the Blessed Qur'an and the Prophet's Esteemed Sunnah, which was designed mostly for senior party members, Saddam established two further religious institutions. The two had wider, state-related responsibilities. The earlier one was Saddam University for Islamic Studies (*jami'at saddam lil-'ulum al-islamiyya*), which opened its doors even before the faith campaign got under way, in November 1989, and fell under the responsibility of the Ministry of Higher Education.[68] The subjects studied were Arabic language, Qur'an sciences, jurisprudence, and "Islamic thinking," designed to undercut the opposition Sunni-Salafi trends. The most important faculty was the one dedicated to *fiqh* (jurisprudence). In June 1998, in the presence of most of the top leadership, the university celebrated the graduation of its sixth class.[69]

Saddam saw the university as his prize Islamic project. He allocated substantial sums to it, the best-known professors and academically inclined clerics were recruited, their salaries were the highest for professorial employees in the land, and the student-teacher ratio (around thirty students per professor) was one of the best, if not the best, in the humanities and social studies. Saddam University for Islamic Studies was a small institution. In the academic year 1992–93, it had only three faculties, twenty-six teachers, and 764 students (including 126 from other countries), but the students were hand-picked, and with a select teaching staff and generous budget, it was indeed an elite school.[70] When the president of the university needed funds, he could go directly to the very top and receive all that he requested.[71] To prepare a suitable student body for this university, beginning in 1991 every year some ten new middle and high-school madrasas were opened in the Sunni areas.[72] These schools, too, provided many well-paying new jobs for Sunni 'ulama. The best graduates could continue their studies at Saddam University for Islamic Studies.[73] In this way the regime was preparing the next generation of Sunni 'ulama Ba'th style or, more accurately, Saddam style.

In 1994 or 1995, the regime established a third institution of higher education, Saddam's College for the Preparation of Imams and Khatibs (preachers). The first class, called "*al-mujahid Saddam Husayn*," graduated from the college in 1998.[74] This was all part of Saddam's plan to eventually populate with his own Islamic clones all the Sunni religious institutions, from mosques, through state courts (which included 'ulama as *qadhi*s), to local muftis, who provided religious jurisprudence. (By this time, there was no longer a Grand Mufti of Iraq.) It was a systematic and hugely expensive scheme or industry, one that drew on all the resources of the state, and it had a good chance of success, but it was stopped in its tracks by the American invasion.

The Faith Campaign and Barbaric Penalties

Beginning in 1991, the deepening economic crisis gave birth to a strikingly high level of crime. The economic disintegration led to inflation, which in turn led to price hikes that the government was unable to control. In both cases, the regime's response was extreme violence, in part explained in terms of a claim to shar'i legitimacy. Theft and robbery became so rampant that the party established a special branch called The People's Guards (*nawatir al-Sha'b*). The Guards patrolled the streets and reportedly succeeded in arresting thieves, who were summarily executed.[75] Reports about widespread official bribe offenses, too, became routine.[76] It is hardly surprising that the government found a scapegoat on whom to blame the runaway inflation: the merchants. Almost daily cartoons in the press showed the fat merchant "*abu jasha' al-hisari*" ("the Father of Greed from the Boycott") being chased by the good, hard-working people.[77] In 1992, twenty-one merchants were hanged on their own businesses' doors by 'Uday 's bodyguards for profiteering without any legal procedure.[78] Crime, fictional crime, and moral offenses were the issues over which the faith campaign showed its sinister face. In a closed-door cabinet meeting in August 1994, Saddam admitted that his humanism was misplaced when he had at first rejected the suggestion of his colleagues in the "leadership" to do as the Qur'an orders: "Cut off the hand of the male and female thief" (*iqta'u yad al-sariq wal-sariqa*).[79] The "leadership" also suggested a non-Islamic punishment, to cut off an ear of a military deserter, and if he deserted again, to cut off his second ear. The mutilations were to be performed with a knife, apparently on the spot under field conditions. Saddam initially objected because "I knew that we shall kill between five and six thousand persons [this way]," but eventually, he relented. Returning to his favorite theme, Saddam argued that, like God, he too realized that without deterring punishments, people would misbehave. God created heaven, but this did not suffice, so he then created hell, together with severe punishments in this world. People needed a brutal threat to behave. The president reported that the new law was crowned with great success, as thousands of army deserters immediately reported for duty. He was happy to hear from a minister that the gory punishments were displayed on television to increase their deterrence value.[80] Saddam was happy, but the reports he received may have been exaggerated. Owing to the general chaos and the regime's relatively weak control in the southern provinces, many deserters probably managed to slip through the government's dragnet.

RCC Decree No. 59 of June 4, 1994, was the first in a host of shar'i laws to be introduced, with the result that the Iraqi Penal Code was largely transformed. According to the new law, with very few exceptions the punishment for robbery and car theft would be amputation of the hand at the wrist. "In case of repetition, the left foot should be amputated at the ankle."[81] This was actually to be seen as great leniency; just before that, the punishment for car theft was death.[82] A few days after the first enactment, the government decided that unauthorized money changers were, in fact, thieves, and as such they too were to be punished in the same way.[83] Later, Decree No. 92 of July 21, 1994, stipulated that forgers of official documents, too, being the same as thieves, would be punishable by life imprisonment or amputation.[84] By July 1994, the amputation of the right hand was applied to more cases of "thieves," such as profiteering bakers.[85] To differentiate between a war hero and a car thief, both having lost a hand or a leg, on August 18, 1994, the RCC issued Decree No. 109 to the effect that any thief whose hand was amputated "shall be [also] tattooed between his eyebrows." As befitted a civilized regime, the amputation and branding by knife were to be replaced by hospital operations.[86] In March 1994, prostitution was outlawed: all parties engaged in prostitution were to be executed.[87] This, too, may serve as indication that the phenomenon had existed on a fairly wide scale. Saddam's elder son 'Uday, who owned a newspaper, a magazine, and a television station, was conspicuous among the supporters of the amputation and execution laws. 'Uday's enthusiasm for draconic punishments was further demonstrated when, a few weeks after the prostitution law was enacted, he complained that the new law, according to which not only the "working girls" but also the "madam" of a "house of ill repute" (*bayt al-da'ara*) ought to be executed, had never been applied. He demanded actual death sentences and executions.[88] Indeed, on August 27, 1994, the RCC enacted a new Decree No. 118, repeating the previous decree punishing by death anyone "organizing a group" for prostitution.[89] Earlier, in the spring of 1990, the RCC had issued a short-lived decree allowing the killing of women by male relatives to defend the family's honor.[90] In 1994, 'Uday's lust for blood was not satisfied before he mourned the abrogation of the 1990 law and called for its reinstitution. Accordingly, he demanded the killing of adulteresses (though not adulterers), as this would "reflect our age-old Iraqi family tradition, which makes us, as Iraqis, stand out among our [Arab] brethren."[91] In other words, 'Uday was not ready to leave the murders to individual fathers, brothers, or cousins of the "offending" woman, as was the tribal tradition; he wanted the state to do the killings. In the second half of the 1990s, whenever 'Uday felt an urge to taste blood, his private militia, Saddam's *Fida'iyyin*, would round up young women, whom they would then accuse of prostitution and behead in public, often in front of the women's homes. Sometimes, representatives of the General Union of Iraqi Women would be present. This practice gained wide notoriety in Iraq, as it was meant to do, and served as a powerful deterrent against any opposition activity. Most people believed, probably correctly, that the girls were not prostitutes at all, but rather that some of their male relatives were active in the opposition.[92]

The Treatment of Sunni 'Ulama and Activists

Beginning in 1970, the ruling party created an extensive security system designed to watch over both Sunni and Shi'i clerics and activists.[93] A 1980 "top-secret" memorandum from the Bureau of the North Organization (*maktab tanzim al-shimal*) to the Bureau of the Regional Leadership (*maktab amanat al-qutr*) detailed ideas for implementing decisions that had been made by an extraordinary meeting of the Supreme Council for State Security (*al-majlis al-a'la li-amn al-dawla*) to exercise more stringent control over people (other than 'ulama) with religious inclinations. Chiefly, the memorandum suggested regularly following college and university students who had expressed "religious inclinations [*muyul diniyya*]," and also any peasants and workers so inclined. When such were identified, the recommendation was "to limit and influence the more outstanding elements among them"—in other words, limit their unhelpful activity—and then "to attract them [*kasbuhum*] to the ranks of the party." The party should collect all available information about each of these people: their families, personal history, political and social background. The party's Student Bureaus would be instructed to befriend those people and help them with solving their material problems, and in this way draw them into "patriotic" (*wataniyya*) activities, that is, secular Ba'thi activities. Those elements that had an extremist religious orientation (*ittijah dini mutatrrif*) and therefore could not be "won over" were to be "neutralized" (*tahyid*) and moved out, or treated even more severely. It was suggested to pay special attention to "the professors, lecturers and teachers who have extremist religious inclinations and to distance them from . . . teaching." Finally, it was suggested to sow doubts among the negative elements and create mistrust between them. This would weaken them and help the party.[94]

Even at the height of Saddam's faith campaign the regime's suspicion of all clerics, as well as of non-'ulama religious activists, real and perceived, remained as before, if not more so. The Iranian and Saudi regimes and the movements they sponsored were openly hostile to Ba'thi Iraq and perceived it as representing a real danger. They could not be reconciled under any circumstances. This approach was realistic, but sometimes it reached a paranoid level. An example of an unrealistic phobia is a 2000 party memorandum that warned that a rapprochement (which never materialized) between Iran and Saudi Arabia presented the danger of collusion inside Iraq between the Da'wa and local Wahhabis.[95] When it came to Sunni religious activists, the regime's internal security organs were inclined to package all Sunni fundamentalists together as Saudi-supported Wahhabis. In the same vein, in 2001 the Ministry of Endowments and Religious Affairs (the establishment of which in itself had been one of the signs of Islamization) held a conference for academics and clerics as well as security analysts to discuss how to fight Wahhabism.[96] The fear that Saudi Arabia was financing Wahhabism in Iraq was real, and, as always under the Ba'th, it trickled down to the level of the individual citizen. A presidential order sent to all party branches in 2001, when the faith campaign was in full swing, instructed them to obtain from every mosque imam in their area a signed document declaring Wahhabism an infidel movement. Anyone who refused to sign was to be promptly removed from his job.[97] This Wahhabi scare had reached absurd proportions in 1995, when even some Baghdad merchants were characterized as "Wahhabis."[98] These men may have demonstrated more religiosity than most others, but the possibility that they were Wahhabis was extremely remote. Those were the years when, because of the economic crisis and price hikes, merchants were accused of inflating prices and of profiteering from the population's great suffering.[99] Likewise, during the early 1990s 'Uday Saddam Husayn was arresting and hanging Baghdadi merchants to deter them from competing with him in selling contraband goods. Accusing merchants of Wahhabism was a good way of getting rid of them.[100]

There can be little doubt that both the regime's domestic security organs and the clerics understood that "Wahhabism" was not necessarily Wahhabism but rather a generic term or a code word for any organized Sunni Islamists who were not fully coordinated with the regime and with Saddam's concepts of what revived Islam was. In view of Saddam's alliance with some parts of the Muslim Brotherhood, it was far more convenient to accuse disloyal clerics or ardent mosque-goers of Wahhabism than of Salafi inclinations. Sometimes, though, the security officials described the suspicious elements more honestly—and more accurately—as "men of religion with religious-Salafi, Wahhabi, Muslim Brotherhood inclinations" (*ittijahat diniyya salafiyya, wah-habiyya, ikhwan muslimun*).[101] All, however, were seen as dangerous.

More than others, mosque personnel had to be carefully monitored, controlled, and purged. In 1995, the party organized a committee in every province that included the secretary of the *far'*, the head of General Security, and the director of *awqaf* (religious endowments) to evaluate all the religious functionaries. All the functionaries were apparently to evaluate each of their colleagues according to the colleague's political and religious leanings, connections with opposition movements, family relatives who had escaped from Iraq, and, finally, whether he "prayed for Mr. President" in his sermons.[102] A stream of documents produced by party and state security bodies in subsequent years show systematic spying on practically every religious functionary and group to make sure they were loyal to the regime, or at least not hostile to it.[103] In addition to monitoring all Friday sermons in all mosques, every appointment by the Ministry of Endowments to any religious institution had to undergo party security approval.[104] Clerics were usually partitioned by the party security into categories of those who were members or at least closely associated with the party, sympathetic independents, and some to be put on the watch list as a result of rumors that they had mixed with "suspicious and Wahhabist elements."[105] Unreliable imams were removed, arrested, or even sent to psychiatric hospitals.[106] The party's security organs were even concerned with Salafi groups in Kurdistan, an area much of which since 1991 was de facto independent under American and British military protection. Their activities were reported in detail. Cadres of *al-Haraka al-Islamiyya* were reported to have been encouraging their members to go and fight in Chechnya, and by January 2000 they had already sent more than 150 men there and were paying them salaries. They were strong in Talabani's areas, while Barzani were killing them. In Irbil, some men grew beards so that they could join those groups that had their own mosques, and their local leader was reported to be one 'Abd al-Rahman Muhyi al-Din. The security bodies were clearly concerned about a spillover from Kurdistan into Iraq.[107]

The Shi'i Shrines, Rituals, and 'Ulama

When it came to all Shi'i expressions of religiosity during the faith campaign, the regime was facing more acute dilemmas than before. The campaign used the clerics as intermediaries with the public, mainly as Qur'an teachers but also more directly as political pawns, but after the 1991 revolt the regime trusted the Shi'i clerics even less than it did before. In view of the regime's commitment to Islam, preventing the public from praying in the mosque was unthinkable. Forbidding Friday communal prayers, which were prone to antiregime protests, was embarrassing. (As will be shown below, in 1997 it was allowed for the first time under the Ba'th.) Limiting religious commemorations, which often turned into staging grounds for protests, was awkward. And yet the Ba'th remained the Ba'th: security had to be maintained at all costs. Between 1993 and 2003, therefore, the regime adopted a mix of policies. It both supported the 'ulama more than before and kept them under surveillance, killing those whom it considered dangerous. It both supported the main shrines and kept strict watch over mosque-goers. During important commemoration days, it allowed certain ceremonies to go forward, forbade others, and then changed its mind, but it always had large security forces in the holy cities, with well-structured duties and strict orders. Participants in religious commemorations and festivals and mosque functionaries were always kept under close watch.

The Central Shi'i Shrines

As part of the faith campaign, considerable material support was extended to the central Shi'i shrines (*'atabat*), far less to ordinary Shi'i mosques, *husayni-yyat*, and madrasas. Since the 1970s, the strategy had been to better control the masses by channeling them to central places. Government support for the main Shi'i shrines after the 1991 revolt was an important element in the effort to normalize the regime's relations with the community it had just devastated, but it also fitted well into the president's faith campaign. To begin with, during the revolt the revolutionaries took shelter in the shrines of Najaf and Karbala and the religious schools around them. The regime had no qualms about bombarding the buildings. The damage was extensive, and something had to be done about it. The community itself started the repairs, and the regime joined in. The media gave wide publicity to the president's personal interest and contribution. The reconstruction included gilding parts of the shrines' domes, contributions of "expensive chandeliers," fixing the glazed colored tiles on the outside walls, and laying marble tiles on the floors, as well as many other massive repairs and improvements. Until the mid-1990s, the president ordered close to a ton of pure gold and far larger quantities of pure silver to be allocated for the repairs. Expensive government contributions were made throughout the 1990s almost every year: they included repairs and refurbishing of madrasas and the development of pilgrimage-support sites.[108] Though on a far smaller scale than in the Sunni areas and Baghdad, the regime also renovated some mosques and tombs of Shi'i lesser saints, and even built some brand-new mosques.[109] The media never told the public that those minor holy tombs were of the supporters of the Shi'i Imams, but the regime could rest assured that the Shi'is understood it well.

The Shi'i 'Ulama and the Strange Case of Sadiq al-Sadr

In the Shi'i arena too, monitoring of all mosque functionaries and any organized religious group was a central duty of the party and state security bodies. A good example that demonstrates that any religious behavior deviating from what the regime could tolerate immediately galvanized the security organs into action in the Shi'i areas too was the case of the Imam al-Hasan Shi'i mosque in Saddam City. In one of his Friday sermons, the mosque's imam spoke out against women working in shops because in doing so, they would meet with men. In another sermon, he praised schools in which almost all the girls wore the hijab. Furthermore, the mosque imam was critical of tribal chiefs, whom he accused of making decisions based on tribal traditions rather than on the shari'a.[110] Needless to say, this Shi'i imam was not a Wahhabi: Wahhabism is hostile to the Shi'a. In November 1998, the influence of Ayatollah Muhammad Muhammad Sadiq al-Sadr (henceforth: Sadiq al-Sadr) in Saddam City was tremendous. At the time, he was still seen as a collaborator. The regime turned a blind eye when he expanded his control over religious schools and launched for the first time under the Ba'th communal Friday prayers in a few Shi'i towns in the south. A study of Sadr's fatwas shows very clearly that the opinions expressed by the imam reflected Sadr's teachings.[111] The mosque imam whose sermons were reported was clearly his disciple. Sadr still appeared quite loyal to the regime. The sermons did not go contrary to Saddam-inspired Islam. The preacher did not demand compulsory hijab attire. Women's work outside the home was already in the process of becoming unpopular with the party, and returning to the shari'a was the regime's new credo. Still, preaching for Sadr's principles was sufficient to turn on all the red lights in the regime's security system.

If only possible, the regime preferred to attract the 'ulama to the party and its interpretation of Islam as well as to collaborate with the internal security rather than to alienate them.[112] Some 'ulama were lured or coerced, or both, into expressing support for the regime.[113] Many more were quietly rewarded through the campaign's policy of recruiting teachers for Qur'an and Hadith courses from the state schools and various adult classes, even in some mosques. The campaign elevated their social and economic status. At the same time, however, the regime looked for ways to curb their power. For example, a mild measure was adopted in the mid-1990s when the regime no longer allowed 'ulama to received donations and use them to buy medicines and distribute them to the needy through their religious charities. The public was instructed to make all donations and contributions to the Ministry of Health.[114] A brutal way to weaken the Shi'i leadership was to weed out influential figures, Ba'th style. Thus, in July 1994 regime agents assassinated Muhammad Taqi al-Kho'i, another son of the late Grand Ayatollah Abu al-Qasim al-Kho'i.[115] The son was not a renowned clergyman (he was only *Hujjat al-Islam*), but he did command respect from the Shi'i community and had some financial clout because he managed his late father's bequest inside Iraq. In 1998, regime agents assassinated Ayatollah Murtada Borujerdi, and in that same year also assassinated Ayatollah Mirza 'Ali Gharawi together with his Lebanese brother-in-law the cleric Muhammad 'Ali al-Faqih and two companions on the Najaf-Karbala road.[116] At the time, it was widely believed that, following the death in 1992 of Grand Ayatollah Kho'i, these assassinations had been designed by the regime to clear the way for the ascendancy of a more cooperative ayatollah, Sadiq al-Sadr, a first cousin of Muhammad Baqir al-Sadr, who had been executed in 1980. Sadiq al-Sadr did indeed create the impression that he was collaborating with the regime. As the Iraqi government daily reported later, "The Iraqi leadership . . . had supported him in becoming a religious authority [*marja' taqlid*]."[117] Nevertheless, in February 1999 he too was assassinated. But by whom, and why? Was Sadiq al-Sadr a regime collaborator or a revolutionary?

No one disputes the fact that at least for a while, he served, or pretended to serve, as a regime agent. The dispute regards his long-term intentions. His detractors believe that he served the regime faithfully until, at a later stage, when he had lost all respect in the community, he changed his mind and became more confrontational. Sadiq al-Sadr himself reported that, following the death of Grand Ayatollah Kho'i, to delegitimize him the regime leaked that he, Sadr, was its "agent" and an intelligence employee "who was appointed by Baghdad" as an Arab Iraqi counterweight to the Persian "Sayyid al-Sabzavari so there would not be a Farsi *marja'*." As a result, he confessed, "Contacting me [was claimed to be] forbidden [*haram*] and of course it would not meet the approval of Allah . . . because . . . the agent is a devil and the devil is in hellfire. . . . They also did indeed disperse the people around me . . . but Allah gradually acted on my behalf and cleared [my name]."[118]

His supporters are convinced that he was intent from day one of his collaboration with the Ba'th in the early 1990s to confront the regime, but that to gain influence and power (possibly also money) he first had to deceive Saddam by pretending to be a collaborator. In 1997, Sadiq al-Sadr was allowed to lead Friday prayers in some southern towns, and in 1998 in his Kufa Friday mosque close to Najaf. Until then, and for almost two hundred years, Friday communal prayers had been a rare sight in Shi'i Iraq, and under the Ba'th this prayer was not practiced at all. Historically, the Shi'a have found it difficult to fully recognize the legitimacy of any ruler until the return (*al-raj'a*) or appearance (*al-zuhur*) of the Imam Mahdi, whenever he reveals himself. Since the preacher (khatib) of the Friday prayer is expected to recognize the ruler, this fact explains the lackluster character of the Friday prayers even in a Shi'i country like Iran. In Iraq, the Ba'th regime insisted that in the Friday sermon the preacher had to pay homage to the leader, and the Shi'i clerics were reluctant to do so. The Ba'th regime also feared Shi'i religious mass gatherings, with the result that both sides did not support Friday prayers.

If the assassinations of more senior 'ulama were designed to clear the way for Sadiq al-Sadr, then the regime's plan is widely believed to have backfired. Sadr was criticized for his close cooperation with the regime by Ayatollah Muhammad Baqir al-Hakim, the leader of the Iran-based Supreme Assembly of the Islamic Revolution in Iraq (SAIRI). According to opposition sources, by 1998 Sadr and other mosque imams seemed to take this criticism to heart.

Sadr refused to cancel his Friday prayers as he had been ordered to do by the regime, and openly demanded the release of his religious representatives (or "agents," *wukala*) from prison. In his sermons he was careful to mention the government in a respectful way, and when the government asked him to tell people not to march to Karbala on the Arba'in he did just that, but he also told people that in each similar case they must obey only him. In other words, he implied that he, not the Ba'th regime, was the leader of the community. Worst of all, he was believed by many to have declared that the Ba'this needed to perform "repentance" (*al-tawba*). However, I failed to find this call in the collection of all his Friday sermons.[119] Very likely, it was just a rumor and he never uttered those dangerous words, but the rumor was sufficient to set off red lights and sirens in the *mukhabarat* (secret police) offices in Baghdad and the south. By implication, it meant that the Ba'this were sinners, and that all their attempts to demonstrate repentance as part of the faith campaign were futile as long as they did not do so explicitly, preferably in front of Sadr himself. The regime became concerned as well when Sadr managed to win the hearts and minds of some of its Shi'i security agents in Saddam City. Sadr's activity in the tribal areas of the south was endorsed by the regime, as they saw him as a docile collaborator, but when he showed some independence, these activities and popularity became a risk. Finally, 1998 was a bad year for a regime that had become more paranoid than before. Sadr, however, also burned his bridges with the main religious authorities in Najaf, with the Hakims in Tehran, and with 'Abd al-Majid Kho'i in London. Since at least 1998, vitriolic hatred had been the hallmark of relations between Sadr's camp and SAIRI. On February 19, 1999, Sadr and his two sons were gunned down in their car near Najaf.[120] After his assassination, Sadr's supporters in Qom (Iran) attacked SAIRI's leader, Ayatollah Muhammad Baqir al-Hakim, during his mosque sermon.[121] After the demise of the Ba'th regime, the rivalry between the Sadrists and SAIRI became far more devastating. Indeed, it became a hallmark of Shi'i politics, involving assassinations, assassination attempts, military confrontations, and political acrimony.[122]

The regime fiercely denied responsibility for Sadiq al-Sadr's assassination and accused Iran of committing the crime.[123] Judging by the 1998–99 correspondence between the Ba'th Party's Najaf branch (*far*) and the higher echelons, the Najaf branch saw in Sadr a clear and present danger. They admitted that, when 10,000 to 12,000 flocked to the Kufa Friday Mosque, controlling them was becoming impossible. "Gatherings are difficult to control, security-wise," the branch reported, "and if any error occurs, deliberately or unintentionally, it will lead to the killing of thousands."[124] This meant that the branch officials understood well that Sadr's activities were tolerated by the regime. They were mystified, and suspected that Sadr was actually supported by the regime, and yet their objection was clear: had anything gone wrong, they would have been held responsible. The Najaf branch also complained that, in his Friday sermons, Sadr did not show sufficient Iraqi patriotism. He demanded the freeing of his imprisoned "agents" and students, and this infuriated the party. Various ideas were brought up for how to isolate him and limit his influence including preventing admirers from outside Najaf from entering the city and forcing Sadr to pay explicit tribute to Saddam in his sermons. From the correspondence, it seems that the lower the party level, the greater the anxiety, but even the Najaf branch was treating the subject with restraint, only vaguely suggesting that someone might make a tragic mistake. Party officials were aware that any conflagration would damage the regime. Saddam and the senior party levels did not authorize forcing Sadr to pay explicit homage to the president; at least there is no documented evidence of it. Yet, apparently to hedge his bets, the ayatollah did go halfway.[125] Assassination was never mentioned as a solution, nor is there any evidence in the party documents of such a decision.[126] Still, much as the possibility that the decision to recruit Sadr was made by two or three people at the very top and kept in total secrecy (see below), the order to kill him could have come from the very top, without any recorded consultation. In such a case, to avoid public protest, the order could have been kept on a limited, need-to-know basis and carried out by a very small intelligence unit.

However, the assassination was as likely an Iranian operation as a Ba'thi one. The Iranians saw in Sadr a threat, for he openly challenged Khamenei's authority. Not even recognized yet as a grand ayatollah, Sadr brazenly claimed for himself the title of *wali amr al-muslimin*—Leader of [all] the Muslims, Sunnis and Shi'is, Iraqi, Iranian, and others. Until then, this title had been reserved for Khomeini and, after his death, for Khamenei. Not surprisingly, the office of the Sadr family in Iran was closed as a result. Sadr's relations with Tehran deteriorated to a crisis level in 1997–99.[127] The Iranian regime knew that the usual suspect in assassination cases of senior Shi'i clerics was the Ba'th regime. There was therefore little that Iran stood to lose by sending a small and well-trained team to murder Sadr. Finally, Sadr attacked the most senior clerics of Najaf in an unprecedented way: he accused them of cowardice and corruption. As far as may be judged by the restrained nature of his criticism of the Ba'th regime, it is not clear that he crossed the threshold that would "require" an assassination. He did demand the release of religion students from jail, but he did so politely, and in fact a regime decision to set the students free could endow him with the aura of one who had dared and won, an image he could indeed use to serve the regime best if he was a collaborator. The paranoid Ba'th regime might have felt threatened, but Sadr's death could also have been the result of any of his other rivalries as well.[128] Still, the Shi'i population had little doubt that it was Saddam's *mukhabarat* agents who had assassinated him. In this way, they could still support both the Najaf-based and Qom-based *marja'iyya* and other Shi'i power centers and retain reasonable community cohesion.

Was Sadr a regime agent, then? There are at least four different possibilities. The most obvious one is that the regime always hated Sadr and feared his influence, but until November or December 1998 it avoided a confrontation with him because any limits on his religious activities could be interpreted as limits on religion itself. This could have been embarrassing in the midst of Saddam's faith campaign. In the end, when he crossed their red line, they had him killed. Another possibility is that there was no "deal," but the top regime figures, perhaps just Saddam, 'Izzat Ibrahim, and one or two additional officials, saw Sadr (as their media claimed after his death) as a good candidate to become the next *marja'*. Sadr could fit well into the Ba'thi mold of an Arab and Iraqi citizen who could replace the Persian ayatollahs as chief source of emulation. As will be recalled, in the 1980s 'Izzat Ibrahim warned against Sadr. Perhaps he figured out that the very idea of an Arab *marja'* was dangerous, because such a *marja'*, if not fully trusted by and supportive of the regime, could strew havoc in the Shi'i areas, as his communication with his flock would have been far more effective than that of his Persian colleagues. The example of Baqir al-Sadr, who was only a young ayatollah, should have served as ample warning.

By 1997–98, though, this lesson was forgotten, and Sadiq al-Sadr was allowed surprising freedom of action. Probably this was the case because, until 1998, he was a quietist. His family relationship to Muhammad Baqir al-Sadr was a great asset: what could be a better choice than a Sadr who accepts the Ba'th? In 1997, he was allowed to conduct Friday prayers in Nasiriyya and other southern cities, and in 1998 this permission (or tolerance) was extended to the very central Kufa Friday Mosque. In 1998, the regime also turned a blind eye when he took over a few religious schools. There is no doubt that the regime could have prevented all those steps. This is clear from the fact that, for whatever reason, Saddam ordered one school to be taken from Sadr and given back to the Hakim family.[129] The regime also stopped the communal prayer at the Friday Mosque of Nasiriyya, which prompted Sadr to demand its reopening.[130] It is quite possible that, without any actual agreement between Sadr and the regime in place, Sadr's activities were tolerated in the hope that he would reciprocate in kind.

Another possibility is that there was indeed a secret agreement between the regime and Sadr but that neither the Kufa *shuʻba* or above it the Najaf *farʻ*, nor the Middle Euphrates Bureau or even most of the members of the All-Iraqi Regional Leadership, were aware of this. Some may have suspected it—hence the careful language used by the Najaf *farʻ* when protesting the great freedom allowed to Sadr—but they could not know for sure what their bosses really had in mind. The principle of "need to know" was Saddam's trademark, and even his most senior officials and generals knew that they did not know far more than they did know. The senior Baʻthis were fully aware that any sign of collaboration with the regime would destroy the reputation of any ayatollah in the eyes of the Shiʻi community. Any connection, therefore, between a good candidate and the regime had to be concealed at all costs; hence the need to keep such collaboration secret even from very senior officials. Furthermore, any such a candidate for *marjaʻ* status had to demonstrate a degree of independence and, as long as he did not offend Saddam or the Baʻth, even some defiance. This was precisely what Sadr did. He demanded the release of the students and the reopening of the Nasiriyya Friday Mosque, and he also tried to establish himself as the supreme religious (and possibly political) authority of the community. This pattern was subversive, but it never even remotely approached his older cousin's defiance: Muhammad Baqir al-Sadr had declared the Baʻth infidels and called for an Islamic revolution. Also, by demanding for himself religious leadership, Sadr became useful when he ordered his followers to obey the regime's dictate and refrain from marching on the Arbaʻin. But he did more. He severely criticized Saddam's enemies, the Wahhabi Saudis, the British and Americans, and, obviously the "Zionists." Finally, by declaring himself to be *wali amr al-Muslimin*, he challenged the authority of Saddam's nemesis, Iran's Ayatollah Khamenei.[131]

Yet another interpretation of Sadr's activities may be that at first, with or without an agreement, he took advantage of the relative leniency of the regime during the faith campaign and paid the price by remaining politically passive. When he realized that this had turned him into a pariah in the eyes of the Shiʻi community, as he seemed to have admitted, he changed his course and adopted a more aggressive posture. Finally, it may also be that his supporters were right, and that from day one he intended to confront the Baʻth, but he needed time and some power before he could launch his attack, thus remaining docile until he felt strong enough.

The limitations that the regime imposed on Sadr in 1998–99, such as trying to prevent people from reaching Kufa and later an order to stop the Friday prayers altogether, may similarly be interpreted in two different ways. One way, they represented a true wish to limit and isolate him, as demanded by the Najaf *farʻ*. Even if he was a regime agent (let alone if he was not), the flocking of 10,000 young men on Fridays to his mosque could be seen even by Saddam as too risky. Another way, the limitations may have been an attempt to convince the public that Sadr was not a collaborator. The available documentation does not provide a definite answer. Whatever the case, Sadr's conduct during the last year of his life was a dance on a dangerous tightrope. He tried not to cross the regime's red lines, but he still alienated many Baʻthis, especially the Najaf *farʻ*; he antagonized the Iranian regime; and he greatly irritated his more senior colleagues at the *hawza*. The last years of his life exposed the rivalries within the Shiʻi religious leadership. Far more important, the final year of his life sheds a harsh, bright light on the highly complex and often tragic interrelations between the Shiʻi religious leadership and the Baʻth regime.

A paradox of Baʻth policy regarding the senior ʻulama of both sects was that in a Sunni-controlled state, the Sunnis lost the few senior religious leaders they had. Under the Ottomans and the monarchy there were still some religious leaders, just as under the British rule the Sufi ʻAbd al-Rahman al-Kaylani (al-Gaylani) and his nemesis, the Wahhabi-inclined Mahmud Shukri al-Alusi, had been retained. After World War II, Iraq still had influential Sunni clerics, such as Amjad al-Zahawi, Qasim al-Qaysi, and Najm al-Din al-Waʻiz. They were well known and represented the (conservative) Sunni religious opinion.[132] Already under the monarchy, however, and more so under the ʻArifs, this leadership was in decline, and under the Baʻth rule it disappeared as a nationally recognized authority. What was left was some local religious leadership at the level of local mosque imams, but none on an all-Iraqi level. The Shiʻi losses in this respect were sustainable. Despite the numerous executions, assassinations, and arrests, the four grand ayatollahs that the American forces found in Najaf in 2003, led by ʻAli al-Sistani, had only to avoid a confrontation with the Baʻth regime to survive, and so they did. Thus the Shiʻi community still had a religious leadership that, in the moment the regime disappeared, achieved a prominence unknown since the Ottoman era.

Regime-Shiʻa Confrontations, 1998–2003

Fear of a New Revolt and Its Consequences

Following the suppression of the 1991 revolt, the Shiʻi population was in a state of shock. Unrest began again in the spring of 1998. The reason seems to be that with the renewed tension with the United States over weapons inspections, the regime became more nervous and the Shiʻi activists gained self-confidence. The state security forces' operations in the south suddenly surged. The crackdown started with a large-scale operation against the Bani Hujaym tribe near Nasiriyya, which resulted in executions and arrests.[133] Between August and November 1998, the south saw a rise in antigovernment activities and the Republican Guard attacked villages and small towns around Nasiriyya, Suk al-Shuyukh, Basra, and ʻAmara. The tribes attacked included Juwaybar, al-bu Salih, the ʻAsakira, al-bu Hasan, and al-Shumaysh. There were executions, and many were arrested, including women and children. On November 22, 1998, hundreds of young men were arrested in Karbala, apparently as they were preparing to celebrate the birthday of the Imam Mahdi in the Islamic month of Saʻban. During the military operations, whole villages were wiped out. On January 6, 1999, the center of Grand Ayatollah Bashir al-Najafi was attacked while he and members of his seminary were praying. Qusay Saddam Husayn and his uncle, ʻAli Hasan al-Majid, issued the orders for these operations.[134] Beginning in March 1999, there were again numerous reports of an upsurge in antiregime activities in the Shiʻi areas. Some of the activity, though not all of it, was the Sadrists' response to the assassination of their *marjaʻ*. Some was in response to the authorities' attempt to prevent the newly introduced Friday prayers.[135] Yet since 2000, no meaningful regime-Shiʻi confrontations had been reported.

Beginning in the early 1990s, Saddam held numerous closed-door meetings with his lieutenants to prepare for a new mass revolt in the south. The planning was usually quite sensible. Thus, for example, in a high-level discussion with his generals in 1992, the officers described likely Iranian military options against Iraq. They assigned a very high probability to a combination of Iranian support for (Shiʻi) riots in the south. The solution was to finish off the domestic riots first, so as to prevent contact between the local "trouble-makers" (*mushaghibin*) and the Iranian forces. The places to which Saddam gave the highest priority were Baghdad, then Hilla, then Kut, and "Basra must not be forgotten." He emphasized that "this high priority" for Maysan and

Basra was designed to prevent "splitting Iraq," an Iraqi nightmare and a strategic Iranian interest.[136] A new Shiʻi revolt remained very high on Saddam's list of threats until 2003. In reality, though, all the revolts of 1998–2003 were small in scale and uncoordinated, and all failed completely. And yet they were sufficient to arouse Saddam's paranoia, which in 2003 resulted in a fateful strategic mistake. After the American invasion, Saddam's fear of a repeat of the 1991 Shiʻi revolt reached an absurd level and hastened his demise. Fearing that his tanks would be unable to reach the south and put down a new revolt, he rejected the urgent pleadings of his generals to allow them to blow up all the bridges between Basra and Baghdad and to flood vast areas in the south. Such a strategy would have delayed the American advance to a crawl. This could have given the defending forces time to get more intelligence about the main American effort (Saddam believed that the US forces were coming mainly from Jordan) and to better prepare Baghdad's defenses. Saddam personally would have had more time to prepare his escape and the guerrilla war. His paranoia cost him his life.

Security during Religious Rituals

With relative tranquility in the south and the faith campaign ongoing, in the early and mid-1990s Shiʻis were allowed to perform some of the religious ceremonies that had been forbidden to them since 1977. They included a mass pilgrimage to Karbala on the birthday of the Imam Mahdi, which were, however, subject to meaningful security limitations. Still, the security apparatus kept harassing the people.[137] Some ʻAshura rituals were allowed again. For example, the distribution of free rice and broth in the streets was again allowed. After 1977, the practice had been forbidden because the free food attracted many to those politically charged gatherings. As long as they did not arrive in groups, mosque-goers usually were not interrogated, but surveillance continued. After the 1998–99 confrontations in the south, strict limitations on Shiʻi ceremonies were reintroduced. Security measures were stringent. All those who attended the ceremonies were to provide their personal details. The regime's security warned against weddings in which poems were recited to protest the assassination of Sadiq al-Sadr. People who stayed in hotels and who had come for some religious occasion had to be reported. Thursday night visitations to the holy sites in Karbala were to be discouraged because they often resulted in mass protests. Shiʻi clerics were called on to fight such "deviations" from Islam.[138] This was strange: here, the party conveniently adopted a Wahhabi approach. Traditional visitations that, as late as 1992, Saddam himself considered to be common ground uniting Sunnis and Shi'is suddenly became idolatry. There is no evidence that any Shi'i cleric supported this attack on the Shi'a, but neither did any opposition activity that could endanger the regime result from it.

Islamic Education in School Textbooks

The Qur'an and Islamic Values

In the early and mid-1990s, the Ministry of Education issued two new series of textbooks, *The Blessed Qur'an* (*Al-Qur'an al-Karim*), designed to teach the Qur'an to primary school pupils, and *Islamic Education* (*al-Tarbiya al-Islami-yya*), a more general series teaching wider Islamic subjects. The two were part of the faith campaign, even though the earlier of the two versions came out a few months before the campaign was officially announced. To rub in the cause of Jerusalem rather than the Ka'ba, the front page of *The Blessed Qur'an* showed Jerusalem's Dome of the Rock. One would expect al-Aqsa Mosque, but the Dome is more grand and unique.[139] The bizarre aspect of this whole textbook is that the authors chose the very last *suras* because they are the shortest ones, without regard for content (the language throughout the Qur'an is difficult, anyway). The authors simply followed the Qur'anic order of *suras* from the 93rd to the 114th, with not one *sura* or *aaya* missing. Most *suras* are impossible for children to understand. *Sura* 96, for example, "the Clot" (*al-'Alaq*), speaks about the creation of man, but it also threatens the sinners with hell. The same threat of hellfire is even more explicit in *Sura* 98, "the Clear Proof" (*al-Bayyina*), *Aaya* 6. The *sura* of "the Calamity" (*al-Qari'a*, *Sura* 101) talks about "a day wherein mankind will be as thickly scattered moths" (*Aaya* 4) and the mountains will become "as carded wool" (*Aaya* 5), and people who are not protected will be destroyed. "The Palm-Fiber" (*al-Masad*, *Sura* 111) describes the fate of Abu Lahab, half-brother of the Prophet's father, who opposed the Prophet. It reads: "The power of Abu Lahab will perish and he will perish* his wealth and gains will not exempt him* he will be plunged into flaming fire* and his wife the wood carrier* will have upon her neck a halter of fiber." The *sura* of "The Daybreak" (*al-Falaq*, *sura* 113*) is not less frightening for a small child.[140]

The textbook for teaching the Qur'an to the second graders has precisely the same approach.[141] The textbook for the fourth grade[142] starts with

Sura 58, "She who Disputeth" (*al-Mujadala*), and goes all the way to *Sura* 66, "Banning" (*al-Tahrim*). Again, it follows diligently the Qur'anic order of *sura*s. Two of the *sura*s, 58 and 65, deal with men's right to divorce their wives and their duties in such cases, a subject totally mystifying for a small child. It gets even more perplexing when the "Divorce" *sura* (65, *al-Talaq*) goes into the details of menstruation (*Aaya* 4). This is definitely not suitable for ten-year-olds. The series is a pedagogical disaster.

A far better-written and better-produced series for primary schools, *Islamic Education* (*al-Tarbiya al-Islamiyya*), was issued in 1991, and a new edition was printed every year. The book for the first grade[143] is written in large letters, and it is easier for a child to understand. The book is replete with high-quality photographs and drawings in full color. Even the paper is of very good quality. It opens with a straightforward explanation of "the essence of Islam," to wit: "God is our Lord [*rabbuna*], Muhammad is our Prophet, Islam our religion, the Qur'an our Book, the *Ka'ba* our Direction of Prayer, the Muslim males our brothers and the Muslim females our sisters." A beautiful drawing of nature scenery, including many animals, is accompanied by an explanation: "God . . . is our Lord, the Creator of everything." "I am a Muslim, I obey God and his Messenger, I love God, the Exalted, and his blessed Prophet." And so on. A problem arises, though, when the pillars of Islam are being taught. The first pillar, the *shahada*, provides "testimony that there is no God but Allah and that Muhammad is the Messenger of Allah." Here the Shi'a add the principle of the Imamate: "and 'Ali is the Friend of Allah" (*wa 'Ali wali Allah*), but there is no mention of it in the book.[144] The Ministry of Education's dilemma was a difficult one: with no ill intent on their part, many Shi'i parents could be offended all the same. Until the 1990s, Qur'an classes were few and far between, but in the faith campaign they became very prominent, and with them came the dilemma of the *shahada*.

The Sectarian Balance in Textbooks: How to Pray?

The Sunni-Shi'i difference stands out more when *al-Tarbiya al-Islamiyya* textbook for the first grade teaches the pupils how to pray. It shows in pictures the various phases of preparing for prayer, praying, and ending the prayer. The problem arises when it comes to the different prayer practices of Sunnis and Shi'is. According to the textbook, one has to wash one's hands before prayer from the fingers to the elbow, starting with the right hand. The Shi'is, however, are shown washing their hands from the elbow to the fingers, starting with the left hand. Also, while the book shows how one washes one's ears before prayer, this is something that Shi'a usually do not do. Finally, the book demonstrates the Sunni way of washing both feet fully and meticulously, even between the toes, while the Shi'i way is just to wipe the feet with one's wet hand (*mash al-qadamayn*). When praying, Sunnis kneel and prostrate themselves, touching the floor or the prayer mat with their forehead, and this is what the book shows. Shi'is touch with their forehead a stone or a brick of clay from Karbala or Najaf, or a piece of paper on the mat or the floor if it is not a stone floor. All these are small differences, but in a country where slightly over 50 percent of the population is Shi'a, this book had the potential to create a sense of alienation between the child and the school, because in religious homes the child is taught to pray differently.[145]

An interesting aspect of all these textbooks is that all the girls shown in prayer are wearing scarves, while in other situations their hair is usually exposed. Boys and girls study in the same class, even though boys sit on one side of the room and girls on the other. But during prayer, there is a complete separation of the sexes.[146] In the first years of the campaign, there was indeed no gender separation in school, but in the mid-1990s this too was imposed. Veils, though, were never imposed wholesale.

Some textbooks from the secular era survived the faith campaign. The earlier version of the same series, issued for the first time in 1978, during the Ba'th secular era, but used also during the faith campaign, is very different. There are no veils at all, and the series does not show how to pray, though it does provide the pupil with some details about the Friday prayer, as well as the prayers for the two most important festivals ('Id al-Fitr, 'Id al-Adhha). It does not impose on little children many difficult *sura*s, and it concentrates on telling the stories of Islam during the lifetime of the Prophet, where Sunni-Shi'i differences can easily be papered over.[147] The 1978 version does not escape the Sunni-Shi'i differences, though, as it discusses at some length the history of the first four Rightly Guided Caliphs, the first three of whom the Shi'a detest, but in the book they appear Sunna-style, in a very positive light.[148] Still, because in the 1970s and most of the 1980s very little attention was paid to religious studies, this problem was very marginal.

The Sectarian Balance in Textbooks: The Caliphate

Another central series, *Arab-Islamic History* (*Al-Ta'rikh al-'Arabi wal Islami*), could not avoid mention of the four first caliphs as well as other controversial historical personalities and events. The series was first issued during the Iran-Iraq War, but the same books appeared in new editions until 2003. The first three caliphs and their contribution to Islam are described in some detail and in a very positive way. All three, as well as the fourth, 'Ali, are described as being among the ten who were promised paradise. Their extensive marriage interconnections and marriage connections with the Prophet are detailed, too. These details are in no way coincidental: they are designed to demonstrate to the Shi'i student that relations between the Prophet and his four replacements, as well as relations among the four caliphs, were very close. This is supposed to disarm the Shi'a and make it difficult for them to claim that 'Ali was wronged by the first three caliphs. To avoid intersectarian friction, the tragic dispute surrounding the assassination of 'Uthman ('Uthman's family accused 'Ali and his supporters of the murder) is not mentioned. To balance the positive account of the first three caliphs, the authors give a particularly glowing (though not unusual in Sunni tradition) account of 'Ali, who is also the only one to receive the title "Imam."

Things get tougher when the authors discuss the Umayyad era. Mu'awiya's picture is shown and he appears in a positive light, and the Umayyad contribution to the Islamic state, including the "Arabization" of the state bureaucracy, is described in detail. The book does not devote a single word to the bitter dispute and war between 'Ali and Mu'awiya. It is hardly surprising that the Shi'i student whose book I received in 2004 crossed out the page describing Mu'awiya. (He did this, though, with a pencil—that is, in a way that could be reversed. The books were given out free at the beginning of the academic year and collected again at the end of the year.) The authors made a concession to the Shi'a in that they omitted any mention of Yazid, the caliph under whose rule Imam Husayn was murdered.[149] Much more praise is showered on 'Ali in a book by the same authors for the second grade intermediate school that came out for the first time two years later. 'Ali "became the source of trust for the three Caliphs who preceded him: they consulted with him over the rules of the shari'a and over political issues, and 'Umar in particular consulted him." 'Ali's close family relations with the first three caliphs are presented in some detail. Finally, Mu'awiya's picture vanished.[150] Perhaps someone in the Ministry of Education received instructions from the Presidential Palace to tweak the Sunni-Shi'i balance a little more toward the Shi'a. Saddam's attempt to create an ecumenical Islam was represented here too, but the book was still written using a Sunni approach.

When it came to Sunni-Shi'i balance, thus, the writers of the textbooks were confronted with the same problem faced by Sati' al-Husri, Iraq's first director of education (1921–27), an educator and a pan-Arab ideologue. When confronted with anti-Sunni instruction in a primary-school-level madrasa in Karbala, he concluded that the whole issue of Sunni-Shiʻi theological and historical dispute had to be addressed, and appropriate textbooks had to be written. He suggested a number of solutions, but in the end he admitted that none of them was satisfactory.[151] In practice, he opted essentially for the Sunni approach, except that ʻAli received somewhat more praise than in most other Arab countries. This was done not only to try to bridge the Sunni-Shiʻi gap but also as an expression of Iraqi pride: ʻAli's capital city was Kufa, in today's southern Iraq. The Baʻth continued this tradition. The problem under the Baʻth, therefore, was not unique in Iraqi history. However, the paradoxical result of Saddam's faith campaign was that, because it catapulted religious studies to unprecedented heights, the theological aspect of the Sunni-Shiʻi divide became much more visible. The number of hours per week dedicated to these studies increased immensely, as did their status. This meant that the same problematic texts that previously were marginal became central overnight. Saddam's 1977 warning that if the Baʻth were to turn Islamic the Sunni-Shiʻi chasm would grow deeper came back to haunt him.

The Sectarian Balance in Post-Baʻth Textbooks

The same dilemma is still not easy to resolve in the post-Baʻth new Iraq. This time Shiʻi parties form the largest political bloc and the prime minister is Shiʻi. Yet Sunnis (Arabs and Kurds) represent almost 50 percent of Iraq's population, and, culturally speaking, Iraq is a part of the largely Sunni Arab world. A delicate and sensitive balancing act therefore has been necessary. The post-Baʻth textbooks of Islamic history that were written by a committee of three, at least one of whom was a Shiʻi, had an innovative approach. Had the same textbooks been issued by a Sunni-dominated regime, they would still have caused Shiʻi unease. Still, since the responsibility for the books is that of a Shiʻi-controlled Ministry of Education and government, the Shiʻis of Iraq may see this as a necessary concession to their Sunni counterparts. The versions of early Islamic history that appear in all the textbooks for all age groups are very similar. Probably the best example is the textbook *Arab-Islamic History for the Fifth Grade, Primary School.*[152] The book elevates ʻAli, the first Shiʻi Imam, by mentioning a *hadith* that had never been mentioned before in Iraqi textbooks. According to this *hadith,* when the Prophet wanted to create brotherhood between the people of al-Madina and *al-muhajirin,* those who had migrated with him from Mecca, he "held the hand of Imam ʿAli bin Abi Talib and said, 'This is my brother in this world and the next.'"[153] More problematically, the book mentions the famous instance of the Prophet returning to al-Madina from his last *haj* to Mecca, knowing this was his farewell pilgrimage (*hujjat al-widaʿ*). While the group rested near a hot spring he spoke to his supporters, "clarifying the essence of the Islamic religion." The textbook does not explain what this "essence" was, but it does report that on the same occasion, a very important Qurʾanic verse came down from God: "Today I completed for you your religion" (*surat al-Maʾida, Aaya* 3).[154] In other words, at that moment God sealed the Qurʾan. What the textbook does not say but every Shiʿi child knows is that according to a *hadith* regarded as reliable by both Sunnis and Shiʿis, on that same occasion the Prophet also said, "He whose *mawla* [or *mawlan*] I am, ʿAli is his *mawla*." A Shiʿi child understands this declaration to be the "essence of the Islamic religion" because the Shiʿa interpret the expression "*mawla*" as "master." They believe that on that occasion, near Hot Spring (Ghadir Khumm), by saying this Muhammad publicly appointed his cousin and son-in-law ʿAli as his heir. Sunnis dispute the meaning of "*mawla*" because they do not think that Muhammad ever appointed ʿAli his immediate heir. Shiʿis also believe that ʿAli's appointment is precisely the moment when and the reason why God told the believers that their religion was now complete. Needless to say, the Sunnis do not consider this particular Qurʾanic verse to be connected in any way to the Prophet's words at Ghadir Khumm.

The new textbook avoids an open clash with the Sunna by only hinting at the Prophet's appointment of ʿAli, but it does include the connection between the important Qurʾanic verse and whatever happened at Ghadir Khumm. To Shiʿi children, this means that God approved of ʿAli's appointment. Sunni children who are not acquainted with *Hadith al-Ghadir* may not understand the connection and thus may miss the Shiʿi point that God ordered the community to follow ʿAli after the Prophet's death.

The textbook provides a sympathetic description of the achievements of the three Rightly Guided Caliphs who ruled before ʿAli. This, therefore, is an attempt to show respect for Sunni values. Very much like the Baʿth-era textbooks, the new books heap special praises on the fourth caliph, ʿAli, something that was acceptable to most Sunnis, certainly in Iraq. Yet the book introduces something that represents total innovation to the Sunnis. It provides the names and deeds of five rather than four Rightly Guided Caliphs (*al-khulafa al-rashidun*). The fifth one is none other than Imam ʿAli's elder son, al-Hasan. According to the textbook, he received the *bayʿa* (oath of allegiance) from the community in Kufa, his father's capital city. He then decided, according to the textbook, to abdicate in favor of the governor of Damascus, Mu'awiya the Umayyad. According to the textbook, he did so in order to prevent a civil war and bloodshed.[155] This is the Shi'i way of interpreting history, but it is not offensive to the Sunnis. Declaring Imam Hasan the fifth of the great caliphs may be seen by Sunnis as a small price to pay for Shi'i acceptance of the first three caliphs as legitimate—indeed, as great historical figures. As for the Shi'i Ministry of Education, if attacked by Shi'i diehards for this theological concession, the ministry could quote none other than the "First [Latter-Day] Martyr," the great revolutionary Ayatollah Muhammad Baqir al-Sadr, who in 1979 declared two of the first three caliphs to be pious Muslims.[156]

A soft indication in the post-2003 textbooks that the Umayyads were illegitimate was the critique directed at Mu'awiya. The textbooks explain that according to the Prophet's legacy, the heir of any caliph must be chosen through a consultative assembly (*shura*). Mu'awiya decided instead that his son would inherit him. "This initiative, which goes contrary to the Prophet's approach . . . created a powerful reaction among the Muslims," the book explains. Eventually, this led to the "mighty opposition led by Imam Husayn bin 'Ali bin Abi Talib against Yazid bin Mu'awiya." This opposition "resulted in his [Imam Husayn's] martyrdom on the tenth of Muharram . . . and those with him . . . in Karbala. The Umayyad authorities applied the most brutal means against the revolutionaries. And this is why the battle of Karbala astounded the whole Islamic world, as in it Imam Husayn performed the most magnificent of all heroic exploits in terms of sacrifice and death for God which history eternalized."[157] This is the Shi'i approach, but this too is not offensive to Sunnis, especially in Iraq, where the Syrian-based Umayyads are not very popular. At the same time, however, the book describes correctly and with appreciation the achievements of the Umayyad Caliphate.[158] Likewise, the achievements of the 'Abbasids are described well and without rancor, nor is there any mention of the Shi'i belief that some 'Abbasids caused the death of some of their imams.[159]

A remarkable aspect of the historiography of the Arabs in the modern age is a hostile attitude toward the Safawids (or Safavids, *al-Safawiyyin*), who conquered parts of Iraq "out of a greedy lust for its riches."[160] The Safawids were a Shi'i Sufi dynasty, believed to be descendants of the Prophet, who conquered Iran in the early sixteenth century and forced Shi'i Islam on it. It is unexpected that a Shi'i-controlled Ministry of Education would present them in a negative light. The reason why this was done is apparently that many Shi'i Arabs are distrustful of the Persians even though they share the same sectarian affiliation. But there seems to be a further reason to this negative attitude: many Sunnis in Iraq often describe Shiʿis, or some of them, as "Safawids," or Persian Shiʿis. This is a very offensive term. The Ministry of Education made it clear, therefore, that the Shiʿis of Iraq are Arabs and Iraqi patriots and have nothing to do with Persian expansionist ideas, if such exist.

A Party Revolt: Is Baghdad Becoming Riyadh?

The Islamization campaign clashed head-on with the heart of the party's original identity and raison d'être. This had to be disturbing to many party members, but after the 1991 Gulf War and the Shiʿi revolt that followed, the party was demoralized, blamed by the leader for its failure to nip the revolt in the bud.[161] The party was less capable than ever of opposing Saddam. But in the last analysis, while party tenets of faith mattered, some even a great deal, regime survival mattered more. In all the sources available, either in the Iraqi public media or in closed-door leadership discussions, although I could find many remnants of the old rational and secular discourse, I found no open opposition to the new party line. No one openly opposed the enforcement of the study of the Qurʾan and the Sunnah, or the gigantic sums spent on building mosques while at least 10 percent of the population lacked housing. I found no objection to the new sharʿi system of punishment, either. In fact, it seems that the latter was received with satisfaction by party and state officials. The minister of *awqaf* (religious endowments), for example, commended the new law mandating severing the right hand and the left leg of thieves, explaining that the advantages of such a punishment accrued from its being "in line with God's Book and the provision of the Islamic law and in harmony with God's words: 'As to the thief, both male or female, cut off their hands'" (*Sura* 5, *al-Maʾida, Aaya* 38). The minister had also a utilitarian, nonreligious explanation, reminiscent of the "old" party thinking: the sharʿi punishments were the most effective because they were the best deterrent.[162] The new decree was in fact supported enthusiastically by all of the Iraqi media. The government daily conducted a poll of judges, officials, and citizens, all of whom supported the new law for a variety of reasons. An official in the Ministry of Endowments regarded it as positive simply because it placed the shariʿa "at the center of life." Judges remained secular, as they felt that shame and the prospect of physical injury would serve as effective deterrents. Simple citizens were reported by the government daily to be thinking along similar lines when they expressed satisfaction, in the hope that the new law would reduce the property crime that bedeviled their lives.[163] A columnist in the party newspaper, however, was worried not because of the draconian nature of the law but rather that people might confuse a war hero with a common thief, both having lost a hand or a leg. To remedy the situation, he suggested branding thieves with a small cross on their cheek.[164] The regime demonstrated its democratic nature when eventually this led to the branding of a large cross on the thief's forehead.

The attitude to the limits on entertainment, betting and the banning of public consumption of liquor was very different, though. Since they came to power in 1968 the senior party officials had been drinking in private meetings, as well as in social clubs such as the 'Alwiya, the Hunting Club (*Nadi al-Sayd*), and the Horsemanship Club. Army officers, too, used to drink when they met socially, for example in the Air Force Sports Club, in *al-Nadi al-Bahri* (the Navy Club), and *al-Nadi al-'Askari* (the Army Club). It is not clear whether this kind of social drinking at the top of the party leadership was stopped. Interviews with a former general indicate this social drinking was stopped, though officers usually kept whiskey bottles in the drawers of their office desks. Whether or not the party luminaries continued drinking in their expensive clubs until 2003, the mid-level party members who could not afford the exclusive clubs were seething. In late 1989, as part of a high-level debate among the party leadership, members pointed out that the party, including the various candidate and supporters' levels, in one way or another reached almost the whole Iraqi nation. They were proud that the whole nation was now in support of the party. Referring to the middle level, Saddam retorted angrily, "Among our *cadres* there are such who don't read the newspapers seriously! They complete their party chores and then put in front of them the [liquor] glass and [drink] from sunset to midnight until they are picked up under their armpits, and it is all over."[165] Saddam was not speaking against drinking but rather against getting drunk and neglecting duties beyond clear-cut obligations. He was well aware of his comrades' habits and must have realized that stopping drinking altogether was more than he could do without paying a hefty price.

Many members were deeply concerned as well by a few other aspects of the faith campaign. This concern was given vent by the only person in Iraq who could write against the president's policy with impunity. One year into the faith campaign, *Babil*, 'Uday's daily paper, came out with a sensational leading article. The daily warned that any attempt to plant an alien fundamentalist

"Islamic heart" into a "pan-Arab [secular] body" would inevitably lead to the body's death. Iraq's "enemies" were asking in delighted anticipation, "Does this mean that we [Iraqis] will put on veils and that [Harun] al-Rashid's Baghdad with all its history and its various sects will turn into a city similar to Saudi cities?"[166] Going Islamic, 'Uday warned, quoting his father's 1977 caution, could create divisions among the various Islamic sects, whereas religious pluralism was Iraq's lifeline. "Whatever attire the Islamic [fundamentalist] trend dons in Iraq, [it] will bring us disaster because we are not one Islamic sect or community," 'Uday wrote. Finally, and again like his father in 1977, 'Uday warned that whatever the party did by way of returning to Islam, it would not be accepted as legitimate by the Islamic fundamentalists, and thus the whole effort was in vain.[167]

In 1994, *Babil* published a letter it had allegedly received from an anonymous worried citizen in which the latter explained the danger of a burgeoning "Wahhabi" movement in Iraq led by one Muhammad Nasir al-Din al-Albani. Reportedly, the movement was receiving financial support from Saudi Arabia. Members managed to influence the youth and "even our old people," the citizen complained. The Wahhabis' poisonous ideas would lead to civil war, apparently because of their hatred of the Shi'a. They used the mosques to spread their heresies, and they had also infiltrated the Iraqi (Sunni) theological colleges. Most 'ulama did not dare confront them, either out of fear or because of (presumably Saudi) bribery. They were, however, easy to identify because they all wore the same clothes and looked the same. This meant that they all obeyed orders from one center. "The party and security organs do not seem to be aware" of their activities. "Does this mean [official] consent? If this is so, then let the issue come into the open and let us all join this movement."[168] The anonymous writer declared that the relevant state ministries (mainly the Ministry of the Interior) "lack the daring, youthful and revolutionary vision. . . . They rely on red tape, nepotism and personal and tribal factors, and . . . at best the issue would be delegated to a committee." Turning to 'Uday, the writer declared, "We are putting these questions before you and we are confident that your responsibility towards the youth and the Iraqis . . . makes us hopeful of getting decisive answers." The editors added "an observation": "We have information on the centers and places where the Wahhabis are staying. If the security organs [General Security under 'Uday's uncle Watban Ibrahim Tikriti] so require, we can supply the necessary information." Shielding himself against accusations of disloyalty to the president and his campaign, the anonymous citizen professed his allegiance solely "to Islam, the Ba'th and Iraq."[169]

A few days later, a leading columnist in *Babil* launched a vicious attack against anonymous politicians in high places in Iraq who gave support to people who hatch "conspiracy." These conspirators were "wearing the garb of godliness and [religious] piety," and those politicians who supported them "embellish the bad and dirty and denigrate the devout and competent ones."[170]

Were those mentioned really Wahhabis? More likely, they were Sunni Salafis. Even during the faith campaign, the party's internal security bodies followed and reported the activities of Salafis in Iraq. They were suspected but still tolerated under the faith campaign. But for 'Uday and *Babil* and those party members who resented important aspects of the campaign, they were an easy target through which they could criticize 'Uday's rival, his maternal uncle, Interior Minister Watban Ibrahim Tikriti, and through him the president. These conclusions are supported by the enigmatic and vitriolic column. As for the senior politicians behind the "Wahhabis," according to an American intelligence source, at the instigation of Watban Ibrahim Tikriti, a group of "fundamentalists" demonstrated in late 1993 in front of 'Uday's television station *Sawt al-Shabbab Min Dar al-Salam* (The Voice of Youth from the Abode of Peace—that is, Baghdad). They protested against the American and other "corrupt" films shown by this station. Indeed, 'Uday's channel was showing American films, some of them quite promiscuous, that many party members enjoyed but that were seen by religious circles as un-Islamic. A short while afterward, the station, together with 'Uday's Radio Youth station, was closed down by the Ministry of the Interior, on the pretext that no operating license had been issued. The Iraqi media (including the party daily) called for the reopening of 'Uday's radio and television stations, after the "technical and operational mistakes" had been corrected. The stations did indeed reopen after two weeks.[171] The president's son had been competing for influence with his uncle, but there is no reason to doubt the wider resentment in the party's circles as well, in view of the "Wahhabization" of Iraqi public life. Pampering the "men of religion" and allowing the mosque to become more central in the citizen's life came at the expense of the party, and members could hardly be happy with such a change. According to one report of a foreign visitor, by 2001 this cultural party "revolt" had won the day. Despite the official ban on nightclubs, a nightclub culture of belly dancing and similar erotic performances had become quite widespread on private and semiprivate occasions observed in restaurants, at least in Baghdad. Likewise, in the late 1990s Iraqi TV broadcasts included both calls for prayer and reports on such erotic shows.[172]

Islamization and Foreign Policy

Relations with the Islamic World

In a private meeting with the Sudanese minister of agriculture in April 2002, Saddam gave vent to his frustration that his faith campaign had failed to achieve its foreign policy goal: "In the faith campaign in Iraq, our experience went through a form of continuity and tranquillity," he reported. However, since the campaign went so smoothly without opposition, he complained, "our Muslim and Arab brothers did not realize the extent of change we accomplished in Iraq." As a result of the campaign, "Students in Iraq learn about religion from the first grade to high school, and all the judges studied the Qur'an and the life of the Prophet. Anyone who failed was fired." Furthermore, "This applied to the party cadres as well," and "everyone's fate was determined regardless of position." To further impress his Islamist guest, he added, "The latest thing we decided is for businessmen to study the [Qur'anic] art of dealing and take a test. Based on that [test], the decision is made whether to allow them to practice business."[173] As befitting a leader with pan-Arab and now also pan-Islamic horizons, Saddam also invited visitors from Arab countries to participate in his Qur'an teaching courses. Because of financial limitations, the number of such visitors was small, but the direction was clear.[174] Still, Saddam's own assessment of the benefits of his campaign in the Arab and Islamic worlds was gloomy. Since it involved no mass arrests and torture, let alone any high-profile executions, the Islamization campaign ran along below the radar screens of the Islamic countries. This seems to have been Saddam's conclusion because, in the last analysis, all his courting of the Islamic world did not win him sufficient support to end the international embargo and to prevent the American attacks in 1991 and 2003. And yet his Islamic initiatives abroad did produce some positive results in the Sunni world. A main purpose of the 1986 love offensive directed at the Sudanese and Egyptian Muslim Brotherhood was to improve Iraq's foreign relations. Relations with Islamist-controlled Sudan were indeed improved: as mentioned above, the leader of Sudan's Islamist movement visited Baghdad soon after the 1991 Gulf War. Following the invasion of Kuwait in 1990 the Egyptian Muslim Brotherhood was cautious, trying not to antagonize the regime, which supported the United States. After a brief period of indecision, the Brotherhood eventually adopted a position that objected to American involvement. As we are told by an Egyptian scholar,

"Once Iraq began to rely heavily on Islamic propaganda and Saddam began to project himself as a reborn Muslim, they [the Muslim Brotherhood] came to see the invasion as an expression of hostility between two Islamic forces. They continued to condemn the invasion and ask for Iraqi withdrawal, however now within the context of settling the conflict . . . between Iraq and Kuwait."[175] However, as Tariq ʿAziz predicted in 1986, the alliance with the Muslim Brotherhood affected relations with Cairo.

Islamic Conferences

Beginning in 1983, every few years the Ministry of Endowments and Religious Affairs hosted a few hundred Sunni "men of religion" and Islamic intellectuals from all over the Muslim world, including countries with Muslim minorities, at a Popular Islamic Conference (*al-muʿtamar al-islami al-shaʿbi*). The conferences usually were convened when Iraq was in particular need of support. In April 1983, the first congress was convened after the Iraqi withdrawal from Khuzestan. As this was a government ministry that convened and hosted a religious gathering, it was one of the indications that Baʿthi Iraq no longer believed in the separation of religion from politics. During the Iran-Iraq War, the Popular Islamic Conferences became a vehicle to recruit support against the Iranian enemy. A few days before January 15, 1991, the deadline for the American ultimatum to Iraq to withdraw from Kuwait, a time when Iraq was bracing for war, the Ministry of Endowments convened yet another Popular Islamic Conference, this time to support Iraq against the United States and its allies, including Saudi Arabia, Egypt, and Syria. A few conferences were convened in the 1990s to mobilize the Islamic world against the international embargo. The congresses and other initiatives abroad, like the building of Islamic centers in various countries and the allocation of stipends to attract foreign students to government-sponsored Islamic institutes of education in Iraq, won Iraq some support in the Sunni world.[176] However, because few governments supported Iraq, in the end, none of those projects was sufficient to make a decisive contribution. All international Islamic efforts to expedite the end of the Iran-Iraq War or to prevent American-led offensives or to end the international embargo failed. The faith campaign, though, had a profound if bizarre effect on Iraq's relations with the Vatican.

The Pope's Visit to Iraq That Never Was

In September 1999, the Vatican made public Pope John Paul II's wish to visit Ur of the Chaldeans, or what is known as Tall al-Maqyar, in southern Iraq where the first Hebrew, the Patriarch Abraham, was born. In the official explanation, no connection between Abraham and Arabism or Islam was mentioned. The general consensus in the scientific community in the West is that if Abraham existed, he lived in the eighteenth century BCE, some eleven centuries before the Prophet Muhammad was born, and that he was a "Hebrew," while Arabs, or "Aribu," are mentioned for the first time in an Assyrian tablet from the ninth century BCE. A group of "Iraqi intellectuals" set out immediately to correct the papal mistake. They criticized the pope for not being forthcoming in defending Iraq against the United States, but his historical mistakes bothered them more. They defined Abraham as "the first Muslim" and an "ancestor of the Arabs." The former could be correct only if one interpreted "Muslim" as "monotheist," which medieval Islamic sources do, but the Iraqi intellectuals failed to do. Regarding the latter, according to Islamic sources the intellectuals were correct, but the Bible does not consider Ishmael an Arab. The intellectuals argued also that the Patriarch "was born in the land of the Arabs," in Sumerian Ur. When he was chased out of his birthplace, "Abraham began his struggle tour of the lands of the Arabs: . . . Harran, Palestine . . . Mecca. . . . He united believers . . . and formed the Muslim cult." All this, they complained, was not mentioned by the pope. The Iraqi intellectuals also protested the papal use of terms like "the Temple," "the children of Israel" (who actually appear often in the Qur'an as *Banu Isra'il*). They felt that this was nothing short of the "glorification of Israel." The pope apparently did not believe, they pointed out, that Jews wanted to kill Jesus twenty centuries ago, but God saved him by making one of his disciples look like him and be crucified. Finally, the Iraqi intellectuals addressed the pope directly: "You seek to strengthen fruitful dialogue with the Jews and form a full partnership with them and you forget their cries in Jerusalem [2,000 years ago]: 'Crucify him, crucify him! His blood must be spilled by us and by our children.'"[177] In the face of meek objection on the part of Tariq 'Aziz and the Foreign Ministry's experts to Saddam's insistence that the pope had first to correct his mistakes, Iraq rejected the pope's request, and the papal visit to Iraq was canceled. Such a visit could have helped Saddam in his efforts to lift the international embargo. At least, it would have eased his isolation. Its cancellation dealt a further blow to Iraq's international standing.

Chapter 7
What Kind of Islam?

The Renewal of Faith: A Quasi-Ecumenical Arab Sunni-Shi'i Islam

Some two years after the Kuwait war, Saddam told a gathering of Arab intellectuals that "Iraq's power today stems, in the first place, from faith in God." The Arabs won their historic battles because they strongly believed in the Islamic principles, he explained. However, he observed that in Iraq just then, "our faith is based on a kind of renewing of the [Islamic] Message [*tajdid al-risala*] and not just on inheriting . . . rites from the past."[1] This was not the first time he had presented himself as a Sunni-style Mahdi, but it was the first time Saddam had used 'Aflaq's perfectly secular nationalist term "*risala*" to denote the *Islamic* Message. Saddam betrayed his guru shamelessly. Thankfully, 'Aflaq was dead and could not object. Renewing Islam and rejecting inherited rites could sound Ikhwan style or even Wahhabi. Yet this was not the case.

The most ambitious and comprehensive definition of his roles as both the Reviver of Islam and the One Who Knows What God Wants came in Saddam's speech on Victory Day in 1994, celebrating the anniversary of the end of the Iran-Iraq War in 1988. It was a creative synthesis of a Ba'thi revolutionary anticlerical and anti-Islamist sentiment with his newfound religiosity. Saddam compared his religious approach to that of Ayatollah Khomeini and his regime. By implication, he also related his approach to that of the Sunni and Shi'i clerics and to Islamist movements of all colorations. The Iranians, he said, were attaching to Islam all "the sins of politics" and were using Islam as a political tool. Worse still, their approach to Islam was petrified, immune to the demands of the new age. "God Almighty does not like repetition," Saddam knew. Rather, God supported "innovation, improvement and change." Indeed, God himself had introduced changes from Adam through Noah, Abraham, and Moses to Muhammad. In each age a new prophet was sent with a new message, one that was suitable for the new circumstances. Muhammad was *khatam al-anbiyaa*, the Seal of the Prophets, he admitted. Yet extraordinary men still had a monumental role to play: "God . . . did not end the world after the new message." Rather, "God has left for Man the door wide open for *ijtihad* [interpretation of the Qur'an and Sunna] for life, in the light of faith." What was necessary now, Saddam argued, was "to renew the meanings and the ways for a more robust faith among the Muslims everywhere." "A Believing [Islamic] Arabism is the new road to faith and to rescuing the [Islamic] nation," he concluded.[2] In other words, Saddam's role as he saw it was the renewal and revival of Islam by way of the Arabs, Sunna and Shi'a alike, the role of an Arab Mahdi. This is an Islam more open to the world, more modern and flexible, in which the 'ulama will not be as central as in the "petrified" version. A typical product of his faith campaign and of the general trend toward Islamization was "Abu Muhammad," a nineteen-year-old anti-American insurgent from Tikrit who in 2004 claimed to be leading twenty fighting men. As the young fighter put it, all of them believed in "a mix of Islam and pan-Arabism."[3] Even though he was affiliated with a clear-cut Sunni insurgent group, one of whose goals was to prevent a Shi'i takeover under the American wing, "Abu Muhammad" did not mention the sectarian issue. In other words, he internalized Saddam's new semi- or quasi-ecumenical Sunni-Shi'i Arab Islam that was de facto preserving Sunni Arab hegemony.

The 'Ulama

How did Saddam see the role of the 'ulama? In his 2001 private meeting with Dr. Najmah Hibbat Allah, deputy president of the Upper House of India's Parliament, Saddam uttered his punch line: "Government affairs are too important to be left in the hands of mullas." In other words, both the Iranian approach of the rule of the *faqih* (religious jurist) and Taliban system of Mulla Omar's Afghanistan[4] were unacceptable. Saddam also explained to his guest that while in Iraq, every pupil and student studied Islam, including the Qur'an and Hadith, in school at every level, "we are not wasting our time on what the mullas are wasting their time [on]."[5] To judge from the context, by this statement he meant fanatical fatwas issued by radical muftis and would-be muftis, petrified jurisprudence detached from the reality of modern life. He also meant, apparently, the Shi'i sectarian theology and interpretation of history. Saddam never trusted the 'ulama of either sect: his *mukhabarat* (intelligence services) kept a watchful eye on each mosque and its personnel. He needed them to buttress his shaky legitimacy, but at the same time he was preparing a new generation of Sunni 'ulama to replace them, a generation of young, Ba'thi-educated 'ulama. If anything, his being forced to pamper them during his faith campaign only increased Saddam's hatred of the 'ulama of the old school. He often hinted at his dislike for and disapproval of the clerics, nowhere more clearly than in his instructions to the party on the eve of the American invasion. On January 23, 2003, the Presidential Office issued top-secret instructions to all security services, military intelligence, and other intelligence services. This was a time when an American invasion was almost certain. "God forbid if the Iraqi command falls to the Coalition Forces. . . . To all associates in your offices . . . work according to the following instructions: 1. Demolish and burn all the state offices and departments in the country [*nahb wa kharq kaffat dawa'ir al-dawla*]." 2. "Sabotage electrical power stations," as well as "water stations." Then "disrupt domestic and external communications." Then came an enigmatic instruction: "Recruit dependable elements and direct them to the mosques." Then, "associate with the Islamic religious university [*hawza 'ilmiyya*] in Najaf." No less puzzling was the instruction to "associate with . . . the Islamic parties," for those were precisely the parties the regime was trying to eliminate. Finally, there was a very strange instruction: "Assassination of the imams and preachers of the Friday mosques and [ordinary] mosques [*ightiyal a'imma wa khutaba al-jawami' wa'l masajid*]."[6] Maybe befriending the fundamentalists and the clerics was to be a step toward their assassination. Saddam always disliked competition.

Shari'a "Lite"

Even though he aligned himself with the Syrian and Sudanese Muslim Brotherhood, Saddam's newfound Islam was not similar to theirs, let alone that of the Wahhabis, al-Qa'ida, the Taliban, or any other Salafis. In his last message to the Iraqi people between June 1979 and April 1980, Saddam's nemesis Muhammad Baqir al-Sadr warned all Iraqi Muslims, Shi'is and Sunnis alike, of the regime's deviations both from 'Umar's and Abu Bakr's Islam and from 'Ali's Islam. He warned against Saddam's "oppression and tyranny" and his isolation from the people, protected by his *mukhabarat*, while the Rightly

Guided Caliphs were living among their people. He accused Saddam of monopolizing power "on a tribal basis." All these accusations were credible, but they represented Saddam's ruling style more than non-shar'i practices. It may equally credibly be argued that, except for the tribal component, Sadr's champion, Ayatollah Khomeini, ruled Iran in a similar fashion. Sadr, however, also accused Saddam of unambiguous shar'i sins: Saddam "dropped the religious ceremonies," apparently meaning the regime's limitations on Shi'i rites, and "fill[ed] the land with alcoholic drinks, pigs' fields, and all kinds of abominations." Also, Sadr claimed, Saddam did not derive his ideals "from our Islamic Message," as a legitimate leader should do, and he did not impose "the justice of Islam."[7] Whether or not Saddam paid attention to those accusations, his newly acquired Islam seemed to show that he was trying to demonstrate attachment to the shari'a. However, what he considered to be shar'i obligations that had to be enforced by the government was different from the interpretation of the Muslim Brotherhood, and very different from that of the various Salafi groups. Surprisingly, in his hateful and bitterly critical message of June 1979, Baqir al-Sadr did not accuse Saddam of deviating from Islam when it came to socioeconomic policies. The reason for that is not clear: after all, in Ba'thi Iraq in the 1970s the banking and taxation systems and many other aspects of the economy were a mix of Western and Soviet styles. In the early 1960s Sadr wrote his *Iqtisaduna* (*Our Economy*).[8] When it came to the philosophical foundations, the differences between Ba'thi Iraq and Sadr's vision of the correct Islamic economy were profound. However, the de facto main contours of the socioeconomic policies of the Ba'th state which came under the definition of "socialism" eerily resembled the main outlines of Sadr's Islamic social justice. The massive oil revenues in the second half of the 1970s enabled the regime to develop the infrastructure at such a breakneck speed and subsidized food, health services, education, energy, and so many other aspects of the economy that any scathing criticism would have been seen as irrelevant. As for not paying *zakat* (alms), the Islamic tax, taxes were so low that this, too, was of little relevance to most people. Sadr therefore chose his battles carefully.

One difference between Saddam's and the Muslim Brotherhood's Islam was that Saddam, while extremely proud of the myriad mosques he had ordered built, also boasted that he had built new churches.[9] Whether true or not, this was not exactly Muslim Brotherhood style. Another difference was that while imposing meaningful limitations on the sale of spirits, he still allowed it. Forbidding it altogether would have guaranteed a violent reaction from the military officers and deep resentment among party members. Interestingly, as of November 2012, alcohol in Muslim Brotherhood–controlled Egypt was still available under the same system as during Mubarak's era. Technically, one could buy spirits only in "tourist governorates," but those included Cairo, Alexandria, Giza, and other cities—in other words, most of the country. And yet the Muslim Brotherhood government chose to leave things as they were. As for pigs, here too former president Muhammad Mursi of Egypt did not interfere with the Christians' right to raise the animals.[10] Saddam did the same during his faith campaign. It may be that Mursi was waiting for the right moment when he could eliminate all spirits from Egypt and impose other shar'i rules, but a year into his presidency he still had not done this.

It is not clear what Sadr meant by "corruption." If Sadr meant that a dress code, including the hijab, was not imposed, Saddam went halfway. In one of the first salvos in his faith campaign he called on the Popular Councils (*majalis al-sha'b*), party-affiliated bodies spread across the country, to use their influence to persuade young women to dress in a modest fashion. However, as befitting a perfectly democratic leader, he made suggestions but refrained from imposing them:

> I have an opinion I want to share with you. This concerns the fact that some girls are wearing clothes that influence other girls. Let us go to the families of these girls . . . and tell them: We would like to see your women dress properly before God and the people. . . . Do not ask the authorities to do everything for you.[11]

And yet there was no imposition of any particular rules regarding dress code: under Ba'th rule Baghdad never saw Iranian-style morality police. Is the hijab covered by the shari'a? This depends on interpretation, and at least Muhammad 'Abduh, Grand Mufti of Egypt (1899–1905), ruled that the hijab was not a shar'i obligation. Saddam also ridiculed the Saudis for prohibiting women from driving cars.[12] If by "corruption" Sadr meant sexual promiscuity, then here too Saddam went halfway: the capital punishment law for prostitution demonstrated an intention. In practice, though, it was implemented very discriminately, when it served the regime's political needs.[13] If by "corruption" Sadr referred to photographs of scantily dressed foreign female film stars and fairly open discussions of sex issues, all those continued to appear in the regime's media. Under his faith campaign, Saddam also did not change the Law of Personal Status back to the monarchy status quo as demanded by the 'ulama, nor did he annul the role of the civil courts in this realm. The draconian punishments for stealing and related crimes were practiced more generally. This could somehow be seen as imposing "the justice of Islam," as Sadr demanded, but it is not at all certain that this was what Sadr intended. If by "the justice of Islam" Sadr meant forbidding usury or even interest payments, then here too Saddam went halfway. In a government meeting in December 1996, Saddam objected to usury and interest payments, and the press supported this Islamic approach.[14] Yet no laws or regulations were ever introduced outlawing interest payments. Sadr accused the Ba'th of ignoring the religious "ceremonies," apparently meaning the limitations they imposed on the Shi'i days of commemoration. Indeed, between 1977 and 1991 such limitations were severe, but between 1992 and 1999 most of the limitations were removed, to be reimposed again as a result of Shi'i civil unrest. In other respects, mosque-going remained relatively unhindered. Finally, Sadr protested against the "pigs' fields," but why should Christians be prevented from raising pigs? The Ba'th regime never mentioned this issue. Interestingly, post-Mubarak Egypt under the hegemony of the Muslim Brotherhood did not touch this issue either. It has to be said that while Sadr's shari'a-inspired complaints against the Ba'th rule were nebulous, some of the faith campaign's enactment could be seen as a response to his last message. Still, Sadr's main focus was on general religiosity and on the ecumenical message, as was Saddam's in his faith campaign. Sadr's religiosity was genuine. Saddam's, at least at first, was cynical, but whether or not he eventually became a born-again Muslim, he did go through some Islamic motions.

Not being a mulla himself, Saddam naturally objected ferociously to the Iranian concept of "the rule of the [religious] jurist." He also strongly objected to the Saudi way of running the state, meaning, apparently, the right of the 'ulama to veto the decisions of the political leadership. While it is true that in certain realms Saddam did introduce what he himself called an "[Islamic] upheaval in the lives of the Iraqis,"[15] he did not impose Qur'an or Hadith studies on his military officers, or even on all civilian party members. Such courses were imposed only on the more senior cadres: members of the Regional Leadership, the *makatib tanzim* (organization bureaus) and the *furu'* (branches).[16] Sadr demanded a rule inspired by "the Islamic Message." Rhetorically speaking, in the faith campaign the Ba'th indeed exchanged their secular message for the Islamic Message. And yet Saddam's message was shari'a "lite."

Gender Issues: Islamist Inspiration, Ba'thi Practice

The Law of Personal Status

Despite his Islamization steps, Saddam did not Islamize the secular 1963 law that was based on General 'Abd al-Karim Qasim's 1959 law, nor did he reverse the pro-female amendments of 1978 and those of the mid-1980s. The reason seems to have been that annulling the law would have meant returning all matters of personal status to the shar'i courts. This would have greatly strengthened the 'ulama, far beyond what Saddam had to do and had already done as part of his faith campaign. As a result of his strong dislike for and competition with the religious establishment, Sunna and Shi'a alike, the realm of personal status issues, among the most important ones in Islam, remained essentially secular to the very end. That the clauses relating to inheritance were close to the Shi'i shar'i law was a legacy from the Ba'th rule of 1963 and had nothing to do with the faith campaign.

Women in the Workforce and the Leadership

During the 1990s, Saddam declared a few times that women should give up paid employment and support their families by working from home, for example by producing clothes. In 2000, he reportedly ordered women out of government jobs, arguing that "keeping women at home gives the highest meaning to humanistic values." This call was supported by the General Union of Iraqi Women (GUIW).[17] This was clearly an attempt on Saddam's part to stroke the male ego, the result of both religious and tribal values that saw men as superior. But even Saddam was unable to change reality. He could not fire women en masse from government jobs, and he could not prevent girls from enrolling in institutions of higher education. Had he done the former, he would have had to hire unqualified men and pay them more. Had he done the latter, it would have been such a shocking departure from party tradition and tenets of faith that it would have caused an uproar. Between the early 1980s and at least until 1997, when unemployment in Iraq was very high, especially among men, the situation changed very little. Statistics on the education sector show a gradual increase in the percentage of women as students and as teachers. More generally, there was no decline in women's share in the salaried workforce.[18]

Furthermore, at the same time that Saddam declared that women should stay home, he and the state-run media also acted in the opposite direction.

For example, at least until 2000, professional women, mainly in technical and engineering professions, but also managers, journalists, and even judges, still appeared fairly regularly in the Iraqi press.[19] Likewise, in the party's Regional Leadership elections of May 2001, the scientist Dr. Huda Salih Mahdi 'Ammash became the first woman ever to enter the Regional Leadership. Her election was a generous gesture toward her father, General Salih Mahdi 'Ammash, who was one of the five members of the first Revolutionary Command Council (RCC) under Ba'th rule (1968–70) and who had been ousted by Saddam. It was also a gesture toward all Iraqi women. This certainly was no Riyadh, nor was it Tehran or Khartoum. But soon after the demise of the Ba'th regime in 2003, the new "democratic" regime introduced by the Americans quickly caught up with Tehran when it decided to fire all female judges because, according to Islam, a judge must be a male.

Another area in which the Ba'th regime pretended to imitate Tehran and Riyadh but did not quite do so concerned the dress code for women. In official photographs, senior party women adopted a peculiar dress code. Thus in 1997, GUIW chairwoman Manal Yunis was shown in the press wearing a hijab.[20] On the Regional Leadership, Dr. Huda Salih Mahdi 'Ammash similarly made a point of appearing in her official photographs wearing a khaki-colored veil to go with her military uniform.[21] Since the mid-1990s, the president's wife, too, appeared regularly wearing a scarf. However, in all those cases the scarves were merely symbolic. They left the hair at the front of the head fully exposed, as if to say, "See, I am covering my hair to demonstrate piety, but Iraq is not Iran; here, a woman's hair should be seen."

Female Sexuality

In another cultural sphere in its last decade, the attitude toward sexuality, in particular female sexuality, the Ba'th regime exhibited baffling inconsistency or confusion. Generally speaking, the early seventies saw a fairly open discussion in the Iraqi media of sex issues in a way that reflected Western liberal influences.[22] Short stories about romantic relationships between young men and women appeared in the magazines. For many years, one could find in the Iraqi press media photographs of scantily dressed young women in seductive poses, even though from the mid-1970s on, most were foreign models, not Iraqi or Arab. This was a subtle compromise with public opinion, as it allowed the media to continue to demonstrate the Ba'th disdain for the clergy and their "fossilized" religious values without being criticized for degrading Arab women. Here, as in the case of expressions of atheism, the mid-1970s represented the first watershed: the sociocultural conservative backlash worked only to a limited degree. Expressions of both sexual liberalism and atheism disappeared, but only the most blatant ones. Under the faith campaign, sexual promiscuity should have disappeared altogether, but it did not. Prostitution was rampant, at least in Baghdad. This was the result of the economic depression and the existence of many war widows who had to provide for themselves and their children. Western male reporters who spoke to me after returning from Baghdad on condition of anonymity reported that the *mukhabarat*, too, contributed to this social affliction by hiring the services of young women to spy on visitors.[23] 'Uday Saddam Husayn's beheadings of those accused of prostitution hardly helped solve this problem.

The 1990s saw a great deal of internal regime contradictions regarding female sexuality. Regime spokespersons attacked women who used cosmetics, yet the Iraqi press implied praise of independent women who chose their own lovers. There was open discussion of the fact that by stopping sex education in schools as part of the faith campaign, Iraq was sinking into the swamp of venereal diseases and unplanned pregnancies.[24] In 1994, 'Uday Saddam Husayn publicized in his daily newspaper the performances of a troupe of Egyptian transvestites in Baghdad.[25] How could Saddam have allowed this? In addition to religious considerations, it should be remembered that in his 1991 meeting with tribal shaykhs, he urged them to kill all transvestites.[26] It seems that Saddam could tolerate the public display of transvestitism because it ridiculed Egyptian rather than Iraqi men. Religiously speaking, though, it was indeed an abomination. Baghdad was not Riyadh.

Family Planning: Confusion Ruling the Waves

An inexplicable inconsistency—or confusion—was revealed in the 1990s in the realm of the regime's demographic policy. In the 1970s the regime established a large number of centers of family planning (*tanzim al-usra*). In those days, the term meant mainly birth control.[27] In June 1981, in an initial response to the casualties of the war and the growing alarm over the strategic implications of the demographic gap between Iraq and Iran, the RCC issued Ordinance No. 632. It promised substantial economic incentives to Iraqis who married before they reached age twenty-two. These incentives included a loan of 500–750 Iraqi dinars (around $1,500–$2,250), a grant of 500 Iraqi dinars, free lodging for students, free travel all over Iraq, and priority in receiving government-sponsored homes.[28] A few years later Saddam announced, "Each family [should] produce five children. . . . The family that does not produce at least four children deserves to be harshly reprimanded. . . . Procreation is one of the most essential factors of strength."[29] In the failed battle of February–March 1986 to regain the Faw Peninsula, Iraq lost more than 50,000 men during the forty days of fighting, and in the successful defense against the huge Iranian offensive in the Basra area between December 1986 and March 1987, Iraq again lost tens of thousands of young men. In response to those horrendous losses, in late 1987 the regime launched a new campaign to increase fertility.[30] The surprising aspect of the public pro-reproduction campaign in the 1980s, though, was that with the exception of the president's speeches, it lacked the high-profile Islamic trademark, already prevalent in other areas in those days.[31] Clearly, the senior party officials and professionals did not yet share their president's wish to placate the religious circles. This approach changed radically during the faith campaign.

As part of the faith campaign, in mid-1994 the GUIW organized a conference at which clerics and "experts" explained the intimate connection between fertility (*injab*) and the fulfillment of "religious duties" (*al-furudh al-diniyya*). They urged all Iraqis to increase fertility and praised the president for his "unlimited support" for encouraging more Iraqi births. The conference warned against "limiting the birth rate" (*tahdid al-nasal*) because it was "an unforgivable crime" against society and Islam. The conference announced that babies were gifts from God and that Islam did not allow "killing a soul," that is, using contraceptives.[32] Indeed, despite the economic strife the government made efforts to encourage an increase in the birth rate. In 1993, it decided, for example, to provide electrical appliances at reduced prices for young couples as part of the effort to encourage people to marry young, so that they could have more children.[33] A few months later, Saddam allocated 10 million Iraqi dinars for young married couples in the Shi'i governorates of Maysan ('Amara) and Dhi Qar (Nasiriyya). In each of the governorates, more than 250 couples were supposed to receive this stipend.[34] The press dedicated space to the notion that Iraq was one of those countries furthest from the danger of a "population explosion" and that there was thus every reason to encourage population growth.[35] At a symposium on population growth, Minister of Planning Dr. Samal Majid Faraj emphasized the great efforts made by the government to encourage the birth rate, and vowed that the Iraqi population would indeed continue to grow by leaps and bounds. Strangely, the conference was organized in cooperation with the United Nations.[36]

A closer look at the Iraqi media reveals that the Ministry of Health worked at cross-purposes to Saddam's messages and to the warning not "to kill a soul." In June 1993, the ministry decided to open a number of clinics in maternity hospitals in Baghdad, Ninneweh (Mosul), and Basra, to advise women about family planning. These centers were instructed to provide to the public birth control devices at subsidized prices.[37] A family planning clinic was opened in the maternity hospital of Karbala. A similar clinic was opened in Diwaniyya, and it was reported that the clinic would deal with *tanzim wa tahdid al-nasal* (organizing and limiting fertility).[38] "Preventing pregnancy" (*man' al-hamal*) was announced as an official policy, and the Iraqi Association for Family Planning started special courses for female physicians.[39] The ministry organized a conference in cooperation with the Association of Family Planning (*Jam'iyyat Tanzim al-Usra*). At the conference, the minister of health emphasized the importance of family planning to reduce maternal deaths, a politically sensitive term for reducing the number of births per woman.[40] This inconsistency is evidence that, at least into the mid-1990s, despite the official ideology of Islamization and despite Saddam's expressed wish to keep women at home as wombs in the service of the nation, many party officials and health professionals continued the secular policies of the 1970s. In defiance of Saddam's demand, the birth rate actually fell. This was mainly the result of a decrease in the number of marriages owing to economic difficulties, and married couples tending to have fewer children out of a general sense of insecurity.[41]

Pagan Cultures: No to the Taliban

"What Happened in Afghanistan Is Damage to Islam"

Although any hint of atheism and any explicit mention of secularism disappeared from the cultural and intellectual spheres, some central components of the Ba'th Party's antireligious posture remained unchanged under the faith campaign. Paramount among those elements was Saddam's obsession with pre-Islamic (*Jahili*) civilizations: to his last day, he was proud of the pagan civilizations of Mesopotamia and profoundly disdainful of the approach of the 'ulama and religious fundamentalists of all colorations to culture and to the needs of the modern age. "What happened in Afghanistan is damage to Islam" (*isa'a lil islam*), he said in a private meeting with the Muslim deputy president of the Indian Senate on her visit to Baghdad. "They destroyed the Buddha monument [at Bamiyan] 1,400 years after the existence of Islam, as if Islam expects Mulla Omar to do this! Does this mean that it is our duty here in Iraq to destroy the civilization of Babylon? . . . Does it mean that this Mulla Omar is the only one who understands Islam? . . . Government affairs are too important to be left in the hands of mullas."[42]

Another example underscoring Saddam's attachment to the glory that was pagan Mesopotamia, despite his Islamization campaign, was his reformulating past glories to legitimize present governance. In his annual speech on Victory Day in 1999, celebrating the end of the Iran-Iraq War, Saddam dwelled on the historical riddle that, despite the occupation of Babylon by the Persians in 539 BCE and the leveling of Baghdad at the hands of the Mongols in 1258 CE, the "Iraqi man's spirit" remained solid. How was it, he wondered, that the Iraqi man was able to rise again from the ashes, as he did under the Ba'th after eight hundred years of slumber? Since the dawn of history, he answered himself, the Iraqis had always strived to reach the summit, never settling for a place in the middle and never accepting mediocrity, and they had always found the right leadership to guide them to greatness. Alluding to himself, he explained:

> Sumer, Babylon, Baghdad, Assyria . . . and Ur did not live in the middle, between the bottom and the peak. When they eye the peak and when they are sure of the guide's sincerity and honesty . . . they make their way to the peak to occupy it and serve as the highest beacon . . . sending out a light . . . guiding other people . . . who cannot find their way.[43]

Even as he was settling his rhetorical account with a hostile Iran, Saddam could not forget Iraq's ancient history. The Elamite (Persian) king Schuturk-Nachonettihad, he reminded his people, stole from Babylon the Hammurabi obelisk on which the first codex of laws was inscribed because he himself could not create such a marvel, and felt envious. He even tried to erase Hammurabi's name from the stele, showing the hate (for the Iraqis) that he had inherited from his Persian forefather. Hundreds of years later, the Persian king Cyrus destroyed Babylon, the pearl of the world's civilization at the time. He did this in collaboration with the Jews. Why? This was an "expression of blind and stupid inability" on the part of the Persians, Saddam said.[44] (In fact, Cyrus did not destroy Babylon after he conquered it.) In a speech to (mainly Shi'i) party members and policemen who had fought bravely against the Shi'i revolutionaries in Maysan ('Amara) in March 1991, the president emphasized that "in the ancient books" there was always "one Iraq." When the West "lived in caves without civilization," Iraq as a united nation had already created the Sumerian, Babylonian, and Assyrian civilizations, in a long and glorious succession.[45] In a lecture to the Iraqi Students Union, implying the Shi'i-Sunni divide, he reminded the budding intellectuals that their national history extended for six or seven thousand years, and that this long and glorious history had been created by all Iraqis, not just by one or two groups.[46]

Indeed, even during his faith campaign, Saddam's court intellectuals continued to present him as the human incarnation of the long and heroic history of pre-Islamic Mesopotamia in the same style of personality cult as before the campaign. Thus, for example, Dr. Fawzi Rashid discussed the month Tammuz (July) and the Mesopotamian fertility god of the same name, whose meaning in Sumero-Akkadian is "the Good Son." He explained that "the ancient Iraqis" understood well the critical importance of the "leader-hero." As a result, they deified a leader whose name was Tammuz. When asked whether the modern Iraqis too understand this imperative, he answered, "Yes! If we observe the modern history of Iraq until our day, the day of the leader Saddam Husayn, we find out that there is a strong connection between the month of Tammuz and the appearance of the hero-leader [who is] a good son to his people and nation."[47] In another interview, Rashid compared Saddam to the ultimate Mesopotamian ruler, Gilgamesh. Like Saddam, like Gilgamesh, the court intellectual emphasized, the leader united the nation, and like all other "ancient Iraqi kings" Saddam, too, deeply loved and was loved by the people.[48] Saddam himself mentioned pre-Islamic Iraqi history with great pride both in public and in private discussions with his elite. In a closed-door discussion with his government in 1993, for example, he insisted that the annexation of Kuwait was Iraq's undeniable right because "this has been part of our land since the Sumerians."[49] On Revolution Day in 1994, Saddam expressed a wish to be seen by the Iraqis as their god. He told his people:

> Some 5,000 years ago, the Iraqis produced Tammuz, the man and the leader, who took good care of the needs of his people. . . . They greatly honored him and placed him in the highest possible rank in life in accordance with the standards of that time [declaring him god]. . . . The people called Tammuz the Virtuous Son [the translation from Sumerian of the name Du-mu-zi]. Since the . . . July 1968 Revolution, Tammuz [read: Saddam as his reincarnation] returned to the field of responsibility . . . after a long absence . . . of 700 years . . . . Tammuz returned as

a leader of the people and a Virtuous Son. Tammuz is back to protect the weak from themselves [read: to save the Shiʻa and the Kurds from themselves] . . . to nourish the elements of virtue in their minds, and to straighten the elements of weakness and evil within them. He is back to protect them from the others, the wolves of the foreigner and the wolves of their [own] kin. . . . Tammuz is back, a faithful son of the people and the country and a wise, experienced leader with his new principles, adopted by his glorious revolution of . . . July 1968. . . . You [Iraqis] have proven for over 3,000 years that you are a loyal people. You have given Du-mu-zi/Tammuz the trait of a Faithful Son and you highly cherished him. . . . [The Iraqis] are qualified to play their [leading] role within the [Arab] nation.[50]

By the return of Tammuz, Saddam could mean the Baʻth Party that came to power in Tammuz (July) 1968, but far more likely, he meant that he was as great as, or even the reincarnation of, the Sumerian-Akkadian-Babylonian god of plenty. Either way, this meant that his Islam did not see anything negative in pre-Islamic cultures. Maybe he even saw a mild flaw in Islam in the sense that under Islam, the deifying of humans was no longer allowed.

Sufi Islam in Iraq

Historical Background

The regime's attitude toward Sufi Islam may serve as further evidence that Saddam's interpretation of Islam was very different from Salafi or Wahhabi Islam. The Islamic mystical trend known as Sufism has deep roots in what is today Iraq. No figure in early Sufism is more controversial than Abu al-Mughith Husayn ibn Mansur Baydawi, known as al-Hallaj (c. 858–922). Islamic orthodoxy regarded him as a dire heretic, though the Sufis were inspired by certain aspects of his approach to religion, emphasizing the emotional over the intellectual way to God. In the modern age, the great French Orientalist Louis Massignon (1883–1962) studied him in great depth.[51] Al-Hallaj was executed in ʻAbbasid Baghdad for heresy.

Baghdad served as the center of classical Sufism in the eleventh century, whence the mystical discipline spread as far as central Asia and India.[52] According to an April 2004 report from Falluja, one of Iraq's most orthodox

Sunni Iraqi cities,[53] along with the strength of orthodox institutions there one could also find strong Sufi networks. The London-based newspaper *al-Hayat* found that most of the Falluja anti-American insurgents were affiliated with the orthodox Muslim Brotherhood, and some with a Wahhabi trend, but in addition the Sufi orders of the Qadiriyya, the Naqshbandiyya, the Rifa'iyya, the Shadhiliyya, the Darqiyya, the Badawiyya, and the Halabiyya were represented among the insurgents. There was no contradiction between orthodoxy and Sufism there: Sufi orders occasionally met for *halaqat al-dhikr* (circle of prayer, or literally "circles of mentioning God") in the mosques after the orthodox afternoon ('asr) or evening (al-'asha) prayer, implying that the purist Wahhabi total rejection of Sufism had little sway in town.[54] According to an academic Iraqi source, Iraq also had a limited representation of the Bektashi order, whose main base is in Turkish Anatolia.[55]

In the twentieth century the single most important Sufi order in Iraq was the Qadiriyya, established in Baghdad in the late twelfth century by Shaykh 'Abd al-Qadir al-Kaylani (al-Gaylani). Ever since, their main center has remained in Baghdad, even though their teachings spread throughout the Islamic world. Early on in their existence they became the target of criticism from Islamic orthodox purists. The practice of visiting their *'khalwa* (a hermitage) was sharply criticized by Ibn Taymiyya. Some other practices, too, were frowned upon, such as the use of musical instruments in their *dhikr* ceremonies.[56] Since the rise of the Hanbali purist orthodox movement of Ibn 'Abd al-Wahhab in Arabia, later to be known as the *Wahhabiyya* (Wahhabis) or *al-Muwahhidun*, "the Monotheists," rivalry between them and the Qadiriyya has been a constant feature in Baghdad. There is almost no Qadiri religious practice that the Wahhabis do not denounce, and almost no unique Wahhabi tenet of faith that the Qadiris do not reject. When the British forces seized Baghdad from the Ottomans in1917, the few Wahhabi 'ulama in town, led by a member of the Alusi family, presented ferocious opposition to the new regime, while the Qadiris, led by the elderly Shaykh 'Abd al-Rahman al-Kaylani (or al-Gaylani), concentrated on returning life to normalcy and using the British to advance the country's interests (such as including Mosul and Kirkuk in Iraq).

The history of the Iraqi Naqshbandiyya begins with Shaykh Dhiya' al-Din Khalid (1776–1827), a Kurd from the Shahrizur district. At that time, the leading Sufi order among Kurds and Arabs alike was the Qadiriyya. Shaykh Khalid traveled to Delhi to study under Shah Ghulam 'Ali of the Naqshbandiyya-Mujaddidiyya order. Then he returned to Iraq as Shah Ghulam's top emissary in the Ottoman realm. Shaykh Khalid trained a large body of elite scholars, who went on to form the critical mass of the Naqshbandiyya order in Iraq and Syria. His teaching stressed that the practice of mysticism (*tasawwuf*) was complementary to but not a substitute for orthodox religious knowledge (*'ilm*). His followers were expected to master the science of traditional jurisprudence at the same time as they embarked on spiritual quests under the guidance of a Sufi master.[57] As a result of this initiative, disciples of the Naqshbandiyya were better trained than those of the Qadiriyya. Unlike the latter, who preached among the underprivileged, the Naqshbandis generally belonged to middle-class or well-to-do sections of society.[58] Shaykh Khalid instructed his followers to support the Ottoman sultan, and asked God to "destroy the Jews, the Christians, the Zoroastrians [*majus*], and the Persian Shi'is [*rawafidh al-a'ajim*], devastate and destroy the heretics and the accursed *Khawarij*." By *Khawarij*, he apparently meant the Wahhabis. The dual trends within Islam that most threatened the Naqshbandiyya were, on the one hand, unorthodox Sufi orders that the Naqshbandis regarded as deviant, and on the other, puristic orthodox zealots who rejected Sufism entirely. Sheikh Khalid died in Damascus in 1827. Despite his attempt to maintain his disciples' unity after his death, no figure was acknowledged as sole successor.[59]

With the authority of the Naqshbandi order diffused among numerous 'ulama throughout Iraq and Syria by the late nineteenth century, local notables were able to convert their status as tribal leaders (*aghas*) into religious authority that was passed, like tribal leadership, from father to son. The most significant example of the mobilization of Naqshbandi Sufism into political power was the rise of the Barzanis in Kurdistan. The Barzani shaykhs' religious and spiritual erudition attracted followers of various origins, some tribal and some nontribal peasants, to a new movement that was internally egalitarian and willing to accept new converts, but "in the course of conflict with surrounding tribes came to behave very much like a tribe."[60] By the 1920s, the quasi-tribal Barzanis had become the standard-bearers of Kurdish national resistance to Baghdad's assertions of control over the north. At the same time the Talabani clan, affiliated with the older Qadiriyya, built its own base of support in Sulaymaniyya, driven by a long-standing enmity with the Barzanis. The rivalry between these two Sufi-inspired clans would become the basis of the most salient schism in Iraqi Kurdish society, the division between Barzani's Kurdish Democratic Party and Talabani's Patriotic Union of Kurdistan.[61] Shaykh Khalid also had a strong influence on the Arabs of Iraq.[62] Nonetheless, the older Sufi orders, mainly the Qadiriyya, continued to predominate in mainly Arab central and southern Iraq. In 2003, Shaykh Bakr al-Samarra'i, the imam of the Kaylani mosque, the center of the Qadiriyya, estimated that there were 80 million members of the order worldwide, including two million Iraqis. If correct, this would make the Qadiriyya the largest religious order in the country.[63]

The Sufis under the Ba'th

As in other aspects of religious life in Iraq, the Ba'th infiltrated and exerted control over the Sufi networks. When Saddam embarked on his faith campaign, part of this campaign was support for Sufi orders. The regime considered the Sufis politically an innocuous outlet for the growing religiosity of Iraqis.[64] Indeed, Sufi Islam was seen as a counterweight to the Salafis and Wahhabis and as such a very useful tool in the faith campaign. In exchange for official support, the Sufis were expected to toe the Ba'th political line or remain apolitical, which they did. The rejuvenation of Sufi life was overseen by 'Izzat Ibrahim al-Duri, vice chairman of the RCC, who was a member of the Qadiriyya and Rifa'iyya Sufi orders.[65] From time to time in the 1990s, certain Sufi orders were mentioned favorably in the regime's media and even given some academic attention. One such Sufi order is the Kasnazaniyya, a subdivision of the Qadiriyya. Most of the members are Kurds, and their main center is in the Kirkuk area. Like its mother organization, this particular subdivision made its peace with the Ba'th regime soon after the latter came to power in Baghdad. Under the Ba'th, they were not political, but they agreed to make 'Izzat Ibrahim al-Duri one of their shaykhs as a gesture to the regime.[66] A small group belonging to that order was sometimes invited to parties organized by the president's family, on which occasions they would stage a highly dangerous and unusual performance for the benefit of their hosts. They would stick knives and swords through their bodies, even in their heads, and in one case one of the performers allowed 'Uday Saddam Husayn to pull out a sword from his body (very slowly and carefully). This amazing feat was recorded on a video cassette that was shown by CBS in 1997. The shaykh of the order regularly fulfilled his duty of congratulating the president on important occasions. The media gave such homage publicity, and in this way implied regime recognition of the legitimacy of Sufi activities.[67] The Kurdish shaykh of the Kasnazaniyya, Muhammad al-Shaykh 'Abd al-Karim al-Kasnazani al-Husayni, was known to have lived in Baghdad as recently as 1996.[68] Saddam himself showed a great deal of respect for and attention to the Kasnazaniyya.[69] Other Qadiri branches, too, won official recognition. Thus, for example, Shaykh Sa'd al-

Din Hatim Salih was reported in 1993 to be the shaykh of al-Qadiriyya al-Hiyaliyya.[70] In 1992, the shaykh of the Rifaʿi order, al-Sayyid Muhammad Daʾud Khazam al-Samarraʾi, died. The regime's press made public the fact that a special meeting of members of the order would take place in the order's *takiya* (monastery) in al-Madaʾin to commemorate the first year of his departure.[71] The regime occasionally urged the Sufi orders to participate in celebrations designed to provide the leader and regime with a semblance of public support. For example, as part of the celebrations of *Salamat al-Watan wal-Qaʾid* (The Wholeness of the Homeland and the Leader-Commander) in the Sunni neighborhood of al-Aʿzamiyya of Baghdad, it was announced that the neighborhood's Sufi orders would participate by organizing *dhikr* ceremonies, as well as *al-madih al-sharif* (The Noble Tribute) in support of "the personality of the *Sayyid* President."[72] On occasion, sympathetic learned articles in the press discussed the various Sufi orders in Iraq. Such an accurate article appeared in early 1993, dwelling on the three main orders in Iraq, the Qadiriyya, the Rifaʿiyya, and the Naqshbandiyya.[73] Because under the faith campaign the political atmosphere was Sufi-friendly even more than it was orthodox Islam-friendly, Sufi influence was everywhere in the Sunni areas. It is likely, therefore, that government and even party officials and military officers emulated Saddam's Deputy Commander in Chief ʿIzzat Ibrahim al-Duri[74] and joined Sufi *tariqa*s, but both the open sources and the internal documents remain silent about it.

During a March 2002 state visit to Damascus, ʿIzzat Ibrahim al-Duri toured the tomb of the revered Sufi saint Muhyi al-Din Ibn al-ʿArabi. The announcer made sure that the religious connotation of the visit would not be lost on the viewers.[75] A similar message of connection between the regime and Sufi groups was sent in August 2002, when the Sufi Shaykh Bakr ʿAbd-al-Razzaq al-Samarraʾi delivered a Friday sermon from the Abu Hanifa mosque, the most important Sunni mosque in Baghdad. He urged "all Muslims in the world, and Arabs in particular, as well as the followers of the noble Sufi schools . . . [to] strike at British and American interests."[76] Through this statement, al-Samarraʾi legitimized both the Baʿth and the Sufi practices, which were anathema to the Salafi and Wahhabi extremists. Sayyid Ahmad al-Kaylani, a descendant of Shaykh ʿAbd al-Qadir al-Kaylani and custodian of his shrine, who under Saddam served as Iraq's ambassador to Pakistan, struck an even stronger pro-Saddam and pro–faith campaign chord. In an interview with *Asia Times* just before the Second Gulf War, he defended Saddam's regime as having "fully implemented Islamic rules in letter and spirit," contrary to the hostile interpretations of the campaign by the

Wahhabis and the Muslim Brotherhood.[77] On the whole, the Sufis fulfilled the role assigned to them by the regime.

The Sufis after the Ba'th

In its final days, the Ba'th regime may have reconsidered its faith in the Kasnazaniyya. Sufi leaders told the Americans that they had been plotting with Kurdish leaders for the downfall of the regime. Indeed, the Kasnazaniyya was originally the Kurdish branch of the Qadiri order in Kurdistan. During the last days of the regime, witnesses reported that government forces had rounded up and executed at least forty men from the Sufi Kasnazan mosque south of Baghdad. In April 2003, American forces uncovered the bodies of dozens of Sufis in Baghdad.[78] After the regime had fallen, there was speculation that 'Izzat Ibrahim al-Duri himself was coordinating anti-American resistance through the Kasnazaniyya network.[79] This information was never confirmed, and the Kasnazaniyya order was in fact sympathetic to the new system. The most important orders, the Qadiris and Rifa'is, were not actively opposed to the American occupation.[80] This may explain the attacks on Sufi centers by al-Qa'ida-affiliated Salafi terrorists, who had two scores to settle with the Sufis, their nonorthodox Islam, and their passive support for the post-Ba'th order.[81]

Insurgents belonging to a variety of small Sufi groups were individually involved in anti-American operations in al-Anbar already by 2003, but until the summer and fall of 2006 no major Sufi order was officially active militarily. Then the first group appeared, the Squadrons of Shaykh 'Abd al-Qadir al-Kaylani (Gaylani). In February 2007 another Sufi insurgent group declared itself the Army of the Naqshbandi Order (*Jaysh al-Tariqa al-Naqshbandiyya*). They issued a statement along with a video posting of an attack, explaining their decision to join the insurgency. Citing growing sectarianism and injustice committed by the "despicable Bush . . . and the surrogate sectarian [Shi'i] government," the group declared its resolve to fight against the "racist crimes" of the "Safawi" power. By this they adopted the vocabulary of the Sunni insurgents, be they ex-Ba'this or Islamists: the Shi'i-hegemonic government in Baghdad was accused of being an Iranian puppet. "The Army of the Men of the Naqshbandi Order," they added, "fights the occupying infidels and their surrogates . . . in order to prove to the whole world that the *mujahidin* are . . . Iraqis and are not, as portrayed by our enemies, foreigners." Finally, they lamented the execution of Saddam Husayn, whom they referred to as the "great president, our *mujahid* leader."

They also made clear their nationalist character by stating, "Our hands were never smeared with Iraqi blood."[82] In other words, they were averse to killing Shi'is for being Shi'is, a different approach from that of al-Qa'ida affiliates like Abu Mus'ab al-Zarqawi.

The main reasons why those Sufi orders joined the insurgency were the eruption of a full-fledged civil war following the destruction of *al-'Ataba al-'Askariyya*, the tomb of the tenth and eleventh Shi'i Imams, in Samarra in February 2006, and the execution of Saddam Husayn in December 2006. Being both Sufi and purist Sunni orthodox, the Naqshbandiyya are the most likely to continue the struggle against the new Shi'i-hegemonic system. On April 23, 2013, a Naqshbandiyya group attacked a military roadblock at the town of Huweija. The army attacked the Naqshbandi center (*takiya*) and anyone in the vicinity, and fifty-three people, including women and children, were killed. This started a series of confrontations that, owing to al-Qa'ida's involvement, by mid-2014 had resulted in thousands of deaths.[83] In June 2014, the Naqshbandiyya, under the leadership of 'Izzat Ibrahim and in cooperation with the militant group Islamic State of Iraq and Syria (ISIS), led an onslaught on Mosul that continues at the time of this writing.

The Effect of the Faith Campaign on the Shi'i and Sunni Communities

Even though attending the mosque frequently, especially in groups, was still a sure way to draw the attention of the internal security services, people were more comfortable than at any time since 1970 attending the prayers and commemoration days. The increased attendance added to the clerics' social standing. This process was given a boost when the government increased the clerics' salaries, as well as their employment and media exposure. Islam was suddenly omnipresent: in the schools, in the university, in the media, in the legal system, even in Ba'th Party branch meetings. By jumping on it the regime gave the moving Islamic wagon an additional push, and with it upgraded the status of all the 'ulama. While the senior Shi'i 'ulama had already been comfortable economically and highly respected by their flock, those who benefited most from the faith campaign were mainly the local Sunni 'ulama and the Shi'i lower-rank clerics. Mosque functionaries in both sects, the leaders of prayer (imams) and preachers (khatibs), as well as other religious functionaries such as the teachers of religion in religious madrasas and in state schools and the Shi'i *sada*, saw their socioeconomic status going up. Suddenly they found themselves in leadership positions they had never had in Iraq. To some extent they eclipsed the secular party officials because, as Saddam had predicted in 1977, when it came to Islam, the clerics were far better equipped. As the mosque became more central to community life, it threatened the power of the party centers. Moreover, some people did not stop at the state-sponsored moderate Islamization. On the Shi'i side the anti-Da'wa law took care of it, but on the Sunni side the 1990s saw the slow rise of Iraqi Salafi circles, which represented a long-term threat to the regime. The regime was aware of it and monitored the clerics and religious groups, but it was unable to put an end to it.

On the eve of the American invasion in 2003, Iraq was a new country, no longer a moderately religious society with a large number of secular individuals and a modernizing secular ruling elite, but a country on the way to deep religiosity and under the powerful influence of local mid-level and junior clerics. This was the seniority level of the clerical leadership of both the Sunni anti-American insurgency and Muqtada al-Sadr's Saddam City–based Mahdi Army (*Jaysh al-Mahdi*). In other words, this was the clerical level most closely involved in leading the anti-American insurgency. Later on, when the civil war of 2006–8 flared up, the same clerical level on the Shi'i side in Baghdad led the anti-Sunni bloodletting. No information on the role of the Sunni clerics in that respect has become generally available.

Whereas the president's faith campaign won him some support among the Sunnis, in the Shi'i community the faith campaign had a very different effect. The relative relaxation of security rules regarding visits to the mosques and ceremonies encouraged people to participate more in religious activities. At the same time, the off-and-on limitations on commemorating the 'Ashura and other important days frustrated the Shi'i community. The Shi'is could easily identify severe discrimination in the regime's treatment of religious occasions in the Shi'i and Sunni areas, as no limitations at all were imposed on the Sunnis. (All the Sunni festivals, such as Ramadan, the two main 'Ids, and the Prophet's birthday, are general Islamic ones and did not serve as occasions for antiregime political demonstrations.) This discrimination, seen by the regime as an act of self-preservation, was seen by the Shi'is as hypocrisy. The Shi'is were well aware that under the faith campaign the regime was far more lenient toward Sunni Salafis than it was toward their Shi'i counterparts. To them this discrimination cast the campaign as an empty shell.

The shock of the March 1991 revolt and its brutal suppression left an indelible mark on the rest of the decade. Frequenting the mosque and participating in the commemoration days turned out to be much more than fulfilling a religious obligation. It became a way of expressing a political no less than a religious Shi'i identity and an opposition to the regime that often was translated into anti-Sunni sentiment. This was the case even though many Ba'th Party members and some generals who had helped put down the revolt were themselves Shi'is. In 1992, the regime's press reported that one million pilgrims visited Karbala to celebrate 15 Sha'ban, the day on which the Prophet moved the direction of prayer (*al-qibla*) from Jerusalem to Mecca.[84] What really happened had nothing to do with the change of the *qibla*. In reality, one million Iraqi Shi'is visited Imam Husayn's shrine to celebrate a birthday and commemorate the 1991 revolt. The revolt erupted on 15 Sha'ban, the Imam Mahdi's birthday. Indeed, many Shi'is referred to the revolt as *al-Thawra al-Sh'baniyya*, "the Sha'ban Revolution." One million people celebrated the birthday of the Imam Mahdi, something the Ba'thi media could not admit, as Sunnis do not revere the Imam Mahdi and do not believe in his return. At the same time, though, the million people also commemorated the deaths of tens of thousands of Shi'i revolutionaries precisely one Islamic year before. Every Shi'i knew that. The regime's dilemma was whether to allow the celebration and secure relative tranquility or prevent it and incur further Shi'i wrath. Having decided to allow it, the regime had to find an elegant way to explain it, which it did. But there is no mistaking the paradox: by allowing more religious freedom without solving the core issues, the regime won some breathing space but also encouraged the Shi'i identity. As limited as it was, the greater religious latitude allowed to the Shi'a thus did not get the Shi'a in any way closer to the regime. If anything, it allowed them to express more than before their opposition through mosque attendance and, when allowed, through commemoration days, and thereby hardened the crust around the community and accentuated the political gulf separating them from their Sunni compatriots.[85] In his 2000 diary, Barzan Tikriti, Saddam's half-brother, noted that he had spoken a few times to his elder brother about the danger of the Islamization campaign. In those conversations, he quoted to Saddam a chapter from his 1977 lecture in which the president warned that by adopting religion as its ideology, the party would drive a wedge between Sunnis and Shi'is.[86]

Saddam's attempt to win the Shi'i community's support through his quasi-ecumenical Islamization campaign had at best scant chances of bridging this gulf. In the event, the results were paradoxical. It seems that even though it tried to keep to the common denominators of the Qur'an, Hadith, and some shari'a, when the government imposed Islamic studies in schools in heavy doses, it inadvertently increased Shi'i displeasure. Even presumably innocuous classes teaching pupils how to pray risked sectarian tension. In most towns of the south, at least 90 percent of pupils in each class were Shi'is. Being taught to pray in the Sunni style could not endear to them the Ministry of Education. Thus, on the Shi'i side, the Islamization campaign backfired completely. Since 1997–98, the regime had allowed Muhammad Sadiq al-Sadr, Muqtada Sadr's father, to conduct communal Friday prayers in Kufa and a few other southern towns. To the regime's dismay, however, rather than winning it Shi'i support the Friday prayers exposed the potential of Shi'i power and opposition, especially among the younger generation. Whoever assassinated Sadr, the Ba'th regime was held responsible and suffered a further public setback.

Among the Sunni Arabs of Iraq, the Islamization campaign had a very different effect. In the case of the most extreme Salafis, no regime concessions could possibly satisfy their expectations and demands. Any reform short of a total return to Salafi Islam would have been regarded by them as a fraud. A good example of this brand of Islamist was the Falluja-born Salafi 'Umar Husayn Hadid.[87] However, less radical Muslims found the campaign rewarding, and it reduced their reservations with respect to the secular Ba'th regime. At the very minimum, such people could far more easily coexist with the regime, and even serve loyally in its administration. A few Muslim Brothers were allowed to return to Iraq and were even employed by the state. A good example of the new brand of Ba'thi-style Muslim activists is a 2005 insurgent whose nom de guerre is Abu Dhi'b (Father of the Wolf). He was born in a small Sunni Arab town in the mid-1960s. His father was an illiterate peasant. He lived almost his entire life under Ba'th rule. He graduated from the Faculty of Law with flying colors and then joined the Institute of National Security, an elite academic hub that produced high-quality security cadres for the regime, mainly drawn from the Sunni Arab population. He then joined *al-Amn al-'Amm* (General Security), the largest internal security body in Iraq, where he served until sometime in 1991. The 1991 Gulf War shattered his faith in regime and leader, as well as in the party's ideology. He asked for a leave, and spent the next four years at an Islamic religious school in Iraq. At the Islamic school he became acquainted with the writings of Ibn Taymiyya, probably the single most extreme puritanical theologian of medieval Islam and the source of inspiration for the most radical modern Arab Islamist, the Egyptian Sayyid Qutb (executed by Gamal 'Abd al-Nasir in 1966), but he did not become a "Qutbi." He graduated as an *'alim*, or cleric, and despite his disenchantment with Saddam and the Ba'th, he rejoined General Security. He continued to serve leader and regime faithfully there until April 2003.

After the downfall of the Baʿth regime, he donned the Salafi *dishdasha* (traditional ankle-length garment), grew a beard, and became a Salafi of sorts, but to make it easier to sneak in and out of Baghdad for his clandestine activities he eventually shaved his beard. Probably the most telling part of the discussion between the insurgent and the journalist was when the former, despite his admiration for al-Qaʿida foreign fighters in their struggle against the Americans, also admitted that differences between them and most of the Iraqi insurgents were deep. As he put it, "Al-Qaʿida believes that anyone who doesn't follow the Qurʾan literally is a *kafir* [apostate or infidel] and should be killed. . . . This is wrong. We can't take Islamic theory from the time of the Prophet and implement the same rules in the twenty-first century."[88] This view is strangely reminiscent of Saddam's 1977 "shariʿa is *passer de mode*" lectures. Much has changed since then, but the rejection of Salafi-style shariʿa imposition remained. Now it was yes to Islam in politics, but no to its more extreme forms. And yet Barzan Tikriti's fear that if his elder brother continued the campaign much longer, the Salafis would eventually destroy him and the regime could not be dismissed easily.

Was the Islamic Faith Campaign Antireligious?

Was Saddam's Islamic faith campaign in fact antireligious? Was it a seamless continuation of his staunch secularism of the 1970s? Did his faith campaign represent a barely disguised continuation of his opposition to involving Islam in the nation's political life? Could it be that Saddam's strong and explicit rejection of any role for the shariʿa in the modern age remained intact even during the faith campaign? Or alternatively, is it possible that both the party and the president became born-again Muslims?

According to a study based on the recently released classified Iraqi documents, in the 1990s and until the end of the Baʿth regime "the files clearly indicate that the regime remained to the end . . . obsessed with *all religious movements*, be they Wahhabism or Shiʿism, and wanted to infiltrate them to ensure its control."[89] This observation is correct, but only in part. It is true that, to his last day in power, Saddam did his best to prevent any activities by any opposition religious personalities, organizations, or movements, Sunni and Shiʿi alike.[90] However, he was not at all "obsessed with all religious movements." On the contrary: he encouraged and financed people and institutions that toed *his* religious line. He simply created his own "movement" in Iraq and abroad, which he supported generously. At least *he* considered it—or presented it—as religious.

As for repressing all other religious interpretations, while he allowed much more freedom to nonconfrontational ʿulama, Saddam did indeed suppress or at least monitored and sometimes limited all other Islamic activities, but there was nothing new or surprising about his actions, either in other Islamic regimes or in Baʿthi Iraq. In terms of his approach to power, Saddam remained Saddam: just because he decided to take party, regime, and country with him when he jumped on the Islamic bandwagon did not mean that he had decided to give up his control system. From his first day as czar of internal security in late 1968, he was obsessed with control, and gradually built a massive system of intelligence services that spied on the population and on each other. All the Islamists—real and perceived—were under constant surveillance, and many were banished, arrested, tortured, and killed. This remained Saddam's hallmark until 2003. However, from the early 1990s, as distinct from protecting a secular regime from its Islamist rivals and other powers, the same domestic security system was charged with protecting Saddam's Islamic project against any Islamic competition. Only Saddam's version of Islam was to be allowed. His interpretation of Islam was indeed an unusual one, very different from those of the Muslim Brotherhood, al-Qaʿida, the Taliban, or the Daʿwa. Yet whatever the view of Western scholars, Saddam believed or wanted the nation and the Islamic world to believe that it was indeed Islam, and the correct interpretation at that. In his mind, or at least in his media treatment of the issue, the fact that his interpretation was the only correct religion legitimized eliminating any other interpretation.

Saddam was not alone in this approach. The same applied to Iran's Ayatollah Khomeini, who, within the Shiʿi community of Iran, repressed the ayatollahs Muhammad Kazim Shariʿat-Madari and Husayn Ali Montazeri, as well as the Hojjatiye circle, which challenged his "rule of the jurist." Likewise, he arrested or killed any member of the *Mujahidin Khalq*—the Islamic socialists who had supported the shah's ouster but who became part of the left-wing opposition to Khomeini's regime—whom he could reach. The Saudi regime, for its part, repressed all opposing interpretations of Islam: its fight against the Muslim Brotherhood and al-Qaʿida are two contemporary examples. Likewise, in Sudan, ʿUmar al-Bashir has been imposing a version of Islam that incorporates the views of both Hasan al-Turabi and the Muslim Brotherhood as well as his own. Indeed, the idea of going Islamic and then suppressing all other Islamic interpretations came from none other than the Sudanese Muslim Brother Hasan ʿAbd Allah al-Turabi, who was instrumental in institutionalizing the Islamist regime in Sudan in 1989. His visit to Baghdad in 1991 as an official guest and his meeting with Saddam were signs of the coming change. In the secret Pan-Arab Leadership meeting in 1986, to placate those who opposed a rapprochement with the Sudanese Brothers, Saddam promised that if they came to power, the Baʿth would fight them. In 1989, they seized power in a coup d'état. Yet in 1991, Turabi was Saddam's welcomed guest. Turabi advised Saddam, *"in al-dawla nafs-ha qadat al-irshad al-dini, limadha alʿaan yekun hizb Islami?"* (If the state itself is leading the religious guidance, for what [reason] then is [or: should there be] a religious party?). Saddam muttered that he was proud of everything he *had* done, but did not object to the idea of implementing Turabi's idea *in the future*.[91] Saddam adopted this advice lock, stock, and barrel when he declared his faith campaign. Until then, he felt he had a national-revolutionary legitimacy to ban any Islamic body or activity that he considered a threat. Now, he probably believed that he had full *Islamic* legitimacy to do the same, and he had very good examples in other contemporary Islamic regimes. In other words, whether Saddam's Islam was "true" Islam or not had nothing to do with his repression of any other interpretation of Islam in Sunni Iraq. The Shiʿi ʿulama were beyond his theological reach, and politically most of them were quietists anyway, but any Shiʿi political party could be and was outlawed. However, it would seem that to use Islam as a cover, he had no choice but to go Islamic at least in part, at least outwardly, by demonstrating Islamic piety in public life—which he later did.

It has also been argued that "the [Baʿth] regime publicly launched a faith campaign but . . . behind the scenes, *continued to be antireligious and to repress any sign of religiosity.*"[92] And again, it is argued that because he repressed "all religious movements," Saddam "remained to the end . . . *suspicious of all religious activities.*"[93] I see Saddam's faith campaign differently. As argued above, repressing all (Sunni) "religious activities" other than his own or those that did not clash with his own is no proof that his own activities were non-Islamic, let alone "antireligious," or that he remained "to the end" "suspicious of all religious activities." According to Sassoon's definition, the current Iranian and Saudi regimes are also "antireligious" because they too repress all other Islamic "religious activities," but I do not think that this is necessarily the case, nor was this the case in Saddam's Iraq. As I understand it, for Saddam the defining question was *whose* religious activities were to be targeted. Turabi's example had given him a license to crush his competitors, and in doing so

Saddam simply protected the legitimacy of his rule, which since the early 1990s included his interpretation of Islam, against any such competition.

Saddam believed, or claimed to believe, or first claimed to believe and then believed, that the religious activities he supported were indeed Islamic, and he supported many such activities. But were those activities really Islamic? With regard to Sunni-Shi'i relations, his interpretation pretended to be a Sunni-Shi'i ecumenical brand but, as suggested above, in reality it was a soft Sunni approach. Even though the precise details of the five pillars of Islam (*arkan al-islam*)[94] are not fully agreed on by all Muslims, these rules still represent an approximate common ground over which Muslims agree.[95] To these precepts, Muslims add *al-nahi 'an al-munkar* (forbidding that which is forbidden). What did Saddam do about it? When it came to the pillars, at least outwardly Saddam implemented them, even if not fully in all cases. He declared his belief in God and the Prophet (*al-shahada*) publicly on every advertised visit to a mosque or a shrine. Beginning in the early1980s he even tried to impress foreign diplomats with his daily prayers.[96] Moreover, Saddam affixed the *takbir* ("*Allahu Akbar*," "God is Great") on the national flag. This too may be seen as a religious practice connected with prayer: Muslims open all daily prayers with the *takbir* as an expression of intent (*niya*). The pillars do not include the duty to establish mosques, but by building many Friday mosques he encouraged community prayers, an important duty in Sunni Islam. Saddam also introduced *al-zakat*, the collecting of alms, as a state activity, even though he did not enforce it. The government subsidized the *haj*, the pilgrimage to Mecca, and Saddam himself went on the pilgrimage. Also, rather than keep the young generation away from the mosques, as he tried to do in the 1970s, in the 1990s he pushed students to spend time in the mosques even during their summer holiday in order to study the Qur'an and Hadith with the 'ulama. He ordered the printing of millions of Qur'ans and forced Qur'an studies on much of Iraqi society and even on the top Ba'th officials, traders, and judges. Some of these studies were traditional madrasa-style studies led by 'ulama: some were led by university professors. Much as Saddam disliked the 'ulama, he also elevated their status. These policies are not part of the pillars, but they certainly encouraged "religious activities."

As for forbidding the forbidden, from the early 1990s Saddam enforced much stricter, shari'a-inspired limits on public behavior, such as enforcing Ramadan fasting and limiting alcoholic drinks and entertainment. Saddam also imposed other "explicit scriptural injunctions" like shar'i punishments, which meant a partial imposition of the *hudud*, a class of fixed punishments for crimes that are considered to be crimes against God. These included capital punishment for prostitution and amputation as punishment for theft.[97] This meant a revolution in the Iraqi penal code. His rhetoric, too, was thoroughly Islamized, and state symbolism was transformed. In most of those areas, he struck what appeared to be a middle course, somewhere between his secularism of old and Khomeini's Iran (or Numayri and Bashir's Sudan).[98] However, most of Saddam's steps were not extreme. In the same way that in the 1970s, however reluctantly, he and his colleagues had to support some Islamic practices, in the 1990s he had to allow some non-shar'i practices to continue in order to avoid a clash with his complaining party members and with the military. In other fields, too, he had to take into account security and economic needs. He did little to enforce his view that women should stay home, because the Iraqi economy needed the female workforce. While expressing concern that it might aid women in being unfaithful to their husbands, he still encouraged women to join the party because women had easy access to other women in the general public and therefore served as useful informers, and they could frisk a female suspect without offending her and her family. Likewise, he did not abolish the more or less secular Law of Personal Status because handing this crucial responsibility exclusively to the 'ulama would have given them too much power. On the cultural level, his personal taste was also important. He did not force women to wear the hijab not only because the party might have protested, but also because he considered it to be a primitive and backward practice, and one that would present him as an appendix to the Muslim Brotherhood. He despised the Taliban and remained fascinated by the heathen civilizations of Mesopotamia.

And yet whether or not the steps that Saddam took toward Islamic traditions were to be a push for Islamization, they certainly represented a U-turn in the practice of the Ba'th regime. As discussed in the first two chapters, the point of departure of the regime's ideology, rhetoric, culture, and symbolism was secular in the extreme, with whiffs of atheism. If God was mentioned, it was in order to shield the party from accusations of outright atheism. With respect to culture, the 1972 larger-than-life monument of the wine poet Abu Nuwas on Abu Nuwas Street, where numerous restaurants and bars could be found, may best exemplify the original Ba'thi frame of mind.[99] Saddam's 1977 declaration that the shari'a was irrelevant to modern life summed up the party's original approach to Islam as a living religion. The strategic commitment was rather to the ideal of a national, secular, united Arab megastate. Saddam's subsequent introduction of the shari'a, partial as it was; his endeavor to thrust party and nation into his version of Islam; and his and the Pan-Arab Leadership's new concept of an Islamic mega-state signaled the Islamization of Baʿthi Iraq. This could not happen as long as Baʿth Party founder Michel ʿAflaq was alive, but after ʿAflaq died in 1989 and was post-humously converted to Islam, the main obstacle was removed. Even though the fear, voiced by some party members, that Baghdad was becoming Riyadh never materialized, these steps nonetheless represented a profound change in the regime's public behavior. It seems, therefore, that Saddam could hardly have been "suspicious of all religious activities." He was not at all suspicious, provided those activities were his.

Initially, Saddam embarked on the Islamization of the country out of polit-ical calculation rather than because of a newfound faith. At the July 1986 meeting of the Pan-Arab Leadership, Saddam explained that "men of religion" were becoming very influential, and that this necessitated a new approach (see chapter 4). In addition, what he did would not have satisfied the Daʿwa or Baqir al-Sadr, the Wahhabis or the Muslim Brotherhood, let alone the Taliban. And yet, Islam is a communal religion, not just a personal faith. Regardless of how "truly" religious Saddam and the Baʿth Party were, in Islam the public sphere is of crucial importance, and in the 1990s to a significant extent Saddam Islamized public life in Iraq. Under the Baʿth, the contrast between the 1970s and the 1990s was stark. These two observations—the regime's public policies and the departure from party ideology and practice—should serve as the main yardsticks for the historian.

To what extent was Saddam's pretense to interpret Islam, or imagine his version of Islam and then impose it, at all legitimate? This is in the eyes of the beholder, but he was not the first leader in the modern age to do so. The highest-profile modern leader to do so before Saddam was of course Ayatollah Khomeini. In addition to the very principle of "the rule of the jurist," in itself a controversial interpretation of Shiʿi Islam, Khomeini introduced a far-reaching interpretation of the authorities of the religious jurist-ruler (*vali*). In January 1988, after Iran's Constitution Guardians' Council vetoed on Islamic grounds a few laws passed by his government, a furious Khomeini rebuked the Council, insisting that the government was not constrained by Islamic rules. To him, the government, or the rule (*hukumet*), was an "absolute authority" (*wilaya mutlaqa*), bestowed by God on the Prophet and following him on the ʿulama. Because the government is one of God's most important ordi-nances (*ahkam-e-ilahi*), it has a priority over all God's secondary or ancil-lary ordinances (*ahkam farʿiyya ilahiyya*), including pillars of Islam such as prayer, fasting and *haj*. As a result, the Islamic government can temporarily prevent any ritual ordinance if it goes contrary to government interests. In other words, the Islamic government can suspend certain religious duties if doing so serves an important political motive. It can prevent the *haj* temporarily, or even destroy mosques. In another fatwa, Khomeini added that "the preservation of the Islamic Republic is a Godly duty above all other." Finally, Khomeini assured his flock that he could do much more, but he preferred to remain silent about his assurances at that stage. 'Ali Khamenei, the then-head of the Constitution Guardians' Council, hurriedly atoned for the veto: "the ordinances of the *vali-e-faqih* [ruler-jurist] [Khomeini] are . . . similar to those of God himself."[100] As shown earlier (see chapters 5 and 6), Saddam, too, was not particularly shy about his new role in the Islamic world and humanity, but he was a modest man by comparison, and never explicitly claimed an authority equal to that of God.

Khomeini's interpretation, according to which for reasons of state he could suspend the shari'a or much of it, was highly controversial in both Shi'i and Sunni circles, yet Western scholars did not consider him "antireligious." The modern era has shown other similarly extraordinary interpretations of religion. In the Sunni world, the Ahmadis in the late nineteenth century came up with a radically peaceful interpretation of Islam that forbade jihad, and in the twentieth century the Taliban of Afghanistan came up with a radically repressive interpretation of the shari'a (for example, toward women and culture) and a radical commitment to jihad. Yet, at least Khomeini was a very senior Shi'i cleric, a *mujtahid*, and the founders of both the peaceful and extremist Sunni movements were experienced clerics. By comparison, Saddam was a layman who had little, if any, knowledge of Islamic jurisprudence.

Who did Saddam think that he was to offer an interpretation of Islam? How did he dare? As James Piscatori sees it, after the Prophet, "[in Sunni Islam] no mediator exists between God and man and thus . . . there is no priestly cast endowed with esoteric wisdom or sacramental powers."[101] In the modern age, some new Islamic movements that came with independent interpretations were led by laymen. The Muslim Brotherhood and al-Qa'ida are the best-known examples; the Brotherhood has even had anticlerical tendencies. Other lay heads of state who preceded Saddam had imposed their interpretations of Islam. Saddam, for his part, delineated the broad conceptual outlines of his interpretation. The rest he left to the many 'ulama who worked for him in the plethora of religious institutions he established and financed. He did not feel the need to be a jurist himself.

Did the party and the president eventually become born-again Muslims? There is no evidence that the party changed this way. The attitude in the Iraqi Ba'th Party's internal documents to the Islamization is pragmatic. Rather than explaining the teaching of Qur'an to party cadres, for example, as a way to please God, as a true born-again Muslim would do, the documents explain it in terms of benefit to the regime or strengthening the "steadfastness and patience [al-sumud wal-sabr]" and other pre-faith-campaign values of the party's cadres.[102] Furthermore, at the same time that Saddam announced that the party no longer objected to a pan-Islamic state, the party retained its original secular slogans: "Unity, Freedom, Socialism" and "One Arab nation with an eternal message." They appeared on all its documents, and the latter was chanted in unison in party congresses. Moreoever, unlike the senior leadership, the available evidence indicates that the party's rank and file did not have to go through Qur'an and Hadith courses.[103] The "acculturation" (or indoctrination) courses, planned and supervised by the central *madrasat al-'i'dad al-hizbi* (the Ba'th Party Preparatory School) in Baghdad, seem to have been a throwback from a more secular era, with the only additions of Saddam's personality cult and contemporary political developments like the 1980–88 Iraq-Iran War and the 1991 Gulf War. Similar courses were also given to those 10 percent or fewer of the party's "active members" (*'udhu 'amil*).[104] And yet, as shown above, during the faith campaign many among the most senior leadership members were going through "faith courses," including extensive Qur'an and Hadith studies at another party institute, Saddam's Institute for the Study of the Holy Qur'an. Both institutions were an organic part of the party's structure.

Why did Saddam's Qur'an courses stop at the senior level? After all, he did push the whole Iraqi nation into aspects of the shari'a, and brought Qur'an studies, often in the mosque, into the state education system. Why not do the same with the party's more junior member levels? As reported by the party, the number of junior members in 2002 was close to 3.7 million.[105] This figure looks greatly inflated, but even if the number was only half that, there were too few reliable 'ulama or professors who could be trusted to teach such numbers of party members. As we have seen in the discussion of the religious universities (*hawza*), the party leaders admitted in the late 1980s that the party had only two senior and a few scores of junior supportive 'ulama. As part of his faith campaign, Saddam established institutions designed to create such 'ulama, but this is a process that takes many years to complete. Although 'ulama taught at all school levels as part of the faith campaign, inviting those whose support might be questionable to teach in the party as well was unthinkable to Saddam. He did not trust the ideological commitment of the wide membership base. Unleashing regular 'ulama among his flock of party members could easily result in complete disaster, as many of them were at risk of sliding or gliding into the "real" thing: Salafi Islam for Sunnis, "Khomeinism" for Shi'is. With his version of Islam, Saddam was on the razor's edge: he was open to challenge from Sunni and Shi'i *mutadayyinin* (religious devotees) on the one hand and from his secular-minded senior members on the other.[106] The religion of the bearded, *dishdasha*-wearing Salafis was a Sword of Damocles hanging over his head. Survival therefore came first. For the time being, 'Aflaq's equivocal language could be manipulated sufficiently to demonstrate to the rank and file that the Ba'th Party was a God-fearing party that admired the Prophet. But more than that, at school the party's younger generation had been exposed to the Islamic campaign like everyone else. Even by merely studying Saddam's speeches, a party obsession, the members were made fully aware of the faith campaign. Although party indoctrination was limited to some two hours once a week, almost all of the information that members received came from the party daily *al-Thawra* and other state media, which were full of news about the religious campaign. The younger members were therefore inundated by Saddam's Islamic campaign. The party also informed all members of the extensive Qur'an studies of the senior leadership, using them as a shining example. It can only be guessed that between the secular tradition (which was still alive in the party meetings and courses) on the one hand and the faith campaign on the other, the party's younger generation was confused. As for the senior cadre, they accepted Saddam's dictates for practical reasons, rather than as a result of a profound religious metamorphosis. Many may have relented in order to keep their jobs and perks. For others, challenging the president was impossible after so many years of strict party discipline, especially in a time of great perils like economic ruin and the dangers of another Shi'i revolt, another war with Iran, or another confrontation with the United States. Unity was the only guarantee of perpetuating party rule, and Saddam was the only guarantee for party unity.

And yet the very fact that the party performed such a U-turn in its ideology and public policies meant that whatever the personal conviction of the individual member, as a collective body it was no longer the same party. The Ba'th was a highly ideological party. In the July 1986 Pan-Arab Leadership, Saddam compared with great pride the Ba'th Party's modern, elaborate, and sophisticated ideology and the primitive, even retarded ideology of the Muslim

Brotherhood, whose members held the Qur'an in their hands and claimed that this was their ideology. The party remained in power, but by adopting even part of the Muslim Brotherhood's once-despised platform, it lost its soul. The young people who joined the party in the 1990s could probably live with the Islamization, and many may have even liked it. Yet to the party old-timers, the Islamization of Ba'th ideology and public policies represented nothing short of a humiliating surrender. There was no way they could accept the lame arguments they found in the party's literature—open and internal alike—justifying the change. They must have been able to see through those empty phrases and discern that, to stay in power, the party had betrayed 'Aflaq's "message," *al-risala*, or that it had jettisoned all its beliefs under a whimsical order from the leader, or both. It may be argued that Saddam "Ba'thized" Islam by emptying it of some of its shar'i contents, but this will be correct only if one defines "true" Islam exclusively as the Islam of the Wahhabis or of Sayyid Qutb and any other extreme Salafis. In such a case, Saddam indeed created a compromise by moving the regime and the country only part of the way toward Islam. And yet, even more so, Saddam Islamized the Ba'th, and in doing so he turned 'Aflaq's world on its head. In the 1940s, Michel 'Aflaq had Ba'thized Islam by moving it away from a religion of injunctions of "thou shalt do" and "thou shalt not do" into a purely spiritual and personal religion that expected no prayer, no fasting, no rites, not even dutiful visits to the mosque. At first, Saddam posthumously converted his father figure, the Christian 'Aflaq, to Islam. Then he dragged the country into the mosque, imposing upon it the Qur'an, Islamic education, Islamic duties, and even the stringent punishments prescribed by the *hudud*.

The party's strong exoskeleton survived the slings and arrows of outrageous fortune, but it lost its ideological compass. Even though until the 1990s the members realized that national secular Arab unity, the apple of the Ba'th eye, would have to wait for a long time, they still could believe that their party had the long-term solution for all the Arab problems and that in Iraq, at least some of the party's principles had been implemented. Saddam's faith campaign catapulted them into another universe. It can be assumed that many of the party old-timers suffered an acute cognitive dissonance and were dispirited, but very few could challenge the president over his faith campaign. One of those few was his elder son 'Uday, and another was his half-brother Barzan Tikriti, but they were powerless to change his course. In sum, all the indications are that the party Islamized its outward conduct as much as Saddam wanted it to do, but did not change its secular worldview.

And yet, follow-up studies of Ba'thi-inspired insurgent anti-American groups between 2003 and 2006 expose a twilight situation Now, when there was no longer anyone to tell them how to think, the Ba'thi insurgents could snap back to their secular roots of the 1970s, but those of whom I found some information did not quite do that. According to Ahmed Hashim, the group under the command of 'Izzat Ibrahim al-Duri seemed to have made "religious faith an element of its new ideological stance. . . . [T]he Ba'thists have thus drawn closer to those nationalist-Islamist elements of the insurgency that have not shown irrevocable hostility to the former regime and its ideology." Hashim adds, "The new emphasis on Islam among some Ba'thists . . . reflects the growth of religious sentiment among party members, particularly during the years of occupation." Finally, he reports that some Ba'this who drew closer to the "nationalist-Islamists and even to some Iraqi Salafists" still objected to al-Qa'ida's wanton killing of Shi'i Iraqis as well as to their goal of "creating a Sunni theocracy."[107] All of this sounds much like Saddam's interpretation of Islam. A slightly earlier study reached relatively similar conclusions when discussing a Ba'thi-inclined insurgent group, *al-mujahidin*. In its communiques, this group used a combination of secular content and Islamic openings and endings.[108] From this, I conclude that the origins of the religious sentiment among the young Ba'this were to be found earlier than what Ahmed Hashim thought. It began in the Iran-Iraq War, as we are told by the party's 1982 congress and by Saddam's assessment in 1986, then the 1991 Gulf War and the suffering resulting from the embargo. Then came Saddam's faith campaign and the 2003 American occupation. It would seem, then, that some of Saddam's Islamic faith campaign had rubbed off on some of its members. Other than that, though, there is no evidence that the Islamization had truly penetrated into the middle and senior echelons of the Ba'th Party. But what about the leader?

Did Saddam Become a Born-Again Muslim?

The course charted over the next few pages puts aside any attempt at psychological profiling and focuses instead on one facet only: Saddam's religiosity. Moreover, the conclusions, which must remain largely speculative, are based on limited information. That said, Saddam's public record is very clear. A comparison of his numerous public speeches in the 1970s with those from the 1990s shows a clear shift toward expressions of Islamic religiosity. Whether in the openings, with or without the religious formula (the *basmala*), or the endings, again with or without some religious formula (mostly God is Great, *allahu akbar*), or in the content of the speech, almost all the speeches of the 1990s contain Islamic components that are absent from the speeches of the 1970s. In his public policies, too, Saddam demonstrated a clear religious shift. By any quantitative measure, Saddam's public policy moved decisively toward Islamic religiosity.[109] However, while the content of public speeches may be seen as cynical window-dressing, crucial in ideological terms but short of true conviction, a better understanding may be gained through additional information regarding Saddam's behavior behind the scenes. The problem is that even his secret audiotapes and other highly classified documents that were recently made available to researchers provide only a very partial image. Yet in early 2014, this is the available information, and despite its limitations, it does provide some important indications. My conclusion, though tentative, is that from the early or mid-1990s Saddam became a "born-again" Muslim of sorts. If true, then for him this represented nothing short of a "conversion" from extreme secularism with a whiff of atheism to religiosity.

In December 1999, when it became clear that this was to be a year of drought, Saddam ordered that in all parts of Iraq, people were to pray for rain. The media explained that since the days of the Prophet such a prayer had been practiced, obeying "an order from *Wali al-Amr*," or the Ruler of the Muslim Community. This year the order came from the president, "the Commander of the Congregation of the Believers." Saddam was shown on the first page of the newspapers praying, though in a private capacity rather than in a mosque.[110] More than a convincing demonstration of religiosity, this prayer looked like part of a public relations campaign designed to accentuate the president's piety and devotion to the Prophet and his tradition, and his claim to be the Prophet's replacement. Indeed, it seemed that Saddam had no limits when it came to manipulating history and ideology, even his own identity, to serve political expediency or his megalomania. He reinvented himself as a *sayyid*, an offspring of the Prophet, and as a latter-day Caliph al-Mansur and Salah al-Din (Saladin).[111] He reinvented the ancient Mesopotamians, Akkadians, Babylonians, and Assyrians as Arabs and Iraqis, and himself as a latter-day Nebuchadnezzar, Sanneherib, Sargon the Akkadian, and Hammurabi. He even reinvented the Hebrew patriarchs and the Jewish prophets and Jesus as Arabs.[112] In late 1991, in the midst of the economic suffering brought on by the United Nations embargo, the president rejected calls in Iraq (most significantly from his prime minister, Sa'dun Hammadi, a US-educated economist) to accept fully all the UN disarmament demands. His winning argument was that God had wished for some of his "messengers and prophets" great sufferings before they won the day, and some prophets even died. The present suffering was, thus, inspired by God's will. "The generation that goes through the greatest sufferings and tribulations," he assured his long-suffering listeners, "will eventually enjoy a suitable and prominent place with God."[113] All this created again the strange impression that Saddam believed he had a direct line to God, and intimate and exclusive knowledge of God's political will.[114] To the very end of the Ba'th regime, many in Iraq considered this line of argument to be a cynical tactic. This impression was supported by the fact that the communication line between Saddam and God became progressively busier as the war against the Allied forces in Kuwait approached, and during the course of the war. The themes of an "innovator" or "reviver" of Islam and a latter-day Messenger of God similarly outlasted the occupation of Kuwait and became the main component behind his domestic policy. Indeed, the faith campaign became seen by many, especially in the lower and middle echelons of the party, as a rational, even cynical tactical step that Saddam undertook to win the support of the conservative circles in a moment of crisis.

But is it possible that over the years, with the crisis deepening, when he felt that a hostile world was closing in on him, Saddam underwent a psychological metamorphosis and became a sort of true believer? When his public record is read together with his confidential conversations and documents, it appears that eventually he began to believe all those inventions. After the invasion of Kuwait he claimed for the first time a direct line to God. This was indeed likely done at first as a cynical way to avoid criticism. As will be shown below, as the crisis progressed, however, and as Saddam progressively charged God with more responsibility for everything that happened, he seems to have evolved. A few additional lines of evidence support this proposition.

Personality Change

There is some evidence that after the war with Kuwait and the Shi'i revolt, Saddam went through a personal metamorphosis. He began to spend long periods writing poems and novels. Three of the books, the most famous one being *Zabibah wal-Malik* (Zabiba and the King) were published. The author remained anonymous, but the Presidential Palace's secret instructions to print and disseminate the first two novels, *Zabibah* and *The Fortress*,[115] are contingent evidence that he was indeed the author. A fourth one was complete but not yet in print. In interviews after the 2003 war, some of Saddam's generals disclosed that after the defeat in Kuwait and, following it, the March 1991 Shi'i revolt, he had "lost his trust in the Iraqi people and his paranoia deepened." After his cousin and son-in-law Husayn Kamil defected to Jordan in 1995, he became depressed because such a member of his closest circle and his family had betrayed him in the most humiliating way. For Saddam, coming from a tribal background, the family was the innermost circle of trust and the core of power. Husayn Kamil defected with his younger brother, Saddam, and their wives, Saddam's daughters. This was an even more crushing blow. Because of the ease with which a man can unilaterally divorce his wife in Sunni Islam, daughters always owe their first allegiance to their fathers, for if they are divorced they may need to return to the father's home. That his daughters followed their renegade husbands represented a profound humiliation for Saddam. As some of his officers reported to the Americans, as a result of the betrayal "he isolated himself from everyone. Rarely did he go out among the people. He no longer trusted his senior officers." He even ceased visiting the Republican Guard, his pride and joy. Some senior cabinet ministers did not see him for two years. With regard to the American attack of March 2003, he had "thoroughly unrealistic expectations" of his military, being unable "to connect reality with his own hopes and dreams."[116] This impression is exaggerated: Saddam did pay attention to the military preparations, but he was a different man all the same.

There is evidence that part of this metamorphosis was manifested as a growing religiosity. His reaction to the calamities that befell Iraq as a result of his policies was a growing reliance on God and a belief that if his military failed to do so, God would extricate him from his predicament. In Islamic terms, he became progressively more attached to the concept of reliance on God (*al-tawakkul*). This reliance can be traced back to the occupation of Kuwait, but in the last three or four years of his rule it became more pronounced. At the same time, though, he managed to partition his psyche, one part of it remaining perfectly rational and calculating. Thus, for example, in June 2002, in a closed-door conversation with Iraqi nuclear scientists, very rational people indeed, he justified his faith campaign first in purely spiritual and then in perfectly rational terms: "What is more expensive than gold is the feeling inside of you that [you] please God," he said, but then he switched on his rational personality, explaining that religiosity would also "enlarge you in people's eyes."[117] In other words, if you are seeking people's respect, go religious, or at least fake it.

Magic, Miracles, Prophecies, and Visions

A central feature of Saddam's speeches during the Kuwait crisis was invoking early Islamic traditions of miracles and supernatural events that saved pre-Islamic Mecca and, later, the fledgling Muslim community. By harping on those ancient myths, the Iraqi president created the impression that he knew something his baffled officers and soldiers did not know, perhaps that his scientists had achieved some technological breakthroughs capable of neutralizing the American military superiority. In early September 1990, the Iraqi president made use of the Qur'anic tale of Abraha, the Ethiopian military commander who, according to tradition, tried to conquer Mecca. On the year when the Prophet was born, Abraha came with war elephants, but God sent "swarms of flying creatures" that "pelted them with stones made of baked clay," and the whole army and its elephants were thus "like green crops" devoured by the cattle (*Surat al-Fil*, The Elephant, No. 105). Saddam implied that the American technological advantage would be eliminated by some heavenly means that the Iraqis would employ.[118]

Some other ancient tales of miraculous deliverance rushed through Saddam's feverish mind. One was the miracle of Badr, a small town southwest of al-Madina at which the army of the Prophet defeated the far larger one of the Meccan idol worshippers in the year 624 CE. "When the battle of Badr between the gathering of the faithful Muslims and the gathering of the infidels intensified," Saddam related, "God's Messenger . . . threw a handful of dust in the air toward the enemies, repeating his known prayers invoking God to grant the Muslims victory." The result was that "God responded, and the gathering of infidels was defeated." The Badr miracle was recorded by God in the Qur'an when he said: "When thou throwest a handful of dust, it was not thy act, but God's." Amazingly, Saddam again promised his listeners some kind of a technological miracle: "Thus, to make the weapons of the Zionists and the Americans ineffective, we only need, God willing, to throw sand in their eyes, blinding them. For an elephant to leave [in panic] it only needs some sand to enter its nose, ear or eye."[119] Saddam's listeners were probably hovering between hope that Iraq indeed possessed a new weapon and a rising dread that their president was getting progressively more delusional. My impression is that in his desperation, while preparing for war as best he could, Saddam also found consolation in the belief that God cannot forsake him.

There were additional facets to Saddam's growing faith in God. Two days before the UN ultimatum elapsed, he donned the mantle of a prophet of

332

redemption, a latter-day Isaiah:

> Only the worthy will be preserved. You will see how the seats of power
> will fall. . . . You will also be glorious and triumphant. . . . Victory will
> be for you. . . .Not only Kuwait but Palestine will be coming, the Golan
> and Lebanon [will be free from Syrian occupation], God willing.[120]

Three days after the beginning of the war, he resorted to a bizarre prophetic-poetic style that exposed either a desperate attempt to boost the troops' morale or divorce from reality. Strangely, the first and last sentences were clear references to the return of the Shi'i Redeemer, the Imam Mahdi:

> The skies in the Arab homeland will appear in a new color and a sun of
> new hope will shine. . . . Then the door will be wide open for the libera-
> tion of beloved Palestine, Lebanon and the Golan. . . . The Ka'ba [in
> Mecca] and the tomb of the Prophet [in al-Madina] . . . will be liberated
> [from Saudi occupation] . . . and God will bestow [riches] upon the
> poor and the needy.[121]

When Iraq entered the fourth week of the war, after thousands of allied forces' bombing raids had created havoc at the front, Saddam resorted to another bizarre imagery that baffled many in Iraq. When the crescent of the new moon appeared, he created an association between that Islamic symbol of renewal and hope and the situation on the battlefield:

> The light of every new moon at the beginning of a new month is a sign
> of a great and certain victory for the struggling gathering of believers...
> and (the crescent) is absolute proof . . . that God is alive, capable and
> great. . . . With God's help and through a miracle coming from God
> more than 1,400 years after the appearance of the . . . Islamic Message,
> you strugglers have proved that . . . when God permits, the oppressed
> can score victory over tyranny.[122]

Is it possible that the Iraqi president was not told of the total chaos on the front? Or was it that the Islamic symbolism of the new moon captivated his imagination to such a degree? After the Kuwait war and the mass revolt against his regime, Saddam felt isolated. He was indeed surrounded by powerful ene-mies: the Western-imposed no-fly zone in the north, the Iranian threat in the east and the international embargo, and the domestic threat of another Shi'i revolt. Saddam resorted to visions to comfort himself and his people. In a speech in May 1991 he told his listeners that before the war he had had a "vision" (*ru'ya*). In this vision, he was walking with a few friends in an open area when suddenly a flock of mad dogs surrounded them. The besieged men found a tree, broke off a few branches, turned them into clubs, and beat and killed some of the dogs and chased away the others.[123] No doubt this vision related to the lost war, the revolt, the postwar troubles, and Saddam's survival. And yet it demonstrated that, while still a rational man, the Iraqi president was finding refuge in metaphysical images and scenarios. In a few cases Saddam also told his lieutenants of optimistic dreams he had had. There is no reason to believe they were impressed. Tariq 'Aziz, though, tried it on President Akbar Hashimi Rafsanjani when, in a visit to Tehran following the invasion of Kuwait, he suggested a united Iraqi-Iranian front against the United States. 'Aziz told one of Rafsanjani's assistants that before his journey to Iran, his (Christian) wife had visited the tomb of Imam Musa Kazim in Kazimayn (Baghdad). She then had a dream in which the seventh Imam came and told her that her husband's mission to Iran would be crowned with success. On hearing of it, Rafsanjani burst out laughing. His reply to 'Aziz was that the Americans were an Iraqi problem.[124]

That Saddam was not faking a process of growing religiosity of some kind seems to be borne out by evidence coming from close associates. In 2000, Saddam's half-brother Barzan noted in his private diary that his brother, the president, had undergone some kind of psychological metamorphosis. "For a few years now," Barzan wrote, "the way the president thinks, unfortunately, is similar to the way of thinking of a monk who is sitting in a sanctuary and worshiping [God] [*tafkir rahib jalis fi mihrab wa yata'abbad*]. . . . I told the president . . . of the danger of an alliance with the religious trend domestically and externally." Domestically, Saddam had aligned himself with Sunni Islamists, something that "will arouse Shi'i fears." Internationally, Barzan believed this would alienate the secular Arab regimes and "even Saudi Arabia." Eventually, the Sunni fundamentalists would topple the regime, Barzan warned. Saddam remained silent.[125] Another bit of internal evidence comes from Culture Minister Latif Nusayyif Jasim, who in 1995 in a private discussion with a colleague that was apparently recorded without his knowledge disclosed that Saddam was becoming very religious. Once, Jasim said, the president asked why God had been punishing him so severely (since 1991). Saddam told Jasim, though, that no matter what punishments God might unleash against him, he would never waver in his love for God.[126] Saddam must have liked it when he listened to the secret recording, but that this discussion was never made public might mean that it represented Jasim's genuine impression. Saddam as a latter-day Job does not sound very credible, but his public speeches as well as his words in closed-door meetings and his top-secret military communiqués since 1999–2000 imply a similar change. In the face of the lethal danger from the United States, he apparently felt that he had done all that he could, and now it was God's responsibility to deliver him and Iraq. His most devout lieutenant, RCC deputy chairman 'Izzat Ibrahim, was infected. In 2002, congratulating the Iraqi military over a successful maneuver, in a message to the minister of defense that was also delivered to the whole political and military leadership, Ibrahim's main topic was "reliance on God" (*al-tawakkul 'ala allah*). Ibrahim promised his military commanders: "Allah loves those who rely on him [*al-mutawakkilin*]!" Therefore, "since Allah loves *al-mutawakkilin*, will he betray them to the Americans?" For some reason, rather than choosing the Prophet's victories he chose the example of Moses and the Children of Israel. Before they entered "Palestine" many were afraid of the local people, whom they saw as giants, but they were told to "rely on God if you are believers." And they prevailed. After further Islamic argument that God always rewarded "men who fulfilled what they promised God," he had no doubt: "We shall achieve victory, God willing."[127] Since the Ba'th came to power Ibrahim was known to be religious, with special ties to Sufi organizations, but his speeches in the 1970s and 1980s were never in this spirit of reliance on God.

On Revolution Day of 2002, Saddam's speech was very unusual for him, but it was a speech that could be expected from a born-again Muslim. About 20 percent of the speech was one long prayer to God that sounded more like an incantation designed to ward off the American devils. For example, after a few opening paragraphs he turned to address God:

Lord! You are our highest and most supreme God; you created us and protected us for a purpose that you have intended. You are our God and the God of our fathers, of our sons, of our ancestors, and of our grandchildren after us. You are the God of him [read: me] who worships you. . . . Yet, you destroy the defiant [the Infidel American] . . . he suffers the consequences of his rebellion [against God] and disbelief; he will perish. . . . There is no God but you, our Lord, we seek in you refuge from Satan. . . . Lord! We submit to you with faith and love. We bow to you in worship.

And so on and so on. And the president ended his incantation: "Make us victorious oh our Lord over the infidel nation as you made us victorious in our goals and actions and guarded us from obliteration on the days of . . . July, 1968 . . . and what came later" (*fansurna rabbuna ʿala al-qawm al-kafirin mithlma nassartana fi ahdafina wa fiʿlina wa hafaztana min kull tahlika . . . min tammuz ʿam 1968 wama . . . baʿdaha*).[128]

Some six weeks before the onset of Operation Iraq Freedom in 2003, Saddam chose a very depressing historical case to prop up his troops' morale, the trauma of the Mongol conquest of Baghdad in 1258 CE. Under the leadership of Hulagu (1256–1265), the grandson of Genghis Khan, the Mongols devastated Baghdad and executed the ʿulama and the literati. Saddam described the coalition forces as latter-day Mongol hordes, warning his people that the United States was bent on doing the same to Baghdad, but he promised them that this time "the Mongols of our age" would be stopped and crushed at the gates of Baghdad. The Iraqi army was ready for war, he promised, and also: "How can a new Hulagu destroy . . . the great Iraq . . . after God has ordained this nation to rise again?"[129]

In the second half of the 1990s the then-Russian foreign minister (1996–98) Yevgeny Primakov, an observant analyst whose Arabic is quite good, reached the conclusion that all the Russian attempts to save Saddam from himself might fail: "It has to be said that Saddam continued to believe in his lucky star, in his own foresight and ultimately in Allah, who would save him from harm."[130] Primakov could have been fooled by Saddam, of course, but for what purpose? Primakov was not a Sudanese Islamist or an Indian Muslim politician. He was a former communist and an atheist immune to religiosity, and the meetings were not supposed to—nor did they—become known to the Iraqi public. Furthermore, had Saddam intended to impress, claiming divine protection could only send the opposite message: that the Iraqi president was losing his grip on reality. Primakov was the foreign diplomat who met with Saddam more than any other, and he was the last foreign diplomat to see him, a few days before the start of the 2003 war. His testimony adds weight to the impression that Saddam underwent some kind of religious metamorphosis.

By late March 2003, after the coalition forces had invaded Iraq, when giving instructions to his soldiers Saddam was shrill:

> Hit now . . . according to what God has ordered you to do! . . . Those who are believers will be victorious. . . . We have been promised by God in our struggle with the enemies of humanity that God will support his

soldiers and they [the enemy] will be defeated. . . . We are the soldiers of God. . . . The victory of God is very close. . . . Have courage . . . because your place with God is very, very strong and very high indeed. . . . God is great! God is great! And long live our country! Long live Palestine, free and Arab. Long live Iraq! Long live Iraq! Long live Iraq the country of jihad and virtue! . . . God is great! God is great![131]

This demonstration of total reliance on God to deliver him and Iraq was received with dismay by his commanders. A few days later, Saddam sent his troops his last message. It was brief, and much of it was again mere Islamic incantations and promises of God's guaranteed victory. It started with "fight them and God will torture them by your hands [*yu'adhdhibuhum allah biaydikum*]*." Then came simple instructions on how to prepare ambushes, and in the end a long incantation promising the Iraqi soldiers that if they relied on God and believed in him they would be victorious, because their enemy believed in "infidelity and atheism and crime."[132]

A Letter to God

The most telling evidence that Saddam may have become a believer of sorts was a 2002 letter he sent to God. The letter was never made public, and indeed, until 2012–13 no Iraqi had ever heard of it. It was to be cast in pure gold letters that were to be affixed to a tablet of granite. The tablet was to be encased in a massive steel and lead box with an unbreakable glass front, which would be placed inside one of the walls of Saddam's magnificent *umm al-ma'arik* mosque. This letter to God was designed to endure any disasters, the lead internal wall securing the box content against radiation. One more item was to be placed in the big box: a smaller stainless steel box, one wall of which would also be made of glass. In that box would rest a few hairs from Saddam's mustache. In his letter, Saddam explained to God that "throughout their . . . history the Arabs . . . regarded their men's mustaches as a criterion of their commitment and a sign of their readiness to bear their gender's responsibility." (In days of old in Iraq, a hair from a man's mustache sometimes served as a guarantee, much like a handshake among diamond dealers in the West.) He besought God "to protect the hairs of these mustaches, together with protecting Iraq." The letter was signed by Saddam on May 22, 2002. Saddam's handwriting is disorderly and agitated, quite unlike his usual handwriting. It would seem that he was stressed and anxious when he wrote it.

"Today, I put these hairs from my mustache as trust [*wadiʿa*] with you," he wrote to God, "and by doing this I want that you will remember my history together with all the meanings that I placed with you,"[133] by which Saddam meant his Islamization measures, including the project of mosque building. In exchange, he wanted deliverance. There is no certainty that the letter was meant to remain a secret. The glass windows could have been intended to allow mosque-goers to see the content, or they may have been planned for God's benefit alone. However, because the project was never made public, there is reason to believe that the letter was meant to remain private, between Saddam, a few of his closest lieutenants, and God.

There is some reason to believe, therefore, that in his own way, toward his end Saddam became a believer. The combined pressures of eight years of war against Iran, then a crushing defeat in the first Gulf War, then the total surprise of the Shiʿi and Kurdish revolts, then the seemingly endless years of the embargo and the defection of Husayn Kamil, which ended with the murder of the fathers of his grandchildren, and then, finally, the unmistakable threat of an American assault, may have pushed him to return to the safety of the Islam of his childhood. His initial faith campaign was most likely a cynical step, designed to win popular support, but he rejected all attempts to change it even though it alienated at least some of the party. His alliance with the Islamists scared his closest supporters. True, he and his security men took some precautions by infiltrating the Islamic extremist groups, and from time to time they arrested and even executed some of them.[134] And yet Saddam pursued this partnership. It would seem that he believed that this partnership, as well as the wider faith campaign and even a very personal sacrifice such as his contribution of many liters of his blood toward the writing of a Qurʾan, would win him grace not only in the eyes of the religious circles in Iraq and the Muslim world but also in the eyes of the Lord.

Conclusion and Postscript

Religiosity Out of Hardships and the Revealed Power of Islam

When the Ba'th Party assumed power in Baghdad in 1968, it established a secular regime that made some concessions to Islam. To avoid a complete breach with the popular masses, during the first twelve to fourteen years of its rule in Baghdad the Ba'th regime followed the example of equivocation set by the party's founding ideologue, the Syrian Christian intellectual Michel 'Aflaq. Still, wherever it did not expect a meaningful public backlash, the regime adhered to its original, strictly secular party doctrine. There could be no doubt as to where the party members' hearts were: they saw themselves as a modernizing elite, an enlightened avant-garde whose mission was to educate the masses along secular pan-Arabism lines and wean them of "superstitions," meaning traditional Islam. They were bent on creating the New Iraqi Man. Thus, they adopted secular policies in education, law, culture, and intellectual activity, and tried to push the 'ulama to the periphery of political, social, legal, educational, and cultural life. In all this, they were similar to the Ottoman reformers of the second half of the nineteenth century, who "wanted to remove the 'irrational' barriers to progress that Islamic institutions were taken to be."[1] As the reforming Ottomans saw it, "Society had to be opened for the technological, administrative, economic and political changes that these groups saw as necessary for the establishment of a reformed social order . . . [through] the secularization of the state in ideology, law, education and bureaucracy" and pushing the 'ulama to the fringe.[2]

When the party reached the end of its tether in 2003, Bagdad was ruled by a regime that tried hard to look Islamic even though it retained some of its secular traditions. Deviations from an important tenet of faith, or "bargains" with society, occur often in the case of radical political movements after they come to power. Usually such a deviation is explained away as tactical and momentary retreat. Vladimir Lenin's New Economic Policy is just one example, if the most glaring one, of such a tactical or would-be tactical retreat. In the 1986 secret meeting of the Pan-Arab Leadership, Saddam did the same. The difference was that in the case of the Ba'th, this became what 'Aflaq had feared: a path of no return. Because of the profound identity and policy ramifications of this particular U-turn, the senior Ba'this clung tenaciously to their secular worldview. They clung to it far beyond their attachment to 'Aflaq's principle of egalitarian and amalgamative pan-Arabism, which they abandoned in favor of the Mesopotamian-origin narrative. The recruitment of the tribes and their shaykhs, too, came to them far more easily than abandoning the party's secularism. In the end, however agonizingly, they consciously sold their souls for what they hoped would be society's support in Iraq and popularity in the Islamic world.

Saddam's judgment and political expediency eventually swept away the party members' reservations and protests. Most of the senior echelons of the party did not become true Muslim believers simply because looking like a Muslim believer was expedient. And yet, in public, the Ba'th Party put on religious dress. The transformation was incremental. In the early 1980s, the regime admitted that the Iraqi public and even some party cadres had begun to turn to the mosque. This was the result mainly of two mutually reinforcing developments. One was the hardships experienced by most Iraqis during the Iran-Iraq War in the 1980s. The other was the soaring prestige of Khomeini and his Islamic regime and the Iranian victories in the Iran-Iraq War. This created the impression that a return to Islam could unlock great energies hitherto untapped.

Certain large-scale historical shifts underlay the Ba'th Party's change in strategy. The demise of the Ottoman Empire in World War I shattered Islam's image as a source of power and cast Western, including communist secular, systems as the new models to be emulated in the quest for power and dignity. Beginning in the 1920s, most new ruling elites, whether they were monarchies, as in Iraq and Jordan, or republics, as in Syria and Tunisia, were essentially secular. The revolutionary elites of the 1950s and 1960s, military officers and civilian activists alike, who replaced the old regimes were equally if not more secular. The 1967 defeat of Egypt and Syria, the champions of secular pan-Arabism, at the hands of Israel in the Six-Day War was the first demonstration that the secular god had feet of clay. In 1979 in Iran, vibrant political Islam and power suddenly fused, and the Iraqi public took notice.

There was an additional reason for the change. Mark Neocleous has suggested that the state can become overpowering even when it lacks absolute power if it manages to co-opt parts of society, that is, create a wide societal coalition. In this way, a regime can suspend a certain social and political situation and protect itself against forces, even strong ones, that seek change.[3] This was essentially the case in Iraq between 1968 and 2003. To freeze the reality of power relations, the forces that the regime coopted had to represent a critical mass. Just as previous regimes had done, the Baʻth managed to attract the support of most Sunni Arabs. With almost 20 percent of the total population behind it, the Baʻth regime cast a wider net as it quickly recruited a few large Kurdish and Shiʻi tribal groups. In the 1970s and 1980s, the regime was also successful in coopting many other Shiʻis as bureaucrats, even military officers. No less important, beginning in the mid-1970s, with huge new oil revenues propping up its self-confidence and also its ability to reward, the party started expanding at breakneck speed. Through recruitment and cooptation, the regime managed to acquire the critical mass of supporters—some enthusiastic, others reluctant—that was needed to perpetuate the Sunni hegemony. At the same time, however, such a massive recruitment had a dialectical result in that it exposed the party to outside influences more than ever before. The new recruits, most of them Shiʻis, were not particularly dedicated party members. They represented a cross-section of Iraqi society, and in the 1980s and 1990s Iraqi society was embracing Islam. Not only that, but the party's effort to indoctrinate the new members into a more secular stance failed. Quite the opposite: however meekly and below the party's official radar screen, the new members challenged the party's worldview and added thrust to the U-turn the regime would soon commence.

The destruction and inconclusive end of the Iran-Iraq War, the defeat in the 1991 Gulf War, the March 1991 Shiʻi revolt, and the international embargo further encouraged the public to attend the mosque, but also dealt more blows to the regime's morale and confidence. Between 1986 and 1992, Saddam stood with one leg on the horse of Islam, the other on the horse of the party's traditional secularism. In 1993, finally, he had to jump. Taking the regime with him, he committed himself to Islam.

While Baghdad never became Riyadh or even Tehran, it went a long way in that direction. Saddam, however, never contemplated the possibility of turning over some of his power to the ʻulama or to any of the old Islamist movements. Rather, the party and the *mukhabarat* were assigned the same roles as before, serving as Saddam's angels of death, coercion, reward, indoctrination, education, mass mobilization, and information. Now, however, they were in addition the "supporters," *al-sahaba*, protecting the new Messenger, or Mahdi, and spreading his Message. This was a message of a unique kind of Islam, and yet a kind of Islam it was. Personally, Saddam became more withdrawn, "like a hermit in a sanctuary, worshipping [God]." The president did not neglect to prepare his military forces for war, he did not stint in his efforts to erode the international embargo, but he seemed to have believed that if worse came to worst, his program of Islamization would win him some kind of heavenly insurance. He seemed to hope that if he changed his ways—built many mosques, imposed Qur'an and Hadith studies, donated his blood for writing a Qur'an, and even introduced the Shari'a in some walks of life in Iraq—God would show his appreciation and reward him with victory, or at least survival. This was a new Saddam.

Party Dictatorship and Its Limitations

The fiercest dictatorship in the Arab world was forced, first, to recognize its domestic limitations, and then to adapt its ideology and policies accordingly. Having realized that it was extremely unpopular with most Iraqis, along with intimidation and terrorization policies unprecedented in Iraq, the Ba'th regime also looked for ways to win hearts and minds, or at least to defuse public hostility. Partly to ameliorate Shi'i and Kurdish concerns, Saddam made great efforts to mold an Iraqi identity that would mean both partial separation from the Arab world and the future leadership of it. When he introduced the national founding myth of Mesopotamian origin, he met with some opposition: for some party members, this was sacrilege. Yet Saddam personally relished this endeavor. There was nothing he enjoyed more than to be compared favorably with Sargon the Akkadian, Hammurabi, and Nebuchadnezzar, alongside al-Mansur, Harun al-Rashid, and Salah al-Din.

Coopting the tribal shaykhs was also controversial. Most of the leadership came from the urban lower middle class. The party elite went through the state educational system, where most teachers saw tribalism through Western (liberal democratic or communist) eyes, as a primitive and exploitative remnant of the premodern past. To them, tribal shaykhs, much like the 'ulama, were a competing elite.[4] Saddam, though, combined in his personality a modernizing nationalist with a tribal man. He felt equally comfortable in the gilded-hems garb of a tribal shaykh—even though his was not a shaykhly

342

family—or in an expensive three-piece Western suit.[5] Here, too, while to the party this was a difficult and unnatural transformation, to him the "tribalization" of the Ba'th was gratifying.

The third metamorphosis was the most profound and the only one painful to Saddam personally, as it was to his party. Islamizing the party and Iraq was not only humiliating; it meant a change of identity. It is true that almost every Muslim Arab, even the most secular one, is attached to Arab Islamic history. (This is no different from, for example, the attachment of secular and atheistic Jewish Zionists of the first half of the twentieth century to Jewish history.) The great Arab Islamic golden age is part of the identity of virtually all Muslims. An abstract belief in God and admiration for the Arab Prophet were legitimate, too, but "ordering what is right and forbidding the forbidden" did not apply to most party members. When 'Aflaq suggested that party members "may not be seen" among those who prayed and fasted, he knew that most cadres did not see themselves as bound by Islamic injunctions, rules, and rites. He also knew that his young disciples rejected the "men of religion." Going Islamic, therefore, was not easy.

The painful discussion at the July 1986 meeting of the Pan-Arab Leadership may serve as evidence of how agonizing it was for the party leaders to decide on an about-face and embrace the Muslim Brotherhood. They seemed to understand well what this meant, and for those who perhaps did not, Tariq 'Aziz elaborated what it would do to the party, and secretary-general Michel 'Aflaq made it clear when he predicted that this was a decision whose ramifications would extend for decades to come.

Islamization represented the most profound admission of failure on the part of the Ba'th dictatorship. The regime had more control than any previous regime; it could assassinate or execute without trial anyone it wanted to; it could arrest and torture anyone on a whim, and did so; and it had near total control of the media and the educational system, but all this power to coerce and indoctrinate, combined at least until the early 1980s with a robust economic ability to bribe and buy off people, failed to produce the desired result.

Worse still, while it may be said that Joseph Stalin's dictatorship failed to transform the people of the Soviet Union into atheistic, let alone selfless, communists, Stalin at least did not return to capitalism, nor did he present himself as (or become) a born-again Orthodox Christian, or try to force the Soviet Communist Party onto the Orthodox Church. In this vein, Hitler was arguably more successful than Stalin, as he seems to have turned much of the German nation into Nazis or Nazi sympathizers. This was still the case despite his crushing defeats in the war, beginning with the shocking surrender in Stalingrad on January 31, 1943, of German field marshal Friedrich Paulus and his Sixth Army. Saddam, too, was definitely a dictator, and his party made colossal efforts to impose a totalitarian system, with some success. Saddam's was a fierce coercive machine in control of a massive indoctrination system. And yet not only did it fail in its mission, but it surrendered almost unconditionally to the ideology of the Ba'th Party's worst enemies, the Islamists—"almost" because the regime's Islam was different from that of both the fundamentalist Sunnis and the Shi'is. And yet the defeat was still monumental.

Why did the Ba'th regime under Saddam Husayn fail in its secular enterprise? There is no simple answer to this question, but it would seem that religiosity in the Arab world is deeper than the Ba'th activists had believed. By 2014, other "republican" authoritarian secular regimes in the Arab Islamic world had lost, too, and the most secular or atheistic parties, the communists and Antun Sa'ada's Syrian Social Nationalist Party, never even achieved power. After an era of secular ruling elites in the Islamic Arab world, the twenty-first century, especially since the so-called Arab Spring, ushered in a time in which secularism became a burden. By 2014, even the future of the secular legacy of the great Mustafa Kemal Atatürk in Turkey was uncertain. Because Saddam had confronted Khomeini's Islamist regime, which found fertile soil in the Shi'i population of Iraq, he had already identified this sea change in the 1980s, far earlier than other "republican" rulers. Presidents Husni Mubarak of Egypt, Zine El Abidine Ben Ali of Tunisia, Bashar al-Asad of Syria, and others learned the same lesson in 2011. When compared with the relative stability of the Islamist regime of 'Umar al-Bashir in Sudan, this may mean that in the twenty-first century, secular, authoritarian nonmonarchies that have very limited economic resources can exist in the Arab Islamic world only with great difficulty.

At the same time, the events of June 30 to July 3, 2013, in Egypt and the protests followed by some secular constitutional developments in Tunisia seem to indicate that extreme Islamic impositions, Muslim Brotherhood style, are also unacceptable to the masses in those countries that had experienced life under more or less secular systems. Even after Saddam became or appeared to become a born-again Muslim, in his interpretation of Islam he tried to steer a middle course between the secular worldview of his youth and his secular party elite and security establishment, on the one hand, and the growing religiosity of the Iraqi people (and himself) on the other.

There was yet another reason for the failure of the Ba'th dictatorship to mold the Arab Muslim into the New Arab Man. From day one, the party had prepared for itself a safety hatch. The founders were timid and doubtful of their eventual success, and refused to burn their bridges. Even the choice of terminology in the single most important slogan of the party, "One Arab nation with an eternal message," reflected uncertainty and the fear of failure. Whereas the communists chose for "nation" a perfectly secular term, *sha'b*, the Ba'th could have chosen the same or the religiously neutral term *qawm*—"tribe" in classical Arabic, though by the 1940s *al-qawmiyya* was already recognized as meaning "nationalism," so *qawm* could be used for nation. Instead, Ba'th chose *umma*, the heavily charged Islamic term. And while the communist slogan spoke of "a happy nation" or "a happy people" (*sha'b sa'id*), the Ba'th Party slogan spoke of a "message" (*risala*), which created a chain of associations leading to the Message of the Messenger of God (*rasul allah*). Almost everything Michel 'Aflaq uttered regarding the connection between Arabism and Islam was equivocal and misleading. This was even the case when he spoke in one-on-one meetings with religiously inclined members. Fukayki reports a typical case of a young party recruit who wanted to be certain that the party did not clash with Islam. While Fukayki himself knew better, he fulfilled this young recruit's request and arranged for him to see 'Aflaq in 1959 in Beirut. 'Aflaq indeed assured the young man of "the connection between the Ba'th and Islam and the [Ba'th] fear of God" (*al-taqwa*).[6] What "connection" really meant was Islam as history, and by *taqwa* 'Aflaq meant a spiritual, ethereal faith in some higher entity that involved neither "thou shalt" nor "thou shalt not." But the new recruit had no way of seeing through this deception. Over time, the new recruits were expected to become properly indoctrinated.

For purely tactical reasons, by 1963 the party already had betrayed its "message." Fukayki severely criticizes his colleagues for abandoning party tradition when, on coming to power, they published Communiqué Number One, which called on the Iraqis to fight the communists, "God's and your enemies."[7] They also partially succumbed to the demand of the 'ulama to abolish former prime minister General 'Abd al-Karim Qasim's secular Law of Personal Status: though they did not abolish it, they incorporated into it some of the clerics' demands. When in 1989 the party insisted that Michel 'Aflaq had converted to Islam before his death, this strange feat marked the end of the party's original secular identity. And when in the 1990s, Saddam and his lieutenants took full advantage of 'Aflaq's intended ambiguity and began to interpret the party's message as an *Islamic* one, the final coup de grâce was delivered to the party ideology. To stay in power, the bloody dictator surrendered almost unconditionally to the belief system of his oppressed people. If ever there was a paradoxical totalitarian dictatorship, this was it.

The Effect of the Faith Campaign on Post-Ba'thi Iraq

When the regime was toppled by the coalition forces in April 2003, the secular exiled Iraqi returnees were taken aback by the degree of Islamic religiosity they encountered and the tremendous political weight of the clerics in both the Sunni and Shi'i parts of the country. With the all-powerful Ba'th Party gone with a bang, the only local sociopolitical leaderships that remained were the tribal shaykhs and the clerical class. Many tribal shaykhs were Saddam's appointees, while the local clerics were considered to be more independent and therefore enjoyed greater popularity. Saddam Husayn had made sure that no other political elite remained. The middle class was decimated. Nasserists, communists, pro-Syrian Ba'thists, liberals, active antiregime Islamists—all were dead or in exile. In the Sunni areas, the previously docile clerics now became important local leaders of the resistance, sometimes of violent insurgency.[8] In the Shi'i areas, the clerics who under the Ba'th had made an effort to remain below the regime's radar assumed the traditional pre-Ba'th role of political community leaders. Some, like *marja' taqlid* Grand Ayatollah 'Ali Sistani, instructed their followers to refrain from violence. Others, such as the junior cleric Muqtada al-Sadr, ordered their supporters to fight the Americans.

Either way, the leadership of the Shi'i 'ulama and *sada* was unchallenged, and the legitimacy of all the lay Shi'i politicians, most of them returnees, depended on some form of clerical approval. For an example of the culture shock experienced by many returnees, we may turn to the words of a secular Basra-born and -bred American Iraqi engineer who had fled his hometown for Saudi Arabia in March 1991 after the collapse of the Shi'i revolt. On returning to Basra in the late spring of 2003 he could not believe his eyes: "The 'ulama and *sada*, these ignorant and primitive people who know nothing about the world, have suddenly become the community leaders, and their word is law."[9] This was the result of the political and socioeconomic crises of the 1980s and 1990s and Saddam's faith campaign.

The expatriate newcomers were also taken aback by the strong show of sectarian identity. Between the shock of the horrendous suppression of the Shi'i revolt of 1991 and the decade of the faith campaign, the Sunni-Shi'i divide in Iraqi society was further accentuated. The first and in itself relatively innocuous display of sectarian identity that was suddenly allowed to surface was sufficient to produce a powerful shock wave. By the end of April 2003, some two weeks after the final collapse of the Ba'th regime, the Shi'i community commemorated the fortieth day (*al-arba'in*) of the 680 CE death of Imam Husayn at the hands of the Umayyads. Two or three days before this day, Shi'is traditionally march in mass processions to Karbala, where Imam Husayn is buried. On that day in April 2003, a throng of some 10,000 young Shi'i men from the huge shantytown of Saddam City, led by their low- and mid-level clerics, staged a mass procession in Baghdad. They hardly knew how to express themselves, so they simply chanted in unison at the top of their voices the religious chants they had learned at home and in the mosque since childhood. They did not scream for democracy, nor did they extol Iraqi nationalism, not even Arabism, Islam, or freedom. They roared in total ecstasy Shi'i and anti-American slogans: "*Abadan wallah / ma nansa husayna / Ya Husayn ya Husayn!*" (By God, we shall never forget our Husayn / O Husayn, O Husayn!); "*Maku wali illa 'Ali*" (There is no lord but 'Ali); "*Kull arwahna li Husayn nafdihi*" (All our souls for Husayn; we shall redeem him); "*Ya Husayn ya shahid*" (O Husayn, O Martyr); "*Law qata'u arjulana wal-yadayn / na'tika zahfan sayyidi ya Husayn*" (If they cut off our legs and hands / we shall reach you crawling, my lord O Husayn!).

While the demonstrators' anti-American slogans were very disturbing to the new overlords, in terms of Sunni-Shi'i relations the procession-demonstration seemed innocuous enough. At least on the surface, and possibly deeper down, the participants were expressing a purely religious-communal elation. Yet many Sunnis heard in this demonstration an ominous anti-Sunni rumbling. In the chants, they seemed to hear echoes of a deep-seated protest against many centuries of what Shi'is see as Sunni injustice and oppression, and the newly gained confidence that the tables were about to turn. Some Shi'i leaders, though not Ayatollah Sistani and his close associates, later did their best to turn this elation into anti-Sunni ire. When the American Civil Administration dismissed the military and initiated a sweeping de-Ba'thification process, the Sunnis interpreted these actions as anti-Sunni measures. This created palpable fear in the Sunni community of American intentions, and of the Shi'a and their connection to Iran.[10] The powder keg of civil war had been prepared. The explosion at the Shi'i 'Askari Shrine in Samarra in February 2006 set it alight. For two years, Iraq was torn by the worst sectarian violence since the establishment of the state. Unlike the government suppression of the 1991 revolt, this time no Shi'is supported the other camp: this was no longer a regime-versus-Shiʻi but a clear-cut Sunni-versus-Shiʻi confrontation. In 2013, severe Sunni-Shiʻi violence erupted again. The renewed violence led many to believe that between the marauding operations of movements like the Sunni Islamic State of Iraq and Syria, known as ISIS, and the Shiʻi *Asaʼib Ahl al-Haqq* (League of the Righteous, or Brigades of the People of God), another civil war was in the making.

At the same time, though, there are indications that many Iraqis would like to retain Iraq as a united, nonsectarian country, separate from its neighbors, be they Sunni or Shiʻi, Arab or Persian. There are differences between those who prefer a decentralized Iraq with regions retaining broad authority and those who insist on a highly centralized state, at least for the Sunni and Shiʻi Arabic-speaking population, but both want a distinct Iraqi state.[11] By 2013–14, there were also indications that a nonsectarian, all-Iraqi intellectual elite was being born. Some of them, like the novelists Fuʼad al-Takarly, Muhammad Khudayr, and Taha Hamid al-Shabib, were active under the Baʻth but because of regime censorship took refuge in an allegorical style that was extremely difficult to decipher. After 2003 they began to write freely. Younger novelists such as ʻAli Badr (since 2009 residing in Belgium), Najm Wali (living in Germany), Maysalun Hadi, Saʻd Salum, Nasif Filk, Ahmad Saʻdawi, ʻAbd al-Karim al-ʻUbaydi, Nazim al-ʻUbaydi, and Taha Hamid al-Shabib have been publishing their literature in Iraq for a large audience of avid readers. New intellectual magazines such as *Masarat* and *ʻImda*, and old ones under mostly new editorial boards, such as *Afaq ʻArabiyya, al-Aqlam*, and the communist *al-Thaqafa al-Jadida*, appear regularly. The future of Iraq depends on the balance between heavily armed, bigoted, violent sectarian movements and sect-hegemonic politicians on the one hand, and liberal, all-Iraqi intellectuals armed with computers and printing presses on the other. A new Iraq cannot and does not need to eliminate sectarian differences. Shiʻis will remain Shiʻis, Sunnis will remain Sunnis, and the Kurds already have their clear-cut autonomy. A new Iraq will need to find a way for its communities not just to coexist but to achieve a far more ambitious goal: national integration, which will eventually enable a unifying national identity to emerge. So which will it be: A civil war and the break-up of Iraq along sectarian and ethnic lines, or a new spirit of a unified national identity?

Appendix
Ba'th Party Membership and Organization[1]

Membership

From its inception, the Ba'th Party was a hierarchical organization. In its first years, this hierarchy was rudimentary, but when it came to power in Iraq in 1968 the party already had a fairly well-developed membership and organizational system. By the early to mid-1970s, the system of membership ranks had reached its full form. At the very bottom was the "follower" (*mu'ayyid*). At that level, a new recruit was expected mainly to participate in weekly meetings, in which he or she was indoctrinated in party beliefs and philosophy. A "follower" who proved to be reliable and disciplined was promoted one stage to the higher level of "supporter" (*nasir*). At that level, a member would sometimes participate with security operations or help organize public proregime rallies. The next level was "advanced supporter" (*nasir mutaqaddim*), followed by "candidate" (*murashshah* or *murashih*). The "candidate" could then become a "trainee member" (*'udhu mutadarrib*), which was the step right before full membership. A person who reached the status of "full" or "active member" (*'udhu 'amil*) could begin to climb the party's organizational ladder. On average, the length of time required to become an "active member" was between five and ten years, but for those who showed dedication and talent or had the right connections, a reasonable timespan was closer to five years.

This system did not apply to close relatives of the party's senior leaders. Some of them entered the party and became full or active members almost immediately, and then climbed the administrative ladder at a breakneck speed. The party documents never mention this fast track. Usually, however, people were promoted according to their dedication, which was expressed by regular meeting attendance and help with the party's outreach, time invested, energy and industriousness, loyalty, discipline, organizational skills, and intelligence—except that intellectual originality and integrity were not particularly encouraged. Higher education was, however, appreciated. A safe way to ascend was to conform to all party political analyses, ideals, and policies; to be well acquainted with Saddam's aphorisms, political theory, and philosophical deliberations; and to faithfully deviate from them according to the new party line. This advice, too, cannot be found in the party documents. When it came to suggesting better ways to strengthen the regime, some independent thinking was tolerated at the highest levels of the organizational pyramid.

A Pyramidal Organization[2]

The lowest echelon of Ba'th Party organization during the 1940s and 1950s was the "circle" (*halaqa*), a Sufi term describing the circle of prayer. By the time the party came to power in Baghdad in the 1960s, the name had already been changed to the secular "cell" (*khaliya*), a term representing one unit in a honeycomb. New recruits joined the party at this level. During the years of clandestine activity in Iraq, Syria, Lebanon, and Jordan, the number of members in each "circle" or "cell" was small, usually no more than seven. Only the secretary of the cell should know party members outside of the cell, ideally just of the higher level above his own cell. This meant that if a cell member was interrogated by the authorities, he could only report on his colleagues in his own cell. This was a Leninist technique that the party founders learned when they were close to the French Communist Party during their studies in Paris. In reality, though, this system of secrecy did not work well, and many members knew each other. When the Ba'th became the ruling party, the system changed in principle and a cell in Ba'thi Iraq could include around thirty members. Each cell had a secretary who was responsible for its activities and represented his cell at the higher level, the "division" (*firqa*, plural *firaq*). In the 1950s, the division did not exist, but it was added apparently in 1963 when the party came to power for the first time and received an influx of new members. The secretary of the cell was always a more veteran party member, an active member. The division, too, had a secretary who by definition was at least also a member of the higher level, the "section" (*shu'ba*, plural *shu'ab*). A member who excelled could be promoted to become a section member. One level higher was the "branch" (*far*, plural *furu'*). When the party came to power for nine months in 1963, it established five of these branches: Baghdad, North, Center (Ramadi, Ba'quba, Kut), Middle Euphrates (Najaf, Diwaniyya, Hilla), and South (Basra, Nasiriyya, 'Amara). Soon after it came to power again in 1968, the party's ranks swelled once more. By 1976, it had eleven branches: Baghdad, Diyala, Anbar, Ninneweh, Salah al-Din, Ta'mim, North, Wasit, Dhi Qar, Babil, and Basra. This number remained constant until 1980, when a Karbala branch was added. By 1982, the number of branches went up to sixteen, and by 1989 the number of branches had increased again to twenty-three. Until 1982, two or three provinces could be lumped together in one branch, but afterward in some cases a single province (Baghdad, for example) was partitioned geographically into two branches.

At the beginning of Ba'th rule in Iraq, right above the branch (*far'*) was the Regional Leadership (RL, *al-qiyada al-qutriyya*), but by 1981, as the party expanded considerably, a new level was introduced between the branch and the RL, the "organization bureau" (*maktab tanzim*, plural *makatib tanzim* or just *makatib*). There were five such bureaus (*makatib*): South, Euphrates, Baghdad, Center, and North. Each bureau was responsible for a few branches. In November 1992, at the Tenth Congress of the Iraqi Ba'th Party, this level was reorganized: the five bureaus became ten "organizations" or "structures" (*tanzimat*), each responsible for a smaller number of branches (*furu'*). This was a lesson learned from the Shi'i uprisings of March 1991: the leadership felt the need to improve control over the membership, especially at the lowest rung. All ten organization secretaries were also integrated into the higher (and the highest) party level, the RL, being another indication of the leadership's recognition of the need to improve the connection between the top and the bottom of the party pyramid. This arrangement remained the same until the party lost power in the spring of 2003.

Becoming a member of a division (*firqa*) was not automatic upon becoming an active member: only a minority of active members was promoted above the active member level to membership of divisions, sections, and branches. (The higher levels of bureaus, organizations, and the RL needed to be and were very small bodies.) This Ba'thi arrangement created a steep hierarchy even among active members. According to internal documents from 1986, active members represented only some 2.5 percent of the total party membership, and by 2002 this percentage had risen to only around 7 percent.[3] This again meant a very steep pyramidal structure, separating the active members from the masses at the lower rungs.

Above the cell, division, section, branch, and organization bureau levels came the RL. This was the second most important decisionmaking authority in Iraq after the Revolutionary Command Council (RCC) and before the government. All but one of the RCC members were drawn from the RL, but most of the time not all RL members were also RCC members. Whereas the RL was a clear-cut Ba'th Party body, the RCC was a state institution that did not officially belong to the party. Still, crucial political decisions were usually made by joint meetings of both institutions. The president of Iraq was also the RCC chairman and the RL secretary-general.

From the time it came to power in Iraq, the Ba'th Party oscillated between the uncontrollable urge to increase the number of members at the lower echelons and the ever-present fear that the new recruits were not sufficiently loyal and imbued with the party's ideals. As a result, party expansion took place in fits and starts, and at least once, following the shocking double-impact of the 1991 Shi'i revolt and its suppression, the party contracted. Still, despite the doubts regarding the true nature of the membership at the base, the party expanded. The administrative way to solve the dilemma was to keep a small, better-indoctrinated elite, the active members, as guides and supervisors, but the dilemma was never fully resolved.

In terms of the broader Ba'th Party organization, there was one body that was theoretically above the RL, the Pan Arab Leadership (PAL, *al-qiyada al-qawmiyya*). It was headed by a secretary-general and consisted of the leaders of the Ba'th branches from all the Arab countries where such party branches existed. Iraqis were the highest percentage of PAL members. Until 1989, the PAL secretary-general was Ba'th Party founder and chief ideologue Michel 'Aflaq. Following his death, Saddam Husayn took his place. The PAL had little weight when it came to political decisions that involved only Iraq. However, when crucial ideological or even political decisions that applied to the party branches in the whole Arab nation were concerned, they had to be debated by and decided by the PAL. Theoretically the PAL was sovereign to make any decision, but in reality the president of Iraq (who until 1989 was always also the deputy secretary-general of the PAL) could get it to make decisions that suited his strategic goals. In cases of conflict, the PAL would not express its view and the Iraqi president and under him the RCC and the RL would make the decision and sometimes would come out with a communique declaring it. This happened, for example, in September 1970, when 'Aflaq and some other PAL members demanded that the party support the Palestinian organizations against the army of King Husayn of Jordan. The decision was made by the president of Iraq and the RCC, and in protest Secretary-General 'Aflaq left for Lebanon. In 1973, 'Aflaq also pleaded for the life of a very senior party member, 'Abd al-Khaliq al-Samarra'i, after Saddam accused him of participating in a coup d'état. Saddam spared his life at the time, but kept him in prison and later executed him. 'Aflaq did not protest the execution publicly, and from then on he followed Saddam's line.

Alongside the pyramidal structure, since at least the late 1950s the Ba'th Party also had headquarters *makatib* (bureaus), the most important one being *makatib amanat sir al-qutr* (the Country [i.e., Party] Secretariat), which served also as the Bureau of the Secretary-General. Other bureaus were *maktab al-fallahin* (Peasants' Bureau), *maktab al-'ummal* (Workers' Bureau), the *maktab al-'askari* (Military Bureau), and other bureaus devoted to finances, youth and students, culture, and foreign relations. In the 1970s, those bureaus were reorganized, and in the 1990s the Ba'th Party *makatib* were the Party Secretariat, the Professional and Popular Bureau, the Bureau for Foreign Relations, the Military Bureau, and the Bureau of Youth and Students.

Notes

Introduction

1. Saddam Husayn, *Muqtatafat Min Ahadith Saddam Husayn* [Excerpts from Saddam Husayn's speeches] (Beirut: Dar al-Taliʿa, 1979), 31.

2. See, for example, Qanun 97 of 1985, *al-Maʿhad al-Islami al-ʿAli Li Iʿdad al-Aʾimma Wal Khutaba*, in *al-Waqaʾiʿ al-ʿIraqiyya* no. 3080, January 13, 1986, 10–11.

3. See, for example, Document 476-97, *Mashruʿ khuttat ʿamal li-tansiq bayna al-munazamat al-hizbiyya wal-jamahiriyya fi majal tabʾith al-mujtamaʿ* [Action plan for the coordination between the party and popular organizations in the realm of the Baʿthification of society], in the Baʿth Regional Command Collection (BRCC) in the Hoover Institution document collection.

4. See, for example, Saddam in a closed-door discussion with the Revolutionary Command Council (RCC) in June 1981 on the Israeli raid on the nuclear reactor, complaining that the Israelis were trying to "destroy the New [Iraqi] Man" of science and progress, CRRC SH-SHTP-A-000-571. See also his intention "to achieve a total change in society," Husayn, *Muqtatafat Min Ahadith Saddam Husayn*, 13, 163. This Baʿthi ambition is reminiscent of the ambitions of social movements from an earlier era, such as the idea of creating the "new Soviet man" and the "new Hebrew [or Jewish] man."

5. Saddam in a closed-door discussion of the Pan-Arab Leadership on January 25, 1995, CRRC SH-SPPC-000-660.

6. See, for example, a videotape from January 1, 1992, CRRC SH-RVCC-V-001-402.

7. *Babil*, July 19, 1994.

8. See also John F. Devlin, "The Baʿth Party: Rise and Metamorphosis," *American History Review* 96, no. 5 (December 1991):1396–1407.

9. See the *Encyclopaedia Britannica* entry on dictatorship at http://www.britannica.com/EBchecked/topic/162240/dictatorship (last accessed September 13, 2013). For a comprehensive history of ruling regimes in the Middle East, see Roger Owen, *State, Power and Politics in the Making of the Modern Middle East* (London: Routledge, 2008). For Saddam's repression system, see Kanʿan Makiya's (Samir al-Khalil's) seminal *Republic of Fear: The Politics of Modern Iraq* (London: Hutchinson Radius, 1989). For an analysis of Saddam's dictatorship, see Isam al-Khafaji, "State Terror and the Degradation of Politics in Iraq," *Middle East Report (MERIP)* 176 (May–June 1992): 15–21.

10. See the *Encyclopaedia Britannica* entry on totalitarianism at http://www.britannica.com/EBchecked/topic/600435/totalitarianism (last accessed September 13, 2013).

11. Toby Dodge, *Inventing Iraq: The Failure of Nation-Building and a History Denied* (New York: Columbia University Press, 2003), 157.

12. Sa'dun Shakir and 'Izzat Ibrahim in a party discussion as reported by *al-Yom al-Sabi'*, January 22, 1990.

13. Joseph Sassoon, *Saddam Hussein's Ba'th Party: Inside an Authoritarian Regime* (Cambridge: Cambridge University Press, 2012), 50.

14. See Saddam announcing it in 1976: Saddam Hussein, *Social and Foreign Affairs in Iraq* (London: Croom Helm, 1979), 57.

15. See Fatima Mohsen, "Cultural Totalitarianism," in *Iraq since the Gulf War: Prospects for Democracy*, ed. Fran Hazelton (London: Zed Books, 1994).

16. See Ibrahim al-Marashi, "Iraq's Security and Intelligence Network: A Guide and Analysis," *Middle East Review of International Affairs (MERIA)* 6, no. 3 (September 2002): 1–13; al-Marashi, "An Insight into the Mindset of Iraq's Security Apparatus," *Intelligence and National Security* 18, no. 3 (Autumn 2003): 1–23.

17. Sassoon's *Saddam Hussein's Ba'th Party* devotes considerable space to this punishment and reward system; see esp. 98–161, 193–226.

18. See Kevin M. Woods and James Lacey, *Iraqi Perspectives Project: Saddam and Terrorism: Emerging Insights from Captured Iraqi Documents*, 5 vols. (Alexandria, VA: Institute for Defense Analysis, 2007).

19. For economic and other travails since the 1980s, see Sami Zubaida, "Une société traumatisée, une société civile anéantie, une économie en ruine," in *Le livre noir de Saddam Hussein*, ed. Chris Kutchera (Paris: Oh! Edition, 2005); Abbas al-Nasrawi, "Economic Consequences of the Iraq-Iran War," *Third World Quarterly* 8, no. 3 (July 1986): 869–95; al-Nasrawi, "Iraq: Economic Consequences of the 1991 Gulf War and Future Outlook," *Third World Quarterly* 13, no. 2 (June 1992): 335–52; Nimah Mazaheri, "Iraq and the Domestic Political Effects of Economic Sanctions," *Middle East Journal* 64, no. 2 (Spring 2010): 253–68.

20. Antonio Gramsci, *Selections from the Prison Notebooks* (London: Lawrence and Wishart, 1971), 244–63.

21. Pierre Darle, *Saddam Hussein . . . Maître des mots: Du langage de la tyrannie à la tyrannie du langage* (Paris: L'Harmattan, 2003), 160.

22. Achim Rohde, *State-Society Relations in Ba'thist Iraq: Facing Dictatorship* (Abingdon, UK: Routledge, 2010), 12.

23. See Amatzia Baram, "*Qawmiyya* and *Wataniyya* in Ba'thi Iraq: The Search for a New Balance," *Middle Eastern Studies* 19, no. 2 (April 1983):188–200.

24. For the party's explanations as to why unification with Syria failed, see the RCC Communiqué, published in *al-Thawra* and *al-Jumhuriyya*, October 2, 3, 1978; *al-Jumhuriyya*, October 18, November 27, 1978, February 3, 1979; *al-Hawadith*, July 27, 1979. Syria was expected to admit that its policies were close to treason and that Baghdad's ideological champion, Michel 'Aflaq, was the only legitimate ideologue, which would mean that the Syrian Ba'th was a fake. For the Mesopotamian trend, see Amatzia Baram, *Culture, History and Ideology in the Formation of Ba'thist Iraq: 1968–1989* (London: Palgrave Macmillan; New York: Martin's Press, 1991).

25. See Baram, *Culture, History and Ideology*; Baram, "Mesopotamian Identity in Ba'thi Iraq," *Middle Eastern Studies* 19, no. 4 (October 1983): 426–56; Baram, "*Qawmiyya* and *Wataniyya* in Ba'thi Iraq"; Ofra Bengio, *Saddam's Word: Political Discourse in Iraq* (New York: Oxford University Press, 1998), 92, 137, 166–68; Eric Davis, *Memories of State: Politics, History, and Collective Identity in Modern Iraq* (Los Angeles: University of California Press, 2005).

26. See Amatzia Baram, "Neo-Tribalism in Iraq: Saddam Husayn's Tribal Policies 1991–1996," *International Journal of Middle Eastern Studies* 29, no. 1 (February 1997): 1–31. Later, this subject was revisited in its wider Middle East context by Faleh A. Jabar and Hosham Dawod in their edited volume, *Tribes and Power: Nationalism and Ethnicity in the Middle East* (London: Saqi Books, 2002).

27. See Amatzia Baram, "Re-inventing Nationalism in Ba'thist Iraq 1968–1994: Supra-Territorial and Territorial Identities and What Lies Below," *Princeton Papers: Interdisciplinary Journal of Middle Eastern Studies* 5 (Fall 1996): 29–56.

28. See Bengio, *Saddam's Word*, esp. 176–91.

29. Rohde, *State-Society Relations in Ba'thist Iraq*, esp. 75–118.

30. See Amatzia Baram, "From Militant Secularism to Islamism: The Iraqi Ba'th Regime 1968–2003," Woodrow Wilson International Center for Scholars Occasional Paper (Washington, DC: Woodrow Wilson International Center for Scholars, 2011); and later Sassoon, *Saddam Hussein's Ba'th Party*, 259–68.

31. See, for example, CRRC SH-PDWN-D-000-590, Presidential Decree 840 from November 4, 1986, punishments for offending the president and the party; SH-IDGS-D-000-268 and 576, reports from 1979–84 on arrests of people who cursed Saddam and who "offended the regime"; SH-BATH-D-000-364, January 15, 1998, 'Uday Saddam Husayn, defining for what one should be executed.

Chapter 1

1. See, for example, Sami al-Jundi, *Al-Ba'th* [The Ba'th] (Beirut: Dar al-Nahar, 1969), 22–27. Fichte's *Addresses to the German Nation* (1808), speeches delivered in Berlin under the French occupation, were particularly popular with secular Arab intellectuals. In those lectures, Fichte urged the German people to "have character and be German." A corollary to his idea of German identity was anti-Semitism: he argued that making Jews free German citizens would hurt the nation. Fichte defined German identity in terms of what he saw as the long historical continuity of the German language, but also in terms of the virtues of historical "Germania" and German heroism as represented by Arminius. Fichte was considered by his critics to be an atheist. He denied it, but his concept of religion was far closer to intellectual spirituality than it was to conventional religiosity.

2. For more details, see, for example, the excellent account by John Devlin, *The Ba'th Party: A History from Its Origins to 1966* (Stanford, CA: Stanford University Press, 1976, 1979), 1–45. See also Yitzhak Oron, "Mifleget Ha Thiya Ha Aravit Ha Sotzialistit" [The Resurrection Arab Socialist Party], *Ha Mizrah He Hadash* 9, no. 4 (1959): 241–63.

3. By far the best account of the personal and organizational history of the Ba'th in Iraq in the 1940s and 1950s is by Ronen Zeidel, "The Iraqi Baath Party 1948–1995:

Personal and Organizational Aspects" [in Hebrew] (master's thesis, University of Haifa, 1997), esp. 20–102.

4. In December 1970, 'Aflaq was still in Beirut, from where he advised his followers in Baghdad on Arab relations. See *al-Hawadith*, December 25, 1970.

5. See, for example, *Sawt al-'Iraq*, July 1982, 4; *al-Da'wa Chronicle* no. 17, September 1981, 7; no. 5, September 1980, 2; no. 37, May 1983, 4, 6; Hizb al-'Amal al-Islami [Islamic Labor Party], *Saddam Husayn Warith al-Shah* [Saddam Husayn, heir of the shah] (Tehran: Author, 1981).

6. CRRC Records, SHTP-A-000-835, Saddam in a secret meeting on September 16, 1980. The next day, Saddam declared the Iranian-Iraqi Algiers Agreement of 1975 null and void. Five days later, Iraq invaded Iran. Six days later, Saddam declared victory. The war lasted eight more years.

7. See 'Aflaq defined as "Un-Identified Male 1" (UM1), CRRC SH-A-001-167, July 1986. For details, see chapter 4. Until his death, 'Aflaq remained silent regarding the increase in Islamic rhetoric in the regime's media. He died before Saddam officially launched his Islamic "faith campaign."

8. Baghdad Voice of the Masses in Arabic, June 24, 1989, in FBIS-NES, June 26, 1989, 10.

9. Qur'an, for example, *Sura 7, al-a'Raf, Aaya*s 62, 79; *Sura 5, al-Ma'ida, Aaya* 67; *Sura 6, al-An'am, Aaya* 24.

10. Qur'an, *Sura 3, Aal 'Imran, Aaya* 110.

11. Qur'an, *Sura 23, al-Mu'minun, Aaya* 52.

12. 'Aflaq tried at least once to differentiate: "We consider Israel a basis for imperialism. . . . Israel is also an expression of the force of world Zionism. . . . What represents a danger to the Arab nation is the existence of Israel as a State, not the presence of a Jewish minority in the Arab homeland." See his 1957 lecture, "As'ila wa ajwiba" [Questions and answers], in his *Fi Sabil al-Ba'th* [On the way of resurrection] (Beirut: Dar al-Tali'a, 1974; first published 1959), 223–24.

13. 'Aflaq in a 1955 lecture, "Qawmiyyatuna al-mutaharrara amam al-tafriqa al-diniyya wal-'unsuriyya" [Our free nationalism facing religious and racist division], ibid., 175–77.

14. Ibid., 174–76.

15. See, for example, Devlin, *The Ba'th Party*, 28–31.

16. Al-Jundi, *Al-Ba'th*, 22–23.

17. Ibid., 27.

18. Ibid., 27.

19. Hitler's *Mein Kampf* and *The Protocols of the Elders of Zion* were widely available in Arabic in bookstores all over the Arab world since the 1940s, except that the parts of Hitler's work that contained derogatory references to the Arabs were omitted. In Ba'thi Syria, blood-libel stories about Jews using the blood of non-Jewish people for the unleavened Passover bread and wine were officially disseminated. See, for example, Mustafa Talas, *Fatir Sahiyyun* [Zion's unleavened bread] (Damascus: Talas Lil-Dirasat Wal-Tarjama Wal-Nashr, 1986).

20. For example, CRRC SH-PDWN-D-000-812, 19; CRRC SH-PDWN-D-000-855, 22; CRRC SH-PDWN-D-000-724, 9.

21. See, for example, the party's publication *Nidhal al-Ba'th* 1: 230, reporting a communiqué from January 1947, as reproduced in the Iraq internal Ba'thi magazine *al-Thawra al-'Arabiyya* 6–7 (1973): 67.

22. See, for example, Hani al-Fukayki, *Awkar al-Hazima: Tajribati fi Hizb al-Ba'th al-'Iraqi* [The sources of defeat: My experience in the Iraqi Ba'th Party] (London and Cyprus: Riad el Rayyes Books, 1993), 62–63.

23. 'Aflaq in a 1950 lecture, "Al-'Arab bayna madhihim wa mustaqbalihim" [The Arabs between their past and future], in *Fi Sabil al-Ba'th*, 164–67, esp. 165.

24. 'Aflaq in a 1943 lecture, "Dhikra al-rasul al-'Arabi" [The memory of the Arab messenger], in *Fi Sabil al-Ba'th*, 131–32. The speech was delivered at Syrian University.

25. Interview conducted in Europe, September 30, 1990. The activist, a very senior member, initiated the interview as he wanted the history of the movement to be known but asked that his name not be mentioned, fearing that his own party members in Europe would ostracize him for being interviewed by an Israeli historian.

26. Ibid., 134.

27. Fukayki, *Awkar al-Hazima*, 279, describes a classic instance in 1963 when the figurehead president 'Abd al-Salam 'Arif, a religious man, briefly left a meeting with his Ba'thi colleagues to perform a duty prayer (apparently the afternoon prayer), but his Ba'thi colleagues did not even remotely considered joining him. Instead, they took advantage of his absence to discuss how to oppose him.

28. *Al-'Iraq*, August 9, 1979.

29. Audio recording, CRRC SH-PDWN-D-00-028, Saddam's discussion with the General Staff, recorded on August 25, 1981. See also from later years SH-SHTP-A-000-631, a discussion with senior officers in July or August 1988; SH-SHTP-D-000-757, Saddam and senior officers discussing the Arab way of war, sometime in 1993; SPPC-D-000-660, a press report covering articles that appeared between January 1995 and November 2001 on the *Rashidun*, and others.

30. See, for example, SH-PDWN-D-000-724, press reports from 1995.

31. 'Aflaq, "Al-'Arab bayna madhihim wa mustaqbalihim," 164–67.

32. Ibid., 166–67.

33. Shibli al-'Aysami, *Fi al-Thawra al-'Arabiyya* [On the Arab revolution], 4th ed. (Beirut: Dar al-Tali'a, 1973), 150–51, 173–74.

34. Hizb al-Ba'th al-'Arabi al-Ishtiraki [Arab Ba'th Socialist Party], "*Dustur Hizb al-Ba'th al-'Arabi al-Ishtiraki, April 7, 1947*" [The Constitution of the Arab Ba'th Socialist Party, April 7, 1947], in *Nidhal Hizb al-Ba'th al-'Arabi al-Ishtiraki 'Abra Mu'tamaratihi al-Qawmiyya 1947–1964* [The struggle of the Arab Ba'th Socialist Party through its Pan-Arab Congresses] (Beirut: Dar al-Tali'a, 1971), 27.

35. Fukayki, *Awkar al-Hazima*, 272–73. In the 1960s, Fukayki was a member of the Iraqi Regional Leadership and a member of the party's politburo (ibid., 274).

36. Ibid., 62. Fukayki complained that party leaders also had little general education (168, 172).

37. Ibid., 83.

38. Ibid., 83–84. Fukayki reported that even members of the Communist Party participated in these rites, and even practiced serious self-flagellation.

39. Ibid., 79.

40. Ibid., 63.

41. Al-Jundi, *Al-Ba'th*, 26–27.

42. Hizb al-Ba'th al-'Arabi al-Ishtiraki, *"Dustur Hizb al-Ba'th al-'Arabi al-Ishtiraki, April 7, 1947,"* 30.

43. Ibid., 30.

44. 'Aflaq, "Al-Risala al-'Arabiyya al-Khalida," [The eternal Arab message], *Fi Sabil al-Ba'th*, 100. The speech was made in 1946.

45. Hizb al-Ba'th al-'Arabi al-Ishtiraki, *"Dustur Hizb al-Ba'th al-'Arabi al-Ishtiraki,"* 25.

46. 'Aflaq, "Al-Risala al-'Arabiyya al-Khalida," *Fi Sabil al-Ba'th*, 98–99. Some thirty years later, Shibli al-'Aysami, deputy secretary general of the Baghdad-based party's Pan-Arab Leadership and a leading party ideologue close to 'Aflaq, would express the same views through the party's Beirut-based publishing house. See Shibli al-'Aysami, *Risalat al-Umma al-'Arabiyya* [The message of the Arab nation] (Beirut: Dar al-Tali'a, 1978), 97–98.

47. 'Aflaq in a 1940 lecture, "Al-qawmiyya hubb qabla kull shay'" [Arab nationalism is love before anything else], in *Fi Sabil al-Ba'th*, 112–13.

48. 'Aflaq, "Dhikra al-Rasul al-'Arabi," ibid., 126, 133.

49. Ibid., 133.

50. 'Aflaq in a 1950 lecture, "The Arab Ba'th Is Revolution," in *Fi Sabil al-Ba'th*, 65. See also a July 1955 lecture, "The Connection between the Organization and Revolutionary Action," in *Fi Sabil al-Ba'th*, 90, 95; and a 1950 lecture, "Al-Sila bayna al-'uruba wal-haraka al-inqilabiyya" [The connection between Arabism and the revolutionary movement], in *Fi Sabil al-Ba'th*, 75.

51. 'Aflaq in a 1946 lecture, "About the Arab Mission," in *Fi Sabil al-Ba'th*, 100.

52. Ibrahim Khalas, "Al-Tariq li-Khalq Insanina al-'Arabi al-Jadid" [The path to creating our new Arab man], *Jaysh al-Sha'b* 749, April 2, 1967, as reproduced in Mordechai Kedar, "In Search of Legitimacy: Asad's Islamic Image in the Syrian Official Press," in *Modern Syria: From Ottoman Rule to Pivotal Role in the Middle East*, ed. Moshe Ma'oz, Joseph Ginat, and Onn Winckler (Brighton: Sussex Academic Press, 1988), 18–19.

53. See, for example, Robert N. Bellah, "Civil Religion in America," in "Religion in America," Special Issue, *Dædalus* 96, no. 1 (Winter 1967): 1–21.

54. 'Aflaq, "Fi al-qawmiyya al-'Arabiyya" [About Arab nationalism], in *Fi Sabil al-Ba'th*, 111.

55. Al-Jundi, *Al-Ba'th*, 26–27.

56. Fukayki, *Awkar al-Hazima*, 78–79.

57. Ibid., 79.

58. Benedict Anderson, *Imagined Communities: Reflections on the Origin and Spread of Nationalism* (London: Verso, 1983), 19.

59. Anthony D. Smith, *The Ethnic Origins of Nations* (Oxford: Blackwell, 1989), 179.

60. Ibid., 136, 175–76.

61. Michael Gilsenan, *Recognizing Islam: Religion and Society in the Modern Arab World* (New York: Pantheon Books, 1982), 11.

62. Ibid, 12–13.

63. For details, see Amatzia Baram, *Culture, History and Ideology in the Formation of Ba'thist Iraq* (London: Palgrave Macmillan; New York: St. Martin's Press, 1991); Elie Podeh, *The Politics of National Celebrations in the Arab Middle East* (Cambridge: Cambridge University Press, 2011), 129–55.

64. CRRC SH-BATH-D-000-144.

65. CRRC SH-RVCC-V-001-402, circa 1992.

66. Kan'an Makiya (Samir al-Khalil), *Republic of Fear: The Politics of Modern Iraq* (London: Hutchinson Radius, 1989), 212.

67. Fukayki, *Awkar al-Hazima*, 274. Fukayki described his fear of being regarded as "sectarian" if he should arrange for Grand Ayatollah Hakim to meet with the government at the cleric's request. Fukayki also complained of an anti-Shi'i attitude of General 'Abd al-Salam 'Arif, a typical Sunni pan-Arab military officer under the monarchy (273–74).

68. See, for example, ibid., 83.

69. Interview with a senior member of the Da'wa Islamic Party who had left Iraq in 1979, Europe, September 1990.

70. Hanna Batatu, *The Old Social Classes and the Revolutionary Movements of Iraq* (Princeton, NJ: Princeton University Press, 1978), 742. Batatu based his report almost exclusively on Iraqi monarchy police files, but the police did not know of many members.

71. Zeidel, "The Iraqi Baath Party 1948–1995," 33–51. Zeidel based his information mainly on the archives of the Iraqi Ba'th Party that were reproduced, including the original documents, in the Iraqi press over a few years, mainly in the early 1990s. The authenticity of these documents is beyond doubt: many of the members mentioned were later purged, even executed, by Saddam, and some were accused of high treason, but their names and contributions to party and nation in the early years were reported in full. In this, Saddam was very different from Joseph Stalin.

Chapter 2

1. The first Provisional Constitution, Law No. 38 of September 21, 1968, was published in *al-Waqa'i' al-'Iraqiyya* no. 1625, September 21, 1968, and *Weekly Gazette* no. 38, September 17, 1969, 2–6. For the second Provisional Constitution, see *Al-Dustur al-Mu'aqqat* (Baghdad: Mudiriyyat al-I'lam al-'Amma-Matba'at al-Hukuma, 1970), 3–4, 15–16, Resolution No. 792 of July 16, 1970. For an English-language version, see "Interim Constitution," *Iraqi Weekly Gazette* no. 10, March 13, 1971, 3–4, 7. For the Constitution of 1990, see below.

2. For 'Arif's provisional constitution, see *Al-Dustur al-Mu'aqqat*, published in *al-Waqa'i' al-'Iraqiyya* no. 949, May 10, 1964.

3. League of Nations, *Constitution of 'Iraq (Organic Law)* (Geneva, February 20, 1929), Article 13.

4. Republic of Iraq, Ministry of Guidance, Directorate General of Guidance and Broadcasting, *Interim Constitution* (Baghdad: Government Press, 1959), Article 4. First published in *al-Waqa'i' al-'Iraqiyya* no. 2, July 28, 1958.

5. Another Ba'thi politician, President Hafiz al-Asad of Syria, learned his lesson the hard way when he omitted "Islam is the state religion" from his 1973 Constitution. Mass demonstrations and confrontations with the regime's security forces resulted, mainly in Damascus and in the northern cities of Homs and Hama (see Raymond A. Hinnebusch, *Authoritarian Power and State Formation in Ba'thist Syria: Army, Party and Peasants* [Boulder,

CO: Westview Press, 1990]), 292–93). Asad then changed direction. In a letter of partial surrender addressed to his rubber-stamp parliament, he explained that he was changing the constitution to make it better suit "the needs of the masses . . . [and] their wishes and [to be] in harmony with their true interests." "There is a wish," Asad explained, "among segments of the [Syrian] people, that the Permanent Constitution will stipulate that the religion of the president of the republic is the Islamic religion" (*al-Thawra* [Damascus], February 21, 1973). This was not exactly what the demonstrators demanded, but to avoid total humiliation, this is what Asad could offer. The March 13, 1973, Syrian Permanent Constitution included this sentence (for an English-language text of the constitution, see Peter B. Heller, "Document: The Permanent Syrian Constitution of March 13, 1973," *Middle East Journal* 28 [1974]: 53–66). Asad still had some difficulty convincing the majority Syrian Sunnis that his religious sect, the 'Alawites-Nusayris, were Muslims, but at least in the constitution the issue was settled. There is no evidence that the Iraqi Ba'th regime ever contemplated the removal of the "Islam is the state religion" clause, but if it did, then the Syrian Ba'thi experience served as a sufficient warning.

6. See, for example, Law No. 129 of 1968, the 5th Amendment to the Liquor Law No. 3 of 1931, signed on October 5, 1968, *Weekly Gazette* no. 12, March 19, 1975, 2; Law No. 14 of 1971, 7th Amendment to Liquors Law No. 3 of 1931, *Weekly Gazette* no. 30, July 28, 1971, 14; Law No. 15 of 1971, 13th Amendment to Liquor Excise Duties Law No. 17 of 1937, *Weekly Gazette* no. 30, July 28, 1971, 15; Law No. 219 of 1970, The Establishment of the New Ahliyya Beer Company, *Weekly Gazette* no. 35, September 1, 1971, 11; Law No. 80 of 1980, *Weekly Gazette* no. 47, November 19, 1980, 2, relating to owners of taverns, instructing them not to allow in anyone under the age of eighteen, under the punishment of six months in jail; Instruction No. 1 of 1981, *Weekly Gazette* no. 46, November 18, 1981, 9–10, on the establishment of tax-free shops in Baghdad where people entering Iraq, both Iraqis and foreigners, could buy one liter of "spiritual liquors," one of champagne, one of wine, a box of beer, etc.; Law No. 9 of 1982, Regulating the Taxes and Duties Imposed on Beer, *Weekly Gazette* no. 10, March 10, 1982, 2, and many more.

7. See, for example, Yasin al-Nasir, *Shari' al-Rashid: 'Ayn al-Madina wa Nazim al-Nass* [Al-Rashid Street: The city's eye and the composer of text] (Beirut: al-Mada, 2003), 107–8.

8. Badr Shakir al-Sayyab, *Diwan* [A poetry collection] (Beirut: Dar al-'Awda, 1971), 1:449–52, *Al-Mabgha*.

9. Conversations with scores of Jewish Iraqis in Israel, London, and Washington, D.C., between 1977 and the late 1990s.

10. Uriel Dann, *Iraq under Qassem: A Political History 1958–1963* (New York: Praeger, 1969), 56.

11. *Al-Jumhuriyya*, March 27, 1994. General Dhanun was the first to call for "expos[ing] the suspect places from a moral point of view" in order to "uproot this phenomenon [prostitution] that is alien to our people's Arab habits and traditions." The general also reported that a few such places were closed down, with everybody there arrested and soon to face a just trial.

12. Saddam Husayn, in *Muqtatafat Min Ahdith Saddam Husayn* [Excerpts from Saddam Husayn's speeches] (Beirut: Dar al-Tali'a, April 1979), 12–13.

13. Ibid., 18–19.

14. League of Nations, *Constitution of 'Iraq (Organic Law)*, 1929, Articles 73, 76, 77.

15. Law No. 188, Law of Personal Status, of 1959, *al-Waqaʾiʿ al-ʿIraqiyya* no. 280, December 30, 1959.

16. J. N. D. Anderson, "A Law of Personal Status for Iraq," *International and Comparative Law Quarterly* 9 (October 1960): 561–63. See also Noga Efrati, "The Marriage Contract and Women's Roles in the Family: Iraq 1958–1988" [in Hebrew] (master's thesis, University of Haifa, 1995), 24–25, 34. For more on gender history in Iraq, see Yasmin Husein al-Jawaheri, *Women in Iraq: The Gender Impact of International Sanctions* (London: I. B. Tauris, 2008); Nadje Sadig al-Ali, *Iraqi Women: Untold Stories from 1948 to the Present* (London: Zed Books, 2007); Marion Farouk-Sluglett, "Liberation or Repression? Pan-Arab Nationalism and the Women's Movement in Iraq," in *Iraq: Power and Society*, ed. Derek Hopwood, Habib Ishow, and Thomas Koszinowski (Reading, UK: Ithaca Press, for St. Anthony's College, Oxford University, 1993), 51–73; Jacqueline S. Ismael and Shereen T. Ismael, "Living through War, Sanctions and Occupation: The Voice of Iraqi Women," *International Journal of Contemporary Iraqi Studies* 2, no. 3 (2008): 409–24.

17. Under the monarchy, the constitution stipulated that "shariʿa courts alone shall be competent to deal with actions relating to the personal status of Muslims and . . . *waqf* foundations" (Article 76). Justice was to be administered there "according to the terms of the shariʿa doctrine of each of the Islamic sects" (Article 77). See League of Nations, *Constitution of ʿIraq (Organic Law)*.

18. For the party dispute, see Hani al-Fukayki, *Awkar al-Hazima: Tajribati fi Hizb al-Baʿth al-ʿIraqi* [The sources of defeat: My experience in the Iraqi Baʿth Party] (London and Cyprus: Riad el Rayyes Books, 1993), 129–30.

19. For the law (Law No. 11 of 1963, Amending Personal Status Law No. 188 of 1959), see *Weekly Gazette* no. 30, 1963. The Arabic version was published in *al-Waqaʾiʿ al-ʿIraqiyya* no. 785, March 21, 1963. For an analysis of a religious conservative close to Ayatollah al-Hakim, see Muhammad Bahr al-ʿUlum, *Adhwaʾ ʿala Qanun al-Ahwal al-Shakhsiyya al-ʿIraqi* [Illuminating the Iraqi law of personal status] (Najaf: Matbaʿat al-Nuʿman, 1963), 9–10, as quoted in Efrati, "The Marriage Contract and Women's Roles in the Family." For the amendment, see Law No. 11 of 1963, published in *al-Waqaʾiʿ al-ʿIraqiyya* no. 785, March 21, 1963. And see an analysis by Chibli Mallat, "Siʿism and Sunnism in Iraq: Revisiting the Codes," in *Islamic Family Law*, ed. Chibli Mallat and Jane Connors (London: Graham and Trotman, 1990), 71–91.

20. Bahr al-ʿUlum, *Adhwaʾ ʿala Qanun al-Ahwal al-Shakhsiyya al-ʿIraqi*, 8, 242–46, 249–56.

21. N. J. Coulson, *Succession in the Muslim Family* (Cambridge: Cambridge University Press, 1971), 142.

22. Khalid ʿAbd al-Munʿim al-ʿAnni, *Mawsuʿat al-ʿIraq al-Hadith* [The encyclopaedia of modern Iraq] (Baghdad: Arab Encyclopaedia House, 1977), 3:1506.

23. Hizb al-Baʿth al-ʿArabi al-Ishtiraki [Arab Baʿth Socialist Party], *Thawrat 17 Tammuz al-Tajriba wal-Afaq* [The 17 July Revolution Experience and Horizons: The Resolutions of the Eighth Regional Congress] (Baghdad, January 1974), 153–54. See also an English-language version: Arab Baʿth Socialist Party, *The 1968 Revolution in Iraq: Experience and Prospects: The Political Report of the 8th Congress . . . January 1974* (London: Ithaca Press, 1979), 115–16.

24. Bushra Bustani, "Al-mar'a al-'Arabiyya wal-fikr al-mutakhallaf" [The Arab woman and the retarded thought], *al-Muthaqqaf al-'Arabi* 7, no. 1 (1975): 59–69.

25. Saddam Hussein, *On Social and Foreign Affairs in Iraq* (London: Croom Helm, 1979), 30–31.

26. Law No. 21 of 1978, published in *al-Waqa'i' al-'Iraqiyya* no. 2639, February 20, 1978.

27. Law No. 57 of 1980, published in *al-Waqa'i' al-'Iraqiyya* no. 2766, March 31, 1980.

28. See 'Izzat Ibrahim in a secret meeting of the RCC, CRRC SHTP-A-000-835, September 16, 1980.

29. Law No. 189 of 1980, published in *al-Waqa'i' al-'Iraqiyya* no. 2804, November 24, 1980, quoted in Efrati, "The Marriage Contract and Women's Roles in the Family," 43–46.

30. Resolution 147, published in *al-Waqa'i' al-'Iraqiyya* no. 2870, February 8, 1982, quoted in Efrati, ibid., 43–46.

31. Law No. 51 of 1985, published in *al-Waqa'i' al-'Iraqiyya* no. 3052, July 1, 1985, quoted in Efrati, ibid., 50–51.

32. Qirar 1708 of December 17, 1981, published in *al-Waqa'i' al-'Iraqiyya* no. 2865, January 4, 1982, 4–5.

33. Resolution No. 3066, published in *al-Waqa'i' al-'Iraqiyya* no. 3066, October 7, 1985; Resolution No. 1529, published in *al-Waqa'i' al-'Iraqiyya* no. 3081, January 20, 1986.

34. See www.iraqipapers.com. An English-language version is available through BBC Monitoring, January 16, 2004.

35. Shafiq al-Kamali, anthem, *al-Thawra*, July 12, 1981. Translation by Raymond Stock.

36. Reeva S. Simon, *Iraq between the Two World Wars: The Creation and Implementation of a National Ideology* (New York: Columbia University Press, 1986), 162–63. A pro-Nazi, anti-British revolt with strong pan-Arab coloration that erupted in Baghdad in April–May 1941 demonstrated to the British military commanders and embassy staff in Baghdad the danger posed to their interests by the radical pan-Arab educational system they had allowed since 1921. Concentrating on Sumer, Akkad, Babylon, and Assyria seemed far safer because it held the promise of creating an Iraqi identity at the expense of the pan-Arab one that pushed the Iraqi educated and lower middle classes toward deep involvement in the Palestine issue and anti-British struggle.

37. Baghdad Voice of the Masses in Arabic, August 2, 1990, 0410 GMT, in FBIS-NES, August 2, 1990, 26. The Arabic-language broadcast was made on Baghdad Voice of the Masses (*Sawt al-Jamahir*), August 2, 1990, 04.10 GMT. See also the text of the party's Pan-Arab Leadership, Baghdad Domestic Service in Arabic, August 3, 1990, in FBIS-NES, August 3, 1990, 28, 29.

38. For a discussion of the strategic-political shift since 1970, see Amatzia Baram, "*Qawmiyya* and *Wataniyya* in Ba'thi Iraq: The Search for a New Balance," *Middle Eastern Studies* 19, no. 2 (April 1983): 188–200. For the cultural process, see Amatzia Baram, *Culture, History and Ideology in the Formation of Ba'thi Iraq* (London: Palgrave Macmillan; New York: St. Martin's Press, 1991); Baram, "Culture in the Service of Wataniyya: The Treatment of Mesopotamian-inspired Art in Ba'thi Iraq," *Asian and African Studies* 17 (Fall 1983): 265–313.

39. *Al-Thawra*, July 26, 1979.

40. *Afaq 'Arabiyya* no. 12, August 1976, 43.

41. For details, see Baram, *Culture, History and Ideology.*

42. *Al-Thawra*, May 19, 1981.

43. For details, see chapter 6.

44. *Al-Thawra*, September 22, 1972.

45. A series of interviews with a retired Iraqi general, Washington, D.C., 2010–2011.

46. Fukayki, *Awkar al-Hazima*, 69, 109.

47. *Hurras al-Watan*, April 1988.

48. See, for example, an advertisement for the American film *The Avengers and the Police*, featuring an actress in minimal lingerie in "natural colors," for the benefit of party members reading the party daily *al-Thawra*, July 20, 1972. Austrian actress Sybil Danning exposes most of her breasts to the Iraqi reader while in a seductive pose in the government daily *al-Jumhuriyya*, January 14, 1981.

49. 'Abd Tufiq al-Hashimi, *Al-Tarbiya al-Islamiyya fi al-Marahil al-Dirasiyya al-'Iraqiyya* [Islamic education in the Iraqi school levels] (Baghdad: al-'Anni Press, March 1974), 50–51.

50. Ibid., 76–77.

51. Ibid., 90, 101.

52. Ibid., 75.

53. Saddam Husayn, speech at the Ministry of Public Education, July 10, 1976, in Husayn, *Muqtatafat Min Ahadith Saddam Husayn*, 9.

54. Saddam Husayn, speech to the Youth Union, February 15, 1976, ibid., 12.

55. Hashimi, *Al-Tarbiya al-Islamiyya fi al-Marahil al-Dirasiyya al-'Iraqiyya*, 15.

56. Ibid., 19–20.

57. Ibid., 19–20.

58. Ibid., 17.

59. Ibid., 20–26, 50–51.

60. Mahir al-Qaysi (or, in the English version, al-Kasey), *Youth Education in Iraq and Egypt* (Helicon CESO (Seminar of Comparative Education)—K.U.L., 1981), 135.

61. Ibid., 142.

62. Ibid., 152–53.

63. Ibid., 126.

64. For example, Wizarat al-Tarbiya [Ministry of Education], *Al-Tarbiya al-Qawmiyya wal-Ishtirakiyya lil-Saff al-Rabi' al-'amm* [Pan-Arab and socialist education for the fourth general grade] (Baghdad: Republic of Iraq, 1990).

65. Ibid., 7–13. See also 23–29.

66. Ibid., 81–83.

67. See Arab Ba'th Socialist Party—Iraq, *Revolutionary Iraq 1968–1973: The Political Report Adopted by the Eighth Regional Congress of the Arab Ba'th Socialist Party—Iraq, January 1974* (Baghdad, 1974), 181–82.

68. Halaf Nassar al-Hiti, *Al-Qiyam al-Sa'ida fi Sahafat al-Atfal al-'Iraqiyya* [The dominant values in Iraqi children's magazines] (Baghdad: Manshurat Wizarat al-Thaqafa wal-Funun, 1978), 12.

69. Ibid., 110–111.

70. Ibid., 113–15.

71. Ibid., 117–18.

72. Husayn Qasim al-'Aziz, "Al-Asas al-Maddi li Tatawwur Minaj al-Bahth al-Ta'rikhi" [The materialist basis for the development of historical research], *al-Muthaqqaf al-'Arabi* [The Arab intellectual] 6, no. 1 (January 1974): 87–92.

73. Ibid., 90–92.

74. Mu'ayyad al-Talal, "Al-'Abath wal-Huriyya" [Futility and freedom], *al-Aqlam* 9, no. 5 (1973): 2. The magazine, published in Baghdad, is dedicated to education and sent free to senior teachers.

75. Ibid., 3–4.

76. Ibid., 21. See also Ilyas Farah, "Hiwar ma'a al-duktur Ilyas Farah" [Discussion with Ilyas Farah], *Afaq 'Arabiyya* 1, no. 1 (September 1975): 44–45. Farah was at the time a member of the Baghdad-based Pan-Arab Leadership of the Ba'th.

77. Nur al-Din al-Hakim, "Mushkilat al-huriyya al-insanayya wal-qanun al-'ilmi" [The problem of human freedom and the scientific law], *al-Muthaqqaf al-'Arabi* 7, no. 6 (June 1975): 85–94.

78. Nur al-Din al-Hakim, "Hawla mushkilat al-huriyya al-insaniyya" [On the problem of human freedom], *al-Muthaqqaf al-'Arabi* 6, no. 6 (August 1974): 16–30.

79. 'Abd 'Ali Salman, *Al-Mujtama' al-Rifi fi al-'Iraq* [The countryside society in Iraq] (Baghdad: Ministry of Culture and Information, Dar al-Rashid lil-Nashr, 1980), 18. Emphasis added.

80. For an excellent overarching historical documentation and analysis of Iraq's secular national days from the 1920s, see Elie Podeh, *The Politics of National Celebrations in the Arab Middle East* (Cambridge: Cambridge University Press, 2011), 108–55.

81. *Dalil al-Mamlaka al-'Iraqiyya li Sanat 1935–6 al-Maliyya* [Guide for the Iraqi Kingdom for the budget year 1935–36] (Baghdad, 1936), 56, 772; see also 58, official holidays for Jews and Christians.

82. Law No. 10 of 1963, *Qanun al-'Atalat al-Rasmiyya* (*al-Waqa'i' al-'Iraqiyya* no. 782).

83. See how the greatest anthropologist of modern Iraq, 'Ali al-Wardi, relates to the 'Ashura processions in the government's daily, *al-Jumhuriyya*, February 28, 1972, 12 Muharram 1398. Wardi himself was Shi'i.

84. Law No. 110 of 1972, *Official Holidays*, published in *Weekly Gazette* no. 39, September 27, 1972, 6. And see Law No. 49 of 1973 amending Law No. 110 of 1972 (*Weekly Gazette* no. 40, October 3, 1973, 10). The Sabean community was granted two days' holiday at Easter, one on the small holiday, two days for the holiday of Banja, and one day for the birthday of the Prophet Yahya.

85. See, for example, full-page drawings showing Saddam as the bearer of the party's torch, a latter-day Imam Husayn, the incarnation of all the Arabs but also the reincarnation of Gilgamesh and of Tammuz, the Sumero-Akkadian god of fertility and resurrection: *al-Thawra*, April 28, 1986; and Saddam as the Life-Giver to all the Arabs (the latter appearing as a six-year-old girl), *al-Thawra*, April 28, 1987.

86. See, for example, Foreign Minister 'Abd al-Karim al-Shaykhali organizing a *Ma'dubat Iftar* (Fast-Breaking Dinner), *al-Jumhuriyya*, December 3, 1968; a party for *Jam'iyyat al-Aadab al-Islamiyya* on *Laylat al-Qadar*, sponsored by the president in Baghdad, whose message was read there and televised, *al-Jumhuriyya*, December 17, 1968 (27 Ramadan); a similar occasion a year later at al-Kaylani's mosque, fully televised again, *al-Jumhuriyya*, December 6, 1969; senior officials making speeches on Badr Day, 17 Ramadan, *al-Thawra*, September 2, 1977; at the president's instruction, the Ministry of Awqaf organizing an *iftar* dinner for senior party members, 'ulama, "and citizens" at the tombs of the Shi'i Imams 'Ali al-Hadi (the tenth Imam, died 254 *Hijri*) and al-Hasan al-'Askari (the eleventh Imam, died

260 *Hijri*) in Samarra, *al-Jumhuriyya*, June 25, 1984; and a similar occasion at Kazimayn for party members and "masses," *al-Jumhuriyya*, June 24, 1984; and the party's branch (*shuʿba*) The Hero of Liberation at *Farʿ* Saddam in Saddam City (a Shiʿi shantytown in northeast Baghdad, today Sadr City) holding an *iftar* dinner for members "as part of a series of Ramadan evenings" organized by the party, *al-Thawra*, May 29, 1985.

87. For Ramadan, see, for example, *al-Jumhuriyya*, November 13, 1968, 21 Shaʿban 1388; *al-Jumhuriyya*, November 5, 1969, 24 Shaʿban 1389; *al-Jumhuriyya*, October 29, 1970, 28 Shaʿban 1390; *al-Jumhuriyya*, October 7, 1972, 28 Shaʿban 1392; *al-Jumhuriyya*, August 12, 1977, 27 Shaʿban 1397; *al-Thawra*, June 30, 1981, 28 Shaʿban 1401; *al-Jumhuriyya*, April 11, 1988, 24 Shaʿban 1408. For Muharram, see, for example, *al-Jumhuriyya*, March 19, 1969, 30 Dhu al-Hijja 1388; *al-Jumhuriyya*, March 6, 1970, 28 Dhu al-Hijja 1389; *al-Jumhuriyya*, February 15, 1972, 30 Dhu al-Hijja 1391; *al-Jumhuriyya*, February 2, 1973, 29 Dhu al-Hijja 1392; *al-Jumhuriyya*, January 14, 1975, 1 Muharram 1395.

88. Qurʾan, *Sura 2, al-Baqara, Aaya* 185.

89. *Al-Jumhuriyya*, November 13, 1968, 21 Shaʿban 1388. And compare to the ʿArif period, for example: *al-Jumhuriyya*, December 26, 1964, 22 Shaʿban 1384.

90. *Al-Jumhuriyya*, November 6, 1969, 25 Shaʿban 1389.

91. See, for example, *al-Jumhuriyya*, October 29, 1970, 28 Shaʿban 1390.

92. See Communiqué of Ministry of Labor, *al-Jumhuriyya*, October 7, 1972, 28 Shaʿban 1392, and compare to the more lenient instruction by the Baghdad governor Khayr Allah Talfah (Saddam Husayn's maternal uncle), *al-Jumhuriyya*, October 4, 1972, 25 Shaʿban 1392.

93. See, for example, *al-Thawra*, August 23, 1976, 27 Shaʿban 1396; *al-Jumhuriyya*, August 15, 1977, 30 Shaʿban 1397.

94. *Al-Thawra*, June 30, 1981, 28 Shaʿban. See also *al-Thawra*, May 31, 1983.

95. *Al-Jumhuriyya*, April 10, 1988, 23 Shaʿban 1408.

96. For example, *al-Thawra*, March 3, 1992, and February 2, 1993.

97. CRRC SH-SHTP-A-000-835, September 16, 1980.

98. CRRC SH-SHTP-A-001-167, July 24, 1986.

99. Interviews with the retired Iraqi general, United States, 2011.

Chapter 3

1. Joyce Wiley, *The Islamic Movement of Iraqi Shiʿas* (Boulder, CO: Lynne Rienner, 1992), 94.

2. For details, see Amatzia Baram, "Neo-Tribalism in Iraq: Saddam Husayn's Tribal Policies 1991–1996," *International Journal of Middle East Studies* 29, no. 1 (February 1997): 7–10. See also a confidential discussion between Saddam and his generals in which the generals reluctantly agreed to employ Shiʿi tribes along the Iranian border to prevent infiltration and sabotage coming from Iran, CRRC SH-RVCC-D-000-610, a meeting on February 29, 1992.

3. Achim Rohde dedicates some space to this debate. See his *State-Society Relations in Baʿthist Iraq: Facing Dictatorship* (Abingdon, UK: Routledge, 2010), 10–11.

4. For Kurdish history and the Ba'th regime–Kurdish relations, see, for example, Michael Eppel, "The Demise of the Kurdish Emirates: The Impact of Ottoman Reforms and International Relations on Kurdistan during the First Half of the Nineteenth Century," *Middle Eastern Studies* 44, no. 2 (2008): 237–58; Eppel, "State Building and Social Ferment in Kurdistan," *Journal of South Asian and Middle Eastern Studies* 31, no. 4 (2008): 70–77; Eppel, "Kurdish Leadership in Post-Saddam Iraq: National Challenges and Changing Conditions," in *Iraq between Occupations: Perspectives from 1920 to the Present*, ed. Amatzia Baram, Achim Rohde, and Ronen Zeidel (New York: Palgrave Macmillan, 2010), 79–102; Ofra Bengio, *The Kurds of Iraq: Building State within a State* (Boulder, CO: Lynne Rienner, 2012); Gareth Stansfield, *Iraqi Kurdistan, Political Development and Emerging Democracy* (London: Routledge/Curzon, 2003); David Romano, *The Kurdish Nationalist Movement: Opportunity, Mobilization and Identity* (Cambridge: Cambridge University Press, 2006); Michael Gunter, *The Kurdish Predicament in Iraq: Political Analysis* (New York: St. Martin's Press, 1990); Kerim Yildiz, *The Kurds in Iraq: The Past, Present and Future* (London: Pluto Press, 2004); Robert Olson, *The Goat and the Butcher: Nationalism and State-Formation in Kurdistan-Iraq since the Iraq War* (Costa Mesa, CA: Mazda Publishers, 2005); and David McDowall, *The Modern History of the Kurds* (London: I. B. Tauris, 2005).

5. For a concise discussion of the revolt and its consequences, see Phebe Marr, *The Modern History of Iraq*, 3rd ed. (Boulder, CO: Westview Press, 2011), 23–28. For an analysis of that revolt, see Abbas Kadhim, *Reclaiming Iraq: The 1920 Revolution and the Founding of the Modern State* (Austin: University of Texas Press, 2012).

6. Abu Khaldun Sati' al-Husri, *Mudhakkirati fi al-'Iraq al-Juz' al-Awwal. 1921–1927* [My memoirs in Iraq. Part 1, 1921–1927] (Beirut: Dar al-Tali'a, 1967), 87–89. For the best analysis of the British policies in Iraq and British-Hashimite relations under King Faysal, see Peter Sluglett, *Britain in Iraq: Contriving King and Country, 1914–1932* (New York: Columbia University Press, 2007).

7. 'Abd al-Razzaq al-Hasani, *Ta'rikh al-Wizarat al-'Iraqiyya* [The history of the Iraqi governments] (Sidon: al-'Irfan, 1953), pt. 3, 286–93.

8. Hanna Batatu, *The Old Social Classes and the Revolutionary Movements of Iraq* (Princeton, NJ: Princeton University Press, 1978), 26.

9. See, for example, Husri, *Mudhakkirati fi al-'Iraq, 1921–1927*, 271–78, 321–33, 585–602.

10. Etan Kohlberg, "The Evolution of the Shi'a," *Jerusalem Quarterly* 27 (Spring 1983): 125; Michael Gilsenan, *Recognizing Islam: Religion and Society in the Modern Arab World* (New York: Pantheon Books, 1982), 58–61.

11. Gilsenan, *Recognizing Islam*, 59–60, 68–71; Kohlberg, "The Evolution of the Shi'a," 125.

12. Batatu, *The Old Social Classes*, 398–99.

13. Kohlberg, "The Evolution of the Shi'a," 109–13.

14. Ibid., 109–13.

15. Gilsenan, *Recognizing Islam*, 61.

16. Ibid., 59.

17. Batatu, *The Old Social Classes*, 978, 983. Those were the Shi'i poorest of the poor, so their Shi'i identity was only one component. They came from al-Thawra slum (later Saddam City), al-Shawwaka, al-Kreimat, al-Shu'la, and similar working-class neighborhoods. Many also came from 'Aqd al-Akrad, a Kurdish-Shi'i-Faily quarter.

18. *Liwa' al-Sadr*, 7 Jamadi II, 1409 (1988), 6.

19. Hamid Bayati, *The Shia of Iraq between Sectarianism and Suspicions in British Secret Documents, 1963–1966* (London: Dar al-Rafid, 1997), 94ff.

20. Arnold Wilson, *Loyalties, Vol. 2: Mesopotamia 1914–1917* (London: Oxford University Press, 1930), 2:238; Richard Coke, *The Heart of the Middle East* (London: Butterworth, 1925), 196; *Baghdad Yearbook* (Baghdad: al-Iraq Press, 1923), 1:38.

21. Religious Statistics for Iraq, August 1, 1932, FO 406/70, quoted in Yitzhak Nakash, *The Shi'is of Iraq* (Princeton, NJ: Princeton University Press, 1994), 13.

22. For an analysis of the results of the three campaigns, see Amatzia Baram, *Iraq Past, Present and Future: Arabic-Speaking Iraqis between the Tribes, the Sunnah and the Shi'ah*, Middle East Institute Perspective Series (Singapore: National University of Singapore, 2009), 19–36.

23. For slightly different assessments, see, for example, Helen Chapin Metz, ed., *Iraq: A Country Study* (Washington, DC: Federal Research Division, Library of Congress, and Headquarters, Department of the Army, 1990), 80–86.

24. See, for example, Fadil al-Ansari, *Sukkan al-'Iraq* [The population of Iraq] (Damascus: University of Damascus Press, 1970), esp. 24–34, 108–17. See also Riyadh Ibrahim al-Sa'di, *Al-Hijra al-Dakhiliyya Lil-Sukkan fi al-'Iraq 1947–1965* [Internal migration of the population in Iraq, 1947–1965] (Baghdad: Baghdad University Press, 1976), e.g., 123, 250–54. For an analysis based on the census results of 1947, 1957, and 1965, see Plate 16 in Iraq, Ministry of Planning, Central Statistics Organization, *Annual Abstract of Statistics*, 1970 (Baghdad: Iraq, Ministry of Planning of the Republic of Iraq), 46.

25. See, for example, Middle East Watch, *Human Rights in Iraq* (New Haven, CT: Yale University Press, 1990), 69–75; Michael M. Gunter reports of Kurdish complaints in this respect, *The Kurds of Iraq: Tragedy and Hope* (New York: St. Martin's Press, 1992), 17, 73; Saddam's own admission of fairly large-scale deportations from "strategic areas," *Times*, July 27, 1976, as reproduced in Ofra Bengio, *The Kurdish Revolution in Iraq* [in Hebrew] (Tel Aviv: Ha-Kibbutz ha-Meuhad, 1989), 172. On more recent deportations from the Kirkuk area throughout the late 1990s, see United Nations, Commission on Human Rights, "Questions of the Violation of Human Rights and Fundamental Freedoms in Any Part of the World: Situation of Human Rights in Iraq," Report submitted by the Special Rapporteur, Mr. Max van der Stoel, in accordance with Commission Resolution 1998/65 (United Nations Economic and Social Council, New York, 55th session, February 26, 1999), 7–8.

26. "Sijillat al-Ahwal al-Madaniyya," *al-'Iraq*, February 25, 1984, 4; Yahya Zaki, *al-Jumhuriyya*, February 17, 1983, 4.

27. A calculation based on Saddam Husayn's report to the effect that, in early 1980, the capital's population numbered 3 million, *al-Jumhuriyya*, April 2, 1980. Also *Statistiches Bundesmat Statistik Des Auslandes, Iraq 1982* (Stuttgart: Statistiches Bundesmat Statistik Des Auslandes, 1982), 13, citing for Baghdad in 1980 (end of the year) 3.3 million.

28. For example: Kazimiyya, where two important Shi'i imams are buried, houses around 6 percent of Baghdad's population; al-Karimat, al-Shakiriyya, al-Shawaka, al-Shu'la.

29. Ya'akov Rosen, "Ha Shi'im Be 'Iraq Me'az 1968" [The Shi'is in Iraq since 1968] (master's thesis, Hebrew University of Jerusalem, 1985).

30. CRRC SH-RVCC-D-000-610, a meeting on February 29, 1992. See also Saddam and tribal shaykhs from Saddam City, SH-SHTP-A-000-891, late 1991.

31. ʿA(li) Najaf (pseud.), *Al-Shahed al-Shahid* [The witness, the martyr] (Tehran, 1981), 27.

32. Reporting the atmosphere in Iraq in 1979, *Liwaʾ al-Sadr*, February 9, 1983, 5–7, 10; *Imam* 2, nos. 3–4 (April–May 1982), 59–60.

33. An interview with four young Iraqi exiles, Boston, May 1995. See also Faleh A. Jabar, "Why the Intifada Failed," in *Iraq since the Gulf War: Prospects for Democracy*, ed. Fran Hazelton (London: Zed Books and CARDRI, 2004), 108; Jabar, "Why the Uprisings Failed," in *Middle East Reports (MERIP)* 176 (May-June 1992): 2–14.

34. For example, Order No. 835 of November 15, 1972, published in *al-Waqaʾiʿ al-ʿIraqiyya*, November 22, 1972, 12. Similar earlier limitations were reported to me, but no mention of them was found in the Iraqi codex of laws.

35. *Al-ʿAmal*, June 27, 1968. The last Grand Mufti was Najm al-Din al-Waʿiz.

36. Bashar al-Faydhi, an interview in *al-Sharq*, March 2, 2005; Muhammad Bashar al-Faydhi, *Al-Sarab: Hisad al-ʿAmaliyya al-Siyasiyya fi zill al-Ihtilal al-Amriki* [The mirage: The harvest of political action in the shadow of the American occupation] (Amman: Dar al-Jil al-ʿArabi, 2007), 71.

37. An interview in Haifa, Israel, 2006.

38. For Musa Sadr, see Moshe Maʿoz, *Asad: The Sphinx of Damascus* (London: Weidenfeld & Nicholson, 1988); Patrick Seale, *Asad of Syria: The Struggle for the Middle East* (London: I. B. Tauris, 1988). For Ayatollah Hasan al-Shirazi and his activities in Syria, see *Tariq al-Thawra* no. 29, February–April 1983, 15–17; no. 25, May 1982, 9–11; *Saddam Husayn Warith al-Shah* (Tehran, 1979, 1981), 45–46; *al-Nashra* no. 5, December 1983, 23–25; *al-Mukhtar al-Islami*, June 17, 1981, 71–72.

39. See Abu Bilal, the Daʿwa representative in Damascus, *al-Jihad*, December 10, 1990, and a visit to Damascus by the president of the Tehran-based Supreme Assembly of the Islamic Revolution in Iraq, Ayatollah Muhammad Baqir al-Hakim, *Liwaʾ al-Sadr*, 18 Rabiʾ al-Awwal 1409.

40. The Baʿth twins, Iraq and Syria, went through a rapprochement in the second half of the 1990s, but Damascus did not expel the Daʿwa activists. For details, see Amatzia Baram, *Building toward Crisis: Saddam Husayn's Strategy for Survival* (Washington, DC: Washington Institute for Near East Policy, 1998), 87–96.

41. For example, ʿAbd al-Husayn al-Dujayli, a madrasa teacher in Najaf; Ibrahim al-Fadhili, head of the Najaf Committee for Religious Indoctrination (*Lajnat al-Tawjih al-Dini*), *al-Jumhuriyya*, June 13, 1969; the *marjaʿ* al-Sayyid Kamil Ibn Salih al-Daraji, imam of the Radhawi Mosque in Baghdad, denouncing those who hid behind religion and spread dissent, *al-Jumhuriyya*, June 16, 1969.

42. *Al-Jumhuriyya*, July 28, 1969.

43. *Al-Jumhuriyya*, Saturday supplement, August 20, 1977.

44. See, for example, high-profile support for the president in his just war against "the hostile Iranian enemy" by Shiʿi clerics in Najaf, *al-Jumhuriyya*, February 19, 1984. And see a government appointee-made-grand ayatollah, ʿAbd al-Karim Aal ʿAli Khan al-Madani, and his son, *al-Thawra*, May 5, 1991. See below for details on what looked like collaboration with the regime by Ayatollah Muhammad Sadiq al-Sadr, 1992–1998.

45. For details, see below. And see Fadhil al-Kilidar, the *sadin* (sexton) of the Najaf shrine, who often supported the regime, and Muslim al-Sayyid Husayn al-Musawi, *murshid* (guide) of the Kazimiyya shrine, denouncing the 1991 revolt, *Babil*, May 16, 1991.

46. Report from Party Secretariat to Deputy Secretary General of the Party, September 30, 2002, BRCC 009-2-5 (002-003), in Joseph Sassoon, *Saddam Hussein's Ba'th Party: Inside an Authoritarian Regime* (Cambridge: Cambridge University Press, 2012), 267.

47. This delusional thinking comes through loud and clear, for example, in a highly classified meeting between Saddam and his senior military commanders on February 29, 1992. See CRRC SH-RVCC-D-000-610.

48. See, for example, *al-Jumhuriyya*, August 20, 1977, the minister of *awqaf* reporting that (since the riots of early 1977) the government's spending on the Shi'i shrines had tripled; and *al-Jumhuriyya*, January 10, 1980; February 19, 1984; and *Alif Ba*, March 6, 1996, 7.

49. See, for example, *al-Jumhuriyya*, January 10, 1980; and more extensive reporting in 'Abd al-Wahhab 'Abd al-Razzaq Marzuq, *Al-'Iraq Balad al-Turath Wal Muqaddasat al-Islamiyya* [Iraq, the land of heritage and Islamic holy places] (Baghdad: Ministry of Awqaf and Religious Affairs, 1987).

50. *Al-Quds al-'Arabi*, January 10, 2001, 3.

51. The ministers of *awqaf* (religious endowments) and religious affairs from the mid-1980s were 'Abd Allah Fadhil 'Abbas al-Samara'i, from the late 1980s to 1993 (*al-Thawra*, August 11, 1991) and 'Abd al-Mun'im Ahmad Salih al-Tikriti (*al-'Iraq*, September 15, 1993; *al-Qadisiyya*, June 7, 1994) from 1993 until 2003.

52. *Al-Thawra*, May 5, 1991.

53. *Al-Thawra*, August 31, 1992.

54. For the theological differences and conflicts, see a succinct analysis by Kohlberg, "The Evolution of the Shi'a." See also Moojan Momen, *An Introduction to Shi'i Islam: The History and Doctrine of Twelver Shi'ism* (New Haven, CT: Yale University Press, 1985).

55. *Al-'Iraq*, August 9, 1979.

56. CRRC SH-SHTP-A-000-891. The meeting took place sometime between September and December 1991.

57. CRRC SH-BATH-D-000-325, July 8, 1999.

58. CRRC SH-BATH-D-000-474, a number of documents from 1994 to 2002.

59. See chapter 2. For a comprehensive study of national days in much of the Arab world, see Elie Podeh, *The Politics of National Celebrations in the Arab Middle East* (Cambridge: Cambridge University Press, 2011).

60. For example, *al-Jumhuriyya*, February 13, 1973 (10 Muharram 1393H); January 23, 1975 (10 Muharram 1395H); October 18, 1984 (11 Muharram 1404H).

61. *Al-Jumhuriyya*, August 6, 1979, a celebration of 'Ali's birthday in Karbala.

62. For example, 'Izzat Ibrahim reading Saddam's message, *al-Thawra*, March 15, 1987.

63. *Al-'Iraq*, April 5, 1985, 'Ali's birthday; *al-'Iraq*, May 6, 1984, al-Husayn's birthday; *Alif Ba*, March 25, 1987; al-Husayn's birthday; *al-Thawra*, March 15,1987, 'Ali's birthday; *al-Thawra*, March 10, 1987, 'Ali's birthday; March 4, 1988, 'Ali's birthday; *al-Jumhuriyya*, February 21, 1988, 'Ali's birthday; March 23, 1988, al-Husayn's birthday.

64. *Al-Thawra*, February 20, 1987.

65. *Al-Jumhuriyya*, April 6, 1987; March 23, 1988; 'Ali's birthday, *al-Thawra*, November 2, 1998.

66. *Al-Thawra International* (in Arabic), March 4, 1988; 'Ali's birthday, *al-Thawra*, November 2, 1998.

67. For example, *al-Thawra*, November 21, 1982.

68. For example, Saddam's visit to Najaf, *al-Thawra*, May 5, 1976; Taha Yasin Ramadhan in Najaf, *al-Thawra*, June 9, 1985.

69. See the first publication, initiated by Saddam's maternal uncle, Khayr Allah Talfah, no doubt in consultation with his nephew and with President Bakr, Ahmad al-Rujaybi al-Husayni, *Al-Nujum al-Zawahir fi Shajarat al-Sayyid al-Amir Nasir* [The bright stars in the (family) tree of the sayyid emir Nasir] (Baghdad: Matba'at al-Ma'arif, 1971).

70. *Al-'Iraq*, August 9, 1979.

71. See his meeting with Shi'i tribal shaykhs in Saddam City (Baghdad) in late 1991, CRRC SH-SHTP-A-000-891.

72. CRRC SH-PDWN-D-000-724, pp. 41–43 in the original text, January 12, 1995, Saddam in a cabinet meeting.

73. For example, the Shi'i cleric *'alama* Sayyid Husayn al-Rufay'i, in charge (*sadin*) of 'Ali's Tomb in Najaf, *al-Jumhuriyya*, February 19, 1984.

74. RCC Decision No. 2006, November 27, 2000, BRCC B001-1-7 (015), cited in Sassoon, *Saddam Hussein's Ba'th Party*, 264. The real meaning of this absurd decision is not clear. As I did not see this document, I cannot confirm that it was correctly understood.

75. CRRC SHTP-A-001-404, 0:40:00 minutes into the meeting.

76. CRRC SH-SHTP-A-000-714, a meeting sometime in the mid-1990s.

77. CRRC SHTP-A-001-404, 0:40:00 minutes into the recording.

78. Iraqi TV Baghdad in Arabic, August 8, 1997, reported by BBC, August 11, 1997.

79. CRRC SHTP-A-001-404, between 0:55:00 and 1:18:00 minutes into the recording.

80. Lorenzo K. Kimball, *The Changing Pattern of Political Power in Iraq, 1958 to 1971* (New York: Robert Speller and Sons, 1973), 148. For an analysis of that event in the context of the regime's intimidation of the general population, see Ken'an Makiya (Samir al-Khalil), *Republic of Fear: The Politics of Modern Iraq* (London: Hutchinson Radius, 1989), 46–58.

81. *Al-Ahram*, February 1, 1969; *al-Kifah*, February 3, 1969.

82. *Nida al-Watan*, February 1, 1969.

83. President Ahmad Hasan al-Bakr, *al-Jumhuriyya*, May 17, 21, 1969, and interview with Sawt al-Fallah (Baghdad), *al-Jumhuriyya*, May 18, 1969; Nadim Ahmad Yasin, *al-Thawra*, June 23, 1969, 9; the Regional Leadership Communiqué, *al-Thawra*, April 25, 1969; cartoon showing the United States removing a large rock from Israel's shoulders using an Iranian rope, *al-Thawra*, May 11, 1969; Pan-Arab Leadership communiqué, *al-Jumhuriyya*, November 22, 1969.

84. See Ahmad Hasan al-Bakr, a speech delivered in his name in Najaf on the occasion of Imam Husayn's birthday, "Kalimat al-Ra'is bi Ihtifal al-Najaf" [The President's word in the Najaf celebration], October 23, 1969, in *Masirat al-Thawra fi Khutab wa Tasrihat al-Sayyid al-Ra'is* [The road of the revolution in the lectures and announcements of the Sayyid the president] (Baghdad, 1971), 136–38. For more, in Karbala celebrating 'Ali's birthday on September 27, 1969; his speech in Najaf on the birth of al-Husayn, October 23, 1969; his speech in Karbala to celebrate the Prophet's birthday on May 21, 1970, see ibid., respectively 21–22, 132–33, 193–95.

85. A secret meeting of both the RCC and the Regional Leadership on September 16, 1980, CRRC SHTP-A-000-835.

86. *Tariq al-Sha'b*, July 7, 1977, interview with Minister of Planning 'Adnan Husayn.

87. See *al-Jumhuriyya*, February 26, 1979

88. CRRC SH-SHTP-A-001-400, July 1979–September 1980, mainly 0:30:00 to 0:35:00 minutes into the discussion.

89. CRRC SHTP-A-000-835. And see below.

90. Mohammed Mahdi Salih, *Ba'th Socialism and Regional Development* (Baghdad: Dar al-Mamun, 1982), esp. 13, 25–35. For more, see chapter 5 in this book.

91. See Sassoon, *Saddam Hussein's Ba'th Party*, 2–3.

92. For a detailed discussion of the denominational structure of the party, see Amatzia Baram, "The Ruling Political Elite in Ba'thi Iraq, 1968–1986: The Changing Features of a Collective Profile," *International Journal of Middle East Studies* 21, no. 4 (November 1989): 447–93.

93. For a full analysis of the Iraqi ruling elite between1968 and 1986, see ibid.

94. Baghdad Radio, December 12, 1990, reproduced in FBIS-NES-DR, December 12, 1990, 25.

95. For details, see Baram, "The Ruling Political Elite in Ba'thi Iraq."

96. Ronen Zeidel, "The Iraqi Baath Party 1948–1995: Personal and Organizational Aspects" [in Hebrew] (master's thesis, University of Haifa, 1997), 333–36. For the opposition's confirmation that Shi'is were to be found in the party's middle level, see, for example, broadcast reports of the capture, interrogation, and killing of such people in Voice of the Iraqi Islamic Revolution (in Arabic), April 18, 30, 1995, in FBIS-NES-DR, April 19, 1995, 3, and May 2,1995, 42, respectively.

97. Zeidel, "The Iraqi Baath Party 1948–1995," 180–85, based on some fifty issues of the dailies *al-Thawra* and *al-Jumhuriyya*.

98. Batatu, *The Old Social Classes*, 1078.

99. Marr, *The Modern History of Iraq*, 1st ed. (1985), 227.

100. Sassoon, *Saddam Hussein's Ba'th Party*, 52.

101. *Al-Yawm al-Sabi'*, January 22, 29; February 5, 12, 19, 1990.

102. Ibid.

103. See the discussion in chapter 4 in the section titled "The Last Stand of Fortress Secularism."

104. See Baram, "Neo-Tribalism in Iraq"; Faleh A. Jabar and Hosham Dawod, eds., *Tribes and Power: Nationalism and Ethnicity in the Middle East* (London: Saqi Books, 2002).

105. Najaf, *Al-Shahed al-Shahid*, 135–38; *al-Qa'id al-Shahid*, 14–19; *al-Da'wa Chronicle* no. 3, July 1980, 2.

106. Kohlberg, "The Evolution of the Shi'ah."

107. See *Hadith al-Dar* in Muhammad Baqir al-Sadr, "Tasdir" [Introduction] to 'Abd Allah al-Fayyadh, *Ta'rikh al-Imamiyya wa Aslafihim min al-Shi'a* [The history of the Imami Shi'a and their forebears] (Baghdad: Matba'at As'ad and Baghdad University, 1970), 21.

108. Muhammad Baqir al-Sadr, *Muqaddimat fi al-Tafsir al-Mawdu'i lil-Qur'an* [Introductory notes to the objective interpretation of the Qur'an] (Beirut, 1980), 216–18.

109. Sadr, "Tasdir," in Fayyadh, *Ta'rikh al-Imamiyya wa Aslafihim min al-Shi'a*, 16–21.

110. Ibid., 24–25.

111. Muhammad Baqir al-Sadr, *Lamha Tamhidiyya 'an Mashru' Dustur al-Jumhuriyya al-Islamiyya* [A preliminary glimpse at the proposed Constitution of the Islamic Republic] (Beirut, Dar al-Ta'aruf Lil-Matbu'at, February 1979), 13, 20. For more details, see Amatzia

Baram, "The Radical Shi'ite Opposition Movements in Iraq," in *Religious Radicalism and Politics in the Middle East*, ed. Emmanuel Sivan and Menachem Friedman (New York: State University of New York Press, 1990), 107–23.

112. See, for example, Muhammad Baqir al-Hakim, head of SAIRI, emphasizing the common goals of Shi'is and Sunnis, *Bayan al-Quwa al-Mu'aradha al-Islamiyya al-'Iraqiyya, al-Jihad*, September 17, 1990. See also Muhammad Baqir al-Hakim promising that the future rule in Iraq would be "neither Shi'i nor Sunni nor sectarian," *Liwa' al-Sadr*, October 28, 1990, 1. See also *al-Jihad*, July 9, 1990.

113. See, for example, the promise to correct the historical wrong and give the Shi'i majority their full rights after they were discriminated against, communiqué of the Islamic Movements, *Bayan al-Quwa al-Mu'aradha al-Islamiyya al-'Iraqiyya, al-Jihad*, September 17, 1990. See Muhammad Baqir al-Hakim's speech to his soldiers, *Liwa' al-Sadr*, February 24, 1991. Hakim even mentioned the need to ensure the success of the "Imams' practice" in Iraq, that is, of Shi'i supremacy. And see Shaykh al-Aasifi, *al-Jihad al-Duwali*, December 11, 1989, on the need to implement the "Imami" policy, and "Abu Jihad" in *al-Jihad*, November 12, 1990. That the Islamic (Shi'i) opposition deserved to play the leading role because it had paid with the most blood, *al-Jihad*, July 9, 1990; *al-Jihad*, November 19, 1990.

114. Kazim al-Husayni al-Ha'iri, *Labina Awwaliyya Muqtaraha li Dustur al-Jumhuriyya al-Islamiyya fi al-'Iraq* [An initial suggested brick for the Constitution of the Islamic Republic in Iraq] (Qom: Maktab al-Marja' al-Dini Samahat Ayat Allah al-'Uzma al-Sayyid Kazim al-Ka'iri, 1424H).

115. Kazim al-Husayni al-Ha'iri, *Mabahith al-Usul, Taqriran li-Abhath Samahat Ayat Allah al-'Uzma al-Shahid al-Sayyid Muhammad Baqir al-Sadr* [Studies of the sources: An account of the studies of Ayatollah al-'Uzma al-Shahid al-Sayyid Muhammad Baqir al-Sadr] (Tehran, 1986), vol. 2, pt. 1,151–53; *al-Da'wa Chronicle* no. 3, July 1980, 2.

116. For more, see Baram, "The Radical Shi'ite Opposition Movements in Iraq," 102–7.

117. *Al-Jumhuriyya*, March 8, 1985. For more information on the Shi'i movements, see Faleh A. Jabar, *The Shi'ite Movement in Iraq* (London: Saqi Books, 2003)

118. For more on the history of the Islamic movements of Iraq, see Mu'min 'Ali, *Sanawat al-Jamr: Masirat al-haraka al-Islamiyya fi al-'Iraq 1957–1986* [The embers years: The journey of the Islamic movements in Iraq] (London: Dar al-Masira, 1993).

119. Interview with a senior Da'wa activist in Europe, September 1990. The man joined the party in 1966.

120. When riots erupted, to defuse the situation the regime put the new legislation on hold until 1974. See an RCC decree of December 15, 1974, assigning the "management of all religious schools" to the Ministry of Education, *Arab Report and Record*, December 1–15, 1974, 545.

121. *Al-Jarida*, June 29, 1969. *Al-Hayat*, June 22, 1969, Shi'i clergy in Lebanon, under the leadership of Musa Sadr, denouncing the Ba'th regime for trying to involve the Shi'i clergy of Iraq in international political disputes.

122. Middle East News Agency (Cairo), in a dispatch from Baghdad, June 11, 1969, on a television interview with Midhat al-Hajj Sirri, Baghdad's ex-mayor, saying that Hakim was present in meetings between conspirators (including the ex-mayor himself) and the CIA. For the confiscation of Mahdi al-Hakim's property, see *al-Nahar*, June 24, 1969.

For Shirazi, see *al-Hayat*, June 26, 1969. For more information, see Amatzia Baram, "The Impact of Khomeini's Revolution on the Radical Shiʻi Movement of Iraq," in *The Iranian Revolution and the Muslim World*, ed. David Menashri (Boulder, CO: Westview Press, 1990), 131–54. See also Amatzia Baram, "Two Roads to Revolutionary Shiʻi Fundamentalism in Iraq," in *Accounting for Fundamentalism: The Dynamic Character of Movements*, ed. Martin E. Marty and Scott Appleby (Chicago: University of Chicago Press and the American Academy of Arts and Sciences, 1994), 531–90; Baram, "The Radical Shiʻite Opposition Movements in Iraq," 95–126.

123. Interview with "Abu Layth," an ex-Daʻwa member who, when he left Iraq in 1976, was not yet a senior member of the party, Washington, D.C., May 30, 1994. (For a few more years, the Jesuit College remained a good school mainly thanks to its new principal, the father of Mithal al-Alusi, and some quality teachers he chose.)

124. For example, Middle East News Agency, in a dispatch from Baghdad, June 7, 11; *al-Nahar*, June 24, July 5, September 26, 1969; *al-Hayat*, June 2, 11, 22, 23, 26, 27, July 12; August 2, 1969; *Nida al-Watan*, July 21, 1969.

125. Najaf, *Al-Shahed al-Shahid*, 27.

126. Ibid., 14–15.

127. *Al-Hayat*, July 2, 1969; *al-Safa*, July 19, 1969.

128. This alleged or real fatwa was quoted by the Iranian broadcasting station of Ahvaz. The denial came in Lebanon within a few hours. See *al-Hayat*, June 30, July 1, 1969.

129. *Al-Hayat*, June 23, 27, July 11, 12, 1969; *al-Nahar*, July 5, 1969; *Nida al-Watan*, July 21, 1969.

130. *Al-Nahar*, September 26, 1969.

131. *Al-Jumhuriyya*, June 23, 1970.

132. An interview with Yusif al-Khoʻi, London, July 8, 1997. The interviewee had to leave Iraq in 1976.

133. *Al-Jumhuriyya*, November 7, 8, 1969. See also November 12, 1969.

134. See Baram, "The Impact of Khomeini's Revolution on the Radical Shiʻi Movement of Iraq," 139.

135. For example, Najaf, *Al-Shahed al-Shahid*, 11, 13, 26; *al-ʻAhd*, November 20, 1987. And see Sadr's notes to Muhsin al-Hakim, *Minhaj al-Salihin* (Beirut, 1980).

136. *Al-Jumhuriyya*, June 11, 1969.

137. See Abbas Kadhim, "The Hawza under Siege: A Study in the Baʻth Party Archive," Occasional Paper 1 (Boston: Boston University Institute for Iraqi Studies, June 2013), 26. Most documents referenced in Kadhim's study are found in the Baʻth Party Archive, Baʻth Regional Command Collection (BRCC), at the Hoover Institute, Box 023-4-7.

138. *Al-Jumhuriyya*, July 6, 1969. Other clergy whose names were mentioned were Abu al-Qasim al-Khoʻi, Muhammad al-Shahrudi, Muhammad al-Hasani al-Baghdadi, and ʻAbd Allah al-Shirazi.

139. *Al-Jumhuriyya*, July 8, 1969.

140. *Al-Jumhuriyya*, October 23, 1969.

141. For more details, see Amatzia Baram, "From Radicalism to Radical Pragmatism: The Shiʻite Fundamentalist Opposition Movements of Iraq," in *Islamic Fundamentalism and the Gulf War*, ed. James Piscatori (Chicago: University of Chicago Press and the American Academy of Arts and Sciences, 1991), 30–34. See also Abdul-Halim al-Ruhaimi, "The

Da'wa Islamic Party: Origins, Actors and Ideology," in *Ayatollahs, Sufis and Ideologues: State, Religion and Social Movements in Iraq*, ed. Faleh A. Jabar (London: Saqi Books, 2002), 151–52. The two sources reach similar conclusions based on largely similar sources.

142. For a history of the Iraqi Communist Party, see John Franzén, *Red Star over Iraq: Iraqi Communism before Saddam* (New York: Columbia University Press, 2011).

143. Interview with a very senior Da'wa member, London, September 1990.

144. For example, Reuters, in a dispatch from Tehran, February 1, 1972; Associated Press, January 8, 1972; *al-Da'wa Chronicle* no. 10, February 1981, 9; no. 30, October 1982, 3; *al-Mukhtar al-Islami* no. 25, June 17, 1981, 74–75.

145. *Al-Jihad*, September 10, 1990; Najaf, 28–29.

146. *Al-Jumhuriyya*, February 11 through March 6, 1974.

147. *Al-Jihad* no. 52, September 6, 1982, 7.

148. For example, on the population of Karbala, and Jasim al-Rikabi, the Shi'i governor of the Shi'i province of Qadisiyya, *al-Jumhuriyya*, February 11, 1974; lead article, *al-Jumhuriyya*, February 13, 1974; the "[Shi'i] masses" in Wasit, *al-Jumhuriyya*, February 15; development plans in Karbala and Qadisiyya, *al-Jumhuriyya*, February 7, 11, 19, 1974; the Popular Council in the name of the "masses of Karbala" to the president, against the "agent" Iranian regime and in praise of the promised raise in the standard of living, *al-Jumhuriyya*, February 21, 1974; *al-Jumhuriyya*, February 19, 1974; the Shi'i religious Saykh 'Abd al-Latif al-Daramy, a letter to the president castigating the Iranian aggression, *al-Jumhuriyya*, February 20, 1974.

149. Interviews with David Karon, who from 1968 to 1974 was in charge of the Kurdish file in the Mossad, Israel, *Kibbutz Kfar Menachem*, March 1993.

150. *Guardian*, December 16, 1974; *Imam*, April–May 1982, 56–61; Najaf, *Al-Shahed al-Shahid*, 29.

151. Hizb al-'Amal al-Islami, *Saddam Husayn Warith al-Shah* [Saddam Husayn, heir of the shah] (Tehran: Hizb al-'Amal al-Islami, 1981), 47–48.

152. *Al-Shira'*, August 1, 1986; *al-Massar*, October 28, 1987, 13.

153. *Al-Jumhuriyya*, February 7, 11, 12, 13, 14, 16, 1974.

154. *Al-Jumhuriyya*, March 15, 1974.

155. On a few occasions annually, Shi'i pilgrims flock to Karbala. The main days are the 'Ashura, on 10 Muharram, commemorating al-Husayn's death; the Arba'in, commemorating the fortieth day after his death; and Nisf Sha'ban (Mid-Sha'ban), celebrating the birthday of the twelfth Imam (or the Expected Imam) al-Mahdi, Muhammad al-Qasim.

156. Marr, *The Modern History of Iraq*, 2nd ed. (2004), 173.

157. Interview with Yusif al-Kho'i, London, July 8, 1997. The interviewee had to leave Iraq in 1976.

158. Ibid.

159. Ibid.

160. Wiley, *The Islamic Movement of Iraqi Shi'as*, 52

161. See, for example, *al-Da'wa Chronicle* no. 10, February 1981, 9; February 22, 1982, 4; October 30, 1982, 3; Hizb al-'Amal al-Islami, *Saddam Husayn Warith al-Shah*, 48–49; *al-Shahada*, 16 Safar 1404H.

162. *Al-Jumhuriyya*, February 11, 12, 1977; also *al-Jumhuriyya*, February 10, 14, 16, 19, 21, 22, 1977.

163. For example, *al-Jumhuriyya*, February 11, 12, 14, 15, 1977, quoting Shi'i clerics, among others.

164. The 'Alawites are a syncretic sect, combining Islamic elements but also some Neo-Platonic elements. Until the twentieth century this community was called the Nusayris. According to many Muslims, they actually left Islam in the ninth to tenth centuries.

165. *Al-Hawadith*, April 8, 1977.

166. *Al-Jumhuriyya*, February 25; Hani Wahib, *al-Thawra*, March 6, 1977.

167. *Al-Thawra*, March 24, 1977.

168. For details, see Baram, "The Ruling Political Elite in Ba'thi Iraq," 447–93.

169. Based on interviews with five men who fled the Shi'i south following the suppression of the March 1991 uprising, Boston, May 1995. This information is supported by Sayyid Farqat al-Qazwini, director of the Hilla-based University for Humanitarian, Scientific and Religious Studies; see his interview with David Shelby and Hilary White, *Special to the Washington File*, February 26, 2004. And see security instructions for the party branch (*far'*) of Karbala before 'Ashura, CRRC SH-BATH-D-000-159, April 22, 2002.

170. *Al-Thawra*, December 14, 1977.

171. Husayni, *Al-Nujum al-Zawahir Fi Shajarat al-Sayyid al-Amir Nasir.*

172. Saddam Hussein, "A View of Religion and Heritage," in *On History, Heritage and Religion* (Baghdad: Translation and Foreign Languages Publishing House, 1981), 28–29. See also Hasan Tawalba, ed., *Muqtatafat Min Ahadith Saddam Husayn* [Quotations from the talks of Saddam Husayn] (Beirut: Dar al-Tali'a, 1979), 175–86. An identical approach is expressed in early 1980 by *al-Thawra al-'Arabiyya*, the internal party organ, disseminated to members only, when it attacked Khomeini's Islam. See "Al-'Ilmaniyya wa Jawhar al-Mawqif al-Ba'thi Min al-Din" in the issue of July 1980, 13–18.

173. Hussein, "On Writing History," in *On History, Heritage and Religion*, 13.

174. Hussein, "A View of Religion and Heritage," 24, 27–28.

175. Ibid., 30–31.

176. Shibli al-'Aysami, *Risalat al-Umma al-'Arabiyya* [The message of the Arab nation] (Beirut: Dar al-Tali'a, 1978), 49–53, 56, 61, 67–70, 79.

177. Dr. Mundhir Ibrahim, minister of justice, to *al-Thawra*, March 6, 1979.

178. CRRC SH-SHTP-A-000-751, 3, Saddam meeting with military officers in late 1980s, 00:17:20–00:25:29 minutes into the recording.

179. Faruq 'Umar Fawzi, "Al-Babikiyya wa Fikr al-Qaran al-'Ishrin [The Babikiyya and the thought of the twentieth century], *Afaq 'Arabiyya* 2, no. 5 (January 1977): 88.

180. Ibid., 77–89, quotation at 86. Faruq 'Umar is referring to a new book written by the Iraqi Marxist of Shi'i background Husayn Qasim al-'Aziz, *Al-Babikiyya, Intifadat al-Sha'b al-Adhirbijani dhidd al-Khilafa al-'Abbasiyya* [The Babikiyya (Kharamiyya): The intifada of the Azerbaijani people against the 'Abbasid caliphate] (Baghdad: Maktabat al-Nahdhah; Beirut: Dar al-Farabi, 1974). The book was an adaptation of a doctoral dissertation prepared in Moscow under Professor Bonyatov at the Institute for Eastern Languages.

181. Faruq 'Umar Fawzi, "Al-Haraka al-Kharamiyya fi al 'asr al-'abbasi bayna al-dughmatiyya wal-mawdhu'iyya" [The Kharamiyya movement in the Abbasid era: Between dogmatism and objectivity], *Afaq 'Arabiyya* 10 (June 1977): 94–99.

182. Fawzi, "Al-Babikiyya wa Fikr al-Qaran al-'Ishrin," 77–89, esp. 81.

183. Faruq ʿUmar Fawzi, "Al-Haraka al-Kharamiyya fi al ʿasr al-ʿabbasi bayna al-dughmatiyya wal-mawdhuʿiyya." As far as is known, though, Dhu al-Nafs al-Zakiyyah, a descendant of Imam al-Hasan (the second Imam), declared himself the legitimate Imam of his time. After his death some of his followers, the Muhammadiyya, believed that he vanished into an occultation, from which he would emerge one day to fill the earth with justice. See Momen, *An Introduction to Shiʿi Islam*, 50.

184. Faruq ʿUmar Fawzi, "Harakat al-Mukhtar al-Thaqafi" [The Mukhtar al-Thaqafi movement], *Afaq ʿArabiyya* 3, no. 1 (September 1977): 76–82.

185. Ibid., 81.

186. Faruq ʿUmar Fawzi, "Abu Muslim al-Khurasani wa Usturat al-Batal al-Munqidh" [Abu Muslim al-Khurasani and the myth of the delivering hero], *Afaq ʿArabiyya* 10, no. 4 (June 1979): 42–47.

Chapter 4

1. *Al-Zahf al-Akhdhar*, January 20, 1981, 15; *Liwaʾ al-Sadr*, February 9, 1983, 5–7. 10; Imam 2, nos. 3–4 (April–May 1982): 59–60; *al-Daʿwa Chronicle* no. 3, July 1980, 3; no. 37, May 1983, 1, 8; Hizb al-ʿAmal al-Islami, *Saddam Husayn Warith al-Shah* [Saddam Husayn, heir of the shah] (Tehran: Hizb al-ʿAmal al-Islami, 1981), 51; *al-Mukhtar al-Islami*, June 17, 1981, 75; *al-Ahram*, August 5, 1979.

2. *Imam* 2, nos. 3–4 (April–May 1982): 59–60.

3. Ibid., 59–60; *Liwaʾ al-Sadr*, February 9, 1983, 5–7, 10.

4. *Liwaʾ al-Sadr*, February 9, 1983, 5–7, 10.

5. Ibid., 5–7. For a Baʿthi admission that religiosity, real or simulated, had became a problem among party members, see Arab Baath Socialist Party Iraq, *The Central Report of the Ninth Regional Congress, June 1982*, trans. SARTEC, Lausanne (Baghdad, January 1983), 279–83.

6. ʿA[li] Najaf (pseud.), *Al-Shahed al-Shahid* [The witness, the martyr] (Tehran, 1981), 63–64, 131–32; *Imam* 2, nos. 3–4 (April–May 1982): 61–62; Associated Press, dispatch from Tehran, June 14, 1979.

7. Najaf, *Al-Shahed al-Shahid*, 62.

8. Associated Press, dispatch from from Tehran, June 14, 1979; *Imam* 2, nos. 3–4 (April–May 1982): 61–62; Najaf, *Al-Shahed al-Shahid*, 131–32.

9. *Al-Zahf al-Akhdhar*, January 20, 1981, 15; *Liwaʾ al-Sadr*, February 9, 1983, 5–7. 10; *al-Daʿwa Chronicle* no. 3, July 1980, 3; no. 37, May 1983, 1, 8; Hizb al-ʿAmal al-Islami, *Saddam Husayn Warith al-Shah*, 51; *al-Mukhtar al-Islami*, June 17, 1981, 75; *al-Ahram*, August 5, 1979. Hizb al-Daʿwa al-Islamiyya, *Istishhad al-Imam Muhammad Baqir al-Sadr* [The martyrdom of the Imam Muhammad Baqir al-Sadr] (Beirut: Hizb al-Daʿwa al-Islamiyya, 1981), 38–30; Najaf, *Al-Shahed al-Shahid*, 56–65; *Imam* 2, nos. 3–4 (April–May 1982): 59–61.

10. *Al-Jumhuriyya*, February 27, 1979.

11. CRRC SHTP-A-001-404, and see below.

12. Najaf, *Al-Shahed al-Shahid*, 131–32; *al-Qaʾid al-Shahid*, no date, 11–13.

13. Najaf, *Al-Shahed al-Shahid*, 135–38; *al-Qaʾid al-Shahid*, no date, 14–19; *al-Daʿwa Chronicle* no. 3, July 1980, 2.

14. *Alif Ba*, April 9, 1980. See also a later law to the same effect, published in *al-Waqaʾi al-ʿIraqiyya*, January 2, 1984, 3.

15. *Al-Daʿwa Chronicle* no. 10, February 1981, 9; *al-Thawra*, April 5, 6, 1980; *Fajr al-Thawra al-Islamiyya* [The dawn of the Islamic revolution] (Tehran: Echo of Islam, 1982), 57; *Impact International*, April 25–May 8, 1980, 5–6.

16. Amatzia Baram, "From Radicalism to Radical Pragmatism: The Shiʿite Fundamentalist Opposition Movements of Iraq," in *Islamic Fundamentalism and the Gulf War*, ed. James Piscatori (Chicago: University of Chicago Press and American Academy of Arts and Sciences, 1991), 36–37.

17. For more details, see ibid., 36–37; Amatzia Baram, "The Radical Shiʿite Opposition Movements in Iraq," in *Religious Radicalism*, ed. Emmanuel Sivan and Menachem Friedman (Albany: State University of New York Press, 1990), 96–98; Phebe Marr, *The Modern History of Iraq*, 3rd ed. (Boulder, CO: Westview Press, 2011),172.

18. *Alif Ba*, April 16, 1980, 15.

19. Ali Babakhan, "The Deportation of Shiʿis during the Iran-Iraq War," in *Ayatollahs, Sufis and Ideologues: State, Religion, and Social Movements in Iraq*, ed. Faleh A. Jabar (London: Saqi Books, 2002), 198, 200; Marion Farouk-Sluglett and Peter Sluglett, *Iraq since 1958: From Revolution to Dictatorship* (London: KPI, 1987), 258.

20. Arab Press Service 13, no. 19 (November, 1980): 5–12.

21. SHTP-A-001-404; SHTP-A-000-835, and see below.

22. *Al-Daʿwa Chronicle* no. 38, June 1983, 8; no. 39, July 1983, 3; no. 40, August 1983, 8; *Sawt al-Iraq*, September 1983, 4; *al-Nahar*, June 25, 1983; statement of Tariq ʿAziz to Reuters in Kuwait, July 20, 1983, confirming the execution.

23. *Al-Daʿwa Chronicle* no. 3, July 1980, 4.

24. *Al-Daʿwa Chronicle* no. 49, May 1984, 6–7.

25. *Imam* 3, no. 1 (January 1983): 30; admission of Saddam Husayn's success in deterring people from demonstrating, *al-Daʿwa Chronicle* no. 16, August 1981, 4.

26. A personal interview with a senior Iranian SAVAK official in Haifa, Israel, 2005.

27. CRRC SHTP-A-001-404, most likely June 1979, around 0:27:00 minutes into the recording.

28. See Amatzia Baram, "The Ruling Political Elite in Baʿthi Iraq, 1968–1986: The Changing Features of a Collective Profile," *International Journal of Middle East Studies* 21, no. 4 (November 1989): 455, 473.

29. CRRC SHTP-A-001-404, around 0:50:00 minutes into the recording.

30. CRRC SHTP-A-001-404, around 0:15:00 minutes into the recording

31. CRRC SHTP-A-001-404, around 0:53:00 minutes into the recording.

32. It is not clear whom Iraq supported in 1976; probably those were anti-Asad Baʿthis or Muslim Brothers.

33. CRRC SHTP-A-001-404, around 0:35:00 minutes into the discussion.

34. CRRC SHTP-A-001-404, around 0:41:00 minutes into the recording.

35. CRRC SHTP-A-001-404, around 1:18:00 minutes into the recording.

36. CRRC SHTP-A-001-404, around 1:28:00 minutes into the recording.

37. CRRC SHTP-A-001-404, 0:45:00–0:54:00 minutes into the recording.

38. CRRC SHTP-A-001-404, around 1:15:00 minutes into the recording.

39. Ibid., around 1:18:00 minutes into the recording.

40. CRRC SHTP-A-000-835, Saddam in a secret meeting on September 16, 1980.

41. Alexander Haig, Top Secret/Sensitive, "Talking Points" for meeting with the President, ca. April 1981, National Security Archives, George Washington University, Washington, D.C. I am grateful to Ms. Shuli Bina for this reference.

42. See Amatzia Baram, "Saddam Husayn and Nasirism: 1968-2000," *Orient* 41, no. 3 (September 2000): 461–72.

43. CRRC SHTP-A-000-835, transcript, p. 21.

44. Ibid.

45. CRRC SH-BATH-D-000-300.

46. See, for example, CRRC SH-GMID-D-000-620.

47. For a history of the war, see Anthony H. Cordesman and Abraham R. Wagner, *The Lessons of Modern War, Vol. II: The Iraq-Iran War* (Boulder, CO: Westview Press, 1990); Dilip Hiro, *The Longest War: The Iran-Iraq Military Conflict* (London: Routledge, 1991); Shahram Chubin and Charles Tripp, *Iran and Iraq at War* (Boulder, CO: Westview Press, 1988).

48. See the report by the Iraqi Islamic Party about persecutions under the Ba'th, *Bayan al-Hizb al-Islami al-'Iraqi*, April 20, 2003, at www.iraqi.com (last accessed December 3, 2003).

49. CRRC SHTP-A-001-404.

50. The RCC's National Security Council meeting, December 31, 1979, BRCC 003-1-1 (411–412), in Joseph Sassoon, *Saddam Hussein's Ba'th Party: Inside an Authoritarian Regime* (Cambridge: Cambridge University Press, 2012), 268.

51. The Hoover Institute's Document Center, 003-1-1-0409, a memorandum sent from the Supreme Council for State Security at the RCC to the Regional Leadership of the party, the Bureau for State Security. The meeting was convened on December 4, 1979.

52. CRRC SHTP-A-000-835, 'Izzat Ibrahim to Saddam in a secret meeting on September 16, 1980.

53. CRRC SH-SHTP-A-001-167, July 24, 1986.

54. Saddam Hussein, "A View of Religion and Heritage," in his *On History, Heritage and Religion* (Baghdad: Translation and Foreign Languages Publishing House, 1981), 25, 35. See also 37.

55. Hizb al-Ba'th al-'Arabi al-Ishtiraki, al-Qutr al-'Iraqi [Arab Socialist Ba'th Party—Iraq], *Al-Taqrir al-Markazi lil-Mu'tamar al-Qutri al-Tasi', Haziran, 1982* [The central report of the Ninth Regional (Iraqi) Congress, June 1982] (Baghdad, January 1983), 293–300. The following quotations are from the official English-language translation: Arab Ba'th Socialist Party—Iraq, *The Central Report of the Ninth Regional Congress, June 1982* (Baghdad, January 1983, trans. SARTECH, Lausanne, 1983), 245–83.

56. Ibid., 271.

57. Ibid., 272–73.

58. Ibid., 274–75.

59. Ibid., 274–75.

60. Ibid., 279–80.

61. Ibid., 280–81.

62. CRRC SH-RVCC-D-000-610, p. 1. Saddam meeting with military commanders to discuss security issues in the mid-1990s.

63. CRRC SH-SHTP-D-000-614, March 1991.

64. For example, CRRC SH-MISC-D-000-729, March 20, 1985. For an extensive and innovative analysis of the regime's policy vis-à-vis the marsh Arabs, see Ariel I. Ahram, "From Hearts and Minds to Ashes and Mud: Development, Counterinsurgency, and the Destruction of the Iraqi Marshes," a paper presented at a meeting of the American Political Science Association, Chicago, September 1, 2013.

65. See, for example, CRRC SH-MISC-D-000-310, a report about executions of Daʿwa members from 1983. On executions of marsh Arabs, see CRRC SH-PDWN-D-001-029, May 11, 1983.

66. CRRC SPPC-D-000-448, a meeting on August 21, 1994, pp. 9–11 in the text. It is not sufficiently clear whether Saddam is talking about the Iran-Iraq War or the years following it.

67. See, for example, Regulation (*Qirar*) No. 1370, published in *al-Waqaʾiʿ al-ʿIraqiyya* no. 2974, January 2, 1984, 3, specifying the death penalty for defection to the enemy's camp, desertion, shirking military service, plotting against the state, espionage, and membership in the Daʿwa Party.

68. For the treatment of this issue in Iraqi literature, see Ronen Zeidel, "The Shiʿa in Iraqi Novels," *Die Welt des Islams* 51 (2011), esp. 21–31.

69. See the funeral of his mother, Salma, *al-Thawra*, April 17, 1994.

70. *Al-Sharq al-Awsat*, December 9, 1999, 1.

71. *Al-ʿArabi*, January 8, 1987.

72. *Al-Thawra*, May 26, 1993; April 18, 1994.

73. *Al-Thawra*, February 17, 1993.

74. *Al-Qadisiyya*, April 17, 1995.

75. *Al-Qadisiyya*, December 1, 1987.

76. Other well-known Shiʿi general officers were ʿAbd al-Zahra Shakara (*al-ʿIraq*, October 28, 1984); ʿAla Kazim al-Janabi, ʿAbd al-Karim Mahmud al-ʿIthawi, Niʿma Faris al-Mihyawi (*al-Qadisiyya*, August 9, 1991); Barik ʿAbd Allah al-Hajj Hanta; Jiyad (or Chiyad) Rashash al-Amara (during the March 1991 Intifada he defected to Iran); and Kanʿan Mustafa al-Kanʿan, the shaykh of Banu Tamim in Basra, who was executed in 1995, after which his brother, a navy general, Muzahim Mustafa Kanʿan, was placed under house arrest by the regime (based on an interview with a Shiʿi man from the Banu Tamim who participated in the Intifada in Basra, Washington, D.C., August 2004). Others were Tariq Sadiq ʿAbd al-Husayn (*al-Thawra*, July 25, 1993; *al-Qadisiyya*, January 8, 1994), Shakir Husayn ʿAlaywi (*al-ʿIraq*, August 24, 1993), Hamid Ahmad al-Ward (*al-Thawra*, April 22, 1986), Usama Mahmud al-Mahdi, Zayd Jawad Hasan al-Rubayʿi (*al-Jumhuriyya*, January 19, 1984), ʿAbd al-Amir ʿUbays al-Sabah, ʿAbd al-Amir Jasim ʿAlwan al-Taʾi (*Alif Baʾ*, March 17, 1985), Muhammad Khalaf al-Khafaji (*al-Qabas*, March 22, 1999), Khudhayr ʿAbbad Ghadhban of the Najaf-based Karamitha tribe (*Babil*, February 17, 1993), and Sinan ʿAbd al-Jabbar Abu Kalal, who hailed from the Najaf-based Abu Kalal tribe (*al-Thawra*, March 3, 1994). Their full service details are in my possession.

77. *Al-Daʿwa Chronicle* no. 38, June 1983, 8; no. 39, July 1983, 3; no. 40, August 1983, 8; *Sawt al-Iraq*, September 1983, 4; *al-Nahar*, June 25, 1983; Tariq ʿAziz to Reuters in Kuwait, July 20, 1983, confirming the executions.

78. Saʿdun Shakir in a high-level party committee meeting, August 30, 1987.

79. Abbas Kadhim, "The Hawza under Siege: A Study in the Ba'th Party Archive," Occasional Paper 1 (Boston: Boston University Institute for Iraqi Studies, June 2013), 12–35. Most documents referenced in Kadhim's study are found in Box 023-4-7 of the Ba'th Party Archive, Ba'th Regional Command (in this book called the Regional Leadership) Collection (BRCC) in the Hoover Institution at Stanford University, California.

80. In a study from 1984, for example, the officials were happy to report that the numbers of participants in the 'Ashura festivities decreased markedly to 120,000—half the average participation of previous years. Less happily it was reported that the number participating in the Arba'in ceremonies had increased slightly to 450,000 (see Kadhim, "The Hawza under Siege," 18–19, for the Central Bureau communication to the Presidential Office on August 22, 1984). The party also looked for ways to control the crowds that did assemble for the commemorative ceremonies. Sa'dun Hammadi, the impressive Shi'i Ba'thi intellectual, observed that "there is a category, men and women who recite the *ta'ziya* [lamentation, consolation]. . . . It is necessary to create a group of those supportive of the state; they are after the money" (Hammadi in an August 30, 1987, high-level meeting, quoted in Kadhim, "The Hawza under Siege," 25). This was one Shi'i who had little respect for the religious Shi'i masses. Internal documents from the last few years of the Ba'th regime show that his cynical advice was implemented (see chapter 6).

81. Deliberations of a committee chaired by 'Izzat al-Duri to decide the fate of the *hawza*, August 30, 1987, quoted in Kadhim, "The Hawza under Siege," 27.

82. An undated memo from the director general of the Central Bureau, Kamil Yasin Rashid, to the secretary general of the Ba'th Party, ibid., 34.

83. The August 30, 1987 meeting, quoted in Kadhim, "The Hawza under Siege," 25–27.

84. Ibid., 27–28

85. Ibid., 26.

86. From the Director General of the Central Bureau to Saddam, March 9, 1988, ibid., 29.

87. Kadhim, "The Hawza under Siege," 26.

88. Ibid., 26–27.

89. Ibid., 27.

90. Ibid., 28–29.

91. Ibid., 26–27.

92. Ibid., 27–28. And see Memorandum from the President's Secretary for Party Affairs to Saddam Hussein on August 28, 1984; Memoranda from the Central Bureau to the regional organizations on September 16, 1984; Memorandum from the Euphrates Organization to the Central Bureau on November 4, 1984, ibid., 30–33.

93. CRRC SH-SHTP-A-000-665, a leadership meeting in 1989.

94. CRRC SH-BATH-D-000-300, an orientation report produced on February 11, 1987.

95. *Al-Jumhuriyya*, December 6, 1984,

96. L. Veccia Vaglerii, "Al-Kadisiyya," in *Encyclopaedia of Islam*, New Edition, 5:384–87; G. R. Hawting, "Sa'd b. Abi Wakkas," ibid., 8:696–97.

97. *Al-'Iraq*, September 22, 1980: "We are with the Arab regardless of our view of the non-Arab: We cannot remain friends with a [non-Arab] friend who affects Arab sovereignty."

98. See Amatzia Baram, "Saddam Hussein: A Political Profile," *Jerusalem Quarterly* 17 (Fall 1980): 141–42. The journal was issued in early September 1980. The article was written in May–June 1980.

99. *Al-ʿIraq*, September 17, 1980. And see a nice illustration of the Spartans under Leonidas beating the Persians in the battle of Thermopylae, *al-ʿIraq*, September 20, 1980; Qadisiyya youth camp: *al-Jumhuriyya*, August 19, 1980.

100. *Al-Jumhuriyya al-Usbuʿiyya*, September 21, 1980; *al-Jumhuriyya*, September 22, 1980.

101. See *al-Jumhuriyya*, September 30, 1980, "The Victory of the Iraqi Army in the Battle of *Qadidiyyat Saddam*"; *al-ʿIraq*, September 30, 1980; *al-ʿIraq*, October 7: "*Qadisiyyaht Saddam Husayn*—Pride for the Arabs and Arabism," ibid., October 11, 1980.

102. *Al-ʿIraq*, September 30, 1980.

103. See, for example, awarding the Sword to Qusay Saddam Husayn, Supervisor of the Republican Guard, together with al-Rafidayn (the Twin Rivers) Medal 1st Order, Mother of Battle Medal, and a few other decorations, for his contribution to "defending the honor and sovereignty of great Iraq, and the Arab nation's dignity and security," Baghdad Republic of Iraq Radio Network in Arabic, December 23, 1999, in FBIS-NES-DR JN2312212299, December 23, 1999.

104. See, for example, interviews with Iraqi historians in which they discuss Saddam and the role of the hero in history, comparing him to Gilgamesh, Sargon the Akkadian, and the ʿAbbasid caliph Abu Jaʿfar al-Mansur, the founder of Baghdad, *al-Thawra*, April 29, 1984. See also Faruq ʿUmar Fawzi, *Al-ʿIraq Wal-Tahaddi al-Farisi* [Iraq and the Persian challenge] (Baghdad: Dar al-Shuʿun al-Thaqafiyya al-ʿAmma-Aafaq ʿArabiyya, 1987); Fawzi, *Hukkam Bilad Faris Wal-ʿUdwan ʿAla al-ʿIraq Khilal al-ʿAsr al-ʿAbbasi* [The rulers of the lands of Persia and the aggression against Iraq in the ʿAbbasid era] (Baghdad: Dar al-Shuʿun al-Thaqafiyya al-ʿAmma-Aafaq ʿArabiyya, 1988).

105. For a discussion of many of the sources and their versions, see Joseph Sadan, "Death of a Princess: Episodes of the Barmakid Legend in Its Late Evolution," in *Story Telling in the Framework of Non-Fictional Arabic Literature*, ed. Stefan Leder (Wiesbaden: Harrassowitz Verlag, 1998), 130–57.

106. J. Hurovitz, "ʿAbbasa," in *Encyclopedia of Islam*, New Edition, 1:14; See also "The Wizara and Fall of the Barmakids," ibid., 1:1034–36.

107. Saddam's interview with *al-Anba*, April 27, 1983, 13.

108. Tawfiq Sultan al-Yuzbaki, "Al-Umma al-ʿArabiyya fi Muwajahat al-Ahqad al-ʿUnsuriyya al-Farisiyya" [The Arab nation in confrontation with the racist Persian hatred], *Aadab al-Rafidayn* 14 (September 1981): 15–18.

109. Fawzi, *Al-ʿIraq Wal-Tahaddi al-Farisi*, 60–62. See also Saʿdun Hammadi, the most senior Iraqi Baʿth ideologue and a member of the Regional All-Iraqi Party Leadership, *al-Thawra*, August 26, 1987.

110. Faruq ʿUmar Fawzi, *Al-Khilafa al-ʿAbbasiyya Fi ʿAsr al-Fawdha al-ʿAskariyya 861–946* [The ʿAbbasid caliphate in the era of military civil war] (Baghdad: Manshurat Maktabat al-Muthanna, 1977), 22–25.

111. And see a similar U-turn in Faruq ʿUmar's view of Abu Muslim al-Khorasani, the Persian leader of the revolutionary ʿAbbasid movement in Khorasan who was assassinated by the second ʿAbbasid caliph, al-Saffah: compare Fawzi's *Al-Khilafa al-ʿAbbasiyya Fi ʿAsr al-Fawdha al-ʿAskariyya*, 15–16, with his 1987 *Al-ʿIraq Wal-Tahaddi al-Farisi*, 57–59.

112. ʿAbd al-Rahman al-ʿAnni and Hasan Fadhil Zuʿayn, *Al-Taʾrikh al-ʿArabi al-Islami lil-Saff al-Thani al-Mutawassat* [Arab-Islamic history for the second grade, intermediate school], 13th ed. (Baghdad: Ministry of Education, 2002), 96. See the same approach also in the same authors' book for the fifth primary grade, *Al-Taʾrikh al-ʿArabi al-Islami lil-Saff al-Khamis al-Ibtidaʾi* [Arab-Islamic history for the fifth grade, primary school], 16th ed. (Baghdad: Ministry of Education, 2003), 48.

113. Hasan Fadhil Zuʿayn et al., *Al-Taʾrikh al-ʿArabi wal-Islami lil-Saff al-Khamis al-Ibtidaʾi* [Arab-Islamic history for the fifth grade, primary school], 1st ed. (Baghdad: Ministry of Education, 1987 [16th ed., 2003]), 48.

114. Al-ʿAnni and Zuʿayn, *Al-Taʾrikh al-ʿArabi wal-Islami lil-Saff al-Thani al-Mutawassat*, 13th ed., 68. See also Hasan Fadhil Zuʿayn, ʿAbd al-Rahman ʿAbd al-Karim, and ʿAbd al-Amir ʿAbd Daksan, *Al-Taʾrikh al-ʿArabi wal-Islami lil-Saff al-Khamis aql-Ibtidaʾi* [Arab-Islamic history for the fifth grade, primary school], 16th ed. (Baghdad: Ministry of Education, 2003), 45.

115. Wizarat al-Tarbiya [Ministry of Education], *Al-Taʾrikh al-Hadith wal-Muʿasir lil-Watan al-ʿArabi lil-Saff al-Sadis al-Ibtidaʾi* [The modern and contemporary history of the Arab homeland for the sixth grade, primary school] (Baghdad: Ministry of Education, 1988), the part on Saddam's Qadisiyya, at 61–68. In another series, Wizarat al-Tarbiya [Ministry of Education], *Al-Tarbiya al-Wataniyya lil-Saff al-Rabiʿ al-Ibtidaʾi* [Patriotic (National-Iraqi) education for the fourth grade, primary school] (Baghdad: Ministry of Education, 1990), 52. See also ʿAbd al-Rahman al-ʿAnni et al., *Al-Taʾrikh al-ʿArabi wal-Islami lil-Saff al-Thani al-Mutawasat* [Arab-Islamic history for the second grade, intermediate school], 13th ed. (Baghdad: Ministry of Education, 2002), 55–61.

116. CRRC SH-SHTP-A-000-751, Saddam meeting with military officers in late 1980, 00:17:20–00:25:29 minutes into the recording.

117. *Official Gazette* no. 39, September 24, 1980, 3.

118. For example, *al-ʿIraq*, July 5, 1987; *al-Jumhuriyya*, December 12, 1987. Among the names mentioned as supporting the regime openly were al-Sayyid Muhammad Tahir al-Musawi, the *sadin* of the Kazimiyya Shrine in Baghdad, who described the Iranian leadership's positions as *al-kufr wa al-ilhad* [apostasy/infidelity and atheism]. Shaykh Mahdi al-Rufayʿi, the imam of the Friday Mosque al-Imamayn in Karbala, Shaykh Khalil Ibrahim, a member of *lajnat al-tawʿiya al-diniyya* (Religious Indoctrination Committee), and also imam and khatib of the Friday Mosque Albu Hajim in Diwaniyya, and Shaykh Nuri Salih Ahmad, imam and khatib of the Great Friday Mosque in al-Hilla, all supported the regime openly in the above newspapers.

119. See, for example, Deputy Prime Minister Taha Yasin Ramadan to a Shiʿi audience, *al-Thawra*, September 3, 1981; accusing Tehran of falsifying the Qurʾan, *al-Thawra*, June 11, 1981; a telegram from the anonymous participants in the celebrations to mark the Prophet's birthday, *al-Jumhuriyya*, December 6, 1984; and unnamed ʿulama in a visit to the battlefront calling Khomeini's regime "the regime of apostasy" (*al-nizam al-murtadd*), *al-Qadisiyya*, October 13, 1987; congratulations to the president from the "men of religion" and visitors to Karbala, *al-Thawra*, February 13, 1988. No names were mentioned; and see *al-Thawra*, January 24, 1988; *al-Jumhuriyya*, December 12, 1987.

120. Al-Muʿtamar al-Islami al-Shaʿbi al-Thani, *Muqarrarat al-Muʿtamar al-Islami al-Shaʿbi al-Thani* [Resolutions of the second popular Islamic conference] (Baghdad, April 1985), mainly 27–28.

121. For example, *al-Jumhuriyya*, December 6, 1984; *al-Qadisiyya*, October 3, 1987. See also *al-Thawra*, January 24, 1988.

122. *Al-Thawra*, August 26, 1987, 2 Muharram 1408; a*l-Thawra*, May 2, 1991.

123. *Al-Jumhuriyya*, May 23, 1981.

124. An interview with "'Umar," an Iraqi engineer hailing from a Sunni family with ties to the Ba'th Party who left Iraq in 1990, Washington, D.C., February 10, 1994. In 2005 "'Umar" was representing his country as a senior diplomat in the West.

125. On the eve of the war the most important party magazine still called for "secularism." See, for example, "Al-'Ilmaniyya wa Jawhar al-Mawqif al-Ba'thi Min al-Din" [Secularism and the essence of the Ba'th position vis-à-vis religion], in *al-Thawra al-'Arabiyya*, the internal party magazine, disseminated to members only, July 1980, 13–18. This term disappeared later.

126. Saddam Husayn, *Al-'Iraq Jaysh tahta al-silah* [Iraq, an armed military] (Baghdad: Dar al-Huriyya, 1982), 5, 42, 43, 48.

127. *Al-Jumhuriyya*, December 6, 1984, a telegram to Saddam from a group celebrating the Prophet's birthday.

128. *Al-Thawra*, November 4, 1981.

129. See Etan Kohlberg, "The Evolution of the Shi'ah," *Jerusalem Quarterly* 27 (Spring 1983): 121.

130. Moojan Momen, *An Introduction to Shi'i Islam* (New Haven, CT: Yale University Press, 1985), 169, based on al-Nu'mani's *al-Ghayba* and on al-Majlisi's *Bihar al-Anwar.*

131. Kohlberg, "The Evolution of the Shi'ah," 116.

132. Minister Nuri Faysal al-Shahir to *al-Dustur*, 11, September 28, 1981, 28–29. See also *Muqarrarat al-Mu'tamar al-Islami al-Sha'bi al-Thani*, mainly 27–28.

133. *Al-Thawra*, May 19, 1981. For an earlier and softer version of the same thesis, see Saddam in speeches in the Shi'i south soon after Khomeini's return to Tehran, "Al-Islam taklif li inqadh al-umam 'an tariq al-'arab" [Islam, a duty to save the nations via the Arabs], *al-Diyar*, 246, February 26, 1979. For Saddam's source of inspiration, see Khayr Allah Talfah, his maternal uncle, in whose home he grew up, *al-Jumhuriyya*, February 24, 1983. And see Shi'i 'ulama in Maysan, *al-Thawra*, July 2, 1981; a cable from a celebration on the eve of the new Islamic year, *al-Thawra*, March 25, 1983; Saddam for Christmas, *al-Thawra*, December 25, 1980; 'ulama to Saddam, *al-Thawra*, December 12, 1987.

134. Excerpts from Saddam's speech, "President Saddam Husayn's Speech on the 9th Anniversary of (The Great Victory Day) marking the end of the war with Iran," Iraqi TV in Arabic, August 8, 1997, BBC, August 11, 1997, also published on an official Internet site, http://196.27.0.22/iraq/victory1.htm.

135. The information in this section is based in part on Pesah Malovany, *Milhamot Bavel ha-Hadashah: 'Aliyato u-Nefilato shel ha-Tzava ha-'Iraqi* [The wars of modern Babylon: The rise and fall of the Iraqi military] (Tel Aviv: Ma'rachot, 2009), 109–509, and partly on the author's personal files.

136. For example, *Ruz al-Yusuf*, May 1, 1989, 28.

137. *Al-Jumhuriyya*, February 8, 1976.

138. Law No. 37 of 1981, *Mizaniyyat Wizarat al-Awqaf wal-Shu'un al-Diniyya 1981*, published in *al-Waqa'i' al-'Iraqiyya* no. 2731, May 25, 1981, 478, Article 1. Article 3 is not

very clear, but it seems to provide some additional 18 million Iraqi dinars to help with the ministry's expenses. For the detailed allocations, see 479–89.

139. Qanun 97 of 1985, *Al-Ma'had al-Islami al-'Ali Li I'dad al-A'imma Wal Khutaba,* published in *al-Waqa'i' al-'Iraqiyya* no. 3080, January 13, 1986, 10–11.

140. Minister Nuri Faysal Shahir to *al-Dustur* no. 11, September 28, 1981, 29.

141. Ibid.,

142. *Al-'Iraq,* April 8, 1984.

143. See reports about investments in the economy of Karbala as well as in the two shrines there, *al-Thawra,* May 9, 1981. For reports about presents from the president to the *sadana* of the two shrines in Karbala, *al-Thawra,* July, 16, 1981. A report of one million Iraqi dinars for projects for expanding and beautifying the Karbala shrines, including air conditioning, *al-Thawra,* September 20, 1981; and an amazing report by the governor of Karbala according to which, during one year of war, various projects in his governorates had been completed for 113.7 million Iraqi dinars, and additional projects costing 70.1 million dinars were being pursued. These projects included both economic ones and investments in the shrines; *al-Thawra,* October 17, 1981.

144. *Al-Jumhuriyya,* February 19, 1984.

145. 'Abd al-Wahab 'Abd al-Razaq Marzuq, *al-'Iraq Balad al-Turath,* 60–61.

146. Minister Nuri Faysal Shahir to *al-Dustur* 11 (September 28, 1981): 29.

147. For example, on fairly large investments in 1987–88, see *al-Qadisiyya,* November 4, 1987; on the opening of a Saddam mosque in Birmingham, UK, see *al-Thawra,* April 26, 1988; on the minister of *awqaf* (endowments) calling for faster expansion and renovation of the Karbala shrines, and the press providing the full scale of the renovation, see *al-Thawra,* February 22, 1988.

148. CRRC SH-SHTP-A-001-167, July 24, 1986.

149. CRRC SH-SHTP-A-001-167, July 24, 1986.

150. See CRRC SH-SHTP-D-000-864, late September 1982.

151. See CRRC SH-SHTP-D-000-864, late September, 1982.

152. CRRC SH-SHTP-A-001-167, July 24, 1986. There are a few indications that identify UM1 clearly as 'Aflaq, for example, that he is chairing the meeting and that all address him, and only him, as "Professor" (*ustadh*). I am grateful to Chris Khouri for drawing my attention to the latter fact.

153. CRRC SH-SHTP-A-001-167, 40–46 minutes from the beginning of the conversation.

154. Saddam in a closed-door discussion with the Pan-Arab Leadership on January 25, 1995, CRRC SH-SPPC-000-660.

155. See, for example, a videotape from January 1, 1992, CRRC-SH-RVCC-V-001-402.

156. CRRC SH-SHTP-A-001-167, ibid, around 00:50:00 minutes into the discussion. The discussion is in a mix of literary and demotic Arabic.

157. Michel 'Aflaq, *Fi Sabil al-Ba'th* [On the way of resurrection], 11th ed. (Beirut: Dar al-Tali'a, 1974), 111–13, "Al-qawmiyya hubbun qabla kull shay'," a lecture delivered in 1940.

158. See Avivah Shusmann, "The Attitude of the Egyptian Press to the Shi'a on the Background of the Islamic Revolution in Iran" [in Hebrew], *Ha Mizrah He Hadash* 31 (1986): 140–41.

159. See *al-Daʿwa*, August 1979; January, July, October 1980; December 1983; *Liwaa al-Islam*, September 1987; April, July, August, September, December 1988; and other sources as quoted in Liad Porat, "The Egyptian and Syrian Muslim Brothers and Their Struggle against the Secular Arab Regimes . . . 1970 to the Early 1990s" [in Hebrew] (PhD diss., University of Haifa, April 2008), 250–55.

160. CRRC SH-SHTP-A-001-167, time in discussion between 0:39:22 and 0:41:07 minutes.

161. Ibid., time in discussion between 0:39:22 and 0:41:07 minutes, emphasis added.

162. Ibid., time in discussion between 0:58:00 and 0:59:13 minutes, emphasis added.

163. Strangely, Joseph Sassoon seems to take Saddam's words here at face value (*Saddam Hussein's Baʿth Party*, 260). By 1986 Saddam had already demonstrated that survival trumped ideological conviction every time, and befriending the Muslim Brotherhood was a matter of survival to him.

164. CRRC SH-SHTP-A-001-167, beginning about one hour into the discussion to the end.

165. Saddam's impression is confirmed by a number of interviews with Iraqis who lived in the south and in Baghdad at the time.

166. CRRC SH-SHTP-A-001-167, mainly from 01:22:00 to the end.

167. An audio recording of the meeting between Saddam and Turabi on July 18, 1991, CRRC SH-SPPC-D-000-217.

168. The *shuʿubiyya* was a ninth- to tenth-century Persian-Islamic movement that demanded equality between Arab and Persian Muslims. Some of its leaders were indeed anti-Arab, but they were relatively unimportant. In Arab tradition, though, this movement became identified with Persian anti-Arab sentiments.

169. Saddam Hussein, *Religious Political Movements and Those Disguised with Religion* (Baghdad: Dar al-Maʾmun, 1987), 8, 11, 12, 13.

170. Ibid., 19–22, 27.

171. Baghdad Voice of the Masses in Arabic, June 24, 1989, in FBIS-NES, June 26, 1989, 10.

172. Interview with Ambassador April Glaspie, Tel Aviv, March 29, 1995.

173. Interview in a European capital, September 1990.

174. INA in Arabic, January 14, 1991, in FBIS-NES, January 14, 1991, 38.

Chapter 5

1. See Amatzia Baram, "The Iraqi Invasion of Kuwait: Decision-Making in Baghdad," in *Iraq's Road to War*, ed. Amatzia Baram and Barry Rubin (New York: St. Martin's Press, 1994), 5–36.

2. For details, see Ofra Bengio, *Saddam's Word: Political Discourse in Iraq* (New York: Oxford University Press, 1998), 62–68.

3. See *al-Jumhuriyya*, July 30, 1990.

4. See, for example, Saddam's speech on the Prophet's birthday, *al-ʿIraq*, October 12, 1989; Baghdad Radio, September 14, 1991; *al-Qadisiyya*, January 21, 1992; *al-Thawra*, October 11, 22, 1992.

5. Pesach Malovany, *Milhamot Bavel ha-Hadashah: 'Aliyato u-Nefilato shel ha-Tzava ha-'Iraqi* [The wars of modern Babylon: The rise and fall of the Iraqi military] (Tel Aviv: Ma'rachot, 2009), 560–615.

6. See *al-Jumhuriyya*, July 30, 1990.

7. Sa'd al-Bazzaz in his two-day lecture in the United States following his defection to the West, on August 16–17, 1995; see also Bazzaz, *Harb Talidu Ukhra: Al-Ta'rikh al-Sirri li Harb al-Khalij* [A war that gives birth to another war: The secret history of the Gulf War] (Amman: al-Ahliyya lil-nahsr wal-Tawzi', 1992–1993), 50.

8. Interview with an Iraqi brigadier general in London through a Norwegian academic colleague, June 1999.

9. CRRC SH-PDWN-D-000-724, 42–44 in the original transcript.

10. Bazzaz lecture, August 16–17, 1995; see also Bazzaz, *Harb Talidu Ukhra*, 50; Tariq 'Aziz in an interview with Milton Viorst, *New Yorker*, June 24, 1991, 64–67; 'Aziz to Milliyet (Ankara), May 30, 1991.

11. CRRC SH-SHTP-A-000-632, August 4, 1990.

12. CRRC SH-SHTP-A-001-233, a conversation with senior officers, August 7, 1990.

13. See, for example, a meeting with senior advisers around October 1990, CRRC SH-SHTP-A-000-670.

14. On Saddam ordering his generals to prepare for a defensive war, CRRC SH-SHTP-A-001-233, August 7, 1990. Iraqi sources indicate that Saddam deployed fifty-five of his sixty-six divisions to the Kuwaiti theater, and he dug them in deep, with plentiful artillery and armor reserves, and the Republican Guard in depth behind them all, in exactly the manner that Iraq had learned to use to stymie Iranian offensives in the 1980s. Saddam even instructed his military commanders to plan for an early occupation of the oil-rich Saudi eastern shore. See Malovany, *Milhamot Bavel ha-Hadashah*, 534–60.

15. CRRC SH-SHTP-A-001-233, August 7, 1990.

16. Text of CNN Interview with Saddam Husayn, INA in Arabic, October 31, 1990.

17. INA in Arabic, November 3, 1990, FBIS-SERIAL JN 0311165890, 15.

18. CRRC SH-SHDP-D-000-830, a Pan-Arab Leadership meeting sometime in 1992. Saddam loved the report, but regarding the Syrian Ba'th he retorted with disgust, "*Wa hal al-sulta hunak ladayhim hizb?*" (Does the regime there [in Syria] have a party at all?).

19. See CRRC SH-SHTP-A-001-233, August 7, 1990, Saddam was certain that US aerial attacks would create a refugee problem, and that would they cause protests "from the Arab West to the Arab East." Also, in his meeting with his lieutenants on September 16, 1980, he believed that a successful Iraqi offensive against Iran would bring him Arab support that would twist the hands of unsympathetic Arab regimes, CRRC SH- SHTP-A-000-835.

20. Speech on Army Day, Baghdad Domestic Service in Arabic, January 6, 1991, in FBIS-NES, January 7, 1991, 25.

21. "Text of CNN Interview with Saddam Husayn," INA in Arabic, October 31, 1990, in FBIS-NES, November 1, 1990, 18. "Saddam Responds to Mubarak," Baghdad Domestic Service in Arabic, August 23, 1990, in FBIS-NES, August 24, 1990, 28. See also a remarkably meek disclosure: "I am Saddam Husayn, [merely] a Worshipper of God. . . . [Merely] one of God's worshippers," in "Japanese TV Interviews Saddam on Gulf Situation," Tokyo NHK General TV Network, October 22, 1990, in FBIS-NES, October 23, 1990, 25.

22. "Letter to America," INA in English, September 26, 1990, in FBIS-NES-DR, September 26, 1990, 26.

23. SH-SHTP-A-001-236, as reproduced in Kevin M. Woods, David Palkki, and Mark E. Stout, *The Saddam Tapes: The Inner Workings of a Tyrant's Regime, 1978–2001* (New York: Cambridge University Press, 2011), 181–82. In the secret meeting of September 16, 1980, too, Saddam believed he would immediately capture 20,000 Iranian soldiers.

24. "Saddam Message to President Bush," Baghdad Domestic Service in Arabic, January 17, 1991, in FBIS-NES, January 17, 1991, 17–18.

25. INA in Arabic, February 10, 1991, in FBIS-NES, February 11, 1991, 23.

26. CRRC SH-BATH-D-000-324, a secret memorandum from Saddam, February 16, 1991. See also CRRC SH-SPPC-D-000-448, 9–11.

27. CRRC SH-PDWN-D-000-406, a message sent on February 24, 1991.

28. CRRC PDWN-D-000-406, February 25, 1991. See also Baghdad Domestic Service in Arabic, February 26, 1991, in FBIS-NES-DR, February 26, 1991, 14–15, and based on the author's own listening.

29. "Saddam Sends Open Message to King Fahd," Baghdad Domestic Service in Arabic, January 14, 1991, in FBIS-NES, January 15, 1991, 27. See also Saddam quoting from the Qur'an a verse that promises *al-Janna* (paradise) to those who die in *jihad*, Baghdad Domestic Service in Arabic, January 20, 1991, in FBIS-NES-DR, January 22, 1991, 36. And see, in the middle of the war, Saddam's message to the Iraqis, Arabs, and Muslims, INA in Arabic, February 10, 1991, in FBIS-NES-DR, February 11, 1991, 23.

30. "The gate of paradise is open for all the good ones and all . . . those who worked with faith," Saddam Husayn, *al-Thawra*, May 13, 1994; *al-Thawra*, July 18, 1993.

31. *Al-Thawra*, July 18, 1993.

32. *Al-Thawra*, April 7, 1993.

33. *Al-Thawra*, December 1, 1993.

34. See, for example, the Sunni fundamentalist Indian-Pakistani thinker (died 1979) Abu al-A'la al-Mawdudi, *Mujaz Ta'rikh Tajdid al-Din wal-Hayat: Waqi' al-Muslimin wa Sabil al-Nuhudh Bihim* [A concise history of the innovation of religion: The state of the Muslims and the way to reviving them] (Beirut: Mu'assasat al-Risala [Institute of the Message], 1975), 44–53, esp. 50–53.

35. "Saddam Addresses Union Group," Iraqi News Agency (INA) in Arabic, November 3, 1990, in FBIS-NES JN1311165890, November 3, 1990, 15–16. "Saddam Husayn Addresses Islamic Delegation," INA, December 15, 1990, in FBIS-NES, December 17, 1990, 14–15. See also "Saddam Calls Arab Muslims to Save Mecca," Baghdad Domestic Service in Arabic, August 10, 1990, in FBIS-NES, August 13, 1990, 45–47; "Saddam Addresses Ba'th Party Congress," Baghdad Radio Network in Arabic, October 6, 1992, in FBIS-NES, October 7, 1992, 20–23.

36. "Saddam Calls on the Arabs and Muslims to Save Mecca," Baghdad Domestic Service, August 10, 1990, and a National Assembly statement, ibid., August 11, 1990, in FBIS-NES, August 13, 1990, 45–47. For the story of the shaykh and his daughter, see "Letter to America," INA in English, September 26, 1990, in FBIS-NES, September 26, 1990, 25; for *Qaruniyyin*, see, for example, *al-Thawra*, January 22, 1991.

37. "Saddam Husayn Addresses Islamic Delegation," INA, December 15, 1990, in FBIS-NES, December 17, 1990, 14–15.

38. "Saddam Addresses Arab Youth Seminar," Baghdad Domestic Service in Arabic, November 29, 1990, in FBIS-NES, November 29, 1990, 18.

39. "Saddam Addresses Popular Islamic Delegation," Baghdad Domestic Service in Arabic, September 24, 1990, in FBIS-NES, September 25, 26–27.

40. *Al-Thawra*, January 13, 1991. See also a National Assembly statement, ibid., August 11, 1990, in FBIS-NES, August 13, 1990, 45–47.

41. "Saddam Calls on the Arabs and Muslims to Save Mecca," Baghdad Domestic Service, August 10, 1990, and a National Assembly statement, ibid., August 11, 1990, in FBIS-NES, August 13, 1990, 45–47.

42. "Saddam Calls on the Arabs and Muslims to Save Mecca," Baghdad Domestic Service, August 10, 1990; "Saddam Repeats Call for Jihad," Baghdad Domestic Service in Arabic, September 5, 1990, in FBIS-NES, September 6, 1990, 28; INA in Arabic, December 31, 1990, in FBIS-NES, January 3, 1991, 23.

43. Sa'd al-Bazzaz, *Babil*, April 13, 1992.

44. *Babil*, November 21, 1993.

45. "Saddam Husayn Addresses Islamic Delegation," INA in Arabic, December 15, 1990, in FBIS-NES, December 17, 1990, 16.

46. *Al-Thawra*, December 3, 1990, quoted in Bengio, *Saddam's Word*, 84.

47. Husayn al-Shahbali, *al-Thawra*, November 20, 1990. For some allusions by the mid-1980s that Saddam was equal to the Prophet, see Bengio, *Saddam's Word*, 84.

48. CRRC SPPC-D-000-586, February 2002.

49. See, for example, reports of interrogations, trials, and executions of real and perceived Da'wa members, CRRC SH-IDGS-D-000-311, 1984–1990; SH-IDGS-D-000-578, 1982–1991; CRRC SH-MISC-D-000-310, June 1983.

50. SH-IDGS-D-000-232, April 23, 1984.

51. See decisions by Saddam on the forced evacuations of many villages on the Iranian border near Basra, CRRC SH-MISC-D-000-729, March 20, 1985; reports on the situation in the Ahwar marsh areas, CRRC SH-BATH-D-000-518, January 1984–May 1885.

52. See Saddam's speech at the Tenth Regional Ba'th Party Congress, *al-Thawra*, October 7, 1992.

53. See an internal Ba'th document, a February 1987 lecture by a senior official to the party's Culture Bureau, SH-BATHY-D-000-300, and Saddam's public speech, *al-Thawra*, March 16, 1991.

54. *Al-Thawra*, July 28, 1991.

55. The revolt erupted on 15 Sha'ban, the Imam Mahdi's birthday.

56. Faleh 'Abd al-Jabbar, "Why the Intifada Failed," in *Iraq since the Gulf War: Prospects for Democracy*, ed. Fran Hazelton (London: Zed Books, 1994), 106–7.

57. *Al-Ahram*, September 4, 1991, as quoted by Ronen Zeidel, "The Iraqi Baath Party, 1948–1995: Personal and Organizational Aspects" [in Hebrew] (master's thesis, University of Haifa, June 1997), 191, 201.

58. See, for example, a description by the regime of the murder of doctors, *al-Qadisiyya*, January 18, 1992, and other pointless killings, *al-Jumhuriyya*, March 4, 1992; *al-'Iraq*, March 31, 1992. These reports were well founded.

59. See, for example, Kan'an Makiya, *Cruelty and Silence: War, Uprising and the Arab World* (London: Penguin, 1993), 68–71. See also Fanar Haddad, *Sectarianism in Iraq:*

Antagonistic Visions of Unity (London: Hurst; New York: Columbia University Press, 2011), 65–87. For the repression of the Kurdish population, see Human Rights Watch, *Bureaucracy of Repression: The Iraqi Government in Its Own Words*, February 1, 1994, www.hrw.org/en /reports/1994/02/01/bureaucracy-repression (last accessed October 1, 2013).

60. Bazzaz, *Harb Talidu Ukhra* [A war that gives birth to another war], 449.

61. Makiya, *Cruelty and Silence*, 78, 91, 93; Jabar, "Why the Intifada Failed," 111.

62. Makiya, *Cruelty and Silence*, 90.

63. A collective interview, Boston, May 1994.

64. Based on an interview with a central activist of the Da'wa Party, London, September 1991.

65. Interviews with Shi'i revolutionaries and American officials, 1994.

66. Makiya, *Cruelty and Silence*, 74–75, 97.

67. *Al-Qadisiyya*, October 20, 1991. In reality, Mahir was a very mediocre military officer.

68. Makiya, *Cruelty and Silence*, 97. The regime's secret documents do not mention this belief.

69. Ibid., 99.

70. Some 25,000, according to Human Rights Watch, *Endless Torment*, 29. General Wafiq al-Samarra'i, ex-chief of military intelligence who defected in 1994, assessed no fewer than 100,000 casualties; interview, in FBIS-NES-DR, December 20, 1994.

71. *Al-Thawra*, October 22, 1991.

72. For a detailed account, see Amatzia Baram, "Neo-Tribalism in Iraq: Saddam Husayn's Tribal Policies 1991–1996," *International Journal of Middle East Studies* 29, no. 1 (February 1997): 7–9.

73. SH-PDWN-D-000-328, March 16, 1991.

74. An interview with the US general who commanded a division in the war, Washington, D.C., 1994.

75. CRRC SH-PDWN-D-000-328, March 16, 1991.

76. CRRC SH-SHYTP-A-000-891.

77. *Al-Thawra*, August 31, 1992.

78. *Al-Thawra*, August 31, 1992.

79. For the theological differences and historiographic conflicts. see a succinct analysis by Eitan Kohlberg, "The Evolution of the Shi'a," *Jerusalem Quarterly* 27 (Spring 1983): 109–26. See also Moojan Momen, *An Introduction to Shi'i Islam: The History and Doctrines of Twelver Shi'ism* (New Haven, CT: Yale University Press, 1985).

80. See, for example, *al-Thawra*, December 17, 18, 1992; February 26, 1993; July 11, 1993; November 6, 1995.

81. INA, September 14, 1991, as reproduced in FBIS, NES, DR, September 16, 1991, 16–20.

82. *Al-Thawra*, September 15, 1991.

83. Zeidel, "The Iraqi Baath Party, 1948–1995," 287–88.

84. Joseph Sassoon, *Saddam Hussein's Ba'th Party: Inside an Authoritarian Regime* (Cambridge: Cambridge University Press, 2012), 52. See also Ba'th officials in *al-Yom al-Sabi'* (Paris and Beirut), January 22, 1990.

85. This information comes from Shi'i revolutionary, academic, and Ba'thi sources. See, for example, *al-Jihad*, June 5, 1991; *Liwa' al-Sadr*, September 29, 1991; Phebe Marr, *The*

Modern History of Iraq, 3rd ed. (Boulder, CO: Westview Press, 2011), 243–48; Makiya, *Cruelty and Silence*, 57–105; Haddad, *Sectarianism in Iraq*, 65–87; and my interviews with young revolutionaries from Hilla, some of whom had traveled all over the south at the beginning of the revolt, Boston, May 1995. *Alif Ba*, March 18, 1992.

86. *Al-Qadisiyya*, March 14, 1992. See also an implied such admission, *al-Thawra*, March 4, 1992.

87. And see a vague reference to the senior party officials in the south, SH-SHTP-A-000-830, 1992, implying such blame.

88. Sassoon, *Saddam Hussein's Ba'th Party*, 143, 155.

89. Many were killed, some badly tortured first; see Makiya, *Cruelty and Silence*, 57–105; *al-Qadisiyya*, January 18, 1992; *al-Jumhuriyya*, March 4, 1992; *al-'Iraq*, March 31, 1992; Human Rights Watch, *Endless Torment: The 1991 Uprising in Iraq and Its Aftermath* (Washington, DC: Human Rights Watch, June 1992), 46–50. From the opposition side, see Voice of Iraqi Islamic Revolution in Arabic, April 18, 30, 1995, in FBIS-NES-DR, April 19, May 2, 1995.

90. In his speech at the October 1992 Ba'th Regional Congress, Saddam himself reported a serious problem of members (both Sunnis and Shi'is) leaving the party. See FBIS-NES-DR, October 7, 1992, 15.

91. Sassoon, *Saddam Hussein's Ba'th Party*, 52.

92. Some members asked to be redrafted into the military for economic reasons (*al-Thawra*, May 30, 1993). Others received modest help from a "Party Mutual Help" (*al-takaful al-hizbi*) escrow fund that was opened especially for such cases in some branches (*al-Qadisiyya*, March 16, 1993). Many received medals that came with economic benefits (*al-Thawra*, February 14, 1993; *al-Jumhuriyya*, February 27, 1993; *al-Qadisiyya*, March 16, 1993).

93. See Lt. Gen. 'Abd al-Wahid Shanan Aal Ribbat, Commander of the Fourth Corps, *al-Thawra*, February 17, 1993; see also Lt. Gen. Tariq Sadiq 'Abd al-Husayn, who replaced him, *al-Qadisiyya*, January 8, 1994.

94. See *al-Qabas*, March 22, 1999, in FBIS-NES-DR LD2203181399, March 22, 1999.

95. The interview was conducted on my behalf by a colleague in London in 1999. Colonel Zaydi claimed that Shi'i pilots represented no more than 5 percent of all pilots in the Iraqi Air Force but that Shi'is represented a very high percentage among the technical crews. See (Staff Col.) Ahmad al-Zaydi, *Al-Bina al-Ma'nawi lil-Quwat al-Musallha al-'Iraqiyya* [The essential structure of the Iraqi armed forces] (Beirut: Dar al-Rawda, 1990), 168.

96. Sassoon, *Saddam Hussein's Ba'th Party*, 2–3.

97. Ibid., 2–3.

98. Some 25,000 were killed in the Shi'i areas, according to Human Rights Watch, *Endless Torment*, 29. General Wafiq al-Samarra'i, ex-chief of military intelligence who defected in 1994, assessed no less than 100,000; interview, in FBIS-NES-DR, December 20, 1994. In 2009, officials at the Iraqi Ministry of Human Rights indicated that there may be around 270 unopened known mass grave sites in Iraq. See United Nations Assistance Mission for Iraq, *Human Rights Report*, January 1–June 30, 2009, "Mass graves," 10.

99. All of the above account means that when analyzing the internal Ba'thi documents, researchers should adopt a critical stance. Archival documents, especially the Ba'thi ones, cannot be regarded as the holy grail of openness, candor, and the naked truth of what the

Ba'th regime was up to. If not read critically, the documents can be misleading. This is particularly the case with Sunni-Shi'i relations: what the documents say is very important, but what they are silent about is equally important. Here, the internal documents need to be integrated with open sources.

100. The most serious Sunni tribal revolt erupted when Saddam returned the body of Brigadier General Muhammad Mazlum al-Dulaimi to his family. A prominent member of the Dulaym Confederation's al-bu Nimr tribe, his body bore marks of horrible torture, and sections of al-bu Nimr rose in open revolt in response. Other Dulaymis staged an insurrection at the Abu Ghraib military base in June. The information is based on interviews, but the Ba'th regime itself implied that something very serious happened with al-bu Nimr. See Baram, "Neo-Tribalism in Iraq," 6; Faleh Jabar, "Sheikhs and Ideologues: Deconstruction and Reconstruction of Tribes under Patrimonial Totalitarianism in Iraq, 1968–1998," in *Tribes and Power: Nationalism and Ethnicity in the Middle East*, ed. Faleh Jabar and Hosham Dawood (London: Saqi Books, 2003), 99–105.

101. See his bitter denial of and attack on those who criticized his regime for discrimination against Shi'is in terms of government jobs and development funds and that he preferred his hometown Tikrit, *al-Thawra*, August 31, 1992. During the Iran-Iraq War, see CRRC SH-SHTP-D-000-607, between February 25 and July 31, 1985, Saddam complaining about a substantial (Shi'i) fifth column in Iraq.

102. See, for example, CRRC SH-GMID-D-001-326, 1982.

103. Ariel I. Ahram, "Militarized Development and the Destruction of the Iraqi Marshes: From Hearts and Minds to Ashes and Mud," unpublished study, November 1, 2013. (An earlier version was presented as a paper at the September 1, 2013, meeting of the American Political Science Association in Chicago under the title "From Hearts and Minds to Ashes and Mud: Development, Counterinsurgency, and the Destruction of the Iraqi Marshes.")

104. Ibid., 22–24. See also CRRC SH-PDWN-D-001-029, May 11, 1983.

105. Abbas Kadhim, "The Hawza under Siege: A Study in the Ba'th Party Archive," Occasional Paper 1 (Boston: Boston University Institute for Iraqi Studies, June 2013); Ahram, "Militarized Development and the Destruction of the Iraqi Marshes."

106. SHTP-A-001-404, May or June 1979.

107. Sassoon, *Saddam Hussein's Ba'th Party*, 2–3. Sassoon misquotes me. According to him, I reported that "the late 1980s" saw "the near disappearance of the Shi'i element from the first rank of its [the party's] leadership." In my research, however, I have never suggested it. In fact, based on Batatu's *The Old Social Classes* and on my study of official biographies in the Ba'thi dailies between 1968 and 1986, I have argued that such a development took place, but not "by the late 1980s." Rather, I reported that it took place a whole generation earlier: "between November 1963 and 1970." Compare Amatzia Baram, *Culture, History and Ideology*, 14–15, with Joseph Sassoon, *Saddam Hussein's Ba'th Party*, 2–3, and 3n5. I also showed that after 1977, Shi'is in fact became quite prominent in the Ba'th leadership. See my "The Ruling Political Elite in Ba'thi Iraq, 1968–1986."

108. For example, a secret memorandum, CRRC SH-PDWN-D-000-328, 26–27.

109. SH-PDWN-D-000-328, March 16, 1991. Only in his 1992 speech (*al-Thawra*, August 31, 1992) did Saddam gather enough civil courage to discuss the Sunni-Shi'i dichotomy explicitly. I could not find a subsequent repeat of this candor.

110. CRRC SH-IISX-D-000-404, October 15, 1991.

111. SH-SHTP-A-000-830, 1992.

112. CRRC SHTP-A-001-404, May or June 1979, ca. 0:40:00 minutes into the meeting. For more, see below.

113. CRRC SH-SHTP-D-000-714, a government meeting in the mid-1990s.

114. Peter Ford, "The Men Who Shot Uday Hussein," *Christian Science Monitor*, September 26, 2003.

115. See *al-Qadisiyya*, February 3, 1994; April 11, 1994; *al-'Iraq*, April 2, 1994, for reports about the "Mother of Battles River," designed ostensibly for the "irrigation of 600,000 dunams of desert regions." The operation was entrusted to the Military Industrialization Organization. It included digging and dumping more than five million cubic meters, employing 6,000 people, and using 4,000 to 5,000 trucks and pieces of heavy mechanical equipment. The river, flowing between Dhi Qar and Basra governorates, is 108 to 120 kilometers long and 16 meters deep, and between 65 and 118 meters wide. All this was achieved within six months. Even more impressive is "Saddam's River," ostensibly designed to irrigate six million dunams and extending from Yusufiyya (40 kilometers south of Baghdad) to Basra—565 kilometers altogether. It is 100 meters wide at the surface and 50 meters wide at the bottom. In September 1992—within 180 days—the project was completed, having employed 6,000 workers, 2,200 heavy digging machines, and "hundreds" of cranes. See INA, September 3, 1992; December 7, 1992, in FBIS-NES-DR, September 4, 1992, 27; December 8, 1992, 31; Baghdad Radio, December 7, 1992, in FBIS-NES-DR, December 7, 1992, 31.

116. See a series of satellite photographs: Central Intelligence Agency (CIA), *The Destruction of Iraq's Southern Marshes*, publication NESA 94-10021, RTT 94-10054 (Washington, DC: CIA, August 1994); Marr, *The Modern History of Iraq*, 276.

117. Marr, *The Modern History of Iraq*, 276.

118. For details, see Baram, "Neo-Tribalism in Iraq," 1–31.

119. SH-RVCC-D-000-610, February 29, 1992.

120. For more, see Baram, "Neo-Tribalism in Iraq," 1–31. See also Faleh A. Jabar and Hosham Dawod, eds., *Tribes and Power: Nationalism and Ethnicity in the Middle East* (London: Saqi Books, 2002).

121. Top Secret and Personal, Cc: Ministry of Defense, Air Force Command, Commander's Aides, Operations, CRRC, SH-PDWN-D-000-329, 7, March 29, 2003.

122. SH-SHTP-A-000-891. The meeting took place sometime between September and December 1991.

123. As far as I am aware, no such 'Ali tradition or fatwa exists.

124. SH-SHTP-A-000-891.

125. See also Salah al-Mukhtar, editor in chief, *al-Jumhuriyya*, November 17, 1993; January 5, 1994.

126. See, for example, an oath by 586 Shi'i tribal shaykhs from the Hilla area to turn in "infiltrators," "saboteurs," "deserters," and other criminals, *al-Thawra*, March 7, 15, July 14, 1993; *al-Jumhuriyya*, May 25, 1993.

127. CRRC SH-IISX-D-000-404, 1–5.

128. CRRC SH-IISX-D-000-404, 1–5.

129. An analysis from 1995 describing the political splits within the Da'wa and its history, CRRC SH-GMID-000-622, 9–11, December 11, 1995.

130. See Saddam's clear instructions: weapons first, only later Frigidaires, because the danger to Iraq was partition, as in Lebanon. CRRC SH-SHTP-D-000-757, 1993.

131. See, for example, the distribution of 330 plots in Suwayra, and a promise for an additional 400 for (Shi'i) fighters from the same area in the Popular Army, and plots and homes for soldiers and officers from Amara, *al-Qadisiyya*, May 29, 1993. On 20,000 dinars for a bereaved family instead of a car, see *al-Qadisiyya*, July 11, 1993.

132. CRRC SH-SHDP-D-000-830, a Pan-Arab Leadership meeting sometime in 1992.

133. CRRC SH-BATH-D-000-325, July 8, 1999.

134. CRRC SH-BATH-D-000-159, April 22, 2002. For less extensive reports of security measures, see: Party Secretariat to heads of *tanzimat*, "Religious Occasions," March 12, 2000; Party Secretariat to Ali Hasan al-Majid, February 22, 2000, BRCC 004-4-3 (209–12); Party Secretariat to all heads of *tanzimat*, March 29, 1997, BRCC 003-4-4 (470–72), in Sassoon, *Saddam Hussain's Ba'th Party*, 263–64.

Chapter 6

1. Kim Ghattas, "Iraqis Seek Refuge in Religion: Regime Has Co-opted Growing Religious Mood," BBC, April 25, 2002; Washington Kurdish Institute, April 26, 2002.

2. *Al-Qadisiyya*, May 31, 1994.

3. For example, *Babil*, May 28, 1994, reminded its readers that in early September 1993 the dollar was worth 54 Iraqi dinars, whereas a year later the dollar was worth 510 dinars.

4. INA, September 25, 1994, in FBIS-SERIEL JN 2509132994, September 25, 1994; *al-Malaff al-'Iraqi* 34 (October 1994):36; *Babil*, September 28, 1994.

5. *Al-Thawra*, July 21, 1994.

6. *Babil*, December 28, 1995.

7. See, for example, *al-Jumhuriyya*, January 14, 1996; *Alif Ba*, January 17, 1996, in FBIS-NES, March 19, 1996, 40–41.

8. For more details, see Amatzia Baram, *Building toward Crisis: Saddam Husayn's Strategy for Survival* (Washington, DC: Washington Institute for Near East Policy, 1998), 65–86.

9. Ghattas, "Iraqis Seek Refuge in Religion."

10. Ibid. For details about the mosque-building policy in the 1990s, see below.

11. Ibid.

12. See Moojan Momen, *An Introduction to Shi'i Islam* (New Haven, CT: Yale University Press, 1985), 172–73.

13. Ibid., 76–77, 81.

14. *Al-Thawra*, April 7, 1993.

15. *Al-Qadisiyya*, June 15, 1993.

16. *Al-Jumhuriyya*, June 19, 1993.

17. *Al-Thawra*, November 17, 1991.

18. *Al-Thawra*, November 17, 1991; July 29, 1992.

19. *Al-Thawra*, August 17, 1992.

20. *Al-Qadisiyya*, April 6, 1993.

21. *Al-Qadisiyya*, July 9, 1994.

22. For example, Ma'sum Sa'di in *Alif Ba*, March 2, 1994, 16–18; Nabil 'Abd al-Qadir, *al-Thawra*, January 9, 1994.

23. *Babil*, June 16, 18, 1994.

24. *Al-Qadisiyya*, July 31, 1994.

25. *Al-'Iraq*, December 3, 1998.

26. *Al-Jumhuriyya*, July 13, 1993.

27. *Al-Qadisiyya*, December 12, 1993.

28. Republic of Iraq Radio Network in Arabic, October 11, 1993, in FBIS-NES, October 13, 1993, 45. See also *Babil*, October 12, 1993.

29. *Babil*, June 1, 1994.

30. A written message from a major general in Saddam's army, July 19, 2012.

31. *Alif Ba*, October 24, 2001.

32. *Al-Jumhuriyya*, June 23, 1993. Particular names mentioned in support in this issue include Husayn al-Musawi, the *murshid* (guide) of the al-Kazimiyya (Shi'i) Mosque and 'Abd Allah al-Shaykhali, imam and preacher of the al-Imam al-A'zam (Sunni) Mosque.

33. CRRC SH-SHTP-A-001-167.

34. Announcement by Hatim Hamdan al-'Azzawi, head of the Presidential Office, on August 4, 1994, *al-Thawra*, August 5, 1994.

35. CRRC SH-BATH-D-000-474. No precise date is provided, but the context implies the timing.

36. A written message from a major general in Saddam's army, July 19, 2012.

37. CRRC SH-PDWN-D-000-409, 23. The meeting took place between April 27 and May 7, 2002. See also CRRC SH-PDWN-D-000-812, 195.

38. CRRC SH-PDWN-D-000-409, no pages in the Arabic text, English text p. 21, between April 27 and May 7, 2002.

39. See Saddam's meeting with his government on April 21, 2002, CRRC SH-PDWN-D-000-409, English text p. 23.

40. *Al-Jumhuriyya*, July 21, 1998.

41. *Al-Thawra*, October 19, 1998.

42. Only a "full" or "active" member could become a member of *firqa*, *shu'ba*, *far'*, and higher hierarchical levels.

43. A party internal update April 2, 2002, BRCC, 004-2-3, 085, as reproduced in Joseph Sassoon, *Saddam Hussein's Ba'th Party: Inside an Authoritarian Regime* (Cambridge: Cambridge University Press, 2012), 266. Dean of Saddam Institute to Presidential Diwan, July 10, 2002, BRCC 004-4-6(123); a document produced by the institute, August 21, 2001, BRCC 012-3-4 (073-074); Presidential Diwan, December 1, 2001, BRCC 004-2-3 (195); Dean of Saddam Institute to Party Secretariat, April 25, 2002, BRCC 004-2-3 (155). For the curriculum of the 1998 academic year, see BRCC 012-3-4 (074). For dissertations of excellence, see BRCC 004-2-3 (056), in Sassoon, *Saddam Hussein's Ba'th Party*, 266–67.

44. See Sayyid Qutb, *Fi Zilal al-Qur'an* [In the shadow of the Qur'an], 17th ed. (Cairo: Dar al-Shuruq, 1992).

45. *Al-Jumhuriyya*, July 21, 1998.

46. Ibrahim on October 16, 2001, BRCC 004-2-3, 244-256, quoted in Sassoon, *Saddam Hussein's Ba'th Party*, 266.

47. Saddam in a closed-door discussion of the Pan-Arab Leadership on January 25, 1995, CRRC SH-SPPC-000-660.

48. "Saddam Husayn Article on the Prophet's Birthday," *al-Jumhuriyya*, September 21, 1991, in FBIS-NES, September 26, 1991, 21–23.

49. *Al-'Iraq*, October 26, 1992.

50. *Al-Qadisiyya*, October 29, 1991. For more information about the sums collected as *zakat* and how they were distributed, see, for example, *al-Thawra*, March 27 and 30, 1992; *al-'Iraq*, March 11, 1992.

51. *Babil*, June 16, 1994. For the actual beginning of Qur'an classes for teachers as the centerpiece of the campaign, see "Koranic Teaching Program in Schools Explained," *al-'Iraq*, August 28, 1993, 5, in JPRS-NEA-93-112 30 93AE0623A, November 1993. For the opening in Najaf one year later, see *Babil*, August 1, 1994.

52. *Al-Jumhuriyya*, September 11, 1993. See also Decree No. 82 of July 7, 1994, published in *al-Thawra*, July 8, 1994, very conspicuously on the front page.

53. Interview with a retired general, Washington, D.C., July 2011.

54. *Al-Thawra*, August 20, 1994. See also instructions by Minister of the Interior Watban Ibrahim Hasan, Saddam's half-brother, *al-Thawra*, July 10, 1994.

55. *Al-Qadisiyya*, May 27, 1993.

56. See a cornerstone ceremony for a similar mosque in al-Salman, in Muthanna governorate in the south, *al-Thawra*, April 19, 1993.

57. Philip Smucker from Baghdad, *Daily Telegraph*, July 29, 2001. See also Ghattas, "'Iraqis Seek Refuge in Religion."

58. *Al-Thawra*, May 16, 1994; *al-'Iraq*, May 21, 1994; *al-Qadisiyya*, November 4, 1987.

59. A written message from a major general in Saddam's army, July 19, 2012.

60. *Al-Thawra*, May 18, 1994.

61. See, for example, a mosque named after 'Izzat Ibrahim, deputy chairman of the RCC and deputy commander in chief of the armed forces, in his hometown of Dur, *al-'Iraq*, February 20, 1992.

62. *Al-Jumhuriyya*, April 7, 1992.

63. Ghattas, "'Iraqis Seek Refuge in Religion." For details about the mosque-building policy in the 1990s, see below.

64. CRRC SH-PDWN-D-000-855, January 2002.

65. For example, *al-Thawra*, December. 25, 1995.

66. Qanun 97 of 1985, *Al-Ma'had al-Islami al-'Ali Li I'dad al-A'imma Wal Khutaba*, published in *al-Waqa'i' al-'Iraqiyya* 3080, January 13, 1986, 10–11.

67. 'Abd al-Wahab 'Abd al-Razaq Marzuq, *Al-'Iraq Balad al-Turath Wal-Muqaddasat al-Islamiyya* [Iraq, the land of heritage and Islamic holy places] (Baghdad: Ministry of Awqaf and Religious Affairs, 1986), 60–61.

68. *Al-Thawra*, November 23, 1992.

69. *Al-Qadisiyya*, June 28, 1998. See also *al-'Iraq*, March 2, 1992; *al-Thawra*, January 24, 1993.

70. See, for example, INA, October 14, 1992, in FBIS-NES, October 14, 1992; *Al-Thawra*, January 24, 1993, and interviews with Iraqi officials in Washington, D.C., summer 2004. Children of regime luminaries attended, too, an indication of the great prestige of the university. See a lecture by a student, Ibrahim 'Izzat Ibrahim, son of the

deputy chairman of the RCC and deputy commander in chief of the armed forces, *al-Qadisiyya*, March 16, 1993.

71. See, for example, his request to ʿUday Saddam Husayn for help and ʿUday's contribution of 100,000 Iraqi dinars toward scholarships, *al-Thawra*, March 31, 1993.

72. For example, *al-ʿIraq*, December 10, 1991; *al-Thawra*, July 30, 1992.

73. *Al-Jumhuriyya*, June 19, 1993.

74. *Al-Thawra*, October 21, 1998.

75. *Al-Thawra*, December 4, 7, 1992.

76. *Al-Thawra*, July 13, 1992.

77. *Al-Thawra*, May 13, 1991, July 28, 1992, August 10, 1992, *Alif Ba*, May 25, 1994.

78. See, for example, a report of twenty-one hangings of merchants by ʿUday's bodyguards for profiteering, *L'Express*, August 13–19, 1992, 24–34; and vicious attacks on the merchants for robbing the people, *Babil*, December 25, 1993.

79. CRRC SH-SPPC-D-000-448, 9–11. The meeting took place on August 21, 1994. The Qurʾan says, "As to the thief, both male and female, cut off their hand" (*Sura* 5, *al-Maʾida, Aaya* 38).

80. CRRC SH-SPPC-D-000-448, 9–11.

81. Republic of Iraq Radio Network in Arabic, June 4, 1994, in FBIS-SERIAL JN0406194294, June 4, 1994.

82. Ten car thieves sentenced to death, *al-Thawra*, December 4, 7, 1992.

83. Republic of Iraq Radio Network in Arabic, June 13, 1994, in FBIS-SERIAL JN1306125394, June 13, 1994.

84. Decree No. 92 of July 21, 1994, published in *al-Thawra*, July 24, 1994, in FBIS SERIAL JN3007140294, July 30, 1994.

85. *Al-Jumhuriyya*, July 6, 1994.

86. *Al-Thawra*, August 26, 1990, in FBIS-SERIAL JN 0109143394, September 1, 1994.

87. *Al-Jumhuriyya*, March 27, 1994. General Dhanun, the first called to "expose the suspect places from a moral point of view" in order to "uproot this [prostitution] phenomenon that is alien to our people's Arab habits and traditions." The general also reported that a few such places were closed down and everybody there was arrested and soon to face a just trial.

88. "Abu Sirhan," *Babil*, June 5, 1994.

89. *Al-Thawra*, September 4, 1994, FBIS-SERIAL JN1309162594, September 13, 1994. Law No. 8 of 1988 had already defined what "prostitution" was.

90. See the website www.fas.harvard.edu/~irdp, file 1 0935 687, March 28, 1990, reported by Achim Rohde, *State-Society Relations in Baʿthist Iraq: Facing Dictatorship* (Abingdon, UK: Routledge, 2010), 102. See also Ofra Bengio, *Saddam's Word: Political Discourse in Iraq* (New York: Oxford University Press, 1998), 241n9.

91. "Abu Sirhan," *Babil*, June 5, 1994.

92. "Extra Judicial Executions," in Amnesty International, *Amnesty International, 2001 Annual Report on Iraq*, http://www.atour.com/news/international/20010710l.html. In October 2000, dozens of young women accused of prostitution were beheaded without any judicial process in Baghdad and other cities. Men suspected of procurement were also beheaded. The killings were reportedly carried out in the presence of Baʿth Party representatives. Members of *Fedaʾiyyi Saddam* used swords.

93. An interview with a senior Da'wa activist in London, September 1990. Until 1970, the party was free to organize religious festivals and commemoration days at the university, but then the activist was warned that such activities would land him in jail, as actually happened.

94. BRCC 003-1-1-0371, June 12, 1980, a top-secret memorandum (*sirri lil-ghaya*) from the Northern Organization Bureau.

95. Al-Karkh, *tanzim* to all heads of party branches in the district, "Activities of Wahhabis," June 18, 2001, BRCC 004-3-1 (388), in Sassoon, *Saddam Hussein's Ba'th Party*, 261.

96. Party Secretariat to heads of *tanzimat*, September 8, 2001, BRCC 004-4-4 (070), in Sassoon, *Saddam Hussein's Ba'th Party*, 261.

97. Party Secretariat to all branches, "Guidance," July 23, 2001, BRCC 004-4-6 (231-235), in Sassoon, *Saddam Hussein's Ba'th Party*, 261.

98. Suspicion of Baghdad merchants, BRCC 005-1-2 (097-098), November 30, 1995, in Sassoon, *Saddam Hussein's Ba'th Party*, 161.

99. See Latif Nusayyif Jasim in *al-Qadisiyya*, April 13, 1992; *al-Thawra*, May 13, 1991; July 28, 1992; August 10, 1992.

100. Twenty-one hangings of merchants for profiteering, *L'Express*, August 13–19, 1992, 24–34; vicious attacks on the merchants for robbing the people, *Babil*, December 25, 1993.

101. Hoover Institution Archive, Stanford, California, an uncatalogued report from July 22, 1995, directed to a secretary of a party "branch" (*amin sir qiyadat far'*).

102. Party Secretariat to All Secretaries of Branches, "Evaluation," December 28, 1995, BRCC 103-1-5 (054, 189), in Sassoon, *Saddam Hussein's Ba'th Party*, 263.

103. See Sassoon, *Saddam Hussein's Ba'th Party*, 261–62.

104. Party Secretariat to the Deputy Secretary of the Party, April 10, 1996, BRCC 119-4-8 (254), in Sassoon, *Saddam Hussein's Ba'th Party*, 261.

105. Salah al-Din branch to Party Secretariat, November 18, 1998, BRCC 093-4-4 (024-026) in Sassoon, *Saddam Hussein's Ba'th Party*, 262.

106. SSO to Presidential Diwan, April 2, 1996, BRCC, B 001-2-1 (180-181), in Sassoon, *Saddam Hussein's Ba'th Party*, 262.

107. See, for example, report from January 28, 2000, by the Ba'th Bureau of the North, CRRC SH-BATH-D-000-066; From *Tanzimat Muhafazat* Ninneweh, Duhuk, and Irbil, to *Imanat Sirr al-Qutr*, January 27, 2000, CRRC SH-BATH-D-000-144. See also Hoover Institution Archive, Stanford, California, an uncatalogued report from July 22, 1995, directed to a "secretary of a branch" (*amin sir qiyadat far'*) regarding "men of religion with religious-Salafi, Wahhabi, MB [Muslim Brotherhood] inclinations" (*ittijahat diniyya salafiyya, wahhabiyya, ikhwan muslimun*).

108. *Al-'Iraq*, September 2, 1991; *Babil*, October 6, 1991; *al-Qadisiyya*, January 20, 1992; *al-Thawra*, February 23, 1992; *al-Qadisiyya*, March 1, 1992; *al-Thawra*, July 1, 1992; *al-Thawra*, April 15, 1992, on opening of three new gates in the Friday Mosque of Sadiq al-Sadr in Kufa; *Babil*, October 14, 1993; *al-Qadisiyya*, May 19, 1994. See also a report of a visit to Karbala by John Lancaster, *Washington Post*, February 16, 1995; *Alif Ba*, March 6, 1996, 7; *al-Qadisiyya*, December 23, 1996, and more.

109. For example, *al-'Iraq*, September 16, 1993; *al-Thawra*, February 18, 1994; *al-Jumhuriyya*, March 30, 1994.

110. Saddam Party Branch to Party Secretariat, November 6, 13, 1998, BRCC 093-4-4 (077-079), in Sassoon, *Saddam Hussein's Ba'th Party*, 262.

111. Muhammad Sadiq al-Sadr, *Fiqh al-'Asha'ir: Hiwar Fatawa'i Ma'a Marja' al-Muslimim Za'im al-Hawza al-'Ilmiyya Samahat Ayat Allah al-'Uzma al-Sayyid Muhammad al-Sadr* [The tribes' jurisprudence: A religious edicts debate with the source of the Muslims' leader of the religious university, Grand Ayatollah M. (M. Sadiq) al-Sadr], (Beirut: Dar al-Najwa, 1997).

112. Party Secretariat to all Branch Secretaries, October 8, 1998, BRCC 093-4-4 (001), in Sassoon, *Saddam Hussein's Ba'th Party*, 262.

113. See, for example, a government appointee-made-Grand Ayatollah, 'Abd al-Karim Aal 'Ali Khan al-Madani, and his son, *al-Thawra*, May 5, 1991.

114. International Crisis Group, "Iraq's Shi'ites under Occupation," Middle East Briefing 8 (Baghdad and Brussels: International Crisis Group, September 9, 2003), 5.

115. Reuters, July 22, 1994; IRNA (in English from Tehran), July 22, 1994.

116. *Mid-East Mirror*, June 22, 1998; *al-Watan al-'Arabi*, July 3, 1998, in FBIS-NES-DR JN0607192298, July 6, 1998.

117. *Al-Jumhuriyya*, February 27, 1999, in FBIS-NES-DR, March 2, 1999. And see below.

118. Abbas Kadhim, "The Regime and 'The Vocal Hawza': Ba'th Party Communication on Al-Sadr's Friday Prayers at the Kufa Mosque (1998–1999)," in his "The Hawza under Siege: A Study in the Ba'th Party Archive," Occasional Paper 1 (Boston: Boston University Institute for Iraqi Studies, June 2013), 36–51, and see Appendix II, p. 67.

119. See Isma'il al-Wa'ili, ed., *Dustur [Muhammad Muhammad Sadiq] al-Sadr* [Al-Sadr's Constitution] (Najaf: Mu'assasat Baqiyyat Allah linashr al-'Ulum al-Islamiyya, Maktabat Dar al-Mujtaba, 2004 CE/1434 H).

120. For example, an interview with Bayan Jabr, member of the Central Council of SCIRI in Syria and Lebanon, *al-Hadath*, March 1, 1999, in FBIS-NES-DR, March 1, 1999. The content of some of Sadr's sermons and Hakim's attack were reported to me by Iraqi Shi'is in the United States in 1999 and 2003–2004. See also a good report of the rivalry between Sadr, on the one hand, and the Hakims, Kho'i, and Sistani on the other in Patrick Cockburn, *Muqtada al-Sadr and the Battle for the Future of Iraq* (New York: Scribner, 2008), 96–99.

121. Cockburn, *Muqtada al-Sadr*, 109, and reports by Shi'i interviewees, Washington, D.C., 1999, 2004.

122. For details. see Amatzia Baram, "Sadr the Father, Sadr the Son, the 'Revolution in Shi'ism' and the Struggle for Power in the *Hawzah* of Najaf," in *Iraq between Occupations: Perspectives from 1920 to the Present*, ed. Amatzia Baram, Achim Rohde, and Ronen Zeidel (New York: Palgrave Macmillan, 2010); Cockburn, *Muqtada al-Sadr*, 119–37.

123. *Al-Jumhuriyya*, February 27, 1999, in FBIS-NES-DR, March 2, 1999.

124. Kadhim, "The Hawza under Siege," 43.

125. Baram, "Sadr the Father, Sadr the Son"; Kadhim, "The Hawza under Siege," 46.

126. Kadhim, "The Hawza under Siege," 36–51.

127. See Baram, "Sadr the Father, Sadr the Son," 143–58.

128. Ibid. In a conversation with an Iraqi general who had served under Saddam and whose close friend was in a senior position in Saddam's *mukhabarat* (intelligence services), the general reported that the *mukhabarat* official had sworn to him that the assassination came as a shock to Iraqi intelligence (interview, Washington, D.C., July 2011).

129. Kadhim, "The Hawza under Siege," 44.

130. Najaf Branch Command to the Superintendent of the Najaf, Qadisiyya, and Muthanna Organization, "Friday Prayer" (No. 12/530 on February 8, 1999), in Kadhim, "The Hawza under Siege," 49–50.

131. Baram, "Sadr the Father, Sadr the Son"; Kadhim, "The Hawza under Siege,"48–50.

132. For example, Mir Basri, *A'lam al-Adab fi al-'Iraq al-Hadith* [Eminent men of letters in modern Iraq], 3 vols. (London: Dar al-Hikma, 1994–1999), vol. 2, mainly 339–40, 346; Yunis Ibrahim al-Samarra'i, *Ta'rikh 'Ulama Baghdad* (Baghdad: Ministry of Endowments, 1982), mainly 102–6, 544–45, 686–87.

133. United Nations, Commission on Human Rights, "Report on the Situation of Human Rights in Iraq," April 14, Submitted by the Special Rapporteur, Mr. Max van der Stoel, in accordance with Commission Resolution 1998/65, March 10, 1998 (United Nations, Economic and Social Council, New York, 55th Session, Item 9, June 4, 1999), 8.

134. Ibid., 5–7.

135. *Al-Hayat* (Internet version, in Arabic), May 16, 1999, in FBIS-NES-DR JN1505085999, May 15, 1999. Interview with a senior official at the State Department, Washington, D.C., May 11, 1999; Cockburn, *Muqtada al-Sadr*, 107. For more reports of antigovernment acts, see, for example, John Donnelly and Barbara Demick, "US Targets Already-Shaky Power Base," *San Jose Mercury News*, December 18, 1998; *al-Bilad*, Jeddah, February 22, 1999, in FBIS-NES-DR, February 26, 1999; *al-Sharq al-Awsat*, February 26, 1999, in FBIS-NES-DR; reports of wide-scale arrests of mosque preachers, Sadr's "agents," and a number of students and other clergy following demonstrations and disturbances; *al-Hayat* (Internet version, in Arabic), May 16, 1999, in FBIS-NES-DR JN1605120299, May 15, 1999.

136. CRRC SH-RVCC-D-000-610, February 19, 1992.

137. This happened at least in 2001, as reported to the author by Iraqi Shi'is who visited the United States after the 2003 war (interviews in Washington, D.C., October 2003).

138. Party Secretariat to heads of *tanzimat*, "Religious Occasions," March 12, 2000, BRCC, 004-4-3(032-033); Party Secretariat to Ali Hasan al-Majid, "Negative Phenomenon," February 22, 2000, BRCC, 004-4-3 (209-212), in Sassoon, *Saddam Hussein's Ba'th Party*, 263–64. Party Secretariat to all heads of *tanzimat*, March 29, 1997, BRCC 003-4-4 (470-472), in Sassoon, *The Iraqi Ba'th Party*, 264.

139. Lajna fi Wizarat al-Tarbiya [Committee of the Ministry of Education], *Al-Qur'an al-Karim: Tilawatuhu wa Ma'anihi lil Saff al-Awwal al-Ibtida'i, min Awwal Sura, wal Dhuha, ila Aakhir Sura, al-Nas* [The Blessed Qur'an, its reciting and meanings for the first grade primary school, from the first *sura* . . . to the last *sura* . . .] (Baghdad: Ministry of Education, 1995), 3–5.

140. Ibid., 10–47.

141. Lajna fi Wizarat al-Tarbiya [Committee of the Ministry of Education], *Al-Qur'an al-Karim: Tilawatuhu wa Ma'anihi lil Saff al-Thani al-Ibtida'i, min Awwal Sura, al-Naba, ila Aakhir Sura, al-Layl* [The Blessed Qur'an, its reciting and meanings for the second grade primary school, from the first *sura* . . . to the last *sura* . . .], 5th ed. (Baghdad: Ministry of Education, 1995).

142. Lajna Mukhtassa fi Wizarat al-Tarbiya [Special Committee of the Ministry of Education], *Al-Qur'an al-Karim: Tilawatuhu wa Ma'anihi lil Saff al-Rabi' al-Ibtida'i, min Awwal*

Surat al-Mujadala, ila Aakhir Surat al-Tahrim [The Blessed Qur'an, its reciting and meanings for the fourth grade primary school, from the first *sura* . . . to the last *sura* . . .],7th ed. (Baghdad: Ministry of Education; Jordan: Matba'at al-Nur, 1998). The first edition was printed in 1992.

143. Wizarat al-Tarbiya [Ministry of Education], *Al-Tarbiya al-Islamiyya lil-Saff al-Awwal al-Ibtida'i* [Islamic education for the first grade, primary school], 11th ed. (Baghdad: Ministry of Education; Jordan: Matba'at al-Nur, 2001).

144. Ibid.

145. For example, for the first grade, 'Abd al-Jabbar 'Abd Allah al-Alusi and Rafi' As'ad 'Abd al-Halim, *Al-Tarbiya al-Islamiyya lil-Saff al-Awwal al-Ibtida'i* [Islamic education for the first grade, primary school], 12th ed. (Baghdad: Ministry of Education, 2002), 39–44; for the second grade, 'Abd al-Hakim al-Sa'di, *Al-Tarbiya al-Islamiyya lil-Saff al-Thani al-Ibtida'I* [Islamic education for the second grade, primary school] (Baghdad: Ministry of Education, 2003), 47–50.

146. See, for example, Muhammad Ridha 'Abd al-Jabbar and Idris Mustafa 'Aziz, *Al-Tarbiya al-Islamiyya lil-Saff al-Thalith al-Ibtida'i* [Islamic education for the third grade, primary school],11th ed. (Baghdad: Ministry of Education, Ibn Khaldun Press, 2002), 23, 49, 74, 99; 'Abd al-Hakim al-Sa'di and Ahzan Yasin al-Duri, *Al-Tarbiya al-Islamiyya lil-Saff al-Thani al-Ibtida'i*, 6th ed. [Islamic education for the second grade, primary school], 6th ed. (Baghdad: Ministry of Education, 1996), 24, 59, 68.

147. Ahmad 'Ali al-Khatib et al., *Al-Tarbiya al-Islamiyya lil Saff al-Khamis al-Ibtida'i* [Islamic education for the fifth grade, primary school], 23rd ed. (Baghdad: Ministry of Education, 2001), 44.

148. Ibid, 46–50.

149. Hasan Fadhil Zu'ayn, 'Abd al-Rahman 'Abd al-Karim al-'Anni, and 'Abd al Amir 'Abd Daksan, *Al-Ta'rikh al-'Arabi al-Islami lil-Saff al-Khamis al-Ibtida'i* [Arab-Islamic history for the fifth grade, primary school], 16th ed. (Baghdad: Ministry of Education, 2003), 25–45; Hasan Fadhil Zu'ayn, 'Abd al-Rahman 'Abd al-Karim al-'Anni, et al., *Al-Ta'rikh al-'Arabi al-Islami lil-Saff al-al-Thani al-Mutawassat* [Arab-Islamic history for the second grade, intermediate school], 13th ed. (Baghdad: Ministry of Education, 2002), 48–49.

150. Zu'ayn et al., *Al-Ta'rikh al-'Arabi al-Islami lil-Saff al-Thani al-Mutawassat*, 74–84.

151. Sati' al-Husri, *Mudhakkirati fi al-'Iraq al-Juz' al-Awwal: Part 1, 1921–1927* [My memoirs in Iraq: Part 1, 1921–1927], 1st ed. (Beirut: Dar al-Tali'a, 1967), 323–26.

152. Hasan Fadhil Zu'ayn, 'Abd al-Rahman 'Abd al-Karim al-'Anni, and 'Abd al-Amir 'Abd Daksan, *Al-Ta'rikh al-'Arabi al-Islami lil-Saff al-Khamis al-Ibtida'i* [Arab-Islamic history for the fifth grade, primary school], 24th ed. (Baghdad: Republic of Iraq, Ministry of Education, 2011).

153. Ibid., 21.

154. Ibid, 39.

155. Ibid., 34–36.

156. See a full reproduction of his last message to the Shi'i masses of Iraq, *al-Da'wa Chronicle* no. 3, July 1980, 2.

157. Ibid., 48.

158. Ibid., 48–53.

159. Ibid., 56ff. For a similar approach, see Hasan Fadhil Zu'ayn, 'Abd al-Rahman 'Abd al-Karim al-'Anni, and 'Abd al-Amir 'Abd Daksan, *Al-Ta'rikh al-'Arabi al-Islami lil-Saff*

al-Thani al-Mutawassat [Arab-Islamic history for the second grade, intermediate school], 23rd ed. (Baghdad: Republic of Iraq, Ministry of Education), 21, 31, 41–47, 65–67, 68ff.

160. ʿImad ʿAbd al-Salam Raʾuf, Nuri ʿAbd al-Hamid Khalil, Tariq Nafiʿal-Hamdani, and ʿAbd al-Sattar ʿAbd al-Wahid ʿAli, *Al-Taʾrikh al-Hadith wal-Muʿasir lil-Watan al-ʿArabi lil-Saff al-Sadis al-Ibtidaʾi* [Modern and contemporary history of the Arab homeland for the sixth primary grade], 22nd ed. (Baghdad: Republic of Iraq, Ministry of Education, 2011), 7.

161. See, for example, *al-Thawra*, May 5, 1991; February 27, 1992; *Babil*, July 11, 1992; *al-Jumhuriyya*, November 24, 1992.

162. Republic of Iraq Radio Network in Arabic, June 5, 1994, in FBIS-JN0406194294, June 4, 1994.

163. *Al-Jumhuriyya*, June 7, 1994.

164. *Al-Thawra*, June 9, 1994, in FBIS-SERIAL JN1606101994, June 16, 1994.

165. *Al-Yom al-Sabiʿ*, reporting on internal discussions at the top of the party leadership, January 29, 1990.

166. *Babil*, July 19, 1994.

167. Ibid.

168. *Babil*, June 12, 1994, 12, in FBIS-NES-DR JN1606122494, June 16, 1994.

169. Ibid.

170. ʿAbd al-Jabbar Muhsin, "Lies and Hypocrisy," *Babil*, July 6, 1994, FBIS-SERIAL JN1307102694, July 7, 1994.

171. Interview, Washington, D.C., June 1994. And for the closure of ʿUday's radio and TV stations in late December 1993 or early January 1994, and their reopening on January 10 in response to "public demand," see *al-Thawra, al-Jumhuriyya*, January 8, 1994; Baghdad Republic of Iraq Radio in Arabic, January 10, 1994, in FBIS-NES, January 14, 1994, 34.

172. Pierre Darle, *Saddam Hussein . . . Maître des mots: Du langage de la tyrannie à la tyrannie du langage* (Paris: L'Harmattan, 2003), 56–66, as quoted in Rohde, *State-Society Relations in Baʿthist Iraq*, 117–18.

173. CRRC SH-PDWN-D-000-409, April 21, 2002, 21.

174. See a Jordanian family invited by the Ministry of Endowments who took part in the eighth class of Qurʾan reciting (*hafz al-Qurʾan*), *al-ʿIraq*, December 3, 1998. The course took place in the Shiʿi south.

175. Gehad Auda, "An Uncertain Response: The Islamic Movement in Egypt," in *Islamic Fundamentalisms and the Gulf Crisis*, ed. James Piscatori (Chicago: American Academy of Arts and Sciences with the Fundamentalism Project, 1991), 118.

176. For 1990–91, see a good survey in Piscatori, *Islamic Fundamentalisms and the Gulf Crisis*, mainly 1–27, 70–198,155–85. Iraq had no meaningful success among the Shiʿa; ibid., 28–51, 52–69.

177. *Al-Thawra*, September 29, 1999, in FBIS-NEW-DR, October 11, 1999.

Chapter 7

1. *Al-Thawra*, December 11, 1992.

2. *Al-Thawra, al-Jumhuriyya*, August 9, 1994.

3. Amatzia Baram, "Who Are the Insurgents? Sunni-Arab Rebels in Iraq," Special Report (Washington, DC: US Institute of Peace, April 2005), 15–16.

4. Mulla Muhammad Omar (or 'Umar), the spiritual leader of the Taliban, was Afghanistan's de facto eleventh head of state, from 1996 to late 2001, with the official title "Head of the Supreme Council." He held the title Commander of the Faithful (*Amir al-Mu'minin*) of the Islamic Emirate of Afghanistan, which was recognized by only three nations: Pakistan, Saudi Arabia, and the United Arab Emirates.

5. CRRC SH-PDWN-D-000-509, January 9, 2001.

6. CRRC SH-PDWN-D-000-012, January 23, 2003. Top-secret communiqué no. 549, from the Presidential Office.

7. *Al-Da'wa Chronicle* no. 3, July 1980, 2.

8. The book came out in print for the first time in 1982. For a recent Internet version in English, see *Iqtisaduna—Our Economics* (Tehran: World Organization for Islamic Services, March 10, 2012), http://www.hajij.com/library/component/k2/item/187-iqtisaduna-our -economics.

9. CRRC SH-PDWN-D-000-855, mid-January, 2002.

10. Internet interview with Steve Negus in Cairo, November 18, 2012. The same approach remained until July 3, 2013, when Mursi was toppled.

11. "Saddam Addresses al-Ta'mim Delegation," Baghdad Republic of Iraq Radio–First Program Network in Arabic, September 25, 1991, in FBIS-NES, October 1, 1991, 17.

12. *Baghdad Observer*, July 10, 1994.

13. In the Qur'an, the punishment for immoral sexual conduct (*al-fahisha*) is "detention" for life at home (*Sura* 4, *Aaya*s 15–26) or, in a later version, for unlawful sexual intercourse (*al-zina*) such as prostitution, 100 lashes (*Sura* 24, *Aaya*s 2–4). In the Hadith, the punishment is stoning. On adultery and prostitution, see R. Peters, "Zina," in *Encyclopaedia of Islam* 2, 11:509–10.

14. *Al-'Iraq*, December 6, 1996, 5.

15. CRRC PDWN-D-000-409, 21, a meeting with a Sudanese cabinet minister sometime between April 27 and May 7, 2000.

16. Email communication from a major general in Saddam's army, at the time in Washington, D.C., to me in Haifa, Israel, July 19, 2012.

17. Achim Rohde, *State-Society Relations in Ba'thist Iraq: Facing Dictatorship* (Abingdon, UK: Routledge, 2010), 105.

18. Between the academic years 1983–84 and 2001–2, the representation of women among academic teaching staff increased from 22.1 percent to 34.1 percent. Teaching staff in secondary schools, too, became more feminized, rising from 54.8 percent in 1992–93 to 61.3 percent in 2000–1. The representation of women among primary school teachers remained stable throughout the 1990s at around 71–73 percent. See Rohde, *State-Society Relations in Ba'thist Iraq*, 102.

19. Ibid., 199n215. For female judges and barristers, see *Alif Ba*, July 13, August 23, 2000.

20. *Al-Thawra*, March 3, 1997. As reported in Rohde, *State-Society Relations in Ba'thist Iraq*, 104.

21. Her latest photograph appears on the red five of hearts card of the American military's most-wanted cards packet.

22. Rohde, *State-Society Relations in Ba'thist Iraq*, 76.

23. Interviews in Washington, D.C., 1989–90, 1994–95, 1997–99, 2002.

24. For example, *Alif Ba*, April 14, 21, 28, 1993; June 21, 1995, as reported in Rohde, *State-Society Relations in Ba'thist Iraq*, 115–16; and interviews.

25. *Babil*, January 13, 1994, reproduced in Rohde, *State-Society Relations in Ba'thist Iraq*, 116–17.

26. CRRC SH-SHTP-A-000-891.

27. See, for example, *al-Jumhuriyya*, May 22, 1979.

28. Qirar 632, *al-Waqa'i' al-'Iraqiyya* 2832, 508–9.

29. "Saddam Husayn Addresses Iraqi Women," *al-Jumhuriyya*, May 4, 1986, in BBC, May 8, 1986, E1. See also a call to women to produce children as part of the Iraqi war effort, *Alif Ba*, August 3, 1988, 58; *al-Thawra*, January 14, 1988; official encouragement to marry young, by helping with the payment of dowry by men under age twenty-two, *al-Thawra*, December 17, 1987; and an attempt to convince fathers not to demand high dowry for their daughters, *al-Thawra*, October 14, 1988.

30. *Al-Thawra*, October 27, 1987.

31. See a debate among professionals that preceded the fertility campaign, discussing the country's ability to absorb a wave of new births, headed by RCC member and head of the Council for the Study of Demographic Increase Dr. Sa'dun Hammadi, *al-Thawra*, May 12, 1987. See also *al-Jumhuriyya*, May 13, 1987; *al-Jumhuriyya*, January 23, 1988; *al-Thawra*, February 28, 1988; *Alif Ba*, April 12, 1988.

32. *Al-Jumhuriyya*, May 16, 1994.

33. *Al-Thawra*, July 5, 1993.

34. *Al-Thawra*, November 21, 1993.

35. *Al-Thawra*, June 10, 1994.

36. *Al-Thawra*, January 16, 1994.

37. *Al-Qadisiyya*, June 3, 1993.

38. *Al-'Iraq*, February 18, 1994; *al-Qadisiyya*, February 22, 1994.

39. *Al-Thawra*, January 26, 1994.

40. *Al-'Iraq*, December 10, 1993. See also the annual conference of the association, in which no fewer than 450 male and female doctors participated, *Babil*, February 27, 1994.

41. Amatzia Baram, "The Effect of Iraqi Sanctions, Statistical Pitfalls and Responsibility," *Middle East Journal* 54, no. 2 (2000): 194–223.

42. CRRC PDWN-D-000-507, 46, January 9, 2001.

43. Baghdad Iraq TV Network in Arabic, August 8, 1999, in FBIS-NES JN0808133799, August 8, 1999.

44. Ibid.

45. *Al-Thawra*, September 9, 1992.

46. *Al-'Iraq*, August 31, 1993.

47. *Al-Jumhuriyya*, July 1, 1993. See also a poem by Abd al-Razzaq 'Abd al-Wahid, "O Great Iraq" ("Ya 'Iraq al-Kubar"), *al-Qadisiyya*, January 18, 1994; a poem by Kazim Nasir al-Sa'di, "The Love of Iraq" ("Hubb al-'Iraq"), *al-'Iraq*, January 17, 1994; a musical produced by *al-Ashbal* (the Lions' Cubs) school in Baghdad inspired by the Prophet's message, Arab values, and the civilizations of Mesopotamia, *al-Qadisiyya*, January 17, 1994; and a poem by Majid al-Shara', "The Sun of Iraq" ("Shams al-'Iraq"), in *Babil*, June 6, 1994.

48. *Babil*, December 23, 1993.

49. CRRC SHTP-D-000-757, 1993.

50. Baghdad Republic of Iraq Radio Network in Arabic, July 17, 1994, FBIS-Serial JUN1707094594, July 19, 1994. For a pre-Islamic-faith-campaign drawing by Wisam Murkus of Saddam on his birthday as the reincarnation of Tammuz, see *al-Thawra*, April 28, 1986.

51. Louis Massignon, *The Passion of al-Hallaj: Mystic and Martyr of Islam* (Princeton, NJ: Princeton University Press, 1994). This is an abridged edition.

52. Itzchak Weismann, *Taste of Modernity: Sufism, Salafiyya, and Arabism in Late Ottoman Damascus* (Boston: Brill, 2001), 23.

53. *Al-Hayat*, Internet version, April 19, 2004.

54. *Al-Hayat*, Internet version, April 19, 2004.

55. *Al-Jumhuriyya*, January 19, 1993.

56. D. S. Margoliouth, "Naqshbandiyya," in *Encyclopaedia of Islam*, New Edition (1971), 4:382.

57. Ibid., 4:382; Weismann, *Taste of Modernity*, 26–31.

58. Helkot Hakim, "The Origins of the Naqshbandiyya Order," in *Ayatollahs, Sufis and Ideologues*, ed. Faleh A. Jabar (London: Saqi Books, 2002), 143.

59. Weismann, *Taste of Modernity*, 53–54, 75–80.

60. Martin van Bruinessen, "The Kurds and Islam," Working Paper 13, Islamic Area Studies Project, Tokyo, 1999.

61. *Al-Hayat* (London), February 2, 2000, FBIS FTS20000203000649, February 3, 2000.

62. Tarik Hamdi al-Azami, "The Emergence of Contemporary Islamic Revival in Iraq," *Middle East Affairs Journal* 3 (1997): 126.

63. Syed Saleem Shahzad, "Bin Laden Gives Iraq an Unlikely Unity," *Asia Times Online*, February 28, 2003, www.atimes.com.

64. Jean-Pierre Tuquoi, "Le soufisme, mystique de l'islam, reste vivace en Irak," *Le Monde*, June 14, 1996.

65. *Al-Quds al-'Arabi* (London), February 4, 2004, FBIS GMP 2004020000117; Shahzad, "Bin Laden Gives Iraq an Unlikely Unity."

66. According to one of their leaders, 'Izzat Ibrahim's entire family belonged to the Kasnazaniyya. His uncle was one of its Guides (*murshidin*), and he himself joined before the Ba'th came to power. The order was established by 'Abd al-Karim al-Kasnazani, and its leader in 2007 was Shaykh Muhammad al-Kasnazani. The interviewee defined his order as "a spiritual rather than a political system," but after 2003 they established a political party, Hizb al-Tajammu' al-Watani al-'Iraqi. See Nehru al-Kasnazani in *al-'Arab al-Yawm*, July 20, 2007.

67. See, for example, a congratulatory letter addressed to Saddam from Shaykh Muhammad 'Abd al-Karim al-Kasnazani al-Husayni, the head of the Kasnazaniyya Qadiriyya in the world, *al-'Iraq*, August 31, 1993.

68. "Muslims, Islam and Iraq," website maintained by Alan Godlas, University of Georgia.

69. See, for example, Saddam's decision to send his senior bodyguard, Arshad Yasin, to the funeral of the wife of the order's sheikh, 'Abd al-Karim, who was buried in Kirkuk, *al-Thawra*, September 7, 1992.

70. *Al-Jumhuriyya*, January 10, 1993.

71. *Al-Thawra*, May 30, 1993.

72. *Al-Jumhuriyya*, January 16, 1993.

73. *Al-Jumhuriyya*, January 19, 1993; see also a report about a master's thesis dealing with al-Imam al-Rifaʿi, the founder of the order, *al-ʿIraq*, December 15, 1995. The journalist ʿAbd al-ʿAziz al-Rawi points out that "our generation and the next ones are in dire need of such studies." And for a series of lectures on Sufism planned by Saddam University for Islamic Studies, see *al-Thawra*, March 31, 1993.

74. ʿIzzat Ibrahim was made a four-star general, even though he had never served in the armed forces.

75. Baghdad Republic of Iraq Television in Arabic, March 13, 2002, FBIS GMP20020313000223.

76. Report on Friday Sermons, Baghdad Radio in Arabic, August 30, 2002, FBIS GMP 20020901000033.

77. Sayed Saleem Shahzad, "The Saddam Branch of Islam," *Asia Times Online*, February 8, 2003, ; Shahzad, "Bin Laden Gives Iraq an Unlikely Unity."

78. *Times* (London), April 24, 2003.

79. *Guardian*, October 31, 2003; Baghdad Al-Yawm al-Akhar in Arabic, November 3, 2003, FBIS GMP 20031104000257.

80. A closed-door talk given by a very senior Qadiri Sufi shaykh, Washington, D.C., February 2004.

81. For example, a murderous attack on a Rifaʿi *takiya* in Baghdad, Ashraf Khalil, "ʿIraq's Sufi Community Shaken by Deadly Attack," *Los Angeles Times*, June 5, 2005; Lydia Khalil, "New Sufi Group Joins the Iraqi Insurgency," *Jamestown Foundation* 4, no. 2 (February 20, 2007), on attacks by the precursor to Abu Musʿab al-Zarqawi's group, Ansar al-Islam, on Sufi shrines and tombs of the Naqshbandi order in Kurdistan.

82. Khalil, "New Sufi Group Joins the Iraqi Insurgency." See also http://www.islammemo.com/cc, December 30, 2006; and http://www.iraqoftomorrow.org/index/72305.htm, September 19, 2009.

83. See, for example, *Gulf Times*, April 25, 2013; telephone interview with a foreign correspondent in Huweija, April 24, 2013.

84. *Al-Thawra*, *al-Jumhuriyya*, February 19, 1992.

85. For a seminal study of sectarianism and sectarian identity in Iraq from 1997 to 2007, see Fanar Haddad, *Sectarianism in Iraq: Antagonistic Visions of Unity* (London: Hurst; New York: Columbia University Press, 2011). It is based not only on written sources but on field interviews with Iraqis. Haddad examines the intricate relations between sectarian identity and national Iraqi identity and sectarianism and state, and suggests some patterns of sectarian activity in Iraq: passive, assertive, and banal. He also examines the construction of the memory and heritage of the Shiʿite Intifada of 1991 into contemporary Iraqi Shiʿite historiography and identity. Another noteworthy book that deals with similar issues through the 1920 revolt is Harith al-Qarawee, *Imagining the Nation* (New York: Rossendale Books, 2012).

86. Barzan's diary, last entry, dated October 21, 2000, CRRC SH-MISC-D-000-950, 4 (p. 65 in the original diary).

87. Hadid blew up his town's cinema in the mid-1990s for showing Western and Egyptian "promiscuous" films. Unwilling to look un-Islamic, the regime did not rebuild the

cinema. He killed a Baʻthi official there, was sentenced to death, and fled Iraq. Returning in 2003, he later joined Abu Musʻab al-Zarqawi's Salafi terrorist group. More detailed information may be found in Baram, "Who Are the Insurgents?," 12–13. Hadid was killed in the battle of Falluja, Operation Phantom Fury, in December 2004.

88. See report of a series of discussions with "Abu Dhiʼb" by Ghaith Abdul-Ahd, *Washington Post*, October 27, 2005, A1, A10.

89. Joseph Sassoon, *Saddam Hussein's Baʻth Party: Inside an Authoritarian Regime* (Cambridge, Cambridge University Press, 2012), 260–61. Emphasis added.

90. As was shown above, there is information confirming this fact in the open sources, and Sassoon (ibid., 260–64) provides more such information from classified Baʻth documents.

91. CRRC SH-SPPC-D-000-217, July 18, 1991.

92. Sassoon, *Saddam Hussein's Baʻth Party*, 3. Emphasis added.

93. Ibid., 260–64. Emphasis added.

94. The *Shahada* (Evidence) that there is only one God and Muhammad is His Messenger; prayer; alms (*al-zakat*); fasting (*al-som*) during Ramadan; and going on pilgrimage (*al-haj*).

95. Dale F. Eickelman, *The Middle East: An Anthropological Approach*, 2nd ed. (New York: Prentice Hall, 2002), 262–66; see also 267–83.

96. An interview with a Western ambassador to Baghdad, who met with Saddam twice and reported that in 1988 he stopped the meeting to pray the noon prayer (*al-zuhr*). Whether or not he did this as mere show, he wanted people to know that he was praying; beginning in the early 1980s his praying image often appeared in the press.

97. Other punishments in this class include penalties for illicit sexual activity, consumption of alcoholic drinks, and apostasy.

98. See Gabriel R. Warburg, "Islam and State in Numayri's Sudan," *Africa* 55, no. 4 (1985), 400–13, especially 407, 409–10. In Sudan, Numayri banned alcoholic drinks altogether and imposed the Islamic *hudud*.

99. See the picture of the monument in Amatzia Baram, *Culture, History and Ideology in the Formation of Baʻthist Iraq: 1968–1989* (London: Palgrave Macmillan; New York: St. Martin's Press, 1991), plate 13.

100. *Ettelaʻat*, January 7, 1988; *Keyhan*, January 10, 1988, as reproduced in Meir Litvak, "The Rule of the Jurist (*Velayat-e-Faqih*) in Iran: Ideal and Implementation" [in Hebrew], *Ha Mizrah He Hadash* 42 (2001), 171.

101. James P. Piscatori, *Islam in a World of Nation States* (Cambridge: Cambridge University Press, 1986), 4–9; Bernard Lewis, *Islam in History: Ideas, People, and Events in the Middle East* (Chicago: Open Court, 1993), 263–64.

102. For example, CRRC SH-BATH-D-000-474, probably 2002.

103. Joseph Sassoon, "The Iraqi Baʻth Party Preparatory School and the 'Cultural' Courses of the Branches," *Middle Eastern Studies* 50, no. 1 (January 2014): 27–42.

104. Sassoon, "The Iraqi Baʻth Party Preparatory School", 30.

105. Calculated from Sassoon, *Saddam Hussein's Baʻth Party*, 52.

106. See (as noted in chapter 4) attacks on his suggestion to end the struggle against the Muslim Brotherhood, CRRC SH-SHTP-A-001-167, July 24, 1986.

107. Ahmed S. Hashim, *Iraq's Sunni Insurgency* (London and Abingdon, The International Institute for Strategic Studies, Adelphi Paper 402, 2009), 27–29.

108. Amatzia Baram, *Who Are the Insurgents? Sunni Arab Rebels in Iraq*, 4.

109. For an early attempt to analyze Saddam "at a distance," see Jerrold M. Post and Amatzia Baram, *Saddam Is Iraq: Iraq Is Saddam*, Counterproliferation Papers, Future Warfare Series 17, USAF Counterproliferation Center, Maxwell Air Force Base, AL, 2002, http://www.au.af.mil/au/awc/awcgate/cpc-pubs/postbaram.pdf. For relevant theoretical sources for the study of leaders' personalities "at a distance" through qualitative and quantitative methods, see, for example, Timothy A. Judge, Joyce E. Bono, and Remus Ilies, "Personality and Leadership: A Qualitative and Quantitative Review," *Journal of Applied Psychology* 87 (2002): 765–80; Ofer Feldman and Linda O. Valenty, eds., *Profiling Political Leaders: Cross-cultural Studies of Personality and Behavior* (Westport, CT: Praeger, 2001); Linda O. Valenty and Ofer Feldman, eds., *Political Leadership for the New Century: Personality and Behavior among American Leaders* (Westport, CT: Praeger, 2002); David G. Winter, "Things I've Learned about Personality from Studying Political Leaders at a Distance," *Journal of Personality*, 73, 557–84; Peter Suedfeld, KarenGuttieri, and Philip E. Tetlock, "Assessing Integrative Complexity at a Distance: Archival Analyses of Thinking and Decision Making," in *The Psychological Assessment of Political Leaders: With Profiles of Saddam Hussein and Bill Clinton*, ed. Jerrold Post (Ann Arbor: University of Michigan Press, 2005), 246–70.

110. *Al-ʿIraq*, December 3, 1999, 1.

111. See, for example, a comparison of Saddam to Salah al-Din in internal party documents, CRRC PDWN-D-000-724, January 12, 1995.

112. "Saddam Delivers a Message on Christmas, New Year," INA in Arabic, December 31, 1990, in FBIS-NES, January 3, 1991, 22.

113. *Al-Thawra*, October 22, 1991. And for similar arguments, see *al-Qadisiyya*, November 12, 1991.

114. See also "Saddam Recommends Releasing German Nationals," Baghdad Domestic Service in Arabic, November 20, 1990, in FBIS-NES, November 20, 1990, 28. And Baghdad Domestic Service in Arabic, January 13, 1991, in FBIS-NES, January 14, 1991, 40.

115. CRRC PDWN-D-000-499, 2002, 24 or 52–54.

116. Kevin M. Woods, Williamson Murray, and Mounir Elkhamri, *Saddam's War: An Iraqi Military Perspective on the Iran-Iraq War*, NDU McNair Paper 70 (Washington, DC: National Defense University, 2009), 17–18.

117. CRRC SH-PDWN-D-000-409, June 26, 2002.

118. "Saddam Addresses Message to Bush, Gorbachev," *INA in Arabic*, September 8, 1990, in FBIS-NES, September 10, 1990, 17–18. For another mention of the story of Abraha, see his call for jihad, Baghdad Domestic Service in Arabic, September 5, 1990, in FBIS-NES-DR, September 6, 1990, 28. See also *al-Jumhuriyya*, September 22, *al-Thawra*, October 9, *al-Qadisiyya*, October 4, 1990.

119. "President, Officials Comment on al-Aqsa Incident," Baghdad Domestic Service in Arabic, October 9, 1990, in FBIS-NES, October 10, 1990, 22–23. For Badr and Abraha, see also Saddam's message to the Iraqis, Arabs, and Muslims, INA in Arabic, February 10, 1991, in FBIS-NES-DR, February 11, 1991, 24.

120. Statement to Iraqi Journalists, INA in Arabic, January 13, 1991, in FBIS-NES, January 14, 1991, 46.

121. Baghdad Domestic Service in Arabic, January 20, 1991, in FBIS-NES, January 22, 1991, 36.

122. "Saddam Delivers Message to Iraqis, Arabs, Muslims," INA in Arabic, February10, 1991, in FBIS-NES, February 11, 1991, 23–24.

123. The speech as reproduced in *al-Thawra*, May 13, 1994.

124. An interview in August 2012 in Europe with a Kuwaiti diplomat, who had received the story from the same assistant on a visit to Tehran.

125. Barzan's diary, last entry, October 21, 2000, CRRC SH-MISC-D-000-950, 4 (65 in the original diary).

126. CRRC SH-PDWN-D-000-642, 25.

127. CRRC RVCC-D-000-315, June 28, 2002.

128. CRRC SH-PDWN-D-000-801, esp. 5-11. See also Saddam's speech for the twelfth anniversary of the Mother of All Battles, January 17, 2002, CRRC SH-PDWN-D-000-855.

129. "Iraq US-Saddam-Speech Second Lead," Agence France-Presse, January 17, 2003, combined with my scribbled notation of the recording of the speech made available to me later.

130. Yevgeny Primakov, *Russia and the Arabs: Behind the Scenes in the Middle East from the Cold War to the Present*, trans. Paul Gould (New York: Basic Books, 2009), 318.

131. "Saddam Remarks Monday," Federal News Service, March 24, 2003.

132. Saddam's communiqué to the troops, March 29, 2003, CRRC SH-PDWN-D-001-096.

133. CRRC SH-PDWN-D-000-499, 43–44 in the original, 22–24 in the translation.

134. BRCC 01-3199-0002-0013, a similar report on 'ulama with "patriotic" inclinations; and CRRC SH-BATH-D-000-066, on Islamic extremists, report from January 28, 2000, from the Party Organization of Ninneweh, Duhuk, and Irbil to the Regional Leadership.

Conclusion and Postscript

1. Michael Gilsenan, *Recognizing Islam: Religion and Society in the Modern Arab World* (New York: Pantheon Books, 1982), 39, 42.

2. Ibid., 39, 42.

3. Mark Neocleous, *Administering Civil Society: Towards a Theory of State Power* (London: Macmillan, 1996).

4. See, for example, Hani al-Fukayki, *Awkar al-Hazima: Tajribati fi hizb al-Ba'th al-'Iraqi* [The sources of defeat: My experience in the Iraqi Ba'th Party] (London and Cyprus: Riad el Rayyes Books, 1993), 272–73.

5. See his discussion with his generals on recruiting and arming the tribes to seal off the Iran-Iraq border, during which he tells them that his understanding of things tribal is far better than theirs, CRRC SH-RVCC-D-000-610, a meeting on February 29, 1992.

6. Fukayki, *Awkar al-Hazima*, 63.

7. Ibid., 267.

8. For details on a few such local clerics, see Amatzia Baram, "Who Are the Insurgents? Sunni-Arab Rebels in Iraq," Special Report (Washington, DC: US Institute of Peace, April 2005), esp. 14–16.

9. Interview, "Ali," Washington, D.C., January 2004.

10. See, for example, General Najim Abed al-Jabouri and Sterling Jensen, "The Iraqi and AQI Roles in the Sunni Awakening," *PRISM* 2, no. 1 (September 16, 2010): 3–7; Baram, "Who Are the Insurgents?"

11. See 'Ali Tahir al-Hamud, *Al-'Iraq Min Sadmat al-Hawiya ila Sahwat al-Hawiyat* [Iraq, from the tragedy of identity to the awakening of the identities] (Baghdad: Masarat, 2012). Based on a master's thesis, this book by a young and promising Iraqi scholar contains the results of a poll conducted by 'Ali Tahir al-Hamud recently in Shi'i, Sunni, and Kurdish neighborhoods in Baghdad examining views on national identity and on neighboring countries. See also Reidar Visser and Gareth Stansfield, eds., *An Iraq of Its Regions: Cornerstones of a Federal Democracy?* (London: Hurst, 2007), a good collection of articles examining the application of the federal model to the Iraqi reality, including regional identities in Iraq, such as the Basra identity and the Tikriti one, as well as a nonethnic regional model for Iraq.

Appendix

1. This appendix is based on information in Yitzhak Oron, "Mifleget Ha Thiya Ha 'Aravit Ha Sotzialistit" [The Resurrection Arab Socialist Party], *Ha Mizrah He Hadash* 9, no. 4 (1959): 241–63 [in Hebrew]; Ronen Zeidel, *The Iraqi Baath Party 1948–1995: Personal and Organizational Aspects* [in Hebrew] (master's thesis, University of Haifa, 1997), 175–286; John F. Devlin, *The Ba'th Party: A History from Its Origins to 1966* (Stanford, CA: Stanford University and Hoover Institution Press, 1979), 16–22; and Joseph Sassoon, *Saddam Hussein's Ba'th Party: Inside an Authoritarian Regime* (Cambridge: Cambridge University Press, 2012), 45–53. It is also based on the Ba'th internal documents at the Conflict Records Research Center in Washington, D.C., and on interviews conducted between 1981 and 2005 with ex-party members who asked that their names not be mentioned. One interviewee who did not ask for anonymity was Talib al-Shabib (1934–97), the Ba'thi foreign minister in 1963 and an Iraqi ambassador in Europe in the 1970s. In 1976, he defected and became a supporter of Ba'thi Damascus. My interview with him was conducted in New York in July 1994.

2. The translation of the Arabic terms here follows mainly John F. Devlin's *The Ba'th Party*, 16–22.

3. Calculated from Sassoon, *Saddam Hussein's Ba'th Party*, 52.

Glossary

aaya: a Qur'anic verse.

Amn al-'amm, al-: General Security, the oldest internal security body in Iraq, preceding the Ba'th regime.

'Ashura: the tenth day of the month of Muharram, in which the Shi'a commemorate the death of Imam Husayn in 680 CE.

'atabat al-muqaddasa, al-: the Shi'i holy shrines in Najaf, Karbala, Kazimayn, and Samarra.

ayat allah: ayatollah (literally, "a sign of God"); a high-ranking Shi'a clerical title.

bay'a: a pledge of allegiance; an Islamic tradition symbolizing acceptance of the ruler's authority and legitimacy.

dajjal: deceiver; a false messiah (the Islamic equivalent of the Antichrist).

da'wa: summons; call; missionary work; religious propaganda; invocation.

dishdasha: a traditional ankle-length garment worn in Arab countries.

faqih: a religious jurist.

far: branch (plural *furu*); a middle-high administrative Ba'th Party level.

fatwa: a religious edict (plural *fatawa*).

firaq: See *firqa*.

firqa: division (plural *firaq*); a lower-middle administrative Ba'th Party level, second from the bottom (above the *khaliyya*).

furu: See *far*.

Hadith: the body of religious oral traditions eventually put into writing that report the teachings, acts, and sayings of the Islmaic Prophet. The Hadith collections inform Islamic jurisprudence.

Halaqa: circle; a Sufi term for a circle of prayer, also used for the lowest level of Ba'th Party organization during the 1940s and 1950s. See also *khaliya*.

hamla al-imaniyya, al-: Saddam Husayn's faith campaign, introduced in full in June 1993.

hawza al-'ilmiyya, al-: the Shi'i religious university, mainly in Najaf (literally, "the territory of learning" or "the territory of religious knowledge").

hizb: political party.

hizb al-Da'wa al-Islamiyy: the Islamic Da'wa Party, the radical Shi'i Islamist party in Iraq established in 1957.

hudud: the class of punishments (literally, "limits") that are fixed in Islamic law for certain serious crimes against God, which include theft, fornication and adultery, consumption of alcohol, and apostasy.

huriyya: "freedom" or "liberty"; part of the Ba'th Party's trinity slogan.

husayniyya: a small neighborhood Shi'i mosque or congregation hall.

'Id: an Islamic festival (plural *a'yad*), the two most important ones being 'Id al-Fitr, the festival of the end of Ramadan, and 'Id al-Adhha, the festival of the sacrifice.

iftar: the fast-breaking evening meal during the month of Ramadan.

'ilmaniyya, al-: secularism.

imam: the leader of prayer in the mosque.

Imam: one of the twelve historical spiritual and political leaders of the Twelver Shi'a, considered infallible.

Imam Mahdi: the Twelfth Imam who, according to the Shi'i tradition, disappeared in the ninth century CE and is expected to reappear and redeem the Shi'a and humanity. (Also referred to as *al-imam al-mahdi*; *al-imam al-gha'ib*, the Hidden Imam; *imam al-zaman*, the Imam of the Generation, *al-imam al-muntazar*, the Expected Imam.)

Imamiyya: the Twelver Shi'a, the largest branch of Shi'a Islam.

intifada: uprising.

Intifadat Sha'ban: the name used by many of the revolutionaries in the 1991 Shi'i uprising against the Ba'th regime that erupted on 15 Sha'ban, the birthday of the Imam Mahdi. (See also *al-Thawra al-Sh'baniyaa*.)

ishtirakiyya: Ba'th-style socialism.

Ja'fari: See *madhhab*.

Jahiliyya: the era of pre-Islamic civilization, seen in Islamic tradition as a negative time of barbarity and idolatry. Applied mainly to Arabia but also to all pre-Islamic (heathen) cultures.

Jumhuriyya: republic.

khaliya: cell (plural *khalaya*); the lowest administrative Ba'th Party level.

khatib: preacher in a mosque (plural khutaba).

khilafa: caliphate.

al-khulafa al-rashidun: the four Rightly Guided Caliphs, the first four leaders of the early Muslim world after the death of the Prophet.

lajnat (plural *lajan*) *al-tawʿiya al-diniyya*: Baʿthi religious indoctrination committees.

madhhab: a Sunni Islamic school of jurisprudence. There are four such schools in Sunni Islam. (The term "*Jaʿfari*" school may also be used to denote the Shiʿa as the fifth school in order to play down the Sunni-Shiʿi difference.)

Mahdi: the Islamic name for the prophesied redeemer, akin to the Jewish or Christian term "messiah."

madrasa: school, specifically an Islamic religious school.

majus: Maji, adherent of Mazdaism, usually referring (by the Baʿth) to Zoroastrians.

makatib tanzim: See *maktab tanzim*.

maktab tanzim: organization bureau (plural *makatib tanzim*); an administrative Baʿth Party level one step above the *farʿ* (branch) and one step below the Regional Leadership.

marjaʿ: the highest source of religious authority in the Shiʿi community (plural *marajiʿ*).

marjaʿ taqlid: "source of emulation"; the full title of the same highest authority.

marjaʿiyya: the collective body of the highest religious authorities in the Shiʿi community, sometimes used to denote just one person.

muʾayyid: "follower"; the lowest level of Baʿth Party membership.

muhafaza: province.

mujtahid: a senior Shiʻi cleric who is authorized to issue religious edicts based on the primary scriptures.

mukhabarat: intelligence agency; secret police.

murashshah or *murashih*: "candidate"; a middle level of Baʻth Party membership.

Naqshbandiyya: one of the two most important Sufi orders in Iraq.

nasir: "supporter"; the second lowest level of Baʻth Party membership.

nasir mutaqaddim: "advanced supporter"; the third lowest level of Baʻth Party membership.

niya: intention, intent, resolve (plural *nawaya*); in the theological sense, relating to the profound intention in prayer.

Qadiriyya: one of the two most important Sufi orders in Iraq.

Qadisiyyat Saddam: "Saddam's Qadisiyya", one of the titles given to the Iran-Iraq War (1980–88). Another was "The Second Qadisiyya"—Qadisiyya being the place of the crucial 636 CE battle between the Arab-Islamic and Persian-Sassanid armies in the south of today's Iraq. The Muslims' victory opened their way to Persia.

qaʼid, al-: the Leader, the Commander. This title, used to describe Saddam Husayn, is the equivalent of Joseph Stalin's title *vojd ozhd*, meaning the supreme leader of the nation. Saddam was regularly addressed as *"al-raʼis al-qaʼid"* (the President Leader) or *"al-qaʼid al-dhurura al-tʼarikhiyya"* (the Leader the Historical Necessity) and similar titles.

qawmiyya: nationalism; in Baʻthi vernacular, relating to Arab nationalism.

qibla, al-: the direction of Islamic prayer toward Mecca.

qiyada al-qawmiyya, al-: The Pan-Arab Leadership (PAL), the highest Baʻth Party body, in charge of relations with Baʻth branches in all the Arab states. Its role was mostly symbolic. The Syrian Baʻth regime had its own PAL.

qiyada al-qutriyya, al-: The Regional Leadership (RL), the highest Ba'th Party body within Iraq, second in its authority only to the Revolutionary Command Council.

rasul: messenger, often used in the context *rasul allah* (Messenger of God).

risala: message, part of the Ba'th slogan "one Arab nation with an eternal message," inspired by the Message of the Prophet Muhammad.

safhat al-ghadr wal-khiyana: "the Pages of Betrayal and Treason"; the label given by the regime to the 1991 Shi'i uprising.

sayyid: an honorific title (plural *sada*) to denote a male descended from the line of the Prophet Muhammad.

sha'biyya: popular, popularity, of the people, as in "popular democracy."

shahada: the Muslim declaration of faith and intent: "There is no God but God and Muhammad is the Messenger of God." (The Shi'a add, "and 'Ali is the friend of God" ["*wa 'Ali wali Allah*"].)

shahid: martyr (plural *shuhada*).

shari'a: Islmac moral and religious laws.

sharif: an honorific title in Sunni tradition to denote a male descended from the line of the Prophet Muhammad.

shu'ba: sections (plural *shu'ab*); the middle administrative Ba'th Party level.

shu'ubiyya: a medieval intellectual movement that demanded equality for Persian Muslims. In its Ba'thi usage, a Persian anti-Arab movement; Shi'i opposition activists were often labeled "*shu'ubis*."

sura: a chapter of the Qur'an.

ta'ifiyya: sectarianism, used by the Ba'thi media as a pejorative term for Shi'is who demanded more rights for their community.

takiya: an assembly place of a Sufi order (plural *takaya*); sometimes translated as "monastery."

tanzimat: literally "organization" or "structure," meaning a "new organization"; since 1991–92, the administrative level that replaced the *maktab tanzim* to improve central control over the party in the provinces.

taqiyya: precautionary dissimulation, often in the form of denying one's faith or otherwise concealing one's religious practices or profession. Regarded by most Shi'i theologians as a must when one's life is in danger; less common in Sunni tradition.

tariqa: a Sufi order.

tawakkul: reliance on God.

ta'ziya: in Shi'i tradition, the rite of mourning the death of Imam Husayn.

thawra: revolution.

Thawra al-Sh'baniyaa, al-: "The Sha'ban Revolution," an alternate name for the 1991 Shi'i revolt. (See *Intifadat Sha'ban*.)

'udhu 'amil: active member, a full Ba'th Party member, the highest level of membership from which a member can begin to climb the party's administrative ladder.

'udhu far': branch member, member of the leadership of a Ba'th Party branch.

'udhu firqa: division member, member of the leadership of a Ba'th Party division.

'udhu mutadarrib: trainee member, one level below active (full) Ba'th Party member.

'udhu shu'ba: section member, member of the leadership of a Ba'th Party section.

'ulama: Islamic men of religion, clerics (singular *'alim*).

umma: nation; in Ba'thi vernacular, used for the Arab nation, including all of the Arabic-speaking countries.

wahda: unity; one of the Ba'th trinity of "unity, freedom, socialism," as in *al-wahdah al-'Arabiyya* (Arab unity).

waqf: religious endowment (plural *awqaf*); usually in the form of land.

wataniyya: patriotism, in the sense of local territorial nationalism.

Arabic-English Transliteration

Arabic	English		Arabic	English
ء	ʾ		ض	*dh*
ب	*b*		ط	*t*
ت	*t*		ظ	*z*
ث	*th*		ع	ʿ
ج	*j*		غ	*gh*
ح	*h*		ف	*f*
خ	*kh*		ق	*q*
د	*d*		ك	*k*
ذ	*dh*		ل	*l*
ر	*r*		م	*m*
ز	*z*		ن	*n*
س	*s*		ة	—
ش	*sh*		و	*w*
ص	*s*		ي	*y, i*

Bibliography

Books and Articles in European Languages

Aburish, Said. *Saddam Hussein: The Politics of Revenge.* New York: Bloomsbury, 2000.

Ahram, Ariel I. "From Hearts and Minds to Ashes and Mud: Development, Counterinsurgency, and the Destruction of the Iraqi Marshes." Paper presented at a meeting of the American Political Science Association, Chicago, September 1, 2013.

Ali, Nadje Sadig, al-. *Iraqi Women: Untold Stories from 1948 to the Present.* London: Zed Books, 2007.

Amnesty International. *Amnesty International, 2001 Annual Report on Iraq,* esp. "Extrajudicial Executions" section. http://www.atour.com/news/international/20010710l.html.

Anderson, Benedict. *Imagined Communities: Reflections on the Origin and Spread of Nationalism.* London: Verso, 1983.

Anderson, J. N. D. "A Law of Personal Status for Iraq." *International and Comparative Law Quarterly* 9 (October 1960): 561–63.

Arab Ba'th Socialist Party. *The 1968 Revolution in Iraq: Experience and Prospects. The Political Report of the 8th Congress . . . January 1974.* London: Ithaca Press, 1979.

———. *Revolutionary Iraq 1968–1973, The Political Report Adopted by the Eighth Regional Congress of the Arab Ba'th Socialist Party–Iraq, January 1974.* Baghdad, 1974.

Arab Ba'th Socialist Party, Regional Leadership. *How the Revolution Confronts the Imperialist Conspiracy: The Report of the Regional Leadership.* Baghdad, November 1972.

Arab Ba'th Socialist Party—Iraq. *The Central Report of the Ninth Regional Congress, June 1982.* Baghdad, January 1983, trans. SARTEC, Lausanne, 1983.

Auda, Gehad. "An Uncertain Response: The Islamic Movement in Egypt." In *Islamic Fundamentalisms and the Gulf Crisis,* edited by James Piscatori, 109–30. Chicago: American Academy of Arts and Sciences with the Fundamentalism Project, 1991.

Azami, Tarik Hamdi, al-. "The Emergence of Contemporary Islamic Revival in Iraq." *Middle East Affairs Journal* 3 (1997): 123–42.

Babakhan, Ali. "The Deportation of Shi'is during the Iran-Iraq War." In *Ayatollahs, Sufis and Ideologues: State, Religion, and Social Movements in Iraq,* edited by Faleh A. Jabar, 183–211. London: Saqi Books, 2002.

Baghdad Yearbook. Vol. 1. Baghdad: al-Iraq Press, 1923.

Baram, Amatzia. *Building toward Crisis: Saddam Husayn's Strategy for Survival.* Washington, DC: Washington Institute for Near East Policy, 1998.

———. *Culture, History and Ideology in the Formation of Ba'thist Iraq: 1968–1989.* London: Palgrave Macmillan; New York: St. Martin's Press, 1991.

———. "Culture in the Service of Wataniyya: The Treatment of Mesopotamian-Inspired Art in Ba'thi Iraq." *Asian and African Studies* 17 (Fall 1983): 265–313.

———. "The Effect of Iraqi Sanctions, Statistical Pitfalls and Responsibility." *Middle East Journal* 54, no. 2 (2000): 194–223.

———. "From Militant Secularism to Islamism: The Iraqi Ba'th Regime 1968–2003." Woodrow Wilson International Center for Scholars Occasional Paper. Washington, DC: Woodrow Wilson International Center for Scholars, 2011.

———. "From Radicalism to Radical Pragmatism: The Shi'ite Fundamentalist Opposition Movements of Iraq." In *Islamic Fundamentalism and the Gulf War*, edited by James Piscatori, 28–51. Chicago: University of Chicago Press and American Academy of Arts and Sciences, 1991.

———. "The Impact of Khomeini's Revolution on the Radical Shi'i Movement of Iraq." In *The Iranian Revolution and the Muslim World*, edited by David Menashri, 131–54. Boulder, CO: Westview Press, 1990.

———. *Iraq Past, Present and Future: Arabic-Speaking Iraqis between the Tribes, the Sunnah and the Shi'ah.* Middle East Institute Perspective Series. Singapore: National University of Singapore, 2009.

———. "The Iraqi Invasion of Kuwait: Decision-Making in Baghdad." In *Iraq's Road to War*, edited by Amatzia Baram and Barry Rubin, 5–36. New York: St. Martin's Press, 1994.

———. "Mesopotamian Identity in Ba'thi Iraq." *Middle Eastern Studies* 19, no. 4 (October 1983): 426–56.

———. "Neo-Tribalism in Iraq: Saddam Husayn's Tribal Policies 1991–1996." *International Journal of Middle East Studies* 29, no. 1 (February 1997): 1–31.

———. "*Qawmiyya* and *Wataniyya* in Ba'thi Iraq: The Search for a New Balance." *Middle Eastern Studies* 19, no. 2 (April 1983): 188–200.

———. "The Radical Shi'ite Opposition Movements in Iraq." In *Religious-Political Radicalism in the Middle East*, edited by Emmanuel Sivan and Menachem Friedman, 95–125. Albany: State University of New York Press, 1990.

———. "Re-inventing Nationalism in Ba'thist Iraq 1968–1994: Supra-Territorial and Territorial Identities and What Lies Below." *Princeton Papers: Interdisciplinary Journal of Middle Eastern Studies* 5 (Fall 1996): 29–56.

———. "The Ruling Political Elite in Ba'thi Iraq, 1968–1986: The Changing Features of a Collective Profile." *International Journal of Middle East Studies* 21, no. 4 (November 1989): 447–93.

———. "Saddam Hussein: A Political Profile." *Jerusalem Quarterly* 17 (Fall 1980): 115–44.

———. "Saddam Husayn and Nasirism: 1968–2000." *Orient* 41, no. 3 (September 2000): 461–72.

———. "Sadr the Father, Sadr the Son, the 'Revolution in Shi'ism' and the Struggle for Power in the *Hawzah* of Najaf." In *Iraq between Occupations: Perspectives from 1920 to the Present*, edited by Amatzia Baram, Achim Rohde, and Ronen Zeidel, 143–57. New York: Palgrave Macmillan, 2010.

————. "Two Roads to Revolutionary Shi'i Fundamentalism in Iraq." In *Accounting for Fundamentalism: The Dynamic Character of Movements*, edited by Martin E. Marty and Scott Appleby, 531–90. Chicago: University of Chicago Press and the American Academy of Arts and Sciences, 1994.

————. "Who Are the Insurgents? Sunni-Arab Rebels in Iraq." Special Report. Washington, DC: US Institute of Peace, April 2005.

Baran, David. *Vivre la tyrannie et lui survivre: L'Irak en transition.* Paris: Mille et une nuits, 2004.

Batatu, Hanna. *The Old Social Classes and the Revolutionary Movements of Iraq.* Princeton, NJ: Princeton University Press, 1978.

Bayati, Hamid. *The Shia of Iraq between Sectarianism and Suspicions in British Secret Documents, 1963–1966.* London: Dar al-Rafid, 1997.

Bellah, Robert N. "Civil Religion in America." In "Religion in America." Special issue, *Dædalus* 96, no. 1 (Winter 1967): 1–21.

Bengio, Ofra. *The Kurds of Iraq: Building State within a State.* Boulder, CO: Lynne Rienner, 2012.

————. *Saddam's Word: Political Discourse in Iraq.* New York: Oxford University Press, 1998.

Bruinessen, Martin van. "The Kurds and Islam." Working Paper 13, Islamic Area Studies Project. Tokyo, 1999.

Burchell, Graham, Colin Gordon, and Peter Miller, eds. *The Foucault Effect: Studies in Governmentality.* London: Harvester Wheatsheaf, 1991.

Central Intelligence Agency (CIA). *The Destruction of Iraq's Southern Marshes.* Publication NESA 94-10021, RTT 94-10054. Washington, DC: CIA, August 1994.

Chubin, Shahram, and Charles Tripp. *Iran and Iraq at War.* Boulder, CO: Westview Press, 1988.

Cockburn, Patrick, *Muqtada al-Sadr and the Battle for the Future of Iraq.* New York: Scribner, 2008.

Coke, Richard. *The Heart of the Middle East.* London: Butterworth, 1925.

Cordesman, Anthony H, and Abraham R. Wagner. *The Lessons of Modern War, Vol. II: The Iran-Iraq War.* Boulder, CO: Westview Press, 1990.

Coulson, N. J. *Succession in the Muslim Family.* Cambridge: Cambridge University Press, 1971.

Dann, Uriel. *Iraq under Qassem: A Political History 1958–1963.* New York: Praeger, 1969.

Darle, Pierre. *Saddam Hussein . . . Maître des mots: Du langage de la tyrannie à la tyrannie du langage.* Paris: L'Harmattan, 2003.

Davis, Eric. *Memories of State: Politics, History, and Collective Identity in Modern Iraq.* Los Angeles: University of California Press, 2005.

Dawisha, Adeed. *Iraq: A Political History from Independence to Occupation.* Cambridge: Cambridge University Press, 2009.

Devlin, John. *The Ba'th Party: A History from Its Origins to 1966.* Stanford, CA: Stanford University Press, 1979.

————. "The Ba'th Party: Rise and Metamorphosis." *American History Review* 96, no. 5 (December 1991): 1396–1407.

Dodge, Toby. *Inventing Iraq: The Failure of Nation-Building and a History Denied.* New York: Columbia University Press, 2003.

Efrati, Noga. *Women in Iraq: Past Meets Present.* New York: Columbia University Press, 2012.

Eickelman, Dale. *The Middle East and Central Asia: An Anthropological Approach.* New York: Prentice Hall, 2002.

Encyclopaedia of Islam, New Edition. Edited by P. J. Bearman, T. Bianquis, C. E. Bosworth, E. van Donzel, and W. P. Heinrichs. London: Brill, 1971.

Eppel, Michael. "The Demise of the Kurdish Emirates: The Impact of Ottoman Reforms and International Relations on Kurdistan during the First Half of the Nineteenth Century." *Middle Eastern Studies* 44, no. 2 (2008): 237–58.

———. "Kurdish Leadership in Post-Saddam Iraq: National Challenges and Changing Conditions." In *Iraq between Occupations: Perspectives from 1920 to the Present,* edited by Amatzia Baram, Achim Rohde, and Ronen Zeidel, 79–102. New York: Palgrave Macmillan, 2010.

———. "State Building and Social Ferment in Kurdistan." *Journal of South Asian and Middle Eastern Studies* 31, no. 4 (2008): 70–77.

Farouk-Sluglett, Marion. "Liberation or Repression? Pan-Arab Nationalism and the Women's Movement in Iraq." In *Iraq: Power and Society,* edited by Derek Hopwood, Habib Ishow, and Thomas Koszinowski, 51–73. Reading: Ithaca Press, for St. Anthony's College, Oxford University, 1993.

Farouk-Sluglett, Marion, and Peter Sluglett. *Iraq since 1958: From Revolution to Dictatorship.* London: KPI, 1987.

Feldman, Ofer, and Linda O. Valenty, eds. *Profiling Political Leaders: Cross-cultural Studies of Personality and Behavior.* Westport, CT: Praeger, 2001.

Franzén, John. *Red Star over Iraq: Iraqi Communism before Saddam.* Oxford: Oxford University Press, 2011.

Gellner, Ernest. *Muslim Society.* Cambridge: Cambridge University Press, 1985.

Gilsenan, Michael. *Recognizing Islam: Religion and Society in the Modern Arab World.* New York: Pantheon Books, 1982.

Gramsci, Antonio. *Selections from the Prison Notebooks.* London: Lawrence and Wishart, 1971.

Gunter, Michael. *The Kurdish Predicament in Iraq: Political Analysis.* New York: St. Martin's Press, 1990.

———. *The Kurds of Iraq: Tragedy and Hope.* New York: St. Martin's Press, 1992.

Haddad, Fanar. *Sectarianism in Iraq: Antagonistic Visions of Unity.* London: Hurst; New York: Columbia University Press, 2011.

Hakim, Helkot. "The Origins of the Naqshbadiyya Order." In *Ayatollahs, Sufis and Ideologues,* edited by Faleh A. Jabar, 140–145. London: Saqi Books, 2002.

Hashim, Ahmed S. "Iraq's Sunni Insurgency," Adelphi Paper 402. London and Abingdon: The International Institute for Strategic Studies, 2009.

Hawting, G. R. "Sa'd b. Abi Wakkas." In *Encyclopaedia of Islam,* New Edition (1971), 8:696–97.

Heller, Peter B. "Document: The Permanent Syrian Constitution of March 13, 1973." *Middle East Journal* 28 (1974): 53–66.

Hinnebusch, Raymond A. *Authoritarian Power and State Formation in Ba'thist Syria: Army, Party and Peasants.* Boulder, CO: Westview Press, 1990.

Hiro, Dilip. *The Longest War: The Iran-Iraq Military Conflict.* London: Routledge, 1991.

Human Rights Watch. *Bureaucracy of Repression: The Iraqi Government in Its Own Words.* Human Rights Watch, February 1, 1994. http://www.hrw.org/reports/1994/iraq/.

———. *Endless Torment: The 1991 Uprising in Iraq and Its Aftermath.* Washington, DC: Human Rights Watch, June 1992.

Hurovitz, J. "Abbasa." In *Encyclopaedia of Islam,* New Edition (1971), 1:14.

Hussein, Saddam. *On History, Heritage and Religion.* Baghdad: Translation and Foreign Languages Publishing House, 1981.

———. *Religious Political Movements and Those Disguised with Religion.* Baghdad: Dar al-Ma'mun, 1987.

———. *Social and Foreign Affairs in Iraq.* London: Croom Helm, 1979.

International Crisis Group. "Iraq's Shi'ites under Occupation." International Crisis Group, Baghdad and Brussels, Middle East Briefing 8, September 9, 2003. http://www .crisisgroup.org/en/regions/middle-east-north-africa/iraq-iran-gulf/iraq/B008-iraqs-shiites-under-occupation.aspx.

Iraq, Ministry of Planning, Central Statistics Organization. *Annual Abstract of Statistics,* 1958–1997. Baghdad: Ministry of Planning of the Republic of Iraq.

Ismael, Jacqueline S., and Shereen T. Ismael. "Living through War, Sanctions and Occupation: The Voice of Iraqi Women." *International Journal of Contemporary Iraqi Studies* 2, no. 3 (2008): 409–24.

Jabar, Faleh A., ed. *Ayatollahs, Sufis and Ideologues.* London: Saqi Books, 2002.

———. "Sheikhs and Ideologues: Deconstruction and Reconstruction of Tribes under Patrimonial Totalitarianism in Iraq, 1968–1998." In *Tribes and Power: Nationalism and Ethnicity in the Middle East,* edited by Faleh A. Jabar and Hosham Dawood. London: Saqi Books, 2003.

———. *The Shi'te Movement in Iraq.* London: Saqi Books, 2003.

———. "Why the Intifada Failed." In *Iraq since the Gulf War: Prospects for Democracy,* edited by Fran Hazelton, 97–117. London: Zed Books, 2004.

———. "Why the Uprisings Failed." *Middle East Report (MERIP)* 176 (May–June 1992): 2–14.

Jabar, Faleh A., and Hosham Dawod, eds. *Tribes and Power: Nationalism and Ethnicity in the Middle East.* London: Saqi Books, 2002.

Jabouri, General Najim Abed, al-, and Sterling Jensen. "The Iraqi and AQI Roles in the Sunni Awakening." *PRISM* 2, no. 1 (September 16, 2010): 1–25.

Jawaheri, Yasmin Husein, al-. *Women in Iraq: The Gender Impact of International Sanctions.* London: I. B. Tauris, 2008.

Judge, Timothy A., Joyce E. Bono, and Remus Ilies. "Personality and Leadership: A Qualitative and Quantitative Review." *Journal of Applied Psychology* 87 (2002): 765–80.

Kadhim, Abbas. "The Hawza under Siege: A Study in the Ba'th Party Archive." Occasional Paper 1. Boston: Boston University Institute for Iraqi Studies, June 2013.

———. *Reclaiming Iraq: The 1920 Revolution and the Founding of the Modern State.* Austin: University of Texas Press, 2012.

Karsh, Efraim, and Inari Rautsi. *Saddam Hussein: A Political Biography.* New York: Free Press, 1991.

Kasey, Mahir, al- (Mahir al-Qaysi). *Youth Education in Iraq and Egypt.* Helicon CESO (Seminar of Comparative Education)—K.U.L., 1981.

Kedar, Mordechai. "In Search of Legitimacy: Asad's Islamic Image in the Syrian Official Press." In *Modern Syria: From Ottoman Rule to Pivotal Role in the Middle East,* edited by Moshe Maʻoz, Joseph Ginat, and Onn Winckler, 17–32. Brighton: Sussex Academic Press, 1988.

Khafaji, Isam, al-. "State Terror and the Degradation of Politics in Iraq." *Middle East Review of International Affairs (MERIP)* 176 (May–June, 1992): 15–21.

Khalil, Lydia. "New Sufi Group Joins the Iraqi Insurgency." *Jamestown Foundation* 4, no. 2 (February 20, 2007).

Khalil, Samir, al-. *See* Makiya, Kanʻan.

Kimball, Lorenzo K. *The Changing Pattern of Political Power in Iraq, 1958 to 1971.* New York: Robert Speller and Sons, 1973.

Kohlberg, Etan. "The Evolution of the Shiʻa." *Jerusalem Quarterly* 27 (Spring 1983): 109–26.

League of Nations. *Constitution of ʻIraq (Organic Law).* Geneva: League of Nations, February 20, 1929.

Lewis, Bernard. *Islam in History: Ideas, People, and Events in the Middle East.* Chicago: Open Court, 1993.

Makiya, Kanʻan. *Cruelty and Silence: War, Uprising and the Arab World.* London: Penguin, 1993.

——— (Samir al-Khalil). *Republic of Fear: The Politics of Modern Iraq.* London: Hutchinson Radius, 1989.

Mallat, Chibli. "Siʻism and Sunnism in Iraq: Revisiting the Codes." In *Islamic Family Law,* edited by Chibli Mallat and Jane Connors, 71–91. London: Graham and Trotman, 1990.

Maʻoz, Moshe. *Asad: The Sphinx of Damascus. A Political Biography.* London: Weidenfeld & Nicholson, 1988.

Maʻoz, Moshe, Joseph Ginat, and Onn Winckler, eds. *Modern Syria: From Ottoman Rule to Pivotal Role in the Middle East.* Brighton: Sussex Academic Press, 1988.

Marashi, Ibrahim, al-. "An Insight into the Mindset of Iraq's Security Apparatus." *Intelligence and National Security* 18, no. 3 (Autumn 2003): 1–23.

———. "Iraq's Security and Intelligence Network: A Guide and Analysis." *Middle East Review of International Affairs (MERIA)* 6, no. 3 (September 2002): 1–13.

Margoliouth, D. S. "Naqshbandiyya."In *Encyclopaedia of Islam,* New Edition (1971), 4:382.

Marr, Phebe. *The Modern History of Iraq.* 3rd ed. Boulder, CO: Westview Press, 2011; previous editions published in 1985 and 2004.

Massignon, Louis. *The Passion of al-Hallaj: Mystic and Martyr of Islam.* Princeton, NJ: Princeton University Press, 1994.

Mazaheri, Nimah. "Iraq and the Domestic Political Effects of Economic Sanctions." *Middle East Journal* 64, no. 2 (Spring 2010): 253–68.

McDowall, David, *The Modern History of the Kurds.* London: I. B. Tauris, 2005.

Metz, Helen Chapin, ed. *Iraq: A Country Study.* Washington, DC: Federal Research Division, Library of Congress, and Headquarters, Department of the Army, 1990.

Middle East Watch. *Human Rights in Iraq.* New Haven, CT: Yale University Press, 1990.

Mohsen, Fatima. "Cultural Totalitarianism." In *Iraq since the Gulf War: Prospects for Democracy,* edited by Fran Hazelton, 7–19. London: Zed Books, 1994.

Momen, Moojan. *An Introduction to Shiʻi Islam: The History and Doctrine of Twelver Shiʻism.* New Haven, CT: Yale University Press, 1985.

Nakash, Yitzhak. *The Shiʻis of Iraq.* Princeton, NJ: Princeton University Press, 1994.

Nasrawi, Abbas, al-. "Economic Consequences of the Iraq-Iran War." *Third World Quarterly* 8, no. 3 (July 1986): 869–95.

———. "Iraq: Economic Consequences of the 1991 Gulf War and Future Outlook." *Third World Quarterly* 13, no. 2 (June 1992): 335–52.

Neocleous, Mark. *Administering Civil Society: Towards a Theory of State Power.* London: Macmillan, 1996.

Olson, Robert. *The Goat and the Butcher: Nationalism and State-Formation in Kurdistan-Iraq Since the Iraq War.* Costa Mesa, CA: Mazda Publishers, 2005.

Owen, Roger. *State, Power and Politics in the Making of the Modern Middle East.* London: Routledge, 2008.

Peters, R. "Zina." In *Encyclopaedia of Islam*, New Edition (1971), 11:509–10.

Piscatori, James P. *Islam in a World of Nation States.* Cambridge: Cambridge University Press, 1986.

———, ed. *Islamic Fundamentalisms and the Gulf Crisis.* Chicago: University of Chicago Press and American Academy of Arts and Sciences, 1991.

Podeh, Elie. *The Politics of National Celebrations in the Arab Middle East.* Cambridge: Cambridge University Press, 2011.

Post, Jerrold M., and Amatzia Baram. *Saddam Is Iraq: Iraq Is Saddam.* Counterproliferation Papers, Future Warfare Series 17. USAF Counterproliferation Center, Maxwell Air Force Base, AL, 2002. http://www.au.af.mil/au/awc/awcgate/cpc-pubs/postbaram.pdf.

Primakov, Yevgeny. *Russia and the Arabs: Behind the Scenes in the Middle East from the Cold War to the Present,* trans. Paul Gould. New York: Basic Books, Group, 2009.

Qarawee, Harith, al-. *Imagining the Nation.* New York: Rossendale Books, 2012.

Rohde, Achim. *State-Society Relations in Ba'thist Iraq: Facing Dictatorship.* Abingdon, UK: Routledge, 2010.

Romano, David. *The Kurdish Nationalist Movement: Opportunity, Mobilization and Identity.* Cambridge: Cambridge University Press, 2006.

Ruhaimi, Abdul-Halim, al-. "The Da'wa Islamic Party: Origins, Actors and Ideology." In *Ayatollahs, Sufis and Ideologues: State, Religion and Social Movements in Iraq,* edited by Faleh A. Jabar, 149–61. London: Saqi Books, 2002.

Sadan, Joseph. "Death of a Princess: Episodes of the Barmakid Legend in Its Late Evolution." In *Story Telling in the Framework of Non-Fictional Arabic Literature,* edited by Stefan Leder, 130–57. Wiesbaden: Harrassowitz Verlag, 1998.

Salih, Mohammed Mahdi. *Ba'th Socialism and Regional Development.* Baghdad: Dar al-Mamun, 1982.

Sassoon, Joseph. "The Iraqi Ba'th Party Preparatory School and the 'Cultural' Courses of the Branches." *Middle Eastern Studies* 50, no. 1 (January 2014): 27–42.

———. *Saddam Hussein's Ba'th Party: Inside an Authoritarian Regime.* Cambridge: Cambridge University Press, 2012.

Seale, Patrick. *Asad of Syria: The Struggle for the Middle East.* London: I. B. Tauris, 1988.

Simon, Reeva S. *Iraq between the Two World Wars: The Creation and Implementation of a National Ideology.* New York: Columbia University Press, 1986.

Sluglett, Peter. *Britain in Iraq: Contriving King and Country, 1914–1932.* New York: Columbia University Press, 2007.

Smith, Anthony D. *The Ethnic Origins of Nations.* Oxford: Blackwell, 1989.

Stansfield, Gareth. *Iraqi Kurdistan, Political Development and Emerging Democracy.* London: Routledge/Curzon, 2003.

Statistiches Bundesmat Statistik des Auslandes. *Iraq 1982.* Stuttgart: Statistiches Bundesmat Statistik des Auslandes, 1982.

Suedfeld, Peter, K. Guttieri, and P. E. Tetlock. "Assessing Integrative Complexity at a Distance: Archival Analyses of Thinking and Decision Making." In *The Psychological Assessment of Political Leaders: With Profiles of Saddam Hussein and Bill Clinton*, edited by Jerrold Post, 246–70. Ann Arbor: University of Michigan Press, 2005.

Tripp, Charles. *A History of Iraq.* 3rd ed. Cambridge: Cambridge University Press, 2007.

United Nations Assistance Mission for Iraq, *Human Rights Report*, January 1–June 30, 2009, "Mass graves."

United Nations, Commission on Human Rights, "Questions of the Violation of Human Rights and Fundamental Freedoms in Any Part of the World: Report on the Situation of Human Rights in Iraq," Submitted by the Special Rapporteur, Mr. Max van der Stoel, in accordance with Commission Resolution 1998/65, February 26, 1999. United Nations, Economic and Social Council, New York, 55th Session, February 26, 1999.

———. "Report on the Situation of Human Rights in Iraq," April 14, Submitted by the Special Rapporteur, Mr. Max van der Stoel, in accordance with Commission Resolution 1998/65, March 10, 1998. United Nations, Economic and Social Council, New York, 55th Session, Item 9, June 4, 1999.

Vaglerii, L. Veccia. "Al-Kadisiyya." In *Encyclopaedia of Islam*, New Edition (1971), 5:384–87.

Valenty, Linda O., and Ofer Feldman, eds. *Political Leadership for the New Century: Personality and Behavior among American Leaders.* Westport, CT: Praeger, 2002.

Visser, Reidar, and Gareth Stansfield, eds. *An Iraq of Its Regions: Cornerstones of a Federal Democracy?* London: Hurst, 2007.

Warburg, Gabriel R. "Islam and State in Numayri's Sudan." *Africa* 55, no. 4: 400–13.

Weismann, Itzchak. *Taste of Modernity: Sufism, Salafiyya, and Arabism in Late Ottoman Damascus.* Boston: Brill, 2001.

White, Hayden. *Tropics of Discourse: Essays in Cultural Criticism.* Baltimore: Johns Hopkins University Press, 1985.

Wiley, Joyce. *The Islamic Movement of Iraqi Shi'as.* Boulder, CO: Lynne Rienner, 1992.

Wilson, Arnold T. *Loyalties, Vol. 2: Mesopotamia 1914–1917.* London: Oxford University Press, 1930.

Winter, David G. "Things I've Learned about Personality from Studying Political Leaders at a Distance." *Journal of Personality* 73, no. 3 (2005): 557–84.

Woods, Kevin M., and James Lacey. *Iraqi Perspectives Project: Saddam and Terrorism: Emerging Insights from Captured Iraqi Documents.* 5 vols. Alexandria, VA: Institute for Defense Analysis, 2007.

Woods, Kevin M., Williamson Murray, and Mounir Elkhamri. *Saddam's War: An Iraqi Military Perspective on the Iran-Iraq War.* NDU McNair Paper 70. Washington, DC: National Defense University, 2009.

Woods, Kevin M., David Palkki, and Mark E. Stout. *The Saddam Tapes: The Inner Workings of a Tyrant's Regime, 1978–2001.* New York: Cambridge University Press, 2011.

Yildiz, Kerim. *The Kurds in Iraq: Past, Present and Future.* London: Pluto Press, 2004.

Zeidel, Ronen. "The Shiʿa in Iraqi Novels." *Die Welt des Islams* 51 (2011).

Zubaida, Sami. "Une Société traumatisée, une société civile anéantie, une économie en ruine." In *Le livre noir de Saddam Hussein*, edited by Chris Kutchera, 601–27. Paris: Oh! Edition, 2005.

Books and Articles in Arabic and Hebrew

ʿAbd al-Jabbar, Muhammad Ridha, and Idris Mustafa ʿAziz. *Al-Tarbiya al-Islamiyya lil-Saff al-Thalith al-Ibtidaʾi* [Islamic education for the third grade, primary school]. 11th ed. Baghdad: Ministry of Education, Ibn Khaldun Press, 2002.

ʿAflaq, Michel. *Fi Sabil al-Baʿth* [On the way of resurrection]. 11th ed. Beirut: Dar al-Taliʿa, 1974; first published 1959.

ʿAli, Muʾmin. *Sanawat al-Jamr: Masirat al-haraka al-Islamiyya fi al-ʿIraq 1957–1986* [The embers years: The journey of the Islamic movements in Iraq]. London: Dar al-Masira, 1993.

Alusi, ʿAbd al-Jabbar, al-, and Rafiʿ Asʿad ʿAbd al-Halim. *Al-Tarbiya al-Islamiyya lil-Saff al-Awwal al-Ibtidaʾi* [Islamic education for the first grade, primary school]. 12th ed. Baghdad: Ministry of Education, 2002.

ʿAnni, ʿAbd al-Rahman, al-, and Hasan Fadhil Zuʿayn. *Al-Taʾrikh al-ʿArabi al-Islami lil-Saff al-Thani al-Mutawassit* [Arab-Islamic History for the second grade, intermediate school]. 13th ed. Baghdad: Ministry of Education, 2002.

———. *Al-Taʾrikh al-ʿArabi al-Islami lil-Saff al-Khamis al-Ibtidaʾi* [Arab-Islamic history for the fifth grade, primary school]. 16th ed. Baghdad: Ministry of Education, 2003.

ʿAnni, Khalid ʿAbd al-Munʿim, al-. *Mawsuʿat al-ʿIraq al-Hadith* [The encyclopaedia of modern Iraq], vol. 3. Baghdad: Arab Encyclopaedia House, 1977.

Ansari, Fadil, al-. *Sukkan al-ʿIraq* [The population of Iraq]. Damascus: University of Damascus Press, 1970.

ʿAysami, Shibli, al-. *Fi al-Thawra al-ʿArabiyya* [On the Arab revolution]. 4th ed. Beirut: Dar al-Taliʿa, June 1973.

———. *Risalat al-Umma al-ʿArabiyya* [The message of the Arab nation]. Beirut: Dar al-Taliʿa, 1978.

ʿAziz, Husayn Qasim, al-. "Al-Asas al-Maddi li Tatawwur Minaj al-Bahth al-Taʾrikhi" [The materialist basis of the development of historical research]. *Al-Muthaqqaf al-ʿArabi* [The Arab intellectual] 6, no. 1 (January 1974): 87–92.

———. *Al-Babikiyya, Intifadat al-Shaʿb al-Adhirbijani dhidd al-Khilafa al-ʿAbbasiyya* [The Babikiyya (Kharamiyya): The intifada of the Azerbaijani people against the ʿAbbasid caliphate]. Baghdad: Maktabat al-Nahdha; Beirut: Dar al-Farabi, 1974.

Bahr al-ʿUlum, Muhammad. *Adhwaʾ ʿala Qanun al-Ahwal al-Shakhsiyya al-ʿIraqi* [Illuminating the Iraqi Law of Personal Status]. Najaf: Matbaʿat al-Nuʿman, 1963.

Bakr, Ahmad Hasan, al-. *Masirat al-Thawra fi Khutab wa Tasrihat al-Sayyid al-Raʾis* [The road of the revolution in the lectures and announcements of the sayyid the president]. Baghdad, 1971.

Basri, Mir. *Aʿlam al-Adab fi al-ʿIraq al-Hadith* [Eminent men of letters in modern Iraq]. 3 vols. London: Dar al-Hikma, 1994–1999.

Bazzaz, Sa'd, al-. *Harb Talidu Ukhra: Al-Ta'rikh al-Sirri li Harb al-Khalij* [A war that gives birth to another war: The secret history of the Gulf War]. Amman: al-Ahliyya lil-nahsr wal-Tawzi', 1992–1993.

Bengio, Ofra. *The Kurdish Revolution in Iraq* [in Hebrew]. Tel Aviv: Ha-Kibbutz ha-Meuhad, 1989.

Bustani, Bushra. "Al-mar'a al-'Arabiyya wal-fikr al-mutakhallaf" [The Arab woman and the retarded thought]. *Al-Muthaqqaf al-'Arabi* 7, no. 1 (1975): 59–69.

Dalil al-Mamlaka al-'Iraqiyya li Sanat 1935–6 al-Maliyya [Guide for the Iraqi kingdom for the budget year 1935–36]. Baghdad, 1936.

Dustur al-Mu'aqqat, al-. Baghdad: Mudiriyyat al-A'lam al-'Amma-Matba'at al-Hukuma, 1970.

Efrati, Noga. "The Marriage Contract and Women's Roles in the Family: Iraq 1958–1988" [in Hebrew]. Master's thesis, University of Haifa, 1995.

Fajr al-Thawra al-Islamiyya [The dawn of the Islamic revolution]. Tehran: Echo of Islam, 1982.

Farah, Ilyas. "Hiwar ma'a al-duktur Ilyas Farah" [Discussion with Dr. Ilyas Farah]. *Afaq 'Arabiyya* 1, no. 1 (September 1975): 44–50.

Fawzi, Faruq 'Umar. "Abu Muslim al-Khurasani wa Usturat al-Batal al-Munqidh" [Abu Muslim al-Khurasani and the myth of the delivering hero]. *Afaq 'Arabiyya* 4, no. 10 (June 1979): 42–47.

———. "Al-Babikiyya wa Fikr al-Qaran al-'Ishrin" [The Babikiyya and the thought of the twentieth century]. *Afaq 'Arabiyya* 2, no. 5 (January 1977): 77–89.

———. "Al-Haraka al-Kharamiyya fi al 'asr al-'Abbasi bayna al-Dughmatiya wal-Mawdhu'iyya" [The Kharamiyya movement in the Abbasid era: Between dogmatism and objectivity]. *Afaq 'Arabiyya* 10 (June 1977): 94-99.

———. "Harakat al-Mukhtar al-Thaqafi" [The Mukhtar al-Thaqafi movement]. *Afaq 'Arabiyya* 3, no. 1 (September 1977): 76–82.

———. *Hukkam Bilad Faris Wal-'Udwan 'Ala al-'Iraq Khilal al-'Asr al-'Abbasi* [The rulers of the lands of Persia and the aggression against Iraq in the Abbasid era]. Baghdad: Dar al-Shu'un al-Thaqafiyya al-'Amma-Aafaq 'Arabiyya, 1988.

———. *Al-'Iraq Fi al-'Asr al-'Abbasi* [Iraq in the Abbasid Era]. Baghdad: Dar al-Shu'un al-Thaqafiyya al-'Amma-Aafaq 'Arabiyya, 1988.

———. *Al-'Iraq Wal-Tahaddi al-Farisi* [Iraq and the Persian challenge]. Baghdad: Dar al-Shu'un al-Thaqafiyya al-'Amma-Aafaq 'Arabiyya, 1987.

———. *Al-Khilafa al-'Abbasiyya Fi 'Asr al-Fawdha al-'Askariyya 861–946* [The 'Abbasid caliphate in the era of military civil war, 861–946]. Baghdad: Manshurat Maktabat al-Muthanna, 1977.

Faydhi, Muhammad Bashar, al-. *Al-Sarab: Hisad al-'Amaliyya al-Siyasiyya fi zill al-Ihtilal al-Amriki* [The mirage: The harvest of political action in the shadow of the American occupation]. Amman: Dar al-Jil al-'Arabi, 2007.

Fayyadh, 'Abd Allah, al-. *Ta'rikh al-Imamiyya wa Aslafihim min al-Shi'a* [The history of the Imami Shi'a and their forebears]. Baghdad: Matba'at As'ad and Baghdad University, 1970.

Fukayki, Hani, al-. *Awkar al-Hazima: Tajribati fi hizb al-Ba'th al-'Iraqi* [The sources of defeat: My experience in the Iraqi Ba'th Party]. London and Cyprus: Riad el Rayyes Books, 1993.

Ha'iri, Kazim al-Husayni, al-. *Labina Awwaliyya Muqtaraha li Dustur al-Jumhuriyya al-Islamiyya fi al-'Iraq* [An initial suggested brick for the Constitution of the Islamic Republic in Iraq]. Qom: Maktab al-Marja' al-Dini Samahat Ayat Allah al-'Uzma al-Sayyid Kazim al-Ha'iri, 1424H [2003 CE].

———. *Mabahith al-Usul, Taqriran li-Abhath Samahat Ayat Allah al-'Uzma al-Shahid al-Sayyid Muhammad Baqir al-Sadr* [Studies of the sources: An account of the studies of Ayatollah al-'Uzma al-Shahid al-Sayyid Muhammad Baqir al-Sadr]. Tehran, 1986.

Hakim, Muhammad Baqir, al-. *Al-Hawza al-'Ilmiyya* [The territory of learning, or the religious university]. Najaf: Mu'assasit Turath al-Shahid al-Hakim, Matba'at al-Zaytun, 2005.

Hakim, Muhsin, al-. *Minhaj al-Salihin.* Beirut, 1980.

Hakim, Nur al-Din, al-. "Hawla Mushkilat al-Huriyya al-Insaniyya" [On the problem of human freedom]. *Al-Muthaqqaf al-'Arabi* 6, no. 6 (August 1974): 16–30.

———. "Mushkilat al-Huriyya al-Insanayya wal-Qanun al-'Ilmi" [The problem of human freedom and the scientific law]. *Al-Muthaqqaf al-'Arabi* 7, no. 6 (June 1975): 85–94.

Hamud, 'Ali Tahir, al-. *Al-'Iraq Min Sudmat al-Hawiya ila Sahwat al-Hawiyat* [Iraq, from the tragedy of identity to the awakening of the identities]. Baghdad: Masarat, 2012.

Hasani, 'Abd al-Razzaq, al-. *Ta'rikh al-Wizarat al-'Iraqiyya* [The history of the Iraqi governments]. Pt. 3. Sidon: al-'Irfan, 1953.

Hashimi, 'Abd Tufiq, al-. *Al-Tarbiya al-Islamiyya fi al-Marahil al-Dirasiyya al-'Iraqiyya* [Islamic education in the Iraqi school levels]. Baghdad: al-'Anni Press, March 1974.

Hiti, Halaf Nassar, al-. *Al-Qiyam al-Sa'ida fi Sahafat al-Atfal al-'Iraqiyya* [The dominant values in Iraqi children's magazines]. Baghdad: Ministry of Culture and Arts, 1978.

Hizb al-'Amal al-Islami [Islamic Action Party]. *Saddam Husayn Warith al-Shah* [Saddam Husayn, heir of the shah]. Tehran: Author, 1981.

Hizb al-Ba'th al-'Arabi al-Ishtiraki [Arab Ba'th Socialist Party]. "*Dustur Hizb al-Ba'th al-'Arabi al-Ishtiraki, April 7, 1947*" [The Constitution of the Arab Ba'th Socialist Party, April 7, 1947]. In *Nidhal Hizb al-Ba'th al-'Arabi al-Ishtiraki 'Abra Mu'tamaratihi al-Qawmiyya 1947–1964* [The struggle of the Arab Socialist Ba'th Party through Its Pan-Arab Congresses]. Beirut: Dar al-Tali'a, 1971.

———. *Thawrat Tammuz al-Tajriba wal-Afaq* [The resolutions of the Eighth Regional Congress]. Baghdad, January 1974.

Hizb al-Ba'th al-'Arabi al-Ishtiraki, al-Qutr al-'Iraqi [Arab Socialist Ba'th Party—Iraq]. *Al-Taqrir al-Markazi lil-Mu'tamar al-Qutri al-Tasi', Haziran, 1982* [The central report of the Ninth Regional (Iraqi) Congress, June 1982]. Baghdad, January 1983.

Hizb al-Da'wa al-Islamiyya [Voice of Islam Party]. *Istishhad al-Imam Muhammad Baqir al-Sadr* [The martyrdom of the Imam Muhammad Baqir al-Sadr]. Beirut: Hizb al-Da'wa al-Islamiyya, 1981.

Hizb al-Islami al-'Iraqi, al- [Iraq Islamic Party]. *Bayan*, April 20, 2003.

Husayn, Saddam. *Al-'Iraq Jaysh Tahta al-Silah* [Iraq, an armed military]. Baghdad: Dar al-Huriyya, 1982.

———. *Muqtatafat Min Ahadith Saddam Husayn* [Excerpts from Saddam Husayn's speeches]. Beirut: Dar al-Tali'a, 1979.

Husayni, Ahmad al-Rujaybi, al-. *Al-Nujum al-Zawahir fi Shajarat al-Sayyid al-Amir Nasir* [The bright stars in the (family) tree of the Sayyid Emir Nasir]. Baghdad: Matba'at al-Ma'arif, 1971.

Husri, Abu Khaldun Sati‘, al-. *Mudhakkirati fi al-‘Iraq al-Juz' al-Awwal, 1921–1927* [My memoirs in Iraq: Part 1, 1921–1927]. Beirut: Dar al-Tali‘a, 1967.

Jundi, Sami, al-. *Al-Ba‘th* [The Ba‘th]. Beirut: Dar al-Nahar, 1969.

Khatib, Ahmad ‘Ali, al-, et al. *Al-Tarbiya al-Islamiyya lil-Saff al-Khamis al-Ibtida'i* [Islamic education for the fifth grade, primary school]. 23rd ed. Baghdad: Ministry of Education, Matba‘at al-Jami‘a al-Namadhujiyya, 2001.

Lajna fi Wizarat al-Tarbiya [Committee of the Ministry of Education]. *Al-Qur'an al-Karim: Tilawatuhu wa Ma‘anihi lil-Saff al-Awwal al-Ibtida'i, min Awwal Sura, wal Dhuha, ila Aakhir Sura, al-Nas* [The Blessed Qur'an, its reciting and meanings for the first grade primary school, from the first *sura* . . . to the last *sura* . . .]. Baghdad: Ministry of Education, 1995.

———. *Al-Qur'an al-Karim: Tilawatuhu wa Ma‘anihi lil-Saff al-Thani al-Ibtida'i, min Awwal Sura, al-Naba', ila Aakhir Sura, al-Layl* [The Blessed Qur'an, its reciting and meanings for the second grade primary school, from the first *sura* . . . to the last *sura* . . .], 5th ed. Baghdad: Ministry of Education, 1995.

Lajna Mukhtassa fi Wizarat al-Tarbiya [Special Committee of the Ministry of Education]. *Al-Qur'an al-Karim: Tilawatuhu wa Ma‘anihi lil-Saff al-Rabi‘ al-Ibtida'i, min Awwal Surat al-Mujadala, ila Aakhir Surat al-Tahrim* [The Blessed Qur'an, its reciting and meanings for the fourth grade primary school, from the first *sura* . . . to the last *sura* . . .], 7th ed. Baghdad: Ministry of Education; Jordan: Matba‘at al-Nur, 1998.

Litvak, Meir. "The Rule of the Jurist (*Velayat-e-Faqih*) in Iran: Ideal and Implementation" [in Hebrew]. *Ha Mizrah He Hadash* 42 (2001): 167–84

Malovany, Pesach. *Milhamot Bavel ha-Hadashah: ‘Aliyato u-Nefilato shel ha-Tzava ha-Iraqi* [The wars of modern Babylon: The rise and fall of the Iraqi military]. Tel Aviv: Ma'rachot, 2009.

Marzuq, ‘Abd al-Wahhab ‘Abd al-Razzaq. *Al-‘Iraq Balad al-Turath Wal-Muqaddasat al-Islamiyya* [Iraq, the land of heritage and Islamic holy places]. Baghdad: Ministry of Awqaf and Religious Affairs, 1986.

Mawdudi, Abu al-A‘la, al-. *Mujaz Ta'rikh Tajdid al-Din wal-Hayat: Waqi‘ al-Muslimin wa Sabil al-Nuhudh Bihim* [A concise history of the innovation of religion: The state of the Muslims and the way to reviving them]. Beirut: Mu'assasat al-Risala [Institute of the Message], 1975.

Mu'tamar al-Islami al-Sha‘bi al-Thani, al-. *Muqarrarat al-Mu'tamar al-Islami al-Sha‘bi al-Thani* [The resolutions of the Second Popular Islamic Congress]. Baghdad, April 1985.

Najaf, ‘A(li) (pseud.). *Al-Shahed al-Shahid* [The witness, the martyr]. Tehran, 1981.

Nasir, Yasin, al-. *Shari‘ al-Rashid: ‘Ayn al-Madina wa Nazim al-Nass* [Al-Rashid Street: The city's eye and the composer of text]. Beirut: al-Mada, 2003.

Oron, Yitzhak. "Mifleget Ha Thiya Ha Aravit Ha Sotzialistit" [The Resurrection Arab Socialist Party]. *Ha Mizrah He Hadash* 9, no. 4 (1959): 241–63.

Porat, Liad. "The Egyptian and Syrian Muslim Brothers and Their Struggle against the Secular Arab regimes . . . 1970 to the Early 1990s" [in Hebrew]. PhD diss., University of Haifa, 2008.

Qaysi, Mahir, al-. *See* Mahir al-Kasey under "Books and Articles in European Languages."

Qutb, Sayyid. *Fi Zilal al-Qur'an* [In the shadow of the Qur'an]. 17th ed. Cairo: Dar al-Shuruq, 1992.

Ra'uf, 'Imad 'Abd al-Salam, Nuri 'Abd al-Hamid Jalil, Tariq Nafi' al-Hamdani, and 'Abd al-Sattar'Abd al-Wahid 'Ali. *Al-Ta'rikh al-Hadith wal-Mu'asir lil-Watan al-'Arabi lil-Saff al-Sadis al-Ibtida'i* [Modern and contemporary history of the Arab homeland for the sixth grade, primary school]. 22nd ed. Baghdad: Ministry of Education, 2011.

Rosen, Ya'akov. "Ha Shi'im Be 'Iraq Me'az 1968" [The Shi'is in Iraq since 1968]. Master's thesis, Hebrew University of Jerusalem, 1985.

Republic of Iraq, Ministry of Guidance, Directorate General of Guidance and Broadcasting. *Interim Constitution.* Baghdad: Government Press, 1959.

Sa'di, 'Abd al-Hakim, al-. *Al-Tarbiya al-Islamiyya lil-Saff al-Thani al-Ibtida'i* [Islamic education for the second grade, primary school]. Baghdad: Ministry of Education, 2003.

Sa'di, 'Abd al-Hakim, al-, and Ahzan Yasin al-Duri. *Al-Tarbiya al-Islamiyya lil-Saff al-Thani al-Ibtida'i* [Islamic education for the second grade, primary school], 6th ed. (Baghdad: Ministry of Education, al-Matba'a al-Wataniyya, 1996.

Sa'di, Riyadh Ibrahim, al-. *Al-Hijra al-Dakhiliyya Lil-Sukkan fi al-'Iraq 1947–1965* [Internal migration of the population in Iraq 1947–1965]. Baghdad: Baghdad University Press, 1976.

Sadr, Muhammad Baqir, al-. *Iqtisaduna—Our Economics.* Tehran: World Organization for Islamic Services, March 10, 2012, http://www.hajij.com/library/component/k2/item/187-iqtisaduna-our-economics.

———. *Lamha Tamhidiyya 'an Mashru' Dustur al-Jumhuriyya al-Islamiyya* [A preliminary glimpse at the proposed Constitution of the Islamic Republic]. Beirut: Dar al-Ta'aruf Lil-Matbu'at, February 1979.

———. *Muqaddimat fi al-Tafsir al-Mawdu'i lil-Qur'an* [Introductory notes to the objective interpretation of the Qur'an]. Beirut: Dar al-Ta'aruf Lil-Matbu'at, 1980.

———. "Tasdir" [Introduction]. In 'Abd Allah al-Fayyadh, *Ta'rikh al-Imamiyya wa Aslafihim min al-Shi'a* [The history of the Imami Shi'a and their forebears], 16–25. Baghdad: Matba'at As'ad and Baghdad University, 1970.

Sadr, Muhammad [Muhammad] Sadiq, al-. *Fiqh al-'Asha'ir: Hiwar Fatawa'i Ma'a Marja' al-Muslimin Za'im al-Hawza al-'Ilmiyya Samahat Ayat Allah al-'Uzma al-Sayyid Muhammad al-Sadr* [The tribes' jurisprudence: A religious edicts debate with the source of the Muslims' leader of the religious university, Grand Ayatollah M. (M. Sadiq) al-Sadr]. Beirut: Dar al-Najwa, 1997.

Salman, 'Abd 'Ali. *Al-Mujtama al-Rifi fi al-'Iraq* [The countryside society in Iraq]. Baghdad: Ministry of Culture and Information and Dar al-Rashid lil-Nashr, 1980.

Samarra'i, Yunis Ibrahim, al-. *Ta'rikh 'Ulama Baghdad* [The history of Baghdad's 'ulama]. Baghdad: Ministry of Endowments (Awqaf), 1982.

Sayyab, Badr Shakir, al-. *Diwan* [A poetry collection]. Vol. 1. Beirut: Dar al-Awda, 1971.

Shusmann, Avivah. "The Attitude of the Egyptian Press to the Shi'a on the Background of the Islamic Revolution in Iran" [in Hebrew]. *Ha Mizrah He Hadash* 31 (1986): 138–59.

Talal, Mu'ayyad, al-. "Al-'Abath wal-Huriyya" [Futility and freedom]. *Al-Aqlam* 9, no. 5 (1973): 2–8.

Talas, Mustafa. *Fatir Sahiyyun* [Zion's unleavened bread]. Damascus: Talas Lil-Dirasat Wal-Tarjama Wal-Nashr, 1986.

Tawalba, Hasan, ed. *Muqtatafat min Ahadith Saddam Husayn* [Quotations from the talks of Saddam Husayn]. Beirut: Dar al-Tali'a, 1979.

Waʿili, Ismaʿil, al-, ed. *Dustur [Muhammad Muhammad Sadiq] al-Sadr* [Al-Sadr's Constitution]. Najaf: Muʾassasat Baqiyyat Allah li-nashr al-ʿUlum al-Islamiyya, Maktabat Dar al-Mujtaba, 2004/1434H.

Wizarat al-Tarbiya [Ministry of Education]. *Al-Quran al-Karim: Tilawatuhu wa Maʿanihi lil-Saff al-Rabiʿ al-Ibtidaʾi, min Awwal Surat al-Mujadal, ila Aakhir Surat al-Tahrim* [The Blessed Qurʾan, its reciting and meanings for the fourth grade primary school, from the first *sura* . . . to the last *sura* . . .]. 7th ed. Baghdad: Baghdad, Ministry of Education; Jordan: Matbaʿat al-Nur, 1998.

———. *Al-Quran al-Karim: Tilawatuhu wa Maʿanihi lil-Saff al-Thani al-Ibtidaʾi, min Awwal Sura . . . ila Aakhir Sura . . .* [The Blessed Qurʾan, its reciting and meanings for the second grade primary school, from the first *sura* . . . to the last *sura* . . .]. 5th ed. Baghdad: Ministry of Education, 1995.

———. *Al-Tarbiya al-Islamiyya lil-Saff al-Awwal al-Ibtidaʾi* [Islamic education for the first grade, primary school]. 11th ed. Baghdad: Ministry of Education; Jordan: Matbaʿat al-Nur, 2001.

———. *Al-Tarbiya al-Qawmiyya wal-Ishtirakiyya lil-Saff al-Rabiʿ al-ʿamm* [Pan-Arab and socialist education for the fourth general grade]. Baghdad: Republic of Iraq, Ministry of Education, 1990.

———. *Al-Tarbiya al-Wataniyya lil-Saff al-Rabiʿ al-Ibtidaʾi* [Patriotic (National-Iraqi) education for the fourth grade, primary school]. Baghdad: Ministry of Education, 1990.

———. *Al-Taʾrikh al-Hadith wal-Muʿasir lil-Watan al-ʿArabi lil-Saff al-Sadis al-Ibtidaʾi* [The Modern and contemporary history of the Arab homeland for the sixth grade, primary school]. Baghdad: Ministry of Education, 1988.

Zaydi, Ahmad, al-. *Al-Bina al-Maʿnawi lil-Quwat al-Musallha al-ʿIraqiyya* [The essential structure of the Iraqi armed forces]. Beirut: Dar al-Rawda, 1990.

Zeidel, Ronen. "The Iraqi Baath Party, 1948–1995: Personal and Organizational Aspects" [in Hebrew]. Master's thesis, University of Haifa, 1997

Zuʿayn, Hasan Fadhil, al-ʿAnni ʿAbd al-Rahman ʿAbd al-Karim, and ʿAbd al-Amir ʿAbd Daksan. *Al-Taʾrikh al-ʿArabi al-Islami lil-Saff al-Khamis al-Ibtidaʾi* [Arab-Islamic history for the fifth grade, primary school]. 16th ed. Baghdad: Ministry of Education, 2003.

Zuʿayn, Hasan Fadhil, ʿAbd al-Rahman ʿAbd al-Karim al-ʿAnni, et al. *Al-Taʾrikh al-ʿArabi al-Islami lil-Saff al-Thani al-Mutawassat* [Arab-Islamic history for the second grade, intermediate school]. 13th ed. Baghdad: Ministry of Education, 2002.

Zuʿayn, Hasan Fadhil, ʿAbd al-Rahman ʿAbd al-Karim al-ʿAnni, and ʿAbd al-Amir ʿAbd Daksan. *Al-Taʾrikh al-ʿArabi al-Islami lil-Saff al-Khamis al-Ibtidaʾi* [Arab-Islamic history for the fifth grade, primary school]. 24th ed. Baghdad: Republic of Iraq, Ministry of Education, 2011.

———. *Al-Taʾrikh al-ʿArabi al-Islami lil-Saff al-Thani al-Mutawassat* [Arab-Islamic history for the second grade, intermediate school]. 23rd ed. Baghdad: Republic of Iraq, Ministry of Education, 2010.

Newspapers and Magazines

Aadab al-Rafidayn, a monthly magazine, Baghdad
Afaq 'Arabiyya, a monthly magazine, Baghdad
'Ahd, al-, Tehran
Ahram, al-, a daily, Cairo
Alif Ba, a monthly, Baghdad
'Amal, al-, a Shi'i magazine, Beirut
Anba, al-, a daily newspaper, Kuwait
Aqlam, al-, a monthly magazine, Baghdad
'Arabi, al-, a daily newspaper, Baghdad
Asia Times Online
Babil, a daily newspaper, Baghdad
Da'wa, al-, a monthly issued by the Muslim Brotherhood, Cairo
Da'wa Chronicle, al-, a weekly issued by the Da'wa Islamic Party, London
Diyar, al-, a daily newspaper, Beirut
Dustur, al-, a daily newspaper, Beirut
Hawadith, al-, an independent weekly, Beirut
Hayat, al-, a daily newspaper, London and Beirut
Hurras al-Watan, a monthly magazine, the Ministry of Defense, Baghdad
Imam, a monthly, issued by the Iranian Embassy in London
Impact International, an international news monthly, London
'Iraq, al-, a daily newspaper, Baghdad
Jarida, al-, a daily newspaper, Beirut
Jihad, al-, a weekly, Tehran
Jihad al-Duwali, al-, a weekly, Tehran
Jumhuriyya, al-, the government daily newspaper, Baghdad
Kifa, al-, a weekly magazine, Beirut
Liwa' al-Sadr, a weekly, issued by SAIRI, Tehran
Malaff al-'Iraqi, al, a monthly magazine, London
Massar, al-, a daily newspaper, Beirut
Milliyet, a daily newspaper, Ankara
Mukhtar al-Islami, al-, a weekly, Cairo
Muthaqqaf al-'Arabi, al-, a monthly magazine, Baghdad
Nahar, al-, a daily newspaper, Beirut
Nashra, al-, a monthly, Cyprus
Nida al-Watan, a daily newspaper, Beirut
Qadisiyya, al-, a daily newspaper issued by the Ministry of Defense, Baghdad
Quds, al-'Arabi, al-, a daily newspaper, London
Rahe Enqelab, a monthly publication in Farsi issued by the Mujahidun, Tehran
Ruz al-Yusuf, a daily newspaper, Cairo
Sawt al-Falla (Voice of the Peasant), a weekly, Baghdad
Sawt al-'Iraq, a Da'wa Islamic Party magazine, Tehran
Sawt al-Jamahir (Voice of the Masses), Baghdad's Arabic-language broadcasts

Shahada, al-, a weekly, Tehran
Sharq, al-, a daily newspaper, Qatar
Sharq al-Awsat, al-, a daily newspaper, London
Shira', al-, a daily newspaper, Beirut
Tariq al-Sha'b, a weekly, Baghdad
Tariq al-Thawra, a monthly of the Mujahidun, Tehran
Waqa'i' al-'Iraqiyya, al-, the official gazette of the Iraqi government, Baghdad
Weekly Gazette, the English-language version of the official gazette, Baghdad
Thawra, al-, the Ba'th Party daily newspaper, Baghdad
Thawra al-'Arabiyya, al-, an internal Ba'th magazine for members only, Baghdad
Al-Zahf al-Akhdhar, a daily newspaper, Tripoli, Libya

Archives

Conflict Records Research Center (CRRC), an archive of Ba'th regime records, housed at the National Defense University, Washington, D.C. Those cited in the text follow ("SH" designates the Saddam Husayn Collection):
———. CRRC SH-BATH: Ba'th Party documents:
D-000-066, 144, 159, 232, 268; 300, 311, 324, 325, 364, 474, 518, 578
———. CRRC SH-GMID: Iraqi General Military Intelligence Directorate:
D-000-620, 622; D-001-326
———. CRRC SH-MISC: Miscellaneous:
D-000-310, 729, 950
———. CRRC SH-PDWN: Presidential Diwan:
D-000-012, 028, 096, 328, 329, 406, 409, 499; 507, 509, 590, 642, 801, 812, 855, 724; D-001-029
———. CRRC SH-RVCC: Revolutionary Command Council:
D-001, 315, 402, 610
———. CRRC SH-SHTP: Saddam Husayn Tapes (mostly audio):
A-000 and D-000: 57, 167, 233, 400, 404, 571, 607, 614, 631, 632, 665, 670, 714, 751, 757, 830, 835, 864, 891
———. CRRC SH-SPPC: Saddam's Personal and Political Correspondence:
D-000-217, 448, 586, 660
Iraq Memory Foundation, a research and education organization that maintains an archive of Ba'th regime documents taken in 1991 from Kurdistan. After the 2003 war, additional documents became available through the Iraq Memory Foundation, the Ba'th Regional Command (in this book: Regional Leadership) Collection (BRCC) from Baghdad. All those documents are housed at the Hoover Institution, Stanford University, CA: www.iraqmemory.org.
National Security Archives, George Washington University, Washington, D.C.
Washington Kurdish Institute, an educational and research organization that advocates on behalf of Kurds and maintains translations of Arab press articles, Washington, D.C.

News Agencies, Broadcast and Print Digests, and Translation Services

al-Malaff al-ʿIraqi, a monthly electronic website
Arab Press Service
Arab Report and Record, publication of Arab Report and Record, London
Associated Press
BBC Monitoring, London, a division of BBC that tracks global news sources for the latest reports and provides translations of Arab broadcasts and newspaper articles
Federal News Service, a company that provides transcripts of news reports in real time on its website, wwwfednews.com
Foreign Broadcast Information Service—Near East and South Asia (FBIS-NES), an open-source CIA compilation of Arab broadcasts
Iran News Agency (IRNA), Tehran
Iraqi News Agency (INA), Baghdad
Joint Publications Research Service—Near East Area (JPRS-NEA), a former US-government-funded organization that provided a monthly collection of articles translated from the Arab press before it was absorbed into the Foreign Broadcast Information Service. Reports from 1957 to 1994 are available from Readex.
Mid-East Mirror, a digest of news and editorials in the Arab, Persian, Turkish, and Hebrew media, London
Middle East News Agency (MENA), Cairo
Reuters News Agency

Index

322–23, 325–327, 345–48; Iran and, 102–3, 150–51, 158, 162–63, 165, 171, 388n19; Iran-Iraq War (1980–88) and, 140–42, 145–49, 152–56, 182–83; Islam and, 185, 187, 206–8, 210–11, 292–96, 339–42; Kurds and, 5, 308–10; Kuwait federation and, 213; Muslim Brotherhood and, 190–92, 197–201, 203–6; nationalism and, 3, 8, 15–19, 25–29, 35–39, 41–45; paganism and, 60–63; prostitution and, 398n87; Qur'an and, 254, 260, 262–64; Saddam Husayn and, 22–23, 216–20, 225, 229–31, 238–42, 244–46; Sadr and, 111–12; schools and, 67–70, 167–70, 283–85, 287; *shu'ubiyya* and, 387n168; sovereignty of, 382n97; Sumer and, 366n85; Sunni-Shi'i relations and, 82–83, 86–89, 91, 94, 98–99, 233–37; tribes and, 239–42, 244–46; 'ulama and, 267–68, 273, 276, 290, 320; women and, 53–56, 302; Zionism and, 104–5, 358n12

Arab Socialist Party, 19

Arab Spring, 10, 49, 197, 344

Arab street, 214–15, 221

Aramaic, 88

Arba'in (Islamic holiday), 14, 184, 201, 274, 287, 347; Ba'th regime and, 122, 124, 126, 128, 131; Karbala and, 376n155; participants in, 382n80; Shi'is and, 84–86, 97, 99–100, 277, 283

'Arif brothers ('Abd al-Salam 'Arif and 'Abd al-Rahman 'Arif), 45, 74, 86–87, 113, 123, 133–35, 361n67; Ba'th Party and, 49, 51–52, 54, 77–78, 90, 107; prayer and, 74–75, 359n27

Armenians, 28

army. *See* military

Army Day, 74, 76

Army of the Naqshbandi Order (*Jaysh al-Tariqa al-Naqshbandiyya*), 313

Arsuzi, Zaki, 18, 21, 25–26

'As, 'Amr bin al-, 30, 31

Asad, Bashar al-, 344

Asad, Hafiz al-, 101–2, 126–27, 198–99; Islamism and, 361n5; nationalism and, 20

Asad regime (Syria), 127, 192–93, 379n32

'Asakira (tribe), 279

'Asa'ib Ahl al-Haqq (League of the Righteous, or Brigades of the People of God), 348

'Ashura (Islamic holiday), 14, 33, 43, 113; Ba'th Party and, 73–75, 82, 85, 98–99, 128; Karbala and, 376n155; medieval historiography and, 133–35; Najaf and, 122–23, 125; participants in, 382n80; Saddam Husayn and, 249, 280, 315

Asia, 308

Asia Times, 312

'Askari, al-Hasan al-, 314, 366n86

'Askari, Ayatollah Murtada al-, 86

Askari Shrine (*al-'Ataba al-'Askariyya, al-*), 314, 347

assassination, 7, 21, 94, 95, 116, 120, 138, 143, 177, 178, 272–74, 276, 278, 279, 280, 284, 297, 317, 343, 383n111, 400n128

Assyrians, 60, 88, 294, 306–7, 329; Nazism and, 364n36

Atatürk, Mustafa Kemal, 16, 26, 344

atheism, 12, 156, 160–61, 179–80, 195, 197; 'Aflaq and, 37–38, 207; Ba'th Party, 80, 104, 119, 126, 130, 133; Fichte and, 357n1; Islam and, 322, 329, 336–37, 343–44; party ideology and, 27–29, 31, 33–34; Saddam Husayn and, 200, 210, 218, 303, 305; secularism and, 41, 50, 60, 65, 69–72, 76

Authoritarian Power and State Formation in Ba'thist Syria: Army, Party and Peasants (Hinnebusch), 361n5

Averroës. *See* Ibn Rushd

awqaf (religious endowments), 59, 268–69, 288, 293, 371n48, 371n51; Karbala and, 386n147; ministry of, 76, 181, 188, 256, 259, 264; monarchy and, 363n17

migration, 88–89

Milhamot Bavel ha-Hadashah (*The Wars of Modern Babylon*) (Malovany), 210

military, 249, 259, 261, 263, 270, 274; alcohol and, 261; Ba'th Party and, 145, 216, 340–42, 344, 347, 352–53; commemoration days and, 98, 100; 1977 crisis and, 123, 126; delusional thinking and, 371n47; deserters and, 266; economic policy and, 392n92; Iran-Iraq War (1980–88) and, 152–55, 161–62, 166, 171–75, 180; Islam and, 279, 289, 297, 299–300, 302, 312–15; Islamism and, 322, 331–32, 335–36; Khomeini and, 143, 150–54, 176, 179; Kurds and, 156, 160, 164, 238; March 1991 revolt and, 223, 225, 228, 232–33, 238–42; nationalism and, 5, 19–20, 30–32, 37, 44; promotions in, 164–65; religious riots and, 132–33; Saddam Husayn and, 204, 210, 212–15, 217, 219, 367n2; secularism and, 53, 59–60, 62, 74, 76, 79–80; Shi'is and, 84, 86–90, 105, 107, 113, 232–33; symbolism in, 183–87; Syria and, 193, 198; tribes and, 239–42, 246

Military Bureau, 353

Ministry of Culture and the Arts, 70

Ministry of Labor and Social Affairs, 77

Ministry of Patriotic Education, 66

miracles, 332

Mizmar, al- (children's magazine), 70

Modern and Contemporary History of the Arab Homeland, The (textbook), 177

Modern History of Iraq, The (Marr), 3

modernization, 110, 193, 206, 261, 342

monarchy, 110, 116, 129–30, 278, 299, 361n70; Ba'th Party and, 59, 73–74, 76, 82–83, 85, 107; nationalism and, 11, 16, 33, 43–44; shari'a and, 363n17

Montazeri, Ayatollah Husayn Ali, 319

Morocco, 49

mosque-state relations, 3, 11, 216, 224, 293, 401n135; Ba'th Party and, 47, 49, 75–77, 80, 181, 208; separation in, 26–28, 31, 38, 82

mosques, 262, 269, 283, 297, 317, 321; building of, 337–38, 342; Husayn and, 189–90; Najaf and, 271–74, 276, 278–79; regime support for, 189–90, 384n118

Mosul, Iraq, 42, 259, 262, 305, 309

"Mother of All Battles," 76, 263

mu'ayyid (follower), 349

Mubarak, Husni, 197, 215, 219, 299–300, 344

Mudarissi Brothers, 143

muhajirin, al- (early followers of the Prophet), 285

Muhammad, Prophet of Islam. *See* Prophet, the

Muharram, 73–74, 77, 125

mujaddid al-din (purifiers), 255

mujahidin (jihadist), 313, 328

Mujahidin Khalq (Islamic socialists), 319

mujtahid (practitioners of *ijtihad*), 43, 54, 92, 95, 324; Shi'is and, 114, 119–21

mukhabarat (Iraqi intelligence services), 10, 52, 142, 146, 172, 204–5, 233, 249; Saddam Husayn and, 214, 237, 247–49, 297, 303, 341; Sadr and, 274, 276, 400n128

Mukhtar, al-Thaqafi al-, 137–38

munafiqun (hypocrites or pro-Western Arabs), 220

Munazzamat al-'Amal al-Islami (the Organization of Islamic Action), 143

murashshah (candidate), 349

Murshid 'Amm (General Guide), 204

Mursi, Muhammad, 14, 299

Musawi, 'Abd al-Hakim al-, 121

Musawi, Abu al-Hasan al-, 121

Musawi, Husayn al-, 370n45, 396n32

Musawi, Muhammad Tahir, 384n118

Musawi, Musa al-, 121

Muslim Brotherhood, 157, 309, 313; 'Aflaq and, 199–201; Ba'th Party and, 2–3, 8, 32, 56, 127; Husayn and,

68, 284; Iran and, 149, 192, 203; "lite" version of, 297–300; monarchy and, 363n17; Qur'an and, 211, 255, 288, 316, 342; religious holidays and, 78, 80; Shi'is and, 103, 113, 115, 129–33, 179, 182; women and, 53–55, 58–59

Sharsh, al- (village), 72–73

Shatt al-Arab, 102, 105, 116, 120–21, 123, 240; Iran-Iraq War (1980–88) and, 146–47, 153–54, 174, 195; nationalism and, 21

Shaykhali, 'Abd Allah al-, 396n32

shaykhs, 218–19, 241–45, 247; Ba'th Party and, 120, 189, 309–13, 340, 342, 346; deserters and, 394n126; Islam and, 253, 261, 263, 303; March 1991 revolt and, 226, 228, 240–42; nationalism and, 25, 39; Shi'is and, 81, 89, 98, 101, 110, 118

Sha'ban Revolution. *See* March 1991 revolt

sha'b ("a people"), 22

Shirazi, Ayatollah Hasan al-, 93, 117, 119, 143

Shirazi, 'Abd Allah al-, 375n138

Shirazi brothers, 121, 143

Shi'is, 81–85, 101–5, 116–20, 126–30, 136–40, 187–89; antiregime activities and, 279–80, 284–88; Arabs and, 2, 9–10, 17, 32–33, 35, 43–45; Badr Day and, 366n86; Ba'th Party and, 12–13, 149–52, 341–44, 346–48, 351–52, 392n99; Ba'th Party membership of, 373n96; Ba'th Party representation in, 231–33; denouncement of Ba'th Party and, 374n121; deserters and, 394n126; discrimination against, 393n101; ecumenism and, 111–15, 295–98, 300; faith campaign and, 253–54, 257, 314–18, 323–24, 326, 328; general officers of, 381n76; Hakim and, 374nn112–13; Imam Husayn and, 183–86; Iran and, 146–47, 367n2; Iran-Iraq War (1980–88) and, 161–65, 171–73, 178–83; Iraqi Air Force and, 392n95; Islamism and, 306, 319–21, 330–34,

338; Karbala and, 91–95, 376n155; Khomeini and, 155–59; Kuwait crisis and, 214; March 1991 revolt and, 221–25, 233–37, 239–42; *marja'* and, 166–70; militias of, 13; Musawi and, 396n32; Najaf and, 121–25; nationalism and, 17, 21, 43–45; Pan-Arab Leadership and, 205–6; Persians and, 176; polls of, 411n11; Qur'an and, 260, 262, 264; RCC secret meeting and, 146–47, 155–73, 178–89, 221–42; regime and, 86–90, 96–100, 106–10, 121–25, 131–35, 141–45; Saddam Husayn and, 226–30, 238–39; Saddam Husayn on, 393n109; Sassoon and, 393n107; secularism and, 53–55, 59, 63, 65, 73–75, 77–79, 205–6; security in South and, 248–49, 361n67; shrines and, 270–74, 276–78, 371n48; support for regime and, 370n45; Syria and, 191, 196–99; textbooks and, 281–85; tribes and, 244, 246–47; Twelvers and, 114, 138; 'ulama and, 267, 274–78; women and, 300–301, 304

Shi'i Najaf University (*al-hawza*). *See hawza*

shrines, 39, 65, 188–89; attacks on, 407n81; *awqaf* and, 386n147; economic policy and, 386n143; financial support for, 238; Husayn and, 188–89; Islam and, 253, 270–71, 312, 316, 321, 347; Karbala and, 91–95; Saddam Husayn and, 230, 238, 249; Shi'is and, 96, 99–101, 126–27, 165, 170, 179; spending and, 371n48

shu'ba (party section), 109, 249, 259, 277, 350

Shumaysh, al- (tribe), 279

shura (consultative council), 211, 287

shu'ubiyya (Persian-Islamic movement), 43, 205, 387n168

Sinai Peninsula, 17

Sistani, 'Ali al-, 95, 169, 224, 254, 278, 346–47; rivalry with Muqtada al-Sadr, 400n120

Six-Day War (1967), 61, 340